LYLE BRYANT

BILL HATFIELD

DUNCAN MACKENZIE

DAVID PANAGROSSO

KENT SHARKEY

STEVE SWOPE

OWEN WILLIAMS

MCSD
TRAINING GUIDE

VISUAL BASIC 5

New Riders

MCSD Training Guide: Visual Basic 5

By Lyle Bryant, Bill Hatfield, Duncan Mackenzie, David Panagrosso, Kent Sharkey, Steve Swope, Owen Williams

Published by:
New Riders Publishing
201 West 103rd Street
Indianapolis, IN 46290 USA

Printed in the United States of America 1 2 3 4 5 6 7 8 9 0

Library of Congress Cataloguing-in-Publication Data

```
***CIP data available upon request***
```

ISBN: 1-56205-850-9

Warning and Disclaimer

This book is designed to provide information about the Microsoft "Developing Applications with Microsoft Visual Basic 5" exam. Every effort has been made to make this book as complete and as accurate as possible, but no warranty or fitness is implied.

The information is provided on an "as is" basis. The authors and New Riders Publishing shall have neither liability nor responsibility to any person or entity with respect to any loss or damages arising from the information contained in this book or from the use of the discs or programs that may accompany it.

New Riders Publishing is an independent entity from Microsoft Corporation, and not affiliated with Microsoft Corporation in any manner. This publication may be used in assisting students to prepare for a Microsoft Certified Professional Exam. Neither Microsoft Corporation nor New Riders Publishing warrants that use of this publication will ensure passing the relevant Exam.

Executive Editor
Mary Foote

Acquisitions Editor
Nancy Maragioglio

Development Editor
Nancy Price-Warner

Technical Editors
Lyle Bryant
Bob Reinsch
Kent Sharkey
Deanna Townsend

Managing Editor
Sarah Kearns

Project Editor
Christopher Morris

Copy Editor
Keith Cline

Software Product Developer
Steve Flatt

Software Acquisitions and Development
Dustin Sullivan

Book Designer
Glenn Larsen

Cover Designer
Dan Armstrong

Indexer
Tim Wright

Production Team
Cyndi Davis-Hubler
Terri Edwards
Donna Martin

About the Authors

Lyle A. Bryant is currently employed with Canada's largest ATEC and technical training company, PBSC Computer Training Centres, an IBM Company, as a full-time software developer.

Lyle has been programming in various languages since his high school days. While completing a two-year business certificate course, he started teaching adult education computer courses for various Winnipeg school divisions and for South Winnipeg Technical Centre. After completing the business program, Lyle opened his own independent software development company, Scorpion Software. Two years later, he took the opportunity to teach technical material with PBSC. He was quickly tracked for MCSD courses and became a Microsoft Certified Trainer. After lots of traveling and teaching across Canada for 1½ years, he also completed various certified courses in the MCSE track.

Future projects for Lyle include his wedding in the summer of 1998, completing both the MCSE and MCSD tracks, and writing more technical books, adding to his current list which includes *Inside Windows NT Workstation 4 Certified Administrator's Resource Edition.*

Bill Hatfield is the author of the bestselling book *Developing PowerBuilder Applications* (Sams), the first book published on PowerBuilder. He is also the author of *Active Server Pages For Dummies* (IDG) and *Creating Cool VBScript Web Pages* (IDG). He's coauthor of the bestselling *Visual Basic 4 Unleashed.*

In addition to writing, Bill is also the editor of Pinnacle Publishing's *Delphi Developer,* a technical journal for professional Borland Delphi programmers. He is a Certified Visual Basic Instructor and a Certified PowerBuilder Instructor and frequently does training and consulting for Internet and client/server development projects.

He works from his home in Indianapolis, Ind., where he lives with his wife Melanie and more computers than any one person should be surrounded by.

Duncan Mackenzie is the owner and lead developer for DM Consulting, specializing in Internet and Database development. He is a Microsoft Certified Solution Developer and much too familiar with Visual Basic 5.0. Currently, his main focus is the development of a web site and software for the PBS television program "The Router Workshop." Duncan can be reached by email at `DuncanM@DMconsulting.mb.ca` or at his web site `http://www.dmconsulting.mb.ca`.

David Panagrosso is a senior systems engineer for Linc Systems Corporation, a leading client/server consulting firm in the Northeast. David is a Microsoft Certified Professional and a Microsoft Certified Solution Developer. He has been in the data processing field for more than 11 years, currently specializing in Microsoft Visual Basic, SQL Server, and Access. David holds a bachelor's and master's degree from Rensselaer Polytechnic Institute, in Troy, New York. He lives in Connecticut with his wife Ellen, and can be reached on the Internet at `dpanagrosso@lincsys.com`.

Kent Sharkey is an MCSD, MCSE, and MCT for F1 Group. He divides his time between consulting and training across North America, sometimes pausing long enough to have a life. He lives in Winnipeg with his wife Margaret, and short, furry "child," Goblin.

Steve Swope is a Microsoft Certified Solution Developer and Microsoft Certified Trainer. He lives in southwest Ohio, where he works as a software development consultant. When he isn't working, he spends much of his time writing and performing music on guitars and woodwinds. He can be reached by email at `73020.1275@compuserve.com`

Owen Williams is an MCDS and MCT for Linc Systems Corp. He lives in Connecticut with his understanding and patient wife Sabine.

About the Technical Editors

Bob Reinsch is an independent contractor, providing services as a Microsoft Certified Systems Engineer and Microsoft Certified Trainer. He has been working on personal computers and networks for almost 20 years, dating back to Commodore Pets with 16 KB of RAM. In his career, he has served as a network administrator on UNIX, Macintosh, Novell, and Windows NT networks. He has been working with Windows NT since 3.1 and has pursued certification since NT 3.5. He has been a trainer since 1994 and has worked with students from Boeing, Chase Manhattan Banks, John Hancock Companies, Cinergy, and the Department of Defense. He has taught classes from Portland, Oregon, to Wiesbaden, Germany.

Bob is husband to Dr. Lisa Friis, Ph.D, and father to Bonnie Reinsch, a beautiful baby girl who learned to whistle when she was eight months old.

Deanna Townsend is a consultant specializing in PowerBuilder development. She has received her MCSD (Microsoft Certified Solution Developer) and CPD (Certified PowerBuilder Developer) certifications. Previous to this book, she has coauthored two MCSE exam guides on SQL Server for New Riders and three PowerBuilder textbooks for Que Education and Training.

Trademark Acknowledgments

Dedications

From Lyle Bryant

I would like to dedicate this, my first book, to the love of my life, Gail Beckett. Your love and support have enabled me to achieve all of my goals. Then, now, and always, 'til we rock on the porch.

From Bill Hatfield

To Technology. Where she leads us, we will follow.

From David Panagrosso

I dedicate this book to my family: my wife Ellen, my parents Lottie and Gerald Panagrosso, and my brother Jerry Panagrosso. Thank you for everything you've done for me.

From Steve Swope

For my family: my wife Wendy, our two dogs (Tally and Cider) and cat (Troubles). They have cheerfully tolerated my abdication from many of our usual activities during this project, and I appreciate it.

From Owen Williams

For Sabine and Luzetta

Acknowledgments

I would like to thank Jason Sirockman for providing me with the opportunity to become a technical editor, an author, and for believing in me and my abilities. I would also like to thank Sean Angus and Nancy Maragioglio for all of their advice, help, and support with editing and writing the two books I have worked on. Also, a special thank you to Nancy Warner for her support and kind words. When additional work became available, she was very encouraging and enabled me to take more work to help complete the book.

—Lyle Bryant

Thanks to Nancy Maragioglio, Nancy Warner, Chris Morris, and all the other folks at Macmillan for their for their help.

—Bill Hatfield

Thanks to my wife Laura for the late-nite cups of hot chocolate when I am behind on a deadline, and to my parents who bought the Commodore 64 that started my programming career.

—Duncan Mackenzie

I would like to thank Nancy Maragioglio and New Riders for allowing me to contribute to this book, and for all the help and support they have provided. I also want to thank Owen Williams, who got me involved with this project in the first place, and to Linc Systems for giving me the opportunity to learn. And finally, thank you to my family for all of the encouragement you have given me through the years.

—David Panagrosso

Thanks to Margaret for putting up with me as I wrote part of this on a vacation, and to Lyle and the Nancys for letting me have the opportunity.

—Kent Sharkey

Many thanks to both Nancy Maragioglio and Nancy Warner for their immense patience with me during the development of this book.

—Steve Swope

Many thanks to my wife for tolerating my long hours at the computer without complaining and thanks for my grandmama for giving me my first computer and my education. I would also like to thank all of the individuals at MCP and Lyle for providing this opportunity. Lastly, I would like to thank my employer Linc Systems, for providing the support and opportunities over the years.

—Owen Williams

Contents at a Glance

Part IV: Distribution Issues   881

Appendixes   1045

Table of Contents

Part II: Coding Issues

Part III: Debugging and Testing Issues

21 Monitoring the Values of Expressions and Variables by Using the Debugging Windows 801

22 Implementing Project Groups to Support the Development and Debugging Process 837

Part V: Appendixes

Introduction

Who Should Read This Book

MCSD Training Guide: Visual Basic 5 is designed for advanced end users and developers who are considering certification as a Microsoft Certified Solution Developer (MCSD). The Microsoft Visual Basic 5 exam ("Exam 70-165: Developing Applications with Microsoft Visual Basic 5") tests your ability to design, develop, and implement solutions based on Microsoft Visual Basic 5.0. This will demonstrate to your customers and colleagues that you have what it takes to design and develop superior custom solutions with Microsoft tools and technologies.

This book is your one-stop shop. Everything you need to know to pass the exam is in here, and it has been certified by Microsoft as study materials. You do not *need* to take a class in addition to buying this book to pass the exam. However, your personal study habits may benefit from taking a class in addition to the book, and buying this book in addition to a class.

This book also can help advanced users and administrators who are not studying for the MCSD exam but are looking for a single-volume reference on Microsoft Visual Basic 5.

How This Book Helps You

This book takes you on a self-guided tour of all the areas covered by the MCSD Visual Basic 5 exam and teaches you the specific skills you need to achieve your MCSD certification. You will also find helpful hints, tips, real-world examples, exercises, and references to additional study materials. Specifically, this book is set up to help you in the following ways:

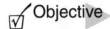 Objective ▶

▶ **Organization.** This book is organized by major exam topics and exam objectives. Every objective you need to know for the "Developing Applications with Microsoft Visual Basic 5" exam is covered in this book; a margin icon is included, like the one in the margin here, to help you quickly locate these objectives. Pointers at different elements direct you to the appropriate place in the book if you find you need to review certain sections.

▶ **Deciding how to spend your time wisely.** Prechapter quizzes are at the beginning of each chapter to test your knowledge of the objectives contained within that chapter. If you already know the answers to those questions, you can make a time-management decision accordingly.

▶ **Extensive practice test options.** Plenty of questions are at the end of each chapter to test your comprehension of material covered within that chapter. An answer list follows the questions so that you can check yourself. These practice test options will help you decide what you already understand and what requires extra review on your part. The accompanying CD-ROM also contains a sample test engine that gives you an accurate idea of what the test is really like.

You also get a chance to practice for the certification exams by using the test engine on the accompanying CD. The questions on the CD provide a more thorough and comprehensive look at what your certification exams really are like. The CD includes the Microsoft Education and Certification Roadmap—a publication from Microsoft that provides a thorough outline of the certification process. The Roadmap Assessment Exam includes the best available examples of the kinds of questions you will find on the certification exam. The Roadmap also includes the Planning Wizard, an online tool that helps you quickly map out a plan for achieving your certification goals.

Note

For a complete description of New Riders' newly-developed test engine, see Appendix D, "All About TestPrep."

For a complete description of what you can find on the CD-ROM, see Appendix C, "What's on the CD-ROM."

Most Roadmap Assessment Exams are based on specific product versions, and new elective exams are available on an ongoing basis. The Microsoft Education and Certification Roadmap is a quarterly publication. You can obtain updates of the Roadmap at any of the following locations:

Microsoft Education: Call 800-636-7544

Internet: `ftp://ftp.microsoft.com/Services/MSEdCert`

World Wide Web: `http://www.microsoft.com/train_cert/default.htm`

CompuServe Forum: `GO MSEDCERT`

The enclosed CD also includes MCP Endeavor, an interactive practice test application designed exclusively for Macmillan Publishing that will help you prepare for the MCSD exams.

This book can help you by serving as a desktop reference for information on Microsoft Visual Basic 5.

Understanding What the Developing Applications with Microsoft Visual Basic 5 Exam Covers

The Developing Applications with Microsoft Visual Basic 5 certification exam goes beyond testing your knowledge of Visual Basic 5. You should have a comprehensive understanding of application programming concepts and procedures, and you should be able to apply these skills to design, develop, and implement solutions based on Microsoft Visual Basic 5. Before taking the exam, you should be proficient in the following job skills.

Design Issues

Design and Create Forms

▶ Create an application that adds and deletes forms at runtime

▶ Use the Forms Collection

Implement Drag-and-Drop Operations Within the Microsoft Windows Shell/Determine When to Use a Specific Event

▶ Implement traditional drag-and-drop operations within the Microsoft Windows shell

▶ Add code to the appropriate form event, such as `Initialize`, `Terminate`, `Load`, `Unload`, `QueryUnload`, `Activate`, and `Deactivate`

Add a Menu Interface to an Application

▶ Dynamically modify the appearance of a menu

▶ Add a pop-up menu to an application

▶ Create an application that adds and deletes menus at runtime

Implement User Interface Controls in an Application

▶ Display data by using the `TreeView` control

▶ Display items by using the `ListView` control

▶ Provide controls with images by using the `ImageList` control

▶ Create toolbars by using the `Toolbar` control

▶ Display status information by using the `StatusBar` control

▶ Create an application that adds and deletes controls at runtime

▶ Use the Controls Collection

Coding Issues

Declare a Variable

▶ Define the scope of a variable by using the `Public`, `Private`, and `Static` statements

▶ Use the appropriate declaration statement

Write and Call `Sub` and `Function` Procedures

▶ Write and call `Sub` and `Function` procedures by using named arguments or optional arguments

▶ Write and call `Sub` and `Function` procedures that require an array as an argument

▶ Call procedures from outside a module

Create and Use a Class Module

▶ Add properties to a class

▶ Add methods to a class

▶ Identify whether a class should be public or private

▶ Declare properties and methods as `Friend`

▶ Set the value of the `Instancing` property

Access Data by Using the Data Controls and Bound Controls

▶ Add data to a table by using the `DBList` or `DBCombo` control

▶ Add data to a table by using the standard `ListBox` control

▶ Display information by using the `DBGrid` control

▶ Display information by using the `MSFlexGrid` control

Access Data by Using Code

▶ Navigate through and manipulate records in a `Recordset`

▶ Add, modify, and delete records in a `Recordset`

▶ Find a record in a `Recordset`

▶ Use the `Find` or `Seek` method to search a `Recordset`

Incorporate Dynamic Link Libraries (DLLs) into an Application

▶ Declare and call a DLL routine

▶ Identify when it is necessary to use the `Alias` clause

▶ Create a DLL routine that modifies string arguments

▶ Pass a null pointer to a DLL routine

▶ Pass an argument by value and by reference

▶ Pass a function pointer to a DLL by using a callback function

▶ Pass a string to a DLL

Build a Microsoft ActiveX Client

▶ Use the `Dim` statement to reference an object

▶ Use the `Set` statement to create an instance of an object

▶ Use the `CreateObject` function to create an instance of an object

Create an Automation Server That Exposes Objects, Properties, Methods, and Events

▶ Define properties for objects by using property procedures

▶ Create a method that displays a form

▶ Create a multithreaded component

▶ Use `App` object properties to control server behavior

▶ Call an object server asynchronously by using a callback mechanism

▶ Create, use, and respond to events

Create and Use an ActiveX Control

▶ Declare and raise events

▶ Create and enable a Property page

▶ Use control events to save and load persistent control properties

▶ Add an ActiveX Control to a web page

Create and use ActiveX Documents

▶ Compare ActiveX Documents to embedded objects

▶ Create an ActiveX project with one or more UserDocument objects

▶ Persist data for an ActiveX Document

▶ Automate an ActiveX Document

▶ Add an ActiveX Document to a web page.

Create Applications That Can Access the Internet

▶ Gain access to the Internet or an intranet by using the Hyperlink object

▶ Create an application that has the capability to browse HTML pages

▶ Create an application that enables connections to the Internet

Implement Error-Handling Features in an Application

▶ Raise errors from a server

▶ Create a common error-handling routine

▶ Display an error message in a dialog box by using the Err object

▶ Use the appropriate error-trapping options, such as Break on All Errors, Break in Class Module, and Break on Unhandled Errors

Implement Help Features in an Application

▶ Set properties to automatically display Help information when a user presses F1

▶ Use the HelpFile property to set the default path for Help files in an application

▶ Use the CommonDialog control to display the contents of a Help file

Debugging and Testing Issues

Select Appropriate Compiler Options

▶ List and describe options for optimizing when compiling to native code

▶ List and describe the differences between compiling to p-code and compiling to native code

Compile an Application Conditionally

▶ Use the #If, #End If, and #Const directives to conditionally compile statements

▶ Set the appropriate conditional compiler flags

Set Watch Expressions During Program Execution

Monitor the Values of Expressions and Variables by Using the Debugging Windows

▶ Use the Immediate window to check or change values

▶ Explain the purpose and usage for the Locals window

Implement Project Groups to Support the Debugging and Development Process

▶ Debug DLLs in process

▶ Test and debug a control in process

Define the Scope of a Watch Variable

Distribution Issues

Use the Setup Wizard to Create an Effective Setup Program

▶ Edit the Setup.inf file

▶ Edit the Vb5dep.ini file

Create a Setup Program That Installs and Registers ActiveX Controls

Manage the Windows System Registry

▶ Use the `GetSetting` function and the `SaveSetting` statement to save application-specific information in the Registry

▶ Register components by using the Regsvr32.exe utility

▶ Register components by using the Remote Automation Connection Manager

▶ Edit the Registry manually

▶ Register a component automatically

Distribute an Application over the Internet

Hardware and Software Needed

As a self-paced study guide, much of the book expects you to use Visual Basic 5 and follow along through the exercises while you learn. Microsoft designed Visual Basic 5 to operate in a wide range of actual situations, and the exercises in this book encompass that range.

Tips for the Exam

Remember the following tips as you prepare for the MCSD certification exams:

▶ **Read all the material.** Microsoft has been known to include material not specified in the objectives. This course has included additional information not required by the objectives in an effort to give you the best possible preparation for the examination and for the real-world network experiences to come.

▶ **Complete the exercises in each chapter.** Exercises in each chapter will help you gain experience using the Microsoft product. All Microsoft exams are experienced-based, and require you to have used the Microsoft product in a real networking environment. Exercises for each objective are placed at the end of each chapter.

▶ **Complete all the questions in the "Review Questions" sections.** Complete the questions at the end of each chapter—they will help you remember key points. The questions are fairly simple. Be warned, however, some questions may have more than one answer.

▶ **Review the exam objectives in the Microsoft Education and Certification Roadmap.** Develop your own questions for each topic listed. If you can make and answer several questions for each topic, you should pass.

▶ **Complete the Roadmap Assessment Exam and visit the relevant topics in the MCP Endeavor application.** Do not make the mistake of trusting all the answers in the Assessment Exams—they're not always correct. Look at this not as a bug, but as a feature to test your knowledge; not only do you have to know you are right, you have to be sure about it, and you have to know why each of the answers is wrong.

> Although this book is designed to prepare you to take and pass the "Developing Applications with Microsoft Visual Basic 5" certification exam, there are no guarantees. Read this book, work through the exercises, and take the practice assessment exams.
>
> When taking the real certification exam, make sure you answer all the questions before your time limit expires. Do not spend too much time on any one question. If you are unsure about an answer, answer the question as best you can and mark it for later review when you have finished all the questions. It has been said, whether correctly or not, that any questions left unanswered automatically cause you to fail. Good luck.

Remember, the object is not to pass the exam, it is to understand the material. After you understand the material, passing is simple. Knowledge is a pyramid; to build upward, you need a solid foundation. The Microsoft Certified System Developer program is designed to ensure that you have that solid foundation.

Good luck!

New Riders Publishing

The staff of New Riders Publishing is committed to bringing you the very best in computer reference material. Each New Riders book is the result of months of work by authors and staff who research and refine the information contained within its covers.

As part of this commitment to you, the NRP reader, New Riders invites your input. Please let us know whether you enjoy this book, whether you have trouble with the information and examples presented, or whether you have a suggestion for the next edition.

Please note, however: New Riders staff cannot serve as a technical resource during your preparation for the Microsoft MCSD certification exams or for questions about software- or hardware-related problems. Please refer to the documentation that accompanies Microsoft Visual Basic 5 or to the applications' Help systems.

If you have a question or comment about any New Riders book, there are several ways to contact New Riders Publishing. We will respond to as many readers as we can. Your name, address, or phone number will never become part of a mailing list or be used for any purpose other than to help us continue to bring you the best books possible. You can write us at the following address:

New Riders Publishing
Attn: Publisher
201 W. 103rd Street
Indianapolis, IN 46290

If you prefer, you can fax New Riders Publishing at 317-817-7448.

You also can send email to New Riders at the following Internet address:

`certification@mcp.com`

NRP is an imprint of Macmillan Computer Publishing. To obtain a catalog or information, or to purchase any Macmillan Computer Publishing book, call 800-428-5331.

Thank you for selecting *MCSD Training Guide: Visual Basic 5*!

P a r t **1**

Design Issues

Chapter

Designing and Creating Forms

This chapter helps you prepare for the exam by covering the following objectives:

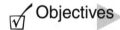

Objectives

▶ Create an application that adds and deletes forms at runtime

▶ Use the Forms Collection

Test Yourself! Before reading this chapter, test yourself to determine how much study time you will need to devote to this section.

1. In a Visual Basic project, the form is used to develop the user interface. Various controls are placed on the form, such as command buttons, text boxes, and picture controls. If the form is moved or resized, all controls on the form are affected. What is the name of the type of control that can have other controls placed on it?

2. When using Form objects in a VB project, the Load statement is used to bring the form into memory. The Show statement is used to display the form onscreen. Are there any other statements that will cause a Form object to be loaded into memory?

3. In Visual Basic, the Unload statement and Hide method are both used to affect forms. Assume a project contained a main form and an options form. Which would be used to ensure that the options form, and all controls on it, could still be referenced after the user had set various options?

4. When a form is created at design time and then saved, what are the file format and file extensions that are used to save the information contained on that form?

5. When creating multiple instances of a form at runtime, what is the keyword used to reference the currently running object?

6. What is the keyword used to create a runtime version of a form that was created at design time?

7. The Forms Collection contains references to Visual Basic Form objects. Does the collection contain references to forms that were created at design time, runtime, or both?

8. In Visual Basic, collection objects usually have various methods and properties that control references in the collection. How many properties and methods does the Visual Basic Forms Collection have? What are their names?

9. The Forms Collection is used to reference all forms that have been loaded into memory. When programming in VB, the individual properties of one Form object might be required. What does the collection provide the programmer with that will enable the control of individual collection members?

Answers are located at the end of the chapter...

This chapter introduces you to the use of Form objects within Visual Basic. The Form object is one of the main "visual" components in VB. It provides the programmer with a simple device to allow interaction with the user. Although Visual Basic offers the programmer additional ways to allow the user to control the program, forms are one of the easiest to develop and work with.

So that you can better understand some of the more advanced concepts covered later in the chapter, the basics are reviewed first. These basics include everything from loading and unloading the form to how design-time forms are stored. This chapter then introduces creating new forms at runtime and working with the Forms Collection.

This chapter covers the following topics:

- ▶ Form basics

- ▶ Loading and unloading forms

- ▶ Showing and hiding forms

- ▶ How forms and related information are stored

- ▶ Creating an application that adds and deletes forms at runtime

- ▶ Creating design-time Form object templates

- ▶ Using the 'ME' object indicator

- ▶ Using the Forms Collection

- ▶ Controlling individual collection members

- ▶ Looping through collections

Form Basics

This section examines the use of VB Form objects within a project. Topics covered include loading and unloading a form into memory, showing and hiding forms from the screen, and how VB Form objects are stored.

When a project is designed and multiple forms are used, it is the programmer's job to ensure a clean, easy-to-use interface. The knowledge of how forms are brought into memory, the effect when forms leave memory, when to expect a form to be displayed, and when it is removed are critical elements in designing a professional-looking application. Also knowing how information is stored at design time will help to ensure forms that can be used throughout various projects or moved from one version of VB to another.

Forms are used to hold other controls for user interaction. When one control has the capability to host other controls, this is known as a Container control. When controls are placed on a form, they are affected when the form is moved or resized. This allows the form to act as the Container control. The `Picture` control is also a Container control that can have other controls placed on it.

This section looks at how to load and unload forms from memory, how to show and hide forms from the screen, and how design-time forms are stored.

Loading and Unloading Forms

Visual Basic projects have a special object that can be automatically loaded when the program is run. This object is referred to as the `startup` object. Figure 1.1 shows an example of a `startup` object. Previous versions of VB allowed forms or `Sub Main` procedures to be used as the `startup` object. With Visual Basic 5.0 (VB5), the `startup` object can now vary depending on the type of project you are creating. A form can be selected, the `Sub Main` procedure, or—new to VB5—nothing. Nothing is used when the program does not require an interface. An example of this type of project might be an ActiveX component or an ActiveX Control.

When forms are used as the `startup` object, the form that has been specified is automatically loaded into memory when the application is started. All other forms are not loaded unless they are referenced in program code or are explicitly loaded into memory. To load a form into memory without directly showing it, the `Load` statement is used. This statement will take only one argument: the name of the object to be loaded. Take a look at the following code:

```
Load Form1
Load frmTest
```

Figure 1.1

Selecting the project startup object.

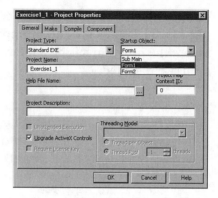

The Load statement accepts a valid object name. This causes the object to be loaded in memory. Although the object is loaded into memory, this does not mean that the object will be visible to the user. This enables the programmer to load multiple forms that may be required and to prepare them with information before display. Once loaded into memory, the form's controls and any program code can be used.

When working with forms in VB, it is important to note that any reference to an object will cause that object to load. The Load statement does not have to be explicitly used before an object can be used. An example of this would be if a form's Caption property was set, as follows:

```
Form1.Caption = "My Notepad"
```

Notice that this is the only line of code that you need to be concerned with. There is no Load statement before the Caption property is set. This code just directly sets the form's property. This single line of code automatically causes the Form1 object to be loaded into memory. This is often referred to as *implicit loading*. Because the object must be loaded to set the property, VB does exactly that.

Implicit loading can often cause problems when working on a multi-form project. The programmer does not notice that one form calls or sets information on another form. The form is then automatically loaded. Then when you attempt to unload all forms you explicitly used, your project continues to run.

The End statement can be used to force all forms to unload, whether they were explicitly or implicitly loaded. This is a fail-safe in case the program missed a reference or miscounted how many forms were loaded.

Note

> The End statement should be used with caution. The End statement will end the program immediately. Any code in a form's Unload event will not run. Similarly, the Terminate event of any classes and forms will not run. Do not use the End statement if you are attempting any code in these events.

When an individual form is no longer required, you can unload it from memory. This will release the graphic components from memory. The form code will still be resident, however. The Unload statement is used to remove objects from memory. The following code is used to unload a form:

```
Unload Form1
Unload frmTest
```

The Unload statement accepts a valid object name. This causes the design-time graphic components of a form to be released. Although the form has been unloaded from memory, it is very important to note that any code related to the form is still in memory. The graphical controls are no longer available, but any form procedures can still be called, depending on their scope.

Load and Unload are used to control the memory status of a form. These two statements always appear before the name of the object to be affected. This is often confused with the Show and Hide methods, which take place after the object name. Show and Hide are used to control whether a form is visible to the user.

Showing and Hiding a Form

Loading and unloading only bring the form into memory or remove the form from memory. If the programmer wants to display the form for the user to interact with, another set of commands must be used. The Show and Hide commands are the methods that can affect the form this way. Unlike the Load and Unload statements, which appear before the selected object, Show and Hide follow the object name and are separated from the object by a period (.).

When a form is to appear onscreen for the user to interact with, the Show statement allows the form to appear. Hide will remove the form from the screen, but allows it to remain in memory.

If the form is to be directly shown to the user, only the Show method is required. The loading of the Form object will take place automatically. The following line of code is only required to both load the form and have it displayed:

```
Form1.Show
frmTest.Show
```

To understand why the form does not have to be explicitly loaded, first always remember that any programmatic reference to an object will cause it to automatically load. That explains why using the object name followed by the Show method causes the form to load first and then display onscreen.

If the form is no longer required to be onscreen, it can be removed from display by just using the Hide method. This keeps the form loaded, but removes it from display. The following code demonstrates this:

```
Form1.Hide
frmTest.Hide
```

The first line of code removes the form named Form1 from the onscreen display. The second line of code removes the object named frmTest. Both prevent user interaction with the form and help you avoid a very busy screen.

Forms can be hidden, which allow the user to set various controls on the form to the required states. If a form is hidden, these states will remain as the user configured them. This allows other forms to reference the form and the controls on that form.

If the form was unloaded, this would re-initialize the controls on the form. Every time the user wanted the settings, they would either have to be loaded from an external source or reset by the user.

Although showing and hiding a form during runtime is vital to the appearance and flow of the application, another important aspect of the form is how the design-time Form object is stored. Knowing how Form objects are stored will allow forms to be moved from one project to another or from one version of VB to another.

Design-Time Storage of Form Objects

After a form has been designed and saved, the information from the form is separated into two components. The first component is a text description of the form itself—all objects contained on the form, all object properties and their values, as well as any code associated with the form and the objects. This text-based information is stored in an ASCII text file with the extension .FRM. Figure 1.2 shows a sample of a text-based .FRM file. Any word processor or text editor can open this file.

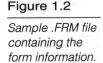

Figure 1.2

Sample .FRM file containing the form information.

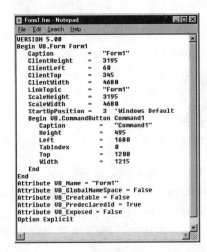

The second file is .FRX. It contains all graphics-related information required by the form. If a `Picture` control or `Image` control is used, and a bitmap graphic is referenced by the control, that image must be stored internally. This information is stored in the separate .FRX file and is in a binary format. The .FRM file will contain references to the .FRX file and a number indicating the image to be referenced for specific controls.

Knowing how the `Form` objects are stored after designing them can be very useful. If a form is taken to another project and doesn't seem to load properly, you could open the text file and determine whether a reference is required for that form. Often, as forms are moved between projects, the references to various controls are not always the same. This gives the programmer the ability to open the file and verify the references that should be included within that project.

Another application of using the form's text file comes up if an old form from a previous version of Visual Basic is to be used within a newer version. By opening the text file with an editor, any problem lines can be removed. The same technique can also be applied when taking `Form` objects from a newer version of VB and going to an older version of the software.

This section has covered how forms are brought into memory and removed from memory. If a form is required to be displayed, the `Show` method is used. Alternatively, the `Hide` method can be called to remove the form from display. The storage of the design-time form is separated into a text-description file, .FRM. Graphics information is stored in an .FRX file. Together, both files create the desired form.

Creating an Application that Adds and Deletes Forms at Runtime

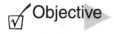 Objective

This section examines the dynamic creation of a VB `Form` object. Topics covered include creating a runtime form, using the dynamic form, and removing the dynamic `Form` object.

The form can be used to create a simple interface to allow user interaction. Programmers can design a project that has multiple forms, with each form having a specific design and purpose. Certain projects will require that users be able to control how many forms they are entering information on. An example of this would be Microsoft Excel, which enables the user to create multiple workbooks. Each workbook has the same design and functionality, but can contain different information. To assist with this process, a form can be designed as a `Template` object. When users require another instance of the form for additional data, they create a new form at runtime. The new form is based on the `Template Form` object. This enables users to create as many forms as they require.

To allow a `Form` object to be used as a `Template Form` object, the programmer must use program code to control a new instance of the form. This instance is created at runtime and is unique from the original `Template` form.

Creating a Runtime Form

If a runtime `Form` object is to be created, the first step is to create a design-time form that will act as a template. Design the form to your requirements, adding all buttons, text boxes, list boxes, and any other controls.

In your program code, you will `Dimension` a new object variable and base it on the `Template` object name. The following code shows the new object variable declaration:

```
Dim x as New Form1
```

In this line of code, x is the new object variable and will be used to control the new runtime object. The keyword `New` tells VB to create a new copy of the `Form1` object.

An example of a project that enables the user to create multiple forms at runtime would be Microsoft Word. When the user is entering text and decides that another letter has to be typed, the user selects File, New. This creates a new instance of a form based on a template form. Microsoft Word uses a special document called Normal.Dot. The .DOT extension is used by Microsoft Word for document templates. This template document contains the default settings as specified by the user. The settings can control the margin settings, the font face and size, and other aspects of the document. When the new form document is created at runtime, it will have all the settings found in Normal.Dot.

To demonstrate creating a runtime instance of a form, perform the following:

1. Create a VB Standard EXE project and have one form with one command button.

2. Open the code window for the command button and enter the following text:

```
Sub mnuFileNew_Click()
     Dim x as New Form1
     x.Show
End Sub
```

Figure 1.3 illustrates a Visual Basic project that creates a dynamic runtime form based on the `Form2 Template` object. The code window displays the `Click` event of the `Command1` button from `Form1`. This code is used to create a new form and set the form's `Caption` property.

Figure 1.3

Project code that will create a runtime form based on another Form object.

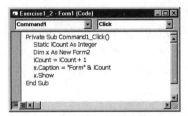

This code will use the `Form1` object and allow other runtime instances of the form to be created. If you continue to click on the Command1 button, new forms will be created as shown in Figure 1.4. Each form will be independent of the others. Use the Visual Basic toolbar and press the End button to quickly destroy all the runtime-created Dorms.

Figure 1.4

*Multiple forms
created at
runtime.*

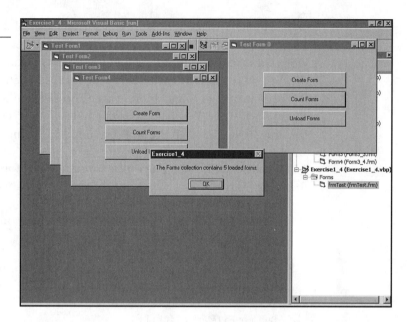

In the preceding code, x is the new object based on Form1. The
keyword New creates another Form object. After the new object has
been created, all properties and methods of the original object
will be available to the user or programmer. To refer to them, just
use the new object variable name and then the property or method, as follows:

```
x.Caption = "My New Form 1"
x.Hide
x.Width = 500
```

The new runtime Form object will operate just like a regular form.
The only difference is that it was created at runtime and is referred to by a different name.

Removing Runtime Forms

After the new object variable has been created and is based on a
Template object, the user or programmer may decide that the
object is no longer required. To remove the runtime form, you
can just Unload the new object.

If you wish to remove a design-time `Form` object from memory, you just refer to the design-time name of the `Form` object and use the `Unload` statement. With runtime objects, this will not work. When the runtime object was created, it used a new name and not the design-time name. If you attempt to use the design-time name, that is the only form that is unloaded. All other runtime forms will remain in memory.

To assist in the removal of a runtime object, a special keyword must be used to reference the object. The keyword `ME` is used to reference the current instance of the object that has the focus. Therefore if the user wants to unload the currently active object, the code would be as follows:

```
Unload ME
```

The object `ME` will unload only the currently active object and leave all other instances intact. The `ME` keyword can be used in many different areas of code where multiple instances of an object may have been declared. This would include using the keyword `ME` on `Form Template` objects as well as when creating a `class` object.

If you have not used the keyword before, it is very easy to apply to current source code. If you want the design-time object to be a template, just replace the design-time object's name with the new keyword `ME`. This ensures that as the object is used to create new instances, the source code does not refer to the specific design-time name. The following code examples demonstrate additional uses of the keyword `ME`:

```
ME.Hide
ME.Show
ME.Caption = "My Notepad"
```

In these code lines, the object name is replaced with the keyword `ME` to allow the currently active object to be used. The first line hides the current `Form` object. The second line shows the current `Form` object. The last line sets the current form's `Caption` property to `My Notepad`. These examples help illustrate how using the `ME` object variable will assist with controlling multiple instances of objects at runtime.

Using the Forms Collection

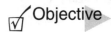 Objective ▶

This section examines using a grouping of objects by Visual Basic, referred to as a collection. Topics covered include using methods and properties of the collection, referencing individual forms, looping through the collection, verifying loaded forms, and unloading forms from the collection.

In Visual Basic, a collection is just a group of objects of the same type. If you have more than one form in a project, you would have a Forms Collection. This collection can be used to easily manipulate all forms or just one specific form. VB offers intrinsic collections as well as user-defined collections. Another example of a collection that is built into VB is the Controls Collection. This collection will return all types of controls contained on the specified form.

When a project is loaded, the Forms Collection will refer to all types of forms within VB. MDI Parent forms, MDI Child forms, and non-MDI forms are all included in the collection. The collection will also include any forms created at runtime.

The Forms Collection will only return a count of the forms that have been loaded. If a project contains multiple forms and only the `Startup` form has been loaded, the collection will only have one item. To be included in the Forms Collection, all forms must be loaded. They do not have to be shown onscreen, only loaded.

If a form is unloaded from the project, that form is no longer part of the collection. The collection will reduce its count by one, and that form will no longer be available.

Using Methods and Properties of the Forms Collection

Most collections have various methods or properties that will return information regarding the collection of objects. The Forms Collection has only one property, `Count`. This property returns the total number of forms loaded by the current project.

To find the total amount of forms in the project, just use the following code:

```
Forms.Count
```

Another example of using the total returned by the Count method would be to include the number in a message box. Refer back to Figure 1.4. This figure illustrated a project with multiple forms loaded and a message box indicating the Count from the Forms Collection.

To test the following code with VB, use a single form and place one command button on the form. Open the code window for the command button and type the following code:

```
Sub Command1_Click()
    Msgbox "The Forms Collection has " & Forms.Count & " forms
    ➥currently", vbInformation, "Forms Count"
End Sub
```

This code will generate a message box with a string that contains the number of forms in the collection. Remember that only loaded forms are in the collection. Any form that has not been loaded or that has been unloaded will not be part of the collection.

Using Specific Items Within the Forms Collection

Each object in the collection can also be referred to by its specific ordinal number. This is an item number automatically assigned as the new items are added to the collection. When referring to the ordinal number of a form, you must always remember that the Forms Collection is 0 based. The first item in the collection will always have the ordinal value of 0. The following code demonstrates using the item value:

```
Forms(0).Caption
Forms(1).Name
Forms(2).Width
```

This code assumes that a VB project has three forms and that all forms have been loaded into memory. The first line will return the `Caption` of the very first item (item 0) in the collection. The second line will return the `Name` property of Form(1). The third line will return the value of the last form's width.

These code examples show how easy referencing specific items in the collection can be. This can be an alternative method to using the specific form names in a given project. With the Forms Collection, you also do not have to know the name of a given form to control it. This will assist in manipulating forms generated at run-time.

Looping Through the Forms Collection

Another way to use the Forms Collection is with various looping techniques. By using `For...Next` statements or `Do...While` statements, the programmer can loop through the collection to affect all the forms, search for specific forms, and search for specific properties or even values. This will assist in searching for information without having to program every form name individually.

A simple example would be to retrieve each form's `Caption`, as follows:

```
Dim iLoop as Integer
For iLoop = 0 to Forms.Count - 1
    MsgBox Forms(iLoop).Caption
Next iLoop
```

This code declares an integer variable for looping, and then sets up the `For...Next` statement. Notice `iLoop = 0`. You must start at 0 because collections are 0 based. Because you will not always know the amount of forms in the collection, you can take the `Forms.Count` and subtract 1 from the total. You must remove 1 because the `Count` starts at 1 and the `Collection` starts at 0. When this sample code is run, a message box displays with the `Caption` property of every form in the collection.

Alternatively, the programmer can loop through the forms collection using the `For Each...Next` statement. The benefit of this statement is that there is no need to read the `Forms.Count` property. Also, there is no need to remember that the Forms Collection is 0-based. The above example could then be rewritten as follows:

```
Dim f as Form
For Each f In Forms
     Msgbox f.Caption
Next
```

Using the Forms Collection to Verify Whether a Form Is Loaded

When a form is referenced in code, it automatically loads the form into memory. One advantage of the Forms Collection is that it only contains forms that have been loaded into memory. This enables the programmer to test for a specific form by looping through the collection and testing the Name property of every item in the collection.

An example of this code is as follows:

```
Sub Command1_Click()
    Dim iLoop as Integer
    For iLoop = 0 to Forms.Count - 1
       If Forms(iLoop).Name = "Form3" Then
            MsgBox "Form3 has been loaded"
         End If
    Next iLoop
End Sub
```

This code declares an integer variable for looping, and then sets up the For...Next statement. Inside the For...Next statement is an If test. With this code, you are looking through each item in the collection and testing the Forms(iLoop).Name property. This allows iLoop to represent every form that is loaded in the collection. If the Name property is equal to Form3, a message box is generated indicating that Form3 has been loaded into memory.

This code sample requires a project with at least three forms. The default form names are expected and the Form_Load event is responsible for loading all forms into memory. Remember that if the forms are not explicitly loaded, they will not be included in the collection.

Using the Forms Collection to Unload All Forms

Another way to use collections and looping is to unload all desired forms by using the collection. This method provides an easy way to step through the collection and unload all members of the collection.

Although looping through the Forms Collection to unload all members might seem like a long way to do the task, it does demonstrate how collections behave. The END statement would be a much faster way of ending the application.

The following code shows how the looping must be controlled. The collection total must be taken first and then reduced by 1 to accommodate for item 0. The collection members are unloaded from the highest member to the lowest. This is due to the collection adjusting the members to fill any space in the collection:

```
Sub cmdClose_Click()
    Dim iLoop As Integer
    For iLoop = Forms.Count - 1 To 0 Step - 1
        Unload Forms(iLoop)
    Next iLoop
End Sub
```

This code assumes at least one form has been loaded in the collection and a command button named cmdClose is on a form. Once run, all forms should be unloaded and the project will terminate if no other forms are in memory.

Exercises

Exercise 1.1: Loading and Unloading Forms

In this exercise, you create a two-form project that will load and unload forms. The Forms Count method will also be used to show the forms that are loaded. This exercise will also show how unloaded form code stays resident in memory.

To create this project, follow these steps:

1. Create a Standard EXE project.

2. Add a second form to the project.

3. On Form1 create five command buttons.

4. Change the Command1 button caption to Show Form2.

5. Open the code window for the Show Form2 button on Form1 and enter the following code:

```
Sub Command1_Click()
    Form2.Show
End Sub
```

6. Change the Command2 button caption to Count Forms.

7. Open the code window for the Count Forms button on Form1 and enter the following code:

```
Sub Command2_Click()
    MsgBox "The Forms Collection contains " & Forms.Count &
    ➥" loaded forms."
End Sub
```

8. Change the Command3 button caption to Unload Form2.

9. Open the code window for the Unload Form2 button on Form1 and enter the following code:

```
Sub Command3_Click()
    Unload Form2
End Sub
```

continues

10. Change the `Command4` button caption to `Form2.Test`.

11. Open the code window for the `Form2.Test` button on `Form1` and enter the following code:

```
Sub Command4_Click()
    Form2.Test
End Sub
```

12. Change the `Command5` button caption to `Form2.Caption`.

13. Open the code window for the `Form2.Caption` button on `Form1` and enter the following code:

```
Sub Command5_Click()
    Form2.Caption = "Hello World"
End Sub
```

14. Open the code window for `Form2`. Under the General Declaration section, enter the following code:

```
Public Sub Test()
    Msgbox "Code from Form2"
End Sub
```

15. Run the project.

16. Click on the `Show Form2` button. `Form2` should be displayed with nothing on it.

17. Return to `Form1` and click the `Count Forms` button. The message box should indicate that the Forms Collection contains two loaded Forms.

18. Click on the `Unload Form2` button. `Form2` should be unloaded from memory at this point.

19. Click on the `Count Forms` button. The message box should indicate that the Forms Collection contains one loaded form.

20. Click on the `Form2.Test` button. The message box should indicate the message `Code from Form2`. Remember that `Form2` has been unloaded at this point.

21. Click on the `Count Forms` button to see how many forms are currently loaded.

22. When the message box appears, it indicates that only one form has been loaded. Procedures are not unloaded from forms. It is only programmatic reference to the form's properties that will cause the load to occur.

23. Click on the `Form2.Caption` button. This will reference `Form2`'s `Caption` property and set it to `"Hello World"`.

24. Click on the `Count Forms` button. The message box should indicate that the Forms Collection has two loaded forms, although `Form2` is not visible.

25. Close `Form1`. Notice that the VB environment is still in runtime. This is due to `Form2` being loaded, but not shown.

26. Press the End button to end the application.

This exercise demonstrated how loading and unloading forms is performed and the effect that unloading has on form-level code. The Forms Collection was used to prove how many forms were present in memory.

Exercise 1.2: Creating and Removing Forms at Runtime

In this exercise, you create a design-time `Form` object. That object will act as the template to create multiple instances of the form at runtime.

To create this project, follow these steps:

1. Create a Standard EXE project.

2. Change `Form1`'s caption to `Create a New Form`.

3. Add a command button to `Form1`.

4. Change the `Command1` button caption to `Add Form`.

continues

5. Open the code window for the Add Form button on Form1 and enter the following code:

```
Sub Command1_Click()
    Static iCount As Integer
    Dim x As New Form2
    iCount = iCount + 1
    x.Caption = "Form" & iCount
    x.Show
End Sub
```

6. Add a second form to the project.

7. Add a command button to Form2.

8. On Form2, change the Command1 button caption to Unload Me.

9. Open the code window for the Command1 button on Form2 and enter the following code:

```
Sub Command1_Click()
    Unload Me
End Sub
```

10. Run the project.

11. Move Form1 to the top-right corner of the screen. This will allow the new forms to be created and not be placed right on top of Form1.

12. Click on the Add Form button from Form1.

13. You should see a new Form with the Caption of Form1, and the form has an Unload Me button.

14. Click on the Add Form button to create as many new runtime forms as you want.

15. When you want to remove a runtime form, just click the Unload Me button of the selected form.

16. Close the Create a New Form window. Notice that if you have other form windows, Visual Basic remains in Runtime mode. Each form must be individually unloaded.

17. On the VB toolbar, use the End button to stop the application and remove all runtime forms.

This exercise demonstrated how to create a design-time Form template object and create a new runtime Form object based on that template. It also covered how to remove runtime instances of the Form object.

Exercise 1.3: Using the Forms Collection

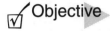 **Objective**

In this exercise, you use the Forms Collection to return information about the forms that have been loaded.

To create this project, use the following steps:

1. Create a Standard EXE project.

2. Add three additional new forms. There should be a total of four forms.

3. Add four command buttons to Form1.

4. Change Command1's button caption to Count Forms.

5. Change Command2's button caption to Show Forms.

6. Change Command3's button caption to Set Captions.

7. Change Command4's button caption to End.

8. Open the code window for Count Forms and enter the following code:

```
Sub Command1_Click()
    MsgBox "The Forms Collection contains " & Forms.Count &
    ➥" loaded forms."
End Sub
```

9. Open the code window for Show Forms and enter the following code:

```
Sub Command2_Click()
```

continues

```
        Form2.Show
        Form3.Show
    End Sub
```

10. Open the code window for Set Captions and enter the following code:

```
Sub Command3_Click()
    Dim iLoop as Integer
    For iLoop = 0 to Forms.Count - 1
        Forms(iLoop).Caption = "I have set Form" & iLoop &
        ➡"'s caption."
    Next iLoop
End Sub
```

11. Open the code window for End and enter the following code:

```
Sub Command4_Click()
    End
End Sub
```

12. Run the project.

13. Move Form1 to the top-right corner of the screen. This will allow the new forms to be created and not be placed right on top of Form1.

14. Click on Count Forms. A message box should indicate that the Forms Collection has only one form.

15. Click on Show Forms. Forms 2 and 3 should now be loaded and displayed, but Form 4 has not been loaded.

16. Click on Count Forms. A message box should indicate that the Forms Collection now has three forms. Form 4 was not loaded and is not part of the collection.

17. Click on Set Captions. This should loop through all forms in the collection, starting at item 0 and increasing to the total amount of forms. Each form should now have a caption with its item number as part of the form name.

18. Click on End and the keyword END will close all forms and end the application.

This exercise demonstrated using the Forms Collection to count the total amount of loaded forms and use an item number to set a specific form's properties.

Exercise 1.4:   Using Runtime Forms and the Forms Collection

 **Objective**

In this exercise, you create runtime forms and use the Forms Collection to control them. Only one form will be created. The form will have three command buttons. The first command button will create a new runtime form based on the design-time form, frmTest. The second command button will use the form's Count property and generate a message indicating how many forms are currently loaded. The third command button will be used to count the total number of forms in the collection and then unload the forms starting from the highest number and counting down to item 0 in the Forms Collection.

To create this project, follow these steps:

1. Create a Standard EXE project.

2. Change the Name property of Form1 to frmTest.

3. Change the Caption property of frmTest to Test Form 0.

4. Create three command buttons on frmTest and ensure they have the following names:

   ▶ The first command button should be named Command1.

   ▶ The second command button should be named Command2.

   ▶ The third command button should be named Command3.

5. Change the Command1 button caption to Create Form.

continues

6. Open the code window for `Create Form` and type the following:

```
Sub Command1_Click()
    Dim x As New frmTest
    x.Caption = "Test Form" & Forms.Count
    x.Show
End Sub
```

7. Change the `Command2` button caption to `Count Forms`.

8. Open the code window for `Count Forms` and type the following:

```
Sub Command2_Click()
    MsgBox "The Forms Collection contains " & Forms.Count &
    ➥" loaded forms."
End Sub
```

9. Change the `Command3` button caption to `Unload Forms`.

10. Open the code window for `Unload Forms` and type the following:

```
Sub Command3_Click()
    Dim iLoop As Integer
    For iLoop = Forms.Count - 1 To 0 Step - 1
        Unload Forms(iLoop)
    Next iLoop
End Sub
```

11. Run the project.

12. Click on the `Create Form` button. A new runtime form should be created. You can create as many new runtime forms as you like.

13. Click on the `Count Forms` button. A message box will produce a message listing the total count of loaded forms in the collection. Add more forms with `Create Form`, and then use `Count Forms` to see the count.

14. Click on the Unload Forms button. (All loaded forms will be unloaded from the collection one by one.) The project should End after pressing this command button. It will end because all forms will be unloaded.

15. Use the End toolbar button in VB, if required.

This exercise demonstrated how to create runtime forms and use the Forms Collection to unload all forms.

Review Questions

1. In the following code, which statement best describes the order of events that happen after this line of code is executed? Assume a VB project with two forms, `Form1` and `Form2`. `Form1` is the `startup` object.

```
Sub Command1_Click()
    Form2.Caption = "Visual Basic Notes"
End Sub
```

   A. When executed, the code will generate `Compile Error: Variable not defined`.

   B. `Form2` is automatically loaded, the caption is set, and `Form2` is shown.

   C. `Form2` is automatically loaded, the caption is set, and `Form2` is not shown.

   D. `Form2` is automatically loaded, the caption is set, and `Form2` is automatically unloaded.

   E. When executed, the code will generate `Compile Error: Method or data member not found`.

2. Visual Basic allows a form to be loaded into memory without directly displaying the form. Which statement can be used to load a form without showing it?

   A. `Load`

   B. `Unload`

   C. `Show`

   D. `Hide`

   E. `Dim`

3. In the following code, which statement best describes the order of events that occur while this code is executing? Assume that the project contains two forms, and that this procedure is in the `Load` event of the startup `Form` object.

```
Sub Form_Load()
    frmSplash.Show
    frmMain.Show
    Unload frmSplash
End Sub
```

A. The `Splash` form shows, `Main` form shows, `Splash` form unloads.

B. The `Splash` form loads, `Main` form loads, `Splash` form unloads.

C. The `Splash` form loads and shows, `Main` form loads and shows and causes a compile-time error.

D. The `Splash` form loads and shows, `Main` form loads and shows, `Splash` form unloads.

E. The `Splash` form shows, `Main` form shows, `Splash` form causes a compile-time error.

4. Visual Basic allows a `Form` object to be removed from the screen, but allows it to stay loaded in memory. This allows other components of the application to refer to controls, properties, and methods of the form. Which statement in VB will remove a form from view, but keep it in memory?

   A. `Load`

   B. `Unload`

   C. `Dim`

   D. `Show`

   E. `Hide`

5. Form objects can be loaded into memory and used by an application. Using the following code, what type of loading is being performed by VB?

```
Sub Main()
    frmSetup.Show
End Sub
```

A. Forced

B. Manual

C. Implicit

D. Inferred

E. Explicit

6. A VB application can define the very first object used when the program is run. This is referred to as the `startUp` object. Where in the VB IDE can the project's `startUp` object be specified?

A. Project, Components

B. Project, Project Properties

C. Project, References

D. Tools, Options

E. Tools, Settings

7. An application can create `Form` objects dynamically at runtime. To create dynamic forms, a `Form` object must be used as the template for the new object. What is the keyword used to create a dynamic runtime form based on another `Form` object?

A. `Me`

B. `The`

C. `Object`

D. `New`

E. `Option`

8. From the following code, select all lines that would create a form at runtime based on a design-time `Form` object template called `frmMainTemplate`. Assume that the project `startup` object is a `Sub Main` procedure and that this line of code will create the first form.

   A. `Dim frmMainTemplate as frmMainTemplate`

   B. `Dim frmMainTemplate as New frmMainTemplate`

   C. `Set x as frmMainTemplate`

   D. `Dim x as New frmMainTemplate`

   E. `Set x = New frmMainTemplate`

9. When a `Form` object is created dynamically at runtime, all properties, methods, and events will be usable. What keyword can be used to refer to the active object rather than the object name?

   A. Me

   B. Friend

   C. You

   D. Var

   E. None of these

10. VB allows a set of similar objects to be grouped together. This allows easier access to the similar objects and also simplifies program code that can affect all members of the group. What is the term used to describe this function grouping?

   A. Friends

   B. Enemies

   C. Procedures

   D. Scopes

   E. Collections

11. Groups of objects simplify control and provide common functions. Which are groups of objects found within Visual Basic?

    A. Variables

    B. Friends

    C. Controls

    D. Variants

    E. Forms

12. When a collection is created in Visual Basic, a property can be used to determine how many objects are in the collection. What property is used to determine this number?

    A. Number

    B. Item

    C. Total

    D. Count

    E. Base

13. The following code sample is missing a line of code. This code is to be used to unload all forms from the Forms Collection. Which line of code will complete this sub procedure best? Assume that the project contains six forms and that this procedure is in a command button on one of the forms:

```
Sub cmdClose_Click()
    Dim iLoop As Integer
    xxxx
        Unload Forms(iLoop)
    Next iLoop
End Sub
```

A. `For iLoop = 0 To Forms.Count Step + 1`

B. `For iLoop = 0 To Forms.Count - 1`

C. `For iLoop = Forms.Count To 0`

D. `For iLoop = Forms.Count - 1 To 0 Step - 1`

E. `For iLoop = Forms.Count To 0 Step - 1`

Answers to Review Questions

1. C. Any reference to an object will cause an implied load in Visual Basic. After `Form2` has been loaded, the `Caption` property is set. The form has been referenced, but the `Show` method was not executed. This form will remain loaded but not shown. For more information, see the section titled "Loading and Unloading Forms."

2. A, D. The `Load` statement can be used to explicitly load a `Form` object into memory. If the `Hide` method of the form is used, an implied `Load` would happen first followed directly by hiding the form. Both could provide the desired result of loading a form into memory. For more information, see the section titled "Loading and Unloading Forms."

3. D. Before a form can be shown it must be loaded into memory. Although the `Load` statement has not been used to explicitly load the form, the `Show` method uses implied loading. This allows the form to be directly shown to the user. The proper order of events would be to load the form, and then show the form. After the two forms are shown, the `Splash` form is then unloaded. For more information, see the section titled "Showing and Hiding a Form."

4. E. The `Hide` statement can be used to remove a `form` object from the screen view, but keep it loaded in memory. The `Unload` statement will remove it from the screen, but will also remove it from memory. For more information, see the section titled "Showing and Hiding a Form."

5. C. If an explicit Load statement is not used before using an object, Visual Basic uses implicit loading. Any programmatic reference to an object will cause that object to be loaded into memory. For more information, see the section titled "Loading and Unloading Forms."

6. B. To specify the startup object of a VB project, the VB IDE provides the Project, Project Properties dialog boxes. The startup object combo box can be found under the General tab. The menu selection Tools, Options is where the startup form could be selected in Visual Basic 4.0. For more information, see the section titled "Loading and Unloading Forms."

7. D. The keyword New is used to create a runtime Form object based on a template form. This instructs VB to create another new object based on the object name following the New keyword. For more information, see the section titled "Creating a Runtime Form."

8. B, D. When dimensioning an object variable it can have any name you choose. The key is to Dim 'var' as New object. The New keyword will create a runtime object from the object name following New. Both answers are correct, but both use a different object variable name. For more information, see the section titled "Creating a Runtime Form."

9. A. The keyword used to refer to the active runtime object is ME. Instead of using the object name, the more generic keyword ME can be used to control and manipulate the active object. Friends are a special type of procedure and are not used for object reference. For more information, see the section titled "Removing Runtime Forms."

10. E. Visual Basic allows groups of similar objects to be used together in a collection. A Friend is a special type of procedure. Procedures are a generic term to classify code. Scope is used to refer to the lifetime of a variable or procedure. These are not related to collections. For more information, see the section titled "Using the Forms Collection."

11. C, E. Similar objects that are grouped together are referred to as collections. Visual Basic provides the Control and form intrinsic collections to keep the similar objects together. Friends are a type of procedures. For more information, see the section titled "Using the Forms Collection."

12. D. The method of a collection used to determine how many objects are in the collection is Count. As objects are added, the Count property is used to keep track of the loaded objects. The Count property is included by default in new collections. Other methods can be programmed in, if required. For more information, see the section titled "Using Methods and Properties of the Forms Collection."

13. D. When the Form Count property is used, it returns that total amount of loaded forms in the collection. This number starts at 1. The collection's first item starts at 0. Therefore you must take the total number of forms ñ 1 and count down to 0. The Step ñ 1 is used to have the for loop count down by one. All other code will produce a subscript out of range error. Collections will always start at 0 and as items are removed, other items are reorganized to lower numbers. Collections require removing the highest number and working down to the lowest. For more information, see the section titled "Using the Forms Collection to Unload All Forms."

Answers to Test Yourself Questions at Beginning of Chapter

1. The name for a control that can "host" other controls is a container control. The container control will allow other controls to be placed on top of itself. This allows the designer more effective groupings of controls as well as allowing the controls to all be affected at the same time. The `Form` control and the `Picture` control are both examples of the container type of control. See "Form Basics."

2. The `Load` statement and `Show` statement will both load a `Form` object into memory. `Load` will load the form, but not show it. `Show` will automatically load the form and display the form onscreen. Another way to load a form into memory is to simply refer to that form. Any programmatic reference to a `Form` object will force VB to load the indicated form. See "Loading and Unloading Forms."

3. The `Unload` method will remove a form from memory. When the form is reloaded, all controls contained on the form will be re-initialized. Therefore the `Hide` method would allow the `Options` form to be set by the user, hide it from the display, and still allow the programmatic reference to the controls as set by the user. See "Showing and Hiding a Form."

4. When forms are created then saved, two files can be generated. The first file is an ASCII text file with an .FRM extension that contains information related to the form, the form's objects, properties of the objects, and any source code for those objects. The second file is a binary file that contains graphic information related to the form. If a picture control is used, an .FRX file will contain the graphics information required by the control. See "Design-Time Storage of `Form` Objects."

5. The keyword used to reference the currently running object is ME. This enables the programmer to reference multiple instances without having to worry about design-time names and runtime object variables. If the design-time name were used, that would be the only object that would be affected. See "Removing Runtime Forms."

6. The keyword used to create a runtime version of an object created at design time is NEW. An object variable is dimensioned as a NEW object. This tells VB to create another instance of the Form object at run time. The following code demonstrates this syntax.

```
Dim x as New Form1.
```

See "Creating a Runtime Form."

7. The Forms Collection contains references to forms that are loaded into memory from both design time and runtime. If a project contains multiple forms, but they are not loaded into memory, the Forms Collection will not contain those form references. See "Using the Forms Collection."

8. The Visual Basic Forms Collection has only one property called `Count`. It returns the total number of forms that have been loaded into memory. See "Using Methods and Properties of the Forms Collection."

9. The collection provides an item number that is an ordinal value assigned to individual objects as they are added to the collection. By using the item number, the programmer can access individual forms and their associated properties for programmatic control. The following code demonstrates using the ordinal item number:

```
Msgbox Forms(1).Caption.
```

See "Using Specific Items Within the Forms Collection."

C h a p t e r

2

Implementing Drag-and-Drop Operations Within the Windows Shell and Using Specific Events

This chapter helps you prepare for the exam by covering the following objectives:

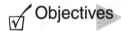 Objectives

- ▶ Implement traditional drag-and-drop operations within the Microsoft Windows shell

- ▶ Add code to the appropriate form event, such as `Initialize, Terminate, Load, Unload, QueryUnload, Activate`, and `Deactivate`

Test Yourself! Before reading this chapter, test yourself to determine how much study time you will need to devote to this section.

1. When a form is shown into memory, which events are fired as the form is loaded and displayed? The following statements are used to load and show the form:

```
Dim x as object
Set x = new form1
x.show
```

2. You have written code in drag-and-drop events that implement drag-and-drop between two list boxes. You need to add code that provides visual cues during drag-and-drop operations. Which event is most appropriate?

3. As the user switches between your application and different Windows applications, which events are fired to notify the form that it loses focus?

4. The DragMode property is used to notify a control to do what?

5. When is the DragOver event fired?

Answers are located at the end of the chapter...

Many Windows applications provide drag-and-drop support to augment the traditional user interface. The Windows desktop, for example, enables the developer to drag and drop a file or folder onto a different folder, resulting in a move operation. The same task can be accomplished by using the DOS prompt or menu items in Explorer. Drag-and-drop closely mimics real-world tasks. Your applications are not required to implement drag-and-drop; however, it makes the application easy to use and more intuitive.

The drag-and-drop operation consists of two phases: the dragging of a item from a source object, and the dropping of an item onto a target object. The *source* is the control, object, or item being dragged. The *target* is the control, object, or item onto which the source is dropped. Visual Basic 5 has two types of drag-and-drop: drag-and-drop within your application, and OLE drag-and-drop. Implementing the two types of drag-and-drop operations in Visual Basic is relatively easy; however, the provided methods and events differ.

You must consider the following factors when deciding on the type of drag-and-drop operation to use in your application:

- ▶ If the data involved in the drag-and-drop operation is primarily data stored in a control's property, traditional drag-and-drop is the best choice. This is valid only if your application will not receive or send dropped data from other applications. Traditional drag-and-drop as implemented by Visual Basic can receive drop data only from controls within the same application.

- ▶ If the target object is a control in the same application instance as the source object, traditional drag-and-drop makes the most sense. If, however, the target can be an object external to your application, OLE drag-and-drop is a better choice.

- ▶ What is the source object when your application is the target? If your application is expecting to receive dropped items from a source other than itself, you should implement OLE drag-and-drop rather than traditional drag-and-drop.

This chapter covers the following topics:

▶ Implementing traditional drag-and-drop support in applications

▶ Managing form events

Implementing Traditional Drag-and-Drop Support in Applications

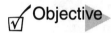 Objective

Most controls provide support for traditional drag-and-drop operations. This means that they provide methods, properties, and events for implementing drag-and-drop. The traditional drag-and-drop support provides two types of drag modes: Automatic and Manual. These drag modes can be set at runtime or design time.

The `DragMode` property is used to control the drag mode. If the `DragMode` property is set to Manual—which is the default—the `Drag` method is needed to start the dragging operation. If the `DragMode` is set to Automatic, a drag-and-drop operation is automatically invoked when the source control is clicked. The following statement enables you to use the `DragMode` property:

```
[control name].DragMode = vbAutomatic
```

The `control name` parameter is the name of the control. It is important to note that a control cannot receive other mouse or keyboard events while it is being dragged.

In addition to the `DragMode` property, each control has a `Drag` method. The `Drag` method is used to start, stop, or cancel the dragging operation. The `Drag` method is valuable only when the `DragMode` is set to Manual. The syntax for the `Drag` method is as follows:

```
[control name].Drag action
```

The `action` parameter can have one of the following three values:

▶ `vbCancel` A value of `vbCancel` cancels the dragging operation.

▶ vbBeginDrag   A value of vbBeginDrag starts the dragging operation.

▶ vbEndDrag   A value of vbEndDrag ends the dragging operation.

Drag Events

Two drag events help controls to respond to drag-and-drop operations. These events are the DragDrop and DragOver events. The DragDrop event occurs when a drag-and-drop operation is completed from dragging a control over the target control and *dropping* the control by using the mouse button or the Drag method. The DragDrop event is defined as follows:

*controlname*_DragDrop(source As Control, x As Single, y As Single)

The source variable is a pointer to a control that was dropped onto the target control. This variable is very useful if you want to accept source controls of a specific type only. An example of this is as follows:

```
Sub txtTarget_DragDrop(source As Control, x As Single, y As
➥Single)
        If typeof source Is textbox Then
                txtTarget.text = source.text
        End if
End Sub
```

The x and y variables contain the location within the target control where the source control was dropped. The location is always expressed in terms of the target control's coordinate system, using the ScaleHeight, ScaleWidth, ScaleLeft, and ScaleTop properties.

The DragOver event occurs after the drag-and-drop operation is in progress. This event can be used to provide visual cues to the user which indicate that the source can be dropped or not dropped onto the target. The event is defined as follows:

```
Private Sub object_DragOver(source As Control, x As Single, y As
➥Single, state As Integer)
```

The source variable is the control from which the data is coming. The x and y variables provide the location within the target control from which the object was dropped. The state variable is used to determine whether the control is being dragged into or out of the target control. This helps by providing visual cues when the dragged item is over the target control. You might change the Mouse icon when the mouse is over the target, for example, and control and change it when the mouse leaves the target control. The following code snippet demonstrates this:

```
Private Sub Text1_DragOver(source As Control, x As Single, y As
➥Single, state As Integer)
    If state = vbEnter Then
    source.DragIcon = LoadPicture("Drop.ico")
    Else
    source.DragIcon = LoadPicture("NoDrop.ico")
    End If
End Sub
```

Changing the Drag Icon

As the drag-and-drop operation proceeds, it is necessary to change the drag icon to provide visual cues to the user. The `drag icon` property can be changed at runtime or design time. The icon can be set at runtime by using the `LoadPicture` function or the `ExtractIcon` method from an `ImageList` collection. The `TreeView` control provides a method called `CreateDragImage`. This method returns a drag icon based on the mode image that is displayed. The following code provides examples of changing the drag icon:

```
txtData.DragIcon = LoadPicture("mydata.ico")
trvView.DragIcon = ImgIcons.ListImages("DragIcon").ExtractIcon
```

Creating a Drag-and-Drop Window

Most standard controls in Visual Basic support drag-and-drop operations. The most common implementation, however, is between list boxes. The Chap2 directory on the CD-ROM contains a sample application, called main.vbp, that demonstrates drag-and-drop between list boxes. The implementation of drag-and-drop can be subdivided into the following two tasks:

▶ Providing visual cues

▶ Responding to drop events

Providing Visual Cues

Visual cues should be provided to a user as the drag-and-drop operation commences. The source control is the first cue that should be provided as the user starts the dragging operation. The `DragIcon` property of the source control is used to determine which icon is used. In this example, the drag icon of the source is set in the `Form_Load` event of the main form. This event is shown as follows:

```
Private Sub Form_Load()
    'Set the Drag icon of the control
    lstOrginal.DragIcon = imgList.ListImages("DRAG").ExtractIcon
End Sub
```

After the drag operation commences with the `lstOrginal` list box as the source, the drag icon from the image list will be used. After dragging has commenced, you may not want the user to drop the dragged item onto certain controls or the form. Your application code can prevent this. You should, however, provide a visual cue to the user to notify him that dropping of the item is not permitted. A common technique is to set the Mouse icon to a No Drop icon.

As the user moves the mouse over a control during a drag operation, the `DragOver` event is fired for the control. The `DragOver` event can be used to change the `DragIcon` property and provide visual cues. The `DragOver` event of the `lstDestination` control is as follows:

```
Private Sub lstDestination_DragOver(Source As Control, X As ○
    ⮕Single, Y As Single, State As Integer)
    'If entering the control then change the icon to drop
    If State = vbEnter Then
        Source.DragIcon = imgList.ListImages("DROP").ExtractIcon
    ElseIf State = vbLeave Then
```

```
'If exiting the control then change the icon to no drop
Source.DragIcon =
➥imgList.ListImages("NODROP").ExtractIcon
        End If
        End Sub
```

The state variable is used to determine whether the user is entering the control or exiting the control. If the user's mouse is *entering* the control, the drag icon of the source is changed to the Drop icon. If the user's mouse is *exiting* the control, the drag icon of the source is changed to a No Drop icon—this means that if the mouse is over the form, the user sees an icon that tells him he cannot drop his data here. Figures 2.1, 2.2, and 2.3 show the different states the Mouse icon goes through during a drag operation.

Figure 2.1

The Mouse icon after the drag operation commences.

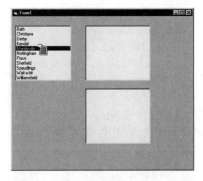

Figure 2.2

The Mouse icon during the drag operation and over the form.

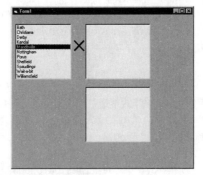

Responding to Drop Events

After the user drops an item onto a target, the user expects some task to be performed. The task itself can vary widely and is based primarily on the relationship between the source and target controls. The task behind dropping an item may result in opening a database connection and copying records, for example. The DragDrop event provides the opportunity to carry out the task. The source parameter supplied as part of the DragDrop event can be used to extract the information needed from the source control. The following code provides an example of this:

```
Private Sub lstDestination_DragDrop(Source As Control, X As
➥Single, Y As Single)
    If Source Is lstOrginal Then
        If Source.ListIndex > -1 Then
            lstDestination.AddItem Source.List(Source.ListIndex)
            Source.RemoveItem Source.ListIndex
        End If
    End If
End Sub
```

To prevent errors, the type of the source control should always be verified. The data from the source control (which is a list box) is copied to the target control (lstDestination is also a list box).

Figure 2.3

The Mouse icon during the drag operation and over a control that can accept the source.

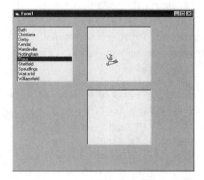

Understanding OLE Drag-and-Drop Support in Visual Basic

Objective

In Visual Basic 5, your applications can accept and send items to other applications by using OLE drag-and-drop. OLE drag-and-drop uses services provided by the Object Linking and Embedding libraries. The aim of OLE drag-and-drop is to provide standard mechanisms to pass data between applications—when a user drags items from one application and drops those items on other applications. With OLE drag-and-drop, you can send and receive much richer data. You could, for example, send a picture or a file during a drag-and-drop operation. With traditional drag-and-drop, you are limited to sending or receiving controls.

Implementing OLE drag-and-drop is very similar to traditional drag-and-drop; basically, a relationship exists between a source and a target. New events have been added to Visual Basic 5 to support OLE drag-and-drop. Table 2.1 lists these events.

Table 2.1

OLE Drag-and-Drop Events

Event Name	Description
OLECompleteDrag (Effect As Long)	Fired when a source object is dropped onto the target. The source is informed with this event to denote whether the drag operation was performed or canceled.
OLEDragDrop(Data As ComctlLib. DataObject, Effect As Long, Button As Integer, Shift As Integer, x As Single, y As Single)	Fired when the source object is dropped onto a target.
OLEDragOver(Data As ComctlLib. DataObject, Effect As Long, Button As Integer, Shift As Integer, x As Single, y As Single, State As Integer)	Fired on the target when its source object is dragged over the control.
OLEGiveFeedback(Effect As Long, DefaultCursors As Boolean)	Fired after the OLEDragOver event. It allows the source to provide visual feedback to the user to indicate what operation will be performed when the user drops the object.
OLESetData(Data As ComctlLib. DataObject, DataFormat As Integer)	Fired on the source object when the target called the GetData method of the source's DataObject. This event is fired when the data for a specified format is not loaded.

Event Name	Description
OLEStartDrag(Data As ComctlLib. DataObject, AllowedEffects As Long)	Fired when the source OLEDrag method is called on, when the OLE drag-and-drop operation is performed, and when the OLEDragMode is set to Automatic. This event is also used to define the data formats and the drop effects that are supported by the source.

As you can see from the table, the implementation of OLE drag-and-drop provides more events than the traditional drop-and-drop approach. In addition to the basic DragDrop and DragOver events, new events notify the start of a drag operation and the event for providing feedback to the client application.

Methods and Properties

In addition to the events shown earlier, you are provided methods and properties to manage the OLEDrag operation. The OLEDrag method has been added. This method aids in the development of OLE drag-and-drop. These methods enable you to manage when an OLE drag-and-drop operation starts.

The OLEDrag method is defined as follows:

```
objectName.OLEDrag
```

The method carries no parameters. When this method is called, the OLEStartDrag event is fired. This allows the source to provide the data needed for the drag operation.

New properties also facilitate the OLE drag-and-drop operations. These properties are OleDropMode, OleDropAllowed, and OLEDragMode.

The OLEDropMode property returns or sets how the target handles the drop operation. The property can have any one of the following values:

▶ vbOLEDropNone   This is the default. The target will not accept OLE drop operations and displays the NO drop cursor.

> ▶ `vbOLEDropManual`   The target component will fire the OLE drop events when the OLE drop operations occur.

> ▶ `vbOLEDropAutomatic`   The target will not fire the OLE drop events and will automatically accept OLE drops if the `DataObject` supplied is in a format it accepts.

The `OLEDropAllowed` property is used to set or return a value that denotes whether the OLE container control can be a drop target. If set to True, the control can receive dropped items. You can drag a Word document from the Windows desktop onto the OLE container control, for example, which would in turn open the document in the control.

The `OLEDragMode` is used to determine whether the programmer or the control is handling the OLE drag-and-drop operation. The `OLEDragMode` property can have one of the two following values:

> ▶ `vbOLEDragManual`   The programmer will handle the OLE drag-and-drop operation.

> ▶ `vbOLEDragAutomatic`   The component will handle all the OLE drag-and-drop operations automatically.

The `DataObject` Object

The `DataObject` is a new object used to represent the data and formats that can be dropped or dragged during a drag-and-drop operation. The `DataObject` is a Visual Basic mirror of the `IDataObject` interface provided in OLE. The objects are an application-independent container for transferring data from a source to a target. The data is stored in a format using methods of the `DataObject`. This `DataObject` object has only one property, called `Files`. The `Files` property is a collection of the type `DataObjectFiles`. The property stores the filenames involved in the drag operation. This usually occurs when the user drags objects to and from the Windows shell. The `DataObjectFiles` collection behaves like a standard Visual Basic collection, but only allows files to be added to its collection.

The `DataObject` has methods that manage the data and format that the `DataObject` holds. Table 2.2 lists these methods.

Table 2.2

Methods of the `DataObject` Object

Method	Description
Clear	Clears the data stored in the `DataObject`.
GetData	Returns data as a variant from the `DataObject`.
GetFormat	Returns a Boolean denoting whether the data in the `DataObject` supports a specific format.
SetData	Inserts data into a `DataObject` using a specific data form.

The GetData method and the SetData method require more explanation. The following sections discuss these methods in greater detail.

The `GetData` Method

During the drag operation, most OLE drag-and-drop events will supply a `DataObject`. In many cases, you need to extract the data from the `DataObject` supplied in the event. The data can be extracted by using the `GetData` method. The `GetData` method is defined as follows:

```
object.GetData (format)
```

The format variable can be a custom format or a predefined standard format. These format types are defined using the constants shown in Table 2.3.

Table 2.3

Constants for the `GetData` Method

Constant	Description
vbCFBitmap	Bitmap (.bmp files)
vbCFDIB	Device-independent bitmap (DIB)

continues

Table 2.3 Continued

Constant	Description
vbCFEMetafile	Enhanced metafile (.emf files)
vbCFFiles	List of files
vbCFMetafile	Metafile (.wmf files)
vbCFPalette	Color palette
vbCFRTF	Rich Text Format (.rtf files)
vbCFText	Text (.txt files)

If the DataObject does not extract the format that is requested, then no data is returned.

The SetData Method

When your application is the target application, you must set the DataObject with the data and the formats that are supported. The SetData method is used to perform this task. The syntax of the SetData method is as follows:

```
object.SetData [data], [format]
```

The data parameter is the data that you want to send to a different application. The format is a constant, as shown in Table 2.3, that denotes the format you want to specify. If you need to specify multiple formats, you can call the DataObject's SetData method multiple times as shown here:

```
DataObject.SetData "Text data", vbCFText
DataObject.SetData "somebitmapfile.bmp" vbCFBitmap
```

Implementing OLE Drag-and-Drop Features in Visual Basic

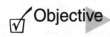

Objective The tasks involved in implementing OLE drag-and-drop in Visual Basic can be broken down into the following three main tasks:

▶ Providing visual cues

▶ Providing data formats

▶ Responding to events as a source and a target

Providing Visual Cues

Visual cues are controlled by using the parameters supplied during certain events. Unlike traditional drag-and-drop, no OLE drag icon can be controlled by the developer. You can specify only the mouse effect that the user will see, not the icon itself. When the drag operation begins, the target has an opportunity to specify which types of effects are allowed in the OleStartDrag event. The event provides a parameter called AllowedEffects that is used by the target to define the effects that can be used with the target during the drag operation. Table 2.4 lists the values for the AllowedEffects parameters.

Table 2.4

Drop Effects	
Drop Effect	Description
vbDropEffectNone	Drop target cannot accept the data.
vbDropEffectCopy	A drop will result in a copy of the data.
vbDropEffectMove	A drop will result in a moving of data from target to source.

A example of implementing this is shown as follows:

```
Private Sub lstOrginal_OLEStartDrag(Data As DataObject,
➥AllowedEffects As Long)
    'Check if a actual item is selected
    If lstOrginal.ListIndex < 0 Then
        Exit Sub
    End If
    'Set the data
    Data.SetData lstOrginal.List(lstOrginal.ListIndex)
    'Set the effects supported
    AllowedEffects = vbDropEffectCopy
End Sub
```

Providing Data Formats

When providing OLE drag-and-drop operations, you can define the data formats supported by your target by using the DataObject. In most cases, your applications will only provide one data format; however, you can use existing data formats or even custom ones.

When the drop operation starts, one of the first events fired is the OLEStartDrag event. In this event, you can set the data and the supported formats. An example of this is shown in the following code:

```
DataObject.SetData "Text data", vbCFText
DataObject.SetData "somebitmapfile.bmp" vbCFBitmap
```

Responding to Events as a Source

The source has to respond to events as the OLE drag-and-drop operation proceeds. The first event of note is the StartDrag event. In this event, the source is allowed to set the data, format, and the drag effects for the drag operation. The event is defined as follows:

```
Private Sub object_StartDrag(Data As DataObject, allowedeffects
➥As Long)
```

When the item is dropped onto a target, the OLECompleteDrag event is fired. This event can notify the source that the item was copied, moved, or not accepted. The event has a parameter called effect, which contains a value that denotes the effect of the drop. The event is defined as follows:

```
Private Sub object_CompleteDrag([effect As Long])
```

If the target requests a specific format that is not loaded, the source's OLESetData event will be fired. This usually occurs when the target calls the GetData method on a DataObject supplied from the source. The OLESetData allows the source to provide the data in the DataObject for the target. The event is defined as follows:

```
Private Sub object_OLESetData(Data As DataObject, DataFormat As
➥Integer)
```

The `DataFormat` parameter is used to denote the `DataFormat` request-ed by the target. The `Data` parameter is the `DataObject` that will contain the data requested.

Responding to Events as a Target

As a target, your perspective is a bit different because you are re-ceiving dropped items. The targets use three primary events to manage OLE drag-and-drop: `OLEDragDrop`, `OLEDragOver`, and `OLEGiveFeedback`. `OLEDragOver` occurs as the user moves an OLE dragged item over the target. The target has the opportunity in this event to decide how to respond. The event is defined as fol-lows:

```
Private Sub object_OLEDragOver(Data As DataObject,
                        Effect As Long,
                        Button As Integer,
                        Shift As Integer,
                        X As Single,
                        Y As Single,
                        State As Integer)
```

The `Data` parameter is the `DataObject`, and can be used to deter-mine what format is being supported. The `Effect` parameter can be changed by the target to denote whether it will or will not ac-cept the data. The `Button`, `Shift`, `X`, and `Y` parameters are used to denote the mouse state and position. The `State` parameter will denote that the mouse was entering, leaving, or moving within the target control. The `OLEDragDrop` event is very similar to the `OLEDragOver` event: It is fired when the target is dropped on the source control. The `OLEDragDrop` event is defined as follows:

```
Private Sub object_OLEDragDrop(Data As DataObject, Effect As
➡Long, Button As Integer, Shift As Integer, X As Single, Y As
➡Single)
```

The `OLEGiveFeedback` event is fired after every `OLEDragOver` event. It allows the source to provide some visual feedback to the user to indicate what operation will occur when the item is dropped. The event is defined as follows:

```
Private Sub object_OLEGiveFeedback(Effect As Long, DefaultCursors
➥As Boolean)
```

The Effect parameter is a long integer set by the target during the OLEDragOver event. This parameter specifies what action is to be performed when the user drops the item. Table 2.5 shows the values for the feedback effects.

Table 2.5

Feedback Effects

Drop Effect	Description
vbDropEffectNone	Drop target cannot accept the data.
vbDropEffectCopy	A drop will result in a copy of the data.
vbDropEffectMove	A drop will result in a moving of data from target to source.
vbDropEffectScroll	Scrolling is occurring or is about to occur in the target.

The DefaultCursors parameter is a Boolean used to determine whether Visual Basic uses the default or custom mouse cursors. If set to True, the default mouse cursors are used.

Managing Form Events

 Objective

As forms are created and destroyed in memory, various events are fired. These events enable the developer to perform different tasks. Such tasks include cleaning up variables, initializing controls, and so forth. The events that center around the creating, loading, unloading, and destroying of forms are listed in the order in which they are fired. Table 2.6 lists these events.

Table 2.6

Form Events

Event Name	Description
Initialize	Fired when an instance of the form is created.
Load	Fired when the form is loaded into memory.

Event Name	Description
Activate	Fired when the form becomes the active window.
DeActivate	Fired when the form becomes the inactive window.
QueryUnload	Fired before the form closes to give you a chance to cancel the unloading of the form.
Unload	Fired when the form is being unloaded.
Terminate	Fired when the form is being removed from memory.

The following sections expand on the information contained in this table.

The Initialize Event

The Initialize event occurs when an instance of a form has been created. The event supplies no parameters and is defined as follows:

```
Private Sub Form_Initialize( )
```

This event is usually fired when the NEW keyword is used to create an instance of a form. In this event, you can write code that will initialize variables to be used at a later stage. You should be careful not to refer to any properties of the form in this event because it will cause the load event to be fired. An example of using the Initialize event is as follows:

```
Private Sub Form_Initialize()
    'Set some module level variables
    m_Conn = 0
    m_default_color = RGB(255,128,0)
End Sub
```

The Load Event

The Load event occurs when the form is loaded into memory. This means that the controls for the form have been created in memory and are accessible. The Load statement or accessing of a form's controls or properties will cause the Load event to be fired. The Load event does not take any parameters and is defined as follows:

```
Private Sub Form_Load( )
```

The Load event is used to initialize controls on the window such as loading list box values, setting the default color, and sizing of the window. An example of using the Form_Load is shown as follows:

```
Private Sub Form_Load( )
    'Load the List box values
    lstState.Additem "CT"
    lstState.AddItem "NY"
    lstState.AddItem "NJ
    'Set a Text box value
    txtName = "<Enter Name>"
End Sub
```

The Activate and DeActivate Events

The form becomes active when the Show or SetFocus methods are used and as a result of user action. This Activate event is fired when the form becomes active and only when the form is visible.

If the form is loaded into memory and not visible, the Activate event will not occur. The Activate and DeActivate event occurs only when moving between forms within the same application. If you move to a different application, the form will not get a DeActivate event. In addition, if the form is being unloaded from memory, a DeActivate event will not occur.

Note that although a form has GotFocus and LostFocus events, these are fired only when the form has child control in itself. The Activate event is fired before the GotFocus, and the DeActivate event is fired before the LostFocus event.

When managing MDI child forms, the Activate and Deactivate event is fired only when the focus is changed between the child forms.

The QueryUnload and Unload Events

When a form is unloaded, two events are fired. The first event is the QueryUnload event. This event gives the form an opportunity to cancel the unload operation. After the QueryUnload event, the Unload event is called. These Unload events usually are called as a result of the Unload statement.

The QueryUnload event has two parameters and is defined as follows:

```
Private Sub Form_QueryUnload(cancel As Integer, unloadmode As
➡Integer)
```

The Cancel parameter can be set to True to prevent the form from being unloaded from memory. The UnloadMode parameter is used to denote where the unload was called from. Table 2.7 shows the enumerated values and descriptions.

Table 2.7

UnloadMode *Constants*	
Constant	Description
vbFormControlMenu	The user choses the Close command from the Control menu.
vbFormCode	The Unload statement was used.
vbAppWindows	The Windows operating system session is ending.
vbAppTaskManager	The Windows Task Manager closed the application.
vbFormMDIForm	The MDI child form is being closed.

The Unload event also enables you to cancel the unloading of the form, but does not tell you who issued the Unload command. The event is defined as follows:

```
Private Sub object_Unload(cancel As Integer)
```

The cancel argument can be set to any nonzero value to cancel the unload operation.

The Terminate Event

The Terminate event is usually fired when the form instance is set to nothing. This can be done explicitly by using a statement such as this:

```
Set objForm = Nothing
```

This statement destroys all the variables associated with the instance of the form. The Terminate event gives you the chance to clean up any variables or objects created that belonged to the form. The Terminate event is defined as follows:

```
Sub Form_Terminate()
```

Exercises

Exercise 2.1: Providing Visual Cues During Drag-and Drop Operations

This exercise gives you a chance to look at providing visual cues during drag-and-drop operations. The Ex2.1 directory on the CD-ROM contains an application that provides drag-and-drop between list boxes, but no visual cues are set up for the items. Drag-and-drop is supported between the list box when the application is executed, but the user is given no cues during the drag-and-drop operation.

You should add code in both list boxes that will change the drag icon during the drag operation. Hint: Use the DragOver event.

The following item has been given to you as a starting point:

An image list with icons with the following keys: DRAG, DROP, and NODROP.

Note that you want to show three sets of icons during the drag operations—one for the start of the drag, one for the drop, and one indicating no drop allowed.

The solution for this exercise is as follows:

```
Private Sub lstDestination_DragOver(Source As Control, X As
➥Single, Y As Single, State As Integer)
'If entering the control then change the icon to drop
If State = vbEnter Then
    Source.DragIcon = imgList.ListImages("DROP").ExtractIcon
ElseIf State = vbLeave Then
    'If exiting the control then change the icon to no drop
    Source.DragIcon = imgList.ListImages("NODROP").ExtractIcon
End If
End Sub
Private Sub lstOrginal_DragOver(Source As Control, X As Single, Y
➥As Single, State As Integer)
If State = vbEnter Then
    Source.DragIcon = imgList.ListImages("DRAG").ExtractIcon
ElseIf State = vbLeave Then
    Source.DragIcon = imgList.ListImages("NODROP").ExtractIcon
End If
End Sub
```

Exercise 2.2:   Providing Visual Cues to the User

In this exercise, you will write code that provides visual cues to the user. You will find a starting point located in the Ex2.2 directory on the CD-ROM.

1. In the OLEStartDrag event, place the appropriate code that will notify the Visual Basic runtime that the target (lstOrginal) supports only copies.

2. In the same event, write the code necessary to fill the data object with the currently selected item in the list box (lstOrginal).

The solution to this is as follows:

```
Private Sub lstOrginal_OLEStartDrag(Data As DataObject,
➥AllowedEffects As Long)
'Check if a actual item is selected
If lstOrginal.ListIndex < 0 Then
    Exit Sub
End If

'Set the data
Data.SetData lstOrginal.List(lstOrginal.ListIndex)
'Set the effects supported
AllowedEffects = vbDropEffectCopy
End Sub
```

Exercise 2.3:   Responding to Events

In this exercise, you will write code that responds to events. To complete this exercise, you must complete Exercise 2.2. You can find a complete solution to Exercise 2.2 in the Ex2.3 directory on the CD-ROM. The following tasks are to be completed:

1. In the OLECompleteDrag event for the lstOrginal list box (the source), write code that will write out a text description of the effect variable to a label called lblcaption.

2. Write the lstDestination's OLEDragDrop event; the event should accept only text data.

The solution to this exercise is as follows:

```
Private Sub lstOrginal_OLECompleteDrag(Effect As Long)

    'Check the ultimate effect
    Select Case Effect
        Case vbDropEffectCopy
            lblCaption.Caption = "Item copied"
        Case vbDropEffectMove
            lblCaption.Caption = "Item cut"
        Case vbDropEffectNone
            lblCaption.Caption = "Nothing occured"
    End Select
End Sub

Private Sub lstDestination_OLEDragDrop(Data As DataObject, Effect
➥As Long, Button As Integer, Shift As Integer, X As Single, Y As
➥Single)

'Check the Data Format
'Only Text format is supported
If Not Data.GetFormat(vbCFText) Then

Else
    'Add the item
    lstDestination.AddItem Data.GetData(vbCFText)
End If
End Sub
```

Exercise 2.4: Using the `Initialize` and `Load` Events

In this exercise, you will write code that uses the `Initialize` and `Load` events of a form.

1. Create a form with the following controls:

   TextBox called txtName

   ListBox called lstState

2. Add some module level variables to the form with the following names and data types:

   m_strDefault as string

   lDefault_Color as long

continues

3. In the `Initialize` event, set the two module level variables to the following values:

   m_strDefault = "Hello World"

   m_lDefault_Color = RGB(100,100,100)

4. In the `Load` event, write the code that will perform the following tasks:

   Load the textbox with the m_strDefault variable

   Load the listbox with the following values, CT, NY, and NJ

   Set the background color to the value of m_lDefault_color

The solution to this is as follows:

```
'General Declarations section
Private m_strdefault As String
Private m_default_color As long

Private Sub Form_Initialize()
        'Set some module level variables
        m_strDefault = "Hello World"
        m_default_color = RGB(100,100,100)
End Sub

Private Sub Form_Load( )
'Load the List box values
lstState.Additem "CT"
lstState.AddItem "NY"
lstState.AddItem "NJ
'Set a Text box value
txtName.text = m_strDefault
me.backcolor = m_default_color
End Sub
```

Review Questions

1. The `QueryUnload` event is fired when which of the following statements is used?

    A. `Unload Form1`

    B. `Form1.Unload`

    C. `Set Form1 to Unload`

    D. This event does not exist.

2. The `DataObject` object is used to manage which of the following tasks?

    A. Contains the data and the format in a drag-and-drop operation.

    B. Contains the data and the format in a OLE drag-and-drop operation.

    C. Is an OLE object that manages dynamic data exchange.

    D. The `DataObject` does not exist in Visual Basic.

3. The `OLECompleteDrag` occurs when

    A. The source received notification from a target that the drag operation is finished.

    B. The target received notification from a source that the drag operation is finished.

    C. The source is dragged onto a target.

    D. Is fired only in Automatic mode.

4. Which of the following statements will check for a text format on a `DataObject` called dt?

    A. `Dt.IsTextFormat`

    B. `dt.GetFormat()`

    C. `Dt.GetFormat(vbCFText)`

    D. The format of a data object cannot be checked.

5. The `OLEGiveFeedback` occurs after which of the following events?

    A. `OLEDragDrop`

    B. `OLEDragOver`

    C. Both the `OLEDragDrop` and `OLEDropOver`

    D. After all drag-and-drop operations

Answers to Review Questions

1. A. The `Unload` statement is used to unload forms. For more information, see the section titled "Managing Form Events."

2. B. The `DataObject` contains both the data and format in an OLE drag-and-drop operation. See the section "The `DataObject` Object" for more information.

3. A. After the OLE dragging operation is completed, the `OLECompleteDrag` event is fired in the source object. For more information, see the section titled "Implementing OLE Drag-and-Drop Features in Visual Basic."

4. C. The `DataObject` object has a function called `GetFormat` that returns the specific data format request if the object supports it. The function has one parameter, which is the desired format. In this case, it is set to the constant used to represent text-based data. For more information, see the section titled "The `DataObject` Object."

5. B. As the dragged item is moved over a target, the `OLEGiveFeedback` is fired. For more information, see the section titled "Responding to Events as a Target."

Answers to Test Yourself Questions at Beginning of Chapter

1. As the form is created, loaded and displayed events are fired in a given sequence. The sequence is `Initialize`, `Load`, and the `Activate` event. The `GetFocus` event of a form is fired only when there are no controls on the form. For more information, see the section titled "Managing Form Events."

2. The `DragOver` event is used to provide visual cues to the user regarding the drag-and-drop operation. The programmer usually sets the MousePointer or sets the `DragIcon` for the source control. For more information, see the section titled "Implementing Traditional Drag-and-Drop Support in Applications."

3. No events are fired. The `Activate/DeActivate` and `LostFocus` events are fired only when switching between different windows within the same application. For more information, see the section titled "Managing Form Events."

4. The `DragMode` property is used to toggle between Automatic and Manual drag modes. For more information, see the section titled "Drag Events."

5. This event is fired when an item is dragged over a control. For more information, see the section titled "Drag Events."

Chapter

Adding a Menu
Interface to an Application

3

This chapter helps you prepare for the exam by covering the following objectives:

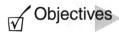 Objectives

- ▶ Dynamically modify the appearance of a menu

- ▶ Add a pop-up menu to an application

- ▶ Create an application that adds and deletes menus at runtime

Test Yourself! Before reading this chapter, test yourself to determine how much study time you will need to devote to this section.

1. Visual Basic forms can be used to host a menu bar. What two methods can be utilized by Visual Basic to create these menus?

2. When designing application menu bars, a variety of terminology is used to refer to the different levels and positions held by a menu item. What is the name of a menu item that appears directly under a window's title bar?

3. When using the Menu Editor, how can the programmer define which menus will be at the top, which will be subitems, and how the order is controlled?

4. Pop-up menus are displayed when the user selects the right mouse button. This displays a menu with options specific to the area that the user has selected. In which event, in Visual Basic, would a programmer trap for the use of the right mouse button?

5. Right-clicking on certain objects provides the user with a menu. What names are used to refer to this menu?

6. Menus can be created dynamically in Visual Basic by declaring a menu array and then loading a new element into the menu array. Once loaded the new menu can have its properties set. True or False?

7. The Unload statement is used to remove menu items created at runtime. Can the Unload statement also be used for removing the design-time menu template that is the first element in the array?

Answers are located at the end of the chapter...

To increase the functionality of a Visual Basic application, menu bars can provide the user with a simple way of controlling the program. The menu bar can be found at the top of a form window in most applications. Visual Basic provides a Menu Editor, which helps to simplify the creation of menus. Once created, these menus can be individually programmed to respond when selected.

Another type of menu that has become quite popular with users is the pop-up menu. This menu can be very specific to certain controls or areas of the application. These menus are often referred to as context-sensitive menus.

To provide the user with customized menu options, menus can also be created at runtime. The Most Recently Used File list is a good example of how dynamic menus are used to customize an application based on the user's needs. These menus provide runtime assistance that can vary depending on a user's preferences.

This chapter covers the following topics:

- ▶ Menu basics

- ▶ Menu terminology

- ▶ Using the Menu Editor

- ▶ Dynamically modifying the appearance of a menu

- ▶ Changing the menu's properties at runtime

- ▶ Adding a pop-up menu to an application

- ▶ Defining the pop-up menu

- ▶ Determining the mouse button

- ▶ Displaying the pop-up menu

- ▶ Controls with pop-up menus

> ▶ Creating an application that adds and deletes menus at runtime
>
> ▶ Creating runtime menu items
>
> ▶ Code for runtime menu items
>
> ▶ Removing runtime menu items

Understanding Menu Basics

Applications use *menu bars* to provide an organized collection of commands that can be performed by the user. Menus can inform the user of the application's capabilities as well as its inabilities. If a program has properly organized menus, the users can easily find common commands as well as features they may not be familiar with. Users can also learn shortcut keys from a well-designed menu structure.

With so many benefits to the user, a programmer should be well-versed in the creation and function that menus can provide. Menus can be created in VB by using two different methods. The first is a built-in Menu Editor dialog box. This editor provides a fast, simple way to generate menus. Once made, all menu objects can have their properties set through program code.

Another method used to create menus with VB involves using the Win32 Application Programmers Interface. The Win32 API is a series of functions that are externally called by VB and are provided by the operating system. By using specialized function calls, a programmer can create menus, set properties of menus, and modify menu structure. Most of the functionality found in the API is also available by using the Menu Editor. Although more difficult to work with, the API does provide enhanced function calls and special capabilities that are not a part of the VB Menu Editor. Using the API is beyond the scope of this chapter.

Knowing Menu Terminology

Knowing how menus operate becomes an important part of the design process. A variety of terminology also relates to menus. Terms such as top-level menu, submenu, and pop-up menu all describe how the menu should behave, as well as where the user can expect to see the menu, as shown in Figure 3.1.

Figure 3.1

The menu terminology and hierarchy.

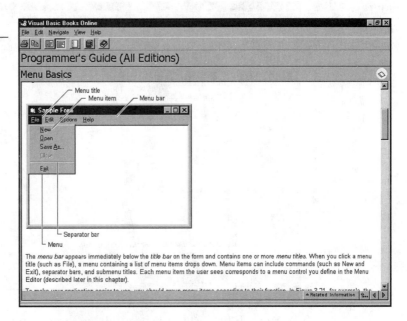

Top-level menus are the items that will be seen on the main part of the menu bar. They appear directly underneath the title bar of the application window. Standard user interface guidelines state that all top-level menus should have at least one submenu.

The submenu appears after a top-level menu has been opened. The submenu can contain a variety of commands that relate back to the top-level menu. One example would be the File menu that can be found in most applications. This would be a top-level menu. Once opened, commands such as New, Open, Save, and Close all relate to actions that affect the file.

Using the Menu Editor

Menus are created in Visual Basic by selecting a form that will host the menu. Menus appear at the top of the form window. After the form has been selected, the programmer can then use the VB Menu Editor, as shown in Figure 3.2.

Figure 3.2

The Visual Basic Menu Editor.

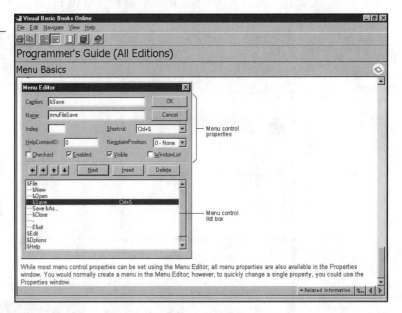

The Menu Editor will only be available when a form is being designed. The Menu Editor is available from the Tools menu in VB5.

The first step in creating a menu is to enter the menu item's caption. The caption can incorporate the ampersand for a shortcut key designation, also known as an accelerator key. This enables the user to see an underlined letter in the menu and use the Alt key along with the accelerator key.

After the caption of the menu item has been set, the menu requires an object name for programmatic reference. The menu name can be any valid object name. It is preferred to use naming conventions to allow for easier reading of source code and quick identification of objects. Menus use the three-letter prefix "mnu" before the selected name.

The remaining task to create a menu is to decide at which level in the menu structure this item will appear. Will the object be a top-level menu item, submenu item, or a sub-submenu item. In the list box at the bottom of the Menu Editor, all top-level menu items are flush with the left side of the list box border. Sub-level menu items will have four small dots preceding the menu caption. Sub-submenu items will have eight dots. The menu items can also be reorganized according to position in the menu.

To control the level and position of the menu item being entered, just use the four direction arrows in the Menu Editor. The up and down arrows allow menu items to be repositioned for order. The left and right arrows allow menu items to be top-level, sub-level, or sub–sub-level.

Menu items can also have their properties set at design time through the Menu Editor. Properties such as Checked, Enabled, Visible, Window List, and a Shortcut Key can all be specified. These properties are also available at runtime. To change the desired property of the menu object, just use the object name followed by the property name and the value.

Dynamically Modifying the Appearance of a Menu

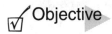 Objective

When a menu system is created at design time, the programmer can control property settings for menu items. After these properties are set, they can be altered at runtime to assist the user in interpreting which selections have been made, which items are turned on, and which commands are available or unavailable.

To dynamically alter the appearance of a menu system, the menu object is referenced along with the desired property to be altered. This syntax is the same for regular controls found on a VB form. The following sections explore the syntax used in setting menu properties.

The following code assumes that Form1 has a complete menu system already defined. The View menu has a submenu item called

Toolbar. This menu item is having the Checkmark property set to True to indicate that the toolbar is visible (see the result in Figure 3.3):

```
mnuViewToolbar.Checked = True
```

Figure 3.3

Sample menu with properties that change at runtime.

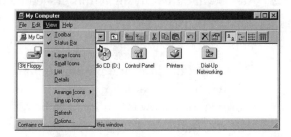

This code uses the same syntax that other objects use: the object name, a period separator, followed by the property to be set, and then the value after the assignment operator.

The following code demonstrates more menu objects and their property settings:

```
mnuViewStatusBar.Checked = True
mnuFileOpen.Enabled = False
mnuFormatFontBold.Checked = True
mnuPopUp.Visible = False
```

In these examples, notice how the use of the menu-naming convention helps in deciphering which menu is to be affected. The object name starts with the mnu prefix, and then the top-level menu item name View, followed by the sub-level menu item StatusBar. This ensures easy readability when going through source code.

Altering application menus at design time is not very different from controlling other objects. The one difficulty that programmers have with menus is remembering to control both the user interface and the menus. The interface can always be seen, but the menus must first be opened to view their states. One common technique used to assist with maintaining a consistent interface is calling a procedure from the menu event, as well as any other location that may affect the menu's state. The procedure will perform the required actions and affect both the interface and required information. This allows various menus to call the same code and keeps the program flow easier to follow.

Adding a Pop-Up Menu to an Application

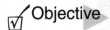Objective

Pop-up menus, also known as context menus, enable the user another convenient way to control the application. Pop-up menus are usually unique for various areas of an application. They can be created in Visual Basic or the operating system, and certain objects provide them.

Microsoft Excel provides an example of pop-up menus, as shown in Figure 3.4. When using Excel, the user has the option to use the main menu bar, shortcut keys, or pop-up menus. Different pop-up menus are found, depending on the object selected. If the user selects a set of cells in the spreadsheet, he gets a specific pop-up menu. If the user right-clicks on a worksheet tab, he gets a different pop-up menu.

Figure 3.4

Pop-up menu for Microsoft Excel.

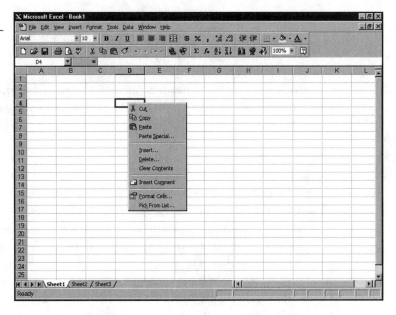

To provide pop-up menus for different parts of the application, various menus must be used. These menus are created as part of the main menu system; they do not have to be visible; and when they are needed, they are called through program code.

Defining the Pop-Up Menu

To create a pop-up menu, a top-level menu item is used. This item can have its visible property set to False so that it does not appear with the regular menu, as shown in Figure 3.5.

Figure 3.5

Design-time view of menu system with a pop-up menu.

All items to appear on the pop-up menu are created as sub-level items of the invisible top-level menu. Each submenu item can have its properties set as required.

When the pop-up menu is needed, the PopupMenu method is called to activate the pop-up menu. The following code demonstrates this:

```
Form1.PopupMenu mnuPopUp1
```

The preceding code calls the PopupMenu method of Form1, as shown in Figure 3.6. The menu item mnuPopUp1 is passed as an argument and is displayed at the current mouse location. This code assumes that a menu system has been created and a menu item named mnuPopUp1 exists.

The PopupMenu method accepts the name of the menu to activate as well as arguments that indicate the orientation of the menu (left, center, and right), as well as the screen coordinates for display and the name of an entry to be displayed in boldface.

Figure 3.6

Runtime view of a custom pop-up menu.

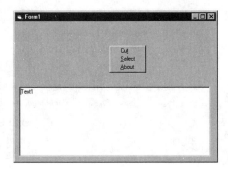

Determining the Mouse Button

After the desired menus have been created, the next step for the programmer is to decide which objects will call which menus. The form, as well as individual controls on the form, can all have pop-up menus specified.

The standard method used to activate an object's pop-up menu is by using the right mouse click. After the right mouse button has been selected, the menu is displayed.

To determine the state of the mouse, the programmer traps the MouseUp event of the object to provide the menu. Using code, the programmer verifies which mouse button the user pressed. To determine which mouse button was activated, the procedure is passed two arguments: Button and Shift. The Button argument contains the mouse button that was pressed. The Shift is used to indicate whether Ctrl, Alt, or Shift was active when the mouse click event occurred.

Note

One of the tricks to learning Visual Basic is to determine which events to use in a given situation. When attempting to determine which mouse button was selected, many new programmers do not see a difference between the MouseUp and MouseDown events. The difference in any event within VB is *when* it occurs. The MouseUp is a preferred place to detect the user's selection of a mouse button. The reason for using the Up

continues

event is to allow the user *forgiveness.* If the user did not mean to click on your object, or has pressed the button and then realized he did not want to, the mouse could still be removed from the object. If the mouse is dragged outside the area of the object, the MouseUp event will not occur. Allowing your program to be forgiving means the user will have an easier time using the software instead of fearing the next mistake.

The following code is found in the form's MouseUp event and determines which mouse button was pressed. A message box is used to display the two arguments Button and Shift:

```
Sub Form_MouseUp(Button As Integer, Shift As Integer, X As
➥Single, Y As Single)
    MsgBox "The user has selected button " & Button & " and
    ➥the pressed key combination " & Shift, vbInformation,
    ➥"Mouse Up Event of Form1"
End Sub
```

The preceding code generates a message box when the user clicks on the form. The message box will indicate a value of 1 for the left mouse button or a value of 2 for the right. The key combination of Ctrl and/or Alt and/or Shift will also be returned as a number. If more than one of the keys are pressed, the value is obtained by adding one key value to the other.

In the MouseUp event, both Button and Shift are integer values. When programming for this event, either the integer value or the constant can be used. Using the constant, however, will help when reading the code later.

Displaying the Pop-Up Menu

When using pop-up menus with forms or controls, you first define the menu, test for the right mouse button, and then display the desired menu.

The following source code puts together these tasks by using the PopupMenu method of the form, at the same time that the mouse button has been pressed.

```
Sub Form_MouseUp(Button As Integer, Shift As Integer, X As
➥Single, Y As Single)
    If Button = vbRightButton Then
        Form1.PopupMenu mnuPopup1
    End If
End Sub
```

In this code sample, a simple If statement provides the check to
see whether the right mouse button has been selected. If the
Button argument equals the vbRightButton constant, the Form
PopupMenu method is called and passed the name of the top-level
menu object to be displayed. Remember that the top-level item
will not be shown, only sub-level items will be.

Any menu can be passed to the PopupMenu method. In the preceding code, a special menu named mnuPopup1 was created and its
visible property was set to False. This hides the top-level menu
from the application menu bar, but allows the menu to be called.
The PopupMenu method will display sub-level menu items, regardless of the top-level menu item's visible property.

The PopupMenu method can only display one menu at a time. A
second call to PopupMenu will be ignored.

Controls with Pop-Up Menus

Not all controls require a pop-up menu to be created. Certain
controls that shipped with Visual Basic, such as the textbox control, already have a pop-up menu built into them, as shown in
Figure 3.7. Visual Basic has no method to disable the built-in pop-
up menus of these controls.

If the PopupMenu method is used with a control that has its own
built-in pop-up menu, the built-in one will always be displayed
first. The custom menu will only be displayed after. Displaying two
separate menus is not usually the desired effect for the user interface.

The benefit of built-in menus is that they do not require program
code for their functionality. The control provides all mouse handling and functions.

Figure 3.7

The built-in pop-up menu of the textbox *control.*

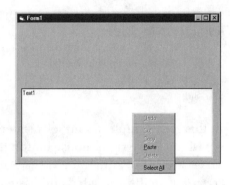

Creating an Application That Adds and Deletes Menus at Runtime

Objective

Runtime menus are created dynamically by the application, as they are required. The runtime menu may list user-selected information, recently used files, or a list of Internet Web sites.

To create runtime menus dynamically, you must use a menu control array. At runtime, the Load statement creates the new menu items, and the Unload statement removes them.

The following sections detail how runtime menus are created and removed from the menu system.

Creating Runtime Menu Items

The three steps to creating a runtime menu item are as follows:

1. Create a design-time menu that will act as the template, as shown in Figure 3.8. Set the Index property of the template item so that a menu control array is created. This array will allow new elements to be created at runtime. These elements can then be controlled like a regular menu item.

Figure 3.8

Creating a template menu item with an index value.

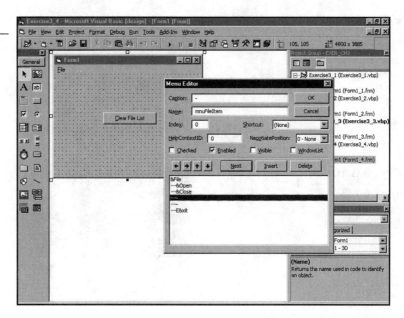

2. Use the Load statement at runtime. The Load statement accepts the name of the object to be loaded and the new item's index. The following is sample syntax:

```
Load mnuFileItem(1)
```

The name of the menu item is based on the design-time item that had the Index property set. To create a new menu, just use the menu name and a unique number that has not been previously used in the array.

3. After the control has been loaded, use the menu name and the index value to refer to the new menu. The menu item can then have all the expected properties set at runtime, as shown in Figure 3.9.

Dynamically created menu items will appear directly under the preceding index item. This must be taken into consideration when incorporating menu items below the array. Menu items below the array will function as expected; however, as the new elements are added to the collection, regular menu items will appear lower on the menu, as shown in Figure 3.10.

Figure 3.9

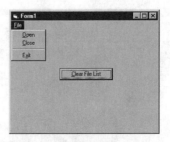

The File menu before runtime items are added.

Figure 3.10

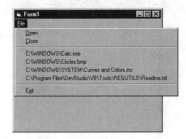

The File menu after runtime items have been added.

Code for Runtime Menu Items

When a menu item has been created at runtime, it is part of a control array. When code is to be associated with the runtime-generated menu, just use the design-time menu item that was the first index number in the array.

The template menu item will have an extra argument in the Click event. The Index argument provides the number used to refer to that control. The following sample code demonstrates how to code for the dynamic menus:

```
Sub mnuFileItem_Click(Index as Integer)
    Select Case Index
        Case 0
            MsgBox "You clicked the first menu item!"
        Case 1
            MsgBox "You clicked the first dynamically created
            ➥menu item!"
        Case 2
            MsgBox "You clicked the second dynamically
            ➥created menu item!"
    End Select
End Sub
```

Removing Runtime Menu Items

You can use two different methods to remove the runtime menus. The first is to hide the newly created item. The second is to unload it.

When hiding a menu item, the user interface will no longer display the item; however, program code can still use the menu and control the properties.

```
mnuFileItem(1).Visible = False
```

If a runtime menu item is unloaded, that control and the associated properties will be removed from memory. If required again, they will have to be loaded.

```
Unload mnuFileItem(1)
```

Only runtime control names and elements can be passed to the Unload statement. If a design-time menu item is passed to Unload, an application error will occur: Can't unload controls created at design time.

Exercises

Exercise 3.1: Creating a Simple Menu

In this exercise, you create a simple menu for the Form object. A standard File menu will be created with common submenu items. A View menu and Help menu will also be created. To create this template, follow these steps:

1. Start Visual Basic 5.

2. Create a Standard EXE project.

3. Select Tools, Menu Editor. Make sure that Form1 is currently selected. Otherwise the editor will not be available.

4. In the Caption text box, type **&File**. Remember that the ampersand is used for shortcut key designation.

5. In the Name text box, type **mnuFile**. The mnu is the three-letter object prefix, and the File is the top-level menu caption.

6. Click on the Next button. Notice the &File appears on the left edge of the bottom list box. This menu item will be a top-level menu because it has not been indented.

7. The caption should now be empty. To enter the next menu, type **&Open** in the Caption property.

8. In the Name text box, type **mnuFileOpen**. The mnu is the three-letter object prefix, the File is the top-level menu, and Open is a submenu of File.

9. Click on the right arrow. Notice that the &Open menu item should now be indented one position under the &File menu. This represents a submenu item.

10. Continue creating the menus by following Table 3.1. Remember to click on Next to create a new menu, and watch the indents.

Table 3.1

Menus to Create

Caption	Menu Name	Position
-	mnuFileSep1	Submenu of File
E&xit	mnuFileExit	Submenu of File
&Help	mnuHelp	Top-level menu
&About	mnuHelpAbout	Submenu of Help

11. On Form1, click on the File, Exit menu item.

12. In the open code window, enter the following code:

```
Sub mnuFileExit_Click()
    Unload Form1
    End
End Sub
```

13. On Form1, click on the Help, About menu item.

14. In the open code window, enter the following code.

```
Sub mnuHelpAbout_Click()
    MsgBox "This is my first application with a Menu",
    ➥vbInformation
End Sub
```

15. Run the project.

16. Select the Help, About menu. A message box should appear.

17. Click on OK to close the message box.

18. Select the File. Notice the Separator line. This appears due to the "-" only being used in the caption of the menu item. Note that this separator still needs a unique name.

19. Choose Exit from the menu. This ends the application.

This exercise demonstrated creating a simple menu system attached to the Form object. Code was also assigned to various menu items so that the code would execute when the menu item was selected.

Exercise 3.2: Dynamically Modifying the Appearance of a Menu

In this exercise, you create a menu that is dynamically modified during runtime. To create this template, follow these steps:

1. Start Visual Basic 5.

2. Create a Standard EXE project.

3. On Form1 create a menu bar with the items in Table 3.2.

Table 3.2

Menu Bar Items

Caption	Menu Name	Position
&File	mnuFile	Top-level menu
&Open	mnuFileOpen	Submenu of File
&Close	mnuFileClose	Submenu of File
-	mnuFileSep1	Submenu of File
E&xit	mnuFileExit	Submenu of File
&View	mnuView	Top-level menu
&Toolbar	mnuViewToolbar	Submenu of View
Status &Bar	mnuViewStatusBar	Submenu of View
-	mnuViewSep1	Submenu of View
&Options	mnuViewOptions	Submenu of View

4. With the Menu Editor open, choose the &Close menu option and remove the check mark from Enabled. This disables the menu by default.

5. Close the Menu Editor.

6. From Form1 select File, Open. In the code window, enter the following code for the menu:

```
Sub mnuFileOpen_Click()
    mnuFileClose.Enabled = True
    mnuFileOpen.Enabled = False
End Sub
```

7. From the code window, find the `FileClose` click event procedure and enter the following code for the menu:

   ```
   Sub mnuFileClose_Click()
       mnuFileOpen.Enabled = True
       mnuFileClose.Enabled = False
   End Sub
   ```

8. From `Form1` select View, Toolbar. In the code window, enter
   the following code for the menu. This code acts as a toggle
   switch. If it is on, turn it off. If it is off, turn it on:

   ```
   Sub mnuViewToolbar_Click()
       mnuViewToolbar.Checked = Not(mnuViewToolbar.Checked)
   End Sub
   ```

9. From `Form1` select View, Status Bar. In the code window, enter
   the following code for the menu:

   ```
   Sub mnuViewStatusBar_Click()
       mnuViewStatusBar.Checked =
       ➡Not(mnuViewStatusBar.Checked)
   End Sub
   ```

10. Run the project.

11. From `Form1` select File, Open. Once clicked, return to the
    File menu. The Open menu should now be disabled, and the
    Close menu should be enabled.

12. From `Form1` select File, Close. Once clicked, the Open menu
    should be enabled, and Close should be disabled.

13. From `Form1` select View, Toolbar. Once clicked, return to the
    View menu. The toolbar should have a check mark beside it.

14. From `Form1` select View, Status Bar. Once clicked, the status
    bar should have a check mark. Notice that the status bar and
    toolbar do not affect each other. One can be on, the other
    off, or both the same.

15. End the application.

continues

This exercise demonstrated simple, dynamical changing of the menu appearance. Although no program code was called, each menu can contain VB commands or calls to other procedures. When changing the appearance of menus, caution should be taken if the code cannot execute or is not successful. The menu appearance should not be altered. By executing code first and changing appearance last, the programmer can better handle the interface needs.

Exercise 3.3:   Adding a Pop-Up Menu to an Application

In this exercise, you create a form that uses a pop-up menu. To create this template, follow these steps:

1. Start Visual Basic 5.

2. Create a Standard EXE project.

3. On Form1 place a text box in the lower portion of the form. Leave half of the form empty. This will provide an area for the custom pop-up menu.

4. On Form1, create a menu bar with the structure in Table 3.3.

Table 3.3

Menu Bar Structure

Caption	Menu Name	Position
MyMenu	mnuMyMenu	Top level
Cu&t	mnuMyMenuCut	Sub of MyMenu
&Select	mnuMyMenuSelect	Sub of MyMenu
&About	mnuMyMenuAbout	Sub of MyMenu

5. With the Menu Editor open, select MyMenu and set the menu to be invisible.

6. Open the code window for Form1.

7. Find the `Form MouseUp` event, and enter the following code:

```
Sub Form_MouseUp(Button As Integer, Shift As Integer, X
➡As Single, Y As Single)
    If Button = vbRightButton Then
        Form1.PopupMenu mnuMyMenu
    End If
End Sub
```

8. Run the project.

9. Click on the form background. Ensure that you are not on the background of the text box.

10. Right-click on the form background. Although no menu bar should appear at the top of the form, your custom pop-up menu should appear. Make sure you use the alternate mouse button to get the menu.

11. The menu items can be clicked, but have no code attached.

12. To see a built-in control pop-up menu, right-click on the `Textbox` control window. Automatically the menu should appear.

13. Type some words into the text box. With the pop-up menu, select to copy and paste some text. Notice that you did not program this functionality.

14. End the application.

This exercise demonstrated how to use both a customized pop-up menu and a built-in, pop-up menu. When customized menus are required, just build them as a regular menu and hide the top-level menu if desired. Built-in menus require no coding or trapping of the mouse, but cannot be overridden in VB.

Exercise 3.4: Creating an Application That Adds and Deletes Menus at Runtime

In this exercise, you create a form that adds and deletes menus at runtime. To create this template, follow these steps:

continues

Exercise 3.4:   Continued

1. Start Visual Basic 5.

2. Create a Standard EXE project.

3. Under the Project menu, choose Components.

4. Check the Microsoft Common Dialog Control. A new tool icon should be added to the toolbox.

5. Add the new tool to Form1. It should appear as a small grey square. This control provides the Open, Save As, Color, Font, Printer, and Help dialog boxes from Windows. The control is invisible at runtime.

6. Change the Name property for the object to CDC1.

7. Open the code window and in the General Declarations section for Form1 enter the following code:

   ```
   Private iItem as Integer
   ```

8. Create the menu structure for Form1 as shown in Table 3.4.

Table 3.4

Form1 Menu Structure

Caption	Menu Name	Position
&File	mnuFile	Top-level
&Open...	mnuFileOpen	Submenu of File
&Close	mnuFileClose	Submenu of File
-	mnuFileItem	Submenu of File
-	mnuFileSep1	Submenu of File
E&xit	mnuFileExit	Submenu of File

9. Using the Menu Editor, select mnuFileItem and set the Index property to 0 and make the menu item invisible. This will be your first element in the menu array, and it will be invisible until an array element has been assigned.

10. Open the File menu while in Design mode. Notice that the Open, Close, Sep1, and Exit are visible, but the first array element—Separator—is not.

11. Select the File, Open menu item. In the code window, enter the following code:

```
Sub mnuFileOpen_Click()
    Dim iLoop As Integer
    cdc1.ShowOpen
    If cdc1.filename <> "" Then
        mnuFileItem(0).Visible = True
        For iLoop = 0 To iItem
            If mnuFileItem(iLoop).Caption =
            ➥cdc1.filename Then
                Exit Sub
            End If
        Next iLoop
        iItem = iItem + 1
        Load mnuFileItem(iItem)
        mnuFileItem(iItem).Caption = cdc1.filename
        mnuFileItem(iItem).Visible = True
    End If
End Sub
```

12. Add a command button to Form1. Change the `Caption` property to **&Clear File List**.

13. Open the code window for the Clear File List button, and enter the following code:

```
Sub Command1_Click()
    Dim iLoop as Integer
    mnuFileItem(0).Visible = False
    For iLoop = 1 to iItem
        Unload mnuFileItem(iLoop)
    Next iLoop
    iItem = 0
End Sub
```

14. Run the project.

continues

15. From Form1 select File, Open. Choose any directory, and then choose any file. The file will not be opened, but the path and filename will appear under the File menu. This is similar to the Most Recently Used list found in many applications.

16. Using File, Open, select as many different filenames as you like. If the path and filename are already in the list, they will not be added again.

17. After you have selected a few different files, use the Clear File List button. This button will use a form-level variable, which indicates the number of menu array elements and unloads each element.

18. After the list is cleared, the Open menu can be used again and then the Clear File List button.

19. End the application.

This exercise demonstrated how runtime menus are created based on a design-time template. The template is the first item in a control array, and new runtimes are loaded as new elements. Unloading the items just requires the array element and the Unload statement to remove the menu from memory.

Review Questions

1. Menus in Visual Basic can have their appearance changed to reflect the state of the application. To change menu items in VB at runtime, which methods can be used?

    A. The Menu Editor

    B. Program code

    C. Program code and the Menu Editor

    D. Menu property of a form

    E. Negotiate property of a form

2. The Menu Editor enables the programmer to create menu objects. These objects can have a variety of properties set and changed. Which property cannot be affected by using the Menu Editor?

    A. Checked

    B. Visible

    C. Picture

    D. Shortcut Key

    E. Enabled

3. In certain applications, objects provide a shortcut menu by using the right mouse button. This pop-up menu can be used to provide common commands for the selected object. Which item best describes the requirements to create a pop-up menu?

    A. Define the top-level and sub-level menu item, trap for the right mouse click, and call the form PopupMenu method

    B. Define the menu items, trap for the right mouse click, and call only the selected menu items

    C. Use the pop-up property of the object

    D. Assign a top-level menu to the pop-up menu property of the object

    E. Use the Menu Editor, define the top-level menu name as pop-up, and in the `mouse click` event call the menu

4. Assume that the Menu Editor has already been used to create a menu structure. For the menus to provide the functionality required, how are the menu items assigned program code?

    A. By using the `ItemCode` property in the editor

    B. By using the `Menu` property in the Properties window

    C. By using the `ItemCode` property in the Properties window

    D. By selecting the menu item from the form and entering code into the opened code window

    E. None of these

5. When a menu control array is created, runtime menu items can be added to the array. When the element's properties are set, where in the menu structure do the new items appear? (Select all appropriate.)

    A. In the order specified by the `NegotiatePosition` property

    B. In the order specified by the array element

    C. Immediately below the preceding array element

    D. At the bottom of the menu specified at design time

    E. None of these

Answers to Review Questions

1. B. The menu items can only be affected by program code at runtime. If an application is to have dynamic menus that reflect the state of the application, the program code will

allow the menu objects to be controlled. The Menu Editor is only available for application forms that have a menu and are in Design mode. For more information, see the section titled, "Using the Menu Editor."

2. C. The `Picture` property cannot be accessed by using the Visual Basic Menu Editor. This property is one of the special features of a menu that requires using the Win32 API. By using a special external call from Visual Basic, a menu can be assigned a picture. The new applications from Microsoft, such as Word 97 and Excel 97, show this capability. For more information, see the section titled, "Using the Menu Editor."

3. A. The top-level menu is created first, and the pop-up menu items are then created as sub-level menu items of the top-level menu. The next step is to test for a right mouse click on the selected object. After the right mouse has been detected, the form `PopupMenu` method is called, and the top-level menu that has been defined is passed as an argument. For more information, see the section titled, "Defining the Pop-Up Menu."

4. D. After the application menu has been created, you select the menu item from the form window it was created on. By using the mouse or keyboard, when the item is selected the code window will open. The code window will contain the name of the menu object and a procedure stub will have been created. The programmer just has to enter the desired code to be run. For more information, see the section titled, "Creating Runtime Menu Options."

5. B,C. When runtime menus are created, they are displayed according to their element number, and they appear directly below the preceding element number. The only exception is if the element is not displayed due to the `Visible` property. Runtime menus will always be on the same menu, directly below the design-time first element. For more information, see the section titled, "Creating Runtime Menu Options."

Answers to Test Yourself Questions at Beginning of Chapter

1. The two methods used by Visual Basic to create menus for an application are the VB Menu Editor and the Win32 API. Both methods can be used from VB to generate menu systems. The built-in Menu Editor is a simple dialog box that enables the user to create a hierarchy of menu items and menu item order. The Win32 API is an external set of functions provided by the operating system, and allows for a wide variety of functions. See "Understanding Menu Basics."

2. The term used to refer to a menu item found directly under a window's title bar is a top-level menu. This menu item is used to group other items into a submenu, which will appear under the top-level item when it is selected. See "Knowing Menu Terminology."

3. When creating menus with the Menu Editor, the programmer uses the left and right arrows. The arrows allow the menu hierarchy to be customized as required. The up and down arrows of the editor allow the items to be ordered from top to bottom. See "Using the Menu Editor."

4. The MouseUp event can be used to determine which mouse button has been clicked. By using a specific object's MouseUp event, the programmer can determine whether the right mouse button was used. If so, the form PopupMenu method can be called. See "Determining the Mouse Button."

5. The menu provided when a user right-clicks on an object has a variety of names. One of the most common terms used is the "pop-up menu." Another term is the "context-sensitive menu." Also used is the "right mouse menu." All terms refer to the same menu. Certain objects and the operating system provide the menu, or they can be created in Visual Basic. See "Adding a Pop-Up Menu to an Application."

6. True. This is one way to allow for the customization of menu items on a menu bar. By setting the index value of one menu item at design time, new items can be dynamically loaded and controlled through code. See "Creating Runtime Menu Items."

7. No. The Unload statement can only be used to remove instances of menu items created at runtime. If the first element in the array—assuming it is the design time item—is passed to Unload, an application error will occur: Can't unload controls created at design time. See "Removing Runtime Menu Items."

Implementing User Interface Controls in an Application

This chapter helps you prepare for the exam by covering the following objectives:

Objectives

▶ Provide controls with images by using the `ImageList` control

▶ Display data by using the `TreeView` control

▶ Display items by using the `ListView` control

▶ Create toolbars by using the `ToolBar` control

▶ Display status information by using the `StatusBar` control

▶ Use the Controls Collection

▶ Create an application that adds and deletes controls at runtime

Test Yourself! Before reading this chapter, test yourself to determine how much study time you will need to devote to this section.

1. If you need to access a particular node of a TreeView control, what two properties of the node can be used to uniquely distinguish it from others in a tree?

2. What are the four ways that items in a ListView can be displayed?

3. What image formats can be loaded together in an ImageList control? For example, can 16×16 icons be loaded with 32×32 icons? Can icons be loaded with bitmaps?

4. What two properties of the ToolBar and Buttons Collections control the availability of Tool Tips?

5. If you include a Panel on a StatusBar control to display the current time, what is the best way to update that time while the application is running?

6. How many Controls Collections are there in a Visual Basic application?

7. If you will be creating TextBox control on a form dynamically at runtime, what two things must you do at design time for it to work?

Answers are located at the end of the chapter...

This chapter describes various 32-bit controls that can be used to enhance your Visual Basic user interface. These controls organize data and provide different ways of presenting information to the user, give you additional means of displaying information about the environment, and also provide the means to you—as a developer—to manipulate data and controls.

All the controls detailed in this chapter are available through the Microsoft Windows Common Controls Library (comctl32.ocx), which can be selected from the project Components dialog box, as shown in Figure 4.1. The `ImageList` control gives you a means of loading graphics files, such as icons and bitmaps, into your application for use with other controls. The `TreeView` and `ListView` controls can be used to organize data in hierarchies and lists respectively. The `ToolBar` control enables you to quickly build toolbars in your application, giving the users an alternative to the menu for performing actions. The `StatusBar` control can be added to an application to present information about the environment to the user, through text messages and progress bars.

Figure 4.1

Adding the Common Controls to a project.

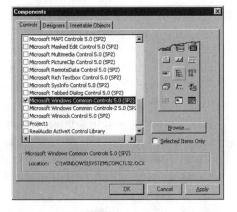

This chapter also discusses the Controls Collection of a form, which Visual Basic provides for manipulating controls without referencing each control by name. Finally, this chapter discusses dynamic controls and how to add controls to a form at runtime and how to remove them when no longer needed.

This chapter examines the following topics:

▶ The `ImageList` control

▶ The `TreeView` control

▶ The `ListView` control

▶ The `ToolBar` control

▶ The `StatusBar` control

▶ Using the Controls Collection

▶ Adding and deleting controls dynamically

Using the `ImageList` Control

 Objective

The `ImageList` is a control that enables you to store graphics images in an application for use by other controls. Both bitmaps and icons can be stored in the `ImageList` control. At runtime, the `ImageList` is invisible, just like a `Timer` or a `CommonDialog` control, so it can be placed anywhere on a form without interfering with the user interface.

After an `ImageList` control has been added to a form, images can be added to the control at design time through the Custom Properties dialog box. The first tab of the dialog box, as shown in Figure 4.2, enables you to change general properties of the `ImageList`. On this tab, you can select the style and size of a graphic that will be included in the `ImageList`. Three of the resolutions, 16×16, 32×32, and 48×48, refer to the resolution of icon files. Custom enables you to include bitmap images into the control, as well as icon images. You do not need to choose a resolution, height, and width for the `ImageList`. As soon as you add an image to the control, Visual Basic automatically determines the properties for you. Also, after you have an image in the control, you cannot change the `resolution` property. It is locked as long as there is an image in the `ImageList` control.

Figure 4.2

The General tab of the Property Pages dialog box for the ImageList control.

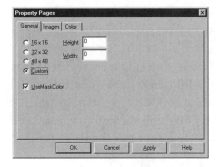

The list of images contained in the `ImageList` control can be managed through the Images tab of the Property Pages dialog box, as shown in Figure 4.3. This tab enables you to add and remove images from the control, as well as set additional information about each image. The Index of each image is assigned by Visual Basic. The Index starts at 1 for the first image, and increments for each additional image. The `Key` property can be used to reference an image in the collection of images for the control. It has a string value that can be used rather than the `Index` property to retrieve an image from the list.

Figure 4.3

The Images tab of the Property Pages dialog box for the ImageList control.

The easiest way to add images to the `ImageList` is to do it from the Images tab at design time. Just click on the Insert Picture button, and you can browse for the *.ico and *.bmp files that you want to add to the control. After you have added images to the `ImageList` control, they are available for your application to use in other controls. Pictures can be loaded into `PictureBoxes` and `Image` controls from the `ImageList`. The images can also be used by the other controls discussed later in this chapter, such as the `ToolBar` and `ListView` controls.

Although you can set up an `ImageList` at design time, and add all the images you may need in your application, there are times when you will have to manipulate these images at runtime. This can be done through the `ListImage` object and the `ListImages` Collection of the `ImageList` control.

`ListImage` Object and `ListImages` Collection

Key Concepts
All the images contained in the `ImageList` control are stored in the `ListImages` Collection. Each icon and bitmap in the collection is a separate `ListImage` object. You can reference each image in the list by index:

```
ImageList1.ListImages(1).Picture
```

or by key value:

```
ImageList1.ListImages("FirstImage").Picture
```

if a key (`"FirstImage"`) was assigned to the `ListImage` object. You can use the `ListImages` Collection to loop through all the images in the list. If you wanted to display all the stored images in a `PictureBox`, one after another, you could use the following code:

```
Dim picImage as ListImage

For Each picImage in ImageList1.ListImages
    Picture1.Picture = picImage.Picture
Next
```

If you knew the image you wanted to move to a `PictureBox`, you could just code this:

```
Picture1.Picture = ImageList1.ListImages(3).Picture
```

Here, the third image in the `ImageList` control would be loaded into `PictureBox` `Picture1`.

Add and Remove Methods

Key Concepts

The Add method of the ListImages Collection is used to add images to the ImageList. The syntax for Add is as follows:

```
ImageList1.ListImages.Add(index, key, picture)
```

Here, ImageList1 represents the ImageList control on your form. Index and Key are optional parameters. If Index is specified, it will be the location at which the image is loaded into the ListImages Collection. If Index is omitted, the new image will be inserted at the end of the collection. Key is a string value that can be used to reference an image in the list without knowing its index value. For example, if an image was added as follows:

```
ImageList1.ListImages.Add (, "folder icon", LoadPicture("folder.ico")
```

you would not know the index value of the new image, but you could still reference it as this:

```
Picture1.Picture = ImageList1.ListImages("folder icon").Picture
```

Using the ListImages key makes your code more readable than if you referenced images by the Index property.

Key Concepts

Images can be removed from the ListImages Collection by using the Remove method. You can use Remove either by specifying the index of the image:

```
ImageList1.ListImages.Remove 1
```

or by providing the key value for the image:

```
ImageList1.ListImages.Remove "key value"
```

Draw Method

You can use the Draw method of the ListImage object to draw an image onto another object. As discussed earlier, an image from the ImageList control can be loaded into a PictureBox by setting the Picture property:

```
Picture1.Picture = ImageList1.ListImages(1).Picture
```

You can also use the Draw method to accomplish the same thing. With Draw, however, you have some additional options. The syntax for Draw is as follows:

```
ImageList1.ListImages(Index).Draw (HDC, x,y, style)
```

where index identifies the image to be drawn. The Key value can be used in place of the Index as well. HDC is the device context ID of the destination device. If you were to draw an image onto a form, for example, you could specify Form1.HDC for the HDC property. This tells Windows where to put an image. The optional parameters, x and y, identify the coordinates within the destination at which the image will be drawn. The Style property can take on the following four values:

- imlNormal (0)   The image will appear normally—with style = 1.

- imlTransparent (1)   The part of the image will appear to be transparent. Transparency is determined by the MaskColor property (set on the Color tab of the Custom Properties dialog box).

- imlSelected (2)   The image will be dithered with the system highlight color.

- imlFocus (3)   The image appears as if it has focus.

Overlay Method

You can use the Overlay method of the ImageList control to combine two images from the ListImages Collection. The method returns the result as a picture. The syntax for the Overlay method is as follows:

```
ImageList1.Overlay(index1,index2)
```

where `index1` and `index2` refer to two images in the `ListImages` Collection. Either the index or the key for a `ListImage` can be used. The resulting picture can be used as any other picture object in Visual Basic. It can be placed on a destination object, such as a `Form` or `PictureBox`, or can even be loaded into an `ImageList` control. The following code

```
Form1.Picture = ImageList1.Overlay(1,2)
```

combines the first and second images from the `ImageList1.ListImages` Collection and places the resulting picture on `Form1`.

ImageHeight and ImageWidth Properties

The `ImageHeight` and `ImageWidth` properties of the `ImageList` control identify the height and width of images contained within the `ListImages` Collection. These properties are read/write at design time (from the Custom Properties window) and at runtime. The Height and Width properties identify the size of an image in pixels.

Key Concepts   Note that after the first image is added to the `ListImages`, all other images must be the same height and width; otherwise an error will occur. If you need to include different-sized icons in an application, you can use multiple `ImageList` controls, one for each size needed.

ListImages Property

The `ListImages` property returns a reference to the collection of `ListImage` objects (`ListImages` Collection) contained within an `ImageList` control.

MaskColor and UseMaskColor Properties

MaskColor is a read/write property used to identify the color that will be used to create masks for the ImageList control. The MaskColor can be set at design time on the Color tab of the Custom Properties dialog box for the ImageList control. It can also be set and read at runtime as follows:

```
ImageList1.MaskColor = vbBlack
```

You can set the MaskColor property by using the Visual Basic color constants, the QBColor function, or by using the RGB function. The MaskColor is used with the Draw and the Overlay methods to determine the parts of an image that will be transparent.

UseMaskColor determines whether the MaskColor property will be used as part of a Draw or Overlay. It takes on either a True or a False value, and is also available at either design time or runtime.

Using the TreeView Control

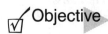
Objective

The purpose of a TreeView control is to display information in a hierarchy. A TreeView is made up of *nodes* that are related to each other in some way. Users can look at information, or objects, presented in a TreeView control and quickly determine how those objects are bound together.

Figure 4.4 shows a good example of TreeView in the Windows Explorer. The left side of Explorer shows information about drives in a hierarchical fashion. Explorer starts its tree with a node called Desktop. From there you can see several nodes indented below the Desktop node. The indentation and the lines connecting nodes show that the My Computer node is a child of the Desktop node. My Computer also has *children*—the A: drive, B: drive, C: drive, and so on. Children of the same parent are often referred to as *siblings*. The A: drive and B: drive, for example, both have My Computer as a parent and are called siblings.

Figure 4.4

Windows Explorer as an example of a TreeView.

The `TreeView` control is available as part of the Common Controls component in Visual Basic. You can use the `TreeView` anytime that you need to display data to a user as a hierarchy.

Node Object and Nodes Collection

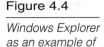
Key Concepts

A `TreeView` is made up of `Node` objects, which are contained in the `Nodes` Collection of the `TreeView`. Just as image information is stored in the `ListImages` Collection for the `ImageList` control, node information is stored in the `Nodes` Collection of the `TreeView` control. Gaining access to a specific node in the tree is done either by referring to that node by index, as follows:

```
TreeView1.Nodes(index)
```

where `index` is an integer identifying a node in the collection, or by referring to the node with a key value, as follows:

```
TreeView1.Nodes("key")
```

where `"key"` is the string value of the node's `key` property. The `Node` object can be used to represent a single node from the `Nodes` Collection:

```
Dim objNode as Node
Set objNode = TreeView1.Nodes(1)
```

After the preceding code executes, objNode will have the same properties as the node identified by TreeView1.Nodes(1).

Add and Remove Methods

Nodes can be added to the TreeView control by using the Add method of the Nodes Collection. The syntax for Add is as follows:

```
TreeView1.Nodes.Add(relative, relationship, key, text, image,
➥selectedimage)
```

All the arguments for the Add method are optional. The Relative parameter tells Visual Basic to which node the new node is related. It also has an impact on the placement of the new node in the tree. This is the Index or the Key value of a node that is already in the Nodes Collection of the TreeView. If the Relative argument is not specified, the new node will be placed at the top level in the tree, after all other existing nodes at that level.

The second argument, Relationship, goes along with the Relative argument in determining the placement of the new node. This argument determines the relationship between the new node and the relative node. The values for the relationship parameter are as follows:

- ▶ tvwFirst (0)   The new node is placed at the same level in the tree as the "relative." It will be added as the first node of that level.

- ▶ tvwLast (1)   The new node is placed at the same level in the tree as the "relative," but will be added after the last existing node at the same level as "relative."

- ▶ tvwNext (2)   The new node will be placed at the same level in the tree as the "relative," immediately following that node.

- ▶ tvwPrevious (3)   The new node will be placed at the same level in the tree as the "relative," immediately preceding that node.

- ▶ tvwChild (4)   The new node will be a child of the "relative" node.

The Key property identifies the new node in the tree. If provided as an argument, it must be a unique string, not used as a key by any other node in the tree. The key is used to retrieve or to find this node, when the index is not known.

 Caution

Throughout Visual Basic, you will find many collections that can be referenced by key, which is a string value. In most of these collections, if you want to use a number as the key, you can just convert the number to a string by using the Str$() function, or by enclosing the number in double quotation marks. You should be aware, however, that the Nodes Collection of the TreeView is an exception to this. Converting a number to a string and attempting to use that string as the key to a TreeView Node object will generate a runtime error.

The last three arguments of the Add method define the appearance of the new node. The text that appears next to a node in the TreeView is specified by the Text argument, a string value. If you want to have icons appear in the TreeView alongside the Text, you must first have an ImageList control on your form. When you set up a TreeView and define its properties through the Property Pages dialog box, you can bind an ImageList to the TreeView. Figure 4.5 shows an example of this.

Figure 4.5

Binding an ImageList to a TreeView control.

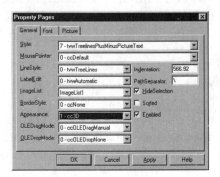

To include an icon with the node text, you can use the `Image` argument. This argument has an integer value, which corresponds to the index of an image in the bound `ImageList` control. The `ImageList` has to be set up first so that the index values are available for use in the `TreeView` control. If you want a node to have a different icon displayed when that node is selected by the user, you can specify a second icon with the `SelectedImage` argument. This is also an integer argument identifying an image in the same `ImageList`.

`EnsureVisible` and `GetVisibleCount` Methods

If at some point during the execution of your program, you need to make sure that a node in the `TreeView` is visible, you can use the `EnsureVisible` method of a specific node:

```
TreeView1.Nodes(23).EnsureVisible
```

This makes the node with an index of 23 visible to the user even if the node is several levels deep in a tree that is completely collapsed. The `EnsureVisible` property expands the tree to make the node visible.

To get the number of nodes visible at any one time, you can use the `GetVisibleCount` method of the `TreeView` control. By using

```
TreeView1.GetVisibleCount
```

you will get a count of nodes visible within the `TreeView`. The count will only include those nodes that are visible, including any nodes partially visible at the bottom of the control. The count does not include any nodes expanded below the bottom edge of the `TreeView` control.

`TreeView` Properties

Numerous properties for the `TreeView` control and for `Node` objects define the appearance of the tree, and give access to nodes within the tree. You can use many of these properties to navigate through a `TreeView`, as follows:

▶ `Child` Returns a reference to the first child of a node. The `Child` property can be used to set a reference to a node:

```
Dim objNode as Node
objNode = TreeView1.Nodes(1).Child
```

This sets `objNode` equal to the first child of the node with index 1. Operations can also be performed directly on the reference to the child:

```
TreeView1.Nodes(1).Child.Text = "This is the first child."
```

This changes the text for the first child node of node 1.

▶ `FirstSibling` Returns a reference to the first sibling of the specified node. `FirstSibling` is a node at the same level as the specified node.

▶ `LastSibling` Returns a reference to the last sibling of the specified node. `LastSibling` is a node at the same level as the specified node.

▶ `Parent` Returns a reference to the parent of the specified node.

▶ `Next` Identifies the node immediately following the specified node in the hierarchy.

▶ `Previous` Identifies the node immediately preceding the specified node in the hierarchy.

▶ `Root` Provides the root node, or top-level node, in the tree for the specified node.

▶ `SelectedItem` Returns a reference to the node currently selected in the `TreeView` control.

▶ `Nodes` Returns a reference to the entire `Nodes` Collection for the `TreeView`.

You can also use the following additional properties to determine the behavior and appearance of the TreeView:

- ▶ Children   Returns the total number of child nodes for a given node.

- ▶ Selected   A True or False value indicating whether a particular node is selected.

- ▶ Expanded   A True or False value indicating whether a particular node is expanded (that is, its child nodes are visible).

- ▶ FullPath   Returns a string value depicting the entire path from the root to the current node. The full path is made up of the text values of all the nodes from the root, concatenated by the character specified by the PathSeparator property.

- ▶ PathSeparator   Identifies the character used as a separator in the FullPath property.

- ▶ LineStyle   Determines the appearance of the lines that connect nodes in a tree. LineStyle can have two values, 0 (tvwTreeLines) and 1 (tvwRootLines). If LineStyle is 0, there will be lines connecting parents to children, and children to each other. If LineStyle is 1, there will also be lines connecting the root nodes.

- ▶ Sorted   A True or False value for the TreeView. If Sorted is True, the root nodes will be sorted alphabetically by the Text property of each node. Child nodes will also be sorted alphabetically within each parent. If Sorted is False, the nodes in the TreeView will not be sorted.

TreeView Events

You can use several events of the TreeView control to code for actions taken by the user or to handle actions caused by code execution. In addition to standard control events such as Click and DblClick, the TreeView control has these following additional events:

▶ Collapse   Generated whenever a node in a TreeView control is collapsed. This event occurs in one of three ways: when the Expanded property of a node is set to False; when the user double-clicks on an expanded node; or when the user clicks on the +/- image for a node to collapse that node. The node that was collapsed is passed in as an argument to the event.

▶ Expand   Generated when a node in a TreeView is expanded. Like the Collapse event, Expand occurs in one of three instances: when the user double-clicks on a node that has children to expand that node; when the user clicks on the +/- image to expand a node; or when the Expanded property for the node is set to True. Expand also has one argument, the node object that was expanded.

▶ NodeClick   Occurs when a Node object is clicked by the user. The node that was clicked is passed in as an argument to the event. If the user clicks anywhere on the TreeView, other than on a node, the Click event for the TreeView control is triggered instead.

Using the ListView Control

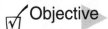 Objective

The ListView control provides a means for displaying lists of information to a user. As with the TreeView, an example of the ListView control can be seen in the Windows Explorer. The left side of Windows Explorer contains a tree of all the directories on a drive. The right side contains a list of items within a directory. To get an idea of the ways in which a ListView control can be used, you just need to look at the way a list of files appears and behaves in Windows Explorer (see Figure 4.6).

Figure 4.6

Example of a
ListView in Win-
dows Explorer,
showing large
icons.

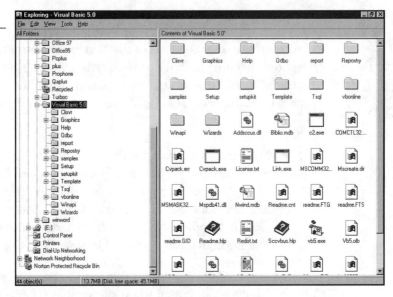

Objects can be displayed in one of four ways with the ListView.
You can use either large or small icons to represent each item in
the list, along with accompanying text information, where multiple items can appear on a single row. You can also display items in
a column listing. Finally, you can show items as a report in the
ListView control, with one item appearing on each line, and
subitem information displaying in additional columns in the control, as shown in Figure 4.7.

As you learn about the ListView, you will see similarities to the
TreeView control. Their behavior and appearance are controlled
in many of the same ways. The major difference that you will notice is that objects in a ListView are not related to each other, as
are objects in a TreeView.

ListItem Object and ListItems Collection

Each item in the ListView is called a ListItem object. If you look
at Figure 4.6, for example, you will see a list of files in the Visual
Basic directory. Biblio.mdb, Readme.hlp, and each of the other
files in the right side of the Windows Explorer is a ListItem.

Figure 4.7

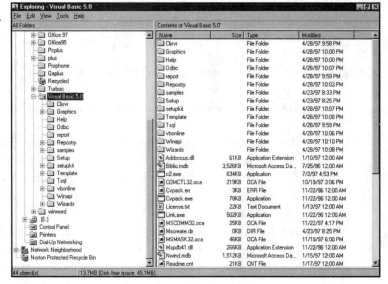

Example of a ListView in Windows Explorer, showing the report style.

The `ListView` control organizes all the `ListItem` objects into a single collection called `ListItems`. This is the same as a `TreeView`, which organizes each `Node` object in a tree into the `Nodes` Collection. The `ListItems` Collection can be used to cycle through all the objects in the control for processing, just as with any other collection:

```
Dim objItem as ListItem
For Each objItem in ListView1.ListItems
    ' do some processing
Next
```

`Index` and `Key` Properties

Items in a `ListView` can be referenced by either the `Index` property or the `Key` property. The `Index` property is an integer expression, typically generated by Visual Basic when a `ListItem` is added to the `ListView`. You can reference a specific item by number:

```
Msgbox ListView1.ListItems(1).Text
```

Alternatively, you can loop through the collection of `ListItems`, referring to each by number:

```
For I = 1 To ListView1.ListItems.Count
    Msgbox ListView1.ListItems(I).Text
Next I
```

Unlike the Index in the TreeView, you have some control over the value of the Index property in the ListView control. Specifying an Index number is discussed later in this section.

A more convenient way to reference an item in the list is by Key. The Key property is a string expression—assigned by you as the developer (or by the user if you desire)—that can also be used to access an item in the list. The Key property is included as part of the Add method (discussed later) when an item is inserted into the list. As a developer, you usually know the value for the Key, and can access a node directly. It is easier to reference the node you want by using a meaningful text string than by using the Index property, which is determined by Visual Basic.

Unlike the TreeView, you can store numbers in the Key property of each ListItem, if necessary. You just have to convert the number to a string by using the Str$() function, and the string value will be accepted as the Key by Visual Basic.

View Property

The appearance of a ListView is determined by the View property. The View property can take on one of the following four values:

▶ lvwIcon (0)   Display item text along with the regular icon, with one or more ListItems per line.

▶ lvwSmallIcon (1)   Display item text along with the small icon, with one or more ListItems per line.

▶ lvwList (2)   Display the small icon, with the text to the right of the icon. One ListItem will appear per line.

▶ lvwReport (3)   Display the small icon, with the text to the right of the icon, and subitem information to the right of the text, displayed in columns. One ListItem will appear per line.

Add and Remove Methods

ListItems are inserted into a ListView by using the Add method. The Add method has the following syntax:

```
ListView1.ListItems.Add(index, key, text, icon, smallIcon)
```

All the arguments for the Add method are optional. The Index argument is an integer value that can be used to specify the position of the new item being added to the list. If the Index argument is omitted, Visual Basic places the new item at the end of the list. The Key property is a unique string that can be used to identify an item in the list, instead of using the Index to that object.

The last three arguments—Text, Icon, and SmallIcon—determine the appearance of the new item in the ListView. If the Text argument is given, that text will appear with the item in the ListView. The Icon and SmallIcon arguments are integers referring to an icon in an ImageList control. As with the TreeView, the ListView needs at least one ImageList control on the form for icons to be displayed. References to ImageLists are set through the Property Pages dialog box for the ListView, as shown in Figure 4.8. You can set references to two different ImageLists for a ListView: one reference for regular icons, and a second list for small icons. Because an ImageList control can only contain images of a single size, two ImageLists are required if you will be using both regular and small icons. Typically, regular icons will be 32×32, and small icons will be 16×16.

Figure 4.8

Setting an
ImageList
reference for a
ListView control.

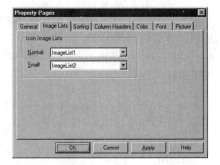

Icon and SmallIcon Properties

After ListItems have been added to a ListView, their references to icons in an ImageList can be read, or set through the Icon and SmallIcon properties. These properties have integer values that correspond to the index value of images in the ImageLists to which the ListView is bound. If you create a form with ListView1, ImageList1, and ImageList2 controls, for example, and you use ImageList1 for regular icons and ImageList2 for small icons, the following:

```
x = ListView1.ListItems(1).Icon
```

returns an integer that corresponds to an index value of an image in ImageList1; while:

```
x = ListView1.ListItems(1).SmallIcon
```

gives you the index of an image in ImageList2.

FindItem Method

After items have been added to a list, you may have a need to find one or more of those items. The FindItem method of the ListView control enables you to search through the items and return the desired ListItem object. FindItem has the following syntax:

```
ListView1.FindItem (string, value, index, match)
```

The string argument, which is required, specifies the string for which you are searching in the list. The value argument tells Visual Basic how to search for the string. Value can be one of the following:

- ▶ lvwText (0)   Search for the String argument in the Text property of the ListItems.

- ▶ lvwSubItem (1)   Search for the String argument in the subitems of the ListItems.

- ▶ lvwTag (2)   Search for the String argument in the Tag property of the ListItems.

The index argument can be used to indicate the start position for the search. This argument can have either an integer or a string value. If the value is an integer, Visual Basic starts the search at the ListItem with an index of that value. If the argument is a string, the search begins at the item, which has a Key value equal to that of the argument value. If the index argument is not specified, the search starts at the first item in the list.

The final argument, match, determines how Visual Basic will select a ListItem that matches the string argument. Match can have the following two values:

▶ lvwWholeWord(0)   A match occurs if the String argument matches the whole word which starts the Text property of the item.

▶ lvwPartial (1)   A match occurs if the String argument matches the beginning of the Text property, regardless of whether it is the whole word.

Arrange Property

The Arrange property of the ListView determines how items are arranged within a list. Arrange can have one of the following three values:

▶ lvwNone (0)   Items are not arranged within the ListView.

▶ lvwAutoLeft (1)   Items are arranged along the left side of the ListView.

▶ lvwAutoTop (2)   Items are arranged along the top border of the ListView.

The ListItem's appearance in a ListView is also determined by the sorting properties.

Sorted, SortKey, and SortOrder Properties

Three properties—Sorted, SortKey, and SortOrder—determine the order of ListItems in a ListView control. The Sorted property can have one of two values, True or False. If Sorted is False, the items in the ListView are not sorted. If the Sorted property is set to True, the ListItems will be sorted, with an order that depends on the other two properties: SortKey and SortOrder. The values of SortOrder and SortKey are ignored unless the Sorted property is set to True.

SortOrder specifies whether the ListItems appear in ascending (lvwAscending) or descending (lvwDescending) order. Ascending order is the default for SortOrder. SortKey identifies on what the items in the list will be sorted. By default, the items in the list will be sorted by the Text property of the ListItems. If your ListView is in a report format with multiple columns, you can sort by using the text value of any of the columns by setting the SortKey property to the desired column. If SortKey is 0, the list will be sorted by the ListItems().Text property. If SortKey is greater than 0, the sort will take place using one of the additional report columns in the control (described in the following section).

ColumnHeader Object and ColumnHeaders Collection

If you want to use a ListView with a report format that has multiple columns for each ListItem, you must work with the ColumnHeaders Collection. ColumnHeaders is a collection of ColumnHeader objects. Each ColumnHeader object identifies one column in a ListView. The ColumnHeaders Collection always contains at least one column for the ListItem itself. Additional columns can be added using the ColumnHeaders.Add method, or removed with the ColumnHeaders.Remove method.

If you look back at the example of the Windows Explorer as an ImageList, you will see that it uses four columns. The first column—the icon and the filename—are the ListItem. This would be the first entry in the ColumnHeaders Collection. Additional columns are included for the file size, type, and modification date.

SubItems Property

Once additional columns have been added to a ListView, those columns can be accessed through the SubItems property of a ListItem. The text that appears in a column for a particular ListItem can be read or set using:

```
Msgbox ListView1.ListItems(1).SubItems(2)
```

For this example, the preceding code will display the text that appears in the second column, SubItems(2), of the first ListItem, ListItems(1).

ItemClick Event

Most code associated with a ListView control appears in either the ItemClick event or the ColumnClick event. The ItemClick event occurs when the user clicks on a ListItem within the ListView control. The ListItem which was clicked will be passed into the event as an argument.

The ItemClick event occurs only when an item in the list is clicked. If the user clicks anywhere in the ListView control, other than on an item, the regular Click event is triggered.

ColumnClick Event

The ColumnClick event is triggered when the user clicks on the column header of the ListView. The ColumnHeader object that was clicked is passed into the event as an argument.

The code that is typically placed in the ColumnClick event is the code to sort the ListItems by that column. This is the normal behavior expected by users in the Windows environment.

Using the `ToolBar` Control

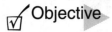

✓ Objective

In earlier, 16-bit releases of Visual Basic, it was difficult to implement a toolbar for your users. You had to place a `PictureBox` control on a form, and then add `CommandButton` controls to the `PictureBox` to simulate the toolbar. With the 32-bit version of Visual Basic 4.0, and now in Visual Basic 5, you have the `ToolBar` ActiveX control that you can add to your forms to easily implement toolbar functionality for your users.

A toolbar is becoming a standard feature of Windows applications. Toolbars provide functionality to a user through an easily accessible, graphical interface. For common functions, the user does not need to navigate through a menu or remember shortcut keys to use an application. Applications are exposing their most common features through buttons on a toolbar.

Setting Custom Properties

The `ToolBar control` is available through the Windows Common Controls, along with the `TreeView`, `ListView`, and `ImageList`. After you have drawn a toolbar on a form, you will usually start by setting properties through the Property Pages dialog box for the control.

On the first tab of the Property Pages dialog box, as shown in Figure 4.9, one of the options you will set most often is the `ImageList`. Like the `TreeView` and the `ListView` controls, the toolbar gets images from an `ImageList` control. If you are building a toolbar that will have graphics on its buttons, you will first need to add an `ImageList` control to the form, and then bind that `ImageList` to the toolbar through the Property Pages dialog box.

Several other properties are unique to the toolbar, and can be set on the General tab. The `ButtonHeight` and `ButtonWidth` properties determine the size of buttons that appear on the toolbar. All buttons will have the same height and width. The number of buttons that can appear on a toolbar is determined by the size of the buttons and the width of the window. If you want the toolbar and buttons to wrap when the window is resized, you can set the `Wrappable` property of the toolbar to `True`.

Figure 4.9

General tab of the custom properties of a toolbar.

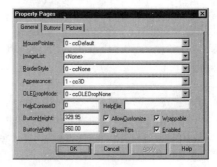

If you want to add Tool Tips to your `ToolBar` control, you must set the `ShowTips` property to `True`. The actual tips that appear are tied to each button. You can allow the user to customize the toolbar by setting the `AllowCustomize` button to `True`. These properties are discussed later in the section titled "Customizing Toolbars."

`Button` Object and `Buttons` Collection

Command buttons on a toolbar are called `Button` objects, and all the `Button` objects are stored in the `Buttons` Collection. This is similar to the way that the `TreeView` `Node` objects are contained in a `Nodes` Collection. Each `Button` object has many properties that control its appearance and functionality. These properties can be set either at design time through the Buttons tab of the Property Pages dialog box (see Figure 4.10), or at runtime.

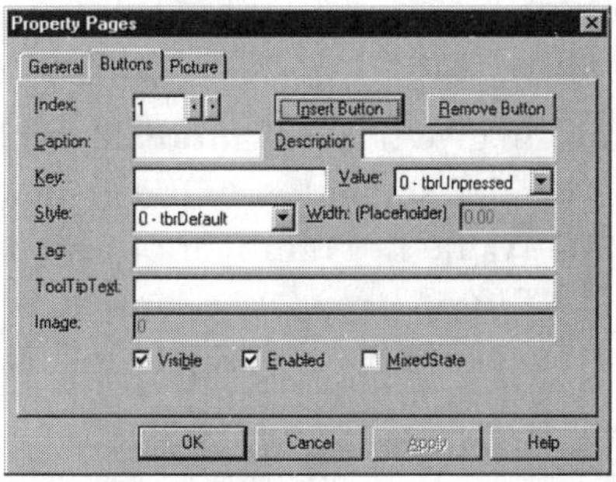

Figure 4.10

Buttons tab of the custom properties of a toolbar.

As with the other controls discussed in this chapter, individual `Button` objects can be referenced by either the `index` property or the `Key` property. The `index` property has an integer value that refers to a button's position on a toolbar. The first button on a toolbar will have an `index` value of 1. The `Key` property is a unique string expression that can be used to access a particular button on a control.

 Caution

> The `Key` property of a `Button` object cannot contain a numeric expression, even if you convert the number using the `Str$()` function first. If you try to use a number converted to a string as the key to a `Button` object, you will receive a runtime error indicating an invalid key value.

`Style` Property

The `Style` property of the `Button` object determines how a button performs on a toolbar. The values that the `Style` property can take are as follows:

▶ `tbrDefault (0)`   The default value for the `Style` property. When buttons have this style, they appear and behave as standard `CommandButton` controls.

▶ `tbrCheck (1)`   The button will function as a check box. This style goes along with the `Value` property (`Pressed` or `Unpressed`). When this button is clicked, it will stay pressed, or indented, until it is clicked a second time.

▶ `tbrButtonGroup (2)`   Buttons with this style function as `OptionButton` controls. Buttons on a toolbar can be grouped together, and all have a style of `tbrButtonGroup` if you want to give the user mutually exclusive options. When the user selects a button in the group, that button will stay depressed (value of 1) until another button in the group is clicked. Button groups are separated from the rest of the buttons in the toolbar by a separator (see following item).

▶ tbrSeparator (3)   If you use this style for a button, it will not appear as a button at all, but as a space between buttons. The space will be a fixed 8 pixels wide.

▶ tbrPlaceholder (4)   This style will allow a button to act like a separator, but the width is adjustable.

Appearance Properties

Several other properties of the Button object control the appearance of each button on the toolbar. The first of these is the image property. The value of image is an integer that maps to the index of an image in an ImageList control. The ImageList used is determined by the ImageList selected on the General tab of the Property Pages dialog box. In addition to an image, you can place a caption on each button of your toolbar by setting the caption property. If you have both an image and a caption on a Button object, the caption will show below the image.

Tool Tips can be added to each button on a toolbar by setting the ToolTipText property. If the ShowTips property of the toolbar is set to True, the ToolTipText of a button will appear to the user when the mouse pointer is rested over that button. This is valuable for new users of an application who do not yet know the purpose of each button.

Add and Remove Methods

Buttons can be added and deleted from a toolbar at runtime by using the Add and Remove methods. The Add method of the Buttons Collection has the following syntax:

```
Toolbar1.Buttons.Add(index, key, caption, style, image)
```

Index is the position at which you want to insert the new button. If you do not specify an index, the new button will appear at the right end of the existing buttons. The key is a string value that can be used to reference the new button. The caption argument will be any text that you want to appear on the new button. Style specifies how a button will behave (as described earlier). Finally, the image argument is an integer value that corresponds to an image in the ImageList connected to the ToolBar control.

To delete an existing button from the toolbar, you can use the Remove method:

```
Toolbar1.Buttons.Remove index
```

where the Index argument is either the integer value for the Index of the Button object you wish to remove, or a string value for the Key of the Button object.

ButtonClick Event

The ButtonClick event for the ToolBar control will trigger whenever a user clicks on a Button object. For each toolbar, there is a single ButtonClick event, not one for each button on the toolbar. The event is triggered as follows:

```
Private Sub Toolbar1_ButtonClick(ByVal button As Button)
```

where the Button argument is a reference to the Button object that has been clicked. You can use this argument to determine which button was clicked by the user, and what to do as a result by using a Select Case statement, such as the following:

```
Private Sub Toolbar1_ButtonClick(ByVal button As Button)

    Select Case button.Key
        Case "Open"
          ' open an existing file
        Case "New"
          ' create a new file
        Case "Exit"
          ' close the application
    End Select

End Sub
```

Customizing Toolbars

Many applications are now allowing users to customize the tool-bars with their own preferences. You can also provide your users the ability to customize the toolbars you create within your application. The first thing you must do before a user can change your toolbar is set the AllowCustomize property to True. As long as AllowCustomize is False, the user cannot make changes.

After AllowCustomize is set to True, customization takes place through the Customize Toolbar dialog box, as shown in Figure 4.11. This dialog box becomes available to the user in one of two ways. The first way is if the user double-clicks on the ToolBar control. The second way is if the Customize method of the toolbar is called.

Figure 4.11

The Customize Toolbar dialog box.

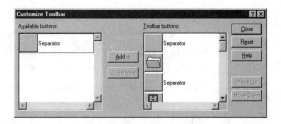

If you will be allowing a user to make changes to a toolbar, you should consider using two additional methods: SaveToolbar and RestoreToolbar. With these two methods, you can save settings from the toolbar in the Windows Registry, and then read them back at a later time to restore the appearance of a toolbar either to the original settings or to the user's personal settings when the application is restarted.

The SaveToolbar method has the following syntax:

```
Toolbar1.SaveToolbar(key As String, subkey As String, value As
➥String)
```

The RestoreToolbar has the following syntax:

```
Toolbar1.RestoreToolbar(key As String, subkey As String, value As
➥String)
```

The key and subkey arguments are the key and subkey of the Windows Registry at which you are storing information, or from where you are retrieving information. The value argument is the information that you are saving or reading.

Using the StatusBar Control

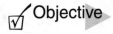 Objective

The StatusBar control is another ActiveX control available through the Windows Common Controls components. With the StatusBar, you can easily display information about the date, time, and other details about the application and the environment to the user.

Panel Object and Panels Collection

A StatusBar is broken into Panel objects, each of which displays different types of information. All the Panel objects are contained in the Panels Collection of the StatusBar. The appearance and purpose of each Panel is determined by the Style property of that Panel. The following styles are available:

▶ sbrText (0)   The Panel will display text information. The information displayed is in the Text property of the Panel.

▶ sbrCaps (1)   The Panel will contain the string "Caps". It will be highlighted if Caps Lock is turned on, or disabled if Caps Lock is turned off.

▶ sbrNum (2)   The Panel will contain the string "Num". It will be highlighted if Num Lock is turned on, or disabled if Num Lock is turned off.

▶ sbrIns (3)   The Panel will contain the string "Ins". It will be highlighted if Insert mode is turned on, or disabled if Insert mode is turned off.

▶ sbrScrl (4)   The Panel will contain the string "Scrl". It will be highlighted if Scroll Lock is turned on, or disabled if Scroll Lock is turned off.

▶ sbrTime (5)   The Panel will display the current time in the system format.

▶ sbrDate (6)   The Panel will display the current date in the system format.

▶ sbrKana (7)   The Panel will contain the string "Kana". It will be highlighted if Kana (a special character set) is enabled, or disabled if Kana is disabled.

Figure 4.12 shows an example of a status bar displaying all the different styles.

Figure 4.12

Different styles of the Panel object.

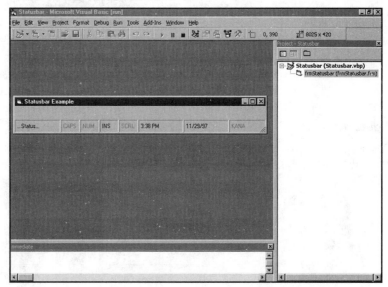

As with the other controls discussed in this chapter, the properties of the StatusBar and the Button objects can be set either through the Property Pages dialog box at design time, or at runtime. The properties of the StatusBar control can be set on the General tab, as shown in Figure 4.13.

The Style and SimpleText properties of the toolbar determine the appearance of the control at runtime. The Style property can have one of two values: Simple or Normal. When the Style property is Simple, only one panel of the StatusBar is visible, and the text in the `SimpleText` property is displayed. When the `Style` property is `Normal`, the `StatusBar` appears with multiple panels.

Figure 4.13

General properties of the StatusBar.

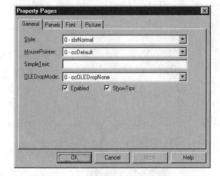

Properties of the `Panel` objects have further control over the appearance of a `StatusBar` control. These properties can be set on the Panels tab of the Property Pages dialog box, as shown in Figure 4.14, or at runtime.

Figure 4.14

Custom properties of the Panel object.

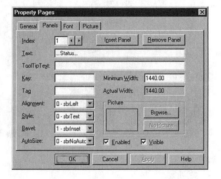

The use of Tool Tips is available to you with the `StatusBar` control. Behavior of Tool Tips for the `StatusBar` is similar to the behavior of Tool Tips for the `ToolBar` control (discussed earlier in "Using the `ToolBar` Control"). An individual `ToolTipText` property is available for each panel of the `StatusBar` control. When the `ShowTips` property of the `StatusBar` is set to `True`, and the user rests the mouse pointer over a panel in the `StatusBar`, the `ToolTipText` is displayed at the mouse pointer.

Several other `Panel` properties affect the appearance of each panel. The `Alignment` property determines whether text displayed in a panel is left justified, right justified, or centered. The `MinWidth` property specifies the minimum width of a panel. The `ScaleMode` of the container on which the `StatusBar` is located determines the units for the `MinWidth`. Each panel also has a `Width` property, which determines the starting width of the object.

The `AutoSize` property of a panel can also have an impact on its width. This property can have the following values:

▶ `sbrNoAutoSize (0)` The panel size will not be changed automatically.

▶ `sbrSpring (1)` If the size of the `StatusBar` increases as the size of the container grows, the width of the `Panel` will also increase. As a `StatusBar` grows smaller, the size of the `Panel` will not go below the `MinWidth` value.

▶ `sbrContents (2)` The `Panel` will be resized to fit its contents, but will never fall below the `MinWidth`.

Another property that affects a panel's appearance is the `Picture`. If you wish to include images—either bitmaps or icons—in a panel, you can add them through the Property Pages dialog box, or at runtime with `LoadPicture`. Unlike the other controls discussed in this chapter, the `StatusBar` does not get images from an `ImageList`. You must specify the image file directly.

Add and Remove Methods

The `Add` method of the `Panels` Collection can be used to add panels to the `StatusBar` at runtime. The syntax is similar to the other `Add` methods discussed in this chapter:

```
StatusBar1.Panels.Add(index, key, text, style, picture)
```

`Index` and `Key` are the unique identifiers that enable you to access a particular `Panel` object. The `text` argument is the text that appears in a panel. How a `Panel` object appears, and what data it contains, is determined by the `Style` argument. Finally, if you want to add an image in the new panel, you can use the `LoadPicture` function in the `Picture` argument to include that image along with any other text that appears.

Panels can be removed at runtime by using the `Remove` method of the `StatusBar`. To remove a `Panel` object, you would use the following:

```
StatusBar1.Remove index
```

where the `index` argument is either an integer equal to the `index` property of the panel, which you are removing, or a string value equal to the `Key` of the panel.

Using the Controls Collection

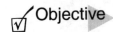
Objective

The Controls Collection is a collection within a form, defined by Visual Basic, which contains references to all the controls on that form. Each member of the collection is a different object on that form—for example, a `TextBox`, `ComboBox`, `ListView`, and so on. Each form in a project has its own Controls Collection that can be used by you, as a developer, to navigate through the different controls on a form. Each control within the collection is referenced as follows:

```
Form.Controls(index)
```

where `Form` is the form name, and `index` is an integer value referring to the desired control. Index values range from 0 through the total number of controls on a form, minus 1. If you have 10 controls on a form, the index values for the Controls Collection would go from 0 through 9.

You will usually use a Controls Collection when you need to process all the controls, or the majority of the controls on a given form. You can loop through a Controls Collection either with a `For Next` loop:

```
For I = 0 To Form1.Controls.Count - 1
    ' process Form1.Controls(I)
Next
```

or with a For Each loop:

```
Dim obj As Control
For Each obj In Form1.Controls
    ' process obj
Next
```

A common use of the Controls Collection is to clear all the controls on a form. If the user wants to reset all the fields on a data entry form, you can code a Clear button with the following code:

```
Private Sub cmdClear_Click()

    Dim objControl As Control
    Dim sTemp As String

    For Each objControl In Me.Controls

        If TypeOf objControl Is TextBox Then
            ' clear the text
            objControl.Text = ""
        ElseIf TypeOf objControl Is ComboBox Then
            ' reset the listindex
            objControl.ListIndex = -1
        ElseIf TypeOf objControl Is Label Then
            ' leave labels as is
        ElseIf TypeOf objControl Is CommandButton Then
            ' leave comboboxes as is
        ElseIf TypeOf objControl Is MaskEdBox Then
            ' clear the masked edit control
            sTemp = objControl.Mask
            objControl.Mask = ""
            objControl.Text = ""
            objControl.Mask = sTemp
        Else
            ' leave any other control alone
        End If
    Next

End Sub
```

This code loops through all the controls on a form, and clears each control based on its type. To clear a `TextBox` control, for example, you would set the `Text` property to a 0-length string. To clear a `CheckBox`, you would set the `value` property to `vbUnchecked`.

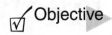 **Key Concepts**

Notice that the preceding code uses an `If` statement to determine the type of control being cleared. You must make sure you know the type of control you reference to avoid runtime errors. Errors will occur if you try to reference a property of a control that is not a valid property. If the first control on a form is a `TextBox`, you can clear that control by using:

```
Me.Controls(0).Text = ""
```

If, on the other hand, the first control is a `CheckBox`, which does not have a `Text` property, with the same code, you will get a runtime error from Visual Basic. The Clear button code example avoids this problem by checking for specific control types within the Controls Collection. The syntax for the `If` statement is as follows:

```
If TypeOf objectname Is objecttype Then
    ' code
EndIf
```

where `objectname` is the object or control (that is, `TextBox`, `ComboBox`, and so forth) on which you are working, and `objecttype` is the class of the object. Using this `If` structure before you reference a control through the Controls Collection will help you avoid runtime errors.

Adding and Deleting Controls Dynamically

☑ **Objective**

Occasionally, you will create forms for which you do not always have a fixed number of controls. You may have to add controls at runtime, or remove some of the controls that you have created. Visual Basic enables you to create and destroy controls dynamically at runtime, based on the needs of your application.

Key Concepts   You must follow several rules to be able to create and remove controls as needed. First, you must have a control of the type you will be creating dynamically placed on the desired form at runtime. If you will be creating `TextBox` controls dynamically on a form, for example, you must have at least one text box drawn on that form at design time. That control can be invisible, and there are no restrictions for the size or placement of that control, but it must be on the form at design time. This control will be the template for dynamically created text boxes.

Key Concepts   The second requirement for using dynamic controls is that the template object you draw at design time must be part of a control array. Usually it is the only control of its type, but has an `Index` value of 0. Continuing with the text box example, you can have a form with only one text box as a template, and that text box must have its `index` property set to 0. If your application required it, you might have additional text boxes with `index` values of 1, 2, 3, and so on. As long as you have a control array with at least one object in it, you can create additional instances of that object dynamically at runtime.

After you have built a form with a control that has its `index` property set to 0 (or higher if you have additional controls in the array), you can create additional controls at runtime. Assume, for example, that you have an application with one form, `Form1`, and one text box, `Text1`. `Text1` has an `index` value of 0. At runtime, you can create additional instances of `Text1` on your form by:

```
Load Text1 (index)
```

where `index` is an integer value that will be used as the index of the new text box. When you run the application, and want to create the first dynamic instance of `Text1`, you would use:

```
Load Text1 (1)
```

because `index` value 0 is already in use by the `Template` control.

After you have loaded the new control on the form, you must set the appearance as desired. You have to set the `Visible` property to

True, if you want the control to appear to the user. Also, the Width and Top properties have to be changed to place the control on the form. Finally, you can change the Height, Width, and any other property that can be altered at runtime.

Code for creating labels dynamically would look like this:

```
' load a new control into the control array
Load lblTemplate(i)

' position the new control on the form and add a caption
lblTemplate(i).Left = lblTemplate(0).Left
lblTemplate(i).Top = lblTemplate(i - 1).Top + _
                     lblTemplate(i - 1).Height + 100
lblTemplate(i).Caption = "This is a new label control with an
➥index of " _
                     & Str$(i)

' make the control visible
lblTemplate(i).Visible = True
```

After you have added dynamic controls to a form, you may need to remove them at some point. To remove a control that you have created dynamically, you simply code the following:

```
Unload Text1(index)
```

where Text1 is the name of the control you loaded previously, and index is the integer value of that control's Index property.

Key Concepts

It is important to remember that you cannot remove the control on the form with an index property of 0 (the template). Also, controls that were added to a form at design time cannot be removed from the form with the Unload statement. Only controls created dynamically can be removed.

Exercises

Exercise 4.1: Using a *ListView* and an *ImageList* Control

In this exercise, you use a ListView and two ImageList controls to display a list of items. The ImageList controls will contain images that will be shown in the ListView. You will bind the controls together and allow a user to add ListItems to the form.

As a reference, use the sections titled "Using the ImageList Control" and "Using the ListView Control."

1. Start a new project in Visual Basic, and create a form like the one shown in Figure 4.15. The form will contain a ListView, two ImageLists, OptionButtons that will be used to change the appearance of the list, text boxes for the user to enter the Key and Index values of the ListItems, and Slider controls to allow the user to select icons.

Figure 4.15

The form for Exercise 4.1.

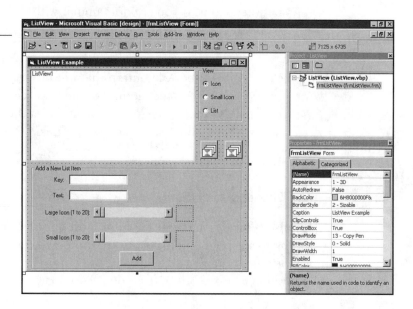

2. Add images to the ImageList controls. Right-click on the first ImageList and select Properties. Choose 32×32, and then click on the Images tab. Now insert several images into the

continues

ImageList. Choose icons (*.ico) files from either the Visual Basic graphics directories, or by selecting any other *.ico files from your PC. This ImageList will contain the regular icons for your ListView. Now repeat the process for the second ImageList (for small icons). This time, however, choose 16×16 as a size before inserting any images.

3. Bind the ListView to the ImageLists. Bring up the custom properties window for the ListView. Click on the Image Lists tab. Select one image list for the normal icons and the other for small icons.

4. Add code to the OptionButtons that will change the appearance of the ListView from Normal to Small Icons, to List. This is done by setting the View property of the ListView.

5. Now code the Slider controls to allow the user to choose between icons. If you are not familiar with the Slider control, you can use text boxes instead to allow the user to enter an image Index.

6. Place code in the Add button that will insert an item into the ListView. Use the Add method of the ListItems Collection to do this. Use the input from the form to set the Key, Text, Normal Icon, and Small Icon properties.

7. Run and test the application.

In this exercise, you create a toolbar, add buttons, and change setting to see how a toolbar appears and performs at runtime. You will be able to standardize buttons, use button groups, and add separators to space out buttons on the toolbar.

This exercise covers information from the section titled "Using the ToolBar Control."

1. Start a new project in Visual Basic. Add an ImageList and a toolbar to the form.

2. Add some icons to the `ImageList` control with the custom properties dialog box (see the section titled "Using the `ImageList` Control" for help). You can select any icons that you have available.

3. Open the Property Pages dialog box for the toolbar. On the General tab, set a reference to your `ImageList`.

4. Go to the Buttons tab, and add a button to the control. Set the `Style` to be the `Default`. Enter an image number and add any text that you wish.

5. Add another button to the control, and set the `Style` to be a `Separator`. Then add three more buttons and set their `Style` to `Group`. For the three buttons in the group, add images and text.

6. Add another separator button, and then add two more buttons. For these two, set the `Style` to `Check`. Again, add images and text to the buttons.

7. Run the application. Click on the buttons one at a time to see how they perform. Click on the buttons in the group. Can you select more than one at a time? Click the button that is a Check button. Does it stay depressed after it is clicked? Click on it again.

Exercise 4.3: Using the Controls Collection

In this exercise, you use the Controls Collection of a form to clear input fields. You will code a `For Each` loop to cycle through all the controls on a form, and you will use the `If TypeOf` statement to clear the value of the controls on the form.

Refer to the section titled "Using the Controls Collection" for help with this exercise.

1. Open a new project in Visual Basic. Add several input controls including `TextBoxes`, `CheckBoxes`, `OptionButtons`, and `ComboBoxes`. Add at least one item to each `ComboBox`.

continues

2. Add a command button to the form. Add code to the command button that will loop through all the controls on the form, using the Controls Collection, and clear each input control that was added in Step 1. Use a For Each loop to navigate through the Controls Collection. Be sure to check the class of each control by using the If TypeOf statement, to make sure you are clearing each one properly.

3. Run the application. Fill in all the input fields. Select values from the OptionButtons and ComboBoxes. Check the CheckBoxes.

4. Click on the Clear button. Did all the controls clear? Did they clear without any runtime errors?

Review Questions

1. If you add nodes to a `TreeView` control that has already been sorted, how do you get the new node to be in the correct sort order?

   A. The new node will automatically be placed in the correct sorted sequence.

   B. Set the `Sorted` property of the `TreeView` to `True`.

   C. Execute the `Sort` method of the `TreeView`.

   D. None of these.

2. What three properties affect the sort order of `ListItems` in a `ListView` control?

   A. `SortKey`

   B. `SortItem`

   C. `Sorted`

   D. `SortOrder`

3. What image file formats can be loaded into the `ImageList` control? (Select all correct answers.)

   A. *.ico

   B. *.gif

   C. *.jpg

   D. *.bmp

4. If you want to have images displayed on the buttons of a toolbar, how do you add these images to the control?

   A. With the `LoadPicture()` function

   B. From an `ImageList` control

   C. From a *.bmp file

   D. All of these

5. What are the areas of a `StatusBar` control in which information is displayed?

    A. `Node` objects

    B. `Status` objects

    C. `ListItem` objects

    D. `Panel` objects

6. If you are removing controls from your form dynamically (at runtime), what controls can you remove?

    A. Controls you have created dynamically.

    B. Any controls on the form.

    C. Any controls that are part of a control array.

    D. You cannot remove controls dynamically.

7. If you are using a Control Collection of a form to loop through and clear control, how do you determine the class of each control?

    A. Using the `Select Case Type` statement.

    B. Checking the `Name` property of each control for standard control prefixes.

    C. Using the `If TypeOf` statement.

    D. You don't need to check the class of a control before clearing it.

8. What type of objects are contained in an `ImageList` control, and what is the collection that holds these objects?

    A. `Image` objects, and the `Images` Collection

    B. `Picture` objects, and the `Pictures` Collection

    C. `Bitmap` objects, and `Bitmaps` Collection

    D. `ListImage` objects, and `ListImages` Collection

9. When you add new nodes to a `TreeView` control, you can specify a `Relationship` argument that determines placement of the new node in relation to the `Relative` argument. Which of these is not a valid relationship?

   A. `tvwFirst`

   B. `tvwNext`

   C. `tvwChild`

   D. `tvwAfter`

10. Values of what data type can be used as the key value for an object in the `ListItems` Collection of a `ListView`?

    A. String

    B. Integer

    C. Long

    D. Variant

11. How are columns added to a `ListView` control?

    A. By incrementing the `Columns` property.

    B. By using the `InsertColumn` method.

    C. By adding `ColumnHeader` objects to the `ColumnHeaders` Collection.

    D. Columns cannot be added to a `ListView` control.

12. Which property of a `Button` object in a toolbar will determine the way in which a button performs (that is, as a separator, part of a group, check, and so forth)?

    A. `Action`

    B. `Style`

    C. `Type`

    D. `Context`

13. If you want to reference all the controls on a form, `Form1`, which two `For` statements enable you to do this?

    A. `For I = 1 to Form1.Controls.Count`

    B. `For I = 0 to Form1.Controls.Count - 1`

    C. `For Each obj in Form1.Controls`

    D. `For Each obj in Form1.Controls.Count`

Answers to Review Questions

1. B. The `Sorted` property must be set to `True`, even if it was `True` when the new node was added. For more information, see the section titled "Using the `TreeView` Control."

2. A, C, D. The `Sorted`, `SortKey`, and `SortOrder` properties determine whether, and how, `ListItems` will be sorted in a `ListView`. For more information, see the section titled "Using the `ListView` Control."

3. A, D. Icons (*.ico) and bitmaps (*.bmp) files can be loaded into the `ImageList` control. For more information, see the section titled "Using the `ImageList` Control."

4. B. Images used by the `ToolBar` control can only come from an `ImageList` control that has been placed on the same form. For more information, see the section titled "Using the `ToolBar` Control."

5. D. Status information is displayed in one or more `Panel` objects on a `StatusBar`. For more information, see the section titled "Using the `StatusBar` Control."

6. A. You can only remove controls you have created dynamically. For more information, see the section titled "Adding and Deleting Controls Dynamically."

7. C. The `If TypeOf` statement can be used to determine the class of an object. It is important to check the type before referencing any properties or method of an object to avoid

runtime errors. For more information, see the section titled "Using the Controls Collection."

8. D. An `ImageList` contains `ListImage` objects. `ListImage` objects are referenced through the `ListImages` Collection. For more information, see the section titled "Using the `ImageList` Control."

9. D. The valid relationships are `tvwFirst`, `tvwLast`, `tvwNext`, `tvwPrevious`, and `tvwChild`. `tvwAfter` is not a valid relationship. For more information, see the section titled "Using the `TreeView` Control."

10. A. Key values of the `ListItems` Collection (and all collections) must be strings. For more information, see the section titled "Using the `ListView` Control."

11. C. The number of columns in a `ListView` control is controlled by the number of objects in the `ColumnHeaders` Collection. For more information, see the section titled "Using the `ListView` Control."

12. B. The `Style` property controls the behavior of a button. Valid values include `tbrDefault`, `tbrCheck`, `tbrButtonGroup`, `tbrSeparator`, and `tbrPlaceholder`. For more information, see the section titled "Using the `ToolBar` Control."

13. B and C. If you use a `For I = ...` statement, the index value of Controls Collection ranges from 0 to n-1, where n is the number of controls on the form. For more information, see the section titled "Using the Controls Collection."

Answers to Test Yourself Questions at Beginning of Chapter

1. The Index and Key properties. Index is an integer value, and Key is a string value. Both are unique within the Nodes Collection, and can be used to retrieve a specific node. See "Using the TreeView Control."

2. The four styles of the ListView are Icon, Small Icon, List, and Report. They are set by using the View property of the object. See "Using the ListView Control."

3. Only a single image format can be used in an ImageList. 16×16, 32×32, 48×48 icons, and bitmaps must be loaded into separate ImageLists. After an image of one format is loaded, images of different formats cannot be loaded. See "Using the ImageList Control."

4. The ShowTips property of the toolbar dictates whether Tool Tips are displayed. The ToolTipText property of the Button object on the toolbar identifies the text that will be displayed when the user rests the mouse pointer over a button. See "Using the ToolBar Control."

5. There is no need to use code that will update the current time in a StatusBar panel. The StatusBar itself will keep the time current while the application is running. See "Using the StatusBar Control."

6. Each Visual Basic application has one Controls Collection per form. Controls Collections are created and maintained for you automatically. See "Using the Controls Collection."

7. To create text boxes dynamically, you must place at least one text box on your form at design time, and you must also set the Index property of that control to 0 to create a control array. See "Adding and Deleting Controls Dynamically."

P a r t **2**

Coding Issues

C h a p t e r

Declaring a Variable

5

This chapter helps you prepare for the exam by covering the following objectives:

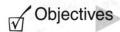 Objectives

- ▶ Define the scope of a variable by using the Public, Private and Static statements

- ▶ Use the appropriate declaration statement

Test Yourself! Before reading this chapter, test yourself to determine how much study time you will need to devote to this section.

1. Variables can be used by just assigning information to a variable name or by having a statement that describes the scope, name, and data type to be used in the source code. What are the names of these two different types of variable declarations used in Visual Basic?

2. Which Visual Basic statement is used to force the programmer to declare all variables before they can be used in the source code?

3. In which part of the source code would a statement be placed that would force the programmer to declare all variables before they are used?

4. Visual Basic uses two keywords to force the programmer to declare variables. These two keywords are required in a certain section within the source code. Does the VB programming environment come with an option that will assist the programmer with automatically inserting these statements into the source code, and if so, where is it located?

5. Visual Basic contains many different data types. Each data type has a unique name that describes the type of information that can be stored as well as the amount of memory that is used. Name at least five different data types for Visual Basic.

6. Programmers can use implicit variable declarations to assign information to a variable. This enables the programmer not to have to specify the type of data being stored in the variable. Of the different data types in Visual Basic, which one is automatically assigned if a data type has not been explicitly declared?

7. A variable declaration can be used to set the scope of a variable as well as the name and data type. What is the keyword used to define a local variable that will retain its value after the procedure has completed execution?

8. What is the keyword used to declare a variable that will be available to all components and for the lifetime of an application?

9. An explicit variable declaration informs the compiler of the scope, name, and data type of a variable before it is used. Implicit declaration does not inform the compiler of the variables before they are used. What is the scope of a variable created by an implicit variable declaration?

10. A form code module can create a public variable by having it declared in the General Declarations section. If a different form had a procedure that required the information from the first form's public variable, how would it be referenced?

11. Assume a procedure call required using the name of the standard module before the name of the publicly scoped variable. What can be determined about the project from this call? Describe the components, variables, and their scope.

12. Public variables can be set by any procedure within a project. To reduce the problems of tracking which procedures change the variable, you can use what other method to provide information when needed?

Answers are located at the end of the chapter...

Variables are a very critical part of any application. By learning how to properly work with variables and how to store information in memory, the programmer can create faster, more efficient programs.

This chapter discusses various aspects of using variables within Visual Basic. The first section of the chapter deals with the proper statements required to declare a variable. The declaration of a variable is reviewed, and the use of scope in a declaration is discussed.

The second section covers the use of variables that have different scope. Scope allows variables to be restricted to different areas of the application. Which variables are available to which applications components is also examined.

This chapter covers the following topics:

- ▶ Overview of variables

- ▶ The two types of variable declarations

- ▶ Declaring a variable

- ▶ Forcing variable declaration with `Option Explicit`

- ▶ Declaring a variable of a certain data type

- ▶ Declaring a variable with different scope

- ▶ Declaring `Local` and `Static` variables

- ▶ Declaring `Private` and `Public` variables

- ▶ Using `Local` and `Static` variables

- ▶ Using `Private` and `Public` variables

Defining the Scope of a Variable

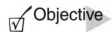√ Objective ▶

Variables are storage locations in memory that are used for a wide variety of data. The variable receives a variable name from the programmer, which allows access to the memory location. The programmer does not have to know the physical memory address of information to retrieve and manipulate it. The variable name is used as a reference to the physical address and reduces the work of the programmer.

After information has been stored, the programmer, application, or user can affect the value held within a variable. Various calculations can be performed on the stored value, or the value can be used in other calculations.

For the operating system to allocate the memory required for a variable, the programmer must decide what type of data the variable will hold. Data comes in many forms and sizes. Small numbers can take very little memory; however, decimal precision can require a lot of memory. Each type of data has a different physical memory requirement. Each programming language has a set of data types, which describe the type of information and how much memory space will be used to hold it. A good programmer will always attempt to use the most effective data type and reduce the memory used by the application.

When the programmer requires a variable, Visual Basic allows two different ways of declaring them. The first method is called *implicit* variable declaration. This method enables a programmer to use a variable anytime he or she requires one. The programmer just has to type a new variable name into the source code and the variable is automatically created by VB. The following line of code uses implicit variable declaration:

```
x = "Hello"
```

In this code sample, the x contains the string value "Hello". Visual Basic automatically created x and selected a default data type for the variable.

The second method of using variables is called *explicit* variable declaration. To use this method, the programmer must first name the variable and describe what type of information will be contained within the variable. The following line of code is an example of explicit variable declaration:

```
Dim x As String
```

In this code sample, before the programmer can use x and assign a value to it, the x must be declared. The `Dim` statement is used to dimension a variable called x. The variable will hold `String` information.

Explicit declarations have the following three parts. The first word is a keyword that determines the scope or lifetime of the variable. The second part is the variable name that will be used in the source code. The third part is the data type of the variable that tells the computer how much memory is required to hold the information.

Both methods of variable declaration can be used with Visual Basic. When working with large projects, or to help reduce source code problems, many programmers use explicit variable declaration. It may require a few extra lines of code, but it can save many hours of frustration and debugging code. When a typo is made on a variable name, the compiler generates an error before running the code. This is due to a special statement that tells the compiler that all variables must be previously declared before they can be used.

The statement `Option Explicit` requires that the programmer inform the compiler of a variable's scope, name, and data type before the variable is used. This statement must appear at the beginning of any type of code module in the General Declarations section. To assist the programmer with explicit declaration, VB has an option that will automatically insert the `Option Explicit` statement into any new code module that is created, as shown in Figure 5.1. Existing code modules will have to have the statement put in manually. To force variable declaration, ensure that the Tools, Options, Editor tab's Require Variable Declaration check box is checked, as shown in Figure 5.2.

Figure 5.1

The General Declarations section with the Option Explicit statement used to force variable declarations.

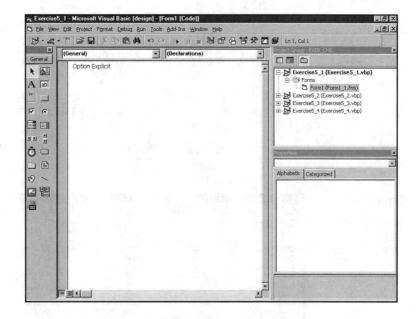

Figure 5.2

The Require Variable Declaration check box will automatically include the Option Explicit statement in the General Declarations section of new code modules.

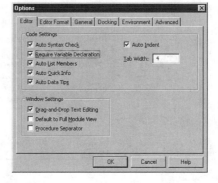

This chapter further examines the requirements of using the explicit variable declaration because it is a more complex and efficient method.

Visual Basic Data Types

Of the three key components to an explicit declaration, the third part—data type—describes the type of information stored within memory. Visual Basic contains many data types. Each data type has a specific name that is used to refer to the information it can hold, as well as to the amount of memory used by that data type.

 Note

For a complete listing of the data types, see Visual Basic Help. Search for "data types," and then look for "data type summary." Figure 5.3 shows the reference page.

Figure 5.3

Visual Basic data type summary.

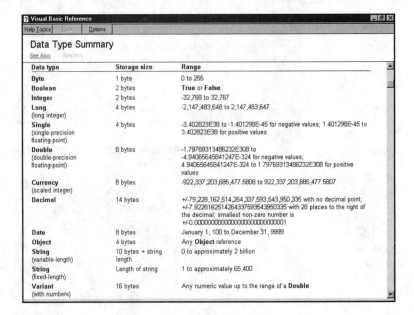

Each data type has been designed to hold a particular piece of information. This allows for optimized memory use. It also enables the programmer to better control the memory requirements and performance of the application.

Visual Basic has many different data types that allow for storage of simple numbers, complex numbers, strings, dates and times, as well as objects. One of the more complex data types in VB is the Variant. This is the default data type of Visual Basic. Variants can be used to store information from any of the other data types. This makes the Variant a very flexible variable but significantly increases the storage requirements. Following are example declarations of various data types:

```
Dim iLoop As Integer
Dim lCounter As Long
Dim strFirstName As String
Dim dblRate as Double
```

The first example declares the variable name of iLoop to store Integer data. The second declares lCounter to store Long numbers. The third variable holds string and the fourth allocates storage for a double number. These samples all use a standard naming convention that describes the type of data they contain by using a special letter prefix followed by the name of the variable. This assists anyone who will be reading the source code so he or she will know the type of data being stored without having to read the declarations. All these code samples have also explicitly declared the type of data to be stored.

When variables are implicitly declared, they do not inform the compiler of which data type will be used. With Visual Basic, the compiler automatically assigns implicit variables with the default data type of Variant. This increases the amount of memory that the application will use. To reduce the storage of information in memory, programmers use explicit declarations. This enables the programmer to inform the compiler of the name and data type of the variable to be used. The compiler then verifies that the correct information is passed to variables.

When incorrect information is assigned to a previously declared variable, a runtime error occurs. The type mismatch is an error that new programmers quickly get accustomed to. To avoid these errors, the programmer must closely monitor how the program assigns information to the variables. When information is manipulated, the programmer must explicitly convert the information before assigning it to a different data type variable. This type of data control requires more attention, but ensures that the application is always doing exactly what it was designed to do.

Scope of Variables

Thus far, you have seen that a variable declaration contains the name of the variable as well as the data type. Another important aspect of a variable declaration is the *scope*. The scope of a variable determines where in the application that variable can be referenced. This allows only certain parts of the program to have access to information and provides security for the data.

The four different types of variable scopes are:

▶ Local

▶ Static

▶ Private

▶ Public

Defining the scope of a variable requires two things. The first is *where* in the project the variable is declared. The second is the *keyword* used in front of the variable name. The following are some code examples of different variable declarations:

```
Dim iLoop As Integer
Static iLoop As Integer
Private iLoop As Integer
Public iLoop As Integer
```

The code samples all declare the same variable name and the same variable type. Notice, however, that the keyword to declare the variable is different for each one.

These four keywords allow the variable being declared to be restricted to certain areas of the application. This enables the programmer tighter control over what information is being assigned to variables. The scope also prevents other procedures from unexpectedly changing the value of the variables.

The keywords Public, Private, Static, and Dim are all used to set the scope. Each has a specific location where it can be used to declare the variable. These keywords must be used in the correct location within the VB source code; otherwise the declaration will not be valid, and a syntax error will occur.

Declaring Local Variables

Local variables are declared within a `Sub`, `Function`, or `Property` procedure. The keyword `Dim` is used in front of the variable name and data type:

```
Dim strFirstName As String
```

Local variables are also referred to as *procedure level* variables. These variables are created and exist only as long as the procedure is executing. When the procedure has completed, the variable is no longer available and will be reset upon the next execution of the procedure:

```
Sub SetFirst()
    Dim strFirstName As String
    strFirstName = txtFirstName.Text
    MsgBox "The first name contains " & Len(strFirstName) &
    ➥" characters.", vbInformation
End Sub
```

Local variables are accessible to the code only within the procedure. Program code outside the procedure cannot use or set a locally scoped variable. This protects the information stored within that variable. The variable can be used by other variables and properties, or it can be passed as an argument to other procedures.

The `Dim` keyword is primarily used within a procedure. VB will allow the use of the `Dim` keyword in the General Declarations section of a code module. When used outside a procedure, the `Dim` statement creates a variable with `Private` scope. The use of the keyword `Private` is preferred over `Dim` in the General Declarations section and has been allowed only for compatibility with previous versions of Visual Basic. The keyword `Private` cannot be used within a procedure.

Declaring Static Variables

Static variables are created within a Sub, Function, or Property procedure. The keyword Static is used before the variable name and the data type:

```
Static X As Integer
```

Static variables are used within the procedure level. The main difference between local variables and static variables is the life span. Static variables retain their values even after the procedure has finished executing. Local variables are reset every time the procedure executes:

```
Sub TestLoop()
    Static X As Integer
    X = X + 1
    MsgBox "The value of X is " & X
End Sub
```

Similar to local variables, a static variable is only accessible to the code within the procedure where the variable has been declared. Program code outside the procedure cannot "see" the variable. This restricts outside code from both using and setting the statically scoped variable. The variable can be used by other variables and properties or passed as an argument to other procedures.

The Static keyword can be used only within a procedure. A compiler error is generated if the Static keyword is used in the General Declarations section of a code module.

Declaring Private Variables

Private variables are created in the General Declarations section of any type of code module. The keyword Private is used in front of the variable name and data type:

```
Private iPage As Integer
```

A privately scoped variable is accessible only to procedures contained within the same code module. If a variable were declared in the General Declarations section of a form code module, procedures from only that form would have access to the variable. Procedures from other form code modules or standard modules would not be able to access the privately scoped variable:

```
Sub Command1_Click()
    iPage = iPage + 1
    MsgBox "There are " & iPage & " pages currently.",
    ➥vbInformation
End Sub
```

The preceding code sample assumes the previous declaration sample has been made in the General Declarations section of the same form code module. The value of the variable is used and set within the Command1_Click procedure. The variable retains its value until the form is unloaded.

When using standard or class modules, variables can also be privately scoped by using a declaration for the variable in the General Declarations section. The privately scoped variable will be accessible only to procedures from the same standard or class module.

Declaring Public Variables

Public variables are created in the General Declarations section of any type of code module. The keyword Public is used in front of the variable name and data type:

```
Public iPage As Integer
```

Public variables are available to all components within the application. The variable is retained for the lifetime of the application.

Publicly scoped variables can be used and set by any code component whether form, standard, or class module.

To reference a publicly scoped variable declared on a form code module, the name of the form must be referenced first, followed by the variable name.

In standard modules, the name does not have to be referenced unless there are multiple modules with the same publicly scoped variable name. Then the module name must be referenced first, followed by the variable name.

Classes must be instantiated before publicly scoped variables of the class can be accessed.

Using the Appropriate Declaration Statement

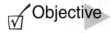 Objective

To protect data that has been assigned to a variable, the programmer can use the scope of a variable to determine where in the application the variable can be accessed. This allows only required parts of the program to be able to change a variable.

One of the most important reasons for using the correct variable scope is to prevent logical errors in the application. A logical error occurs when the program is functioning, but not with the desired results. Logical errors can often be attributed to the programmer expecting a variable to have a certain value when it does not. This "unexpected" value could be caused from a certain procedure within the application changing the variable. Limiting which parts of the application can have access to certain variables can control these logical errors.

This chapter has already discussed the requirements for declaring a variable with certain scope. The following section expands on that information by showing specific uses of local, static, private, and public variables.

Using Local Variables

The keyword Dim is used within a procedure to declare a locally scoped variable.

Note

When an implicit variable declaration is made, the variable will be a `Variant` data type and have local scope. This is another limitation of implicit variable declaration.

Local variables should be used when the value they contain will no longer be required after the procedure has completed execution. The local variable will be reset when the procedure is executed again, thus losing its value.

Some examples of local variable use would be for looping counters, status flags, calculations, and property values. Local variables often have property values assigned and then are manipulated by the procedure. This reduces the work that Visual Basic must perform to resolve object references.

```
Sub Command1_Click()
    Dim iLoop As Integer
    For iLoop = 1 To 100
        Print iLoop
    Next iLoop
End Sub
```

When the preceding code sample is executed, the `iLoop` variable is used to increment the `For` loop and then print the value to the default `Form` object. The variable cannot be altered from outside the `Command1_Click` procedure due to the local scope:

```
Function CountFullName()As Integer
    Dim strFirstName As String, strLastName As String
    Dim iLenFirstName As Integer, iLenLastName As Integer
    strFirstName = frmMain.txtFirstName.Text
    strLastName = frmMain.txtLastName.Text
    iLenFirstName = Len(strFirstName)
    iLenLastName = Len(strLastName)
    frmMain.txtFullName.Text = strFirstName & " " & strLastName
    CountFullName = iLenFirstName + iLenLastName
End Function
```

The preceding code sample demonstrates assigning the value from a property to a locally scoped variable. Then the variable is used to manipulate the information. This reduces the time to have the object reference searched for. The lengths of the first and last names are measured, and then added together, and then used as the return value of the function.

Using Static Variables

The keyword Static is used within a procedure to declare a statically scoped variable.

Static variables should be used when the value they contain is required to remain after the procedure has executed, but the value is not to be altered outside the procedure.

One of the more popular methods to show how a static variable compares to a local variable is a counter loop in a command button, (see Figure 5.4):

```
Sub Command1_Click()
    Dim iLoop1 As Integer
    Static iLoop2 As Integer
    iLoop1 = iLoop1 + 1
    iLoop2 = iLoop2 + 1
    MsgBox "The first value is " & iLoop1 & vbCrLf & "The second
    ➥value is " & iLoop2, vbInformation
End Sub
```

This sample code declares two variables with different scope. The first variable has local scope and the second has static. When the Command1 button is clicked, a message box will appear with two lines of text. The first line of text is the local variable, and the second line of text is the static variable. Which one will continue to increase? The static one will because it will retain the value after the procedure has completed execution and is called again.

Static variables can be used to set persistent status information within a procedure, but are not needed outside the procedure. This can allow the procedure to indicate how many times it has been executed, whether processing is in progress, and other status information.

Figure 5.4

This message box reveals that the value of iLoop2 continues to increase with each click, while iLoop1 remains 1.

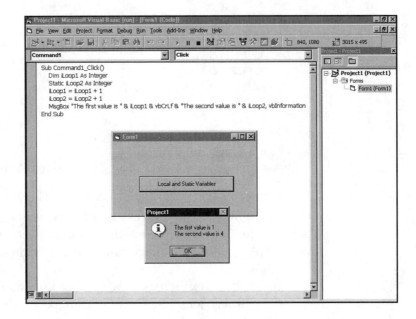

Using Private Variables

Declaring a private variable requires the keyword Private, and the declaration must be located in the General Declarations section of the code module.

Note

> The keyword Dim can also be used in the General Declarations section of the code module. This will also create a privately scoped variable. The preferred method is to use the keyword Private, but Dim has been included for backward compatibility. Private cannot be used in place of Dim.

Private variables should be used when a value is required that can be applied to the entire code component. Private variables can be used for entire form code modules, standard code modules, and classes. All procedures of the code module will have access to the private variable. If required, all procedures can use and / or to alter the value of a private variable.

Private variables require more attention from the programmer to ensure that the value can be changed at any time without a specific value being required by a procedure:

```
Private iPage As Integer

Sub Command1_Click()
    iPage = iPage + 1
    MsgBox "The current page count is " & iPage, vbInformation
End Sub

Sub Command2_Click()
    iPage = iPage - 1
    MsgBox "The current page count is " & iPage, vbInformation
End Sub
```

The preceding code sample uses a form-level private variable declared in the General Declarations section. Two command buttons are placed on the form and then coded as shown:

Command1_Click increases the value of the variable by 1 and then displays a message box indicating the current page count.

Command2_Click decreases the value of the variable by 1 and also displays a message box with the current count.

Both procedures can manipulate the privately scoped variable. If other procedures required the information contained within the variable, they could also use it.

Using Public Variables

Declaring a public variable requires the keyword Public, and the declaration must be located in the General Declarations section of the code module.

Note

In previous versions, this functionality was performed with the Global keyword. This keyword is still available for backward compatibility; however, Public is preferred.

Public variables should be used when a value is required in all parts of the application for the entire lifetime of the application. Public variables require a good deal of consideration by the programmer because any procedure in the application has access to that variable.

When a publicly scoped variable is declared on a form code module, other forms can reference the variable by indicating the form name followed by the variable name. The public variable then looks very much like a custom property of the Form object.

The following code sample uses two different Form objects. Form1 contains a single command button called cmdForm1. Form2 contains a single command button called cmdForm2. Both command buttons have access to the publicly scoped variable of Form1:

```
Public strAppTitle As String

Sub Form_Load()
    strAppTitle = "Big Sample App"
    Form2.Show
End Sub

Sub cmdForm1_Click()
    MsgBox "This application is called " & strAppTitle
End Sub

Sub cmdForm2_Click()
    MsgBox "This application is called " & Form1.strAppTitle
End Sub
```

Notice how Form2's command button must use the name of the form first and then the variable name. Form1 does not require the same qualification, but it is commonly used anyway.

If Form2 does not qualify the variable name with the form name in front, a compiler error will occur (Variable not defined).

When publicly scoped variables are used with standard code modules, the module name does not have to be included to reference the variable. The exception to this rule occurs when more than one code module is using the same publicly scoped variable name. In this case, the reference must indicate which module is to be referenced.

Too many publicly scoped variables can cause logical errors to occur in the application. Most applications will use very few public variables if possible. Another method of passing information from one procedure to another is to use arguments. This is another alternative to using too many public variables and offers better protection of the information.

Exercises

Exercise 5.1: Declaring and Using Local and Static Variables

In this exercise, you create two different types of variables. A single form project that has two command buttons will be created. Each command button will display a message box with a string and a count value. One command button will use a static variable, the other will use a local variable.

To create this exercise, follow these steps:

1. Create a Standard EXE project.

2. Add two command buttons to the form.

3. Change the `caption` property of `Command1` to `Local Variable`.

4. Change the `caption` property of `Command2` to `Static Variable`.

5. Open the code window for `Local Variable` and enter the following code:

```
Sub Command1_Click()
    Dim iLoop As Integer
    iLoop = iLoop + 1
    MsgBox "The variable is now at " &
    ➥iLoop, vbInformation
End Sub
```

6. Open the code window for `Static Variable` and enter the following code:

```
Sub Command2_Click()
    Static iLoop As Integer
    iLoop = iLoop + 1
    MsgBox "The variable is now at " &
    ➥iLoop, vbInformation
End Sub
```

7. Run the project.

8. Click on the Local Variable button three times. Notice that each time you click, the value does not increase beyond 1. This is because the `Dim` statement is used to declare the variable. Every time the procedure is executed, the variable is reset.

9. Click on the Static Variable button three times. Notice that each time you click, the value is increased by 1. This is because the `Static` statement is used to declare the variable. Every time the procedure is executed, the variable's value is left intact.

10. Return to design time.

11. Try to change the declarations and have the buttons reversed. Also try combining a `Static` variable with a `Dim` variable in the same click event.

12. When the procedure is complete, end the application.

This exercise demonstrated how to use local and static variables. Locals are reset with each execution of the procedure. The static variables, on the other hand, retain their values.

Exercise 5.2:   Declaring and Using Private Variables

In this exercise, you create a private variable on a form code module. Two procedures will be used to call the private variable. Both can use and set the variable.

To create this exercise, follow these steps:

1. Create a Standard EXE project.

2. Add two command buttons to the form.

3. Change the `caption` property of `Command1` to `Increase`.

4. Change the `caption` property of `Command2` to `Decrease`.

5. Open the code window for `Form1`.

continues

Exercise 5.2:   Continued

6. From the open code window, go to the General Declarations section of the form code module.

7. Enter the following code. If `Option Explicit` is already there, do not enter it again.

```
Option Explicit
Private iTotal As Integer
```

8. In the `Command1_Click` event, enter the following code:

```
Private Sub Command1_Click()
    iTotal = iTotal + 1
    MsgBox "The current value of the
    ➥Private iTotal variable is " &
    ➥iTotal, vbInformation
End Sub
```

9. In the `Command2_Click` event, enter the following code:

```
Private Sub Command2_Click()
    iTotal = iTotal - 1
    MsgBox "The current value of the
    ➥Private iTotal variable is " &
    ➥iTotal, vbInformation
End Sub
```

10. Run the project.

11. Click on the Increase button. A message box should appear indicating the current value of `iTotal`. This button should increase the private form variable by 1.

12. Click on the Decrease button. A message box should appear indicating the current value of `iTotal`. This button should decrease the private form variable by 1.

13. Continue to use the Increase and Decrease buttons in different sequences. Notice that regardless of the order, the variable is always affected.

14. Return to design time.

15. Experiment by changing the values to increase and decrease the variable. Also try changing the data type.

16. When the procedure is complete, end the application.

This exercise demonstrated how to use a private variable declared on a form code module. Two separate procedures, Command1_Click and Command2_Click, were used to modify the value of the private variable. Both procedures could access and control the value.

Exercise 5.3: Declaring and Using Public Variables

In this exercise, you create an application that uses two Form objects. Form2 will have a public string variable that will be controlled from Form1. Form2 will be used to hold the variable but will not be required onscreen.

To create this exercise, follow these steps:

1. Create a Standard EXE project.

2. On Form1 create one text box and two command buttons.

3. Change the caption property of Command1 to Set Variable.

4. Change the caption property of Command2 to Use Variable.

5. Add a second Form object to the project.

6. Open the code window for Form2 and go to the General Declarations section.

7. Enter the following code. If the Option Explicit is already there, do not enter it again.

```
Option Explicit
Public strWizardName As String
```

continues

Exercise 5.3:   Continued

---

8. Close the code window for `Form2` and close the `Form2` window.

9. Open the code window for the `Set Variable` command button on `Form1`. Enter the following code:

```
Private Sub Command1_Click()
    Form2.strWizardName = Text1.Text
End Sub
```

10. Open the code window for the `Use Variable` command button on `Form1`. Enter the following code:

```
Private Sub Command2_Click()
    MsgBox "The value of Form2's Public
    ➥variable is " & Form2.strWizardName,
    ➥vbInformation
End Sub
```

11. Run the project.

12. In the `Text1` text box, enter the string value `"Setup Wizard"`. You can remove the default `Text1` text.

13. Click on the Set Variable command button from `Form1`. This sets the value of the public variable from `Form2`. `Form2` will not be shown.

14. Click on the Use Variable command button from `Form1`. This uses the value of the public variable in a message box. `Form2` will not be shown.

15. Continue to set and use different values by entering a string in the text box.

16. Return to design time.

17. Try assigning the public variable to `Form1`'s caption property when the Use Variable command button is used. Also try removing the reference of `Form2` from in front of the variable and see the result.

18. When dthe procedure is complete, end the application.

This demonstrated the use of public variables declared on a form code module. The first form was used to set the value of the second form's variable, and then the value of the variable was used in a message box.

Exercise 5.4: Declaring and Using Variables of Different Scope

In this exercise, you create a local variable, a static variable, a private variable, and a public variable.

To create this exercise, follow these steps:

1. Create a Standard EXE project.

2. Add a new standard module to the project.

3. In the open code window for the standard module, enter the following code in General Declarations. If the Option Explicit is already there, do not enter it again.

```
Option Explicit
Public strName As String
Private iTotalPages As Integer
```

4. In the open code window, create this new Sub procedure for the standard module:

```
Sub TotalPageCount()
    ' iTotalPages is a private variable
    ➥of Module1
    iTotalPages = iTotalPages + 1
    MsgBox "The Total page count is now
    ➥at " & iTotalPages, vbInformation
End Sub
```

5. Close the code window for the standard code module.

continues

Exercise 5.4: Continued

---

6. Add three command buttons to Form1.

7. Change the caption property of Command1 to Set Name.

8. Open the code window for Set Name and enter the following code:

```
Private Sub Command1_Click()
    ' strName is a public variable of
    ➥Module1
    strName = InputBox("Please enter the
    ➥name.")

    ' iTimesExecuted is a Static variable
    ➥local to Command1_Click
    Static iTimesExecuted As Integer
    iTimesExecuted = iTimesExecuted + 1
    MsgBox "The Command button Click
    ➥procedure has been executed " &
    ➥iTimesExecuted, vbInformation
End Sub
```

9. Change the caption property of Command2 to Use Name.

10. Open the code window for Use Name and enter the following code:

```
Private Sub Command2_Click()
    ' iLoop is a local variable which is
    ➥reset every time this procedure
    ➥executes
    Dim iLoop  As Integer
    iLoop = InputBox("How many times
    ➥should the message box be shown?")

    For iLoop = 1 To iLoop
        ' strName is a public variable
        ➥from Module1
        MsgBox "You have seen this
        ➥message box " & iLoop & "
        ➥time(s)." & vbCrLf & _
```

```
               "The current name from the
               ➥Module1 variable is " &
               ➥strName, vbInformation
       Next iLoop
    End Sub
```

11. Change the `caption` property of `Command3` to `Total Page Count`.

12. Open the code window for `Total Page Count` and enter the following code:

```
Private Sub Command3_Click()
      ' TotalPageCount is a procedure from
      ➥Module1
      ' which has access to the private
      ➥variable iTotalPages
      TotalPageCount
End Sub
```

13. Run the project.

14. Click on the Set Name button. An input box should be displayed asking for a name. Enter your name and click on OK. `Set Name` sets the public variable of the standard code module.

15. After OK has been clicked, a message box should be displayed indicating how many times that command click procedure has been run. The number of times is tracked with a static variable in the click event.

16. Click on the Use Name button. An input box should be displayed asking how many times the message box should be shown. Enter a value of 3 and click on OK.

17. A message box should indicate how many times you have seen the message box. This is a local variable set by the input box. The second line should be a string indicating the value

continues

of the public variable from the standard code module. The message box will continue looping the number of times you previously entered in the input box.

18. Click on the Total Page Count button. This button calls a procedure from the standard code module that has access to a private variable of the module. The procedure is used to increase the variable and display a message box indicating the value. Every click increases the public variable by one.

19. Return to design time.

20. Try changing the `Total Page Count` to access the variable `iTotalPages` from the standard code module. Can it be done? Also, try including a static variable in the `TotalPageCount` procedure from `Module1` to keep track of how many times the procedure has been executed.

21. When the procedure is complete, end the application.

This exercise has demonstrated using all four types of variables in different situations. A local variable was used for looping. A static variable was used to track procedure execution. A public variable from a standard module was used to hold a string value. A private variable was used on the standard module to hold an integer value controlled by a procedure also defined on the module.

Review Questions

1. Visual Basic provides two different methods that enable the programmer to store information into a variable. What are the names of the two methods that a programmer can use?

   A. Automatic declaration and manual declaration

   B. Required declaration and optional declaration

   C. Implicit declaration and required declaration

   D. Implicit declaration and explicit declaration

   E. Optional declaration and explicit declaration

2. The Visual Basic compiler can generate an error when a variable is assigned a value but the variable has not yet been declared in the source code. Which statement will cause the compiler to generate the error?

   A. `Option Base`

   B. `Require Explicit Variable`

   C. `Option Implicit`

   D. `Require Variable Declaration`

   E. `Option Explicit`

3. Visual Basic can automatically insert a statement into code modules that will force variables to be declared before they are used. Where can the option be found in the Visual Basic Integrated Development Environment?

   A. Project, Project properties

   B. Project, References

   C. Tools, Options, General tab

   D. Tools, Options, Editor tab

   E. Tools, Options, Environment tab

4. Visual Basic contains many different data types. When a variable has been explicitly declared, the data type can be specified. Which are valid data types in VB?

   A. `Integer`

   B. `Float`

   C. `Char`

   D. `String`

   E. `Variable`

5. Visual Basic has a data type that can hold any kind of information. This data type requires much more storage area than other data types and is also the default data type. Which data type has been described?

   A. `String`

   B. `Variant`

   C. `Double`

   D. `Array`

6. An explicit variable declaration contains the scope, name, and data type. If a line of source code assigns the incorrect type of data to the declared variable, what error occurs?

   A. `Expected: end of statement`

   B. `Expected: expression`

   C. `Type mismatch`

   D. `Variable not defined`

   E. None of these

7. Given the following description, define the scope of the variable:

   A declaration for an integer variable is made in a procedure. The variable is assigned a value. The value is used in a calculation. The calculation result is assigned to a text box. The next time the procedure is run, the variable no longer has a value.

What scope has been described?

   A. Private

   B. Public

   C. Local

   D. Static

   E. Friend

8. Given the following description, define the scope of the variable:

The General Declarations section is used to define this variable. The variable will be used by multiple procedures on the same form code module. Other form code modules will not have access to this variable.

What scope has been described?

   A. Private

   B. Public

   C. Local

   D. Static

   E. Friend

9. Given the following description, define the scope of the variable.

A declaration for the variable is made in a procedure. The variable is assigned a data type of Single. The variable is passed to a function for calculation. The variable retains the value after the function has returned and the procedure has completed execution.

What scope has been described?

   A. Private

   B. Public

   C. Local

    D. Static

    E. Friend

10. Given the following description, define the scope of the variable:

    A variable is declared in the General Declarations section of a standard code module. The variable is declared to hold string data. A Sub Main procedure is set as the Startup object for the project and assigns a default value to the variable. The variable is used throughout the different form modules and standard modules of the application.

    What scope has been described?

    A. Private

    B. Public

    C. Local

    D. Static

    E. Friend

11. A variable is declared to hold string data. A command button on Form1 is used to assign a value to the string variable. In the call to assign information to the variable, a different form name is used before the name of the variable. Given this description, where is this variable declared within the project, and what type of scope can be assumed?

    A. Standard module, Private

    B. Form code module, Public

    C. Form code module, Static

    D. Standard module, Public

    E. Form code module, Private

12. A variable is declared to hold integer data. Three different procedures from a standard module use the variable. A procedure from Form1 is also used to assign information to the variable. The call to assign information uses just the variable name. Given this description, where is this variable declared within the project, and what type of scope can be assumed?

   A. Standard module, Private

   B. Form code module, Public

   C. Form code module, Static

   D. Standard module, Public

   E. Form code module, Private

Answers to Review Questions

1. D. The two different methods of variable declaration are known as implicit and explicit declaration. *Implicit* declaration enables the programmer to assign information directly to a variable name without informing the compiler of the variable scope, name, or data type. *Explicit* declaration requires the Option Explicit statement to be placed in the General Declarations section of a code module. Once the statement is in place, the programmer must use a special statement that informs the compiler of the variable's scope, name, and data type before the variable is used in the source code. For more information, see the section titled "Defining the Scope of a Variable."

2. E. The compiler will generate an error when variables are assigned a value before they are declared if the Option Explicit statement appears in the General Declarations section of any code module. This forces the programmer to declare all variables and enables the compiler to check for incorrect variable use or typing errors in the variable name. For more information, see the section titled "Defining the Scope of a Variable."

3. D. To have Visual Basic automatically insert the `Option Explicit` statement into a code module, go to the Tools menu, choose Option, and click the Editor tab. The setting Require Variable Declaration must be checked for VB to automatically insert the statement into only new code modules. Existing code modules must be done manually. For more information, see the section titled "Defining the Scope of a Variable."

4. A, D. Visual Basic can use the `Integer` data type and the `String` data type. `Float` and `Char` are from C/C++, and `Variable` is not classified as a data type. For more information, see the section titled "Visual Basic Data Types."

5. B. The `Variant` is the default data type of Visual Basic. It also requires much more storage to accommodate the wide variety of information that might be assigned. The `Variant` also can hold all the other types of data of VB. For more information, see the section titled "Visual Basic Data Types."

6. C. Type mismatch is used to indicate that information has been passed to a variable that cannot hold the information. Either the information will have to be explicitly converted to the correct data type for the variable, or the variable declaration will have to be changed to accept the data type. For more information, see the section titled "Visual Basic Data Types."

7. C. Local variables will lose their values after the procedure in which they are declared has completed execution. Local variables are declared within a procedure. For more information, see the section titled "Declaring Local Variables."

8. A. Private variables are declared within the General Declarations section of a code module. Private variables can be accessed by all procedures declared on the same code module, but they cannot be accessed by procedures from other code modules. For more information, see the section titled "Declaring Private Variables."

9. D. Static variables retain their values after the procedure in which they have been declared has completed execution. Static variables are declared within a procedure. For more information, see the section titled "Declaring Static Variables."

10. B.Public variables are declared within the General Declarations section. Public variables are available to all components of an application. For more information, see the section titled "Declaring Public Variables."

11. B (Form code module, Public). If one form has a procedure that uses another form name followed by the name of a variable, it is a public variable declared on form code module. For more information, see the section titled "Using Public Variables."

12. D (Standard module, Public). If procedures from a standard module and a procedure from a code module use the variable, the scope is public. If the call to the variable uses only the variable name, the declaration would be on a standard module. Public variables declared on a Form object require the form name when being called. For more information, see the section titled "Using Public Variables."

Answers to Test Yourself Questions at Beginning of Chapter

1. The two different methods of variable declaration are known as *implicit* and *explicit*. Implicit enables the programmer to assign information directly to a variable name. No previous code is required to use implicit variable declarations. Explicit requires the programmer to declare the scope, variable name, and data type of information before the variable is used in the source code. Explicit is the preferred method of declaring variables. It prevents typing mistakes in variable names, reduces the amount of memory needed for storing information, and ensures that the programmer is in control of all information. See "Defining the Scope of a Variable."

2. The statement `Option Explicit` requires that the programmer declare all variables before they are used in source code. This statement forces the programmer to use explicit variable declaration. This helps eliminate typing errors and reduces memory storage for variables. See "Defining the Scope of a Variable."

3. To ensure that explicit variable declarations are used within source code, the programmer is required to place the `Option Explicit` statement in the General Declarations section of all code modules. Whether the code module is a form code module, a standard code module, or a class form module doesn't matter because all contain a General Declarations section that requires the `Option Explicit` statement. See "Defining the Scope of a Variable."

4. The Visual Basic environment does come with an option that automatically inserts the `Option Explicit` keyword into every new code module's General Declarations section. The option can be found under the Tools menu, Options, Editor tab, and it is called Require Variable Declaration. When checked, this option inserts the keyword only on new code modules. Existing code modules must be updated manually. See "Defining the Scope of a Variable."

5. Visual Basic contains many different data types. Here is a list of some variable data types. See "Visual Basic Data Types."

   ▶ Byte   ▶ Double   ▶ Variant

   ▶ Boolean   ▶ Currency

   ▶ Integer   ▶ Date

   ▶ Long   ▶ Object

   ▶ Single   ▶ String

6. Visual Basic allows variables to be used without declaration. If a variable is assigned a value without being declared, VB automatically assigns the `Variant` default data type to the new variable. See "Visual Basic Data Types."

7. `Static` is the keyword used to declare a variable with local scope that will retain its value after the procedure has completed execution. If the `Dim` keyword were used in the declaration, the value of the variable would be reset once the procedure was called again. See "Declaring Static Variables."

8. The `Public` keyword is used to declare a variable that will be available to all program components for the lifetime of the application. See "Declaring Public Variables."

9. Variables created by implicit declaration will always have a `Variant` data type and local scope. Explicit declaration enables the programmer to specify the scope and data type of the variable to be used. See "Using Local Variables."

10. For one form to reference the public variable of another form, the form name containing the public variable must be referenced first, followed by the name of the public variable. See "Using Public Variables."

11. If a procedure call to a public variable on a standard code module requires the name of the module, the following can be determined about the project: It has two standard code modules and two publicly scoped variables with the same name, one per standard module. See "Using Public Variables."

12. To reduce the amount of public variables required by a project, a common method of providing information without using public variables is to use arguments. By passing required information through arguments, the programmer can reduce the need for public variables. This method also reduces the amount of tracking that public variables can cause. See "Using Public Variables."

Chapter

Writing and Calling Sub and Function Procedures

6

This chapter helps you prepare for the exam by covering the following objectives:

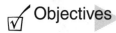 Objectives

▶ Write and call Sub and Function procedures by using named arguments or optional arguments

▶ Write and call Sub and Function procedures that require an array as an argument

▶ Call procedures from outside a module

1. Visual Basic contains a variety of procedure types. A procedure usually contains code all related to accomplishing one task. How many procedure types does Visual Basic have, and what are their names?

2. Of the different types of procedures within Visual Basic, which one will accept arguments and return a value to the calling procedure?

3. Procedures can be called from various areas within an applications source code. When calling a Function procedure, are brackets required to pass arguments?

4. Visual Basic procedures can accept arguments that provide additional information. What are the names of the two methods of calling arguments?

5. With regard to procedure calls and arguments, what symbol is used when passing arguments explicitly by the provided declaration name and then the value?

6. Procedures can have arguments declared to provide additional information to the procedure for processing. What type of arguments can be used to provide a default value to an argument if the procedure call does not provide data for that item?

7. Visual Basic allows for the use of dynamically sizable, multidimensional arrays. What keyword is used, and how are arrays defined within VB?

8. When defining an array, the upper bound is the number used to refer to the highest element value of a dimension. What function is used to determine the upper bound limit of an array?

9. What are the names and how many different types of scopes can be used when declaring a procedure?

10. Event procedures within Visual Basic are private by default. What is the default scope of a general procedure in Visual Basic?

11. When calling a publicly scoped Sub procedure that has been declared on a Form code module, what is required to ensure that the call will be handled by Visual Basic?

12. What is a calling chain used for?

Answers are located at the end of the chapter...

This chapter covers three main objectives. The first objective details different ways arguments of a procedure can be used and how information is passed to a procedure by using positional and named arguments. Optional arguments are also examined. The second objective is using arrays as an argument for a procedure. Declaring and passing arrays and processing array arguments are examined. The third objective details the various scopes of procedures.

This chapter covers Sub and Function procedures in the following sections:

▶ Creating Sub procedures

▶ Creating Function procedures

▶ Passing arguments

▶ Positional arguments

▶ Optional arguments

▶ Named arguments

▶ Declaring arrays

▶ Passing arrays as arguments

▶ Scope of procedures

▶ Calling Sub procedures

▶ Calling Function procedures

▶ Understanding calling chains

Writing and Calling Sub and Function Procedures Using Named Arguments or Optional Arguments

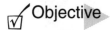 Objective

Procedures are a group of related commands that perform a task. Procedures come in four different types: Sub, Function, Property, and Event. This chapter addresses the use of Sub and Function procedures.

When a task can be used by more than one area of a program or provides a generic task, the Sub or Function procedure can be used to perform the required task. Any part of the application can call a Sub or Function procedure and have the code execute. Command buttons, menu items, or events can all be used to call a procedure.

Both Sub and Function work similarly with one major difference. The Sub cannot return a value to the calling procedure, and the Function can. The use of a Boolean return value can tell the other calling procedure that the code executed successfully or failed. Other values returned from a function could be the result of a calculation.

The following sections detail how to write and use these two powerful procedure types.

Creating Sub Procedures

Sub procedures are used to group commands to accomplish a task. When writing a Sub procedure, ensure that only one task is performed by that procedure. This ensures that different areas of the application can all use the same Sub procedure.

Sub procedures cannot be used to return a value. After the procedure has executed, the program flow returns to the calling procedure. The following is a sample Sub procedure:

```
Sub Login()
    frmLogin.Show
End Sub
```

The preceding sample shows the Sub procedure declaration called Login. Login does not accept arguments because the brackets are empty. The Sub procedure has been designed to just show the login form. The keywords End Sub indicate the end of execution for the procedure.

This sample, although very simple, shows how one task can be performed by the procedure and various parts of the application can all use the same procedure and its functionality.

Sub procedures can accept arguments from a calling procedure. Arguments can be values used by the Sub procedure to perform calculations, set values, or modify information with.

When the Sub procedure is called, information is passed to the Sub by arguments. These are pieces of information that will be accepted and given to the procedure for processing. The following code sample is a Sub procedure declaration with one single argument:

```
Sub CharacterCount(strString As String)
    Dim iLength As Integer
    iLength = Len(strString)
    MsgBox "The String has " & iLength & " characters.",
    ➥vbInformation
End Sub
CharacterCount "Microsoft Visual Basic"
```

From this code, you get the message box shown in Figure 6.1.

The sample Sub procedure accepts one argument that is used to pass a string value. The string value is then measured using the Len() function and the return value of the function is stored in the variable iLength. The message box is used to indicate the information to the user.

The last line in the example is the Sub procedure being called with information being passed as the argument requires.

Procedures can have multiple arguments made up of various data types. When a procedure is called, the information is passed along with the call to the procedure. Arguments are more preferred in an application than public variables—they enable the programmer to have tighter control over where program data is accessed.

Figure 6.1

A sample Sub procedure called from a command button displays the length of a string in a message box.

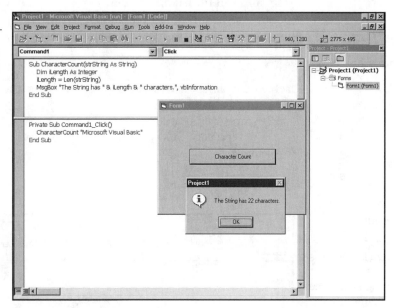

Creating Function Procedures

Like the Sub procedure, the Function is used to group commands to accomplish a task. Functions can be used to perform calculations, alter values, change states, or return a value indicating the success of the task.

Functions can be used to return a value to the calling procedure. After the function has executed, the program flow returns to the next line in the calling procedure and a value can be passed to that line.

Function procedures can accept arguments from a calling procedure. Arguments can be values used by the Function for internal use within the procedure. The information passed can be used to alter properties, change data in a database, or alter the user interface.

The following code sample is similar to the `CharacterCount` `Sub` procedure from the previous section. The difference is that the function offers more use than the `Sub` procedure because of the return value. The `Function` procedure will accept one argument, a string, and will return an integer. The return value is indicated in the `Function` declaration after the last bracket. Notice that the data type of the return value is an `Integer`. Figure 6.2 demonstrates this code.

```
Function CharacterCount(strString As String)As Integer
    Dim iLength As Integer
    iLength = Len(strString)
    CharacterCount = iLength
End Function

MsgBox CharacterCount("Microsoft Visual Basic")
```

Figure 6.2

Function procedure that returns the length of a string passed as an argument.

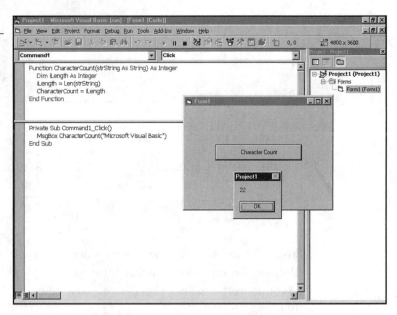

This `Function` has improved the previous `Sub` procedure by providing the calling procedure with a return value that can be further processed. This allows for a more practical use than having a message box display the value. When the `Function` is called, the string is passed, measured using the `Len()` function, and then the value of the length variable is assigned back to the name of the `Function`.

Assigning the value to be returned to the name of the Function indicates return values in Visual Basic. This will pass the calling procedure the indicated value for further processing, if required.

Both Sub and Function procedures accepted a string argument from the calling procedure, but only the function could return the value.

Passing Arguments

When information is passed into a procedure, whether a Sub or Function, it is referred to as an *argument*. The declaration of a Sub or Function procedure is used to indicate the amount of arguments as well as the different data types of the arguments.

When a procedure is called and passed arguments, the information can either be passed directly or a variable can be passed containing the value.

Some programmers find using brackets to pass arguments easier, but it is not required with Sub procedures. Function procedures require brackets if a return value is desired. Notice the following Function procedure calls:

```
MsgBox CharacterCount("Microsoft Visual Basic")
MsgBox CharacterCount "Microsoft Visual Basic"
```

The second example causes a syntax error because the message box requires the return value to be displayed. Consider these two different message box function calls:

```
MsgBox "Hello World", vbYesNo + vbInformation
iResult = MsgBox("Hello World", vbYesNo + vbInformation)
```

The primary difference in these two separate function calls is the use of the brackets. The message box function can be used by itself or with a return value indicating the button selection of the user. If the button is just OK and a return value is not needed, the brackets and variable to hold the return value can be excluded. If the return value is required due to Yes and No buttons, the brackets and a variable to hold the return value are required. The variable can then be tested and processed as required.

When a procedure has declared multiple arguments to be provided during a procedure call, the order they are passed in becomes an important issue. If a procedure expects the first argument to be your first name and the second argument to be your last name, and if they are in a different order, the procedure will not know the difference. If you pass your last name first, the procedure uses it as your first name.

Visual Basic has two different ways of passing arguments to a procedure:

Positional arguments, which are the default, allow arguments to be passed by using comma separators between the arguments. If an argument is not required, just provide an extra comma.

Named arguments allow a special calling convention to be used that explicitly indicates the argument to be provided and the associated value. This gives the programmer more flexibility and ease when using procedures with many multiple arguments.

The following section deals with these two different ways to pass multiple arguments to a procedure.

Positional Arguments

Positional arguments require using the correct order that the procedure expects the information to be passed in. If the information is passed in a different order from the one required, the information is not processed properly.

Consider this Sub procedure declaration with multiple arguments:

```
Sub FullName(strFirstName As String, strLastName As String)
    Dim strFullName As String
    strFullName = strFirstName & " " & strLastName
    MsgBox "Your full name is " & strFullName, vbInformation
End Sub
```

This example has two arguments. The first position argument expects the person's first name. The second position argument expects the person's last name. If the call disregards the importance of the order, the processing of information will be incorrect. The procedure will not know the difference between the first and last name and will join them in the wrong order.

One of the disadvantages to positional arguments can be found when a procedure has many arguments but not all are required. If the first argument must be provided and the programmer wishes to use the ninth argument and nothing in between, for example, commas must be used as place holders even though the other arguments are not used. Figure 6.3 shows the results of using this input box sample code:

```
InputBox "Enter your age", , , , , "c:\windows\help\windows.hlp", 0
```

Figure 6.3

This call to InputBox uses positional arguments to pass information.

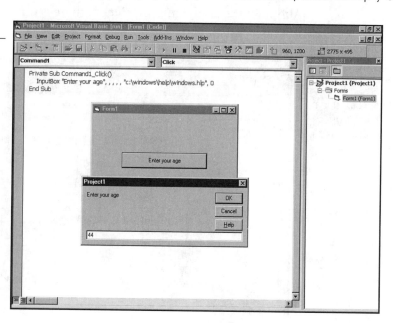

Notice how the extra commas must be provided so that the Help File and Context ID arguments can be provided. To prevent having to count commas, miss commas, and provide improved readability, the second type of argument calling can be used.

Named Arguments

Named arguments are for specific information to be passed into the procedure regardless of the order. This provides the programmer with a sometimes-easier method of calling a procedure with many arguments. It can also increase the readability of less-used functions.

Consider the difference in using named arguments using the input box example again. Notice how named arguments are used. The name of the argument, a colon and equal sign, and the value of the argument:

```
InputBox Prompt:="Enter your age.",
➡HelpFile:="c:\windows\help\windows.hlp", Context:=0
```

This sample code generates the input box found in Figure 6.4. Although the arguments are named, there is no effect on the input box.

Figure 6.4

This call to InputBox uses named arguments to pass information.

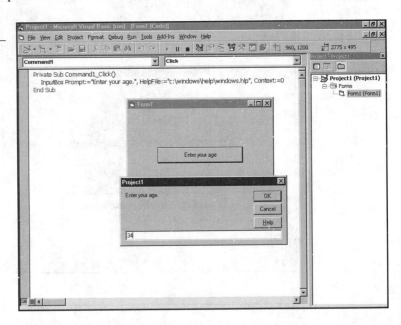

Although a little more typing, it provides a clear way of calling the exact arguments. The arguments can also be placed in any order, and the comma is still used to separate arguments. Consider the following code sample. It performs the same command with a different order. Figure 6.5 shows the results.

```
InputBox Context:=0, HelpFile:="c:\windows\help\windows.hlp",
➥Prompt:="Enter your age."
```

Figure 6.5

This call to InputBox uses named arguments as well, but alters the order that is assigned.

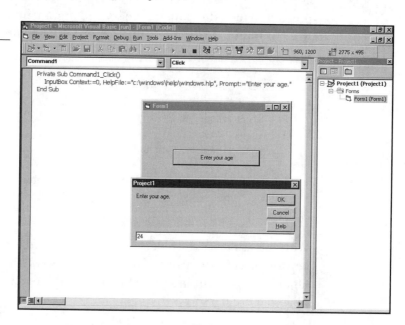

Besides a little extra typing, the correct name of the argument must also be used or a syntax error will be generated. This is not very difficult with the new VB5 parameter information being automatically provided in the form of a tooltip, as procedures are called.

Another interesting issue with named arguments is that not all procedures support named arguments. Certain procedures may not accept this type of calling. The VB Help file has notes regarding some procedures and how named support works.

Optional Arguments

When an argument in a procedure is defined as optional, the procedure does not require information to be passed for that specific item. If not passed in, the optional argument is given a default value within the procedure and then the procedure continues execution with the default value for that argument.

Consider the following revised FullName procedure. The second argument has been declared as an Optional string argument. The procedure tests the value of the second argument; if an empty string is found, due to the string data type, a default value is assigned:

```
Sub FullName(strFirstName As String, Optional strLastName As
➥String)
    Dim strFullName As String
    If strLastName = "" Then
        strLastName = "Newton"
    End If
    strFullName = strFirstName & " " & strLastName
    MsgBox "Your full name is " & strFullName, vbInformation
End Sub
```

With this Sub procedure declaration, the second argument has the keyword Optional in front of the name. VB will also reflect the Optional argument in square brackets in the parameter info tooltip, as Figure 6.6 shows.

Figure 6.6

The Visual Basic parameter info details the procedure name and argument information.

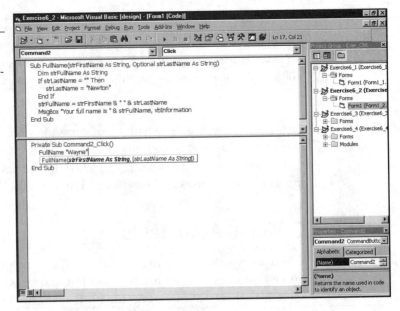

When testing for an optional argument, be sure of the data type used. This determines the value that must be tested for.

After an argument has been declared as optional, all arguments that follow must also be optional or a syntax error will occur.

Writing and Calling Sub and Function Procedures Requiring an Array as an Argument

 Objective ▶

An array can be thought of as a multidimensional variable. Instead of declaring multiple variables to hold information, the array can be used. The array allows for more storage by using the same array name with the addition of elements. The array elements are a numbered storage location. A simple one-dimensional array would have one element number that could be increased, as more storage is required.

Arrays are usually assigned a series of data to be used together in calculations. The most common analogy of an array is the spreadsheet. The rows and columns of a spreadsheet can be used to represent an array. The row would be one dimension of the array. The column would be a second dimension. By indicating which row and column, data can be assigned to that location.

Arrays can become very complex due to the dimensions. Computers can be used to calculate very complex multidimensional arrays that the human mind would be tied in knots trying to comprehend.

The following sections overview declaring arrays and passing them as arguments into procedures.

Declaring Arrays

Arrays are declared using the same keywords as regular variables. The one difference is that the dimension and element numbers follow the array name. Visual Basic then creates an array containing the requested elements. Consider this simple one-dimensional array declaration. Each element in the array will be used to hold only integer-based data:

```
Dim Range(9) As Integer
```

This sample code has declared an array named Range that will contain 10 elements containing integer data. Arrays start at 0 unless otherwise indicated in the declaration. Declarations for arrays can also be more specific.

Visual Basic allows array declarations to specify the range of elements, or bounds. The declaration can specify the lowest number in the array, called the lower bound. The highest number in the array, called the upper bound, can also be specified:

```
Dim Range(1 To 10) As Integer
```

This code sample also declares a one-dimensional 10-element array of integers. The default lower bound of 0 has been explicitly not used in this declaration. The upper bound has been set to 10.

This is a multidimensional array declaration for strings:

```
Dim Clients(1 To 50, 1 To 2) As String
```

This declaration uses two dimensions to separate the clients into regular and prospects. The first dimension can be used to indicate the client's name, and the second dimension can hold a string to indicate the type of client.

Arrays can also be declared as dynamic by not specifying dimensions or elements:

```
Dim Clients() As String
```

Once declared, the array can be re-dimensioned using the keyword ReDim. This allows the array dimensions and elements to be calculated on-the-fly:

```
ReDim Clients(1 To 50, 1 To 2) As String
```

When an array is re-dimensioned, all the contents are lost. To preserve the contents on the original elements, the keyword Preserve is used with ReDim. There are restrictions on how an array can be re-dimensioned. The programmer cannot change the number of the dimensions with ReDim.

Functions can also be used to determine the lower bounds and upper bounds of an array's elements: Lbound and Ubound.

Passing Arrays as Arguments

When a procedure requires an argument, an array can be passed to provide multiple pieces of data. The complete array can be passed and processed by the procedure.

To pass an array, the procedure declaration must define an argument to be an array with the correct data type. The dimensions and elements of the array are not required as part of the declaration. These can be controlled by setting the initial array where required, and then passing the dimensioned array as an argument.

This sample declares a single dimension array with 20 elements, uses a For loop, and populates all elements with a grade of 76. In a real application, these values would all vary, of course:

```
Sub Command1_Click()
    Dim Grade5Class(1 To 20) As Integer
    Dim iLoop As Integer
    For iLoop = 1 To 20
        Grade5Class(iLoop) = 76
    Next iLoop
    MsgBox AverageGrade(Grade5Class())
End Sub
```

The following sample function declaration declares an array argument of integers for processing and returns the class average to the Sub procedure and displays it in the message box:

```
Function AverageGrade(Grades()As Integer)As Integer
    Dim iLoop As Integer, iTotalofGrades As Integer
    For iLoop = 1 To 20
        iTotalofGrades = iTotalofGrades + Grades(iLoop)
```

```
        Next iLoop
        AverageGrade = iTotalofGrades / 20
    End Function
```

The easy part of passing an array as an argument to a procedure is the fact that the dimensions and elements do not have to be specified. This provides more flexibility in passing the information. The Ubound and Lbound functions could then be used within the array to determine the ranges for processing.

Calling Procedures from Outside a Module

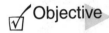 Objective ▶ When a procedure is declared, the programmer can specify the scope, type, name, arguments, and if a function, the return type. The scope of the procedure enables the programmer to specify where in the application the procedure can be called.

Procedure scope is similar to variable scope. It is used to determine which application components can be used to reference the procedure as well as providing protection from having the procedure called from an incorrect component.

The following section describes the different types of scopes that are available to procedures. Examples of calling Subs and Functions, and calling chains, is also discussed.

Scope of a Procedure

There are three different types of procedure level scopes. They are as follows:

- ▶ Public

- ▶ Private

- ▶ Friend

Visual Basic enables the programmer to create a new procedure in two different ways. The programmer can type directly into the code window or the menu Tools, Add Procedure can be used.

If directly created, a general procedure declaration may not indicate the scope. This will allow the procedure to be considered Public by default unless explicitly declared as Private.

Event procedures are Private by default unless explicitly declared as Public.

The simplest type of procedure is Public. The publicly scoped procedure can be called by all components within the application and outside of the application.

Privately scoped procedures can only be called by procedures from the same code module. Other code modules will not have access to the private procedures.

The Friend scope is new to Visual Basic 5. A procedure can be declared with the Friend scope. This allows other procedures from the same project to have access to the procedure, but other applications will not be able to access a Friend scope.

Of the three-procedure scope types, Public and Private are used the most. The Friend scope is limited and used mainly within a class. All scopes can be applied to the various types of procedures: Subs, Functions, and Property procedures.

The next sections examine calling Sub and Function procedures from outside a code module where they have been declared.

Calling Sub Procedures

Sub procedures can be declared with different scope levels to allow various application components to call the Sub procedure.

If a Sub procedure is declared with a Private-level scope, only procedures from the same code module will have access to the Sub. If declared with Public-level scope, procedures from other code components can reference the publicly scoped procedure.

The following code assumes a project has one Form code module and one standard code module. The Sub procedure has been declared on the form object and is to be called by a procedure from the standard code module:

```
Public Sub Greetings()
    frmMain.txtWelcome.Text = "Good Morning Dave."
End Sub
```

The following procedure has been declared on the standard code module and has been declared as Private. When invoked, it calls the Form's publicly scoped Sub procedure and then shows the Form. The Sub Main procedure could not be called from the Form due to the Private scope:

```
Private Sub Main()
    Load frmMain
    frmMain.Greetings
    frmMain.Show
End Sub
```

The Sub Main procedure can be assigned as the project's startup object and will be called first instead of calling a form object. The Main procedure begins by explicitly loading the frmMain form object into memory. Once loaded, the frmMain's public Greetings Sub procedure is called to set a text box on the Form. Then frmMain is shown onscreen.

Notice how the Sub procedure called Greetings has been publicly scoped. This allows procedures from outside the code module, where it has been declared, to access the Sub. To reference procedures declared on a form object, the call must include the name of the form object followed by the public procedure.

If a Sub procedure has been declared Public in a standard code module, the module name is not required as part of the call unless multiple modules use the same publicly scoped Sub procedure name. These are the same rules that apply to publicly scoped variables.

Calling Function Procedures

Function procedures follow the same rules for scope as Sub procedures. Function procedures have Public scope by default, unless explicitly declared as Private.

Public Function procedures declared on a Form code module must be called with the Form name first, followed by the Public Function name.

Functions declared Public in a module do not require the module name as part of the call unless more than one module uses the same publicly scoped Function name.

Understanding Call Chains

Another important aspect of calling procedures is the calling chain. When one procedure is used to call another procedure, the execution of the first procedure has not been completed. Visual Basic keeps track of which procedure is currently executing and which procedure must be returned to when execution has finished.

A *calling chain* is an ordered listing of which procedures have been called by which procedures. The reason this is referred to as a calling chain is because one procedure calls another before it has finished executing. If that procedure then calls another, it has not finished executing either. When the last called procedure has completed execution, the program returns to the previous procedure and completes execution, thus ending the chain.

The *call stack* is a window that displays the latest procedure called at the top of the stack, as shown in Figure 6.7. The procedure to be returned to is listed in the figure. This stack can be useful when determining the order of processing within the procedures. Too many calls can slow down a program and will require optimization.

Figure 6.7

The Call Stack window shows the order of procedures as they are executed.

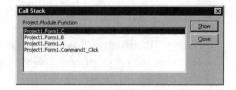

A very simple sample of a calling chain is shown in the following sample code:

```
Private Sub Command1_Click()
    A
End Sub

Public Sub A()
    B
End Sub

Public Sub B()
    C
End Sub

Public Sub C()
    Stop
End Sub
```

The Command button will be the first item in the calling chain. Command1 will call Sub procedure A, placing A at the top of the call stack. Sub A will call Sub B, placing B on top of A and Command1. B calls C, and C is added to the stack and then Stop pauses the VB environment.

Exercises

Exercise 6.1:   Using Positional and Named Arguments

In this exercise, you create two procedures that call the InputBox function and the MsgBox function. The first procedure calls both functions by positional arguments. The second procedure calls both functions with named arguments. To create this template, follow these steps:

1. Create a Standard EXE project.

2. Add two command buttons to Form1.

3. Change the caption property of Command1 to Positional Arguments.

4. Open the code window for Positional Arguments and enter the following code. Notice how information is passed to the InputBox and MsgBox functions:

```
Private Sub Command1_Click()
    Dim strName As String
    strName = InputBox("Please enter your favorite movie.",
    ➡"Movie Title")
    MsgBox strName & " was a great movie", vbExclamation
End Sub
```

5. Change the caption property of Command2 to Named Arguments.

6. Open the code window for Named Arguments and enter the following code. Notice how information is passed to the InputBox and MsgBox functions:

```
Private Sub Command2_Click()
    Dim strName As String
    strName = InputBox(Title:="Movie Title", prompt:="Please
    ➡enter your favorite movie.")
    MsgBox Buttons:=vbExclamation, prompt:=strName & " was a
    ➡great movie."
End Sub
```

7. Run the project.

continues

Exercise 6.1: Continued

8. Click on the Positional Arguments command button. An input box should be displayed asking for your favorite movie. Enter a movie and click on OK.

9. After the input box is closed, a message box should be displayed indicating the name of the movie. Both input box and message box function as expected.

10. Click on the Named Arguments command button. An input box should be displayed the same as the first. The only difference between the first input box and the second is the source code. Enter a movie and click on OK.

11. After the input box is closed, a message box should be displayed indicating the name of the movie. This message box should also appear no different than the last. The source code is the only difference.

12. Return to Design mode.

13. Review the arguments for the `InputBox` and `MsgBox` functions under both buttons. Notice the difference in the readability of the source code.

14. Try changing the order of arguments for both functions in both buttons. Also, try creating a function and using positional arguments and named arguments.

15. When completed, end the application.

This exercise demonstrated using both positional arguments and named arguments in function calls. Regardless of the method used to pass arguments to the function, both work in the expected ways.

Exercise 6.2: Declaring and Using Optional Arguments

In this exercise, you create a procedure that declares optional arguments to a function. If information is not passed to the optional arguments, a default value is assigned. To create this template, follow these steps:

1. Create a Standard EXE project.

2. Open the code window for the Form.

3. Go to the General Declarations section and enter the following Sub procedure. Take a good look at the declaration and notice the use of the Optional statement used in front of the second argument:

```
Sub FullName(strFirstName As String, Optional strLastName As
➥String)
    Dim strFullName As String
    If strLastName = "" Then
        strLastName = "Newton"
    End If
    strFullName = strFirstName & " " & strLastName
    MsgBox "Your full name is " & strFullName, vbInformation
End Sub
```

4. Add two command buttons to Form1.

5. Change the caption property of Command1 to First and Last Name.

6. Open the code window for First and Last Name and enter the following code. Notice the parameter info tooltip that is displayed as the name of the Sub procedure that has been typed:

```
Private Sub Command1_Click()
    FullName "Bob", "Lamontagne"
End Sub
```

7. Change the caption property of Command2 to First Name Only.

8. Open the code window for First Name Only and enter the following code. Notice the parameter info tooltip that is displayed as the name of the Sub procedure that has been typed. Also notice that the second argument is not provided:

```
Private Sub Command2_Click()
    FullName "Wayne"
End Sub
```

continues

9. Run the project.

10. Click on the First And Last Name button. A message box should be generated indicating the name Bob Lamontagne. The Sub procedure was used to concatenate the two arguments into one string. Click on OK to close the message box.

11. Click on the First Name Only button. A message box should be generated indicating the name Wayne Newton. The Sub procedure was used to concatenate the first name provided with a default argument. The Sub procedure tested the second argument and because it was an empty string, provided a default last name.

12. Return to Design mode.

13. Try adding another Optional argument to the Sub procedure FullName. Remember that additional arguments that follow an Optional argument must also be optional. Also try providing a default value if the third argument is not provided.

14. When completed, end the application.

This exercise demonstrated the usefulness of Optional arguments. They allow additional information to be provided to a procedure as well as offering a default value if the information is not specified. This exercise used two command buttons that called the same procedure but with different argument information. The first button provided a first and last name as two separate arguments. The second button provided a first name only, and the procedure provided a default last name.

Exercise 6.3: Declaring and Using Arrays as Arguments

In this exercise, you declare and populate an array. The array will then be passed into a procedure as an argument. The array argument is then used within the procedure. To create this template, follow these steps:

1. Create a Standard EXE project.

2. Add one command button to Form1.

3. Change the caption property Command1 to Declare and Pass Array.

4. Open the code window and go to the General Declarations section. Enter the following Function procedure code. Notice that the Grades() argument uses the brackets to denote a dynamic array. The array has not been dimensioned because the passed-in array will have its own dimensions. Also notice that the array is looped through, each element is read and totaled and then returned as an average:

```
Function AverageGrade(Grades() As Integer) As Integer
    Dim iLoop As Integer, iTotalofGrades As Integer
    For iLoop = 1 To 20
        iTotalofGrades = iTotalofGrades + Grades(iLoop)
    Next iLoop
    AverageGrade = iTotalofGrades / 20
End Function
```

5. Go to the Command1_Click event and enter the following code. Notice how the array declaration has been locally scoped. Nothing outside this procedure has access to the Grade5Class array of integers:

```
Sub Command1_Click()
    Dim Grade5Class(1 To 20) As Integer
    Dim iLoop As Integer
    For iLoop = 1 To 20
        Grade5Class(iLoop) = 76
    Next iLoop
    MsgBox AverageGrade(Grade5Class())
End Sub
```

6. Run the project.

7. Click on the Declare And Pass Array button. A message box should be displayed with the average calculated grade of 76.

continues

Exercise 6.3: Continued

8. When the button is clicked, a local array called Grade5Class is dimensioned with 20 elements to hold integers. A For loop is used to populate the array with one single value, 76. The message box then calls the AverageGrade function, which passes the Grade5Class array. The function then returns the averaged value.

9. Return to Design mode.

10. Try changing the grade value assigned in the For loop. See whether the function returns the correct number. Also, try changing the data type of the array elements. Also, try reducing the size of the array and manually setting values into each element.

11. When completed, end the application.

This exercise demonstrated declaring a local integer array. A For loop was used to populate each element in the array with a grade value. All values were the same for ease of demonstration. The array was then passed to a function. The function accepted the array and then read the value of each element. Each element is totaled and used to calculate the grade average.

Exercise 6.4: Calling Procedures from Outside a Module

In this exercise, you create procedures and use scope to determine from where in the application they can be called. To create this template, follow these steps:

1. Create a Standard EXE project.

2. Add a standard code module to the project.

3. In the open code window for Module1, enter the two following public procedures:

```
Public Sub TimeOfDay()
    MsgBox "The current time is " & Format(Time, "Long
    ➥Time")
End Sub
Public Sub TodaysDate()
    Form1.CurrentDate
End Sub
```

4. Close the code window for Module1.

5. Add two command buttons to Form1.

6. Change the caption property of Command1 to Current Time.

7. Open the code window for Current Time and enter the following code. TimeofDay was previously declared on the standard module and displays a message box with the time:

```
Private Sub Command1_Click()
    TimeOfDay
End Sub
```

8. Change the caption property of Command2 to Current Date.

9. Open the code window for Current Date and enter the following code. CurrentDate was previously declared on the standard module. It calls back to a procedure on Form1, which displays a message box with the date:

```
Private Sub Command2_Click()
    CurrentDate
End Sub
```

10. Open the General Declarations section of Form1 and enter the following procedure:

```
Public Sub CurrentDate()
    MsgBox "Today's date is " & Format(Date, "Long Date")
End Sub
```

11. Run the project.

12. Click on the Current Time button. A message box should be displayed with the current time. Click on OK to close the message box.

13. Click on the Current Date button. A message box should be displayed with the current date. Click on OK to close the message box.

14. Return to Design mode.

continues

15. Try adding a new procedure to Module1 and have another command button on Form1 call the procedure. Also try changing the scope of the Public procedures on Module1 to Private and see whether they can still be called.

16. When completed, end the application.

This exercise demonstrated using procedure level scopes to determine which application components could call the procedures. A form module and standard module were used.

Review Questions

1. Visual Basic provides four different procedure types. Which type of procedure will accept arguments but cannot return a value to the calling procedure?

   A. Property procedure

   B. Event procedure

   C. Friend procedure

   D. Function procedure

   E. Sub procedure

2. Procedures are units of code that combine commands to perform a common task. What are the final keywords used to indicate the completion of execution for a Sub procedure?

   A. End Sub

   B. Exit Sub

   C. End Procedure

   D. Exit Procedure

   E. End

3. From the following code samples, select the correct calls to a Sub procedure with the following declaration:

   ```
   Sub AverageGrade(First As Integer, Second As Integer, Third
   ➥As Integer)
   ```

   A. AverageGrade(First:=80, Second:=76, Third:=55)

   B. AverageGrade 80, 76, 55

   C. AverageGrade(80, 76, 55)

   D. AverageGrade First:=80, Second:=76, Third:=55

   E. AverageGrade First = 80, Second = 76, Third = 55

4. When a procedure call is made, arguments can be passed to the procedure with additional information for processing. What is the name of the method where the procedure call can disregard the order that arguments are passed in?

    A. Optional arguments

    B. Functional arguments

    C. Positional arguments

    D. Ordinal Value arguments

    E. Named arguments

5. Visual Basic provides a tooltip known as the parameter info. This tooltip is a description of a procedure and its arguments. What keyword is used to declare arguments that are surrounded with a square bracket in the parameter info?

    A. `Required`

    B. `Option Explicit`

    C. Optional

    D. Ordinal

    E. Named

6. Visual Basic allows the use of dynamically sizable, multidimensional arrays. From the following declarations, select which static declaration would allow for a single dimensional array with 44 elements that could hold Integer-based data.

    A. `Redim MyArray(44) As Integer`

    B. `Dim MyArray(43)As Integer`

    C. `Redim MyArray(43) As Integer`

    D. `Dim MyArray(44)As Integer`

    E. `Redim Preserve 44 As Integer`

7. Assume that an array has been previously created with two dimensions. The first dimension has four elements and the second dimension has five elements. Within Visual Basic, which keywords are used to retain the currently assigned values while specifying new dimensions for this array?

   A. Preserve

   B. Dimension

   C. Array

   D. Dim

   E. Redim

8. When making a call to a declared procedure, which method of passing arguments requires the position of information being passed to be in the correct order?

   A. Optional arguments

   B. Functional arguments

   C. Positional arguments

   D. Ordinal Value arguments

   E. Named arguments

9. Visual Basic allows procedures to have scopes that determine which application components can call the procedure. What are the three types of scope applicable to procedures?

   A. Friend

   B. Remote

   C. Local

   D. Public

   E. Private

10. Visual Basic allows for three different types of scopes when declaring a procedure. Given the following code sample, select which scope the procedure will have.

```
Function ChangeAccount(iAccount As Integer, iNewNumber As
➡Integer)As Integer
```

    A. Private

    B. Public

    C. Local

    D. Static

    E. Friend

11. Public procedures can be declared on a form code module. Given the following declaration, which syntax can be used to call this Public procedure from frmMain?

```
Function ChangeAccount(iAccount As Integer, iNewNumber As
➡Integer)As Integer
```

    A. ChangeAccount 44, 52

    B. iResult = ChangeAccount(44,52)

    C. iResult = frmMain.ChangeAccount(44,52)

    D. iResult = frmMain.ChangeAccount 44, 52

    E. frmMain.ChangeAccount 44, 52

12. In the Visual Basic IDE, the menu option View, Call Stack displays a window. What information is displayed within the window?

    A. The call order of procedures

    B. The call order of variables

    C. The call order of the environmental stack

    D. The call order of the cpu register stack

    E. The call order of IDE menu selections

Answers to Review Questions

1. E. The Sub procedure accepts arguments and will not return a value to the calling procedure. There are three different types of Property procedures. The Property Let procedure will accept an argument and not return a value, but that was not a choice. Friend is a scope, not a procedure. Functions accept arguments and will return a value. Functions do not have to return a value, but can. For more information, see the section titled "Creating Sub Procedures."

2. A. End Sub are the last keywords used to indicate the completion of a Sub procedure. The keyword End is used to indicate the end of the application and unloads the project. Exit Sub is used to force the completion before the rest of the procedure will execute and reach End Sub. For more information, see the section titled "Creating Sub Procedures."

3. B, D. The procedure can be called by providing the numbers separated by commas or by using the named arguments, the name of the argument, colon, equal sign, and value. Subs are not called with brackets, and equal signs are not used in procedure calls. For more information, see the section titled "Passing Arguments."

4. E. Named arguments allow for the procedure call to disregard the order the arguments are passed in. The other method of passing arguments to a procedure is called positional. Positional requires that a procedure's arguments be passed in the correct declaration order with unused arguments indicated by comma placeholders. For more information, see the section titled "Named Arguments."

5. *C*. ~~B~~. Optional. This keyword is used to declare a procedure argument that is not required when making a call to the procedure. These arguments are surrounded with square brackets in the parameter info tooltip to indicate their optional status. For more information, see the section titled "Optional Arguments."

6. B. `Dim MyArray(43)As Integer`. The `Dim` keyword declares an array called `MyArray` with 44 elements in one dimension, remembering that 0 is an element. The question also asked for a static declaration. Therefore the `Redim` statements would not be valid in this case. They would have to assume that a previous declaration was made. For more information, see the section titled "Declaring Arrays."

7. A, E. The keywords `Preserve` and `Redim` would be required to keep the previously assigned contents of the array while also allowing an increase to the size of the upper bound of the last element. The correct syntax would have them specified as `Redim Preserve`, followed by the name of the array and new size. For more information, see the section titled "Declaring Arrays."

8. C. Positional arguments require the information being passed to the procedure to be in the correct order. Commas separate arguments, and the order indicates which data will be used within the procedure. Named arguments allow for any order provided the name of the argument is provided and the colon equal sign is used when assigning the values. For more information, see the section titled "Positional Arguments."

9. A, D, E. The three different levels of scopes that apply to procedures are `Private`, `Public`, and `Friend`. `Private` allows the procedure to be called only by other procedures declared within the same code module. `Public` allows the procedure to be called from other code modules. `Friend` allows the procedure to be called internally within an application's components, but not externally from the application. For more information, see the section titled "Scope of a Procedure."

10. B. In the declaration of a procedure if the scope is not indicated, the default scope will be used. Procedures have a default scope of `Public` unless explicitly declared different. For more information, see the section titled "Scope of a Procedure."

11. C, E. When calling a Public procedure declared on a form code module, the Form name must be used to reference the procedure name. If the return result is not required, the brackets and variable to hold the returning result do not have to be used. For more information, see the section titled "Calling Sub Procedures."

12. A. The call order of procedures is listed within the Call Stack window. The currently executing procedure is listed at the top and procedures that remain to be executed are listed below. For more information, see the section titled "Understanding Call Chains."

Answers to Test Yourself Questions at Beginning of Chapter

1. Visual Basic has four different procedure types: `Sub`, `Function`, `Property`, and `Event`. The programmer must explicitly call `Sub` and `Function` procedures. `Property` procedures are used to `Get`, `Let`, and `Set` the property of an object. The `Event` procedure is automatically called by Visual Basic when something has happened. The programmer writes code that will respond to specific events of an object. See "Writing and Calling `Sub` and `Function` Procedures Using Named Arguments or Optional Arguments."

2. `Function` procedures are used to return values to `Calling` procedures. The `Sub` procedure can execute commands, but when returning to the calling procedure does not return a value. The `Property Get` procedure can also be used to return a value to the calling procedure, but does not normally accept arguments. The `Event` procedure is automatically handled by Visual Basic and does not return a value. See "Writing and Calling `Sub` and `Function` Procedures Using Named Arguments or Optional Arguments."

3. When a `Function` procedure is called, brackets are required if the return value of the function is needed. If the return value can be disregarded, the brackets surrounding the arguments can be omitted. See "Passing Arguments."

4. The names of the two methods for calling arguments in Visual Basic are Positional and Named. Positional requires arguments to be passed in the correct order as defined by the procedure declaration. Named allows arguments to be specified by name, value, and any order. See "Passing Arguments."

5. The colon and the equal sign are the special symbols used when passing Named arguments. When multiple arguments are specified in a procedure call, the order and position can be overlooked if the name of the argument, the colon equal sign, and value are used. See "Named Arguments."

6. Optional arguments can be used to provide a procedure with a default value if the procedure call does not specify information for that item. The keyword `Optional` is used in front of the argument name and data type. All other arguments following must also then be optional. The procedure can then test the value of the argument to see whether data was provided. If no data can be found, a default value can be set and used within the procedure. Optional arguments will also appear in the parameter info tooltip when the procedure call is coded. See "Optional Arguments."

7. The keyword to define an array in Visual Basic is `Dim`. The difference between dimensioning a variable and an array is the element requirements. An array declaration will have a set of brackets following the array name that will indicate the lower and upper bounds of each dimension within the array. See "Declaring Arrays."

8. The function `Ubound` will return the number of the upper limit of the array. The array named is passed as an argument of the procedure to determine the upper bound limit. See "Declaring Arrays."

9. Three types of scopes can be used when declaring a procedure. `Public`, `Private`, and `Friend` are all used to explicitly set the scope of a procedure. See "Scope of a Procedure."

10. A general procedure has a default scope of `Public`. Unless a procedure declaration has explicitly defined the scope, a procedure will automatically be `Public`. See "Scope of a Procedure."

11. When calling a publicly scoped `Sub` procedure that has been declared on a form code module, the Form name must be used when making the call. This allows Visual Basic to resolve the reference to the object containing the procedure. This is only required for form objects. A standard module name is only required if more than one module uses the same publicly scoped procedure name. See "Calling `Sub` Procedures."

12. A calling chain is used to provide the order in which procedures have been called. The chain details the last procedure called, shown at the top, and all other procedures, which have not completed execution and will be returned to after the top-most procedures have completed. See "Understanding Call Chains."

C h a p t e r

Creating and Using Class Modules

7

This chapter helps you prepare for the exam by covering the following objectives:

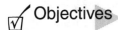

Objectives

- ▶ Add properties to a class

- ▶ Add methods to a class

- ▶ Identify whether a class should be public or private

- ▶ Declare properties and methods as `Friend`

- ▶ Set the value of the `Instancing` property

Test Yourself! Before reading this chapter, test yourself to determine how much study time you will need to devote to this section.

1. You want to create a read-only property. How would you define the Property procedure?

2. Why would you create a property using a Property procedure pair rather than a public variable?

3. How would you create a new method in a class?

4. You have an ActiveX EXE program with a class declared as SingleUse. What effect could this have on the memory of the computer when multiple clients access this object?

5. You are writing the code that takes advantage of an event (Done) fired by another class named SomeTask. What line should you add to the General Declarations section of the module that will respond to the event?

6. What must you do to a class to make it into an interface?

7. Another developer approaches you with a problem. He wants to add a property to a class, but can't remember the syntax. Which of these would add a new property named TaskName to the class?

8. What information about a class is available from the Object Browser?

Answers are located at the end of the chapter...

This chapter covers an important language feature of Visual Basic 5: *classes*. Classes allow for more object-oriented programming. They can help create more maintainable, understandable code. Understanding the fundamentals of creating classes with VB5 is important to understanding development of ActiveX Controls, objects, and documents.

Implementing classes in VB5 can seem a two-edged sword. Initially, it leads to more work because the classes need to be designed. Later, however, the code produced is much more maintainable and extensible. Objects also serve to hide the complexity of code. This allows for the changing of algorithms much more readily. This can also help with group programming, when some of the developers cannot or do not need to understand the entire process.

Designing classes involves defining the properties, methods, and events of an object. *Scoping*—availability of the classes in a project or between objects—plays an important role in their use in ActiveX Objects.

This chapter covers the creation and use of class modules in the following sections:

▶ What is a class?

▶ Adding a class module to a project

▶ Adding a property to a class module

▶ Adding a method to a class module

▶ `Public`, `Private`, and `Friend`

▶ Object Browser

▶ The `Instancing` property

▶ Adding an event to a class module

▶ Creating and using interfaces

Understanding Classes

Class modules in VB5 serve as templates for objects. They can be used in any type of project, but are essential to the creation of ActiveX Objects. An *object* is the combination of data with the procedures that work on that data. An object could include all the data describing an employee (Name, HireDate, Salary, and SSN), for example, and the procedures that work on that data (YearsofService, WritePayCheck, Save, and Load). This is a concept known as *encapsulation*.

Encapsulation is the idea that enables a programmer to hide aspects of their code. The user of an encapsulated object does not need to know how setting the properties and running the methods affects the data. Only the result is important. One example of this is the ListBox in VB5. The List() property of the ListBox stores a number of entries, the items in the ListBox. The user of the List() property does not know how the items in the list are stored. Nor does it matter. The only important fact is that when the List() property is accessed, the correct item is returned. In addition, if the actions performed on the data are complex, as in the case of the API calls described in Chapter 10, "Incorporating DLLs into an Application," encapsulation masks that complexity behind properties and methods. This could allow less experienced developers to use those API calls without needing to know how they work.

One way to try to understand classes and the class modules in them is to compare them with other objects used in the real world and in VB5 programs. Each object has its own data and actions that work on that data, as Table 7.1 shows.

Table 7.1

Objects in the Real World and VB5		
Object	Data	Actions
Coffee cup	Volume	Pour
	Color	Fill
	Quantity	Measure
Form	Left	Move
	Top	Show
	BackColor	Hide

Object	Data	Actions
ListBox	ListCount	AddItem
	List()	RemoveItem
	Text	Clear
Employee	First Name	Work
	Last Name	Go Home
	Salary	Answer Phone
	Hours Worked	

Classes allow for the creation of "black boxes" that can be used repeatedly. By creating them, the programmer is preparing tools for the future. Classes are also essential in the development of ActiveX Objects—a fact that will become more evident in Chapters 11–14.

Adding a Class Module to a Project

Adding a class module to a project is the same as adding any other module in VB5. Choose Add Class Module from the Project menu. A shortcut to this command is also available on the toolbar or by right-clicking on the project name in the project window (see Figure 7.1).

Figure 7.1

Adding a class module using the Project window.

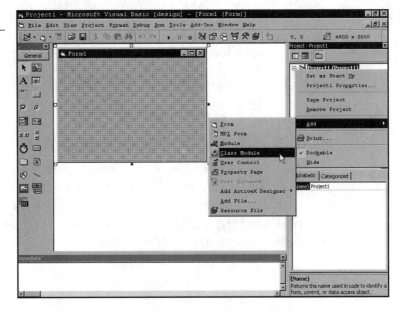

A dialog box will appear, allowing for the creation of a blank class module, the Class Builder Wizard or a previously created template. For the purposes of learning the mechanics of class building, all the examples in this chapter start with a blank class module.

The structure of the newly added class module is midway between the structure of a standard or code module, and that of a form. Similar to a code module, a class module has no visible aspect, unlike a form. In addition, there is no way to add controls to a class, only code. Similar to a form module, however, there is one object associated with a class module: the `Class` object.

The `Class` Object

The `Class` object acts much like the `Form` object in a form module. It has its own collection of properties, methods, and events. Initially, it has no properties or methods. The programmer adds these (as will be seen later). Two events are associated with the `Class` object. Just as code may be added to the events associated with a `Form` object, code may be added to react to the events of a `Class` object.

The events of the `Class` object are as follows:

- ▶ `Initialize`   This occurs when an object of that class first comes into existence.

- ▶ `Terminate`   This occurs when an object of that class is destroyed.

The following section discusses these events in more detail.

Each `Class` object describes a new variable type, such as an integer or string. Declaring an object variable uses the same syntax as declaring a normal variable. If the current project has defined a class module named `Employee`, for example, the following lines of code declare a new variable of that class:

```
Dim emp as CEmployee
Dim emp as New CEmployee
```

This object variable is also referred to as an instance of the class. An *instance* is one specific copy of a class, with its own settings for the properties defined in that class.

The two lines of code just listed differ slightly. Both reserve memory for the new variable, but the second line also has a different meaning. Using the New keyword implicitly initializes the variable. Any use of the variable will automatically create the object. If the variable is not implicitly created in this way, it must be explicitly created before using it.

Assignment of an object variable is also similar to assignment of other variables. However, there is one fundamental difference. A normal variable, like an integer or single, takes up a specific amount of memory. An integer takes two bytes, and a single takes four. There is no way in advance, however, to know how much memory will be taken up by an object variable. Therefore the object variable must be set up to be able to point to any type of object. To assign the object variable, then, you must Set it, as follows:

```
Set emp = New CEmployee
```

This is to identify it as different from the normal Let type assignment done with normal variables.

After the variable is assigned in this way, it is now an instance (or copy) of the class. The properties and methods are now available for use.

To show the difference between implicit and explicit creation of object variables, start a new Standard EXE project in VB5. Add five CommandButtons to the form, and a new class module to the project. Name the objects as shown in Table 7.2. This project is also available on the accompanying CD in the /samples/ch07/ ImpExp directory.

Table 7.2

Objects in the Implicit/Explicit Project

Object	Name	Caption
Form	frmMain	Implicit/Explicit object variables
CommandButton1	cmdCreateImplicit	Create
CommandButton2	cmdNothingImplicit	Is Nothing?
CommandButton3	cmdCreateExplicit	Create
CommandButton4	cmdNothingExplicit	Is Nothing?
CommandButton5	cmdDone	Done
Class module	TestClass	N/A

Add the following code to the form:

```
Option Explicit
Dim objImplicit As New TestClass
Dim objExplicit As TestClass
Private Sub cmdCreateExplicit_Click()
    Set objExplicit = New TestClass
End Sub
Private Sub cmdCreateImplicit_Click()
    Set objImplicit = New TestClass
End Sub
Private Sub cmdDone_Click()
    Unload Me
End Sub
Private Sub cmdNothingExplicit_Click()
    MsgBox objExplicit Is Nothing, , "Is Explicit Nothing?"
End Sub
Private Sub cmdNothingImplicit_Click()
    MsgBox objImplicit Is Nothing, , "Is Implicit Nothing?"
End Sub
```

Notice the two variables declared in the General Declarations section. The objImplicit variable is declared with the As New syntax. It is initialized at this point. Therefore, it is implicitly declared. The `objExplicit` variable is declared without the `As New` syntax. This variable will not be created until the `cmdCreateExplicit` button is clicked, and the following line is executed:

```
Set objExplicit = New TestClass
```

If you click the `cmdNothingExplicit` button before clicking the Create button, this becomes obvious, as the variable is not initialized. Non-initialized object variables are equal to `Nothing`. However, the implicitly defined variable is never equal to `Nothing`.

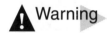 **Warning**

> Implicitly creating a variable may seem like a labor-saving step; however, this can lead to problems later. Any reference to the variable creates it in memory. In the sample application, the implicitly created variable could never be equal to `Nothing`. Expecting it to be later would cause an error. In the same way, a reference later to an implicitly declared variable could cause that variable to remain in memory. This can lead to a memory leak in your program because the variables may not be properly destroyed. You should usually explicitly create an object variable with the `Set VariableName As New ObjectType` syntax.

Initialize and Terminate

When the object variable is first created, the `Initialize` event (if any exists) is executed. This enables the programmer to write any code required by this new object—the creation of dependant objects, for example, or the assignment of default values.

Memory used by an object variable is freed when the variable goes out of scope. This *clearing* of memory can be done at any time by setting the object variable to `Nothing`, for example:

```
Set emp = Nothing
```

At this same time, the `Terminate` event of the class is fired. This is an ideal location for code that *cleans up* after the variable.

Dependant objects may be set to Nothing, for example, or open files may be closed.

A sample program may make the flow of these two events more obvious. Create a new Standard EXE project. Add two class modules to the project. Add six CommandButtons and a ListBox to the form. The names and captions of these objects should be as shown in Table 7.3.

Table 7.3

Initialize/Terminate Explorer

Object	Name	Caption
Form	frmInitTerm	Test Initialize/Terminate
ListBox	lstHistory	N/A
CommandButton1	cmdInit1	Create Class1
CommandButton2	cmdTerm1	Destroy Class1
CommandButton3	cmdInit2	Create Class2
CommandButton4	cmdTerm2	Destroy Class2
CommandButton5	cmdInitLocal	Create Local
CommandButton6	cmdDone	Done

Add the following code to the form module:

```
Option Explicit
Dim c1 As Class1
Dim c2 As Class2
Private Sub cmdDone_Click()
    Unload Me
End Sub
Private Sub cmdInit1_Click()
    frmInitTerm.lstHistory.AddItem "Setting module level
    ➥variable"
    Set c1 = New Class1
    frmInitTerm.lstHistory.AddItem "After setting module level
    ➥variable"
End Sub
```

```
Private Sub cmdInit2_Click()
    frmInitTerm.lstHistory.AddItem "Setting module level
    ➥variable"
    Set c2 = New Class2
    frmInitTerm.lstHistory.AddItem "After setting module level
    ➥variable"
End Sub
Private Sub cmdInitLocal_Click()
    Dim c3 As Class1
    frmInitTerm.lstHistory.AddItem "Setting local variable"
    Set c3 = New Class1
    frmInitTerm.lstHistory.AddItem "After setting local variable"
End Sub
Private Sub cmdTerm1_Click()
    frmInitTerm.lstHistory.AddItem "Destroying module level
    ➥variable"
    Set c1 = Nothing
    frmInitTerm.lstHistory.AddItem "After destroying module level
    ➥variable"
End Sub
Private Sub cmdTerm2_Click()
    frmInitTerm.lstHistory.AddItem "Destroying module level
    ➥variable"
    Set c2 = Nothing
    frmInitTerm.lstHistory.AddItem "After destroying module level
    ➥variable"
End Sub
```

The code added to the classes Class1 and Class2 highlights these two important events in a class' life.

Insert this code into Class1:

```
Private Sub Class_Initialize()
    frmInitTerm.lstHistory.AddItem "Class1 Initialized"
End Sub
Private Sub Class_Terminate()
    frmInitTerm.lstHistory.AddItem "Class1 Terminated"
End Sub
```

Insert this code into Class2:

```
Private Sub Class_Initialize()
    frmInitTerm.lstHistory.AddItem "Class2 Initialized"
End Sub
```

```
Private Sub Class_Terminate()
    frmInitTerm.lstHistory.AddItem "Class2 Terminated"
End Sub
```

If you run the project, the various buttons will be available. Clicking the Create Class# buttons should add a message to the ListBox indicating that an instance of the appropriate class has been created, as seen in Figure 7.2.

Figure 7.2

Running the Initialize/Terminate Explorer.

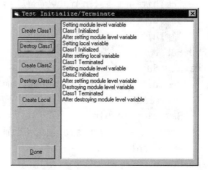

Click on the Create Local button. You should see a message stating that the class was initialized and then terminated immediately. Why does this happen? The c3 variable defined in the subroutine cmdInitLocal_Click is local to this subroutine. The c3 variable goes out of scope and is destroyed when the subroutine ends. This then runs the Terminate event for the class.

 Tip

> Creating a new instance of a variable is a time-consuming task. It may be more efficient to limit how often an object is initialized or terminated. By controlling the scope of the object variables, you can better control when these two events happen. Creating a variable with module level, or global scope may reduce the time required to create and destroy object variables. This is especially true if many procedures access this object variable.

Adding a Property to a Class Module

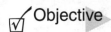 Properties are the changeable characteristics of classes. They represent the data stored in one specific object or instance of the class. They are the adjectives and nouns that describe an object. Examples include `BackColor`, `Name`, and `Height`. Anything variable or changeable about an object can be a property.

You can add a property to a class module in the following two ways:

▶ Create a module-level public variable

▶ Create one or more property procedures

Public Variables

When a module-level (that is, one declared in the General Declarations section of a class module) public variable is added to a class module, a new property is created with the name of the public variable.

This is a quick and easy method of adding a property to a class. However, this technique has a number of problems:

▶ No additional processing of the value passed to the property is possible. This could be a problem in the case of the changed property being needed to determine another, calculated property.

▶ There is no checking of the legitimacy of the data. There is nothing to stop a user from setting a birth date to a date in the future, for example.

▶ The client program must do formatting of the property (if necessary). This reduces the encapsulation of the class, increasing the amount of work that must be done to re-use this class in the future.

▶ Error handling for the property must be done by the client program, again reducing encapsulation.

Tip When adding a property to a class module, avoid using this technique unless you are certain that you will never need to check the data passed to the property.

Property Procedures

A more robust method for adding properties to a class module is to use property procedures.

Property procedures are similar to other procedures such as subroutines and functions. There are three types of property procedures, as follows:

► `Property Get`

► `Property Let`

► `Property Set`

The usual syntax for each of the three is as follows:

► `Property Get PropertyName () as PropertyType`

► `Property Let PropertyName (NewValue as PropertyType)`

► `Property Set PropertyName (NewValue as PropertyType)`

Typically, these procedures are used in pairs. Each property would then be made up of one `Property Get` procedure and either a `Property Let` procedure or `Property Set` procedure.

When using property procedures, a private variable is also needed to store the value of the property. This variable is private to prevent other code from changing it without using the appropriate property procedures. The variable is a private member variable.

Tip
Declare the private variable with a name to make it stand out. One common standard is to prefix the name with the characters "m_". This makes the variable stand out, and reminds the developer not to use it except in the property procedures.

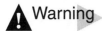 **Warning**
Avoid using this member variable outside of the property procedures, even in the same class. Using the variable in this way sidesteps any validation done in the property procedures and can lead to errors. Always use the property procedures to access the data of an object.

Property Get

A `Property Get` procedure is used when *getting* the value of a property.

For example, from the `Employee` class example:

```
MsgBox theEmployee.Salary
```

Executes the `Property Get` procedure:

```
Property Get Salary() As Currency
    Salary = m_curSalary
End Property
```

Typically, the `Property Get` procedure is used to access some private member variable. If the variable returned is an object variable—for example, a `CEmployee` object—the `Property Get` procedure would be written as follows:

```
Property Get Employee() as CEmployee
  Set Employee = m_objEmployee
End Property
```

Property Let

A Property Let procedure is used to set the value of a property when the property is meant to hold one of the standard Visual Basic data types (for example, an Integer, String, or Date).

For example, from the CEmployee example:

```
FirstName = txtFirst.Text
```

Executes the Property Let procedure:

```
Property Let Salary(NewValue As Currency)
    'can't have a negative salary
    If NewValue > 0 Then
        m_curSalary = NewValue
    End If
End Property
```

The value on the right-hand side of the assignment (txtFirst.Text in the preceding example) is passed to the Property Let procedure as the last parameter. In the case of the preceding example, this would be sNewValue. There can actually be many parameters in the Property Let statement. The last one would always be used in the assignment. For example, if you had a Property Let statement defined as:

```
Property Let HireDate(iDateFormat As Integer, dtNewValue as Date)
```

you would use it:

```
HireDate(vbShortDate) = txtDate.Text
```

However, it should be noted that using multiple parameters like this is rare.

The name of the Property Let statement is derived from the ancient history of BASIC. Back long ago, to assign a value to a variable, you used a line similar to this:

```
Let X = 5
```

Property Set

The `Property Set` procedure is very similar to the `Property Let` procedure. The only difference is that `Property Set` should be used for object variables and variant variables that may hold objects. If you wanted to define a property `Employee` of type `CEmployee`, for example, the `Property Set` statement would be written as follows:

```
Property Set Employee (objNewValue as CEmployee)
  Set m_objEmployee = objNewValue
End Property
```

Because the value passed to the `Property Set` procedure will be an object variable (`CEmployee`), you use a `Set` statement to assign the new value to the private member variable.

To create the `Employee` sample, start a new Standard EXE project. Add a class module and add the following code to the form:

```
Option Explicit
Dim theEmployee As CEmployee
Private Sub cmdCreate_Click()

    Set theEmployee = New CEmployee
    With theEmployee
        .FirstName = txtFirst.Text
        .LastName = txtLast.Text

        If IsNumeric(txtSalary.Text) Then
            .Salary = txtSalary.Text
        Else
            MsgBox "Please enter a number"
            txtSalary.SetFocus
            Exit Sub
        End If

        If IsNumeric(txtHours.Text) Then
            .Hours = txtHours.Text
        Else
            MsgBox "Please enter a number"
            txtHours.SetFocus
            Exit Sub
```

```
            End If

            If IsDate(txtHireDate.Text) Then
                .HireDate = txtHireDate.Text
            Else
                MsgBox "Please enter a date"
                txtHireDate.SetFocus
                Exit Sub
            End If

            lblFullName.Caption = .FullName

        End With

End Sub
Private Sub cmdEnd_Click()
    Unload Me
End Sub
```

To the class module:

```
Option Explicit
Const HOURS_IN_WEEK As Integer=168
'***Private storage for properties
Private m_sFirstName As String
Private m_sLastName As String
Private m_dtHireDate As Date
Private m_curSalary As Currency
Private m_sngHours As Single
'***Properties
Property Get FirstName() As String
    FirstName = m_sFirstName
End Property
Property Let FirstName(NewValue As String)
    m_sFirstName = NewValue
End Property
Property Get LastName() As String
    LastName = m_sLastName
End Property
Property Let LastName(NewValue As String)
    m_sLastName = NewValue
```

```
End Property
Property Get FullName() As String
    FullName = FirstName & " " & LastName
End Property
Property Get HireDate() As Date
    HireDate = m_dtHireDate
End Property
Property Let HireDate(NewValue As Date)
    'can't hire people in the future
    'or more than a century ago
    If (NewValue <= Now) And (NewValue > DateAdd("yyyy", -100,
    ➥Now)) Then
        m_dtHireDate = NewValue
    End If
End Property

Property Get Salary() As Currency
    Salary = m_curSalary
End Property
Property Let Salary(NewValue As Currency)
    'can't have a negative salary
    If NewValue > 0 Then
        m_curSalary = NewValue
    End If
End Property

Property Get Hours() As Single
    Hours = m_sngHours
End Property
Property Let Hours(NewValue As Single)
    'can't work more hours in a week than there
    'are hours in the week, nor a negative number
    'of hours
    If (NewValue > 0) And (NewValue <= HOURS_IN_WEEK) Then
        m_sngHours = NewValue
    End If
End Property
```

(This project is also available on the accompanying CD-ROM in the directory /samples/Ch07/property)

Add the following controls to the form, and name them as listed in Table 7.4.

Table 7.4

Objects in the Employee Properties Example		
Object	Name	Caption
Form	frmEmployee	Employee
Label1	lblFirst	First Name:
TextBox1	txtFirst	N/A
Label2	lblLast	Last Name:
TextBox2	txtLast	N/A
Label3	lblSalary	Salary:
TextBox3	txtSalary	N/A
Label4	lblHours	Hours:
TextBox4	txtHours	N/A
Label5	lblHireDate	Hire Date:
TextBox5	txtHireDate	N/A
Label6	lblFName	Full Name:
Label7	lblFullName	blank
CommandButton1	cmdCreate	Create Employee
CommandButton2	cmdEnd	End

Run the project. It should look similar to Figure 7.3. You should be able to create a new employee. Try not filling in the salary or date fields. You should get an error message. When the Create Employee button is pressed, the full name of the employee should appear on the bottom of the dialog box. This uses the read-only property FullName.

Most of the code in the project is in the class module. Each of the properties has a private storage variable, and Get and Let procedures, except for the FullName property. This is to allow it to be read-only. Validation has been added to ensure that only legitimate data goes into the properties. In a "real-world" program, errors should be created when the data is not correct. In this case, however, you have not raised any errors.

Figure 7.3

Running the Employee properties sample.

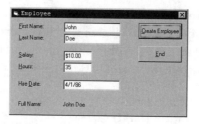

When the Create Employee button is clicked, a new `CEmployee` object is created and the properties assigned. The label on the bottom of the dialog box is filled with the full name of the employee.

Adding a Method to a Class Module

 Objective

Methods are the actions that can be performed by a class. They represent the functions that act on the data stored in an object. To continue the previous analogy, methods are the verbs associated with an object. Examples from some of the standard objects are `Clear`, `AddItem`, `Show`, `Hide`, and `Move`.

To create a new method in a class, insert a new public subroutine or function. If the new method is meant to return a value—for example, the result of a calculation—use a function. In other cases, use a subroutine.

Often the choice of whether to create a property or a method is obvious. When creating a routine designed to open a file, for example, it is more appropriate to create an `Open` method. Occasionally the choice is less obvious. Much of this confusion is caused by the seemingly small difference between property procedures and *normal* procedures.

One way to decide between the two is to consider what the procedure is meant to do:

- ▶ Does it do something?
  (for example, the `Move` method of a form)

- ▶ Does it change the way you describe the object?
  (for example, the `BackColor` property of a form)

In some cases, you may want to create both, to allow the user of your class to choose which is more useful at the time. For example, the Form object has Show and Hide methods that change a property, Visible. Both of these code fragments are equivalent:

```
frmMain.Show
frmMain.Visible = True
```

You will extend the Employee example started earlier to include methods. Create a new project or open the Employee project used in the section titled "Property Set."

Add the following controls to the form, and name them as listed in Table 7.5.

Table 7.5

Objects in the Employee Methods Example

Object	Name	Caption
Form	frmEmployee	Employee
Label1	lblFirst	First Name:
TextBox1	txtFirst	N/A
Label2	lblLast	Last Name:
TextBox2	txtLast	N/A
Label3	lblSalary	Salary:
TextBox3	txtSalary	N/A
Label4	lblHours	Hours:
TextBox4	txtHours	N/A
Label5	lblHireDate	Hire Date:
TextBox5	txtHireDate	N/A
Label6	lblFName	Full Name:
Label7	lblFullName	blank
Label8	lblWge	Wage:
Label9	lblWage	blank

Object	Name	Caption
Label10	lblYoS	Years of Service:
Label11	lblYearsOfService	blank
CommandButton1	cmdCreate	Create Employee
CommandButton2	cmdRaise	Give Raise
CommandButton3	cmdEnd	End

Add the following code to the form:

```
Option Explicit
Dim theEmployee As CEmployee
Private Sub cmdCreate_Click()

    Set theEmployee = New CEmployee
    With theEmployee
        .FirstName = txtFirst.Text
        .LastName = txtLast.Text

        If IsNumeric(txtSalary.Text) Then
            .Salary = txtSalary.Text
        Else
            MsgBox "Please enter a number"
            txtSalary.SetFocus
            Exit Sub
        End If

        If IsNumeric(txtHours.Text) Then
            .Hours = txtHours.Text
        Else
            MsgBox "Please enter a number"
            txtHours.SetFocus
            Exit Sub
        End If

        If IsDate(txtHireDate.Text) Then
            .HireDate = txtHireDate.Text
        Else
            MsgBox "Please enter a date"
            txtHireDate.SetFocus
            Exit Sub
        End If
```

```
            lblFullName.Caption = .FullName
            lblYearsOfService.Caption = .YearsOfService
            lblWage.Caption = Format$(.Wage, "Currency")

        End With

End Sub
Private Sub cmdEnd_Click()
    Unload Me
End Sub
Private Sub cmdRaise_Click()
    Dim Raise As Single
    Dim Msg As String
    Msg = "How much of a raise (in percent)?"
    Raise = CSng(InputBox$(Msg, "Employee Raise", 5))

    If Not theEmployee Is Nothing Then
        theEmployee.AddRaise Raise
        MsgBox "Employee given a raise"
        txtSalary.Text = Format$(theEmployee.Salary, "Currency")
        cmdCreate_Click
    End If

End Sub
```

And to the class module:

```
Option Explicit
Const HOURS_IN_WEEK As Integer = 168
'***Private storage for properties
Private m_sFirstName As String
Private m_sLastName As String
Private m_dtHireDate As Date
Private m_curSalary As Currency
Private m_sngHours As Single
'***Properties
Public Property Get FirstName() As String
    FirstName = m_sFirstName
End Property
Public Property Let FirstName(NewValue As String)
    m_sFirstName = NewValue
End Property
Public Property Get LastName() As String
    LastName = m_sLastName
```

```
End Property
Public Property Let LastName(NewValue As String)
    m_sLastName = NewValue
End Property
Public Property Get FullName() As String
    FullName = FirstName & " " & LastName
End Property
Public Property Get HireDate() As Date
    HireDate = m_dtHireDate
End Property
Public Property Let HireDate(NewValue As Date)
    'can't hire people in the future
    'or more than a century ago
    If (NewValue <= Now) And (NewValue > DateAdd("yyyy", -100,
    ➥Now)) Then
        m_dtHireDate = NewValue
    End If
End Property
Public Property Get Salary() As Currency
    Salary = m_curSalary
End Property
Public Property Let Salary(NewValue As Currency)
    'can't have a negative salary
    If NewValue > 0 Then
        m_curSalary = NewValue
    End If
End Property
Public Property Get Hours() As Single
    Hours = m_sngHours
End Property
Public Property Let Hours(NewValue As Single)
    'can't work more hours in a week than there
    'are hours in the week, nor a negative number
    'of hours
    If (NewValue > 0) And (NewValue <= HOURS_IN_WEEK) Then
        m_sngHours = NewValue
    End If
End Property
Public Function YearsOfService() As Integer
    YearsOfService = DateDiff("yyyy", HireDate, Now)
End Function
Public Function Wage() As Currency
    Wage = Salary * Hours
End Function
Public Sub AddRaise(RaisePercent As Single)
    If IsNumeric(RaisePercent) Then
```

```
        'in case they entered the percentage as a
        'whole number
        If RaisePercent > 1 Then
            RaisePercent = RaisePercent / 100
        End If
        Salary = Salary * (1 + RaisePercent)
    End If
End Sub
```

Much of the code in this project is the same as in the preceding example. New additions to the class module are the two functions YearsOfService and Wage and the subroutine AddRaise. These are public procedures, and therefore, methods. Notice that YearsOfService and Wage could have been created as read-only properties. They were created as methods to demonstrate the small differences between property procedures and normal functions.

Running the project works as it did in the preceding example. The program should appear as shown in Figure 7.4. The main difference is that now there will be two new values displayed when the employee is created, Years of Service and Wage. Clicking the Give Raise button will bring up an input box, enabling the user to enter the percentage of raise. This calls the AddRaise method of the class, adding the raise amount to the salary of the individual.

Figure 7.4

Running the Employee methods example.

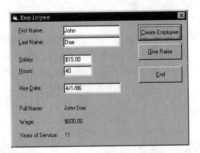

Using Public, Private, and Friend

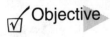

If a property or method is added to a class module, it becomes part of the class. This property or method is usable by other modules in the same project as the class module. It is also available to other projects, as a property or method of objects derived from that class. This is the default setting for the scope of a property or method. There are three other ways of defining the scope of a property or method:

- ▶ Public

- ▶ Private

- ▶ Friend

Using the `Public` Keyword

If the `Public` keyword is used when defining a property or method, the property behaves as though the `Public` keyword is not used. This is because the default scope of a property or method defined in a class module is `Public`.

 Tip

Explicitly defining properties and methods as `Public` when creating them will avoid confusion later because you or another programmer may assume that the scoping is not `Public`. Also, there is the slight (actually, very unlikely) but possible chance that Microsoft will change the default at some later date. This could lead to large sections of your code breaking. Avoid these possibilities and explicitly define properties by using the appropriate scope when you create them.

`Public` properties and methods are available to other modules in the same project as the class module. They are also available to other projects as properties and methods of an object derived from that class module. Most properties and methods will be defined as `Public`.

Consider the following, for example:

```
Public Property Get HireDate() as Date
Public Sub Save()
```

Using the `Private` Keyword

Using the `Private` keyword when defining a property or method creates a property or method private to that class module. Only code in that class module can access the property or method.

 Tip Creating a `Private` property is not necessary. Doing so would only increase overhead because the procedure would have to be run. Use a `private` variable instead. The exception is when you need to execute code when the value is changed or retrieved.

`Private` methods typically support routines used by the properties of a class. For example, you may need some helper routines that perform date calculations.

Consider the following, for example:

```
Private Function NextWorkDay(FromDate as Date) As Date
Private Sub PrintForm(FormName As String)
```

Using the `Friend` Keyword

Using the `Friend` keyword when defining a property or method creates a property or method private to the project containing the class module. Code in the same class module as the procedure can access the property or method. Code in other modules in the same project can also access the property or method. This is useful when creating helper classes that should not be used by other programs.

 Tip When declaring an object that has properties or methods declared as `Friend`, you must declare the object explicitly. If the object is declared `As Object`, the `Friend` properties will not be available for use.

`Friend` properties and methods are often used when a number of classes assist the main class that other programs will use. A class used to write another object to a file, for example, might have two methods: `Load` and `Save`. These methods, declared as `Friend`, would allow the calling object to access them. They would not be available to other projects.

Consider the following, for example:

```
Friend Sub Load(FileName As String)
Friend Function Save(FileName As String) As Boolean
```

By explicitly setting the scope for each of the properties and methods in a class, you can better control how other modules and programs access them. Most properties and methods will be `Public`; however, having access to the `Private` and `Friend` keywords allows for greater control of access.

Object Browser

Keeping track of all the classes built into VB5 and created later can be a difficult task. A single class may have dozens of properties, methods, and events. The Object Browser is designed to help track and identify classes, properties, methods, and events. It is another window that can be opened in the IDE, and can be seen in Figure 7.5.

Figure 7.5

The Object Browser.

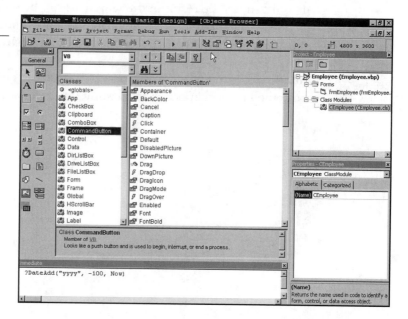

The Object Browser has four main parts. The bottom of the window is dominated by two lists. The one on the left is a list of all the objects currently available to the IDE. Scrolling through this list, many common objects can be seen, such as the Form, Printer, and CommandButton objects. Selecting an object from this list changes the contents of the right ListBox. The right-side ListBox displays the properties, methods, and events of the selected object. The two lists allow then for the browsing of the classes installed and available. Selecting a property, method, or event from the right ListBox displays the syntax and a brief description in the bottom area of the Object Browser. This can help in locating and identifying the correct object, property, method, or event to use in a situation.

Locating the appropriate procedure in the Object Browser can be difficult. This is made worse when more libraries of classes are loaded. To reduce the view and limit it to one library of classes, select the appropriate library from the top ComboBox, as in Figure 7.6. Only the classes of that library will be displayed in the ListBox. Alternatively, the lower ComboBox may be used. This ComboBox is used to search for a specific keyword by name. Type the name, or part of the name in the ComboBox, and then click on the Search button (with the binoculars). A new list will appear. This list shows the result of the search, as can be seen in Figure 7.7. Selecting an item from the Search Results window highlights the appropriate class and procedure in the lower lists.

After the desired procedure has been found, the command can be copied to the clipboard for pasting into a code window.

Figure 7.6

Limiting the libraries shown in the Object Browser.

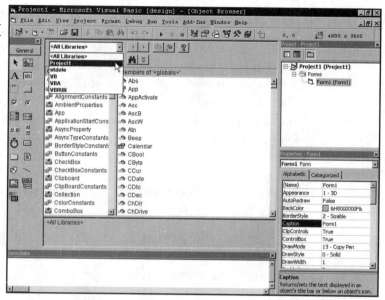

Figure 7.7

Searching in the Object Browser.

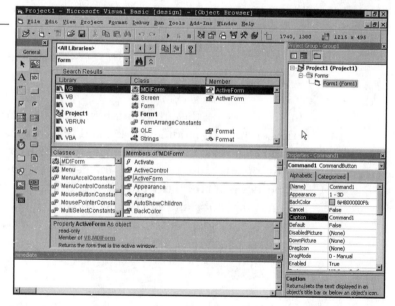

Understanding the Instancing Property

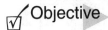

√ Objective

When creating a class for an ActiveX Object, there is a new property available for the class module: the Instancing property. The instancing property defines how other classes and programs can make use of the class. In many ways this is analogous to the scoping of variables. The scope of a variable defines whether one procedure, a module, or every procedure can access its data. In the same way, the instancing of a class may affect how other classes and programs access its properties and methods. Depending on the type of project created, the Instancing property may be set to one of the following:

- ▶ Private

- ▶ PublicNotCreatable

- ▶ MultiUse

- ▶ SingleUse

- ▶ GlobalMultiUse

- ▶ GlobalSingleUse

In Visual Basic 4, this information was actually stored in two properties of the class module: Public and Instancing. The developers of VB5 combined the two properties to reduce confusion. This confusion was caused in part by the fact that if one of the two properties (Public) was set to False, the other (Instancing) had no meaning, but could still be set. The new Instancing property relates to the older Public and Instancing properties as shown in Table 7.6.

Table 7.6

Comparing VB5 Instancing Property and VB4 Public and Instancing Properties		
VB 5 Instancing Setting	VB 4 Public Setting	VB 4 Instancing Setting
Private	False	Any
PublicNotCreatable	True	Not Createable

VB 5 Instancing Setting	VB 4 Public Setting	VB 4 Instancing Setting
MultiUse	True	Createable MultiUse
SingleUse	True	Createable SingleUse
GlobalMultiUse	True	Not available
GlobalSingleUse	True	Not available

Not all the instancing types are available for each of the project types. Table 7.7 shows the valid values for the Instancing property for each of the project types. For ActiveX document projects, the Instancing property may be set as for the appropriate ActiveX project (that is, either EXE or DLL), depending on the object supplying the ActiveX document.

Table 7.7

Availability of Instancing Property by Project Type

Instancing	ActiveX EXE	ActiveX DLL	ActiveX Control
Private	Yes	Yes	Yes
PublicNotCreatable	Yes	Yes	Yes
MultiUse	Yes	Yes	No
SingleUse	Yes	No	No
GlobalMultiUse	Yes	Yes	No
GlobalSingleUse	Yes	No	No

The effect of the various settings is important to the creation of ActiveX Objects.

Instancing Private

This setting is available in any ActiveX project type.

An Instancing setting of Private denotes a class available only to the class module in which it is defined. This is similar to the way that a variable declared as `Private` in a module's General Declarations is only available to be used by routines in that module. Other modules cannot change or read the private variable. Private classes take this to a higher level. Instead of only being accessible from the same module, the `Private` class is only accessible from modules in the same project. Modules in other projects cannot read or set the properties of the class, nor can they execute the methods of the class.

This is useful in the creation of *helper* classes. A helper class is a class not visible outside of its project that provides some support functionality to its project, without other programs needing to access it. A class designed to write logging information, for example, could be added to a number of projects. This class adds to the functionality of the project, but it should not appear in the project's type library. Declaring this class `Private` prevents this. Any of the modules in the project can still access the logging class's properties and methods.

Instancing `PublicNotCreatable`

This setting is available in any ActiveX project type.

An `Instancing` setting of `PublicNotCreatable` denotes a class midway between a `Private` class and a fully `Public` class. A class with this setting appears in the type library for a project. However, other projects cannot create an instance of this class. That is, they cannot use the `as New ClassName` syntax to implicitly or explicitly create an instance of that class. Another class within the same project as the `PublicNotCreatable` class must create the instance. Once created, other programs can access the properties and methods of the class.

`PublicNotCreatable` is useful in the creation of object hierarchies such as the DAO hierarchy examined in Chapter 9 "Accessing Data Using Code." It is possible when using the DAO to create a variable of type `RecordSet`. However, another object must be used to assign the variable to a specific `RecordSet` before using. The following syntax, for example, is invalid:

```
Dim rsEmployees As New RecordSet
```

Although the following is valid (assuming the `theDB` variable is assigned to an open database containing an `Employees` table or query):

```
Dim rsEmployees As RecordSet
Set rsEmployees = theDB.OpenRecordSet("Employees")
```

Using `PublicNotCreatable` to create object hierarchies allows for the control of the creation of objects lower in the hierarchy. They are dependent on the higher objects for creation and assignment.

Instancing `MultiUse`

Available in ActiveX EXE and ActiveX DLL project types.

An `Instancing` of `MultiUse` denotes a class publicly available to other programs. A class with this setting appears in the type library for the project. Other projects can also create new instances of this class by using the `As New ClassName` syntax.

This setting has an effect only when multiple client programs make use of this class. If the `Instancing` property is `MultiUse`, one copy of the class is loaded into memory. This one copy will then provide its functionality to all clients.

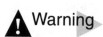 **Warning**

Problems may arise if the task performed by the method or property takes a long time or uses a file or other resource that can only be used by one program at a time. The one copy of the `MultiUse` object can normally only service a single client at a time. Long or resource-dependant tasks can lead to time-outs, as other requests queue up behind the long task. This normally occurs only if the task takes quite a while—the time-out for this is normally about five minutes—or if a large number of clients are being serviced by the class. Avoid using `MultiUse` if the task will take a long time or if it is resource-dependent.

Instancing `SingleUse`

Available in ActiveX EXE project types only.

An `Instancing` of `SingleUse` denotes a class publicly available to other programs. A class with this setting will appear in the type library for the project. Other projects can also create new instances of this class by using the `As New ClassName` syntax.

This setting has an effect only when multiple client programs use this class. If the `Instancing` property is `SingleUse`, a new copy of the server is loaded for each client. Each copy has its own process space, which will not interfere with any other copy of the EXE. The most obvious effect of this technique is that it uses more memory. However, the isolation of servers that this method creates can reduce problems that may occur with long or resource-dependent tasks (as described in the preceding Warning).

Instancing `GlobalMultiUse`

Available in ActiveX EXE and ActiveX DLL project types.

An `Instancing` of `GlobalMultiUse` denotes a class publicly available to other programs. A class with this setting will appear in the type library for the project. Other projects can also create new instances of this class by using the `As New ClassName` syntax.

In many ways, an `Instancing` of `GlobalMultiUse` is identical to that of `MultiUse`. The only difference is that any class defined as `Global` does not require a declaration for its methods and properties to be used. When using the DAO objects as in Chapter 9, for example, variables of type `Database` or `RecordSet` must be declared before being used. A `GlobalMultiUse` class, on the other hand, acts more like the `App` or `Printer` objects in that they are always available.

Tip

When naming objects that have been declared `GlobalMultiUse` (or `GlobalSingleUse`), be careful to make the property and method names unique. If the names are not unique, you must preface the property or method name with the name of the class (not any object of that type), as in `CEmployee.Salary`.

Note

The benefits of a `Global` class only apply to other projects that use the `Global` class. Other modules in the same project must first declare instances of the class before using them.

Instancing `GlobalSingleUse`

Available in ActiveX EXE project types only.

An `Instancing` of `GlobalSingleUse` denotes a class publicly available to other programs. A class with this setting will appear in the type library for the project. Other projects can also create new instances of this class by using the `As New ClassName` syntax.

A class with an `Instancing` property of `GlobalSingleUse` has the characteristics of a normal `SingleUse` class, with the addition of the features of a `Global` class. That is, no variable need be declared before using the properties and methods defined in the class.

Note

By controlling the `Instancing` of a class module, you can limit access to classes in a hierarchy. This allows for the completion of complex hierarchies of objects, forming a natural description of how things react in the real world. Instancing becomes even more important when dealing with code components (as discussed in more detail in Chapters 12–14).

Adding an Event to a Class Module

Events are a new addition to classes in VB5. They allow a class to communicate information to other classes or programs. Creating an event differs from creating properties and methods. Properties and methods are procedures written entirely in the class to define how that class appears to other programs. The class raises events, but the client program contains the code written for that event. The class has little or no control over what the client does when the event is fired. To continue the analogy used earlier, properties are the characteristics you can describe about a class, methods are the characteristics that a class can do, and events are the characteristics that a class responds to. This is similar to the way that a CommandButton object responds to a click event.

A class may generate any number of events. Programs written to use that class may then react to those events. This is the same as the Form object. The form can generate many events (Load, Initialize, and Resize). When using a form, the programmer decides which events to add code to, allowing the program to react to specific events.

Code to create an event is, therefore, different to the code used to create properties and methods. The event is generated by code in the class. The client also needs code to allow it to react to those events.

Creating Events

Creating an event for a class is a two step process. First you must declare the event. Then you must generate the event with the RaiseEvent statement.

The information used to declare an event in VB5 is the name of the event and any parameters that passed to the user of that event.

Tip

Your class is responsible for passing any parameters to the client program. The `KeyPress` event, for example, passes the ASCII value of the pressed key to the client program. This reduces the need for the client program to know what may be affected by the event.

Here is a sample event declaration:

```
Public Event GotPaid()
Public Event WageChanged(NewWage As Currency)
```

Declaring the event in this way is required to allow the information about the event to be available. This information is used later when raising the event, and by the client so that it can identify the events available.

After declaring the event, it may be generated whenever appropriate. To generate an event, use the `RaiseEvent` statement as follows:

```
RaiseEvent WageChanged(NewValue)
```

This would signal any other programs or modules set up to react to the `WageChanged` event.

Reacting to Events

To react to an event, the programmer must first allow VB5 to identify all the events supported by the new object. The declaration of the object in the client program notifies VB5 of this information.

Declaring an object that has events is similar to declaring any other object. To declare and assign an `Employee` object that has events, for example, requires the following code:

```
Dim Emp WithEvents as CEmployee
Set Emp = New CEmployee
```

This notifies the compiler that the `Employee` object generates one or more events. To write code for these events, select the variable name from the object list in a code window, as in Figure 7.8.

Figure 7.8

Adding code to react to events.

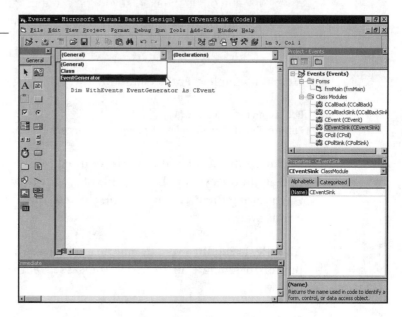

With the object selected, its events appear in the right-hand Proc drop-down list. It is not necessary to write code for all the events. Your class will receive only the events that have code written for them.

Benefits of Events

Events make possible an easy method of object-to-object communication. Without the use of events, objects would need to either poll one another or make use of `CallBack` events to create the same communication. These two methods increase the complexity of the client and often require more code to implement.

Note

Events allow for the creation of communication systems between programs or modules. They are a natural extension of the normal VB way of reacting to program or system occurrences. They allow for asynchronous messaging, identifying when a task is complete or begun.

Create a new, Standard EXE project. Add three CommandButtons to the form and three classes to the project, and then name them as shown in Table 7.8.

Table 7.8

Objects Used in Event Demo

Object	Name	Caption
Form	frmMain	
CommandButton1	cmdCallBack	CallBack
CommandButton2	cmdEvent	Event
CommandButton3	cmdPoll	Polling
Class1	CCallBack	N/A
Class2	CEvent	N/A
Class3	CPoll	N/A

Add the following code to the form:

```
Option Explicit
Dim WithEvents EventGenerator As CEvent
Private Sub cmdEvent_Click()
    Set EventGenerator = New CEvent

    EventGenerator.Start

End Sub
Private Sub EventGenerator_Complete()
    MsgBox "EventGenerator has finished"
```

```
End Sub
Private Sub cmdCallBack_Click()
    Dim CallBackGenerator As CCallBack

    Set CallBackGenerator = New CCallBack

    With CallBackGenerator
        .Register Me
        .Start
    End With

End Sub
Public Sub CallBack()
    MsgBox "CallBack Generator has finished"
End Sub
Private Sub cmdPoll_Click()
    Dim PollGenerator As CPoll
    Set PollGenerator = New CPoll

    PollGenerator.Start
    Do
        DoEvents
    Loop While PollGenerator.StillRunning
    MsgBox "PollGenerator has finished"

End Sub
```

Add the code, as follows, to each of the listed classes.

CCallBack:

```
Option Explicit
Private m_objClient As Object
Public Property Get Client() As Object
    Set Client = m_objClient
End Property
Public Property Set Client(NewClient As Object)
    Set m_objClient = NewClient
End Property
Public Sub Start()
    Dim sngStartTime As Single
    Dim sngDuration As Single

    Randomize Timer
```

```
      'set the duration for 0-10 seconds
      sngDuration = Rnd * 10
      sngStartTime = Timer
      Do
          DoEvents
      Loop Until Timer > sngStartTime + sngDuration
      Client.CallBack

End Sub
Public Sub Register(Client As Object)
      'Client must have a CallBack method
      Set m_objClient = Client
End Sub
```

CEvent:

```
Option Explicit
Public Event Complete()
Public Sub Start()
      Dim sngStartTime As Single
      Dim sngDuration As Single

      Randomize Timer

      'set the duration for 0-10 seconds
      sngDuration = Rnd * 10
      sngStartTime = Timer
      Do
          DoEvents
      Loop Until Timer > sngStartTime + sngDuration
      RaiseEvent Complete

End Sub
```

CPoll:

```
Option Explicit
Public StillRunning As Boolean
Public Sub Start()
      Dim sngStartTime As Single
      Dim sngDuration As Single

      StillRunning = True

      Randomize Timer
```

```
'set the duration for 0-10 seconds
sngDuration = Rnd * 10
sngStartTime = Timer

Do
    DoEvents
Loop Until Timer > sngStartTime + sngDuration

StillRunning = False

End Sub
```

Of the three classes, the CPoll object is the simplest and the most traditional. It sets a flag property to True when the long procedure begins, and to False when done. The client must create a loop to test the StillRunning property. This increases the complexity of the client. This would be especially true if there were more than one property to poll.

The CCallback object requires that any client have a specific method, named CallBack. It uses this method to signal the client when necessary. This creates an obvious problem in that the server (in this case the CCallBack object) must have knowledge of the client. The client is also required to register before starting the server. This gives the server a handle on the client to find the appropriate CallBack method. These two requirements also increase the complexity of the client.

The CEvent object requires the most preparation, but leads to the cleanest implementation at the client end. All the client needs to do is declare the object WithEvents and trap the desired events. The server raises this event when the task is complete.

Creating and Using Interfaces

In the "real world," an interface is the surface where two objects meet. The interface defines how the two objects interact. When using a computer, for example, the human-computer interface is a combination of the keyboard, mouse, and monitor. Normally the user cannot (and probably should not) reach into the case, making and breaking electrical connections to get the computer to work. All the interaction with the computer can then be thought of as the human using the computer's `Computer.MouseMove` and `Computer.KeyboardKeyPress` methods and the computer using the human's `Human.See` and `Human.Hear` methods. This collection of these methods for any class is the interface. Thus in human-computer interaction, there are two interfaces: the computer's and the human's.

For VB5, an interface is a class. However, it is used in a slightly different way than a normal class. In a normal class, code is written to implement the methods and properties of the class. In a class that will be used as an interface, on the other hand, the implementation of the properties and methods are irrelevant. The interface represents the methods and properties, but not the mechanism used by those procedures. The interface serves to gather a number of methods and properties under one name for use in a variety of situations. Other classes may then implement the interface, filling out the actual mechanism used for that particular class.

Gathering a number of methods under one name provides many benefits to the developer:

▶ Allows for the creation of generic communication methods between two or more objects

▶ Allows for the inheritance of the functionality of many objects without the potential confusion that multiple inheritance may lead to

▶ Allows for the development of multiple objects that act in a consistent manner

Generic Communication (Polymorphism)

Polymorphism is a term often used in discussion about object-oriented programming (OOP). The word polymorphism is from the Greek, meaning *many shapes*. The idea behind polymorphism is that many objects can respond to the same signal. Interfaces allow for polymorphism in VB5. The CEmployee class created earlier, for example, could be used as an interface to represent a number of different types of employee, including the following:

▶ UnionEmployee   An employee paid by the hour. If more than 40 hours are worked each week, the employee is paid at 150% of the normal rate.

▶ SalariedEmployee   An employee paid at a fixed rate per week.

▶ Consultant   An employee paid by the hour. No overtime pay is possible.

Creating a traditional program to deal with each of these types of employees (and others that may come up later) would require a number of branches in the code for each of the three types of employee. Instead, each employee type could implement a CEmployee interface. The client program could then use that interface to access the appropriate method or property. For example:

```
Private emp As CEmployee
Set emp = New UnionEmployee
MsgBox emp.WritePayCheck          'Uses the UnionEmployee's
➥WritePayCheck method
Set emp = New Consultant
MsgBox emp.WritePayCheck          'Uses the Consultant's
➥WritePayCheck method
Set emp = New SalariedEmployee
MsgBox emp.WritePayCheck          'Uses the SalariedEmployee's
➥WritePayCheck method
```

Each time, the emp.WritePayCheck executes the appropriate class's method. This is polymorphism at its best, and it is possible through interfaces.

Inheritance

One of the benchmarks of good programming is re-use. Classes and interfaces make this re-use easier. Interfaces in particular can make this easier by allowing a class to contain the functionality of many interfaces. In languages such as C++ and Smalltalk, this is accomplished through the inheritance of one class from another. One class inherits or absorbs all the functionality of a parent class. This may lead to problems when a class needs to inherit functionality from two or more classes. Confusion may arise, caused by properties of the same name in the parent classes. Inheritance with interfaces avoids this problem, as each property and method is associated with a specific class. If you have an interface prepared that allow an object to write itself to disc (IArchive) and another with methods and properties that allow a class to play itself (IPlay), for example, you could implement both the interfaces. After adding code to each of the interfaces' methods and properties, the new object would have the functionality of both interfaces.

Multiple Consistent Objects

Often, some tasks seem very similar but have slightly different results. One such example might be saving the contents of a variable. The value may be saved in a file in one program, the Registry in the next, and a database in yet another. Each of these three programs does the same task, but the mechanics are different. Using an interface can help here.

An interface can represent a common task such as this. The Interface class module could look like the following:

```
Private m_sDestination As String

Public Property Get Destination() As String
End Property
Public Property Let Destination(NewDestination As String)
End Property
Public Function ReadValue(ValueName As String, ValueValue As
➥Variant) As Boolean
End Function
Public Function WriteValue(ValueName As String, ValueValue As
➥Variant) As Boolean
End Function
```

Each class that implements this interface now has a consistent set of procedures to act on. Any clients using classes that implement this interface to save data can change the exact mechanism easily, without needing any change to their code. All they would need is to change to a new class implementing this interface.

Implementing an Interface

After the interface has been defined, the implementation for the interface must be completed. All methods and properties of the interface must be present in any class that implements the interface. If any are missing, a compile-time error occurs. To implement an interface, you add the following (in the General Declarations section of a class module):

```
Implements InterfaceName
```

After the `Implements` statement is added, the interface name appears in the object drop-down list in a code window, as Figure 7.9 shows. The public methods and properties of that interface will appear in the Proc drop-down list.

Figure 7.9

Implementing an interface.

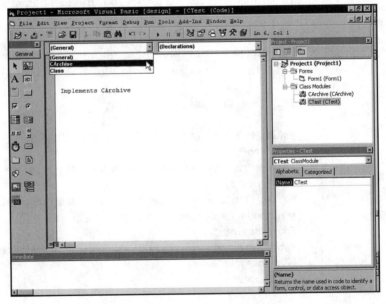

Exercises

Exercise 7.1:   Exploring an Object Hierarchy

To use the Object Browser, complete the following steps:

1. Create a new project in VB5.

2. Choose Object Browser from the View menu.

3. Find the listing for a Form1 object in the left-hand ListBox. It should appear in boldface.

4. Observe the list of properties, methods, and events listed in the right-hand ListBox.

5. Return to the form window by choosing the form name from the Window menu.

6. Add a control to the form (for example, a CommandButton).

7. Return to the Object Browser. Notice that the form now has an entry for the new CommandButton.

Exercise 7.2:   Creating an Object

To create a new class, complete the following steps:

1. Create a new Standard EXE project in VB5.

2. Choose Add Class Module from the Project menu.

3. Rename the Class Module **CAccount**.

4. Look in the Object Browser to find this new class.

Exercise 7.3:   Adding Properties to an Object

To add properties to the class created in Exercise 7.2, complete the following steps:

1. Add two private variables in the General Declarations section of the class module. These will be the private storage for two properties: AccountID and Balance. For example:

continues

```
Private m_sAccountID As String
Private m_cBalance As Currency
```

2. Add the property procedures to access these two properties. The two properties should be available from this or any other project. Balance may be any value, but the `AccountID` must start with the characters "CHQ." For example:

```
Public Property Get Balance() As Currency
    Balance = m_cBalance
End Property
Public Property Let Balance(NewBalance As Currency)
    m_cBalance = NewBalance
End Property
Public Property Get AccountID() As String
    AccountID = m_sAccountID
End Property
Public Property Let AccountID(NewID As String)
    If Left$(NewID,3) = "CHQ" Then
        m_sAccountID = NewID
    End If
End Property
```

3. Observe the new properties in the Object Browser.

Exercise 7.4: Adding Methods to an Object

To add methods to the class created in Exercise 7.2, complete the following steps:

1. Add a new subroutine to the class module. This sub should be publicly available and named **Deposit**. Add code to the new method to increase the `Balance` by a given amount. You should not allow negative deposits. For example:

```
Public Sub Deposit(Amount As Currency)
    If Amount > 0 Then
        Balance = Balance + Amount
    End If
End Sub
```

2. Add a new function to the class module. This function should be publicly available and named **Withdraw**. Add code

to the new method to decrease the `Balance` by a given amount. You should not allow negative withdrawals or a withdrawal that will take the `Balance` below $0. Return the amount withdrawn from the account. For example:

```
Public Function Withdraw(Amount As
Currency) As Currency
    If Amount > 0 Then
        If Amount > Balance Then
            Amount = Balance
        End If
        Balance = Balance - Amount
        Withdraw = Amount
    End If
End Function
```

3. Observe the new methods in the Object Browser.

Exercise 7.5:   Creating a Client for an Object

To create a client to use the `CAccount` object, complete the following steps:

1. Add a form to the project if there isn't one already.

2. Add three labels, a `TextBox` and two `CommandButtons` to the form. Name them as in Table 7.9.

Table 7.9

Objects Used in the `CAccount` Client

Object	Name	Caption
Form	frmAccount	Bank Account
Label1	lblCurBal	Current Balance:
Label2	lblBalance	blank
Label3	lblAmt	Amount
TextBox	txtAmount	N/A
CommandButton1	cmdDeposit	Deposit
CommandButton2	cmdWithdraw	Withdraw

continues

3. Declare a form-level variable of type CAccount in the General Declarations section. It should look like this:

```
Private Acct As CAccount
```

4. In the form's Load event, initialize the form-level variable. Optionally, set a new value for the AccountID and Balance. For example:

```
Private Sub Form_Load()
    Dim sTemp As String
    Do
        sTemp = InputBox$("What is the
        ➥AccountID?")
    Loop Until Len(sTemp)
    Set Acct = New CAccount
    Acct.AccountID = sTemp
    Caption = "Account# " &
    ➥Acct.AccountID
    UpdateBalance
End Sub
```

5. Create a generic private routine that will update the lblBalance with the current balance in the account. This should look something like this:

```
Private Sub UpdateBalance()
    lblBalance.Caption =
    ➥Format$(Acct.Balance, "Currency")
End Sub
```

6. Add code to the Deposit button that executes the Deposit method. Use the value from the TextBox as the amount to deposit. Don't forget to run the UpdateBalance routine. For example:

```
Private Sub cmdDeposit_Click()
    Acct.Deposit txtAmount.Text
    UpdateBalance
End Sub
```

7. Add code to the Withdraw button that executes the Withdraw method. Use the value from the TextBox as the amount to withdraw. Don't forget to run the UpdateBalance routine.

Optionally, display the actual amount withdrawn.

```
Private Sub cmdWithdraw_Click()
    Dim Amt As Currency

    Amt = Acct.Withdraw(txtAmount.Text)
    UpdateBalance
    MsgBox "Withdrawal: " & Format$(Amt,
    ➥"currency")

End Sub
```

8. Run the program. Type an amount in the text box and click on the Deposit button. The displayed balance should increase. Try the Withdrawal button to see whether it debits the account correctly.

Exercise 7.6: Using the `Friend` Keyword

To add a class with a `Friend` method, complete the following steps:

1. Add a new class module to the project. This class module should be named **CArchive**. It will be used to store `Friend` properties and methods of the `CAccount` class.

2. Add a new property to the `CArchive` class. This property will be used to store the `Filename` to save the balance. Declare the property with the `Friend` keyword:

```
Private m_sFilename As String

Friend Property Get FileName() As String
    FileName = m_sFilename
End Property
Friend Property Let FileName(NewFile As
➥String)
    m_sFilename = NewFile
End Property
```

3. Add a new subroutine to the `CArchive` class. This subroutine will be used to save the `Balance`. Open a new file, using the

continues

name in the FileName property created in step 2. Write the value to that file. This should look similar to this:

```
Friend Sub SaveAccount(Value As String)
    Dim hFile As Integer

    hFile = FreeFile
    Open FileName For Output As #hFile
    Print #hFile, Value
    Close #hFile

End Sub
```

4. Add a new function to the CArchive class. This function will be used to load the value from the file. Open the file, using the FileName property created in step 2. Return the value loaded or zero if an error occurs. It should look like this:

```
Friend Function LoadAccount() As String
    Dim hFile As Integer
    Dim sTemp As String

    hFile = FreeFile
    On Error Resume Next
    Open FileName For Input As #hFile
    If Err.Number = 53 Then
        sTemp = 0
    Else
        Input #hFile, sTemp
    End If
    LoadAccount = sTemp
    Close #hFile

End Function
```

5. Add a new private variable of type CArchive to the CAccount class. This declaration should look like this:

```
Private Archive As CArchive
```

6. Add code to the Initialize and Terminate routines of the CAccount class to load and save the Balance to the file. They should be similar to the following:

```
Private Sub Class_Initialize()
    Set Archive = New CArchive

End Sub
Private Sub Class_Terminate()
    Archive.SaveAccount Balance
End Sub
```

7. Add code to the `Property Let AccountID` procedure to name the file to which the `CArchive` will save the account balance. This should be similar to the following:

```
Public Property Let AccountID(NewID As
➥String)
    If Left$(NewID, 3) = "CHQ" Then
        m_sAccountID = NewID
        With Archive
            .FileName = "\" &
            ➥m_sAccountID & ".txt"
            Balance = .LoadAccount()
        End With
    End If
End Property
```

8. Run the program. Make a few deposits and withdrawals, but leave a balance. Exit the program and restart it. The old balance should be loaded. Find the file. It should contain the old balance.

Exercise 7.7: Adding an Event to an Object

To add an event to the class started in Exercise 7.2, complete the following steps:

1. Declare a new event in the class `CAccount`. It should be publicly available, take no parameters, and be named **Over-Drawn**. This declaration should be in the General Declarations section of the class module and look similar to this:

```
Public Event OverDrawn()
```

continues

Exercise 7.7: Continued

2. Add code to the `Withdraw` method that fires the event when the account is overdrawn. It should now look similar to the following:

```
Public Function Withdraw(Amount As
➡Currency) As Currency
    If Amount > 0 Then
        If Amount > Balance Then
            RaiseEvent OverDrawn
            Amount = Balance
        End If
        Balance = Balance - Amount
        Withdraw = Amount
    End If
End Function
```

3. Change the declaration of the `CAccount` variable in the form to allow it to trigger events. This looks like the following:

```
Private WithEvents Acct As CAccount
```

4. Add code to the new `Acct_Overdrawn` event handler. Display a message that the user has overdrawn his account. This should look something like the following:

```
Private Sub Acct_OverDrawn()
    MsgBox "Account Overdrawn",
    ➡vbExclamation
End Sub
```

5. Run the program and try to withdraw more than the balance. The event should run and a message box should be displayed.

Exercise 7.8: Creating and Using an Interface

To use the `CAccount` class started in Exercise 7.2 as an interface, complete the following steps:

1. Add a new class module to the project. This class module should be named **CDepositOnlyAccount**. It will represent a special instance of an account that only allows deposits.

2. Add code to the General Declarations section of the CDepositOnlyAccount to identify the fact that it will implement the CAccount interface. This should look like the following:

```
Implements CAccount
```

3. Implement each of the properties and methods of the CAccount interface. This should be similar to the code used by the CAccount object itself, except for the code in the CAccount_AccountID Property Let procedure, and the CAccount_Withdraw function. It should look similar to this:

```
Private Archive As CArchive
Private m_sAccountID As String
Private m_cBalance As Currency

Public Event Overdrawn()

Private Sub Class_Initialize()
    Set Archive = New CArchive
End Sub
Private Sub Class_Terminate()
    Archive.SaveAccount CAccount_Balance
End Sub

Private Property Let
➥CAccount_AccountID(NewID As String)
    If Left$(NewID, 3) = "DEP" Then
        m_sAccountID = NewID
        With Archive
            .FileName = "\" &
            ➥m_sAccountID & ".txt"
            CAccount_Balance =
            ➥.LoadAccount()
        End With
    End If
End Property

Private Property Get CAccount_AccountID()
➥As String
    CAccount_AccountID = m_sAccountID
End Property

Private Property Let
```

continues

Exercise 7.8: Continued

```
CAccount_Balance(NewBalance As Currency)
    m_cBalance = NewBalance
End Property

Private Property Get CAccount_Balance()
As Currency
    CAccount_Balance = m_cBalance
End Property

Private Sub CAccount_Deposit(Amount As
➥Currency)
    If Amount > 0 Then
        CAccount_Balance =
        ➥CAccount_Balance + Amount
    End If
End Sub

Private Function CAccount_Withdraw(Amount
➥As Currency) As Currency
    MsgBox "Withdrawals not allowed for
    ➥this account"
    CAccount_Withdraw = 0
End Function
```

Note

The AccountID confirms that this is a deposit-only account (identified by the "DEP" in the account ID), and that withdrawals are not permitted.

4. Add code in the Form_Load event of the form to test the AccountID entered and assign the Acct variable to the appropriate type of account. This should make it look similar to the following:

```
Private Sub Form_Load()
    Dim sTemp As String
    Do
        sTemp = InputBox$("What is the
        ➥AccountID?")
    Loop Until Len(sTemp)
    Select Case UCase$(Left$(sTemp, 3))
        Case "CHQ"
            Set Acct = New CAccount
```

```
        Case "DEP"
            Set Acct = New
            ➥CDepositOnlyAccount
        Case Else
            Exit Sub
    End Select
    Acct.AccountID = sTemp
    Caption = "Account# " &
    ➥Acct.AccountID

    UpdateBalance
End Sub
```

Note Notice that the Acct variable may be assigned to either account types because they both implement the CAccount interface.

5. Run the program. Enter a valid checking account number to confirm that this still works as before. End the program and run it again. This time use an AccountID beginning with the characters "DEP" to create a deposit-only account. Deposit some money, and then try to withdraw an amount. You should be refused, and a message box should be displayed.

Note This example is not quite the way it would be done in the "real world." To properly create this pair of account types (and any others that may follow), no code would normally be written in the CAccount interface. All accounts would implement the interface in their own unique ways.

Review Questions

1. You are defining a new property. The property is meant to hold an employee's ID number, which is made up of two characters and four numbers. Which of the following property procedures would you have to define? (Select all that apply.)

    A. `Property Set`

    B. `Property Get`

    C. `Property Let`

    D. `Property EmployeeID`

    E. `Property New`

2. The following line of code is in the General Declarations section of a class module:

    `Public Age as Integer`

    Which of the following is true?

    A. The class defined by the class module will have a new property called `Age`.

    B. All modules in the same project as the class module will be able to access the variable.

    C. An error will occur because this is not a valid declaration.

    D. The value of `Age` can be accessed from any other project that knows about this class.

3. You have designed a class module that will be used as a standalone EXE server. Which of the following is false about the `Instancing` property for the class?

    A. The class cannot be defined `Private`.

    B. A `PublicNotCreatable` class must have another class that provides access to it.

    C. A program using a class defined as `GlobalMultiUse` does not need variables derived from that class to use its properties and methods.

    D. The class cannot be defined as `SingleUse`.

4. You have created a new property in a class module. You have not specified its scope. What scope is it?

    A. `Private`

    B. `Friend`

    C. `Public`

    D. `Global`

    E. None. You must specify the scope for all properties.

5. Which of the following are valid settings for the `Instancing` property of a class? (Select all that apply.)

    A. `GlobalMultiUse`

    B. `Global`

    C. `PublicCreatable`

    D. `SingleUse`

    E. `Private`

6. You have declared a new object variable of type `CAccount`, with the following line:

```
Dim theAccount as CAccount
```

What must you do before using this variable?

    A. Nothing. The variable is ready to use.

    B. `Set theAccount = New CAccount`

    C. `theAccount = New CAccount`

    D. `Set theAccount = CAccount`

7. What action should you not do in a class' Initialize event?

    A. Set default values

    B. Create dependant objects

    C. Set an object variable to a new copy of the class

    D. Open files or other resources to be used by the class

8. What is the syntax to set the return value inside of the Property Get procedure named LastName?

    A. Set Return LastName = ReturnValue

    B. Return ReturnValue

    C. Exit ReturnValue

    D. LastName = ReturnValue

9. What information can you not find by using the Object Browser?

    A. Examples of using an object's properties

    B. Number and type of parameters for the methods of an object

    C. Names of all the properties of an object

    D. Events for an object

10. You are using a program that accesses a SingleUse ActiveX EXE program. After creating a second copy of an object defined by the program, what should you expect to happen?

    A. More memory is used.

    B. Memory is freed.

    C. An error occurs. You can only run one copy of a SingleUse program.

    D. Nothing.

11. What happens if you don't write code to react to all the events an object generates?

    A. A runtime error occurs.

    B. A compile-time error occurs.

    C. No error occurs, but the events you do add code to will not run until you complete all event handlers.

    D. No error occurs, and the events you react to will execute.

12. What happens if you don't write code for all the methods and properties of an interface?

    A. A runtime error occurs.

    B. A compile-time error occurs.

    C. No error occurs, but the methods and properties you do add code to will not run until you complete all `Interface` procedures.

    D. No error occurs, and the methods and properties you have added code for will execute.

13. You try to initialize a new object variable with the following line:

```
Set MyVar = New ClassName
```

but receive an error. What is a possible cause?

    A. You don't need to use the `Set` command here.

    B. You don't have permission to access the class.

    C. `MyVar` has not been declared.

    D. You don't need to use the `New` keyword here.

Answers to Review Questions

1. B and C. Both a `Property Get` and a `Property Let` procedure should be written. This will allow the property to be written to and read. A `Property Set` procedure is not necessary because the variable is not an object variable. For more information, see the section titled "Adding a Property to a Class Module."

2. A. Using a `Public` variable in the General Declarations section of a class module will define a new property for that class. For more information, see the section titled "Adding a Property to a Class Module."

3. D. An ActiveX EXE project may be defined as `SingleUse`, `MultiUse`, `GlobalSingleUse`, or `GlobalMultiUse`. For more information, see the section titled "Understanding the `Instancing` Property."

4. C. The default scope for a property is `Public`. For more information, see the section titled "Using `Public`, `Private`, and `Friend`."

5. A, D, and E. The `Instancing` property of a class may be set to `GlobalMultiUse`, `GlobalSingleUse`, `MultiUse`, `SingleUse`, or `Private`. For more information, see the section titled "Understanding the `Instancing` Property."

6. B. Although the variable has been declared, it has not been initialized. This can be done by setting the variable to a new instance of the class. For more information, see the section titled "Adding a Class Module to a Project."

7. C. Creating a new copy of the class before the class is initialized would lead to an infinite loop because each new class attempts to create a new copy until the computer runs out of memory or resources. For more information, see the section titled "Initialize and Terminate."

8. D. Returning a value from a `Property Get` procedure is the same as returning a value from a function. Set the name of the procedure to the return value in the body of the

procedure. For more information, see the section titled "Adding a Property to a Class Module."

9. A. The Object Browser enables you to view the properties, methods, and events of an object. It does not show any examples of using the properties. For more information, see the section titled "Object Browser."

10. A. Each copy of a `SingleUse` ActiveX EXE program can provide one object. Creating a second object would cause another copy of the EXE to be loaded in memory. For more information, see the section titled "Instancing `SingleUse`."

11. D. You need only to write code to react to the events you wish to deal with. For more information, see the section titled "Adding an Event to a Class Module."

12. B. You must write code for all the methods and properties of an interface. Not doing so will lead to a compile-time error. For more information, see the section titled "Creating and Using Interfaces."

13. C. If a variable is not declared before you attempt to initialize it, you will receive an error. For more information, see the section titled "Adding a Class Module to a Project."

Answers to Test Yourself Questions at Beginning of Chapter

1. Only define a `Property Get` procedure. This is useful when the property is calculated or fixed for an object. See "Adding a Property to a Class Module."

2. Creating a property by using a `Property` procedure pair (`Property Get/Let` or `Get/Set`) allows for error checking, and ensures that the value passed is valid. See "Adding a Property to a Class Module."

3. Create a new `Public` subroutine or function in a class module. See "Adding a Method to a Class Module."

4. Each client gets its own copy of the ActiveX EXE program. Each copy of the ActiveX EXE program uses up memory as the EXE is loaded. See "Understanding the `Instancing` Property."

5. Declare a new variable by using the `WithEvents` keyword. For example, `Private WithEvents theTask as SomeTask`. See "Adding an Event to a Class Module."

6. Nothing. Every class is already usable as an interface. See "Creating and Using Interfaces."

7. Either declare a variable by using the `Public` keyword in the General Declarations section of a class module or create `Property Get/Let/Set` procedures. See "Adding a Property to a Class Module."

8. The Object Browser can be used to identify the properties, methods, and events of a class. See "Object Browser."

C h a p t e r

Accessing Data Using Data Controls and Bound Controls

8

This chapter helps you prepare for the exam by covering the following objectives:

Objectives

- ▶ Add data to a table by using the DBList or DBCombo control

- ▶ Add data to a table by using the standard ListBox control

- ▶ Display information by using the DBGrid control

- ▶ Display information by using the MSFlexGrid control

Test Yourself! Before reading this chapter, test yourself to determine how much study time you will need to devote to this section.

1. Define the terms *bound* and *unbound* when referring to controls.

2. What control is used to connect a VB application to a database and create a Recordset that can be used by other controls to add, modify, and delete information?

3. Visual Basic provides built-in controls for application development. Name four intrinsic controls that can be bound to a data control.

4. Visual Basic allows an application to be connected with a database by using the intrinsic data control. What are the two properties responsible for the connection to the database and the retrieval of the requested Recordset?

5. The data control is used to create Recordset objects for accessing database information. The properties used to create a Recordset can be changed at runtime. What method of the data control must be used to re-create a new Recordset at runtime?

6. When a control is bound to the data control, what are the two common properties used by all controls?

7. The DBList control can be used with a data control to update information stored within a database. Does the DBList control provide a style property to determine the appearance of the visual interface?

8. Does the DBCombo control offer any events that will be fired specifically before information is sent to the database? This would allow the application to provide data validation.

Answers are located at the end of the chapter...

Many applications enable users to work with information provided from an external data source such as a database. Visual Basic has a set of controls specifically designed to simplify database access. These controls also reduce the amount of programming required by handling most of the data-access complexities.

Visual Basic provides many different data-aware controls to assist in developing applications that integrate with a database. This chapter covers using data controls. These controls allow the application to be integrated with a database. After a data control has been connected to a database, data-aware controls allow direct access to the information stored within the database. Five of the more popular data controls that ship with the latest version of Visual Basic are examined.

This chapter covers the following topics:

- ▶ Using data controls for database access

- ▶ Using data bound intrinsic controls

- ▶ Using data bound custom controls

- ▶ Adding and removing custom control reference

- ▶ Adding data to a table by using the DBList or DBCombo control

- ▶ Adding data to a table by using the standard ListBox control

- ▶ Displaying information by using the DBGrid control

- ▶ Displaying information by using the MSFlexGrid control

Using Data Controls and Bound Controls

This section examines connecting an application to a database with special types of controls. Topics covered include defining bound and unbound controls, intrinsic and custom controls, using data controls, and using bound controls.

Visual Basic provides many different ways of accessing information stored within a database. One of the more simplified data access techniques is the data control. The data control allows an application to be directly connected to a database. By using this form-based control, the developer just sets the desired properties and calls the appropriate methods to access the database.

After a data control has been used to simplify the connection to a database, data bound controls are used to pass information to and from the database fields. These data-aware controls also have properties and methods that reduce the need to write program code.

 Note

When controls are used to represent fields from a database, two terms are used to describe how they work: bound and unbound. The term *bound* is used to refer to the fact that these controls automatically handle passing information to and from the database. No program code is required to have these controls perform this data passing. The other term, *unbound*, is used to refer to the lack of automatic updating. These types of controls do not automatically pass information to and from the database. Additional program code is required to have information sent to and from the database. Both bound and unbound controls can be found in the intrinsic and custom controls offered by Visual Basic.

The data control and bound controls are used together to provide one of the easiest ways to utilize the information found within a database. The following is an overview of using the data control and bound controls to access information.

The first step is to connect a data control to the database. This enables the programmer or user to indicate the location, type of database, and table to access. Once set, the data control automatically establishes a connection to the database specified. The connection will then be used to provide the bound controls with information from fields in the specified table.

The second step is to connect the bound controls to a data control. The bound control is set to represent one of the fields from the specified table of the data control. The bound control will handle displaying information from the database as well as writing information to the database.

The following sections detail using the data control to provide access to a database and then connecting a bound control to the data control.

Understanding Intrinsic Versus Custom Controls

Visual Basic provides a wide assortment of controls. These controls are usually divided into two different categories. These categories are used to determine how the controls are added to a project as well as their distribution needs. The first type of control is referred to as an *intrinsic* control and is available by default. This type of control is built in to Visual Basic and is on the default toolbox. Intrinsic controls require only the main distribution files when distributing the application. The second category of control is the *custom* control. Various aspects of custom controls must be understood to use these types of controls in an application. The following is a list of the main issues when using custom controls:

▶ Custom controls must be explicitly added to a project by using the Components dialog box under the Project menu.

▶ Custom controls must be correctly registered with the operating system to be used by the application.

▶ Custom controls require additional files that must be distributed with the final application if the controls are not on the target machine.

▶ Custom controls are registered with the operating system using REGOCX32.EXE, which can be found in the \TOOLS directory.

Although custom controls are more involved than the intrinsic controls, they usually offer more functionality. Many third-party vendors offer a wide variety of controls for Visual Basic.

Using Data Controls

The data control is one of the intrinsic controls of Visual Basic. You can find this control in the default toolbox. Figure 8.1 shows the VB Data Control. It has a series of properties that enable the application developer to specify information required to connect to the desired database. The data control also offers various methods and events that allow for interaction by the application when information is assigned to the database.

Figure 8.1

The Visual Basic Data Control.

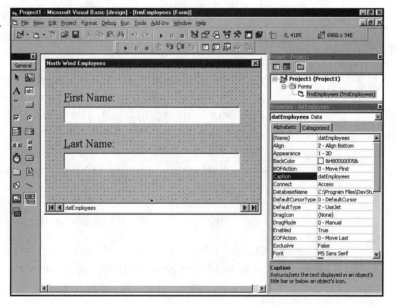

Once added to a form, this control can be used directly by the user or hidden and controlled by program code. The following is a list of the three most important properties of this control. These three properties are the only ones required when connecting to a database.

- ▶ `Connect` Used to indicate the type of database being connected to (that is, Access, dBase, Paradox, FoxPro, Excel, Lotus).

- ▶ `DatabaseName` Used to indicate the path and filename of the database.

- ▶ `RecordSource` Used to indicate the table name that will be used to provide records to the data control. This property can also be an SQL string or a query.

After these three properties have been set, a connection to the database can be established. By using the `Refresh` method of the data control, a `Recordset` object will be created based on the provided information in the `RecordSource` property. This `Recordset` can be directly controlled by the interface of the data control or by methods of the data control's `Recordset` object.

The following code samples demonstrate setting the three main properties of the data control and the `Refresh` method to create a `Recordset` from the database.

The following property is used to determine the type of database being connected to:

```
datNWind.Connect = "Access"
```

The following property is used to determine the path and filename of the database:

```
datNWind.DatabaseName = "C:\Program Files\DevStudio\VB\NWIND.MDB"
```

The following property is used to determine the information that will make up the Recordset. It can be the name of a table, an SQL statement, or the name of a Query from the database:

```
datNWind.RecordSource = "Employees"
```

This method is used to force the data control to create a new Recordset based on the previously set properties:

```
datNWind.Refresh
```

These properties can either be set at design time in the Properties window or at runtime as shown. After these properties have been set and a Recordset has been created, bound controls can be used to display the desired fields.

The following list details other properties of the data control that offer additional control and functionality.

▶ BOFAction   Used to automatically perform an action when the beginning of the Recordset is reached.

▶ DefaultCursorType   Used to indicate the cursor library used by the data control when retrieving the Recordset.

▶ DefaultType   Used to determine the type of data source used by the data control. Either Jet or ODBCDirect data sources can be specified.

▶ EOFAction   Used to automatically perform an action when the end of the Recordset is reached.

▶ Exclusive   Used to indicate whether the database can be opened for single use or multiple use.

▶ ReadOnly   Used to determine whether the Recordset object is read-only and will not automatically update the database.

▶ RecordsetType   Used to determine the type of Recordset generated by the data control (that is, Table, Dynaset, Snapshot).

The data control also has a variety of events that can be used to respond to different activities. These enable the user to be informed of actions completed by the data control. Users can also be given the option of preventing actions from occurring after an action has occurred but before information in the database is altered.

If the information needs to be verified before it is written, the data control has a set of events that are automatically generated as the Recordset is affected. The following list details the three key events of the data control.

- ▶ Validate   Occurs before the current record changes. This event can be used to ensure that correct information is being assigned to the database.

- ▶ Reposition   Occurs after a record becomes the current record. This event is used to update the appearance of the form or to provide additional feedback to the user.

- ▶ Error   Occurs as the result of a data access error. The type of data access error can vary depending on whether information about the database is incorrect or whether rules or relationships of the database are violated.

Using Bound Controls

Bound controls allow direct access to fields of the Recordset created by the data control. These types of controls assist greatly in reducing the overall amount of program code that must be written. Any bound control features the capability to automatically display information when a new record is selected. Bound controls will also write information directly into the specified database field.

The two different types of controls found in VB, intrinsic and custom, both offer different levels of bound control. There are also specifically designed controls that offer an increased level of database control.

In the preceding section, a data control is set to create a `Recordset` based on the Employee table of the NWIND.MDB database. If information from a field is to be displayed, a regular text box can be bound to the data control that created the `Recordset`. The following list shows the two properties found in most controls that allow binding to a data control.

▶ `DataSource`   Used to indicate the name of the data control that contains the `Recordset`

▶ `DataField`   Used to indicate the field to be bound from the `Recordset`

The `DataSource` property must be specified in the Property window at design time because it is not available during runtime.

After the text box has been bound to the data control, information from the `DataField`, shown in Figure 8.2, will be displayed automatically. When the `Recordset` is moved to a new record, the text box will display the new record data.

Figure 8.2

After being bound to a data control, the `DataField` property will list the available fields of the `Recordset`.

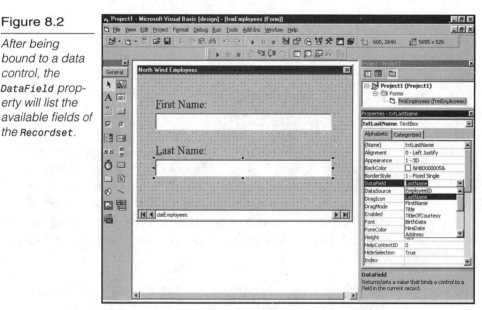

When a text box is bound, it also automatically handles writing information to the `Recordset`. If a user changes information in the text box, when the `Recordset` is moved, the information will be passed to the database.

Many of the Visual Basic controls offer bound properties to reduce the amount of program code required when connecting to and using information from a database. The text box, label, picture, image, check box, list box, and combo box all offer bound properties. VB also includes more powerful data bound controls in the custom controls. The remainder of this chapter examines these.

Adding Data to a Table by Using the DBList or DBCombo Control

Objective

This section examines how these two custom controls can be used to automatically update information within a database. Topics covered include the following:

▶ Additional file requirements for the two controls

▶ Using the DBList and DBCombo control

▶ Differences between the DBList and DBCombo controls

▶ Properties used for information display and for writing information

The DBList and DBCombo controls are additional custom controls that can be added to a project to assist the developer with additional ways of presenting and controlling information.

The DBList presents information in a list format that allows the user to only select from a list of provided values. If an entry is not on the list, the user cannot type in a new entry in the box. Figure 8.3 shows the DBList control.

Figure 8.3

The Visual Basic DBList control.

The DBCombo presents information in a drop-down list format. This requires less user interface space, as seen in Figure 8.4. The DBCombo box also has a style property to determine three different visual interface looks.

Figure 8.4

The Visual Basic DBCombo control.

Both controls must be added to a project before they can be used. Custom controls are added to a project by using the Project, Components dialog box. In the Components dialog box, look for Microsoft Data Bound List Controls 5.0, as shown in Figure 8.5. The file DBLIST32.OCX must be distributed with an application that uses either the DBList or DBCombo custom controls.

Figure 8.5

Adding the DBList and DBCombo controls to a Visual Basic project by using the Components dialog box.

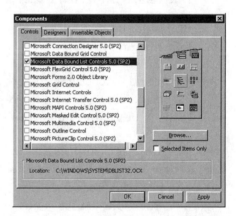

The DBList and DBCombo controls both contain the same five key properties to display and send information into the Recordset of a data control. The five properties are divided into two properties that are used to display the values, and three properties that are used to write the value.

The DBList and DBCombo controls also have events. These events are general to most controls and do not provide specific functionality for the database. The standard Change, KeyUp, KeyDown, MouseUp, and MouseDown can all be used with these controls. If events are required that are specific to database communication, the data control events can be used.

Displaying Information in the DBList or DBCombo Control

The two properties used to display information from a Recordset in the controls are as follows:

▶ RowSource   Sets a value that specifies the data control from which a controls list is filled

▶ ListField   Returns/sets the name of the field in the Recordset object used to fill a control's list portion

These two fields will be used to access the Recordset of the data control and display information from the desired field. The user can then select from the provided list. If a DBCombo box is used, the user may also be able to type an additional entry not in the list. The DBList box will not allow typing.

Writing Information from the DBList or DBCombo Control to a Database

When information is to be written to a database, different properties of the control are used. Three properties are used to indicate the data control to send information to, the field to update, and the field that will contain the information to be written. These properties are as follows:

▶ DataSource   Used to specify the data control that contains the Recordset to be written to

▶ DataField   Used to specify the field to be written to in the Recordset

▶ BoundColumn   Used to specify the source field in a Recordset that will supply the data value to be written

These three different properties are used after the user has selected an item from the provided data list. These properties specify the destination location and data that will be written. Both the DBList and DBCombo controls make use of these properties.

Comparing the DBList and DBCombo Controls

The DBList and DBCombo controls both use the same properties to display and write information. The main difference between these two controls is their visual interface appearance and capabilities.

The DBList box is just a straight list box that provides users with a limited list of options that they can select from.

The DBCombo box has a style property that can be used to alter the appearance of the visual interface component of the control. With the Style property, the developer can specify the following three different styles for the control:

▶ dbcDropdownCombo   Enables the user to select from a drop list or type a new entry

▶ dbcSimpleCombo   Provides a text box with a list below

▶ dbcDropdownList   Enables the user to only select from a list

Each control has a subtly different visual appearance that can be used in different ways when creating an application.

Adding Data to a Table by Using the Standard ListBox Control

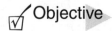

This section examines the use of this intrinsic control for displaying a selection list and adding information to a database. Topics covered include using the ListBox, and properties used for displaying information and writing information to the database.

The ListBox control is one of the default intrinsic controls offered by Visual Basic. This control does not require a custom control reference to be used in the VB design environment. Figure 8.6 illustrates the intrinsic ListBox control. Notice the toolbox in the figure contains no additional controls.

The main difference between the ListBox intrinsic control and the DBList custom control is the source used to provide the control's selection list.

Figure 8.6

The Visual Basic intrinsic ListBox control.

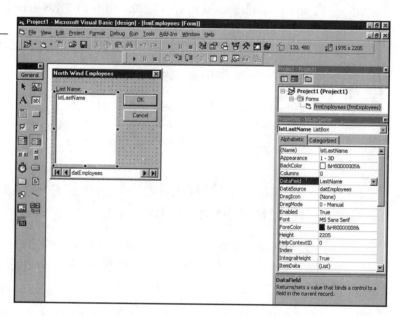

The ListBox control also contains a variety of events. Most of the events for this control are the standard events found in other controls.

The ListBox uses different properties to display and write information into a database. One property is used to provide a selection list. Two properties are used to specify where information is to be written.

Displaying Information in the ListBox Control

To provide the user with a display list of selections, they must be entered into the List property of the control box at design time or by using the AddItem method at runtime.

The AddItem method accepts a string argument and will add the new item to the bottom of the selection list. An optional argument can be used to specify the index of the item if required:

```
lstFirstName.AddItem "Nancy"
lstFirstName.AddItem "Andrew"
lstFirstName.AddItem "Janet"
```

This sample code will be used to add three names to the selection list. After the user has selected an item, other properties will be referenced to update the information to a database.

Writing Information from the ListBox Control to a Database

The ListBox provides two different ways of using information selected. The Text property can be used to return the selected item.

The ListBox can also be bound to a database to store selected information. The DataSource property provides the data control name that will contain the Recordset to be written to. The DataField property will be used to indicate the field to be written to.

The following list details those properties:

▶ DataSource   Used to specify the data control that contains the Recordset to be written to

▶ DataField   Used to specify the field to be written to in the Recordset

The DataSource property must be specified in the Property window at design time because it is not available during runtime.

Displaying Information by Using the DBGrid Control

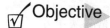 Objective

This section examines a custom control of VB that allows information to be displayed in a grid layout. Topics covered include files required for using the control, display data in the grid, properties of the control, and methods of the control.

The DBGrid is another bound custom control offered by Visual Basic. The DBGrid control is used to display information in a spreadsheet fashion. Information can be positioned in a row and column orientation to assist with presentation. Due to the bound nature of this control, information can be automatically displayed and written to the desired database.

The DBGrid control must be added to a project before it can be used. Custom controls are added to a project by using the Project, Components dialog box. In the Components dialog box, look for Microsoft Data Bound Grid Control, as shown in Figure 8.7. The file DBGRID32.OCX must be distributed with an application that uses the DBGrid custom control.

Figure 8.7

Adding the DBGrid control to a Visual Basic project by using the Components dialog box.

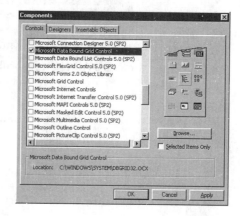

Displaying Data with the `DBGrid`

Due to the nature of the column and row display, only one main property is required to be set when using the `DBGrid` for database access. The control does not have a property for specifying an individual field from the `Recordset`.

The `DBGrid` property `DataSource` is used to indicate the name of the data control that created the `Recordset`. Columns are used to represent all fields from the specified `Recordset`. Rows are used to represent all records from the `Recordset`.

The `DBGrid` also features the option of Retrieve Fields from the database of the specified data control. This can be done at design time to assist with layout. Figure 8.8 illustrates using the Retrieve Fields option at design time.

Figure 8.8

Using the DBGrid's Retrieve Fields option at design time to assist with layout.

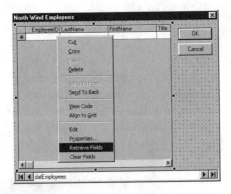

The `DBGrid` can be used to add, modify, or delete information found within the cells. All changes will be reflected in the database specified.

Other properties of the `DBGrid` allow additional capabilities and functionality. The following list details some of these properties:

- ▶ `AllowAddNew` Enables interactive record addition

- ▶ `AllowArrows` Enables use of arrow keys for grid navigation

- ▶ `AllowDelete` Enables interactive record deletion

- ▶ `AllowUpdate` Enables or disables record updatability

Properties are useful for determining how the user can use the grid control. The DBGrid also has a series of events that can be programmed to respond to actions that the control takes. The following section examines some of the events of the DBGrid control.

Using Events of the DBGrid

Events of the DBGrid control can be used to determine whether information should be passed from the database to the DBGrid or from the DBGrid to the database. This allows the application to determine whether correct information is being assigned to the database. Events can also be used to fill in missing information or change the appearance of the VB application depending on the data.

The following list details some of the specific events handled by the DBGrid to assist with validation of data and updating the form as information is assigned, added, modified, or deleted.

▶ BeforeUpdate   Occurs before record changes are written to the database

▶ AfterUpdate   Occurs after record changes are written to the database

▶ BeforeDelete   Occurs before record deletion from grid

▶ AfterDelete   Occurs after record deletion from grid

▶ OnAddNew   Fired when a user action has invoked an AddNew operation

▶ ColEdit   Fired when column data is edited

These events allow the application to respond depending on the actions taken by the user. Before, events can be used to inform the user of an action. After, events can be used to inform the user of the completion of a task.

The following sample code is used to provide the user with a message box asking to confirm the deletion of a record. Figure 8.9 shows the message box asking the user to confirm the deletion. This code assumes that the `AllowDelete` property has been set to True:

```
Private Sub DBGrid1_BeforeDelete(Cancel As Integer)
    Dim iResult As Integer
    iResult = MsgBox("Are you sure you want to delete this
    ➥record?", vbQuestion + vbYesNo)
    If iResult = vbNo Then
        Cancel = True
    End If
End Sub
```

Figure 8.9

Using the DBGrid BeforeDelete event to generate a message box for the user.

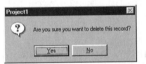

 Note   When using a `DBGrid` control, it is also important to remember that the `DBGrid` is bound to a data control. When information is assigned to the database, both the `DBGrid` and the data control can fire events. In some cases this might be duplication and not be required in both controls.

Displaying Information by Using the MSFlexGrid **Control**

 **Objective**   This section examines another custom control that presents information in a grid layout. Topics covered include files required for distribution, displaying data, using the `MSFlexGrid` without a data control, properties of the control, and using the `MSFlexGrid` with a data control.

The `MSFlexGrid` is another bound custom control that presents information in a row and column fashion. The `MSFlexGrid` offers a different set of capabilities from the DBGrid control covered in the preceding section.

One of the main differences between the MSFlexGrid and the DBGrid is how information is manipulated. The MSFlexGrid is used primarily for displaying information, not modifying it. The DBGrid allows direct access to the cells of the grid and enables the user to enter information directly. The DBGrid's primary design is for accessing information from a database.

The MSFlexGrid control must be added to a project before it can be used. Custom controls are added to a project by using the Project, Components dialog box. In the Components dialog box, look for Microsoft FlexGrid Control 5.0, as shown in Figure 8.10. The file MSFLXGRD.OCX must be distributed with an application that uses the MSFlexGrid custom control.

Figure 8.10

Adding the MSFlexGrid control to a Visual Basic project by using the Components dialog box.

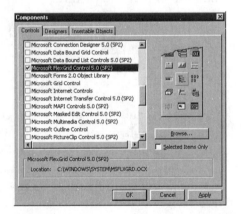

Displaying Data with the MSFlexGrid

The MSFlexGrid can be used alone or it can be bound to a data control. If used by itself, the MSFlexGrid has a wide variety of properties that can be used to assign text, pictures, navigation, formatting, alignment, and other display options.

The MSFlexGrid can also be used to display information from a database when bound to a data control. This information cannot be added, modified, or deleted. The control can be considered read-only due to the inability to change the underlying Recordset.

Information can still be assigned programmatically to the MSFlexGrid but will not affect the underlying information found in the database. The display properties can also be controlled through program code and used to format the appearance of the information provided from the database.

Using the MSFlexGrid Without the Data Control

One of the powerful features of the MSFlexGrid is the capability to programmatically populate information into the cells. This stand-alone method does not require a database or a data control. The MSFlexGrid allows the size of the grid to be set manually or through program code. By navigating the grid with properties, a cell can be selected and information placed in it. Data can be in the form of text or a picture.

The following code sets the size of the grid:

```
MSFlexGrid1.Rows = 5
MSFlexGrid1.Cols = 5
```

This code creates five rows and five columns in the control. By default, the control has one fixed row and one fixed column. These are similar to the column and row headings found in spreadsheets. The FixedCols and FixedRows properties can be set to 0 or increased, depending on the requirements.

The following code is used to navigate the grid. This code selects the second row and the third column:

```
MSFlexGrid1.Row = 2
MSFlexGrid1.Col = 3
```

The following code uses the current cell and sets the Text property with a value:

```
MSFlexGrid1.Text = "44"
```

The following code uses the current cell and sets the `CellPicture` property with an image. The `LoadPicture` function is used to retrieve the file, the same as programmatically assigning a picture to an image control or a picture control. Figure 8.11 illustrates the `MSFlexGrid` control containing both text and picture information:

```
Set MSFlexGrid1.CellPicture = LoadPicture("c:\windows\setup.bmp")
```

Figure 8.11

Using the `MSFlexGrid` *for text and picture data.*

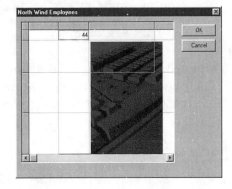

The `MSFlexGrid` can be a very powerful standalone control. The only difficulty when using the control by itself is that information can only be programmatically assigned.

Using the `MSFlexGrid` with a Data Control

When an `MSFlexGrid` control is bound to a data control, information can be displayed from the database. Assuming the data control properties have been set, the `DataSource` property of the `MSFlexGrid` control can be set to the name of the data control.

The `MSFlexGrid` control will use the `Recordset` object created by the data control to display information from the fields into the grid columns and records into the grid rows. Figure 8.12 shows the use of the `MSFlexGrid` control with a data control providing the database connection. Due to the design of the `MSFlexGrid`, information cannot be directly manipulated in the grid. If displayed information from the `Recordset` is programmatically changed, the modification will not be reflected in the data. The `MSFlexGrid` is considered read-only.

Figure 8.12

Using the MSFlexGrid with a data control to display information from a database.

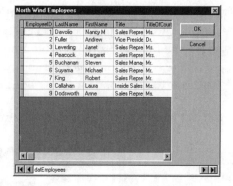

Although read-only, the information in the display can still be effectively formatted through program code. The user will also have the ability to navigate the grid with the mouse or the keyboard.

Exercises

Exercise 8.1:   Using the DBCombo Control

The DBCombo control can be used to simplify data entry and display. In this exercise, the Data Form Wizard is used to create a basic order form from the NWIND.MDB database. An Employee ID is listed in a bound text box control. The DBCombo control will be used to replace the simple text box. This will allow the database to continue to store an ID value while providing the user with a more readable last name. The DBCombo control will also be used to provide a list of employees' last names for easy data entry. An additional data control will provide a connection to the required employee information. To create this exercise, follow these steps:

1. Create a Standard EXE project.

2. Select Project, Components. This dialog box will be used to extend the control selection of the project.

3. From the list, find the component called Microsoft Data Bound List Controls 5.0.

4. Check the item to add the component to the Visual Basic project. This extends the toolbox to include two additional controls: the DBList and DBCombo box.

5. Click on OK to close the dialog box and return to the project.

6. Check the toolbox for the two new controls. Use the tooltip to identify the new items. If the toolbox is not visible, select View, Toolbox.

7. From the Add-Ins menu, choose Data Form Wizard. If the menu is not listed, select the Add-In Manager and choose it from the list.

8. If the wizard is on the Introduction step, click on Next.

continues

Exercise 8.1: Continued

9. From the Database Type, ensure that Access has been selected. Click on Next.

10. Use the Browse button and locate the NWIND.MDB file. It should be in the VB program directory. After the path has been located, click on Next.

11. From the Form Layout, ensure that Single record has been selected. Click on Next.

12. From the Record Source combo box, select the Orders table.

13. From Available Fields, select all fields by using the double right arrows. All fields should now appear in the Selected Fields list box. Click on Next.

14. From Available Controls, ensure that only the Close button has a check mark, and then clear all other check marks. Click on Next.

15. Ensure that the form name is `frmOrders`. Click on Finish.

16. The Data Form Wizard will be used to create a simple data entry form, which you will then modify. Click on OK if required to exit the wizard.

17. Change the startup object to the form `frmOrders`. Use Project, Properties, and change the startup object as required.

18. Run the application.

19. The Orders form should be displayed as created by the Data Form Wizard. If the Orders form is not displayed, check the startup object.

20. Notice that all fields are populated with information retrieved from the NWIND.MDB file. A data control has been used to connect to the database. Use the data control to move from one record to another.

21. Notice the Employee ID as you move from one record to another.

22. Click on Close to end the application. A DBCombo box will be used in place of the Employee ID text box.

23. Move the Employee ID text box, not the label, to the empty space at the side of the form. Reduce the size as required.

24. Add one DBCombo box to the frmOrders form. Place the control in the Employee ID position with the Employee ID text box off to the right side.

25. Change the DataSource property of DBCombo1 to datPrimaryRS. This will connect the DBCombo box to the current Recordset.

26. Change the DataField property of DBCombo1 to EmployeeID. This will connect the DBCombo box to the EmployeeID field of the data control Recordset.

27. Run the application.

28. Move from one record to another. Notice that the DBCombo control reflects the same Employee ID as the text box.

29. Select the drop-down arrow from the Employee ID combo box. Notice that no entries are present. This is due to the properties being set, DataSource and DataField.

30. Stop the application and return to Design mode.

31. Add one data control to the frmOrders form. Move the control to the lower-right corner of the form.

32. Change the Caption property of Data1 to datEmployees.

33. Change the Name property of Data1 to datEmployees.

34. Change the Visible property of datEmployees to False.

35. Change the DatabaseName property of datEmployees to the path of the NWIND.MDB database.

36. Change the RecordSource property of datEmployees to Employees.

continues

37. The data control should now be connected to the Employees table of the NWIND.MDB database.

38. Change the `RowSource` property of `DBCombo1` to `datEmployees`. This will connect the `DBCombo` control to another data control containing only employee information.

39. Change the `ListField` property of `DBCombo1` to `LastName`. This will connect the `DBCombo` control to the last name field of the data control `Recordset`. It will be used for display.

40. Change the `BoundColumn` property of `DBCombo1` to `EmployeeID`. The bound column is used to connect the value of one record to the matching field record in the `datEmployees` control.

41. Run the application.

42. Move from one record to another. Notice the improvement made by using the `DBCombo` control. The employee last name is used rather than the employee ID. This improves readability for the user.

43. Select the drop-down arrow from the Employee ID combo box. Notice that there are now entries present. This is due to the required properties being set.

44. If an employee's last name is selected from the drop-down list, the current order record will be modified with that employee's ID. Verify this by changing an assigned employee. Move to another record and return to the changed record to confirm that the database has been updated.

45. Return to Design mode.

46. Try to change the field displayed by the combo control (perhaps to the employee's first name). Ensure that the record is still being stored correctly and will display as required.

47. When completed, end the application.

This exercise demonstrated using the `DBCombo` control to add information to a database. The `DBCombo` box was used to replace a bound text box. The DBCombo was used to retrieve the current EmployeeID, then use that value and look up the EmployeeID in the datEmployee control. The Last Name was then displayed rather than the EmployeeID, thus increasing readability.

Exercise 8.2:   Using the Standard ListBox Control

The ListBox control can be used to provide the user with a selection list of values. The values found within the ListBox control must be programmatically added to the control. No database properties are offered to populate a selection list. However, the ListBox control can assign information to a database after a selection has been made. Once bound, this control will also highlight a matching entry between the selection list and the current record of the bound data control. To create this exercise, follow these steps:

1. Create a Standard EXE project.

2. From the Add-Ins menu, choose Data Form Wizard. If the menu is not listed, select the Add-In Manager and choose it from the list.

3. If the wizard is on the Introduction step, click on Next.

4. From the Database Type, ensure that Access has been selected. Click on Next.

5. Use the Browse button and locate the NWIND.MDB file. It should be in the VB program directory. After the path has been located, click on Next.

6. From the Form Layout, ensure that Single record has been selected. Click on Next.

7. From the Record Source combo box, select the Orders table.

8. From Available Fields, select all fields by using the double right arrows. All fields should now appear in the Selected Fields list box. Click on Next.

continues

9. From Available Controls, ensure that only the Close button has a check mark, and then clear all other check marks. Click on Next.

10. Ensure that the form name is frmOrders. Click on Finish.

11. The Data Form Wizard will be used to create a simple data entry form, which you will then modify. Click on OK if required to exit the wizard.

12. Change the startup object to the form frmOrders. Use Project, Properties and change the startup object as required.

13. Run the application.

14. Move from one record to another. Notice that the ShipCountry changes as the record changes.

15. Stop the application and return to Design mode.

16. Move the ShipCountry bound text box to empty space on the right side of the form. Resize the text box as required.

17. Add a standard ListBox control to the empty ShipCountry text box area. Resize the ListBox as required.

18. Change the Name property of the ListBox control to lstShipCountry.

19. Change the DataSource property of the lstShipCountry control to datPrimaryRS.

20. Change the DataField property of the lstShipCountry control to ShipCountry.

21. Use the List property of the lstShipCountry control to provide the user with a selection list. In the Property window, enter a country and then use Ctrl-Enter to move to the next line. Each country should be on an individual line.

22. Enter the following data: Argentina, Austria, Belgium, Canada, Denmark, Finland, France, Ireland, Italy, Mexico, Norway, Poland, Portugal, Spain, Sweden, Switzerland, UK, USA, Venezuela.

23. Run the application.

24. Move from one record to another. Notice that the Ship Country list box displays the name of the country. If the country name is in the list box, it will be displayed and highlighted. If the entry is missing, it will show the last value and will not be highlighted. This list box can only display items from the selection list.

25. The original Ship Country text box is still displaying the record value. Find a record with the Ship Country – Germany. Notice that the list box does not display this country.

26. Find another record with the Ship Country – Brazil. Notice that the list box does not display this country.

27. Both Germany and Brazil are countries missing from the list box.

28. Stop the application and return to Design mode.

29. Add the additional countries to the ListBox control: Brazil and Germany. Remember that each country needs to be on an individual line.

30. Run the application.

31. Find a record with the Ship Country – Germany. Notice that the original Ship Country text box is displaying the value; the list box is also displaying the value. This is because the country is part of the selection list.

32. Find a record with the Ship Country – Brazil. Notice the same results.

33. Change the Ship Country for record number 4 by selecting a different country from the list box.

34. Move to another record and then back to record 4. The new country should be displayed. Due to the bound nature of the list box, the record is updated with new information from the selection list.

continues

35. Return to Design mode.

36. Try to add an additional list box to replace the ShipVia field. This will ensure that the user doing data entry will only enter a valid value.

37. When completed, end the application.

This exercise demonstrated the use of a standard list box. The list box was used to provide a selection list to simplify data entry. The list box was bound to a data control to store field information. The list box was also given a selection list by using the List property of the control. After an item was selected from the list, the current record was updated in the appropriate field.

Exercise 8.3: Using the DBGrid Control

The DBGrid control is a very powerful bound control that can be used to display a complete set of fields and records. The control is similar to a spreadsheet and allows for the addition, modification, and deletion of data. This exercise uses a data control and binds it to the North Winds sample database. The DBGrid control will then be bound to the data control. To create this exercise, follow these steps:

1. Create a Standard EXE project.

2. Select Project, Components. This dialog box will be used to extend the control selection of the project.

3. From the list, find the component called Microsoft Data Bound Grid Control.

4. Check the item to add the component to the Visual Basic project. This will extend the toolbox to include the additional control, DBGrid.

5. Click on OK to close the dialog box and return to the project.

6. Check the toolbox for the new control. Use the tooltip to identify the new item. If the toolbox is not visible, select View, Toolbox.

7. Add one data control to the form.

8. Change the `Name` property of `Data1` to `datNWind`.

9. Change the `Caption` property of `Data1` to `datNWind`.

10. Change the `Align` property of `datNWind` to `2 - Align Bottom`.

11. Change the `Visible` property of `datNWind` to False.

12. Change the `DatabaseName` property of `datNWind` to the location of NWIND.MDB. This should be the VB directory.

13. Change the `RecordSource` property of `datNWind` to `Employees`.

14. Add one `DBGrid` control to the form.

15. Size the `DBGrid` control so that the majority of the form is covered by the control. Remember that the data control is invisible and does not require screen space.

16. Change the `Name` property of `DBGrid1` to `dbgEmployees`.

17. Change the `DataSource` property of `dbgEmployees` to `datNWind`.

18. While still in Design mode, right-click on the `dbgEmployees` control and select Retrieve Fields. This will populate the top row of each column with the names of all fields from the data control `Recordset` specified.

19. Run the application.

20. The arrow keys and the mouse can be used to navigate between records and fields. By default, the `DBGrid` control enables the user to modify data. New data cannot be added by default. Both settings are controlled by properties of the control.

continues

21. Modify one of the first names. Notice the far-left column contains a record indicator. When information is changed, a pencil displays.

22. Move to the next row. The information in the preceding row is automatically stored in the database. Notice that the pencil indicator is now a record indicator.

23. Move to the very last row. Notice that a new record cannot be added. This is the default setting of the DBGrid.

24. Stop the application and return to Design mode.

25. Change the AllowAddNew property of the dbgEmployees control to True. This will allow a row at the bottom of the records for creating new records.

26. Run the application.

27. Move to the very last row. It should be an empty row. This row contains a star symbol to indicate a new record. Enter information into each field. The new record will automatically be entered into the database.

28. Stop the application and return to Design mode.

29. Open the code window for the dbgEmployees control.

30. Find the dbgEmployees_BeforeUpdate event and enter the following code:

```
Dim iResult As Integer
iResult = MsgBox("Do you wish to save your changes?",
➥vbQuestion + vbYesNo)
If iResult = vbNo Then
    Cancel = True
End If
```

31. Run the application.

32. Modify one of the records. After you have finished modification, move to another record. The DBGrid control will trigger the BeforeUpdate event.

33. A message box should be displayed asking whether you want to save changes.

34. Answer No to the message box. The information that has been modified will remain, but you cannot move off the record.

35. In the same field with the change, press the ESC key. The pencil indicating modification should change to an arrow indicating a record pointer.

36. Return to Design mode.

37. Try adding a message box to indicate success when information has been successfully written to the database. Use one of the events of the dbgEmployees control. Also, try making the information in the dbgEmployees control read-only, no modification or additions.

38. When completed, end the application.

This exercise demonstrated using the DBGrid control to add, modify, and navigate through a series of records retrieved from a database. The BeforeUpdate event was also used to present a message box and ask whether the changes should be saved.

Exercise 8.4: Using the MSFlexGrid Control

The MSFlexGrid is another control that displays data in a row and column fashion. The MSFlexGrid can be bound to a data control to display record information from a database. When used with a data control, the MSFlexGrid is read-only. To create this exercise, follow these steps:

1. Create a Standard EXE project.

2. Add one data control to the form.

3. Change the Name property of Data1 to datEmployees.

continues

4. Change the `Caption` property of the `datEmployees` control to `datEmployees`.

5. Change the `Visible` property of the `datEmployees` control to False.

6. Change the `Align` property of the `datEmployees` control to `2 - Align Bottom`.

7. Change the `DatabaseName` property of the `datEmployees` control to the location of NWIND.MDB.

8. Change the `RecordSource` property of the `datEmployees` control to `Employees`.

9. Add the Component reference for Microsoft FlexGrid Control 5.0.

10. Ensure the Component has been added to the project by checking for the control `MSFlexGrid` in the toolbox.

11. Add one flex grid to the form.

12. Change the `Name` property of `MSFlexGrid1` to `mfgEmployees`.

13. Change the `Data Source` property of the `mfgEmployees` control to `datEmployees`.

14. Run the application.

15. Move from one cell to another. Notice the `MSFlexGrid` does not have markers on the far-left column to indicate the Data mode.

16. Attempt to change the information in a cell. The `MSFlexGrid` is read-only when bound to a data control.

17. Click on the gray box at the top of a column. This should highlight the column.

18. Click on the gray box at the left of a row. This should highlight the row.

19. Attempt to resize either a column or a row. By default, you should not be able to resize.

20. Stop the application and return to Design mode.

21. Change to `AllowUserResizing` property of the `mfgEmployees` control to `3 - flexResizeBoth`.

22. Change the `Font` property of the `mfgEmployees` control to `Times New Roman - 12 pt`.

23. Run the application.

24. Attempt to resize a column, row, or both. This will enable the user to adjust the columns and rows to best fit the data.

25. Return to Design mode.

26. Try to add a command button to the form that will change the `Font` property of the `mfgEmployees` control.

27. When completed, end the application.

This exercise demonstrated using the `MSFlexGrid`. A data control was connected to the North Winds database and used as the Data Source of the `mfgEmployees` control. The control allows for the browsing of data, but does not allow additions or modification. The `MSFlexGrid` properties were also adjusted to allow for the sizing of rows and columns.

Review Questions

1. The Visual Basic Data Control is used to connect to a database. What is the property used to determine the type of database being connected to?

   A. DatabaseName

   B. Connect

   C. Connection

   D. RecordSource

   E. DataSource

2. An application can use the data control to provide automatic connect to a database. What object is created by the data control to pass information to and from other controls?

   A. RecordSource

   B. RecordList

   C. RecordSet

   D. Record

   E. RecordCollection

3. The data control can have its properties set at runtime to allow for dynamic connections. If the RecordSource property of the data control is changed at runtime, what method must then be executed to force the control to create a new RecordSet object?

   A. Update

   B. Rebuild

   C. Connect

   D. MoveLast

   E. Refresh

4. The RecordSource property of the data control is used to specify the information to be used when creating the RecordSet object. What are the three types of information that can be used in the RecordSource property of the data control?

   A. Table

   B. Form

   C. Query

   D. SQL statement

   E. Index

5. A bound control allows information to be automatically displayed and written to the RecordSet of a data control. What is the name of the common property used to bind a control to the data control?

   A. RecordSource

   B. DataSource

   C. DataField

   D. RecordSet

   E. RowSource

6. Visual Basic provides a wide variety of built-in and custom controls for creating an application. Which control can be used to display information from a database, write information to a database, and uses an expandable and collapsible interface?

   A. ListBox

   B. DBGrid

   C. MSFlexGrid

   D. DBList

   E. DBCombo

7. Which intrinsic control that ships with Visual Basic can be used to provide the user with a selection list? This control can display information from a predefined list, write to a database, and requires some space for display or will provide a scrollbar.

   A. ListBox

   B. DBCombo

   C. DBList

   D. DBGrid

   E. MSFlexGrid

8. Visual Basic allows an application to be distributed to other computers. When creating an application that uses the DBGrid custom control, what additional files must be provided on a computer running the application?

   A. DBGRID.OCX

   B. DBGRID.EXE

   C. REGOCX32.EXE

   D. DBGRID32.OCX

   E. DBGRID32.EXE

9. Information can be automatically assigned from the DBGrid control to a database. What events can be used to validate the information being assigned to the database form?

   A. Validate event of the DBGrid control

   B. Validate event of the data control

   C. Reposition event of the data control

   D. BeforeUpdate event of the DBGrid control

   E. BeforeUpdate event of the data control

10. Visual Basic ships with controls that allow information to be displayed in a grid layout. What grid type control allows information to be directly edited within the cell displaying the information?

    A. MSFlexGrid

    B. VBGrid

    C. DBGrid

    D. MSDataGrid

    E. DBRowColGrid

11. Of the different types of controls providing data in a grid layout, what control allows both text and picture information to be displayed within the grid?

    A. DBGrid

    B. MSFlexGrid

    C. VBGrid

    D. MSDataGrid

    E. DBRowColGrid

12. Controls often provide a variety of properties that can be used to control the formatted display of information. Which grid control allows information within the grid to be formatted for display?

    A. DBRowColGrid

    B. MSDataGrid

    C. VBGrid

    D. MSFlexGrid

    E. DBGrid

13. A grid control allows the display of both text and pictures within the grid. From the listed code, how is a picture assigned to an active cell of the grid?

   A. `Set MSFlexGrid1.CellPicture =`
      `LoadPicture("c:\windows\setup.bmp")`

   B. `Set DBGrid1.CellPicture =`
      `LoadPicture("c:\windows\setup.bmp")`

   C. `Set MSFlexGrid1.CellPicture =`
      `"c:\windows\setup.bmp"`

   D. `Set DBGrid1.CellPicture = "c:\windows\setup.bmp"`

   E. `MSFlexGrid1.CellPicture =`
      `LoadPicture("c:\windows\setup.bmp")`

Answers to Review Questions

1. B. The `Connect` property of the data control is used to determine the type of database being connected to. This property can be used to specify different compatible database formats. The `DatabaseName` property is used for location and filename. The `RecordSource` is used to indicate the Table, Query of the SQL string. `DataSource` is used in data-aware controls to indicate the name of a data control. For more information, see the section titled "Using Data Controls."

2. C. The data control creates the `RecordSet` object to allow information to be read from and written to the database. The `RecordSet` is a reference list to the information stored in the database and can be accessed by other controls. For more information, see the section titled "Using Data Controls."

3. E. After the `RecordSource` property of a data control has been changed at runtime, the `Refresh` method must be used. This method will force the data control to create a new `RecordSet` object based on the new property values. If the `Refresh` method is not used after the `RecordSource` property

has been changed, the old RecordSet object will remain in use by the data control. For more information, see the section titled "Using Data Controls."

4. A, C, D. The RecordSource property can be assigned the name of a Table object from the database, the name of a Query object from the database, or an SQL statement. All three types can be assigned to determine the information to be used to create the RecordSet object of the data control. For more information, see the section titled "Using Data Controls."

5. B. The name of the common property used to bind a control to the data control is the DataSource property. The property is used to indicate the name of a data control located on the same form as the control to be bound. For more information, see the section titled "Using Data Controls."

6. E. The DBCombo control can be used to display information from a database, write information to a database, and has an expandable and collapsible interface. The DBCombo control is a custom control. For more information, see the section titled "Adding Data to a Table by Using the DBList or DBCombo Control."

7. C. The ListBox control is an intrinsic control of VB that can be used to provide a predetermined selection list. The control can also be used to write information to a database and requires display space or will provide a scrollbar. The DBList control is a custom control of VB and uses a database to provide the selection list. The ListBox control must have the selection list added manually. For more information, see the section titled "Adding Data to a Table by Using the Standard ListBox Control."

8. D. The file DBGRID32.OCX must be present on any computer running an application that uses the DBGrid control. If the file is missing or is not correctly registered with the operating system, the application will fail to work correctly. For more information, see the section titled "Displaying Information by Using the DBGrid Control."

9. B, D. Both the Validate event of the data control and the BeforeUpdate event of the DBGrid control can be used to validate the information being assigned to the database. The application developer can choose one or the other. Both events do not have to be used and could conflict if used together. For more information, see the section titled "Using Events of the DBGrid."

10. C. The DBGrid control allows information to be directly edited in the cell used to display the information. The MSFlexGrid can modify the contents of a cell that displays information, but this must be done through programmatic control. For more information, see the section titled "Displaying Information by Using the DBGrid Control."

11. B. The MSFlexGrid control allows both text and picture information to be displayed within the same grid. The DBGrid control can hold text values, but not linked or embedded objects. For more information, see the section titled "Displaying Information by Using the MSFlexGrid Control."

12. D, E. Both the MSFlexGrid and the DBGrid can be used to format information within the grid. This allows the information to be more effectively displayed to the user. For more information, see the section titled "Displaying Information by Using the DBGrid Control" or the section titled "Displaying Information by Using the MSFlexGrid Control."

13. A. The program statement, Set MSFlexGrid1.CellPicture = LoadPicture("c:\windows\setup.bmp"), is used to assign a picture to the active cell in the grid. The LoadPicture function is used for most controls when programmatically assigning a picture to a control. The DBGrid control does not have a CellPicture property and cannot be used to display pictures. For more information, see the section titled "Using the MSFlexGrid Without the Data Control."

Answers to Test Yourself Questions at Beginning of Chapter

1. The term *bound control* is used when referring to a control that automatically handles passing information between a control and a database. By setting special properties of the control, database communication will be controlled without writing additional program code. The term *unbound control* is used when referring to a control that does not automatically handle passing information between a control and a database. Program code can be written that will pass information between the control and the database. See "Using Data Controls and Bound Controls."

2. The data control can be used to connect an application to a database. Once connected, the data control creates a Recordset object that can be utilized by other controls for adding, modifying, and deleting information within the specified database. See "Using Data Controls and Bound Controls."

3. The following is a list of seven intrinsic controls that can be bound to a data control:

   ▶ Textbox   ▶ Picture

   ▶ Label   ▶ List

   ▶ Image   ▶ Combo

   ▶ Checkbox

   See "Using Data Controls and Bound Controls."

4. The two properties of the data control responsible for database connection and creation of the Recordset object are DatabaseName and RecordSource. The DatabaseName is used to indicate the path location and filename of the database to be connected. The RecordSource property is used to indicate the Table, Query, or SQL statement that will be used to create the Recordset for the control. See "Using Data Controls."

5. The method of the data control that will force the creation of a new Recordset object at runtime is Refresh. When the DatabaseName and RecordSource properties are changed at runtime, the Refresh method forces the data control to create a new Recordset based on the updated properties. See "Using Data Controls."

6. When a control is to be bound to the data control, the two common properties used are DataSource and DataField. The DataSource property is used to indicate the name of the data control that will provide the Recordset of information. The DataField property is used to indicate the name of the field to be bound to for displaying and updating information. See "Using Bound Controls."

7. The DBList property does not contain a Style property to determine the visual appearance of the control. Only the DBCombo control provides a Style property for this purpose. See "Adding Data to a Table by Using the DBList or DBCombo Control."

8. The DBCombo control does not provide any events that fire specifically before or after information is transferred to a database. The Change event of the DBCombo control is generic and not specific to database communication. The data control that the DBCombo control is bound to provides these events. See "Adding Data to a Table by Using the DBList or DBCombo Control."

Chapter

9

Accessing Data Using Code

This chapter helps you prepare for the exam by covering the following objectives:

 Objectives

- ▶ Navigate through and manipulate records in a Recordset

- ▶ Add, modify, and delete records in a Recordset

- ▶ Find a record in a Recordset

- ▶ Use the Find or Seek method to search a Recordset

Test Yourself! Before reading this chapter, test yourself to determine how much study time you will need to devote to this section.

1. Visual Basic provides many different methods of database communication and connection. What is the default database engine used by VB5?

2. The Visual Basic IDE can be extended to include additional programmatic objects not included by default. Where in the VB IDE can additional program objects be added?

3. Data Access Objects in Visual Basic allow for database communication. If a "User-defined type not defined" compile-time error occurs when attempting to run an application that uses DAO, what is the first item to check?

4. The Recordset object, provided by DAO, is used to retrieve record information from a database. What Recordset methods can be used to control the location of the current record?

5. When accessing individual records from a database, the Recordset object is used as a reference to the information. What Recordset property can be used to determine the current record number that the set is pointing to?

6. The Recordset object provides various methods for adding and modifying data. What method allows the addition of a new record into the database?

7. Properties can be used to determine the current state of the Recordset object. What property is used to determine the current data entry mode?

8. What is the name of the language used to find and return only specific records within a database?

9. Visual Basic allows the use of special statements to retrieve records from a database. What type of object is stored within the database that contains these statements?

10. Visual Basic Recordset objects can be searched for specific information. What method can be used on a Table type Recordset to find records matching the specified criteria?

11. When searching for information in the records of a Recordset, Visual Basic provides various methods to find matching data. What method can be used on a Snapshot type Recordset?

Answers are located at the end of the chapter...

VB offers the application developer many different options for accessing data within a database. The preceding chapter dealt with using custom controls to access information. This chapter focuses on using program code to access and manipulate information stored within a database.

Although visual controls provide a fast and simplified approach to connecting an application to a database, program code can be a more powerful tool for the developer.

This chapter details the process of connecting to a database and manipulating a Recordset object using program code. The individual records found within the Recordset will also be directly controlled through various properties and methods. Navigation, adding, modifying, deleting, and finding information are all examined in the following sections.

This chapter covers the following topics:

▶ Recordset basics

▶ Using references

▶ Creating a Recordset object

▶ Navigating through and manipulating records in a Recordset

▶ Adding, modifying, and deleting records in a Recordset

▶ Finding a record in a Recordset

▶ Using the Find or Seek method to search a Recordset

Understanding Data Access Basics

This section examines how Visual Basic provides objects that allow the viewing and manipulation of records from a database. Topics covered include DAO basics, setting object references, and creating a Recordset object.

When an application is used to provide information that is stored in an external data source, Visual Basic provides a series of objects, properties, and methods to assist in accessing and using that information.

One of the regularly used methods of connecting a database through program code to a VB application is through the use of Data Access Objects (DAO). This is a predefined object hierarchy used to control information stored within a database. For more information on DAO, see Visual Basic Help and Books Online.

Other methods of connection are also available, such as Remote Data Objects (RDO), Active Data Objects (ADO), Open Database Connectivity (ODBC), ODBCDirect, and more. These additional methods of data access are beyond the scope of this chapter and book.

After a database has been accessed through DAO, the Recordset is the primary object used to retrieve and manipulate a collection of records from the database. The Recordset has a rich set of properties and methods that allow for easy programmatic use of the information. The Recordset object allows for both the display of information as well as the writing of information to the database.

You must be aware of many different issues when using the Recordset—the type of connection to be used, connection options, type of Recordset retrieved, performance and optimization, as well as flexibility. All these issues have different ways of being addressed. Performance and optimization issues of the Recordset object are beyond the scope of this chapter and book.

To utilize Data Access Objects for database manipulation, an object reference must be made in the Visual Basic environment. The next section details using references to extend the VB environment.

Making References

To utilize DAOs in VB5, a special reference must be made for the project to recognize the collection of objects. This reference is similar to the reference required by a custom control.

References use external files to provide the objects and their functionality, which can then be used within the VB IDE. The References dialog box can be found under the Project menu in VB. This dialog box is similar to the Components dialog box; the main difference is the type of information being referenced.

The References dialog box is used to add extended functionality to the program code of Visual Basic. The Components dialog box is used to extend the control selection found within the design-time toolbox.

If a required reference is not found in the dialog box, it may not have been registered with the operating system. A Browse button is offered in the dialog box to locate the files used by the required reference. Figure 9.1 illustrates the References dialog box.

Figure 9.1

The Visual Basic References dialog box.

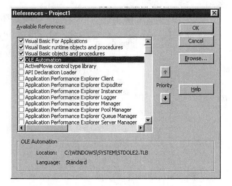

Referencing DAO

When DAO is chosen as the data connection technique, a predefined set of objects, properties, and methods can use a database engine known as the Jet. The Jet belongs to Microsoft and is used for Visual Basic and Access. DAO provides its set of objects to control the Jet and manipulate the desired database.

To include a reference to DAO in your current project, choose Project, References from the VB main menu. Microsoft provides different versions of DAO, which depend on the operating system and the installed version of the Jet. Visual Basic 5 and Access 97 use Microsoft DAO 3.5 Object Library. Figure 9.2 shows this reference being set.

Figure 9.2

Setting a reference to Microsoft DAO 3.5 Object Library.

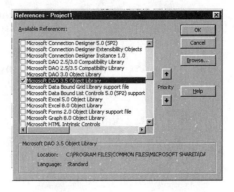

Once included, the project will now have additional programmable objects. VB provides the Object Browser to navigate the various components of a project. Figure 9.3 shows a VB project with default settings and a reference to DAO.

Figure 9.3

The Object Browser can be used to navigate additional references included in a project.

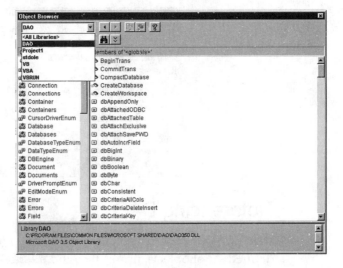

The Object Browser window enables the developer to determine the objects found in various project components. After an object has been selected, related properties, methods, and events are shown. The Object Browser is used to determine how objects are related, to show exposed variables and constants, as well as to provide context-sensitive help if available.

Creating a `Recordset`

Four basics steps are used to create a Recordset. The following list identifies these steps:

1. Set a reference to the DAO Object Library.

2. Declare an object variable for the database and `Recordset`.

3. Use the `OpenDatabase` method to connect to a database.

4. Use the `OpenRecordset` method of the opened database object to create a `Recordset`.

Once created, the Recordset allows access to all requested records from the database. The information within the records can be viewed, modified, or deleted, or can have new data added. The following code demonstrates the creation of a `Recordset` to the North Winds sample database that comes with Visual Basic 5.

```
Dim dbNWind As Database
Dim rsRecordset As Recordset
Set dbNWind = OpenDatabase("c:\program
➥files\devstudio\vb\nwind.mdb")
Set rsRecordset = dbNWind.OpenRecordset("Employees")
```

The first and second lines of code are used to declare two object variables used to reference the database. The third line of code uses the `OpenDatabase` method, passes the path/filename of the database, and sets the object variable for future reference. The fourth line of code uses the `OpenRecordset` method. The argument passed to `OpenRecordset` can be a valid table name, query, or SQL statement. This argument is then used to retrieve the desired records from the database and assign them to an object variable.

After the `Recordset` object has been created, the next step is to use properties and methods of the object to manipulate and view information from the records. The remaining sections detail the use of these various properties and methods.

Navigating Through and Manipulating Records in a `Recordset`

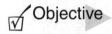 Objective

This section examines various properties and methods used when working with information retrieved from a database. Topics covered include determining the current record number, total amount of records, and repositioning the current record as required.

After a `Recordset` object has been created based on information stored within a database, it can be navigated—to provide data to the application. The navigation of a `Recordset` allows the application to use program code to affect the current location within the collection of records. Navigation also enables the user to move throughout the information as required.

Properties Used for Navigation

You can use various properties and methods to move through the `Recordset`. The position within the `Recordset` can be determined— moving to the next record, moving to the previous record, and even to the beginning and end. This allows the `Recordset` to be manipulated as required by the application or by the user.

The following list describes the key properties used with navigation of a `Recordset`:

▶ `AbsolutePosition`   Sets or returns the relative record number of the current record

▶ `BOF, EOF`   Used to indicate whether the current record in the `Recordset` has reached the Beginning of File or End of File

▶ `Bookmark`   Uniquely identifies a particular record in a `Recordset`

▶ `RecordCount`   Returns the number of records accessed in a `Recordset`

Figure 9.4 shows the use of the Object Browser to determine the properties of the Recordset object.

Figure 9.4

Examining properties and methods of the Recordset object.

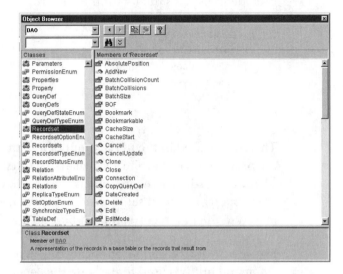

Using the AbsolutePosition Property

The AbsolutePosition property is used to determine the current record being pointed to by the Recordset. The number returned by AbsolutePosition is zero-based. When using the number, a 1 is added to reflect the correct record. The following sample code shows a message box reflecting the current record number:

```
MsgBox "The current record is " & rs.AbsolutPosition + 1
```

The AbsolutePosition property is often used to inform the user of his current position within the Recordset. Usually a Label control on a form will indicate the location or the Caption property of the Data control.

Using the BOF and EOF Property

During the navigation of the Recordset object, the current record must always be pointing to a valid record. If the current record is before the first record in the set, the BOF property will be set to True to indicate no more records. EOF is used the same way to indicate that the "record" just after the last record is current.

If the current record is moved beyond the first or last record in the Recordset, a runtime error will be generated. The following code demonstrates the use of the BOF property:

```
Sub cmdMovePrevious_Click()
    rsEmployees.MovePrevious
    If rsEmployees.BOF Then
        rsEmployees.MoveFirst
    End If
End Sub
```

This code is used in the Click event of a button used to move to the previous record in the Recordset. The first line moves the current record. The second line is used to determine whether the BOF property has been set to True. If so, the Recordset is only moved to the first record and not beyond a valid record.

Figure 9.5 shows a sample application with a set of movement command buttons used to navigate the Recordset object. The command buttons use the BOF and EOF properties to determine the current record position.

Figure 9.5

Using the BOF property of the Recordset object.

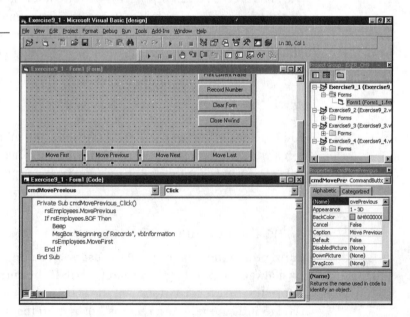

The EOF property can be used in the same way. The only difference is that the EOF property is used to indicate the last record in the Recordset.

Using the Bookmark Property

The Bookmark property uniquely identifies each record within the Recordset. This read / write property can be used to determine the current location and later to return to that same location.

When used to determine the current location, the return value can be stored in a string variable. The following code uses the Bookmark property to return the unique identifier for the current record and stores it in a string:

```
Dim strLocation As String
strLocation = rs.Bookmark
```

After the value of the Bookmark has been stored, actions can be performed on the Recordset object. After the actions have been completed, the Bookmark value can be set to the previous value. The following code sets the Bookmark property to the previously stored value:

```
rs.Bookmark = strLocation
```

The most common use for determining the current location is when a Recordset is being searched. The Bookmark is stored before the search is performed, if the search is not successful, and then the stored value is used to reset the previous Bookmark value. The following code shows this common use:

```
Dim strLocation As String
strLocation = rs.Bookmark
rs.FindFirst "FirstName = 'Andrew'"
If rs.NoMatch = True Then
    rs.Bookmark = strLocation
Else
    MsgBox "Record Found"
End If
```

This code declares a string and stores the current Bookmark value in the string. The Recordset is searched and if NoMatch can be found, the previous Bookmark value is assigned back to the Bookmark property.

Using the RecordCount Property

After a Recordset has been created, the RecordCount property can be used to determine the total amount of records in the Recordset. The type of Recordset created affects the value returned by the RecordCount property. For more information on creating different types of Recordsets, see Visual Basic Help (search for the OpenRecordset method).

During the creation of a Recordset, an additional argument can be specified to determine the type of Recordset created. The type of Recordset determines the level of functionality provided. DAO 3.5 offers five different types of Recordsets: Table, Dynamic, Dynaset, Snapshot, and ForwardOnly. Each type retrieves information in a different way. Depending on the type built, the RecordCount property can return a different value.

When the RecordCount property is used with a Table type Recordset, the property will always indicate the correct number of records. This value will also be up to date if information is added or deleted by other users.

When the RecordCount property is used with the Snapshot, Dynaset, and ForwardOnly types, the property will indicate the amount of records that have been accessed. To determine the accurate number of records, the MoveLast method must be executed on the Recordset. This affects performance when dealing with a network-based database or with a large collection of records.

The following code demonstrates the syntax used with the RecordCount property. The syntax does not change depending on the type of Recordset; only the returning value is affected:

```
lblRSTotal.Caption = rsEmployees.RecordCount & " records"
```

Navigating with the Move Methods

The following list describes the key methods used when navigating in a `Recordset`:

- ▶ `Move`   Moves the position of the current record in a `Recordset`

- ▶ `MoveFirst, MoveLast, MoveNext, MovePrevious`   Moves to the indicated record in the `Recordset`

The `Recordset` has a variety of `Move` methods that can be used to reposition the current record of the `Recordset` as desired.

The `Move` method can accept arguments indicating the amount of records to be moved, both forward and backward.

```
rsEmployees.Move +4
rsEmployees.Move -2
```

The first line moves the current record four rows forward. The second line of code moves the current record two rows backward.

Other methods are included for simple navigation. `MoveFirst` is used to move the current record to the first record in the `Recordset`. `MoveNext` increases the current record by one. `MovePrevious` decreases the current record by one. `MoveLast` is used to position the current record at the very last record in the set.

Adding, Modifying, and Deleting Records in a Recordset

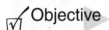 **Objective**

This section examines the methods used to affect the underlying information within a database. Topics covered include using the `EditMode` and `LockEdits` properties. Also covered is the use of the `Edit`, `AddNew`, `Delete`, `Update`, and `CancelUpdate` methods.

The `Recordset` object, provided by DAO, has a set of properties and methods that assist the application in modifying the information within a database. This allows the application to provide functionality to the user that will allow information to be added, modified, and deleted from the collection of records.

Properties Used for Adding, Modifying, and Deleting

When the information contained within the Recordset is to be modified, a series of properties are used to provide feedback on the current state of the Recordset. The following list describes two of these key properties:

- ▶ EditMode   Returns the state of editing for the current record

- ▶ LockEdits   Returns the type of locking in effect during editing

Both can be used to determine what state the Recordset is in while information is being added, modified, or deleted. The following sections show the use of these properties.

Using the EditMode Property

The EditMode property is used as a switch to determine whether information can currently be altered, or is currently being altered.

The EditMode property returns one of three possible values. The value is used to indicate whether the current record is being added or modified, or is not currently in use.

The DAO Object Library defines three constants to represent the values:

- ▶ dbEditNone = 0   No editing in progress.

- ▶ dbEditInProgress = 1   The Edit method was used and the current record is in the copy buffer.

- ▶ dbEditAdd = 2   The AddNew method was used, and the current record in the copy buffer is a new record not yet saved in the database.

The following code is used to determine whether the Edit method has been triggered. If not, the Edit method is used to indicate information will be updated:

```
If rsEmployees.EditMode = dbEditNone Then
    rsEmployees.Edit
End If
```

Using either the Edit or AddNew method of the Recordset object changes the EditMode property. If an attempt is made to change information without using the correct methods, a runtime error occurs.

Using the LockEdits Property

The LockEdits property of the Recordset can be set to control when a lock will be placed on the records. The Jet engine uses a page-level locking system. Each page is 2K in size. This is used to protect the information being entered while in a multi-user environment.

The value of LockEdits can be True or False. This value is used to indicate the type of locking in effect. The Jet engine refers to these values as Pessimistic and Optimistic locking, respectively. The following code shows the use of the LockEdits property of a Recordset:

```
rsEmployees.LockEdits = False
```

This code shows the use of Optimistic locking for this employee Recordset.

If LockEdits equals True, Pessimistic locking is in effect. As soon as a record triggers the Edit method, the page will be locked. When the Update method is used, the page will be unlocked.

If LockEdits equals False, Optimistic locking is in effect. Records being added or modified will be locked only during the update to the database.

Methods Used for Adding, Modifying, and Deleting

When information in the `Recordset` is to be affected, the following list of methods is used to control the state of the `Recordset` being manipulated:

▶ `Edit` Prepares a row of a `Recordset` for editing

▶ `AddNew` Creates a new record in the `Recordset`

▶ `Delete` Deletes a record from a `Recordset`

▶ `Update` Saves changes made with the `Edit` or `AddNew` methods

▶ `CancelUpdate` Cancels any pending `Update` statements

These methods are used together with the previous properties to determine and affect the state of the `Recordset`. The following sections describe the use of these methods.

Using the `Edit` and `Update` Methods

The `Edit` method of the `Recordset` is used to indicate that the current record is to be placed in the copy buffer to be affected as required. The following code shows the `Edit` method being used:

```
rsEmployees.Edit
rsEmployees.Fields("FirstName").Value = "Nancy M."
rsEmployees.Update
```

The first line sets the Edit mode and places the current record in the copy buffer. The second line of code is used to update the `FirstName` field with the new text value. The third line is used to commit the information in the copy buffer and update the database.

Figure 9.6 illustrates an application that restricts user modifications until the `Edit` method has been triggered. Notice that the text box background color is gray. The control also has the locked property set to True to prevent typing in the fields. When the user selects the Edit command button, changes can be made.

Figure 9.6

Data entry is controlled by the use of control properties and command buttons.

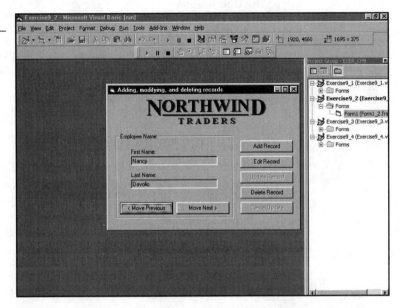

The `Edit` method must first be used before information is changed. After being modified in the copy buffer, the current record then must be updated to the database by using the `Update` method. Alternatively, if the information currently in the copy buffer is to be disregarded, the `CancelUpdate` method can be invoked to clear the copy buffer and reset the Edit mode.

Using the `AddNew` and `Update` Methods

The `AddNew` method is used to create a new record in the `Record-set`. Once triggered, the `EditMode` property is set to `dbEditAdd` to indicate that the copy buffer contains new information not yet placed in the database.

If the `AddNew` method is used, the Edit mode will automatically be set and does not have to be explicitly called. The following code shows the use of `AddNew`:

```
Sub cmdAddNew_Click()
    rsEmployees.AddNew
End Sub
```

Once triggered, information can then be sent to the required fields. Then the Update method can be used to complete the update to the database:

```
Sub cmdNewName_Click()
    rsEmployees.Fields("FirstName").Value = txtFirstName.Text
    rsEmployees.Fields("LastName").Value = txtLastName.Text
    rsEmployees.Update
End Sub
```

Using the Delete Method

The Recordset object provides the Delete method to remove the current record. When used, no warning or message box will be displayed. Messaging must be handled by adding additional program code if desired.

The use of the Delete method is fairly simple. After a record is removed from the set, the current record should be moved to the next record in the set. The following code demonstrates using the Delete method:

```
Sub cmdDelete_Click()
    rsEmployees.Delete
    rsEmployees.MoveNext
    If rsEmployees.EOF = True Then
        rsEmployees.MoveLast
    End If
End Sub
```

This code sample combines the use of the Delete method with the MoveNext method to provide the user with a valid record. To ensure that a valid record is always pointed to, this code also determines whether the end of the Recordset has been reached.

Using the CancelUpdate Method

To complete the process involved in adding and modifying data within the Recordset, the CancelUpdate method provides the means for canceling any pending updates.

When used, the `CancelUpdate` resets the `EditMode` and clears information from the copy buffer. The following code shows the use of `CancelUpdate`:

```
Sub cmdCancelUpdate_Click()
    rsEmployees.CancelUpdate
End Sub
```

Code should also be used to repopulate any controls that may have changed before the `CancelUpdate` was called. This will enable the user to see a valid record rather than controls with incorrect or no data.

The `CancelUpdate` method can be used after the `EditMode` has been set by the `Edit` or `AddNew` methods. If `CancelUpdate` is used without having used `Edit` or `AddNew`, a runtime error occurs.

Finding a Record

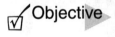 Objective ▶

This section examines the methods used in locating a record that meets the specified criteria. Topics covered include using stored queries and SQL statements.

When viewing and manipulating records from a database, you have many ways of finding a specific record or records. This allows the application, and the user, the ability to deal only with required information.

Two ways of finding information and returning a `Recordset` from a database are by using stored queries and SQL statements. Both enable the user to request only needed information from the database.

The following sections show the use of stored queries from a database, through the use of DAO and the use of Structured Query Language (SQL).

Using Stored Queries

DAO allows the use of stored queries within a database. Using a special language known as SQL, queries can be used to retrieve specific records. This allows only required information to be viewed and manipulated by an application.

Queries are basically SQL statements related to, and stored in, the database. This enables anyone to use the query without being familiar with the SQL language. It also provides the convenience of not having to create the same SQL statements over and over again.

The North Wind sample database contains a series of predefined queries. Figure 9.7 shows the database window viewing the Queries tab.

Figure 9.7

The North Wind sample database queries.

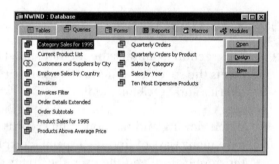

Access provides both a graphics query tool, as shown in Figure 9.8, and a text-based query tool. These two methods can be used to create a query. DAO provides the QueryDef Collection object for the programmatic creation and use of queries within a database.

The first method of calling a stored query from a database is by using the OpenRecordset method. The name of the stored query is passed as an argument. The following code demonstrates the use of this method:

```
Dim dbNWind As Database
Dim rsProductList As Recordset
Set dbNWind = OpenDatabase("c:\program
```

```
➥files\devstudio\vb\nwind.mdb")
Set rsProductList = dbNWind.OpenRecordset("Current Product List")
```

Figure 9.8

Microsoft Access graphics query tool, known as the Query By Example (QBE) Grid.

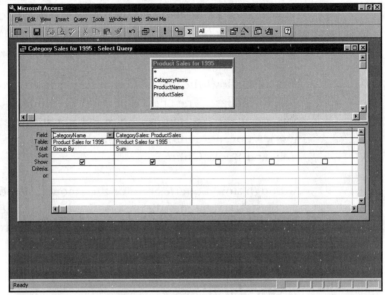

The first line is used to connect to the database. The second line uses the `OpenRecordset` method of the database object. The argument passed is the name of a `Select` query stored in the database. The `rs1 Recordset` object variable will now contain only the matching records.

Another method of calling a stored query from a database is by using the `QueryDef` Collection. `OpenRecordset` is also a method of this object and can be used to retrieve the query results. The following code demonstrates the use of the `QueryDef` Collection:

```
Dim dbNWind As Database
Dim qryProductList As QueryDef
Dim rsProductList As Recordset
Set dbNWind = OpenDatabase("c:\program
➥files\devstudio\vb\nwind.mdb")
Set qryProductList = dbNWind.QueryDefs("Current Product List")
Set rsProductList = qryProductList.OpenRecordset
```

The first three lines of code are for object variable declaration. The fourth line is used to set up the connection to the database. Line five uses the QueryDefs Collection of the database object and references the "Current Product List" stored query. Line six uses the query object variable and executes the OpenRecordset method to retrieve the query results.

DAO also allows the use of Action and Parameter queries from an Access database. The CreateQueryDef method of the database object can also be used for the programmatic creation of stored queries. For more information on these items, see Visual Basic Help and Books Online.

Although stored queries reduce the amount of code required, the use of SQL statements allows specific, dynamic queries to be created as they are required. The following section introduces the basics of using SQL with DAO.

Using SQL

Structured Query Language (SQL) is used on databases to view and modify only relevant information. By reducing the data to only what is needed, the user can focus on important information. Another advantage to using SQL is that it can be generated dynamically for specific needs.

The basic SQL statement is known as a SQL Select. The statement is a string that enables you to specify the fields to be retrieved, the table name containing the fields, and, optionally, a Where clause to act as search criteria. The following code sample demonstrates this:

```
strSQL = "Select * From Products"
Set rsProducts = dbNWind.OpenRecordset(strSQL, dbOpenDynaset)
```

The first line uses the SQL Select statement. The asterisk is used to represent all fields from the specified table. Individual field names could be specified if desired. The second line of code takes the string variable and passes it as an argument to the Open-Recordset method of the database object.

Another code sample demonstrates the use of the `Where` clause to limit the returning records:

```
strSQL = "Select * From Products Where [Category] = 'Beverages'"
Set rsProducts = dbNWind.OpenRecordset(strSQL, dbOpenDynaset)
```

The first line retrieves all fields from the Products table `Where` the `Category` field is equal to `Beverages`. Notice the use of the single apostrophes around the text value of `Beverages`. The second line of code is again used to pass the string to the `OpenRecordset` method.

SQL is not a very difficult syntax to learn and is based on the English language. It can become more complex when dealing with specific fields, relationships, multiple tables, and multiple databases. It allows greater flexibility when used dynamically to find records as needed. For more information and syntax on SQL, see Visual Basic Help and Books Online.

Using the Find or Seek Method to Search a Recordset

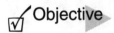
Objective

This section examines two methods used for searching a Recordset. Topics covered include using the `Find` method with a `Dynaset` or `Snapshot` type `Recordset`, and using the `Seek` method with a `Table` type `Recordset`.

Two specific methods of the `Recordset` object that assist with locating information are `Find` and `Seek`. Both methods can be used to locate specified data. Each method is used on a different type of `Recordset`.

The `Find` method can be used only with `Dynaset` and `Snapshot` type `Recordsets`. These two types are more flexible and easier to search.

The `Seek` method can be used only with a very specific type of `Recordset` object. If `Seek` is to be used, the `Recordset` object must return a `Table` type. This limitation is due to the nature of indexing on tables. Indexing is a method of allowing information to be sorted by default.

Using the Find Methods

The Recordset object provides four different Find methods. The following list describes each method:

- ▶ FindFirst   Locates the first record that satisfies the criteria
- ▶ FindLast   Locates the last record that satisfies the criteria
- ▶ FindNext   Locates the next record that satisfies the criteria
- ▶ FindPrevious   Locates the previous record that satisfies the criteria

Each method accepts a string argument that is used to specify the search criteria. The search criteria must have the same syntax as an SQL Where clause. The use of the SQL keyword Where is not required as part of the string.

The following string is an example of an SQL Where clause:

```
'Where [CourseID] = 2480'
```

Notice that the keyword Where is followed by a valid field name, and then the comparison operator, and a value. Just omit the Where keyword and you have a valid search string. For more information on the Where clause, search Visual Basic Help for the Where clause.

This sample code demonstrates finding the first record in a Recordset based on specified criteria.

```
Dim strFind As String
strFind = "[LastName] = 'Fuller'"
rsEmployees.FindFirst strFind
```

The first line declares a string. The second line assigns a string using the LastName field equal to a string value of Fuller. Notice the use of the apostrophe before and after the string value; this is required only with strings. The third line passes the strFind string to the FindFirst method.

Once executed, the Recordset will be searched. If no match can be found based on the criteria, the NoMatch property of the Recordset will be set to True. This allows for testing the success of the search. The following code adds additional lines to generate a message box indicating the results of the search:

```
Dim strFind As String
strFind = "[LastName] = 'Fuller'"
rsEmployees.FindFirst strFind
If rsEmployees.NoMatch = True Then
    MsgBox "No matches found.", vbInformation
Else
    MsgBox "A match was found.", vbInformation
End If
```

Although the Find methods are very useful with Dynasets and Snapshots, the Seek method must be used when dealing with a Table type Recordset. The following section details the use of the Seek method.

Using the Seek Method

When searching for information within a Table type Recordset, the Seek method is used to find records that match the specified criteria.

The Seek method is faster than the use of the Find methods on Dynasets and Snapshots. One of the limitations imposed by using Seek, however, is the requirement of using defined indexes. The Table must have a predefined index that can be used when the search is performed.

The syntax of Seek is different from the Find methods. The first argument passed to the Seek method is a valid comparison operator. The second argument is the value to be searched for in the indexed field. Additional arguments can be passed based on the amount of fields used in the index. The following code demonstrates the use of the Seek with an index:

```
Set rsEmployees = dbNWind.OpenRecordset("Employees", dbOpenTable)
rsEmployees.Index = "LastName"
rsEmployees.Seek "=", "Fuller"
MsgBox rsEmployees.NoMatch
```

The first line is used to create the Table type Recordset. The second line is used to indicate the name of a predefined index. The third line is the Seek method with the first argument being an equal operator and the second argument being the search value of the LastName field.

Similar to the Find methods, the NoMatch property of the Recordset is used to determine the success of the Find or the Seek. If set to False, a match has been found. If set to True, no matching records could be found based on the criteria.

Exercises

Exercise 9.1: Navigating Through and Manipulating Records in a Recordset

The DAO Collection of objects used to control a database contains the Recordset object. It is used to retrieve information from a database and provides various methods and properties that allow the information to be easily navigated. To create this exercise, use the following steps:

1. Create a Standard EXE project.

2. Change the Caption property of Form1 to "Navigating a Recordset".

3. Choose Project, References from the main menu.

4. In the check box selection list, add a reference to Microsoft DAO 3.5 Object Library.

5. Click on OK after the reference is added. The VB IDE will now contain all objects related to the DAO library.

6. In the General Declarations section of Form1, add the following code. This will create two form-level Private variables to assign the database objects to:

```
Option Explicit
Private dbNWind As Database
Private rsEmployees As Recordset
```

7. Increase the size of the form to accommodate buttons on the right side and at the bottom.

8. Add 10 command buttons to Form1. Increase the width of each button four grid units. Decrease the height of each button one grid unit. Use the Shift key and arrow keys after the control is selected as a shortcut. Place six buttons along

continues

the right side and four buttons along the bottom of the form.

9. Change the `Name` property of the top right button to `cmdOpenNWind`.

10. Change the `Caption` property of `cmdOpenNWind` to `"Open Nwind"`.

11. Open the code window for `cmdOpenNWind` and enter the following code. Ensure the path for NWIND.MDB is valid for your installation:

```
Private Sub cmdOpenNWind_Click()
    Set dbNWind = OpenDatabase("c:\program
    ➥files\devstudio\vb\nwind.mdb")
    Print "NWind Opened"
End Sub
```

12. Change the `Name` property of the second right button to `cmdCreateRS`.

13. Change the `Caption` property of `cmdCreateRS` to `"Create Recordset"`.

14. Open the code window for `cmdCreateRS` and enter the following code:

```
Private Sub cmdCreateRS_Click()
    Set rsEmployees = dbNWind.OpenRecordset("Employees")
    Print "Employees Recordset Created"
End Sub
```

15. Change the `Name` property of the third right button to `cmdPrintCurrentName`.

16. Change the `Caption` property of `cmdPrintCurrentName` to `"Print Current Name"`.

17. Open the code window for `cmdPrintCurrentName` and enter the following code:

```
Private Sub cmdPrintCurrentName_Click()
    Print "Employee Name: " &
➥rsEmployees.Fields("FirstName").Value & " " &
➥rsEmployees.Fields("LastName").Value
End Sub
```

18. Change the `Name` property of the fourth right button to `cmdRecordNumber`.

19. Change the `Caption` property of `cmdRecordNumber` to `"Record Number"`.

20. Open the code window for `cmdRecordNumber` and enter the following code:

```
Private Sub cmdRecordNumber_Click()
    MsgBox "The current record number is " &
➥rsEmployees.AbsolutePosition + 1, vbInformation
End Sub
```

21. Change the `Name` property of the fifth right button to `cmdClearForm`.

22. Change the `Caption` property of `cmdClearForm` to `"Clear Form"`.

23. Open the code window for `cmdClearForm` and enter the following code:

```
Private Sub cmdClearForm_Click()
    Form1.Cls
End Sub
```

24. Change the `Name` property of the sixth right button to `cmdCloseNWind`.

25. Change the `Caption` property of `cmdCloseNWind` to `"Close Nwind"`.

continues

Exercise 9.1: Continued

---

26. Open the code window for `cmdCloseNWind` and enter the following code:

```
Private Sub cmdCloseNWind_Click()
    dbNWind.Close
End Sub
```

27. Change the `Name` property of the leftmost bottom button to `cmdMoveFirst`.

28. Change the `Caption` property of `cmdMoveFirst` to "Move First".

29. Open the code window for `cmdMoveFirst` and enter the following code:

```
Private Sub cmdMoveFirst_Click()
    rsEmployees.MoveFirst
End Sub
```

30. Change the `Name` property of the second bottom button to `cmdMovePrevious`.

31. Change the `Caption` property of `cmdMovePrevious` to "Move Previous".

32. Open the code window for `cmdMovePrevious` and enter the following code:

```
Private Sub cmdMovePrevious_Click()
    rsEmployees.MovePrevious
    If rsEmployees.BOF Then
        Beep
        MsgBox "Beginning of Records", vbInformation
        rsEmployees.MoveFirst
    End If
End Sub
```

33. Change the `Name` property of the third bottom button to `cmdMoveNext`.

34. Change the `Caption` property of `cmdMoveNext` to "Move Next".

35. Open the code window for `cmdMoveNext` and enter the following code:

```
Private Sub cmdMoveNext_Click()
    rsEmployees.MoveNext
    If rsEmployees.EOF Then
        Beep
        MsgBox "End of Records", vbInformation
        rsEmployees.MoveLast
    End If
End Sub
```

36. Change the `Name` property of the fourth bottom button to `cmdMoveLast`.

37. Change the `Caption` property of `cmdMoveLast` to "Move Last".

38. Open the code window for `cmdMoveLast` and enter the following code:

```
Private Sub cmdMoveLast_Click()
    rsEmployees.MoveLast
End Sub
```

39. Run the application. If an error occurs, ensure the DAO 3.5 Object Library reference has been checked off.

40. Click on Open NWind. The DAO objects will open the database.

41. Click on Create Recordset. This will create a `Recordset` object based on the NWind Employees table.

42. Click on Print Current Name. This will use the current record's First Name field and Last Name field and will be printed to the background of the `Form` object.

43. Click on Record Number. A message box will be displayed indicating the number of the current record in the `Recordset` object.

continues

44. Click on Move Next. The Recordset will advance the current record by one. No screen change will occur.

45. Click on Print Current Name again. This will again print the first and last name of the current record in the Recordset.

46. Click on Clear Form. This will refresh the background when it becomes too full.

47. Continue using the Move buttons and the Print Current Name button to traverse the Recordset. Use the Record Number button to determine the current record number.

48. When completed with Navigation, click on Close NWind. This will release the connection to the database.

49. Return to Design mode.

50. Try updating the Print Current Name button to include printing the current record number. Also, try adding code that will automatically move the current record after the Print Current Name has been clicked.

51. When completed, end the application.

This exercise demonstrated using properties and methods of the Recordset object to determine the current record location and to move the current record as required.

Exercise 9.2: Navigating, Adding, Modifying, and Deleting Records in a Recordset

When information is contained within a Recordset object, various properties and methods can be used to affect the data. Properties can be used to determine the state of the Recordset. Methods can be used to control the state and add, modify, or delete information as required. To create this exercise, follow these steps:

1. Create a Standard EXE project.

2. Change the Caption property of Form1 to "Adding, modifying, and deleting records".

3. Choose Project, References from the main menu.

4. In the check box selection list, add a reference to Microsoft DAO 3.5 Object Library.

5. Click on OK after the reference is added. The VB IDE will now contain all objects related to the DAO library.

6. In the General Declarations section of Form1, add the following code. This will create two form-level `Private` variables to which to assign the database objects:

```
Option Explicit
Private dbNWind As Database
Private rsEmployees As Recordset
```

7. Increase the size of the form to accommodate buttons on the right side and at the bottom.

8. Add seven command buttons to Form1. Increase the width of each button four grid units. Decrease the height of each button one grid unit. Use the Shift key and arrow keys after the control is selected as a shortcut. Place five buttons along the right side and two buttons along the bottom of the form.

9. Add two `Label` controls and two `Textbox` controls to Form1.

10. Place one label above one text box. Place the second label above the second text box.

11. Change the `Name` and `Caption` properties of the topmost `Label` control to `lblFirstName` and `"First Name:"` respectively.

12. Change the `Name` property of the text box underneath `lblFirstName` to `txtFirstName`. Change the `Locked` property to True and `BackColor` to `Button Face`. Delete any text from the `Text` property.

continues

13. Change the Name and Caption properties of the second Label control to lblLastName and "Last Name:" respectively.

14. Change the Name property of the text box underneath lblLastName to txtLastName. Change the Locked property to True and BackColor to Button Face. Delete any text from the Text property.

15. Adjust the size and layout of the labels and text boxes as required.

16. Change the Name and Caption properties of the top right-most Command button to cmdAddRecord and "Add Record" respectively.

17. Open the code window for cmdAddRecord and enter the following code:

```
Private Sub cmdAddRecord_Click()
    rsEmployees.AddNew
    EditFields
    ClearFields
End Sub
```

18. Change the Name and Caption properties of the second top rightmost Command button to cmdEditRecord and "Edit Record" respectively.

19. Open the code window for cmdEditRecord and enter the following code:

```
Private Sub cmdEditRecord_Click()
    rsEmployees.Edit
    EditFields
    cmdAddRecord.Enabled = False
End Sub
```

20. Change the Name and Caption properties of the third right Command button to cmdUpdateRecord and "Update Record" respectively.

21. Open the code window for `cmdUpdateRecord` and enter the following code. The BirthDate field is filled in here just to prevent any rule violations of the database. This could have been put on the input screen.

```
Private Sub cmdUpdateRecord_Click()
    SaveFields
    rsEmployees.Fields("BirthDate").Value = Format(Date - 5,
➥"Short Date")
    rsEmployees.Update
    rsEmployees.Bookmark = rsEmployees.LastModified
    BrowseFields
End Sub
```

22. Change the `Name` and `Caption` properties of the fourth right Command button to `cmdDeleteRecord` and `"Delete Record"` respectively.

23. Open the code window for `cmdDeleteRecord` and enter the following code:

```
Private Sub cmdDeleteRecord_Click()
    rsEmployees.Delete
    cmdMoveNext_Click
End Sub
```

24. Change the `Name` and `Caption` properties of the fifth right Command button to `cmdCancelUpdate` and `"Cancel Update"` respectively.

25. Open the code window for `cmdCancelUpdate` and enter the following code:

```
Private Sub cmdCancelUpdate_Click()
    rsEmployees.CancelUpdate
    ClearFields
    FillFields
    BrowseFields
End Sub
```

continues

26. Change the `Name` and `Caption` properties of the leftmost bottom Command button to `cmdMovePrevious` and `"< Move Previous"` respectively.

27. Open the code window for `cmdMovePrevious` and enter the following code:

```
Private Sub cmdMovePrevious_Click()
    rsEmployees.MovePrevious
    If rsEmployees.BOF = True Then
        Beep
        rsEmployees.MoveFirst
    End If
    FillFields
End Sub
```

28. Change the `Name` and `Caption` properties of the second bottom Command button to `cmdMoveNext` and `"Move Next >"` respectively.

29. Open the code window for `cmdMoveNext` and enter the following code:

```
Private Sub cmdMoveNext_Click()
    rsEmployees.MoveNext
    If rsEmployees.EOF = True Then
        Beep
        rsEmployees.MoveLast
    End If
    FillFields
End Sub
```

30. In the General Declaration section, add the five following procedures. They are used throughout the command buttons to reduce the amount of code:

```
Sub BrowseFields()
    With txtFirstName
        .Locked = True
        .BackColor = &H8000000F&
        .TabStop = False
    End With
```

```
        With txtLastName
            .Locked = True
            .BackColor = &H8000000F&
            .TabStop = False
        End With
        cmdAddRecord.Enabled = True
        cmdEditRecord.Enabled = True
        cmdDeleteRecord.Enabled = True
        cmdMovePrevious.Enabled = True
        cmdMoveNext.Enabled = True
        cmdUpdateRecord.Enabled = False
        cmdCancelUpdate.Enabled = False
    End Sub

    Sub ClearFields()
        txtFirstName.Text = ""
        txtLastName.Text = ""
    End Sub

    Sub EditFields()
        With txtFirstName
            .Locked = False
            .BackColor = &H80000005&
            .TabStop = True
        End With
        With txtLastName
            .Locked = False
            .BackColor = &H80000005&
            .TabStop = True
        End With
        cmdAddRecord.Enabled = False
        cmdEditRecord.Enabled = False
        cmdDeleteRecord.Enabled = False
        cmdMovePrevious.Enabled = False
        cmdMoveNext.Enabled = False
        cmdUpdateRecord.Enabled = True
        cmdCancelUpdate.Enabled = True
    End Sub

    Sub FillFields()
        txtFirstName.Text =
    ➥rsEmployees.Fields("FirstName").Value
        txtLastName.Text = rsEmployees.Fields("LastName").Value
    End Sub
```

continues

```
Sub SaveFields()
    rsEmployees.Fields("FirstName").Value =
    ➥txtFirstName.Text
    rsEmployees.Fields("LastName").Value = txtLastName.Text
End Sub
```

31. In the Form_Load event, add the following code. This will automatically establish the database connection and create a Recordset object to the Employees table in the NWIND.MDB database:

```
Private Sub Form_Load()
    Set dbNWind = OpenDatabase("c:\program
    ➥files\devstudio\vb\nwind.mdb")
    Set rsEmployees = dbNWind.OpenRecordset("Employees",
    ➥dbOpenDynaset)
    FillFields
    BrowseFields
End Sub
```

32. Run the application. If an error occurs, ensure the DAO 3.5 Object Library reference has been checked off.

33. The FirstName and LastName fields should be grayed out and cannot be typed in. This is a Browser mode to assist the user. An Edit mode exists that will activate the appropriate controls as required.

34. Use the MoveNext and MovePrevious buttons to examine the employees' names. Notice the command buttons that are available and not available.

35. Click on Add Record to prepare the copy buffers. The text boxes should be in Edit mode and will allow data entry. Enter your first name and last name as required. Notice the controls that are available.

36. Click on Update Record to update the information from the copy buffer to the database.

37. Resume Navigation with the Move buttons. Notice your own record entry.

38. Use Add Record to create new records as desired.

39. Move to the first record in the set. It should be Nancy Davolio.

40. Click on Edit Record to switch the controls to the Custom Edit mode.

41. Change Nancy's first name to Nancy M.

42. Click on Update Record to save the changes to the database.

43. Using the Move buttons, confirm that Nancy's first name has been changed. Select another record and then return to Nancy's record.

44. Click on Edit Record to switch the controls to Edit mode again.

45. Change Nancy's first name to Daisy.

46. Click on Cancel Update to clear the changes without writing them to the database.

47. Using the Move buttons, confirm that Nancy's first name has not been changed to Daisy.

48. Using the Move buttons, find your own record entry.

49. Click on Delete Record to remove your own record entry from the database.

50. If you entered additional records, move to them and use the Delete Record button to remove them. Do not attempt to delete any of the default records; a runtime error will occur due to referential integrity rules.

51. Return to Design mode.

52. Try changing the fields being used from the database.

53. When completed, end the application.

continues

This exercise demonstrated using the properties and methods of the Recordset object to add, edit, and remove data from the connected database. The form also has additional procedures to manipulate the controls. These procedures create two different modes for the form: Browse mode and Edit mode. These two modes assist the user in looking for data or modifying it.

Exercise 9.3: Finding and Retrieving Records

DAO allows the use of stored queries or SQL statements to retrieve records from a database. This helps to reduce the amount of records returned and improves performance by limiting the amount of information returned. To create this exercise, follow these steps:

1. Create a Standard EXE project.

2. Change the Caption property of Form1 to "Finding Records using Stored Queries and SQL statements".

3. Choose Project, References from the main menu.

4. In the check box selection list, add a reference to Microsoft DAO 3.5 Object Library.

5. Click on OK after the reference is added. The VB IDE will now contain all objects related to the DAO library.

6. Choose Project, Components from the main menu.

7. In the check box selection list, add a reference to Microsoft Data Bound Grid Control.

8. Click on OK after the control is added. The VB IDE will now contain one additional control in the toolbox. The DBGrid control will be used to view information returned from the database.

9. Add one data control to Form1.

10. Change the `Align` and `Visible` properties to `2 - Align Bottom` and `False`.

11. Change the `Name` and `Caption` properties of `Data1` to `datNWind` and `datNWind` respectively.

12. Change the `DatabaseName` property of `datNWind` to `c:\program files\devstudio\vb\nwind.mdb`. Ensure the correct path/filename for your installation.

13. Leave the `RecordSource` property of `datNWind` blank. A `Recordset` will be programmatically assigned to the data control.

14. Add one `DBGrid` control to `Form1`. Resize the control to take up most of the form's width and ¾ of the form's height. Leave room at the bottom of the form for additional controls.

15. Change the `Name` property of `DBGrid1` to `dbgNWind`.

16. Change the `DataSource` property of `dbgNWind` to `datNWind`.

17. Add one `Label` control and one combo box to the form.

18. Reposition the combo box to be below the `dbgNWind` control on the left-hand side.

19. Change the `Name` and `Text` properties of `Combo1` to `cboQueries` and `Empty` respectively.

20. Reposition the `Label` control above the `Combo` control.

21. Change the `Name` and `Caption` properties of `Label1` to `lblQueries` and `"Find records by stored query:"`.

22. Add another `Label` control and one `Textbox` control to the form.

23. Reposition the textbox to be below the `dbgNWind` control on the right-hand side.

continues

24. Change the `Name` and `Text` properties of `Text1` to `txtSQL` and `Empty` respectively.

25. Reposition the second `Label` control above the `Text` control.

26. Change the `Name` and `Caption` properties of `Label2` to `lblSQL` and `"Find records by SQL statement:"`.

27. Open the code window for the General Declarations section and enter the following code:

```
Option Explicit
Private dbNWind As Database
Private rsNWind As Recordset
```

28. Open the code window for the `Form Load` event and enter the following code:

```
Private Sub Form_Load()
    Set dbNWind = OpenDatabase("c:\program
    ➥files\devstudio\vb\nwind.mdb")

    Dim iLoop As Integer
    For iLoop = 2 To dbNWind.QueryDefs.Count - 1
        cboQueries.AddItem dbNWind.QueryDefs(iLoop).Name
    Next iLoop
    cboQueries.Text = cboQueries.List(0)
    cboQueries_Click
End Sub
```

29. Open the code window for the `cboQueries Click` event and enter the following code:

```
Private Sub cboQueries_Click()
    On Error GoTo ErrHandler
    Set rsNWind = dbNWind.OpenRecordset(cboQueries.Text,
    ➥dbOpenDynaset)
    Set datNWind.Recordset = rsNWind
    Exit Sub
ErrHandler:
    Dim Msg As String, Buttons As Integer, Title As String
    Msg = "An error was encountered while retrieving the
```

```
➥stored query records!" & vbCr & vbCr
    Msg = Msg & "Error Number:  #" & Err.Number & vbCr
    Msg = Msg & "Error Description:" & Err.Description &
vbCr & vbCr
    Msg = Msg & "The Query you selected requires additional
➥information and cannot currently run."
    Buttons = vbOKOnly + vbInformation
    Title = "Error in Stored Query"
    MsgBox Msg, Buttons, Title
End Sub
```

30. Open the code window for the txtSQL KeyUp event and enter
    the following code:

```
Private Sub txtSQL_KeyUp(KeyCode As Integer, Shift As
➥Integer)
    On Error GoTo ErrHandler
    If KeyCode = 13 Then
        If txtSQL.Text = "" Then Exit Sub
        Dim strSQL As String
        strSQL = txtSQL.Text
        Set rsNWind = dbNWind.OpenRecordset(strSQL)
        Set datNWind.Recordset = rsNWind
    End If
    Exit Sub
ErrHandler:
    Dim Msg As String, Buttons As Integer, Title As String
    Msg = "An error was encountered while retrieving the
➥records!" & vbCr & vbCr
    Msg = Msg & "Error Number:  #" & Err.Number & vbCr
    Msg = Msg & "Error Description:" & Err.Description &
vbCr & vbCr
    Msg = Msg & "Please ensure you have the correct SQL
➥statements and punctuation in the textbox."
    Buttons = vbOKOnly + vbInformation
    Title = "Error in SQL statement"
    MsgBox Msg, Buttons, Title
    txtSQL.Text = ""
End Sub
```

31. Run the application. If an error occurs, ensure the DAO 3.5
    Object Library reference has been checked off.

continues

32. The combo box on the left will provide a listing of queries from the database. The text box on the right will be used to type in SQL statements and execute them.

33. From the drop-down list, select the stored query Current Product List. The `Recordset` created from the stored query is assigned to the data control that is used to populate the `DB-Grid` control.

34. Scrollbars should be provided, and you can move through the records as desired.

35. From the drop-down list, select another stored query. Notice that the `DBGrid` is automatically updated with the new selection. Some queries require additional information and may not display. An error message will be generated.

36. In the SQL text box, enter the SQL statements to show all fields from the Employees table.

    ```
    Select * From Employees
    ```

    Pressing Enter in the text box will execute the statements.

37. After the SQL statements have returned records into the `Recordset` object, the `Recordset` is assigned to the data control and then used to populate the `DBGrid` control.

38. In the SQL text box, enter the SQL statements to show only the first name and last name from the Employees table. Select [FirstName], [LastName] From Employees. Press Enter when finished typing.

39. Notice the results of the SQL statement in the `DBGrid` control.

40. In the SQL text box, enter the SQL statements to show all fields from the Products table where the Category field is equal to Beverages.

    ```
    Select * From Products Where [CategoryID] = 1
    ```

41. Continue selecting stored queries from the Query combo box and create new SQL statements. Examine your results. Error handlers have been added to assist with mistakes when creating SQL statements.

42. When completed, end the application.

This exercise demonstrated the use of stored queries to find records in a database. Also demonstrated was the use of SQL statements to retrieve desired records only.

Exercise 9.4: Using the `Find` or `Seek` Method to Search a `Recordset`

When searching for information within a `Recordset`, the `Find` and `Seek` methods are used to locate matching records. To create this exercise, follow these steps:

1. Create a Standard EXE project.

2. Change the `Caption` property of `Form1` to `"Using Find and Seek"`.

3. Choose Project, References from the main menu.

4. In the check box selection list, add a reference to Microsoft DAO 3.5 Object Library.

5. Click on OK after the reference is added. The VB IDE will now contain all objects related to the DAO library.

6. In the General Declarations section of `Form1`, add the following code. This will create two form-level `Private` variables to assign the database objects to:

```
Option Explicit
Private dbNWind As Database
Private rs1Employees As Recordset
Private rs2Employees As Recordset
```

continues

7. In the Form Load event, enter the following code. Ensure the correct path/filename for your installation:

```
Private Sub Form_Load()
    Set dbNWind = OpenDatabase("c:\program
    ➥files\devstudio\vb\nwind.mdb")
    Set rs1Employees = dbNWind.OpenRecordset("Employees",
    ➥dbOpenDynaset)
    Set rs2Employees = dbNWind.OpenRecordset("Employees",
    ➥dbOpenTable)
End Sub
```

8. Increase the size of the form to accommodate one large text box, one label, and two command buttons.

9. Add two command buttons to Form1. Decrease the height of each button by one grid unit. Increase the width of each button by eight grid units. Use the Shift key and arrow keys as a shortcut to resize.

10. Place the two resized command buttons along the bottom center of the form, one on the left and one on the right.

11. Change the Name and Caption properties of the leftmost Command button to cmdFind and "Find [FirstName]" respectively.

12. Change the Name and Caption properties of the rightmost Command button to cmdSeek and "Seek [LastName]" respectively.

13. Add one text box to Form1. Place the text box above the command buttons. Resize the text box to the width of both command buttons. Increase the height of the text box to more than half the size of the form.

14. Change the Name and Text properties of the text box to txtResults and no text respectively.

15. Change the Locked and BackColor properties of txtResults to True and &H8000000F&.

16. Change the `MultiLine` and `ScrollBars` properties of
    `txtResults` to `True` and `2 - Vertical`.

17. Change the `ToolTipText` to `Double Click to Reset the
    Result Window`.

18. Open the code window for `txtResults` and enter the follow-
    ing code into the `txtResults_DblClick` event:

    ```
    Private Sub txtResults_DblClick()
        txtResults.Text = ""
    End Sub
    ```

19. Also, add the following code to the `txtResults GotFocus`
    event:

    ```
    Private Sub txtResults_GotFocus()
        cmdFind.SetFocus
    End Sub
    ```

20. Add one `Label` control to `Form1`. Place the label above the
    text box. Resize the label to the same width as the text box.

21. Change the `Name` and `Caption` properties of `Label1` to
    `lblResults` and `"Results of the Find and Seek methods"`
    respectively.

22. Change the `Align` property of `lblResults` to `2 - Center`.

23. Ensure the form has a good layout with all controls. Also
    ensure enough display space in the `txtResults` text box.

24. Open the code window for `cmdFind` and enter the following
    code in the `Click` event:

    ```
    Private Sub cmdFind_Click()
        Dim strFirstName As String
        strFirstName = InputBox("Please enter the First Name of
        ➥the person you are searching for.", "Using the Find
        ➥method", "Nancy")
        If strFirstName = "" Then
            Exit Sub
        End If
    ```

continues

Exercise 9.4: Continued

```
                    Dim strSQL As String
                    strSQL = "[FirstName] = '" & strFirstName & "'"
                    rs1Employees.FindFirst strSQL

                    If rs1Employees.NoMatch = True Then
                        txtResults.Text = txtResults.Text & vbCrLf & "- No
                        ➥Matching Records Found. -"
                        txtResults.Text = txtResults.Text & vbCrLf & "TRY
                        ➥AGAIN." & vbCrLf
                    Else
                        txtResults.Text = txtResults.Text & vbCrLf & "-
                        ➥Record Matching Criteria Found. -"
                        txtResults.Text = txtResults.Text & vbCrLf & "Title:
                        ➥" & _
                            rs1Employees.Fields("Title").Value
                        txtResults.Text = txtResults.Text & vbCrLf & "Full
                        ➥Name: " & _
                            rs1Employees.Fields("FirstName").Value & " " & _
                            rs1Employees.Fields("LastName").Value & vbCrLf
                    End If
                End Sub
```

25. Open the code window for cmdSeek and enter the following
    code in the Click event:

```
Private Sub cmdSeek_Click()
    Dim strLastName As String
    strLastName = InputBox("Please enter the Last Name of
    ➥the person you are searching for.", "Using the Seek
    ➥method", "Davolio")
    If strLastName = "" Then
        Exit Sub
    End If

    rs2Employees.Index = "LastName"
    rs2Employees.Seek "=", strLastName

    If rs2Employees.NoMatch = True Then
        txtResults.Text = txtResults.Text & vbCrLf & "- No
        ➥Matching Records Found. -"
        txtResults.Text = txtResults.Text & vbCrLf & "TRY
        ➥AGAIN."
```

```
    Else
        txtResults.Text = txtResults.Text & vbCrLf & "-
        ➥Record Matching Criteria Found. -"
        txtResults.Text = txtResults.Text & vbCrLf & "Title:
        ➥" & _
            rs2Employees.Fields("Title").Value
        txtResults.Text = txtResults.Text & vbCrLf & "Full
        ➥Name: " & _
            rs2Employees.Fields("FirstName").Value & " " &
            ➥rs2Employees.Fields("LastName").Value & vbCrLf
    End If
End Sub
```

26. Run the application. If an error occurs, ensure the DAO 3.5 Object Library reference has been checked off.

27. Click on the Find [FirstName] command button. This button uses the FindFirst method of a Dynaset type Recordset object.

28. An input box should be displayed with a default value of Nancy. Just click on OK to accept the default.

29. The Results text box should indicate that a record was found. Both the employee's title and full name should be displayed.

30. Click on the Find [FirstName] command button again. This time, enter the first name "David" in the input box and click on OK.

31. The Results text box should indicate that no match was found and to try again.

32. Click on the Find [FirstName] command button again. This time, enter the first name "Anne" in the input box and click on OK.

33. The Results text box should indicate a matching record.

34. Double-click on the Results text box to clear the previous results.

continues

35. Click on the Seek [LastName] command button. This button uses the Seek method of a Table type Recordset object. The index that is used is LastName.

36. An input box should be displayed with the default value of Davolio. Just click on OK to accept the default.

37. The Results text box should indicate the matching record of Nancy Davolio.

38. Click on the Seek [LastName] command button again. This time, enter the last name "Stock" in the input box and click on OK.

39. The Results text box should indicate that no match was found and to try again.

40. Click on the Seek [LastName] command button again. This time, enter the last name "Fuller" in the input box and click on OK.

41. The Results text box should indicate the matching record of Andrew Fuller.

42. Attempt to find another first name and another last name by using both the Find [FirstName] and Seek [LastName] command buttons.

43. Return to Design mode.

44. Try changing the field searched by the Find command button to EmployeeID. Also, try changing the Seek index and the search field for the Seek command button.

45. When completed, end the application.

This exercise demonstrated the use of the Find method of a Dynaset type Recordset. Also demonstrated was the use of the Seek method of a Table type Recordset object.

Review Questions

1. A Visual Basic application can be developed to communicate with a database for information. What is the name of a set of objects designed to control an MDB database file?

    A. RDO

    B. DRO

    C. DDE

    D. DAO

    E. ADA

2. The DAO Collection provides various objects that can be used to control information from a database. Which DAO object is primarily used for retrieval and manipulation of the records?

    A. DBEngine

    B. Workspace

    C. Recordset

    D. RecordSource

    E. CurrentDB

3. To utilize DAO within the Visual Basic environment, additional information must be specified. What must be set within the VB IDE to allow required DAO functionality?

    A. Object reference

    B. Control reference

    C. Declaration

    D. Resource file

    E. Project properties

4. DAO can be used to extend the functionality of the VB IDE, allowing additional objects for programmatic control. Where in the VB IDE menus are special settings made to have the extra objects?

   A. Project, Project Properties

   B. Tools, Options

   C. Project, Add File

   D. Project, Components

   E. Project, References

5. Visual Basic provides the application developer with an Object Browser window. What is the Object Browser used for?

   A. Examining custom controls for the current project

   B. Examining objects, properties, methods, and events for the current project

   C. Setting a reference to custom controls for the project

   D. Setting a reference to external objects for the project

   E. Adding and removing objects from the current project

6. The `Recordset` object of DAO is used to retrieve and manipulate records from a database. What property is used to indicate the current record in use?

   A. `Position`

   B. `AbsolutePosition`

   C. `RelativePosition`

   D. `Bookmark`

   E. `Index`

7. The `Recordset` is used to retrieve records from the database. What property is used to determine the total number of records that have been retrieved?

    A. `Count`

    B. `TotalRecords`

    C. `AllRecords`

    D. `RecordCount`

    E. `Total`

8. When navigating the `Recordset` object, various methods can be used to control the current record in use. What method is used to move to the last record in the `Recordset` object?

    A. `MoveLast`

    B. `MoveEnd`

    C. `MoveNext`

    D. `Last`

    E. `End`

9. DAO allows for information to be added, manipulated, and deleted from a database. What is the first method of the `Recordset` object used when information is to be changed within the current record?

    A. `EditMode`

    B. `Edit`

    C. `Update`

    D. `CancelUpdate`

    E. `AddNew`

10. When information within the currently selected record has been placed within the copy buffers, what method is used to clear the copy buffers and not write information into the database?

    A. `Update`

    B. `UpdateRecord`

    C. CancelUpdate

    D. Cancel

    E. ClearBuffers

11. When using the DAO Recordset object, only required information from the database can be specified. What two different ways can be used to specify the records to be returned by the Recordset object?

    A. SQL statements

    B. Declarations

    C. Stored queries

    D. Indexing

    E. RPC

12. After a Recordset has been created and contains only the specified records, they can be further searched using additional methods and properties. What method is used to search for records that match specific criteria in a Dynaset type Recordset?

    A. Insert Into statement

    B. Seek

    C. Locate

    D. FindNext

    E. Search

13. What method is used to search for records within a Table type Recordset object?

    A. Insert Into statement

    B. Seek

    C. Locate

    D. FindNext

    E. Search

14. The `Recordset` object can use SQL statements to retrieve records from a database. Which SQL statement will retrieve all fields from the Employees table?

    A. `Select * From Employees`

    B. `Select All From Table Employees`

    C. `Select * Table Employees`

    D. `Select All Table Employees`

    E. `Select * From Table Employees`

15. SQL statements can be used to retrieve records matching a certain criteria. Which SQL statement will retrieve the first and last name of all employees' from New York?

    A. `Select * From 'New York' Employees`

    B. `Select FirstName, LastName From 'NewYork'`

    C. `Select FirstName, LastName Where 'New York' Employees`

    D. `Select FirstName, LastName From Employees Where City = 'New York'`

    E. `Select * From Employees Where City = New York`

Answers to Review Questions

1. D. DAO, Data Access Objects, is a collection of objects used to control an MDB database file. The MDB file is created by the Jet database engine and can also be controlled by DAO. RDO is used for connection to remote databases. This would primarily be a client/server style database, such as Oracle and SQL Server. For more information, see the section titled "Understanding Data Access Basics."

2. C. The `Recordset` object is mainly responsible for the retrieval and manipulation of records from the database. For more information, see the section titled "Understanding Data Access Basics."

3. A. An object reference is used to extend the functionality of the VB IDE. This enables the application developer to include additional program objects as required. For more information, see the section titled "Making References."

4. E. The Project, References menu within the VB IDE is used to set an object reference to extend the application's functionality. For more information, see the section titled "Making References."

5. B. The Object Browser window is used to examine objects, properties, methods, and events found within the current project. It is also used to provide access to any associated help files for the various objects. For more information, see the section titled "Referencing DAO."

6. B. The current record of the `Recordset` is indicated by the `AbsolutePosition` property. This is a zero-based number used to reflect the record in use. The `Bookmark` property is a special value used when moving through the records. It can be set and retrieved, but does not indicate the current record in use. For more information, see the section titled "Using the `AbsolutePosition` Property."

7. D. The `RecordCount` property is used to determine how many records have been accessed by the `Recordset` object. This value can vary depending on the type of `Recordset` created. `Count` is a method used with collection objects. For more information, see the section titled "Using the `RecordCount` Property."

8. A. The `MoveLast` property will reposition the current record in the `Recordset` object to the last record. The `MoveNext` property will increase the position of the current record only by one. For more information, see the section titled "Navigating with the `Move` Methods."

9. B. The `Edit` method of the `Recordset` object is used when information within the current record is to be changed. This triggers the Jet engine to copy the current record into the copy buffers and enables the user to change the required

information. The `EditMode` property is used to determine the current status of the `Recordset`. The `AddNew` method is used to add new information, not change information within the current record. For more information, see the section titled "Using the `Edit` and `Update` Methods."

10. C.`CancelUpdate` is the method used to clear information from the copy buffers without writing the information to the database. The `Update` method is used to take information currently in the copy buffers and write the information into the database. For more information, see the section titled "Using the `CancelUpdate` Method."

11. A and C. Both SQL statements and stored queries can be used to specify the records to be returned from the database by the `Recordset` object. Indexing is used to specify the sort order. For more information, see the section titled "Finding a Record."

12. D. The `FindNext` method will locate the record matching the specified criteria. The four different `Find` methods—`Find-First`, `FindPrevious`, `FindNext`, `FindLast`—can all be used on both `Dynaset` and `Snapshot` type `Recordset` objects. For more information, see the section titled "Using the `Find` Methods."

13. B.The `Seek` method is used on `Table` type `Recordsets` to find matching records. The `Seek` method can only be used on `Tables` due to the use of indexes. The index is a predefined sort order for the records. For more information, see the section titled "Using the `Seek` Method."

14. A.The basic `Select` statement, `Select * From Employees`, will retrieve all fields from the Employees table. The asterisk is used to indicate all fields. For more information, see the section titled "Using SQL."

15. D.The basic `Select` statement can be combined with the `Where` clause to locate only matching records. Only the first and last names were requested, so the asterisk is not used. The `Where` clause requires text strings to be in single quotation marks. For more information, see the section titled "Using SQL."

Answers to Test Yourself Questions at Beginning of Chapter

1. The default database engine used by VB for database communication is Jet 3.5. This is the same database engine used by Microsoft Access. It is used to allow VB to establish communications with Microsoft Access, ISAM data sources, and ODBC data source. A series of programmable objects are also provided for enhanced functionality with Visual Basic. See " Understanding Data Access Basics."

2. The VB IDE can have additional programmable objects by using the References dialog box under the Project main menu. This allows Object Libraries to be used to provide additional objects not provided in VB by default. See "Making References."

3. When using DAO in an application and a compile error indicating user-defined data type not defined, the first item to check is the reference to Microsoft DAO 3.5 Object Library. VB has been told to use an object that it does not understand and must be able to find information on what the object is and how to use it. See "Referencing DAO."

4. The `Recordset` object has various `Move` methods that can be used to control the location of the current record. This allows both the application and the user to control the current record as required. See "Navigating with the `Move` Methods."

5. The `AbsolutePosition` can be used to indicate the current record being pointed to by the `Recordset`. The `Recordset` is zero based and will affect the number returned by the `AbsolutePosition` property. One is usually added to the value for a simplified number. See "Using the `AbsolutePosition` Property."

6. The method of the `Recordset` object that allows for the addition of a new record into the database is the `AddNew` method. This method will clear the copy buffer and prepare the `Recordset` for a new record. See "Using the `AddNew` and `Update` Methods."

7. The property used to determine the current data entry state of the `Recordset` is `EditMode`. This property is used to indicate one of three possible values. Each value specifies whether an edit was triggered by the `Edit` method, the `AddNew` method, or whether no editing is taking place. See "Using the `EditMode` Property."

8. Structured Query Language (SQL) is the name of the special language that can be used to return only records matching a specified criterion. See "Using SQL."

9. The type of object stored within the database that contains special statements for returning records is known as a stored query. The stored query is saved with a unique name and contains SQL statements that can be called repeatedly or by a user who is unfamiliar with SQL. See "Using Stored Queries."

10. The `Seek` method can be used when working with a `Table` type `Recordset`. It can be used to search for information based on specified search criteria. See "Using the `Seek` Method."

11. When using a `Snapshot` type `Recordset` and searching for information, the `Find` methods can be used to locate information. `FindFirst`, `FindLast`, `FindNext`, and `FindPrevious` all accept a string argument in the syntax of an SQL `Where` clause to locate information. See "Using the `Find` Methods."

C h a p t e r

10

Incorporating DLLs into an Application

This chapter helps you prepare for the exam by covering the following objectives:

 Objectives

- ▶ Declare and call a DLL routine

- ▶ Identify when it is necessary to use the Alias clause

- ▶ Pass a null pointer to a DLL routine

- ▶ Pass an argument by value and by reference

- ▶ Pass a function pointer to a DLL by using a callback function

- ▶ Pass a string to a DLL

- ▶ Create a DLL routine that modifies string arguments

Test Yourself! Before reading this chapter, test yourself to determine how much study time you will need to devote to this section.

1. Visual Basic allows the use of external routines to enhance the capabilities of an application. Where in the VB IDE are external routines specified?

2. Additional utilities are provided to enhance the VB IDE. What application can be used to assist with the declarations of external routines?

3. External routines can be used within Visual Basic by declaring information about the routine. What keyword is used to indicate the path/filename of the library providing the routine?

4. Routine names used in other programming languages are not always valid within Visual Basic. What statement allows VB to use routines that might potentially have a name conflict?

5. The `Alias` statement found in an external routine declaration can be used for creating multiple declarations of the same external routine. Why would the `Alias` clause be used to assist with multiple declarations?

6. Most external routines called from Visual Basic are programmed in C/C++. If an argument of the routine will not be providing valid information, a special value is used to indicate an absence of value. When calling external routines from VB, what constant is used to represent an absence of value?

7. Arguments can be passed to external routines in two different ways, by value or by reference. Which way passes a copy of the argument to the external routine for manipulation?

8. In the declaration of an external routine, what keyword is used to pass arguments by reference?

9. Arguments can be passed to external routines in two different ways, by value or by reference. Which way passes the memory address of the argument to the external routine for manipulation?

10. In the declaration of an external routine, what keyword is used to pass arguments by value?

11. When using the Windows API external routines, certain routines require a callback function pointer. What keyword is used to pass a function pointer to an argument?

12. When are strings to be manipulated by an external routine? How are they passed? By value or by reference?

Answers are located at the end of the chapter...

Visual Basic has many built-in programming features and provides extensibility through object references and custom controls. Another method of extending the capabilities of Visual Basic is by using external routines. The operating system, and third party or custom libraries can provide these routines.

External routines are usually located within a special type of file known as a Dynamic Link Library (DLL). This is a file that is connected (linked) to your application at runtime (dynamically) and is used to provide additional functionality. Most DLLs are programmed in either C or C++ languages and can execute more quickly than a VB program.

This chapter deals with the use of external DLL files within a Visual Basic application.

This chapter covers the following topics:

- ▶ Declaration of an external function
- ▶ Calling an external function
- ▶ Using the `Alias` keyword
- ▶ Using the API Text Viewer
- ▶ Passing null pointers
- ▶ Passing arguments by value and by reference
- ▶ Passing a callback function pointer
- ▶ Passing strings
- ▶ Creating reusable DLL routines

Declaring and Calling a DLL Routine

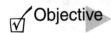 **Objective** This section examines the use of external library functions from with Visual Basic. Topics covered include declaring external routines, passing arguments, and calling external routines.

When Visual Basic and its additional references and components cannot provide required functionality, VB allows the use of external functions.

The Windows operating system provides a wide variety of libraries that can be used to enhance an application. Many of these libraries are also grouped together into a functional set known as an Application Programmers Interface (API). The WIN32 API is the main library of the operating system. Other APIs can also be installed, such as the Telephony API and the Messaging API.

You must follow four general steps when using an external routine within the Visual Basic programming environment:

1. Declare the function to be used in VB.

2. Call the function correctly.

3. Save your work before testing.

4. Test your work.

The following two sections deal with declaring a DLL external function call, and how to call the function from within a Visual Basic application.

Declaring a DLL

Before an external function can be used within a Visual Basic application, information and documentation must be found on the desired routine. The operating system does not provide this information. Many books are written strictly for programmers on APIs and should be consulted if you will be using external routines.

Visual Basic does provide both a text file and a utility that can be used to determine the vast majority of function declarations. The WIN32API.TXT file contains three types of information: declarations, types, and constants. All are used as part of external function calls, as shown in Figure 10.1.

The WIN32API file is strictly used for the declaration of the external routine and does not provide additional information regarding the correct use of the routine.

VB also provides a simple utility, the API Text Viewer, which reads the WIN32API.TXT file and organizes the three types of information, as shown in Figure 10.2. This utility can be used to quickly search for a required declaration. Once found, the declaration can be copied to the VB code, thus reducing typing errors. The API Text Viewer can be found in the Visual Basic program group under the Start menu.

The declaration statement can be placed in the General Declarations section of a form code module. When placed in this location, it must be privately scoped. The declaration can also be declared with a public scope in the General Declarations section of a standard module.

Figure 10.2

The API Text Viewer presents the information found in the WIN32API.TXT in an easy-to-use interface for cutting and pasting.

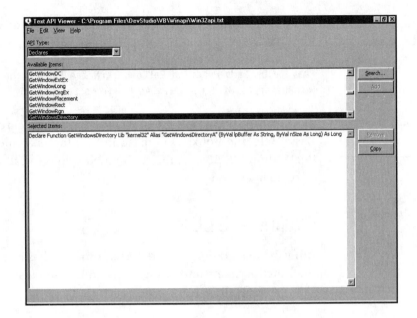

The following code is part of a sample declaration used to determine the computer name of the machine executing the code:

```
Private Declare Function GetComputerNameA Lib "Kernel32"
```

The first keyword is the scope of the declaration. The second keyword is the `Declare` statement, which is used to indicate an external function. The `Function` keyword is used to describe the type of procedure that will execute. The name of the function is `GetComputerNameA`. This function is found in the library (Lib) Kernel32. Notice that this is a file reference and does not contain a path location. The library argument is used to indicate the path and filename where the procedure can be found. If a library is located in the search path of the computer, the path can be omitted. The following code is the remainder of the declaration—the arguments accepted by the function:

```
(ByVal lpBuffer As String, nSize As Long) As Long
```

This function accepts two different arguments: one is a string; the other is a long. The function will also return a long data type value. These arguments are the critical part of the declaration that can make an application crash if not declared and used correctly.

Here is the complete declaration. This would be the complete line that would appear in the code module:

```
Private Declare Function GetComputerNameA Lib "Kernel32" (ByVal
➥lpBuffer As String, nSize As Long) As Long
```

For more information on external declarations, search Visual Basic Help and Books Online for the `Declare` statement. After the declaration has been entered, the next step is to call the function in regular VB code.

Calling a DLL

After the declaration of an external function has been completed, the function name and arguments can be used just like a regular VB function call.

One item of concern when calling an external function is the arguments. Due to the external nature of the function call, VB cannot protect the application if arguments are used incorrectly. In many cases of passing invalid or incorrect information, the function call will cause a General Protection Fault (GPF), and could crash the application, VB, or the operating system.

When arguments are passed to an external DLL routine, the data type must also be correct. Conversion is usually necessary for arguments from C data types to Visual Basic data types. For more information on data type conversion, see Visual Basic Books Online. Under View, select Index and search for C language declaration conversion.

In the preceding section, the `GetComputerNameA` accepts two different arguments. The first is the name of a string to assign the computer name to. The second argument is the length of the string being passed to the function.

The following code demonstrates calling the function and passing in a string for manipulation by the call:

```
lResult = GetComputerNameA(strBuffer, Len(strBuffer))
If lResult <> 0 Then
```

```
      MsgBox strBuffer
   End If
```

Note   Before running any code, save your work. Even experienced programmers have difficulty getting into a good habit of saving their work often. External function calls can cause program Exception errors and General Protection Faults if called incorrectly.

Notice that although this is an external call, the syntax is the same as an internal function call. The first line calls the function and passes a string named `strBuffer`; also passed is the length of the string. The second line is used to test the return value to see whether the call was successful. If so, a message box displays the name of the computer.

The previous example of `GetComputerNameA` has been simplified to introduce the concept of using external functions provided in a DLL. Many other issues must still be discussed to correctly use these powerful, alternative routines.

For more information on using, declaring, and calling external routines, see Visual Basic Books Online. Using the Contents, look under the Component Tools Guide (Pro, Enterprise Only), Accessing DLLs, and the Windows API.

Identifying When It Is Necessary to Use the Alias Clause

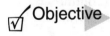

Objective   This section examines the use of the `Alias` keyword in an external routine declaration. Topics covered include identifying when to use the `Alias` clause, and using the `Alias` clause in a declaration.

The `Alias` keyword is an additional component of an external routine declaration. The keyword `Alias` allows the use of external routine names that would conflict with VB naming conventions.

Most external libraries are programmed in the C language and can use characters not allowed in Visual Basic. External routines might also have the same name as reserved or keywords in VB.

To allow the procedure to be used within VB, the declaration can include the `Alias` keyword and allows an alternative name to be used when calling the external routine.

To utilize routines that have illegal names in VB, use VB keywords, or conflict with other routines, you can add the `Alias` clause to a declaration. The `Alias` clause follows the `Lib` clause and is used to indicate the true name of the routine.

The following code shows the `GetComputerNameA` function declaration with an added `Alias` clause:

```
Private Declare Function GCN Lib "Kernel32" Alias
➥"GetComputerNameA" (ByVal lpBuffer As String, nSize As Long) As
➥Long
```

Notice the name of the function has now been named `GCN`. The `Lib` clause indicates the file the routine is located in. After the `Lib` clause, the `Alias` clause is used to provide the true name of the routine found in the external library.

When the `Alias` clause is used in a declaration, the syntax of the call in Visual Basic does not change. The only difference is that the declaration name must be used and not the true name of the routine.

Another use of the `Alias` clause is to provide different declarations for the same external routine. The same external routine might accept different types of data when called. External routines will often indicate that the data type passed could also be `Any`.

By declaring different functions with the `Alias` clause, the specified argument data types can be different. Different argument data types will allow Visual Basic to do type checking on the call and cause a compile-time error rather than a runtime error. This can reduce the chance of the external routine failing and causing GPF errors.

Passing a Null Pointer to a DLL Routine

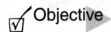 **Objective**

This section examines how nulls can be passed to an external routine when required. Topics covered include declaring a null value and passing nulls.

When passing string arguments to an external routine, often the routine can accept either a string value or a null value. Understanding the difference between these two values becomes very important when using external routines.

A VB string value can contain various characters or it can be empty, with no value. When a string contains no values, it is often referred to as an empty string. However, there is still a memory location ready to accept information.

A *null value* is a special value used to represent absence of value, or nothing. External routines expect this special value, not an empty string or the address of an empty string.

Visual Basic has a predefined constant that can be used when the null value is required. The following section shows an example of using a routine that expects the null value.

When an external routine expects a null value, the predefined VB constant, `vbNullString`, can be used and passed as an argument. This provides the special value of null expected by the external routine.

To demonstrate the use of passing `vbNullString`, the `FindWindow` API call will be used. The following is the declaration for `FindWindow`, provided by WIN32API.TXT:

```
Declare Function FindWindow Lib "user32" Alias "FindWindowA"
➡(ByVal lpClassName As String, ByVal lpWindowName As String) As
➡Long
```

Notice that this declaration automatically uses the `Alias` clause. The function will be called from VB by using `FindWindow`. This will map to the external function name `FindWindowA` in the User32 library.

This function accepts two string arguments and returns a long value. The function requires only one argument to be provided; the other can be set to null. The first argument is the class name of the window being searched for. Often this value is not known and null is passed in this argument. The second string is the window's name, or title bar text of the window being searched for. The return value from this function is a valid handle number for the window. This value can be used to control and pass information to the window.

The following code sample calls the `FindWindow` function. This code will determine if the calculator application is running:

```
MsgBox FindWindow(vbNullString, "Calculator")
```

This code assumes that the `FindWindow` function has been previously declared. The first argument is passed the `vbNullString` constant. This is used to represent the absence of value for the class name. The second argument is a string value of the title bar text of the application window being searched for.

If the function call finds the indicated title bar text and the window it belongs to, the return value will be the handle of that window. This is a unique value dynamically assigned by the operating system to control the window. The window handle is often used by other API calls to control and manipulate desired objects.

Passing an Argument by Value and by Reference

 Objective

This section examines two different ways arguments can be passed to external routines. Topics covered include passing arguments by value, passing by reference, and preventing General Protection Faults.

When an external function call requires additional information, arguments can be used. There are two different ways to pass arguments: the first is by value; the second is by reference.

It is very important when using external routines that the correct method of passing arguments is used. The wrong method of passing could cause the external routine to fail or cause a General Protection Fault.

Passing Arguments by Value

When information is passed by value, a copy of the information is handed to the external routine. This allows the memory space of the original variable holding the data to remain unchanged by the call.

In the argument declaration, the ByVal keyword is used before the name of the argument to be passed by value. The following argument declaration shows the use of the ByVal keyword:

```
(ByVal hWnd As Long, ByVal bInvert As Long)
```

These arguments are taken from the FlashWindow declaration. Notice that both the first argument and second use the keyword ByVal. Only a copy of the information is passed to the routine. This ensures that the original variables responsible for storage are not manipulated and changed in any way.

There is one exception to the ByVal declaration—strings. They are treated differently and are examined later in this chapter.

Passing Arguments by Reference

If an argument is passed to a procedure by reference, the memory address of the variable is given to the routine. This allows direct modification to the contents of the original variable. This is the default passing mechanism for VB.

To declare an argument to be passed by reference, the keyword ByRef is used in the declaration. The following argument declaration shows the use of ByRef:

```
(ByRef lTime As Long)
```

The syntax is similar to ByVal. The main difference is how the call is processed. The memory location of the long variable lTime is passed to the calling procedure.

VB does not require the use of the keyword ByRef. If used, however, it will increase the readability of the source code and procedure calls. ByRef is considered the default passing method.

Passing a Function Pointer to a DLL by Using a Callback Function

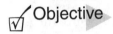 Objective

This section examines the new callback feature of Visual Basic 5. Topics covered include creating a callback function and passing a pointer to the function.

External routines can be given the memory address of a Visual Basic procedure. This address will be called when the external routine has either completed execution or needs to pass information back to the calling application.

The procedure used by the external routine is usually referred to as a *callback procedure*. This enables information to be passed from the external routine into the current application for further processing if required.

The capability to use callback functions is new to VB5. Certain external routines accept the address of a callback function. Special sets of external routines known as *Enumerators* accept callback function pointers. This allows the Enums to return control directly to the specified function. Processing can then continue in the main application.

To take advantage of this powerful new capability, you must perform the following three steps:

1. Declare the required external function.

2. Declare the function to be used for callback. (Ensure that it is created in a standard code module.)

3. Call the DLL routine by using the AddressOf keyword in front of the procedure to be passed as the callback function.

The following code sample shows the declaration of the EnumChildWindows API call:

```
Private Declare Function EnumChildWindows Lib "user32" (ByVal
➥hWndParent As Long, ByVal lpEnumFunc As Long, ByVal lParam As
➥Long) As Long
```

The function accepts three arguments: a parent window handle, the callback function address, and one additional argument. This additional argument is provided for passing information to the callback function to assist the programmer. It is not used by the external function EnumChildWindows itself. The EnumChildWindows returns a long to indicate whether the enumeration has completed.

The following code sample shows the declaration of the callback function used by the EnumChildWindows routine:

```
Public Function CallbackFunction(ByVal hWndChild As Long, ByVal
➥lParam As Long) As Boolean
    CallbackFunction = True
End Function
```

This function declaration must be created in a standard code module. It can be named any valid procedure name. This function has been called CallbackFunction for simplicity. It is passed the handle of a child window and the third parameter from the EnumChildWindows function. Remember that the third argument is not required and is for use by the programmer, not the function.

This callback function also has a return value of Boolean type. It is used to indicate whether the callback should return control to the external routine or complete processing. If the return value is set to True, the Enum function will continue enumeration. If the return value is set to False, the Enum function is halted. The preceding code sample sets the return value to True and allows the Enum to continue until enumeration has completed.

The following code sample shows the call to the function EnumChildWindows:

```
EnumChildWindows Me.hWnd, AddressOf CallbackFunction, 0
```

Notice that the function call is not much different from a regular function call. The function accepts three arguments, as per the declaration. The first is the window handle of the form to be enumerated. The second argument is where the use of the new keyword AddressOf comes into play. It is placed before the name of the procedure that will be used as the callback routine. Visual Basic will handle the address resolution and passing to the external routine. The third argument has been set to 0 because it is not currently being used.

When all three parts have been entered correctly, the function call will pass the window handle to be enumerated. The EnumChildWindows function will then obtain the window handle of every child window found on the main parent window. When the CallbackFunction is called, the child window handle is passed and can be further processed by the custom callback function.

Passing a String to a DLL

 **Objective** This section examines the differences of passing strings to external procedures.

When strings are passed to an external routine, there are extra considerations. Strings receive special treatment due to the differences in storage between VB and C/C++.

There are two main concerns when using strings as arguments. The first concern is how they are passed to the external routines. The second concern is that the string being passed is long enough to hold returned information.

When a string is to be passed as an argument, the ByVal declaration must always be used. Although ByVal indicates to pass a copy of the variable, when used with strings, the memory address is passed instead.

Strings in C/C++ are stored with a terminating character, called null. This special character is used to denote the end of the string contents. Most external routines expect null-terminated strings.

External routines will have the capability to directly modify the contents of the string variable passed. If the string to be assigned is longer than the string passed, the procedure will continue writing past the end of the variable. This will cause very bad results. The program could generate an Exception error or even a General Protection Fault.

To ensure enough space in the string variables passed as arguments, use the following code:

```
Dim strFirstName As String
strFirstName = String(255,0)
```

The first line declares a string variable. The second line uses the String function to populate the variable with zeros. This technique is known as string padding. It ensures that the external routine will not overwrite the variable.

Another method used to ensure a string will provide enough length is to declare a fixed-length string. The following code demonstrates the code:

```
Dim strFirstName As String * 255
```

This line of code declares a string variable named strFirstName and dimensions a size of 255 characters as the maximum for storage.

Either method can be used to ensure a long enough string for use by external routines. The string padding method might be more advantageous because of the capability to remove excess characters. A fixed-length string cannot have its size reduced.

The following declaration shows the use of strings as arguments:

```
Declare Function GetWindowsDirectory Lib "kernel32" Alias
➥"GetWindowsDirectoryA" (ByVal lpBuffer As String, ByVal nSize As
➥Long) As Long
```

Notice how the first argument accepted by this function is a string; the second is a long. When strings are passed by value, the memory location of the variable is given to the external routine, allowing direct change. When other data types are passed by value, only a copy of the variable value is given to the external routine, thus protecting the original variable.

Although string data types are handled differently when passed by value, nothing appears different during the function call.

You should keep two concerns in mind when using strings and external routines. The first concern is that the string being passed to the external routine is long enough to prevent overwriting the memory space of the variable. The second concern is that the external routine is given direct access to the variable; therefore, the original will be changed.

Creating a DLL Routine That Modifies String Arguments

Objective

This section examines creating a reusable DLL routine. The routine can be used to simplify calling external routines.

To reduce the amount of code used in calling an external routine, the application developer can create a reusable Visual Basic procedure. The procedure will encapsulate the external function call and return any required values. This enables the developer to create one fully functional generic routine that can be used in any other application project.

When including generic procedures from one project to another, the developer must ensure that all the correct declarations have been made.

Visual Basic procedures that contain all the required code for calling an external DLL routine can be written. This assists programmers by reducing the amount of coding and simplifies the external call.

The following procedure is an example of encapsulating all required code for an external function call. It contains full documentation and error handling:

```
'' Function:        GetWinDir
''
'' Description:     Used to retrieve the current Windows
'' directory. Includes error handling.
''                  This is a CommonProcedures routine.
''                  Used with the WIN32API standard code module.
''
'' Credits:         Programming - Lyle A Bryant
''
'' Maintenance History:
'' -------------------------------------------------------------
'' Date:          Version:       Developer:           Action:
'' -------------------------------------------------------------
'' 07/20/97       1.0            Lyle A Bryant        Created
''
'' -------------------------------------------------------------
Function GetWinDir() As String
    ' enable error handler
    On Error GoTo ErrHandler
    ' declare local variables
    Dim strWinDir As String
    Dim lLen As Long
    ' pad string for external use
    strWinDir = String(255, 0)
    ' call API routine
    lLen = GetWindowsDirectory(strWinDir, Len(strWinDir))
    ' trim extra 0's from padded string by using the string
    ➥length return value
    strWinDir = Left(strWinDir, lLen)
    ' add one backslash to reflect the directory
    strWinDir = strWinDir & "\"
    ' return strWinDir to calling procedure
    GetWinDir = strWinDir
    ' exit function if no errors encountered
    Exit Function
```

```
         ' error handler section
ErrHandler:
         ' return an error message string if an error is encountered
         GetWinDir = "Error - Unable to retrieve windows directory
         ➥information."
End Function
```

This function can be used to return a string value containing the Windows directory. If an error is encountered while attempting to retrieve the directory, an error string will be returned instead.

The function uses the API declaration GetWindowsDirectory that must also be included either in the same code module or in another code module.

Two variables are used locally within the procedure:

▶ One is a string to hold the return string value from the external function call.

▶ The second is a long variable used to hold the amount of characters of the returned string.

The GetWindowsDirectory call will place the Windows directory location into the local string. GetWindowsDirectory also returns the amount of characters assigned to the string as a return value.

After the string has been populated with the Windows directory, the string is cleaned of extra characters used for padding. Then the string is used as the return value to the calling procedure. An error handler will return an error string if anything goes wrong with the call.

To increase the usefulness of common procedures and reduce the amount of code typing, store all *common* procedures in a standard code module. In a second standard code module, store all *required* API declarations. Figure 10.3 shows the two modules. This allows the generic code and routines to be transferred from one application to another.

Figure 10.3

Using two standard code modules to store generic API declarations and common procedures.

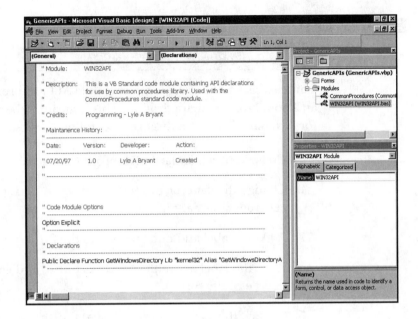

Exercises

Exercise 10.1: Using a Basic DLL Function Call

This exercise demonstrates a very simple API call used to generate an About box for an application. This is meant to be an introductory exercise. To create this exercise, follow these steps:

1. Create a new Standard EXE project.

2. Change the `Caption` property of `Form1` to "`Using a basic DLL function call`".

3. Add one label and one text box to the form.

4. Place the label above the `Textbox` control and center both in middle of the form.

5. Change the `Name` property of `Label1` to `lblApplicationTitle`.

6. Change the `Caption` property of `lblApplicationTitle` to "`Enter the Application Title:`".

7. Change the `Name` property of `Text1` to `txtApplicationTitle`.

8. Clear the `Text` property of `txtApplicationTitle`.

9. Add one more label and text box to the form.

10. Place the label above the text box and center both in the middle of the form, below the first set.

11. Change the `Name` property of `Label1` to `lblCompanyName`.

12. Change the `Caption` property of `lblCompanyName` to "`Enter the Company Name:`".

13. Change the `Name` property of `Text1` to `txtCompanyName`.

14. Clear the `Text` property of `txtCompanyName`.

15. Add one command button to the form.

16. Center the command button below both sets of text boxes.

17. Change the `Name` property of `Command1` to `cmdCreateAboutBox`.

18. Change the `Caption` property of `cmdCreateAboutBox` to `"Create &About Box"`.

19. Open the code window for the General Declarations section and enter the following code:

```
Option Explicit

Private Declare Function ShellAbout Lib
    ➥"shell32.dll" Alias "ShellAboutA" _
    (ByVal hwnd As Long, ByVal szApp As
    ➥String, ByVal szOtherStuff As
    ➥String, ByVal hIcon As Long) As
    ➥Long
```

20. Open the code window for `cmdCreateAboutBox` and enter the following code:

```
Private Sub cmdCreateAboutBox_Click()
    Dim lResult As Long
    lResult = ShellAbout(Me.hwnd, "- " &
    ➥txtApplicationTitle.Text,
    ➥txtCompanyName.Text, 0)
End Sub
```

21. Run the application.

22. In the Enter The Application Title text box, enter a sample name for an application.

23. In the Enter The Company Name text box, enter a sample company name.

24. Select the Create About Box command button. This will use an API call to create a generic About box. Common Microsoft applications, but not MS Office, use this API call.

25. Return to Design mode.

26. Examine the source code again.

27. When completed, end the application.

Exercise 10.2: Declaring and Calling a DLL Routine

Visual Basic allows for the use of external routines. By using a special declare statement, an external procedure can be called and used within an application. To create this exercise, follow these steps:

1. Create a new Standard EXE project.

2. Change the Caption property of Form1 to "Declaring and Calling a DLL routine".

3. Add one label, one text box, and one command button to the form.

4. Place the label and text box on the left side of the form. Ensure that the label is above the text box.

5. Place the command button on the right side of the form.

6. Change the Name property of Label1 to lblWindowTitle.

7. Change the Caption property of lblWindowTitle to "Enter the Window Title Bar Text:".

8. Change the Name property of Text1 to txtWindowTitle.

9. Clear the Text property of txtWindowTitle.

10. Change the Name property of Command1 to cmdFindWindow.

11. Change the Caption property of cmdFindWindow to "&Find Window".

12. Open the code window for the General Declarations section of the form and enter the following code:

```
Option Explicit

Private Declare Function FindWindow Lib
    ➥"user32" Alias "FindWindowA" _
    (ByVal lpClassName As String, ByVal
    ➥lpWindowName As String) As Long
```

```
Private Declare Function FlashWindow Lib
    ➥"user32" _
    (ByVal hwnd As Long, ByVal bInvert As
    ➥Long) As Long
```

13. Open the code window for `cmdFindWindow` and enter the following code:

```
Private Sub cmdFindWindow_Click()
    Dim lHandle As Long
    If txtWindowTitle.Text = "" Then
        MsgBox "Please enter the Title
        ➥Bar text of the Window to be
        ➥found.", vbInformation
        txtWindowHandle.Text = ""
        Exit Sub
    End If

        lHandle = FindWindow(vbNullString,
        ➥txtWindowTitle.Text)

    If lHandle = 0 Then
        MsgBox "Window Not Found. Please
        ➥ensure you have enter the
        ➥correct title bar text from the
        ➥desired window.", vbInformation
        txtWindowHandle.Text = ""
        Exit Sub
    Else
        txtWindowHandle.Text = lHandle
    End If
End Sub
```

14. Add one more label, one more text box, and one more command button.

15. Place the label and text box below the other label and text box set, on the left side of the form.

16. Place the second command button beside the second text box, and on the right side of the form.

continues

Exercise 10.2:   Continued

---

17. Change the `Name` property of `Label1` to `lblWindowHandle`.

18. Change the `Caption` property of `lblWindowHandle` to `"Window Handle to be Flashed:"`.

19. Change the `Name` property of `Text1` to `txtWindowHandle`.

20. Clear the `Text` property of `txtWindowHandle`.

21. Change the `Name` property of `Command1` to `cmdFlashWindow`.

22. Change the `Caption` property of `cmdFlashWindow` to `"F&lash Window"`.

23. Open the code window for `cmdFlashWindow` and enter the following code:

```
Private Sub cmdFlashWindow_Click()
    Dim lResult As Long
    If txtWindowHandle.Text = "" Then
        MsgBox "Please enter the Window
        ➥handle of the Window to be
        ➥flashed.", vbInformation
        txtWindowHandle.Text = ""
        Exit Sub
    End If
    lResult =
    ➥FlashWindow(CLng(txtWindowHandle.Text),
    ➥1)
End Sub
```

24. Run the application.

25. In the text box Enter The Window Title Bar Text, enter the following: **"Declaring and Calling a DLL routine"**. This is the name of the window title bar.

26. Click on the Find Window command button. This will use an API call to find the handle to the window you enter.

27. The gray text box should contain a number, which is the window handle.

28. Click on the Flash Window command button. Another API call will alter the title bar and create a flash effect. Press the command button multiple times to change the title bar.

29. Return to Design mode.

30. Examine the source code again.

31. Try adding a timer to the form. When the user selects the Flash Window command button, the timer will be used to flash the window title bar.

32. When completed, end the application.

Exercise 10.3: Using Strings with DLLs

When passing arguments to external routines, string data types are passed differently than other data types. The following exercise demonstrates the use of string variables with external DLL routines. To create this exercise, follow these steps:

1. Create a new Standard EXE project.

2. Change the Caption property of Form1 to "Using Strings with DLLs".

3. Add one text box and one command button to the form.

4. Place the text box on the left side, and align the command button to the right side of the text box.

5. Change the Name property of Text1 to txtGetComputerName.

6. Clear the Text property of txtGetComputerName.

7. Change the Locked property of txtGetComputerName to True.

8. Change the Background property of txtGetComputerName to Form gray - &H00C0C0C0&.

9. Change the Name property of Command1 to cmdGetComputerName.

continues

Exercise 10.3: Continued

10. Change the `Caption` property of `cmdGetComputerName` to `"Get Computer Name"`. Ensure the button is wide enough to display all the text.

11. Add one more text box and one more command button to the form.

12. Place the second set underneath the first set—text box on the left side, command button on the right side.

13. Change the `Name` property of `Text1` to `txtGetUserName`.

14. Clear the `Text` property of `txtGetUserName`.

15. Change the `Locked` property of `txtGetUserName` to `True`.

16. Change the `Background` property of `txtGetUserName` to `Form gray` - `&H00C0C0C0&`.

17. Change the `Name` property of `Command1` to `cmdGetUserName`.

18. Change the `Caption` property of `cmdGetUserName` to `"Get User Name"`. Ensure the button is wide enough to display all the text.

19. Add one more text box and one more command button to the form. There should be a total of three sets now.

20. Place the third set underneath the second set—text box on the left side, command button on the right side.

21. Change the `Name` property of `Text1` to `txtGetWindowsDirectory`.

22. Clear the `Text` property of `txtGetWindowsDirectory`.

23. Change the `Locked` property of `txtGetWindowsDirectory` to `True`.

24. Change the `Background` property of `txtGetWindowsDirectory` to `Form gray` - `&H00C0C0C0&`.

25. Change the `Name` property of `Command1` to `cmdGetWindowsDirectory`.

26. Change the `Caption` property of `cmdGetWindowsDirectory` to "`Get Windows Directory`". Ensure the button is wide enough to display all the text.

27. Open the code window for the General Declarations section and enter the following code:

```
Option Explicit

Private Declare Function GetComputerNameA
    ➥Lib "kernel32" _
    (ByVal lpBuffer As String, nSize As
    ➥Long) As Long
Private Declare Function WNetGetUserA Lib
    ➥"mpr" _
    (ByVal lpName As String, ByVal
    ➥lpUserName As String, lpnLength As
    ➥Long) As Long
Private Declare Function GetWinDir Lib
    ➥"kernel32" Alias
    ➥"GetWindowsDirectoryA" _
    (ByVal lpBuffer As String, ByVal
    ➥nSize As Long) As Long
```

28. Open the code window for `cmdGetComputerName` and enter the following code:

```
Private Sub cmdGetComputerName_Click()
    Dim strBuffer As String, lResult As
    ➥Long
    strBuffer = String(255, 0)
    lResult = GetComputerNameA(strBuffer,
    ➥Len(strBuffer))
    If lResult <> 0 Then
        strBuffer = Left$(strBuffer,
        ➥InStr(strBuffer, vbNullChar)
        ➥- 1)
        txtGetComputerName.Text =
        ➥strBuffer
    End If
End Sub
```

29. Open the code window for `cmdGetUserName` and enter the following code:

continues

Exercise 10.3: Continued

```
Private Sub cmdGetUserName_Click()
    Dim strUserName As String, lResult As
    ➥Long
    strUserName = String(255, 0)
    lResult = WNetGetUserA(vbNullString,
    ➥strUserName, Len(strUserName))
    If lResult = 0 Then
        strUserName = Left$(strUserName,
        ➥InStr(strUserName, vbNullChar) -
        ➥1)
        txtGetUserName.Text = strUserName
    End If
End Sub
```

30. Open the code window for cmdGetWindowsDirectory and enter the following code:

```
Private Sub
➥cmdGetWindowsDirectory_Click()
    Dim strWindowsDir As String, lResult
    ➥As Long
    strWindowsDir = String(255, 0)
    lResult = GetWinDir(strWindowsDir,
    ➥Len(strWindowsDir))
    strWindowsDir = Left$(strWindowsDir,
    ➥lResult)
    txtGetWindowsDirectory.Text =
    ➥strWindowsDir
End Sub
```

31. Run the application.

32. Select the Get Computer Name command button. The NetBIOS machine name should appear.

33. Select the Get User Name command button. The username should appear if the computer was logged on.

34. Select the Get Windows Directory command button. The drive and path location to the Windows directory should be displayed.

35. At least one of the previous command buttons should have executed successfully.

36. Return to Design mode.

37. Examine the source code again.

38. When completed, end the application.

Exercise 10.4: Using a Callback Function

Visual Basic 5 has introduced a new keyword called AddressOf. This allows the passing of a procedure address as an argument to certain API routines. A special group of functions known as Enumerators can be used and will call a Visual Basic procedure after they have completed execution. To create this exercise, follow these steps:

1. Create a new Standard EXE project.

2. Change the Caption property of Form1 to "Using a Callback function".

3. Add one label, one text box, and one command button to the form.

4. Place the label above the text box on the left side of the form. Place the command button on the right side of the text box.

5. Change the Name property of Label1 to lblWindowTitle.

6. Change the Caption property of lblWindowTitle to "Enter the Window Title Bar Text:".

7. Change the Name property of Text1 to txtWindowTitle.

8. Clear the Text property of txtWindowTitle.

9. Change the Name property of Command1 to cmdFindWindow.

10. Change the Caption property of cmdFindWindow to "&Find Window".

11. Add one more label, text box, and command button.

continues

Exercise 10.4: Continued

12. Place the label and text box on the left side of the form, below the first set. Position the label above the text box and the command button on the right side of the second text box.

13. Change the `Name` property of `Label1` to `lblWindowHandle`.

14. Change the `Caption` property of `lblWindowHandle` to `"Window Handle to be Enumerated:"`.

15. Change the `Name` property of `Text1` to `txtWindowHandle`.

16. Clear the `Text` property of `txtWindowHandle`.

17. Change the `Locked` property of `txtWindowHandle` to True.

18. Change the `Background` property of `txtWindowHandle` to Form gray - `&H00C0C0C0&`.

19. Change the `Name` property of `Command1` to `cmdEnumerateWindow`.

20. Change the `Caption` property of `cmdEnumerateWindow` to `"&Enumerate Window"`.

21. Add another label, one list box, and one more command button.

22. Place the label above the list box, and move them to the left side of the form below the other text boxes.

23. Increase the height of the list box and move the command button to the right side of the list box.

24. Change the `Name` property of `Label1` to `lblEnumerationResults`.

25. Change the `Caption` property of `lblEnumerationResults` to `"Enumeration Results:"`.

26. Change the `Name` property of `List1` to `lstEnumerationResults`.

27. Change the `Background` property of `lstEnumerationResults` to `Form` gray - `&H00C0C0C0&`.

28. Change the `Name` property of `Command1` to `cmdClearResults`.

29. Change the `Caption` property of `cmdClearResults` to "&Clear Results".

30. Open the code window for the General Declarations and enter the following code:

```
Option Explicit

Private Declare Function FindWindow Lib
➥"user32" Alias "FindWindowA" _
    (ByVal lpClassName As String, ByVal
    ➥lpWindowName As String) As Long
Private Declare Function EnumChildWindows
    ➥Lib "user32" _
    (ByVal hWndParent As Long, ByVal
    ➥lpEnumFunc As Long, ByVal lParam As
    ➥Long) As Long
```

31. Open the code window for `cmdFindWindow` and enter the following code:

```
Private Sub cmdFindWindow_Click()
    Dim lHandle As Long
    If txtWindowTitle.Text = "" Then
        MsgBox "Please enter the Title
        ➥Bar text of the Window to be
        ➥found.", vbInformation
        txtWindowHandle.Text = ""
        Exit Sub
    End If

    lHandle = FindWindow(vbNullString,
    ➥txtWindowTitle.Text)
```

continues

```
        If lHandle = 0 Then
            MsgBox "Window Not Found. Please
            ➥ensure you have enter the
            ➥correct title bar text from the
            ➥desired window.", vbInformation
            txtWindowHandle.Text = ""
            Exit Sub
        Else
            txtWindowHandle.Text = lHandle
        End If
    End Sub
```

32. Open the code window for `cmdEnumerateWindow` and enter the following code:

```
Private Sub cmdEnumerateWindow_Click()
    Dim lResults As Long
    lResults =
    ➥EnumChildWindows(txtWindowHandle.Text,
    ➥AddressOf CallbackFunction, 0)
End Sub
```

33. Open the code window for `cmdClearResults` and enter the following code:

```
Private Sub cmdClearResults_Click()
    lstEnumerationResults.Clear
End Sub
```

34. Add one standard code module to the project.

35. In the General Declarations section of the standard code module, enter the following code:

```
Option Explicit

Public Declare Function GetWindowText Lib
➥"user32" Alias "GetWindowTextA" _
    (ByVal hwnd As Long, ByVal lpString
    ➥As String, ByVal cch As Long) As
    ➥Long
```

```
Public Function CallbackFunction(ByVal
➥hWndChild As Long, ByVal lParam As
➥Long) As Boolean
  Dim lLength As Long
  Dim strResult As String

  strResult = String(255, 0)
  lLength = GetWindowText(hWndChild,
  ➥strResult, Len(strResult))
  strResult = Left(strResult, lLength)
  Form1.lstEnumerationResults.AddItem
  ➥strResult
  CallbackFunction = True
End Function
```

36. Run the application

37. In the Enter The Window Title Bar Text text box, type **"Using a Callback function"**.

38. Select the Find Window command button. This will use an API call to retrieve the Window Handle. Once selected, the second textbox should indicate a Window Handle.

39. Select the Enumerate Window command button. This will use an API call to determine all of the child windows (or controls) located on the selected form. The list box will populate with the caption of valid controls.

40. Notice that the list box does not contain Label control text and there is one blank entry used to represent the list box.

41. Using the title bar of another window, repeat this procedure. Try using the calculator, WordPad, or other applications.

42. Return to Design mode.

43. Examine the source code again.

44. When completed, end the application.

Review Questions

1. Visual Basic allows the use of external routines to provide additional functionality. Where in the VB source code are these declarations created?

    A. General Declarations of a form code module

    B. Local procedures

    C. Static procedures

    D. General Declarations of a standard code module

    E. Project, References

2. In the declaration of an external routine, what is the keyword used to indicate the path/file location where the routine is stored?

    A. Alias

    B. Lib

    C. Library

    D. Declare

    E. AddressOf

3. Most external routines called by Visual Basic are written in C/C++. Name rules for procedures are different from VB. What is the keyword used to map the invalid name to a valid Visual Basic name?

    A. Lib

    B. Declare

    C. Alias

    D. Library

    E. AddressOf

4. External routines can accept information in the form of arguments. When using the keyword `ByVal`, what method of argument passing is being used?

    A. The memory address of the variable is passed.

    B. The memory stack of the application is passed.

    C. Only a copy of the variable is passed.

    D. The variable is copied and then the memory address of the original is passed.

    E. None of these.

5. External routines can accept information in the form of arguments. When using the keyword `ByRef`, what method of argument passing is being used?

    A. The variable is copied and then the memory address of the original is passed.

    B. Only a copy of the variable is passed.

    C. The memory stack of the application is passed.

    D. The memory address of the variable is passed.

    E. None of these.

6. From the listed declarations, which one is valid? Hint— Check for syntax.

    A. `Declare Function GetComputerNameA "Kernel32"`
      `(ByVal lpBuffer As String, nSize As Long) As Long`

    B. `Declare Function _GetComputerNameA Lib (ByVal`
      `lpBuffer As String, nSize As Long) As Long`

    C. `Declare Function GetComputerNameA Lib "Kernel32"`
      `As Long`

    D. `Declare Function _GetComputerNameA Lib "Kernel32"`
      `(ByVal lpBuffer As String, nSize As Long) As Long`

    E. `Declare Function GetComputerNameA Lib "Kernel32"`
      `(ByVal lpBuffer As String, nSize As Long) As Long`

7. From the listed declarations, which one is a valid use of the Alias clause?

    A. `Declare Function _GetComputerNameA Alias GCN Lib "Kernel32"`

    B. `Declare Function GCN Alias _GetComputerNameA Lib "Kernel32"`

    C. `Declare Function GCN Alias _GetComputerNameA Library "Kernel32"`

    D. `Declare Function Alias GCN Library "Kernel32"`

    E. `Declare Function _GetComputerNameA Lib "Kernel32" Alias GCN`

8. Visual Basic provides additional utilities to assist the application developer. What utility can be used to reduce typing errors when declaring external function calls?

    A. API Text Viewer

    B. API File Viewer

    C. Application Performance Explorer

    D. Library Routine Explorer

    E. DLL Process Viewer

9. Strings are stored differently in Visual Basic than in C/C++. When passing strings to external routines, what method of argument passing is used?

    A. By alias

    B. By condition

    C. By value

    D. By reference

    E. By address

10. When a string is passed to an external routine for modification, what must be done to the string prior to passing? (Select all appropriate.)

    A. The string must be trimmed.

    B. The string must be declared with a fixed length.

    C. The string must be padded with extra characters.

    D. The string must be measured for length.

    E. The string must be terminated.

11. Which code listed here can be used to pad a string with extra characters?

    A. `Dim strFirstName As String * 255`

    B. `strFirstName * 255`

    C. `strFirstName = 255`

    D. `Dim strFirstName As String = String(255,0)`

    E. `strFirstName = String(255,0)`

12. Which code listed here can be used to create a fixed length string?

    A. `Dim strFirstName As String * 255`

    B. `strFirstName * 255`

    C. `strFirstName = 255`

    D. `Dim strFirstName As String = String(255,0)`

    E. `strFirstName = String(255,0)`

13. Some external routines can accept the address of a function to be called during processing. This is known as a callback function. What is the keyword used to pass the address of the desired function to be used as the callback?

    A. ByRef

    B. ByAddress

    C. ByVal

    D. RefrenceOf

    E. AddressOf

14. Procedures can be created in Visual Basic to be used as callback functions for external routines. What part of the VB source code is used to create procedures to be used as callbacks?

    A. Form code module

    B. Class code module

    C. Standard code module

    D. Resource file

    E. External DLL file

Answers to Review Questions

1. A, D. External procedures can be declared in both the General Declarations of a form code module and the General Declarations of a standard code module. Local and Static procedures cannot contain external declarations. The References dialog box is used for referencing object libraries and not external routines. For more information, see the section titled "Declaring a DLL."

2. B. Lib. The keyword Lib is used to indicate the path/file location where the routine is stored. If the path information is not specified, the default path is searched. The word *Library* is not used as a keyword in the external declaration.

Alias and AddressOf keywords are used for other purposes. For more information, see the section titled "Declaring a DLL."

3. C. Alias. The keyword Alias is used to map the C/C++ invalid name to a valid Visual Basic procedure name. For more information, see the section titled "Identifying When It Is Necessary to Use the Alias Clause."

4. C. Only a copy of the variable is passed. When arguments are passed ByVal, only a copy of the variable is passed to the external routine. This allows the original variable to remain intact and unchanged. For more information, see the section titled "Passing Arguments by Value."

5. D. The memory address of the variable is passed. When arguments are passed ByRef, the external routine is given the memory location of the variable and is allowed to directly change the contents. This allows the application to use the same variable as the external call. For more information, see the section titled "Passing Arguments by Reference."

6. E. Declare Function GetComputerNameA Lib "Kernel32" (ByVal lpBuffer As String, nSize As Long) As Long. Other listed items have a variety of syntactical errors. Check for Missing Lib keyword, missing library filename, missing arguments, and invalid underscore as the first character of the procedure name. For more information, see the section titled "Declaring a DLL."

7. B. Declare Function GCN Alias _GetComputerNameA Lib "Kernel32". This declaration shows the correct use of the Alias clause. The name to be referred to in Visual Basic appears after the procedure type and before the Alias keyword. The actual name of the external procedure appears after the Alias keyword. The keyword Lib is used here to indicate the location of the external file. Library is not the correct keyword. For more information, see the section titled "Identifying When It Is Necessary to Use the Alias Clause."

8. A. API Text Viewer. To assist with external routine declarations, the API Text Viewer can be used to examine the WIN32API.TXT file. The Text Viewer reads the text file and loads three different types of information: declarations, constants, and types. The API Text Viewer assists in finding required declarations and also helps reduce typing errors. For more information, see the section titled "Declaring a DLL."

9. C. By value. When strings are passed to external routines by value, the address of the string is passed. This allows the external routine to directly change the contents of the string variable as required. For more information, see the section titled "Passing a String to a DLL."

10. B, C. The string must be declared with a fixed length or the string must be padded with extra characters. Either method can be used to ensure that the length of the string passed to the external routine will be long enough and that the routine will not overwrite value beyond the length of the string variable. If a string is passed that is not long enough for modification, the external routine will go beyond the length of the string and into unknown memory locations. This could result in an application or even operating system crash. For more information, see the section titled "Passing a String to a DLL."

11. E. `strFirstName = String(255,0)`. This will take the string `strFirstName` and uses the `String` function to pad 255 places in the variable with the 0 character. By padding up to 255 characters, this ensures that the variable will provide enough space for the external routine to write information. For more information, see the section titled "Passing a String to a DLL."

12. A. `Dim strFirstName As String * 255`. This code statement is used to declare a string variable named `strFirstName`. The asterisk is used to create a fixed length string to hold a maximum of 255 characters. For more information, see the section titled "Passing a String to a DLL."

13. E.AddressOf. The keyword AddressOf is used when calling the external routine. AddressOf appears in front of the argument to be passed that will receive the address of the callback function. Visual Basic then handles the resolution and passing of the correct address of the callback function to the external routine. For more information, see the section titled "Passing a Function Pointer to a DLL by Using a Callback Function."

14. C.Standard code module. When creating a procedure in Visual Basic to be used as a callback function, the procedure must be declared within a standard code module. For more information, see the section titled "Passing a Function Pointer to a DLL by Using a Callback Function."

Answers to Test Yourself Questions at Beginning of Chapter

1. External routines are specified in code modules of an application. The keyword `Declare` is used to provide VB with the required information for the routine. The name of the routine, the library location, arguments, and return values are all specified. See "Declaring a DLL."

2. The API Text Viewer can be used to load and organize the WIN32API.TXT file, which contains DLL declarations. Code can be copied from this application into the VB code window. This helps reduce typing errors in external routine declarations. See "Declaring a DLL."

3. The keyword used to indicate the path/filename of the library providing the external routine is `Lib`. In an external declaration, `Lib` is used with the path and or filename of the routine. See "Declaring a DLL."

4. The `Alias` statement allows VB to use routines that might have a naming conflict. It is used in the `Declaration` statement and follows the `Lib` reference. See "Identifying When It Is Necessary to Use the `Alias` Clause."

5. Multiple declarations are created for external routines that can accept more than one data type in an argument. By having multiple declarations using the `Alias` keyword, specific data types can be indicated in the declaration. This allows Visual Basic to perform data type validation within the application before calling the external routine. VB will cause an error if the data type being passed is not valid. This can assist in reducing errors caused from passing incorrect data to the external routine. See "Identifying When It Is Necessary to Use the `Alias` Clause."

6. The constant `vbNullString` is used to represent an absence of value. This is often used when arguments must be passed, but will contain no value for manipulation. This constant is used to represent the null value found in the C/C++ language. Many routines require this value if arguments do not contain valid information. See "Passing a Null Pointer to a DLL Routine."

7. A copy of the argument is passed to the external routine when passing by value. This allows the external routine to manipulate only the copy of the variable and not the original itself. Passing by value ensures the integrity of the original variable. See "Passing Arguments by Value."

8. The keyword used to pass arguments by reference in the declaration of an external routine is `ByRef`. This keyword is used before the argument name and determines that the memory address of the argument is passed to the routine. See "Passing Arguments by Reference."

9. The memory address of the argument is passed to the external routine when passing by reference. This allows the external routine to directly manipulate the memory location and change the original value of the variable. See "Passing Arguments by Reference."

10. The keyword used to pass arguments by value in the declaration of an external routine is `ByVal`. This keyword is used before the argument name and determines that a copy of the argument is passed to the routine. See "Passing Arguments by Value."

11. The keyword used to pass a function pointer to an argument is `AddressOf`. The `AddressOf` keyword passes a pointer of a procedure declared in a VB standard module. This allows the external routine to call the procedure in the standard module when the external routine has completed. See "Passing a Function Pointer to a DLL by Using a Callback Function."

12. When strings are passed to external routines, they are passed by value. When a string is passed by value, Visual Basic passes the address of the string, and not just a copy of the variable. See "Passing a String to a DLL."

Chapter

11

Building Microsoft
ActiveX Clients

This chapter helps you prepare for the exam by covering the following objectives:

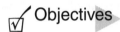 Objectives

- ▶ Using the Dim statement to create object variables

- ▶ Using the Set statement to create an instance of an object

- ▶ Using the CreateObject function to create an instance of an object

Test Yourself! Before reading this chapter, test yourself to determine how much study time you will need to devote to this section.

1. What Visual Basic statement can be used to define an Application object using the Dim statement?

2. Write the statement(s) that will define an object variable and return a valid object reference of type Application?

3. Assume that you have a COM server with an application name of MyApp and an object called Spreadsheet. Write the statement that will create an instance of the Spreadsheet object.

4. If the following code is executed and the server is not running in memory, what occurs?

```
Set objInfo = GetObject("Word.Application")
```

Answers are located at the end of the chapter...

The term ActiveX describes a set of services provided as part of the Windows operating system. The services provided with ActiveX are based on a set of services provided with the Component Object Model (COM). These services that COM provides are summarized as follows:

- Object Management

- Object Persistence

- Structured Storage

- Data Transfer

- Naming and Binding services

COM provides Object Management services by using *reference counting*. With reference counting, COM enables developers to control when object references and their objects are released from memory. In Visual Basic, the management of object references is provided by the Visual Basic runtime engine. In addition, COM provides Object Persistence services that allow objects to be stored in a file. This is particularly important when you wish to extract an application-specific object from a document file.

When objects are stored in files, they are stored using the Structured Storage services provided in COM. With Structured Storage, you can store data in a hierarchical format within a file, very much as files are stored in directories and subdirectories. Structured Storage allows applications to read and save items to files without worrying about restructuring the layout of the file.

COM provides Data Transfer services that enable you to transfer and share data between applications. With Naming and Binding services (Monikers) applications can create, store, and manage objects that provide complex operations such as asynchronous downloading of files. These services are usually not directly accessed by the Visual Basic developer; however, you will use these services via the objects and functions that Visual Basic provides.

COM provides the core services on which ActiveX technology is based. The ActiveX technology provides the following services:

- ▶ ActiveX Documents

- ▶ ActiveX Controls

- ▶ ActiveX Servers

- ▶ ActiveX Automation

ActiveX Documents enable developers to create applications that can host documents in their native format inside other ActiveX Documents. Chapter 14, "Creating and Using ActiveX Documents," provides more detail on ActiveX Documents.

Developers use ActiveX Controls to extend and enhance the services that an application provides. If you need word processing capabilities in your application, for example, you can purchase an ActiveX Control that provides the desired functionality. In addition, you can write your own controls that encapsulate whatever functions you need. Chapter 13, "Creating and Using ActiveX Controls," provides more detail on ActiveX Controls.

Most Microsoft products and commercial vendors' applications provide an ActiveX interface to the services that applications provide. Applications that provide services via an ActiveX interface are usually called ActiveX servers. The client applications that use ActiveX Servers are called ActiveX clients. There are two basic types of ActiveX clients. One type of client is the ActiveX Document container. This type of client application is used to host ActiveX Documents. The other type is referred to as ActiveX clients that are used to communicate with ActiveX Servers that support automation. Chapter 12, "Creating an Automation Server That Exposes Objects, Properties, Methods, and Events," provides more detail on creating ActiveX Servers.

ActiveX Automation enables you to *script* commands to applications. Therefore your client applications can use an ActiveX Server that has *exposed* its objects to the outside world. This chapter

Chapter 13: Creating and Using ActiveX Controls

Objective...	Located Here...
Declare and raise events	*Declaring and Raising Events*, page 523
Create and enable a property page	*Creating and Enabling a Property Page*, page 527
Use control events to save and load persistent control properties	*Saving and Loading Persistent Control Properties*, page 534
Add an ActiveX control to a web page	*Adding an ActiveX Control to a Web Page*, page 536

Chapter 14: Creating and Using ActiveX Documents

Objective...	Located Here...
Compare ActiveX Documents to embedded objects	*Comparing ActiveX Documents to Embedded Objects*, page 564
Create an ActiveX project with one or more `UserDocument` objects	*Understanding the `UserDocument` Module*, page 550
Persist data for an ActiveX Document	*Persistent Data for an ActiveX Document*, page 567
Automate an ActiveX Document	*Automating an ActiveX Document*, page 568
Add an ActiveX Document to a web page	*Adding an ActiveX Document to a Web Page*, page 569

Chapter 15: Creating Applications That Can Access the Internet

Objective...	Located Here...
Gain access to the Internet or an Intranet by using the Hyperlink object	*`Hyperlink` Object*, page 599
Create an application that has the ability to browse HTML pages	*`WebBrowser` Object*, page 605
Create an application that enables connections to the Internet	*Communication Methods and Protocols*, page 580

Chapter 16: Implementing Error-Handling Features in an Application

Objective...	Located Here...
Use the appropriate error-trapping options, such as Break on All Errors, Break in Class Module, and Break on Unhandled Errors	*Setting Error-Handling Options*, page 628
Display an error message in a dialog box by using the `Err` object	*Using the `Err` Object*, page 630
Create a common error-handling routine	*Handling Errors in Code*, page 637; *Using the Error-Handling Hierarchy*, page 645; *Common Error-Handling Routines*, page 647
Raising errors from a server	*Raising Errors From a Server*, page 651

Chapter 17: Implementing Help Features in an Application

Objective...	Located Here...
Set properties to automatically display Help information when a user presses F1	*Implementing Context-Sensitive Help*, page 668
Use the `HelpFile` property to set the default path for Help files in an application	*Referencing Help Through the `HelpFile` Property of an Application*, page 665
Use the `CommonDialog` control to display the contents of a Help file	*Using the `CommonDialog` Control to Display Help*, page 671

Chapter 18: Selecting Appropriate Compiler Options

Objective...	Located Here...
List and describe options for optimizing when compiling to native code	*Compiling to Native Code*, page 708
List and describe the differences between compiling to p-code and compiling to native code	*P-code vs. Native Code*, page 697

Chapter 19: Compiling an Application Conditionally

Objective...	Located Here...
Use the #If...#End If and #Const directives to conditionally compile statements	*Preprocessor Directives*, page 739
Set the appropriate conditional compiler flags	*Compiler Constants*, page 745

Chapter 20: Setting Watch Expressions During Program Execution

Objective...	Located Here...
Set watch expressions during program execution	*Using Watch Expressions and Contexts*, page 776

Chapter 21: Monitoring the Values of Expressions and Variables by Using the Debugging Windows

Objective...	Located Here...
Use the Immediate window to check or change values	*Immediate Window and the* Debug *Object*, page 804
Explain the purpose and usage for the Locals window	*Using the Locals Window*, page 825

Chapter 22: Implementing Project Groups to Support the Development and Debugging Process

Objective...	Located Here...
Debug DLLs in process	*Using Project Groups to Debug an ActiveX DLL*, page 845
Test and debug a control in process	*Using Project Groups to Debug an ActiveX Control*, page 851

Chapter 23: Defining the Scope of a Watch Variable

Objective...	Located Here...
Understand the three levels of scope	*Levels of Scope*, page 867
Choose the appropriate level of scope	*Scope Considerations*, page 873

Chapter 24: Using the Setup Wizard to Create an Effective Setup Program

Objective...	Located Here...
Edit the SETUP.LST file	*Editing the SETUP.LST File*, page 895
Edit the VB5DEP.INI file	*Editing the VB5DEP.INI File*, page 901

Chapter 25: Creating a Setup Program That Installs and Registers ActiveX Controls

Objective...	Located Here...
Create an installation program for ActiveX controls	*Creating a Setup Program for ActiveX Controls*, page 931

Chapter 26: Managing the Windows System Registry

Objective...	Located Here...
Use the GetSetting function and the SaveSetting statement to save application-specific information in the Registry	*Storing Information in the System Registry*, page 980
Register components by using the Regsvr32.exe utility	*Registering Controls—Manually*, page 976
Register components by using the Remote Automation Connection Manager	*Compiling and Distributing Remote Automation/DCOM Clients*, page 972
Edit the Registry manually	*Registering Controls—Manually*, page 976
Register a component automatically	*Registering Controls—Automatically*, page 969

Chapter 27: Distributing an Application over the Internet

Objective...	Located Here...
Prepare for component downloading	*Preparing for Component Downloading*, page 1003
Make use of digital signing	*Making Use of Digital Signing*, page 1005
Guarantee the component is safe	*Guaranteeing the Component Is Safe*, page 1008
Understand your licensing options	*Understanding Your Licensing Options*, page 1010

Objectives List for Exam 70-165: Developing Applications with Microsoft Visual Basic 5

Chapter 1: Designing and Creating Forms

Objective...	Located Here...
Create an application that adds and deletes forms at runtime	*Creating an Application That Adds and Deletes Forms at Runtime*, page 23
Use the Forms collection	*Using the Forms Collection*, page 28

Chapter 2: Implementing Drag-and-Drop Operations Within the Windows Shell and Using Specific Events

Objective...	Located Here...
Implement drag-and-drop operations within the Microsoft Windows shell	*Implementing Traditional Drag-and-Drop Support in Applications*, page 54; *Understanding OLE Drag-and-Drop Support in Visual Basic*, page 59; *Implementing OLE Drag-and-Drop Features in Visual Basic*, page 64
Add code to the appropriate form event, such as Initialize, Terminate, Load, Unload, QueryUnload, Activate, and Deactivate	*Managing Form Events*, page 68

Chapter 3: Adding a Menu Interface to an Application

Objective...	Located Here...
Dynamically modify the appearance of a menu	*Dynamically Modifying the Appearance of a Menu*, page 85
Add a pop-up menu to an application	*Adding a Pop-Up Menu to an Application*, page 87
Create an application that adds and deletes menus at runtime	*Creating an Application That Adds and Deletes Menus at Runtime*, page 92

Chapter 4: Implementing User Interface Controls in an Application

Objective...	Located Here...
Display data by using the TreeView control	*Using the* TreeView *Control*, page 118
Display items by using the ListView control	*Using the* ListView *Control*, page 125
Provide controls with images by using the ImageList control	*Using the* ImageList *Control*, page 112
Create Toolbars by using the Toolbar control	*Using the* Toolbar *Control*, page 134
Display status information by using the StatusBar control	*Using the* StatusBar *Control*, page 140
Create an application that adds and deletes controls at runtime	*Adding and Deleting Controls Dynamically*, page 146
Use the Controls Collection	*Using the Controls Collection*, page 144

Chapter 5: Declaring a Variable

Objective...	Located Here...
Define the scope of a variable by using the Public, Private and Static statements	*Defining the Scope of a Variable*, page 165
Use the appropriate declaration statement	*Using the Appropriate Declaration Statement*, page 174

Chapter 6: Writing and Calling Sub and Function Procedures

Objective...	Located Here...
Write and call Sub and Function procedures by using named arguments or optional arguments	*Writing and Calling* Sub *and* Function *Procedures Using Named Arguments or Optional Arguments*, page 201
Write and call Sub and Function procedures that require an array as an argument	*Writing and Calling* Sub *and* Function *Procedures Requiring an Array as an Argument*, page 211
Call procedures from outside a module	*Calling Procedures from Outside a Module*, page 214

Chapter 7: Creating and Using Class Modules

Objective...	Located Here...
Add properties to a class	*Adding a Property to a Class Module*, page 247

continues

teaches you how to use Visual Basic 5 to write ActiveX clients that use automation.

This chapter covers the following topics:

▶ Creating object references with the `Dim` statement

▶ Early binding versus late binding of ActiveX Servers

▶ Using the `CreateObject` statement

▶ Using the `GetObject` statement

Creating Object Variables with the `Dim` Statement

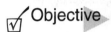 Objective ▶

The `Dim` (Dimension) statement is used to initialize variables. These variables can vary in type from integers to the default Visual Basic data type, Variant. In addition, you can define variables that represent object references. These variables are sometimes referred to as object variables.

A variable defined as an object variable cannot be used until it is pointed to an existing object or a new object. An object variable that does not have a reference to an object is considered to be initialized to `Nothing`. The term `Nothing` is used to denote a variable that does not have an object reference. Object variables can use the following methods:

```
Dim objMyVar as object
Dim objMyVar2 as Form
Dim objMyVar3 as TextBox
```

All three statements will create an object variable that can hold a reference to different object types. The key issue to note is that the variable is unusable until initialized. If you wish to test whether an object variable is not the pointing object, the `Is Nothing` statement can be used in an `If Then` statement. An example of this is as follows:

```
Dim objMyVar as Object
If objMyVar Is Nothing Then
     MsgBox "Object is unutilized"
End If
```

The next code snippets would fail because the objMyVar is not pointing to a valid object:

```
Dim objMyVar as Form
ObjMyVar.Show vbModal 'This statement will fail because the
                     'object variable does not point to an object.
```

To create valid object references, you must use the New keyword or use the CreateObject method. The New keyword's purpose is to allow the developer to create objects that the object variables can use. This keyword may be used as a part of the Dim statement. The New keyword will implicitly create an object and the object variable will refer to the newly created object if the object is createable.

The New keyword cannot be used to create intrinsic data types such as integer, long, strings, and so on. The New keyword cannot be used with the WithEvents keyword. An example of how to use the New keyword follows here:

```
Dim objMyForm as New Form1
```

If you have a Form object called Form1, the objMyForm variable will point to a new instance of Form1. As noted, the New keyword will create a new instance of an object and place a reference of the new object in the variable objMyForm.

Creating an Instance of an Object with the Set **Statement**

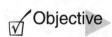
Objective

An alternative to using the New keyword with the Dim statement is to use the Set statement. The Set statement is used to change the object that an object variable is pointing to. Therefore a variable can be defined and initialized as follows:

```
Dim objMyForm as Object
Set objMyForm = New Form1
```

Before the Set statement can be used on a variable, it must first be dimensioned.Using the Set statement is a two-step process. The variable is checked to see if it already points to an object, in which case the object reference is destroyed. Next, the object is assigned to the variable. It is important to note that the variable cannot be used until it is initialized with the Set statement.

The New keyword can only be used to create objects whose libraries are referred to in your Visual Basic project. If a reference is not made to the object libraries that you wish to use, your application will not compile. To create a reference to the Object Library, follow these steps:

1. Choose the Project/References menu item.

2. Select the desired libraries from the References dialog box that appears (see Figure 11.1).

Figure 11.1

The References dialog box.

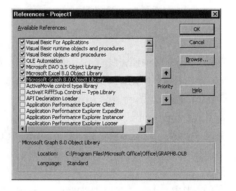

The References dialog box enables you to use different applications' objects that are needed in your application by using a reference to the application's Object Library. An object library is a file that contains information about the objects implemented in an application. The file can be a .tlb (Object Type Library File), a Dynamic Linked Library, an executable, or an ActiveX Control; the type depends on how the creator implemented the server application. After the library is incorporated into your Visual Basic application, the objects in the library are used like any native Visual Basic objects.

The Data Access Object (DAO) library is a commonly used Object Library. This library allows applications to connect to databases using the Jet Engine. With the Object Library reference, Visual Basic will provide syntax checking for methods and properties of the object implemented in your code.

Early Binding Versus Late Binding of ActiveX Servers

The process of binding allows Visual Basic to invoke and use the methods and properties of the object. Your application can use either early or late binding, or both. When you use an Object Library Reference in your applications, the objects used are referred to as early bound objects only if the variables are explicitly dimensioned. The use of early binding has significant performance advantages. At compile, for example, Visual Basic can tell what object a property and method belong to and can look it up in a table of IDs (DISPID's) or use a virtual table of addresses (vtable).

The early binding approach is faster when invoking methods and properties of objects than late biding. When late binding is used, Visual Basic does not know what methods and properties that an object supports, so it has to make extra function calls—which adds overhead—to resolve the object's methods and properties. The differences between late and early binding are derived from how the variables are declared. The following variable declarations show the differences between early and late binding:

```
Dim obj1 as new MyObject
Dim obj2 as Object
Set obj2 = new MyObject
```

Invoking methods and properties using the obj1 object variable is faster that using the obj2 object variable. The overhead of using late binding is quite significant and can take more than 50% of the total invocation time. The following section looks at using the CreateObject statement to create objects.

Using the CreateObject Function

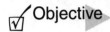
Objective

As seen earlier, you can create instances of objects by using the New keyword. In addition to the New keyword, you can use the CreateObject statement. The CreateObject function is used to create and return a reference to an ActiveX Server component. You can use this with late bound and early bound objects. The CreateObject function syntax is defined as follows:

```
Set ObjectVariable = CreateObject(ProgId)
```

The function will attempt to create an object of a specific type and return a reference. To specify the type of object desired, the ProgID must be passed to the CreateObject statement. The ProgID is a term that refers to a programmatic identifier (ProgID).

Applications that support automation must support at least one object type. This object is usually given a programmatic identifier (ProgID). The syntax for this programmatic identifier is as follows:

```
ApplicationName.ObjectType
```

Both the application name and object type are necessary to make the programmatic identifier (ProgID) complete. This ProgID is supplied as a string argument to the CreateObject statement. An example of this is as follows:

```
Set ObjMyObject = CreateObject("Excel.Application")
```

After an object is created, the programmer is free to use the variable like any other object variable. If you are using CreateObject to create object references, it is not necessary to use object library references in your project unless you intend to bind objects early, or have the Visual Basic compiler ensure that all of the properties and methods are valid. If object references are not used or if the variable is dimensioned as an Object, your objects will be late bound.

The CreateObject function will create a new instance of an object even if the object is already running in memory. To use a currently running instance, the GetObject method can be used. If the object is registered as a single-instance object, only one instance of the object will be running. All CreateObject calls that refer to the single-instance object will just get a pointer to the already running object.

Using the GetObject **Function**

An alternative to using the CreateObject function is to use the GetObject function. The GetObject function, like the CreateObject statement, is used to return an ActiveX Object reference. The syntax of the GetObject function is as follows:

```
Set ObjectVariable = GetObject([pathname] [, class])
```

The pathname is used to specify an ActiveX Document file that contains the objects that you need. The class parameter is used to specify the ProgID (programmatic Identifier) for the object reference desired.

If the server that created the document is running in memory, the document will be loaded and an object reference will be returned to your application. If the application is not running in memory, however, a runtime error will occur. In most cases, it is better to use the CreateObject statement to create object references to servers.

If specific objects within a document are needed, however, the GetObject function is more appropriate. This arises when one document contains multiple objects and you need to obtain a specific object. An example of extracting specific objects from a file is as follows:

```
Dim objWks As Workbook
Set objWks = GetObject(App.Path & "\Ex1104.xls")
```

A Workbook object will be returned from the GetObject statement. Some ActiveX Document servers allow client applications to extract a specific object from a document by using the ! (bang) operator. An example of this is as follows:

```
Dim objWs as SomeObject
Set objWs = GetObject(App.Path & "\MyServer.Doc!SomeObject1")
```

The GetObject statement can also return object references of already running objects. The class parameter is used to specify the ProgID of the desired object. An example of using the class parameter is as follows:

```
Dim objApp as Application
Set objApp = GetObject(,"Excel.Application")
```

An important note regarding the GetObject function is that it cannot be used to return references to objects created with Visual Basic.

Exercises

Exercise 11.1: Defining and Initializing Object Variables

In this exercise, you look at how to define object variables and assign them to objects by using the New keyword. You will create the following types of object variables:

▶ Define a variable called objMyObject of the type Object

▶ Use the New keyword to create a new Form object and assign it to the object variable

▶ Use the Set keyword to create a new Form object and assign it to the object variable

▶ Add and remove the Data Access Object (DAO) Library reference from your project

To perform these tasks, follow these steps:

1. Dim objVar as object. (The statement defines the variable that will hold the object reference.)

2. Dim objVar as New Form1. (This defines the variable and assigns a new object instance to the variable.)

3. Dim objVar as Form 1: Set objVar = New Form1. (Use the Set keyword to assign an instance of the object to the variable after declaring the variable.)

4. To add the Data Access Object (DAO) Library reference to your project, you must choose the Project/References menu item. This menu opens the References dialog box, which enables you to add and remove the Object Library reference.

Exercise 11.2: Late Bound Variables Versus Early Bound Variables

In this exercise, you look at using an early and a late bound object variable. You can find the solution to this exercise in the Ex1102 directory on the CD that accompanies this book. The tasks to be performed are as follows:

▶ Use early binding to create and use Excel Application Objects

▶ Use late binding to create and use Excel Application Objects

To use early binding in your applications, a reference to the Object Library of the desired application is needed in your Visual Basic project. The Object Library to be used in this exercise is Microsoft Excel 8.0 Object Library. The same exercise can be performed with other Object Libraries using different Objects. To solve item 1, follow these steps:

1. Create a new Visual Basic application of project type Standard Exe.

2. Add the Microsoft Excel 8.0 Object Library reference to the project.

3. Add a button (btn1) to the default form (called Form1). In the form, add the click event code for the button for creating an early bound object as follows (note that the variable objEarly is defined as a module-level variable):

```
Dim objEarly As Application
Private Sub btn1_Click()
'Create a new Application Object
Set objEarly = New Application

'Set the Object to be Visible
objEarly.Visible = True

'Create A new Workbook
objEarly.Workbooks.Add

'Send some data
objEarly.ActiveCell = "Hello World"
End Sub
```

With the early binding approach, Visual Basic knows exactly what methods and properties an object supports because the object is defined as an Application object. With late binding, Visual Basic does not know what methods and properties an object supports;

continues

this information must be resolved using a slower process. The `btn2` `click` event demonstrates the use of late binding in creating objects. The code for this event is shown as follows:

```
Dim objLate As Object
Private Sub btn2_Click()
'Create a new Application Object
Set objLate = New Application
'Show the Excel Window
objLate.Visible = True
'Create A new Workbook
objLate.Workbooks.Add

objLate.ActiveCell = "Hello World 2"
End Sub
```

Notice that with late binding the object is defined as an `Object` data type. This allows the variable to have a pointer to any object type. With early binding, however, the object variable is defined as an `Application` object.

Therefore the only types of objects that the object variable can refer to are `Application` objects. The use of early binding allows Visual Basic to perform data type, parameter, and syntax checking on methods and properties at compile time. With late binding, Visual Basic does not provide any syntax checking on methods and properties until runtime.

Exercise 11.3: Creating Objects with the CreateObject Function

In this exercise, you look at creating objects with the `CreateObject` function. The tasks to be performed are as follows:

▶ Use `CreateObject` function to create early bound objects

▶ Use `CreateObject` function to create late bound objects

The key to create early or late bound objects is with the definition of the object variable. You can find the solution for this exercise in the Ex1102 directory on the accompanying CD. To create early bound objects with the `CreateObject` function, follow these steps:

1. Add an Object Library reference to the desired library reference using the References dialog box.

2. Define an object variable of the desired type such as `Application`, `Workbook`, and so on. For example:

```
Dim objVar as Application
```

> **Note** Keep in mind that the object types will vary based on the type of Object Library you are using.

3. Use the `CreateObject` statement to create and return the object reference. For example:

```
Set objVar = CreateObject("Excel.Application")
```

To create a late bound object reference, no Object Library reference is needed. The late bound object reference can be created by following these steps:

1. Define the object variable as `Object` variable type. This can be done as follows:

```
Dim objVar as Object
```

2. Use the `CreateObject` statement to create and return the object reference as follows:

```
Set objVar = CreateObject("Excel.Application")
```

Exercise 11.4: Obtaining Object References with the `GetObject` Function

In this exercise, you look at obtaining object references by using the `GetObject` function. The tasks to be completed are as follows:

▶ Obtain an Excel 8.0 `Workbook` object reference by using the `GetObject` function, using the file Ex1104.xls

▶ Create an Excel `ChartObject` reference

continues

▶ Copy the chart to the Clipboard and paste it to an image control

The solution to this exercise is provided in the Ex1104 directory. Figure 11.2 shows what happens when the application is executed.

Figure 11.2

The sample application solution.

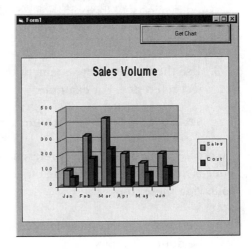

To add an Object Library reference to your project, follow these steps:

1. Select the Project/References menu. This will present the Object Library References dialog box. At this point, you can add or remove Object Library references. For the following code to compile, the reference to the Microsoft Excel 8.0 Object Library must still be included.

2. To open a file with the GetObject function, the following code can be used (assume that the variable has already been defined):

```
Set objVar = GetObject(App.Path & "\Ex1104.xls")
```

3. After the object is returned, a ChartObject can be obtained from it by using the ChartObjects collection.

4. The Chart's graphic information can be copied using the Copy method of the ChartObject.

The code that creates the object variable and copies the ChartObject's image to the image control is as follows:

```
Private Sub btn3_Click()
Dim objWks As Workbook
Dim objWkSheet As Worksheet
Dim objChart As ChartObject

'Get the XL Workbook from the file
Set objWks = GetObject(App.Path & "\Ex1104.xls")

'Get The first worksheet object
Set objWkSheet = objWks.Worksheets(1)

'Get the first chart object
Set objChart = objWkSheet.ChartObjects(1)

'Check if Chart Object is valid
If objChart Is Nothing Then
    MsgBox "No ActiveChart Found"
Else
    'Copy Image to ClipBoard
    objChart.Copy

    'Past the Image Control
    img.Picture = Clipboard.GetData()
End If

End Sub
```

Review Questions

1. Select the types of files that can contain Object Library references?

    A. (.EXE) Executables

    B. (.FRM) Visual Basic files

    C. (.DLL) Dynamic Linked Libraries

    D. (.BAT) Bat files

2. Which of the following statements will create a new `WordDoc` object?

    A. `Dim objMyVar = New WordDoc`

    B. `Dim objMyVar as New WordDoc`

    C. `Dim objMyVar as Object`
       `Set objMyVar = New WordDoc`

    D. `Dim objMyVar as Object`
       `Set objMyVar = GetObject("App.WordDoc")`

    E. All these statements

3. The reference to Object Libraries provides Visual Basic with which of the following information?

    A. It is not used.

    B. A list of objects.

    C. Object types supported by the ActiveX Server and their properties and methods.

    D. Functions for creating object libraries.

4. Which of the following statements will define an object variable and return a valid object reference of type `Application`?

A. Dim x as Object

   Set x = New Application

B. Dim x as new Application

C. Dim x as Application

D. Dim X as Object

   Let X = new Application

5. Assume that you have a COM server with an application name of MyApp and an object called Spreadsheet. Which one of the following statements enables you to access that object?

A. Dim objX as new CreateObject("SpreadSheet")

B. Dim objX as Object

   Set objX = CreateObject("MyApp")

C. Dim objX as Object

   Set objX = CreateObject("MyApp.SpreadSheet")

D. Dim objX as Object

   Set objX = CreateObject("SpreadSheet")

6. If the following code is executed and the server is not running in memory, what occurs?

```
Set objInfo = GetObject("Word.Application")
```

A. The application is loaded into memory and an object reference is returned.

B. A runtime error occurs.

C. The application will not be loaded because the path is not correct.

Answers to Review Questions

1. A and C. Type library references are usually found in type library files, Executables, or Dynamically Linked Libraries. For more information, see the section titled "Early Binding Versus Late Binding of ActiveX Servers."

2. A and C. Both A and C assume that there is a type library reference in the project. If the type library reference is absent, the application will not compile. The other answers would not work under any circumstance. For more information, see the section titled "Early Binding Versus Late Binding of ActiveX Servers."

3. C. The Type Library will provide the information needed for early binding such as the object types, properties, and methods supported. For more information, see the section titled, "Creating Object Variables with the Dim Statement."

4. A and B. Answer A uses late binding to create the object. Answer B uses early binding to create the object. For more information, see the section titled "Early Binding Versus Late Binding of ActiveX Servers."

5. C. The CreateObject statement requires a ProgID that is made up of the application name and the object name. For more information, see the section titled "Using the CreateObject Function."

6. B. A runtime errors occurs because the GetObject requires that a instance of the requested ActiveX Server is running on the machine. For more information, see the section titled "Using the GetObject Function."

Answers to Test Yourself Questions at Beginning of Chapter

1. A variable of the type Application can be defined as follows:

```
Dim objApp as Application
```

If necessary, you can define and create the object as follows:

```
Dim objApp as new Application
```

See "Creating Object Variables with the Dim Statement."

2. Two general methods can be used to define and create the application object. These methods are as follows

```
Dim x as Object
Set x = New Application
```

or

```
Dim x as new Application
```

If the Application is a component in an ActiveX Library, then a programmatic string may also be used to create the object as follows:

```
Dim x as Object
Set x = CreateObject("ApplicationLibrary.Application")
```

if the Application object is located in the ApplicationLibrary application.

See "Creating an Instance of an Object with the Set Statement."

3. The CreateObject statement is used to create the instance of the object. This is done as follows

```
Dim objX as Object
Set objX = CreateObject("MyApp.SpreadSheet")
```

See "Using the CreateObject Function."

4. A runtime error will occur because an instance of the object is not running in memory. See "Using the GetObject Function."

Chapter 12

Creating an Automation Server That Exposes Objects, Properties, Methods, and Events

This chapter helps you prepare for the exam by covering the following objectives:

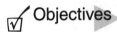 **Objectives**

- ▶ Define properties for objects using property procedures

- ▶ Create a method that displays a form

- ▶ Create a multithreaded component

- ▶ Use the App object to control the server behavior

- ▶ Call an object server asynchronously by using a callback mechanism

- ▶ Create, use, and respond to events

Test Yourself! Before reading this chapter, test yourself to determine how much study time you will need to devote to this section.

1. The text displayed in the Request Pending dialog box can be set using which statement?

2. When implementing automation components, which types of executables can be used?

3. Your programmers are complaining that it takes too long to execute methods of Automation server. You have already determined that the application is already tuned. What can be done to the Automation server to speed up the calls between client and server?

4. What is the purpose of the `WithEvents` keyword? Define a variable that uses it?

Answers are located at the end of the chapter...

In Chapter 11, "Building Microsoft ActiveX Clients," you looked at clients that used Automation servers. This chapter examines creating Automation servers. An Automation server provides its services via COM (Component Object Model) interfaces. In Visual Basic, COM interfaces are hidden from the developer, and the developer will implement his/her Automation server's services via class files. For more information on class files, see Chapter 7, "Creating and Using Class Modules."

Instances of the class modules are passed to the client as object references. The Automation server's object provides its services by using the following techniques:

▶ **Properties**. These are attributes that belong to a given object. A car object can have a `Property` attribute of color, for example. The color property when read would return the current color of the car. In many cases, the value of a property is *modifiable*. A modifiable property is also called a *read/write* property. If needed, the developer can implement read-only properties. It would be better to implement the manufacturer property of a car object as a read-only property because the manufacturer of car once assigned is not changeable.

▶ **Methods**. These are procedures that belong to a given object and perform a task with relation to an object. A *car* object could have a method called *start*, for example, that when executed would start the car. Methods can be either functions or subroutines.

▶ **Events**. User-defined events can be defined for a given object. The firing of events occurs when a specific condition has elapsed. The object that raises (fires) the event is called the *event source*. The objects that implement an event are *event sinks*. When the event source raises the event, the event is fired on all event sink objects that support that event.

This chapter covers the following topics:

- ▶ Creating the Automation server project

- ▶ Adding or modifying classes to the Automation server

- ▶ Adding properties to the Automation server

- ▶ Adding methods to the Automation server

- ▶ Creating a multithreaded Automation server

- ▶ Adding events to the Automation Server

- ▶ Using the `App` object's properties to control server behavior

- ▶ Implementing and using `callback` methods

Creating the Automation Server Project

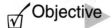 **Objective**

An Automation server can be created from an existing or new project. However, creating an Automation component from a new project is easier. To create a new project that enables you to provide automation services, follow these steps:

1. Choose the File/New Project menu option. The New Project dialog box appears as shown in Figure 12.1

Figure 12.1

The New Project dialog box.

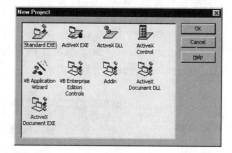

2. Select the ActiveX EXE or ActiveX DLL icon.

You can create the following two types of Automation servers with Visual Basic:

▶ **ActiveX EXE.** A component that can be executed as a standalone application but also provides its services as an Automation server

▶ **ActiveX DLL.** A component that executes as a dynamic link library and cannot be executed as a standalone application

Automation servers that are implemented as Executables will run in their own address space when used by client applications. This means that the calls by client applications are marshalled across the address space to the Automation server. The cost of marshalling can be quite significant in terms of invocation performance.

An alternative is to implement the Automation servers as an ActiveX DLL. When clients access ActiveX DLL, the component will execute in the same address space as the client. This means that the calls made by the client to the Automation server are *not* marshalled across an address space. The performance benefit to this can be significant.

An alternative to creating a new project is to modify an existing one. To change an existing project to an Automation server project, follow these steps:

1. Choose the Project Properties menu items. This menu item opens a dialog box called Project Properties. Figure 12.2 shows this dialog box.

Figure 12.2

The Project Properties dialog box.

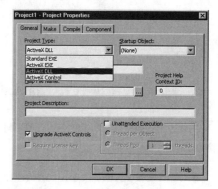

2. On the General tab of the Project Properties dialog box, you can change the project type to an Automation server component. To do this, select either ActiveX EXE or ActiveX.

Adding or Modifying Classes to the Automation Server

After your project has been modified to support automation, you can add or modify class modules; these provide your automation services. The class module has an instancing property that can be set to support automation services. This property can be set only at design time and can have the following values:

- ► 1 – (Private)   This is the default setting. Client applications cannot access the objects of this class. Objects based on this class with this setting can be accessed only from within the automation component.

- ► 2 – (PublicNotCreatable)   Client applications can use the object of this class only if the Automation server creates it. The CreateObject function or New operator cannot be used to create objects from this class.

- ► 3 - (SingleUse)   Client applications can create objects from the class. However, all objects of this class will start a new instance of the Automation server. This option is not allowed in ActiveX DLL projects.

- ► 4 – (GlobalSingleUse)   This is similar to single use; however, the methods and properties of objects of this class are invoked as if they were global functions. This option is not allowed in ActiveX DLL projects.

- ► 5 – (MultiUse)   This allows client applications to create objects from the class. One instance of the Automation server can provide the objects for multiple clients.

- ► 6 – (GlobalMultiUse)   This is similar to MultiUse; however, the methods and properties of the class can be invoked like global procedures.

After setting the class module's instancing property, the methods and properties can be created or modified to make them available to ActiveX clients.

Adding Properties to the Classes of the Automation Server

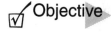 Objective

Properties can be added to a class either by using Property procedures or by using public variables. This chapter first looks at creating properties with public variables. Variables must be declared as public variables to make them directly accessible by automation clients. This is demonstrated by the following variable declarations:

```
Public First_Name as String
Public Last_Name as String
Private Age as Long
```

The variables `First_Name` and `Last_Name` would be accessible by ActiveX clients; however, the `Age` variable would not be accessible. When the ActiveX client changes a public variable, the Visual Basic Automation server is notified that the property has changed.

Therefore, if notification of changes to properties is needed, a `Property` procedure can be used. The `Property` procedure is one of the following three types:

▶ Property Get

▶ Property Let

▶ Property Set

Property Get

The `Property Get` procedure is used to return the current value of a property. This procedure is fired when a client reads a value from a property. When a client reads the `First_Name` property, for example, and if a `Property Get` procedure exists for the `First_Name` property, it would be fired and return the current value. The `Property Get` procedure behaves like a traditional Visual Basic function. The syntax of the `Property Get` procedure is as follows:

```
[Public ¦ Private ¦ Friend] [Static] Property Get name
➥[(arglist)] [As type]
```

An example of implementing the `First_Name Get Property` procedure is as follows:

```
Public Property Get First_Name () as String
'return the first name
First_Name = strFirstName
End Property
```

The `First_Name` `Property` `Get` procedure would be executed when a client executes code that reads the `First_Name` property. An example of this is as follows:

```
Dim strValue as string
strValue = MyObject.First_Name
```

If `MyObject` supports the `First_Name` property, the property procedure would be executed.

Property Let

The opposite of a `Property` `Get` is the `Property` `Let`. This property procedure is called when the property is assigned a value. The `Property` `Let` procedure behaves like a traditional Visual Basic subroutine. The syntax of the `Property` `Let` procedure is shown as follows:

```
[Public | Private | Friend] [Static] Property Let name
➡([arglist,] value)
```

When a client assigns a value to the property, the `Property` `Let` procedure fires and the value is supplied as a parameter. To implement the `First_Name` `Property` `Let` procedure, you can use the following code:

```
Public Property Let First_Name(sName as String)
'store the property value in a module level variable
strName = sName
End Property
```

When a client assigns a value to a property, the procedure is fired and the new value is passed as the `sName` parameter. An example of client code assigning a variable is as follows:

```
MyObject.First_Name = "John"
```

The value of the `sName` parameter of the `First_Name` `Property` `Let` procedure will be "John" when the client code is executed.

Property Set

In many cases, properties need to assign an object reference. When this need occurs, the `Property Set` procedure is used to help clients to assign an object to a property. The syntax of the `Property Set` procedure is shown as follows:

```
[Public ¦ Private ¦ Friend] [Static] Property Set name
➥([arglist,] reference)
```

The behavior of the `Property Set` statement is very much like the `Property Let` statement. A class module can provide an implementation of this procedure if it accepts to receive objects from its clients. A class could accept the assignment of color objects from its clients, for example. An example of implementing such a `Property` procedure is as follows:

```
Public Property Set Color(objColor As Object)
'Store a reference of the color object received from  client
m_objColor = objColor
End Property
```

The client code that calls the `Property` procedure is as follows:

```
MyObject.Color = objMyColorObject
```

`Property` procedures are important because they will notify the automation component when the property has changed in value. In addition, the creator of the automation component can create read-only properties by implementing the `Property Get` and not the `Property Let` procedure. If desired, the programmer can create write-only properties by implementing the `Property Let` procedure only.

Adding Methods to the Automation Server

Methods are functions or subroutines that allow clients to instruct the Automation server to perform variable tasks. Any function or subroutine can become a method by declaring it as `Public`. The following are examples of this:

```
Public Function About() As String
End Function
```

```
Public Sub Load()
End Sub
```

Note that if the procedure is not declared as `Public`, it is assumed that it is a public procedure by Visual Basic. If you want to have procedures that are accessible only by the other procedures within the same class, the procedures must be declared as `Private`. In many cases, you may need to have procedures that are accessible via other classes with the Automation server but not by client code. In this case, the procedure is to be declared as `Friend`. An example of this is as follows:

```
Friend Function X() as long
```

Creating a Multithreaded Automation Server

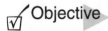✓ Objective

To create multithreaded Automation servers, you must choose the Unattended Execution option. If forms are contained in the Automation server, the Unattended Execution option is not available. You can find the Unattended Execution option on the Project Properties tab.

If Unattended Execution is selected, the Automation server can execute with user interaction. These types of Automation servers cannot have any user interface elements. If there is information that needed attending, it is usually placed in the Event Log.

The Thread Per Object option denotes that each instance of a class defined as `MultiUse` will be created on a new thread. Each thread created will have its own global variables and objects.

The Thread Pool option denotes that all classes defined as `MultiUse` will be created on one of the threads in the thread pool. Each thread has its own set of global variables; however, multiple objects can live on the same thread. The Number of Threads setting defines the maximum number of threads needed for the thread pool. When the maximum is reached, new instances of the `MultiUse` object will be assigned to existing threads.

Adding Events to the Automation Server

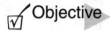 Objective

Events can be added to your Automation server by using the WithEvents keyword. The WithEvents keyword is new with Visual Basic 5. By using events, a client application can be notified when a server task is completed. To define an object that has events, the client uses the WithEvents keyword. Defining a child object that supports events, for example, is done as follows:

```
Private WithEvents m_objectChild As clsChild
```

The statement tells the Visual Basic runtime that the object supports events. The server component (in this case an Automation server) can raise the event when at a certain predetermined point. This would cause an event to be fired in the client application. There are some limitations on the use of events, which are listed as follows:

- ▶ The WithEvents variable cannot be defined as a generic object variable. Hence, you cannot declare the variable as a type object.

- ▶ The WithEvents variable cannot be declared as New. The event object must be created with the Set and New statement or CreateObject statement.

- ▶ The WithEvents variable cannot be declared in a standard code module. The variable can be used only in class, form, or other types of modules that provide class definition.

- ▶ You cannot define arrays of WithEvents variables.

- ▶ WithEvents variables must be module-level variables.

The first step in using events is to define the events in the Automation server's class modules that will fire the events to the client. The Event keyword is used to define the event that will be fired. An example of using the Event keyword is as follows:

```
Public Event BornOn(ByVal dtDateOfBirth As Date)
```

This defines an event called BornOn, which receives one input parameter. This statement does not define the function that will receive the event; it merely declares that the module can fire an event called BornOn.

The next important step is to write the code that will fire the event to the client when necessary. This is accomplished by using the RaiseEvent statement. The syntax for the RaiseEvent statement is as follows:

```
RaiseEvent eventname [(argumentlist)]
```

The eventname is the name of the event to be raised. The argument list will vary based on how the event is defined. An example of this is shown as follows:

```
RaiseEvent BornOn(Now)
```

After the server executes this statement, the client receives this event. The client has to define objects capable of handling the event by using the WithEvents keyword. In addition, the client has to write the event handler that will process the event. An example of this is shown as follows:

```
'Capture the Event
Public Sub m_objectChild_BornOn(ByVal dtDateOfBirth As Date)
MsgBox "Event received on child's date of birth " & dtDateOfBirth
End Sub
```

One of the key issues to note with using events is that they cannot return a value like a function. In addition, events cannot have named arguments, optional arguments, or use ParamArray arguments.

Using the App Object's Properties to Control the Server's Behavior

☑Objective ▶ The App object is a global object that your Visual Basic code can use. The App object has properties that can be used to modify the behavior of an Automation server. These properties are listed as follows:

▶ OLERequestPendingMsgText   Used to set or return the text of the "pending" dialog box displayed when mouse or keyboard input is sent when an automation request is pending.

▶ OLERequestPendingMsgTitle   Used to set or return the property of the text of the "pending" dialog box during an automation request if mouse or keyboard input is sent to the client.

▶ OLERequestPendingTimeout   Returns or sets the number of milliseconds that must pass before the Request Pending dialog box is fired by the mouse or keyboard input when the automation request is pending.

▶ OLEServerBusyMsgText   Sets or returns the text displayed in the default busy dialog box if an ActiveX component rejects the client's request. The OLEServerBusyMsgTitle property is used to set the title of the busy dialog box.

▶ OLEServerBusyMsgTitle   Used to set or read the title for the dialog box displayed when the server is busy and it rejects a client request.

▶ OLEServerBusyTimeout   Used to denote the number of milliseconds that an automation request will continue to be tried before a Busy dialog box is shown.

▶ OLEServerBusyRaiseError   Can be set to True or False and is used to denote that a rejection of a client request will result in a runtime error. If the property is set to True, an error is raised after OLEServerBusyTimeout milliseconds. If the property is set to False, the Server Busy dialog box appears.

Implementing and Using Callback Methods

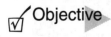 Callback methods can be used to provide notification to clients when a server task is completed. The same effect can usually be achieved with the use of events. The major difference between the

event and the callback approach has to do with the use of sink objects from the client.

When implementing an event, the client declares variables that support the event and also writes the routine that supports the event when it is fired from the server. While in a callback, the client supplies an object to the server, which the server uses to notify the client when it has completed processing.

To implement a callback, follow these steps:

▶ Define a class to manage the notification.

▶ Define a server interface that is used by the client when setting up the callback between client and server.

▶ Write server code to handle the callback object supplied by the client.

▶ Write the client code to provide the callback implementation.

The class that manages the notification is usually called a *manager class*. The class can carry out the work or use worker classes to carry out the work. This class usually provides a method that allows a client to pass the object to the server. The ServerSink.vbp sample application, located in the Ex12.4 directory, provides a class called clsMain that receives notification from clients. The code is listed here:

```
Option Explicit
'Maintain a list of collection
Dim m_colSinks As New Collection
Sub AddSink(objSink As INotify)
'This function is used to change the sink

If Not objSink Is Nothing Then
    'Add the sink to the collection of sinks that are aval.
    m_colSinks.Add objSink
End If
End Sub

Sub Process()
```

```
Dim icount As Long

'Notify client that processing
'has started
Call UpdateSinks("Started")

For icount = 1 To 1000

    'Update the sink
    Call UpdateSinks("Processing ... " & icount)
    DoEvents
Next

'Update the sink
Call UpdateSinks("Ended")

End Sub

Private Sub UpdateSinks(strText As String)

Dim objSink As INotify

'Notify each sink item
For Each objSink In m_colSinks
    Call objSink.Status(strText)
Next

End Sub
```

The AddSink function is used to add the sink object to the server. The client must supply an object that implements the INotify interface. The INotify interface is just a class defined in the server that has no implementation. The use of the "I" prefix is just used as a coding convention to denote interfaces. The INotify class in the server is shown as follows:

```
Option Explicit

Public Sub Status(strStatus As String)
End Sub
```

Notice that the Status subroutine has no code. The client will provide an implementation of the function. The client application is located in the same directory but in a different project called ClientSink.vbp. The application has a class called clsClientSink. The instancing property of clsClientSink is set to PublicNotCreatable. This setting allows the object of this class to be passed to other servers. The code for the class is shown as follows:

```
Option Explicit
Implements INotify

Dim lstInfo As ListBox

'Internal function used to assign
'a list box
Friend Property Set ListControl(lst As Control)
Set lstInfo = lst
End Property

'Implementation of the
'INotify's Status function
Private Sub INotify_Status(strStatus As String)
    'Process the notification
    lstInfo.AddItem strStatus
    DoEvents
End Sub
```

The Implements keyword is used to tell Visual Basic that the class will implement the methods and properties as defined by the interface. The class must provide an implementation of all the properties and methods that an interface has. To write the implementation of a method or property, the procedure must be written using the following syntax:

```
InterfaceName_MethodOrPropertyName
```

Therefore the implementation of the Status function is as follows:

```
Private Sub INotify_Status(strStatus As String)
```

The Status subroutine will be fired when the server application invokes the Status method on the object that supports the INotify interface.

Exercises

Exercise 12.1: Creating Properties with Public Variables

In this exercise, you will look at how to define properties with
`Public` variables. Answer the following questions:

1. Define a property called `First_Name` of the type `String`.

2. Define a property called `Last_Name` of the type `String`.

3. Define a property called `DateOfBirth` of the type `Date`.

The solutions are as follows:

1. `Public First_Name As String`

2. `Public Last_Name As String`

3. `Public DateOfBirth As Date`

Exercise 12.2: Creating Properties with Property Procedures

In this exercise, you will look at how to define properties using
property procedures. Answer the following questions:

1. Define a read/write property procedure called `First_Name` of
   the type `String`.

2. Define a read-only property called `Last_Name` of the type
   `String`.

3. Define a write-only property called `DateOfBirth` of the type
   `Date`.

4. Define a property called `Dependents` that will accept and
   return objects.

The solutions are as follows:

1. Define a module variable in the class that will store the
   `First_Name` property value:

   ```
   'Store the first name in this private
   variable
   ```

```
Dim m_strFirstName As String
'Property procedures to access the first
➥name
'variable
Public Property Get First_Name() As
➥String
    'Return the first name property
    First_Name = m_strFirstName
End Property

Public Property Let First_Name(sName As
➥String)
    'Change the first name property
    m_strFirstName = sName
End Property
```

2. To create a read-only property, a module variable is needed. In this exercise, the name will be m_strLastName:

```
Dim m_strLastName As String
Public Property Get Last_Name() As String
    Last_Name = m_strLastName
End Property
```

3. A module variable called m_dtDateOfBirth must be created to store the DateOfBirth information:

```
Dim m_dtDateOfBirth As Date
Public Property Let DateOfBirth(vNewValue
➥As Date)
    m_dtDateOfBirth = vNewValue
End Property
```

4. The solution is as follows:

```
Dim m_objDependents As Object
Public Property Get Dependents() As
➥Object
    Dependents = m_objDependents
End Property

Public Property Set Dependents(vNewValue
➥As Object)
```

continues

```
        m_objDependents = vNewValue
    End Property
```

You can find the complete solution to the exercise in the Ex12.2 directory. The solution is compromised of two projects. The names of the projects are client.vbp and server.vbp. The client.vbp source code is shown in its entirety as follows:

```
Option Explicit

'Object variable for the server application
Dim m_objPerson As Object


Private Sub Command1_Click()
    'Create the server
    Set m_objPerson = CreateObject("Server1.clsperson")
End Sub

Private Sub Command2_Click()

    'Set the First Name field
    m_objPerson.first_name = txtFirstName.Text

    'Retrieve the last name field
    txtLastName.Text = m_objPerson.last_name

End Sub

Private Sub Command3_Click()
    'Set the date of birth date
    m_objPerson.DateOfBirth = txtDOB.Text
End Sub
```

The server source code is located in the server.vbp project in the class module called clsperson. The code is shown as follows:

```
Dim m_strFirstName As String
Dim m_strLastName As String
Dim m_dtDateOfBirth As Date
Dim m_objDependents As Object
```

```
'Property procedures to access the first name
'variable
Public Property Get First_Name() As String
    'Return the first name property
    First_Name = m_strFirstName
End Property

Public Property Let First_Name(sName As String)
    'Change the first name property
    m_strFirstName = sName
End Property


Public Property Get Last_Name() As String
    m_strLastName = "Hello " & m_strFirstName
    Last_Name = m_strLastName
End Property


Public Property Let DateOfBirth(vNewValue As Date)
    m_dtDateOfBirth = vNewValue
End Property

Public Property Get Dependents() As Object
    Dependents = m_objDependents
End Property

Public Property Set Dependents(vNewValue As Object)
    m_objDependents = vNewValue
End Property
```

Exercise 12.3:   Creating Methods

In this exercise, you will look at how to create methods. Answer
the following questions:

1. Define a method that can be accessed by automation clients.

2. Define a method that can be accessed only by the code of
   the class to which the method belongs.

continues

3. Define a method that can be accessed by code in the entire automation application, but not its clients.

The solutions to this exercise are as follows:

1. `Public Function MyMethod() as Boolean`

2. `Private Sub InternalMethod()`

3. `Friend Sub LocalMethod2()` or
   `Friend Function LoadFunction() as string`

A method provided by an Automation server can perform just about any task that the developer wants. There are some issues, however, when using a GUI (Graphical User Interface) object. When displaying forms, it is preferable to create a new instance of the form and not use the default runtime instance. The new instance may be necessary because the runtime instance may have been used on a previous class. An example of a method displaying a runtime form is shown as follows:

```
Public Sub ShowAbout()
Dim objForm as Form1
Set objForm1 = New Form1
ObjForm1.Show vbModal
End Sub
```

This code is located in the project file called ServerMethod.vbp.

Exercise 12.4:   Creating Events

In this exercise, you will look at how to create events. Answer the following questions:

1. Create a `Public` class and define an event called `BornOn` with one parameter of data type `Date`.

2. Write a routine called `Init` in your new class that will raise an event.

3. Create a client application that will perform the following tasks:

Define and create an object that supports the BornOn object.

Write a procedure that will handle the event for the object.

Write a procedure that will create the new object and call the Init function of the object.

You can find the solution to this exercise in the ServerEvent.vbp file and in Ex1202 directory. The relevant code snippets are also listed here:

1. The Event is declared as follows:

```
Public Event BornOn(ByVal dtDateOfBirth
➥As Date)
```

2. The Init subroutine is as follows:

```
Public Sub Init()

Dim icount As Long
Dim frm1 As New frmProgress

'Show the Window
frm1.Show

'Update the Progress bar
For icount = 0 To 1000

    frm1.pb1.Value = Int(icount / 10)

Next
'Raise the event
RaiseEvent BornOn(Now)
```

continues

Exercise 12.4: Continued

```
'Destory the window
Unload frm1
Set frm1 = Nothing


End Sub
```

3. The client code is as follows:

```
Private WithEvents m_objectChild As
➥clsChild
Private Sub cmdEvents_Click()
'Create a new Child object
Set m_objectChild = New clsChild

'Call the Init Function
m_objectChild.Init

End Sub

'Capture the Event
Public Sub m_objectChild_BornOn(ByVal
➥dtDateOfBirth As Date)

MsgBox "Event received on child's date of
➥birth " & dtDateOfBirth


End Sub
```

Exercise 12.5: Modify Automation Server's Property with the App Object

In this exercise, you will look at how to use the App object to modify the behavior of automation components. Answer the following questions:

1. Set the Text of the Automation Busy dialog box to "Still Processing" and the Title to "MyApp".

2. Set the Request Pending Timeout value to 30 seconds.

The solutions for this exercise are as follows:

1. The solution is as follows:

```
App.OLEServerBusyMsgText = "Still
➥Processing .."
App.OLEServerBusyMsgTitle = "MyApp"
```

2. The solution is as follows:

```
App.OLERequestPendingTimeout  = 30000
```

Exercise 13.6: Create a Callback Mechanism Between Client and Server

In this exercise, you will look at how to create a callback mechanism between client and servers. Complete the following steps:

1. Create an ActiveX project with an interface defined as INotify and a function defined as follows:

```
Sub Status(strStatus as string)
```

2. Create a PublicCreatable class module called clsMain and a function called Process in the ActiveX project that will accept the callback from the client.

3. Create an ActiveX client project that will create an instance of the clsMain and invoke the Process function.

4. Create a class that implements the INotify interface and provides an implementation of the Status function.

You can find the solutions to this exercise in the Ex12.4 directory in two project files: ServerSink.vbp and ClientSink.vbp.

Review Questions

1. Which of the following statements will declare a method correctly?

   A. `Public Function GetCars() as Object`

   B. `Private Function GetCars() as Object`

   C. `Friend Function GetCars() as Object`

   D. `Function GetCars() as Object`

   E. Methods cannot be created in Visual Basic 5.

2. You have an ActiveX Automation server that displays forms. What must be done to have the application run unattended and support multiple threads?

   A. You cannot have unattended Automation servers.

   B. There is nothing that must be done.

   C. Remove the forms and code that refers to forms. Then select the Unattended Execution option.

   D. Add an unattended control to the project.

3. What does the Thread Per Object option provide for an application?

   A. This option is not available in the current release of Visual Basic.

   B. Each `SingleUse` class will get its own thread.

   C. Each `MultiUse` class will get its own thread.

   D. Multiple objects will be in a thread as defined by the object count.

4. You have an `Application` class and a `Workspace` class. The users of your Automation server must be able to create the `Application` but not the `Workspace` class. The only way the user should be able to use the `Workspace` class is through

the use of a function of the `Application` class. How do you achieve this goal?

   A. Define the `Application` class as `MultiUse` and the `Workspace` class as `Private` and return the object via a function of the `Application` class.

   B. Define the `Application` class as `MultiUse` and the `Workspace` class as `GlobalMultiUse`.

   C. Define the `Application` class as `SingleUse` and the `Workspace` class as `GlobalSingleUse`.

   D. Define the `Application` class as `MultiUse` and the `Workspace` class as `PublicNotCreatable`.

   E. Define the `Application` class as `PublicNotCreatable` and the `Workspace` class as `MultiUse`.

   F. This cannot be done in Visual Basic.

5. Which of the following statements will create a read-only property?

   A.
```
Public FirstName as String
```

   B.
```
Property Get FirstName() as string
    ...
End Property
Property Let FirstName(strLast as string)
    ...
End Property
```

   C.
```
Property Get FirstName() as string
    ...
End Property
Property Set FirstName(strLast as string)
    ...
End Property
```

D. `Property Get FirstName() as object`

    `...`

    `End Property`

    `Property Let FirstName(strLast as object)`

    `...`

    `End Property`

E. `Property Get FirstName() as string`

    `...`

    `End Property`

F. `Public ReadOnly FirstName as string`

G. `Friend FirstName as String`

6. Which of the following will correctly set the Request Pending dialog box to "Please Wait Processing"?

    A. `App.OleRequestPendingMsg = "Please Wait`
        `➥Processing"`

    B. `Application.OleRequestPendingMsg = "Please Wait`
        `➥Processing"`

    C. `Set OleRequestPendingMsg = "Please Wait`
        `➥Processing"`

    D. The Request Pending dialog box cannot be changed.

7. Which of the following statements is true about automation components?

    A. They can be implemented only as DLLs.

    B. They can be implemented only as executables.

    C. They are neither executables nor DLLs.

    D. They can be either executables or DLLs.

8. Your programmers are complaining that it takes too long to execute methods of Automation server. You have already determined that the application is already tuned. What can be done to the Automation server to speed up the calls between client and server?

   A. Nothing can be done.

   B. Implement the Automation server as a DLL and run it locally.

   C. Implement the Automation server as an executable and run it locally.

   D. Implement the Automation server as a DLL and run it on a different machine.

9. Which of the following variable definitions using the `WithEvents` keyword is correct?

   A. `Private WithEvents m_obj as object`

   B. `Private WithEvents m_obj as TextBox`

   C. `Private WithEvents m_obj as Variant`

   D. `Private WithEvents m_obj as New TextBox`

10. Which of the following statements is true about the `Implements` keyword?

   A. It does not exist.

   B. It is used to define a C++ interface.

   C. It denotes that the module will provide code to support the interface.

   D. It is used to support implementation inheritance.

Answers to Review Questions

1. A and D. If the `Public` keyword is not used, the function is assumed to be public. For more information, see the section titled "Adding Properties to the Classes of the Automation Server."

2. C. A server that has the Unattended Execution option set cannot have forms. For more information, see the section titled "Creating a Multithreaded Automation Server."

3. A. As instances of the class are created, each instance will execute on its own thread. For more information, see the section titled "Creating a Multithreaded Automation Server."

4. D. The `Workspace` class must be defined as `PublicNotCreatable` and is passed to the client via a function provided in the `Application`. For more information, see the section titled "Creating the Automation Server Project."

5. E. To create a read-only property, the `Property Get` procedure must be defined. For more information, see the section titled "`Property Get`."

6. A. The `App` object enables you to set the Request Pending message text. For more information, see the section titled "Using the `App` Object's Properties to Control the Server's Behavior."

7. D. Automation servers can be implemented as executables or DLLs. For more information, see the section titled "Creating the Automation Server Project."

8. B. When a client uses an Automation server implemented as a DLL, the server runs in the same address space as the client. The invocation overhead is much smaller than calling an executable. For more information, see the section titled "Creating the Automation Server Project."

9. B. The `WithEvents` keyword is used to define a variable that supports events. For more information, see the section titled "Adding Events to the Automation Server."

10. C. The `Implements` keyword is used to specify that a specific module will provide an implementation of a specific interface. For more information, see the section titled "Implementing and Using `Callback` Methods."

Answers to Test Yourself Questions at Beginning of Chapter

1. To change the text shown in the Request Pending dialog box, you can use the following code:

   `App.OleRequestPendingMsg = "Please Wait Processing"`

   See "Using the **App** Object's Properties to Control the Server's Behavior."

2. Automation components can be implemented as either executables or Dynamic Link Libraries (DLLs). See "Creating the Automation Server Project."

3. One of the easiest methods of increasing speed is to implement the component as a Dynamic Link Library (DLL). In addition, you can use Early Binding on the client side to significantly improve function invocation performance. See "Creating the Automation Server Project" and the section "Early Binding Versus Late Binding of ActiveX Servers" in Chapter 11.

4. The **WithEvents** keyword is used to define a variable that supports events. An example of defining a variable that supports events is shown as follows:

   `Private WithEvents m_obj as TextBox`

   See "Adding Events to the Automation Server."

Creating and Using ActiveX Controls

13

This chapter helps you prepare for the exam by covering the following objectives:

 Objectives

- ▶ Declare and raise events

- ▶ Create and enable a Property page

- ▶ Use control events to save and load persistent control properties

- ▶ Add an ActiveX Control to a web page

Test Yourself! Before reading this chapter, test yourself to determine how much study time you will need to devote to this section.

1. Describe how to raise events and why they're necessary when creating ActiveX Controls.

2. Describe the facilities provided in Visual Basic that allow a UserControl to load and write its properties.

3. How does the programmer prevent an ActiveX Control from being visible at runtime?

4. Describe the role of the PropertyBag object.

Answers are located at the end of the chapter...

In Visual Basic 5, the application developer can create ActiveX Controls. In previous versions, this was the exclusive domain of the C++ developers. Writing a control requires a slightly different orientation because controls cannot exist outside the container. In addition, the controls tend to serve two different audiences: the developer using the control, and the end user who uses the final application that has the control.

To enable the developer to create controls in Visual Basic 5, a new code module was created called the UserControl. The UserControl behaves the same way as a class module; the main exception is that it has a user interface and some persistent features.

With Automation servers, multiple classes are defined and made public; therefore, clients can create objects from the public classes. With ActiveX Controls, you define as many UserControls as needed; therefore, the client can use multiple public controls from one file. The file that contains the control usually has an .OCX extension and is referred to as a *control component.*

When instances of a control are created, they must be hosted in a *container object.* The container can vary, but for the most part, it is a Visual Basic form. The process of placing an instance of a control in its container is called *siting.* After the control instance is sited, the event is provided as event procedures in the Code window of the form. In addition, the control has access to container services such as *ambient* properties. Ambient properties are provided by containers. They usually give the control information regarding the best way to display themselves. The Forecolor and BackColor properties are ambient properties, for example. These properties tell the control what color to set its Forecolor and BackColor to make the control appear properly.

As with classes, the UserControl module consists of private and public implementations. However, the UserControl has two public implementations. These public implementations are the appearance of the control and the interface that control provides. The appearance refers to the graphical interface that the control provides. The interface refers to the properties, methods, and events provided to control the instance of the UserControl.

When a Visual Basic developer places a control on a form while designing the form, a design-time instance of the control is created. From the developer's perspective, a control is living on the form; however, only the design-time instance of the control is available. When the form is closed or the project is executed, the design-time instance is destroyed and a runtime instance is created. The runtime instance is created when the form is loaded into memory. The runtime instance of the control is destroyed when the form is unloaded from memory.

As forms are opened and closed at design time, a new design-time instance of the form is created from properties stored in the form's .FRM file. These property settings are stored in the executable, so the runtime instance can be created when the application is executed.

Another way to look at it is that the UserControl module is the canvas where you create your control. The ActiveX Control is made up of the UserControl object and any other controls placed on the UserControl. As with all Visual Basic modules, the UserControl is stored in its own file type. The file has a .CTL extension. If the UserControl has some graphical elements, the data is stored in a .CTX file with the same name as the .CTL file.

These files will define the ActiveX Control's properties, methods, events, and the appearance of the control. A Visual Basic project can have multiple UserControl modules, enabling you to package several controls in one .OCX file.

The UserControl provides its own set of properties, methods, and events. The ActiveX Control that you create can delegate functionality to the UserControl's member methods and properties. These member methods and properties are hidden from your user via encapsulation. Therefore, the UserControl default implementation of code does some of your work.

There are several ways in which controls can be created. One method is to use existing control(s) as a base and add extra features. An alternative is to create your control from scratch. If you create a control from scratch, you have total control over the appearance of the control. Therefore, the Paint event is used to manage the appearance of the control.

Existing controls can be added to your UserControl module and enhanced. This enables you to add your own methods, properties, and events. Changing the appearance of an existing control is more difficult than changing the default behavior of the control because that existing control already has its own painting code that use Windows Messages to paint itself. If your new ActiveX Control uses a standard ListBox control, for example, you may find it difficult to control when and how the ListBox control paints itself.

This chapter covers the following topics:

- ▶ Overview of the UserControl module

- ▶ Creating the control

- ▶ Declaring events

- ▶ Raising events

- ▶ Using properties and methods to raise events

- ▶ Creating a Property page

- ▶ Saving and loading control properties

- ▶ Adding an ActiveX Control to a web page

- ▶ Distributing ActiveX Controls

Understanding the UserControl Module

Creating a new ActiveX Control project is very easy using the UserControl module. To create an ActiveX Control project, follow these steps:

1. Select File, New Project menu.

2. Choose the ActiveX Control Project type and click on OK.

After creating the project, you will have a UserControl module named UserControl1. Figure 13.1 shows the UserControl module.

Figure 13.1

A blank UserControl module.

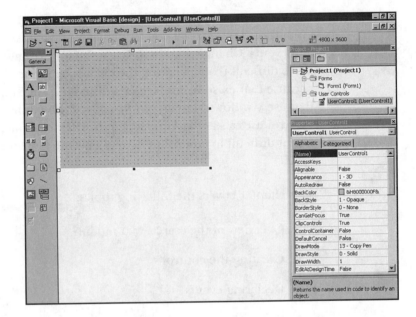

The UserControl module can be seen as a cross between a form module and a class module. It combines elements of both, but has new properties, methods, and events. Table 13.1 summarizes UserControl's new properties.

Table 13.1

UserControl *Properties*

Property Name	Read Only at Runtime	Description
Property AccessKeys As String		Returns or sets a string that defines the hotkeys for the control.
Property ActiveControl As Control	Y	Returns the constituent control that would have the focus if the usercontrol were the active control.
Property Ambient As AmbientProperties	Y	Returns an ambient properties object that contains all the ambient properties for a control.

Property Name	Read Only at Runtime	Description
Property Appearance As Integer	Y	Returns a value (0 or 1) indicating that the control is drawn in 3D at runtime. A value of zero (0) for Flat and one (1) for 3D.
Property AutoRedraw As Boolean	Y	If set to True, allows automatic repainting of a control. The graphics are written to the screen and to a memory area. If the object does not receive paint events, it is painted from the image stored in memory. If set to False, the usercontrol will receive Paint events.
Property BackColor As Long		Returns or sets the backcolor for text and graphics of a control.
Property BackStyle As Integer		Returns or sets the backstyle of a control.
Property BorderStyle As Integer		Returns or sets the borderstyle of a control.
Property ClipControls As Boolean		Returns or sets a value that denotes that the control should repaint the entire display area as opposed to a specific area.
Property ContainedControls As ContainedControls	Y	Returns a collection of controls that were part of the ActiveX Control at design-time or that were added at runtime by the end user.
Property Controls As Object	Y	Returns a reference to a collection of all the controls for an ActiveX Control.
Property Count As Integer		Returns the number of controls for an ActiveX Control.

continues

Table 13.1 Continued

UserControl **Properties**

Property Name	Read Only at Runtime	Description
Property CurrentX As Single		Returns or sets the horizontal positions for the next printing or drawing operation.
Property CurrentY As Single		Returns or sets the vertical position for the next printing or drawing operation.
Property DrawMode As Integer		Returns or sets the DrawMode used by the ActiveX Control.
Property DrawStyle As Integer		Returns or sets the DrawStyle used by the ActiveX Control.
Property DrawWidth As Integer		Returns or sets the DrawWidth used by the ActiveX Control.
Property Enabled As Boolean		Returns or sets the Enabled used by the ActiveX Control.
Property EventsFrozen As Boolean	Y	Returns a value that denotes that the container is ignoring events being raised by the control.
Property Extender As Object	Y	Returns an Extender object that is used to hold properties tracked by the container.
Property FillColor As Long		Returns or sets the FillColor of the ActiveX Control.
Property FillStyle As Integer		Returns or sets the FillStyle of the ActiveX Control.
Property Font As StdFont		Returns the standard Font object for the Control.

Property Name	Read Only at Runtime	Description
Property FontBold As Boolean		Returns True or False indicating whether the font is displayed in a bold face.
Property FontItalic As Boolean		Returns True or False indicating whether the font is displayed in an italic face.
Property FontName As String		Returns the name of the font.
Property FontSize As Single		Returns the size of the font.
Property FontStrikethru As Boolean		Sets or returns True or False indicating whether the font is displayed with strikethru Face.
Property FontTransparent As Boolean		Sets or returns True or False indicating whether the font is transparent so that background images and text can show.
Property FontUnderline As Boolean		Sets or returns True or False indicating whether the font is displayed in an underline face.
Property ForeColor As Long		Returns or sets the ForeColor for text and graphics in the ActiveX Control.
Property hDC As Long	Y	Returns the handle to a device context (hDC) for the ActiveX Control.
Property Height As Single		Returns/sets the height of the ActiveX Control.
Property hWnd As Long	Y	Returns the Windows handle (hWnd) for the ActiveX Control.
Property Hyperlink As Hyperlink	Y	Returns the hyperlink associated with the control.

continues

Table 13.1 Continued

UserControl *Properties*

Property Name	Read Only at Runtime	Description
Property Image As IpictureDisp	Y	Returns a handle to a persistent bitmap.
Property KeyPreview As Boolean		Determines whether keyboard events for an object are processed by the ActiveX Control before the controls that are a part of the ActiveX Control.
Property MaskColor As Long		Returns or sets the color that defines the transparent area in the MaskPicture.
Property MaskPicture As IpictureDisp		Returns or sets the picture that defines the clickable or drawable area of the control when the BackStyle is set to transparent (0).
Property MouseIcon As IpictureDisp		Sets a mouse icon for the ActiveX Control when the MousePointer is set to 99.
Property MousePointer As Integer		Returns or sets the MousePointer for the ActiveX Control.
Property Name As String	Y	Returns the name of the ActiveX Control.
Property OLEDropMode As Integer		Returns or sets the Drop mode of the ActiveX Control.
Property Palette As IpictureDisp		Returns or sets an image that contains the palette used when the PaletteMode is set to Custom.
Property PaletteMode As Integer		Returns or sets the Palette Mode.
Property Parent As Object		Returns the parent of the ActiveX Control.

Property Name	Read Only at Runtime	Description
`Property ParentControls As ParentControls`		Returns a collection of controls that are part of the container where the control is sited.
`Property Picture As IpictureDisp`		Returns or sets the graphic to be displayed in the control.
`Property PropertyPages (Integer) As String`		Returns or sets a string from a array that contains the names of property pages associated with the ActiveX Control.
`Property RightToLeft As Boolean`		Denotes the direction in which text should be displayed on a bi-directional system.
`Property ScaleHeight As Single`		Returns or sets the number of units used for vertical measurement of an ActiveX Control's interior.
`Property ScaleLeft As Single`		Returns or sets the horizontal coordinates for the left edges of an ActiveX Control.
`Property ScaleMode As Integer`		Returns or sets a value that denotes the measurement units for an ActiveX Control. It is used when using graphics methods or moving contained controls.
`Property ScaleTop As Single`		Returns or sets the vertical coordinates for the top edges of the ActiveX Control.
`Property ScaleWidth As Single`		Return or sets the number of units for horizontal measurement of an ActiveX Control's interior.

continues

Table 13.1 Continued

UserControl **Properties**

Property Name	Read Only at Runtime	Description
Property Tag As String		Returns or sets the Tag property of the ActiveX Control.
Property Width As Single		Returns or sets the width of the ActiveX Control.
Property CanGetFocus as Boolean	Y	Returns or sets a value that denotes whether the control can receive focus.
Property ControlContainer as Boolean		Returns or sets a value to denote whether or not the control can support other controls being placed on it.
Property DefaultCancel as Boolean		Is used to notify the container that the control can support being a Default or Cancel button.
Property ForwardFocus as Boolean	Y	Returns or sets a Boolean value that denotes which control will receive focus when an access key for the control is entered.
Property EditAtDesignTime as Boolean		Sets or returns a value that denotes whether the control can be become active during the design time. This is not available at runtime.
Property InvisibleAtRuntime as Boolean		Determines whether the control is visible at runtime.
Property Public as Boolean		Determines whether a control can be shared with another application.

Property Name	Read Only at Runtime	Description
		The default is set to True. If a control cannot be shared, the control can be used only within the ActiveX Control project.
ToolBoxBitmap		This property enables you to set the bitmap shown for the control in the toolbox at design time.

In addition to these properties, the UserControl provides some standard methods used when creating ActiveX Controls. Table 13.2 lists these methods.

Table 13.2

UserControl **Methods**

Method Name	Description
Sub AsyncRead(Target As String, AsyncType As Long, [PropertyName])	Starts reading data from a file or URL asynchronously
Sub CancelAsyncRead ([Property])	Cancels the asynchronous request
Function CanPropertyChange (PropertyName As String) As Boolean	Asks the container whether a property bound to a data source can have its underlying value changed
Sub Circle(Step As Integer, X As Single, Y As Single, Radius As Single, Color As Long, Start As Single, End As Single, Aspect As Single)	Draws circles, ellipses, or arcs
Sub Cls()	Clears the graphics and text created at runtime to restore the control to its design-time look

continues

Table 13.2 Continued

UserControl Methods

Method Name	Description
`Sub Line(Flags As Integer, X1 As Single, Y1 As Single, X2 As Single, Y2 As Single, Color As Long)`	Draws lines, squares, and rectangles
`Sub OLEDrag()`	Starts the OLE drag/drop operation
`Sub PaintPicture(Picture As IPictureDisp, X1 As Single, Y1 As Single, [Width1], [Height1], [X2], [Y2], [Width2], [Height2], [Opcode])`	Draws a graphics file on an ActiveX Control
`Function Point(X As Single, Y As Single) As Long`	Returns a RGB value for a specific point on an ActiveX Control
`Sub PopupMenu(Menu As object, [Flags], [X], [Y], [DefaultMenu])`	Displays a pop-up menu
`Sub PropertyChanged ([PropertyName])`	Tells the container that a property value has been changed
`Sub PSet(Step As Integer, X As Single, Y As Single, Color As Long)`	Sets the pixel at a given location
`Sub Refresh()`	Causes a repaint of the control to occur
`Sub Scale(Flags As Integer, [X1], [Y1], [X2], [Y2])`	Defines the coordinate system used by the ActiveX Control
`Function ScaleX(Width As Single, [FromScale], [ToScale]) As Single`	Converts the X unit of measure value to a different unit of measure
`Function ScaleY(Height As Single, [FromScale], [ToScale]) As Single`	Converts the Y unit of measure value to a different unit of measure
`Sub SetFocus()`	Moves focus to a specific contained control

Method Name	Description
Sub Size(Width As Single, Height As Single)	Sets the size of the UserControl
Function TextHeight(Str As String) As Single	Returns the height of the text string as seen on the ActiveX Control for the current font
Function TextWidth(Str As String) As Single	Returns the width of the text string as seen on the ActiveX Control for the current font

The UserControl module also provides several events that allow the designer's control to respond to events. Table 13.3 lists these events.

Table 13.3

UserControl **Events**

Event Name	Description
Event AccessKeyPress (KeyAscii As Integer)	Fired when the user presses one of the control's access keys or Enter or the Esc key if the Default or Cancel properties are set to True
Event AmbientChanged (PropertyName As String)	Fired when an ambient property has changed
Event AsyncReadComplete (AsyncProp As AsyncProperty)	Fired when the AsyncRead is completed
Event Click()	Fired when the user clicks on the control
Event DblClick()	Fired when the user double-clicks on the control
Event DragDrop(Source As Control, X As Single, Y As Single)	Fired when a Drag/Drop operation occurs
Event DragOver(Source As Control, X As Single, Y As Single, State As Integer)	Fired when an item is dragged over the control

continues

Table 13.3 Continued

UserControl *Events*

Event Name	Description
Event EnterFocus()	Fired when a control enters focus
Event ExitFocus()	Fired when a control exits focus
Event GotFocus()	Fired when a control gets focus
Event Hide()	Fired when the control's visible property is set to True
Event Initialize()	Fired when an instance of the control is created
Event InitProperties()	Fired when the control is created
Event KeyDown(KeyCode As Integer, Shift As Integer)	Fired when the user presses a key when the control has focus
Event KeyPress(KeyAscii As Integer))	Fired when the user presses and releases an ASCII key when the control has focus
Event KeyUp(KeyCode As Integer, Shift As Integer)	Fired when the user releases a key when the control has focus
Event LostFocus()	Fired when the control loses focus
Event MouseDown(Button As Integer, Shift As Integer, X As Single, Y As Single)	Fired when the user presses the mouse button when the control has focus
Event MouseMove(Button As Integer, Shift As Integer, X As Single, Y As Single)	Fired when the user moves the mouse over the control
Event MouseUp(Button As Integer, Shift As Integer, X As Single, Y As Single)	Fired when the user releases the mouse button when the control has focus
Event OLECompleteDrag (Effect As Long)	Fired at the control when a manual or automatic Drag/Drop is completed or canceled

Event Name	Description
Event OLEDragDrop(Data As DataObject, Effect As Long, Button As Integer, Shift As Integer, X As Single, Y As Single)	Fired when data is dropped on a control via an OLE Drag/Drop operation and the OLEDropMode property is set to Manual
Event OLEDragOver(Data As DataObject, Effect As Long, Button As Integer, Shift As Integer, X As Single, Y As Single, State As Integer)	Fired when data is dragged over the control
Event OLEGiveFeedback(Effect As Long, DefaultCursors As Boolean)	Fired at the source control to provide mouse and cursor feedback
Event OLESetData(Data As DataObject, DataFormat As Integer)	Fired at source control when the target requests data that was not provided in the DataObject during the OLEDragStart event
Event OLEStartDrag(Data As DataObject, AllowedEffects As Long)	Fired when an OLE Drag/Drop operation is initiated
Event Paint()	Occurs when the control is moved or changed
Event ReadProperties(PropBag As PropertyBag)	Occurs when the control is asked to read its data from the PropBag parameter
Event Resize()	Fired when the control is resized.
Event Show()	Fired when the control's visible property is set to True
Event Terminate()	Fired when control has been destroyed
Event WriteProperties(PropBag As PropertyBag)	Fired when the control is asked to write properties to the PropBag parameter

As shown in the previous tables, there are many properties, methods, and events to contend with when creating ActiveX Controls. As with most Visual Basic components, you provide code only for the properties, methods, and events of interest and rely on the default implementation provided by Visual Basic. The following sections look at creating and using an ActiveX Control.

Creating the Control

When creating a new control, the easiest method is to use the ActiveX Control Interface Wizard to add the methods, properties, and events that will be supported by the control. The ActiveX Control Interface Wizard is an add-in provided with Visual Basic. The wizard can be invoked by using the Add-in menu. After the wizard is called, you are walked—step-by-step—through the creation of the interfaces for your control. Figure 13.2 shows the first wizard window.

Figure 13.2

The ActiveX Control Interface Wizard—Introduction pane.

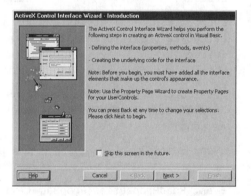

The next window enables you to add or remove standard properties, methods, and events that many controls provide. Figure 13.3 shows this window.

Figure 13.3

The ActiveX Control Interface Wizard—Select Interface Members pane.

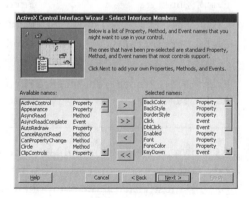

Figure 13.3 shows only the standard interfaces that can be *added* or *removed* from your control. If you want to provide *custom* interfaces, you can add these in the other windows of the wizard. After you select or add the desired interfaces, the next step is to create your own custom member functions. Figure 13.4 shows the window that enables you to add custom member interfaces.

Figure 13.4

The ActiveX Control Interface Wizard— Create Custom Interface Members pane.

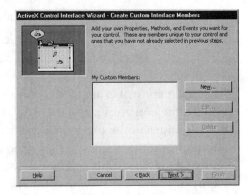

The window shown in Figure 13.4 is used to add and remove custom interfaces for the control. The type of interface is defined when the New button is selected. Clicking on the New button displays the dialog box shown in Figure 13.5.

Figure 13.5

The Add Custom Member dialog box.

In the window shown in Figure 13.5, you can add properties, methods, and events as needed. After the custom interfaces are created, the next step is to map your methods, properties, and events to constituent controls or your ActiveX Control. *Constituent* controls are controls that are a part of your ActiveX Control. You may want to have a list box and command button, for example, as part of your ActiveX Control. The act of mapping your interfaces to constituent controls is an optional one. Figure 13.6 shows the window in which you perform this task.

Figure 13.6

*The ActiveX
Control Inter-
face Wizard—
Set Mapping
pane.*

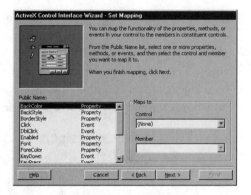

After each control is mapped, you can specify attribute information for the control's interface. The attributes can vary from the
default values to the properties that the control will support. In
addition, you can specify whether the interface members are read-
only or read/write and whether they are available at runtime.
Figure 13.7 shows the window that provides this functionality.

Figure 13.7

*The ActiveX
Control Inter-
face Wizard—
Set Attributes
pane.*

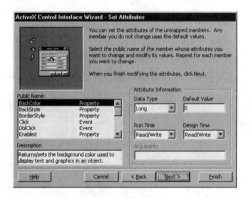

After this window is completed, the ActiveX Control Interface
Wizard makes all the necessary changes to the control. It is important to note that you can make these changes to the control's interface manually, as discussed in the following sections.

Declaring and Raising Events

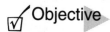 Objective

After your `UserControl` module is created, you can add events to the control. The `Event` keyword is used to define events in a `UserControl` module. Remember that the control's creator is just *defining* the events that are supported. The control's user, on the other hand, will *write* code for the events. Examples of defining events are shown as follows:

```
Public Event About()
Public Event BeforeOpenFile(FileName As String)
Public Event AfterCloseFile(FileName As String)
```

Events are similar to functions and subroutines in that they can be public or private. If it is defined as public, the event is accessible from the control's container.

After the events are defined, the next step is to provide the necessary code that will raise the events to the container. Remember that the container (which may be a Visual Basic form) will provide code to handle the event when it is fired. In the control, the event is fired using the `RaiseEvent` statement. For more information on the `RaiseEvent` statement, refer to Chapter 12, "Creating an Automation Server That Exposes Objects, Properties, Methods, and Events." The `RaiseEvent` statement can be used in any procedure to fire the event.

There is no guarantee that the container will process the event. Remember that the container's programmer will only handle events that are of interest to the programmer. In addition, the container may be in a state in which it cannot handle events, such as Design mode. If the container does not handle the event, the container provides a default mechanism. Examples of raising events are shown as follows:

```
RaiseEvent About()
RaiseEvent BeforeOpenFile("MyFile.txt")
RaiseEvent Event AfterCloseFile("MyFile.txt")
```

Using Properties and Methods to Raise Events

Properties and methods can be added to ActiveX Controls as with any Automation component. The same keywords are used to define properties and methods of an ActiveX Control. For more details on defining properties and methods, refer to Chapter 12. In the Chap13 directory on the accompanying CD-ROM, there is a sample Grid control application called GRID.VBG. This project provides a sample Grid control and a form to test it. When the Grid project is executed at runtime, the window shown in Figure 13.8 appears.

Figure 13.8

An ActiveX Grid control sample at runtime.

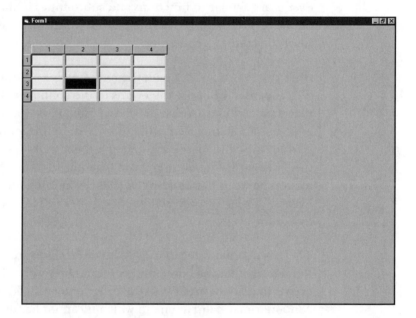

The Grid control at design time is made up of a text box and two command buttons. These buttons are known as *constituent* controls because they are a part of the control. At runtime, the control will dynamically create and lay out controls based on the number of rows and columns specified by the Rows and Columns properties of the control.

The following statements provide some examples of properties and methods of a control. (The code is taken from a sample `Grid` control located in the Chap13 directory on the accompanying CD-ROM):

```
Public Property Get BackColor() As Long
    BackColor = m_BackColor
End Property

Public Property Let BackColor(ByVal New_BackColor As Long)
    m_BackColor = New_BackColor
    PropertyChanged "BackColor"
End Property

Public Sub Refresh()
    Call InitDisplay
End Sub

Public Property Get Rows() As Long
    Rows = m_Rows
End Property

Public Property Let Rows(ByVal New_Rows As Long)
    m_Rows = New_Rows
    Call InitDisplay
    PropertyChanged "Rows"
End Property

Public Property Get Columns() As Long
    Columns = m_Columns
End Property

Public Property Let Columns(ByVal New_Columns As Long)
    m_Columns = New_Columns
    Call InitDisplay
    PropertyChanged "Columns"
End Property
```

As mentioned earlier, the events are raised from procedures by using the RaiseEvent keyword. The ActiveX Control usually raises an event in response to a property change or a method invocation. When the Grid control's cell changes, for example, the container would get CellChanged event notification. To perform this task, the control's programmer must follow these steps:

1. Declare the event.

2. Write the procedure that will fire the event.

3. If providing the container as well, write the code that will handle the event.

Performing step 1 is quite easy and is done with the following code:

```
Public Event CellChange(nCellIndex as long)
```

This code is placed in the General Declaration section of the control.

Step 2 requires writing a new procedure or using an existing one. In this case, you will use an existing one, the txtCell_Change event. The txtCell Change event is fired whenever the text box's data is changed. The necessary code is as follows:

```
Private Sub txtCell_Change(Index As Integer)
    'Raise the event to the container
    RaiseEvent CellChange(Index)
End Sub
```

In step 3, the container's (the form that has the control) code for the event is as follows:

```
Private Sub UserControl11_CellChange(nCellIndex As Long)
    MsgBox "You changed Cell " & nCellIndex
End Sub
```

Once the cell in the grid has been changed, a message box displays as shown in Figure 13.9.

Figure 13.9

The message box shown after the cell has been changed.

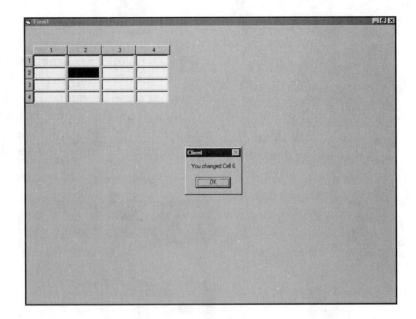

Creating and Enabling a Property Page

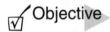Objective

Although Property pages are not a requirement of ActiveX Controls, most controls do provide Property pages. Property pages enable the developer of the container to set property values easily by using a tab-centric interface.

Creating a Property Page

The Property page is usually invoked from the (Custom) property in the Properties window in the Visual Basic environment. Figure 13.10 shows an example of a Property page.

Figure 13.10

An example of a Property page.

The Property page is like a window with some additional methods, properties, and events. The Property page is viewed on a tab at design time and enables a developer to change the characteristics of an ActiveX Control. A control can support multiple Property pages. These can be custom pages or standard pages. There are three standard pages that can be used with any control. The standard Property pages are the StandardFont, StandardColor, and StandardPicture pages. Figure 13.11 shows the StandardFont Property page.

Figure 13.11

The StandardFont Property page.

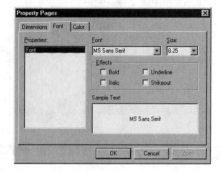

The StandardFont Property page enables the container's developer to change the fonts for properties that use fonts as a value. The StandardColor Property page enables the container's developer to change the color of properties that use color as a value. The StandardPicture Property page enables the container's developer to change the picture and icon properties.

Enabling a Property Page

After Property pages are designed, they should be bound to a given User Control. This allows changes in a Property page to be reflected in the User Control. The User Control provides a collection called the PropertyPages, which maintains the list of pages supported by the control.

Property pages are added or removed from a control by using the PropertyPages property. At design time, you can select the PropertyPages property and add or remove pages from the control, as shown in Figure 13.12.

Figure 13.12

Changing Property pages at design time.

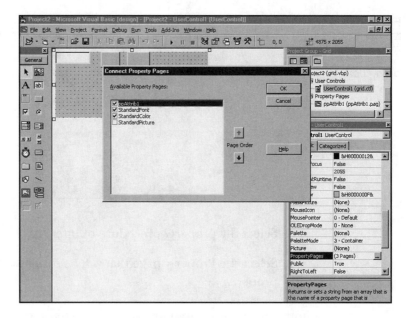

The order of the pages can be arranged and pages can be added or removed as necessary. The Property pages for a control are stored in a string array known as `PropertyPages`. The array can be used to set and modify the pages for the window.

Property pages can be added to individual properties of a control. This is quite common in Visual Basic. When the `Database` property of the `Data` control is selected, for example, a small Ellipsis button appears. If the button is selected, a Property page is shown. To tie a Property page to a control's property, follow these steps:

1. Select the `UserControl` object.

2. Select the Tools/Procedure Attributes menu. This should present a window, as shown in Figure 13.13, after you click on the Advanced button.

Figure 13.13

The Procedure Attributes dialog box.

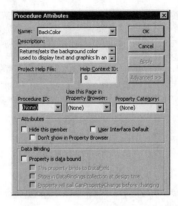

3. Select the property procedure of interest.

4. Select the Property page that will be displayed for the property.

Your can create custom Property pages by using the Property Page module. The Property Page module behaves like a traditional Visual Basic form, but has some additional properties, methods, and events.

To create a Property page, follow these steps:

1. Choose the Project/Add Property Page menu item.

2. The menu will display an Add Property Page dialog box, as shown in Figure 13.14.

Figure 13.14

The Add PropertyPage dialog box.

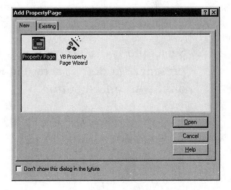

3. At this point you can use a wizard to create either the Property page or a default page.

After the page is created, you can add controls to it and write code to map the controls to the properties of the control. The Visual Basic runtime handles the actions of the OK, Cancel, and Apply buttons.

Opening the Project Group (SampleControl.vbg)

Select the File, Open menu item and choose the SampleControl.vbg file. This project group should contain two projects. When the project group is executed, the main window appears, as shown in Figure 13.15.

Figure 13.15

A sample Control project.

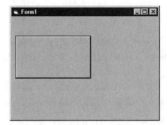

When the button is clicked, a pop-up menu displays. The button is a constituent control of the ActiveX Control in the prjControl project.

Adding a Property Page to the prjControl Project

To add a Property page, use the Project/Add Property Page menu item. Do not use the wizard. A blank Property page will be created that can be customized.

Adding Controls to the Property Page

You can create controls on the Property page, as shown in Figure 13.16.

Tying the Controls to Properties of the ActiveX Control

The Property page has a changed property that is set to True or False depending on whether the controls on the page have been changed. The Change event for the text boxes must set the property to True when they are changed. The following code achieves this task:

```
Private Sub txtCaption_Change()
    Changed = True
End Sub
Private Sub txtBorderStyle_Change()
    Changed = True
End Sub
```

When the Apply button or an OK button is selected, if the changed property is set to True, the ApplyChanges event occurs. The ApplyChanges event allows the Property page to move the values to the ActiveX Control, which uses the control. In addition, when the ActiveX Control's properties change, the Property page will be notified via the SelectionChanged property:

```
Private Sub PropertyPage_ApplyChanges()
    SelectedControls(0).Caption = txtCaption.Text
    SelectedControls(0).BorderStyle = txtBorderStyle.Text
End Sub
Private Sub PropertyPage_SelectionChanged()
    txtCaption.Text = SelectedControls(0).Caption
    txtBorderStyle.Text = SelectedControls(0).BorderStyle
End Sub
```

Figure 13.16

A sample Property page.

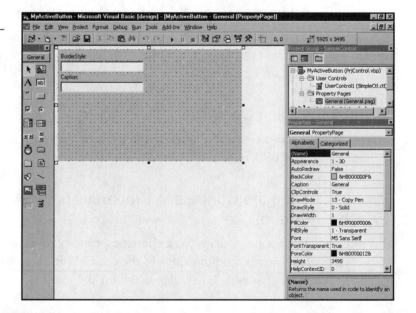

The SelectedControls property is the array of ActiveX Controls currently using the Property page. In most cases, there is only one ActiveX Control. The SelectedControls property is read and set using the two events shown earlier.

Adding the Property Page to the ActiveX Control Property Page Collection

After the Property page is coded, the next step is to add the Property page to a control. This task is accomplished by using the PropertyPages property of the ActiveX Control. The PropertyPages property is an array of pages used by the control. The property can be set or read. At design time, if the PropertyPages property is used, a dialog box is presented, as shown in Figure 13.17.

Figure 13.17

Assigning PropertyPages to a control.

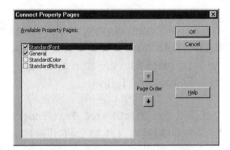

When the control is used on a form and the developer selects the Custom option in the Property window, the developer is presented with the Property window shown in Figure 13.18.

Figure 13.18

An opened Property page.

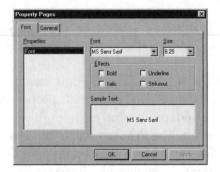

Saving and Loading Persistent Control Properties

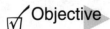

Objective

Controls can be made persistent by saving and loading their properties. When a control is on a form and it saves its properties at design time, the values are stored to the .FRX file of the form. When the form is reopened, the property values are read from the .FRX file for the ActiveX Control. The following three events manage the reading and manipulation of properties:

- ▶ InitProperties

- ▶ ReadProperties

- ▶ WriteProperties

The InitProperties event occurs when a new instance of the ActiveX Control is created. Usually, this event is used to set default values for properties that belong to the control. An example of this is shown as follows:

```
Private Sub UserControl_InitProperties()
    m_BackColor = m_def_BackColor
    m_ForeColor = m_def_ForeColor
    m_Enabled = m_def_Enabled
    Set m_Font = Ambient.Font
    m_BackStyle = m_def_BackStyle
    m_BorderStyle = m_def_BorderStyle
End Sub
```

In this event procedure, the background and foreground color are set to default values along with other properties of interest.

The ReadProperties event is used by the control to read properties into the ActiveX Control's properties. The container that notifies the control to read its properties from a Property Bag fires this event. The Property Bag is an object new to Visual Basic 5. It allows properties to be manipulated by ActiveX Controls. The PropertyBag object has two methods: ReadProperty and WriteProperty. The ReadProperties event provides a PropertyBbag object. An implementation of this event is shown as follows:

```
Private Sub UserControl_ReadProperties(PropBag As PropertyBag)
    m_BackColor = PropBag.ReadProperty("BackColor",
    ↪m_def_BackColor)
    m_ForeColor = PropBag.ReadProperty("ForeColor",
    ↪m_def_ForeColor)
    m_Enabled = PropBag.ReadProperty("Enabled", m_def_Enabled)
    Set m_Font = PropBag.ReadProperty("Font", Ambient.Font)
    m_BackStyle = PropBag.ReadProperty("BackStyle",
    ↪m_def_BackStyle)
    m_BorderStyle = PropBag.ReadProperty("BorderStyle",
    ↪m_def_BorderStyle)
    cmdButton.Caption = PropBag.ReadProperty("Caption", "")
End Sub
```

The ReadProperty method of the Property Bag is defined as follows:

```
ReadProperty(DataName[, DefaultValue])
```

The DataName parameter is a string that represents the string name of the property that wishes to be read. The default value is an optional parameter. If the parameter is specified, it will provide a default value for property.

The control's container will notify the control to write its properties out to a persistent location (in most cases, an .FRX file), using the WriteProperties event. The WriteProperties event provides a PropertyBag used to write the properties out to the persistent location. An example of the WriteProperties procedures is as follows:

```
'Write property values to storage
Private Sub UserControl_WriteProperties(PropBag As PropertyBag)

    Call PropBag.WriteProperty("BackColor", m_BackColor,
    ↪m_def_BackColor)
    Call PropBag.WriteProperty("ForeColor", m_ForeColor,
    ↪m_def_ForeColor)
    Call PropBag.WriteProperty("Enabled", m_Enabled,
    ↪m_def_Enabled)
    Call PropBag.WriteProperty("Font", m_Font, Ambient.Font)
    Call PropBag.WriteProperty("BackStyle", m_BackStyle,
    ↪m_def_BackStyle)
```

```
    Call PropBag.WriteProperty("BorderStyle", m_BorderStyle,
    ➥m_def_BorderStyle)
    Call PropBag.WriteProperty("Caption", cmdButton.Caption, "")
End Sub
```

The `PropertyBag`'s `WriteProperty` is defined as follows:

```
object.WriteProperty(DataName, Value[, DefaultValue])
```

The `DataName` is the name of the property to be saved, and the value is the current value of the property. The `DefaultValue` parameter is an optional parameter; the property value is stored only if it is different from the default value.

Adding an ActiveX Control to a Web Page

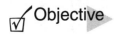Objective

After an ActiveX Control is created, it can be added to an HTML page. This is done by using the `<OBJECT>` `</OBJECT>` tags provided in HTML. The easy method is to use the ActiveX Control Pad. This tool is a simple HTML editor that enables you to add controls to a Web page. When the application is executed, a window appears as shown in Figure 13.19.

Figure 13.19

An ActiveX Control Pad.

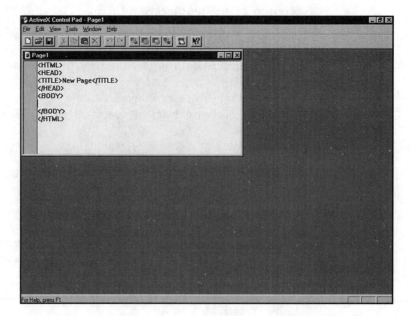

The control has an Edit/Insert ActiveX Control menu option. When this option is chosen, you are presented with the Insert ActiveX Control dialog box as shown in Figure 13.20. The actual items in the list may differ depending upon what controls are loaded on the system.

Figure 13.20

Using the ActiveX Control Pad to insert a control reference.

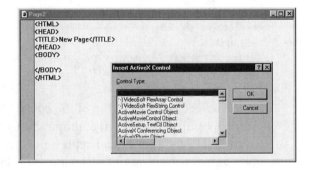

At this point, you can select the desired control. After a control is selected, you can set the properties of the control as shown in Figure 13.21.

Figure 13.21

Using the ActiveX Control Pad to edit the selected control's properties.

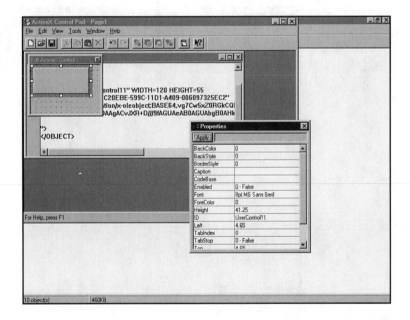

After the control is closed, the Control Pad creates the necessary object tag for the control. The object tag can look like the following code:

```
<OBJECT ID="UserControl11" WIDTH=120 HEIGHT=55
 CLASSID="CLSID:C3C20EBE-599C-11D1-A409-006097325EC2"
 DATA="DATA:application/
➥xoleobject;BASE64,vg7Cw5xZ0RGkCQBg1zJewpOyAABIAAAAAwAIAAvyV0cgAAAAXw
➥B1AHgAdAB1
➥AG4AdAB4AGcMAAAADAAgACvJXR+D///9fAGUAeAB0AGUAbgB0A
➥HkArwUAAA==">
```

In the object tag, the class id of the control is specified. Every ActiveX Control is assigned a unique class id that identifies the control. The DATA parameter represents the binary data used by the control at runtime. The id parameter defines the name that can be used to refer to a control when using VBScript or JScript code. When the HTML page is opened, a web page displays, as shown in Figure 13.22.

Figure 13.22

The web page with the control at runtime.

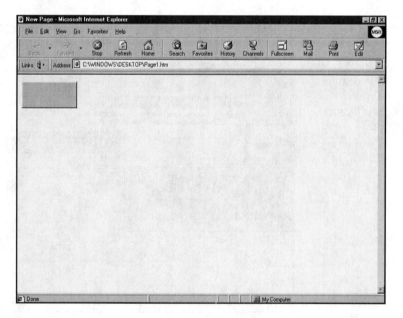

Exercises

Exercise 13.1: Defining Events

In this exercise, you define some events in a control.

1. Create an ActiveX Control project.

2. Define an event procedure called UpdateLocation that takes two parameters: x defined as a long variable and y defined as a long variable.

3. Define a private event procedure called FinishProcessing that takes no parameters.

4. Define an event procedure called ShowObject that has a windows handle as a parameter.

To define the event procedures, use the following code:

```
Public Event UpdateLocation(x as long, y as long)
Private Event FinishProcessing()
Public Event ShowObject(hWnd as long)
```

Exercise 13.2: Raising Events

In this exercise, you raise the following defined events: (Note that the Raise statement must be used within a procedure. The exercise here is only for practice.)

▶ Public Event UpdateLocation(x as long, y as long)

▶ Public Event FinishProcessing()

▶ Public Event ShowObject(hWnd as long)

To trigger the events, use the following code:

```
RaiseEvent UpdateLocation(a, b) 'Assume that a,b are defined
➥variables
RaiseEvent FinishProcessing()
RaiseEvent ShowObject(Me.hWnd)
```

Exercise 13.3: Creating a Property Page

In this exercise, you create a Property page and map its controls to the properties of an ActiveX Control. The project group is located in the Ex13.3 directory on the CD-ROM and consists of two projects: prjMain (testing application for the ActiveX Control) and prjControl (application that creates the ActiveX Control). The name of the project group is SampleControl.vbg. To complete this exercise, follow these steps:

1. Open the project group (SampleControl.vbg).

2. Add a Property page to the prjControl project.

3. Add controls to the Property page.

4. Tie the controls to properties of the ActiveX Control.

5. Add the Property page to the ActiveX Control Property page collection.

Review Questions

1. Which of the following HTML tags will embed an ActiveX Control in a Web page?

   A. `<OBJECT>...</OBJECT>`

   B. `<CONTROL>...</CONTROL>`

   C. `<ACTIVEX>...<ACTIVEX>`

   D. `<VBOBJECT>...<VBOBJECT>`

2. Define an event called `TopClick` with two parameters, x and y.

   A. You cannot define your own events in Visual Basic.

   B. `Event TopClick(x as long, y as long)`

   C. `Event Sub TopClick(x as long, y as long)`

   D. `Event Function TopClick(x as long, y as long)`

   E. `Sub TopClick(x as long, y as long)`

3. Your ActiveX Control needs to fire an event called `TopClick` that has two parameters. The event is defined as follows:

   `TopClick(x as long, y as long)`

   The parameters x and y must each be set to the value of 100. Which of the following statements will accomplish this task?

   A. `Call Event TopClick(100,100)`

   B. `FireEvent TopClick(100,100)`

   C. `RaiseEvent TopClick(100,100)`

   D. `Call TopClick (100,100)`

4. Your ActiveX Control has a Property page that must display the current value of the Caption property in the first control's caption when it is opened. Which of the following code will provide this functionality?

A.
```
Private Sub PropertyPage_SelectionChanged()
    Caption = txtCaption.Text
End Sub
```

B.
```
Private Sub PropertyPage_SelectionChanged()
    SelectedControl.Caption = txtCaption.Text
End Sub
```

C.
```
Private Sub PropertyPage_SelectionChanged()
    Me.Caption = txtCaption.Text
End Sub
```

D.
```
Private Sub PropertyPage_SelectionChanged()
    SelectedControls(0).Caption = txtCaption.Text
End Sub
```

5. Which of the following statements will raise an event called Click with no parameters?

A. RaiseEvent Click

B. Call UserControl_Click

C. RaiseEvent UserControl_Click

D. Raise Click

6. Which of the following code snippets will load the Caption property of a control?

A.
```
Private Sub UserControl_InitProperties()
    Caption = PropBag.ReadProperties("Caption")
End Sub
```

B. ```
Private Sub UserControl_ReadProperties(PropBag As
➡PropertyBag)
    Caption = PropBag.ReadProperties("Caption")

        End Sub
```

C. ```
Private Sub UserControl_Initialize()
        Caption = LoadProperty("Caption")
    End Sub
```

7. You have created an ActiveX Control. The control needs to be hidden from the user at runtime. Which of the following actions will ensure that the control is hidden at runtime?

   A. Setting the visible property to `False` in the `Initialize` event of the control.

   B. Setting the `InvisibleAtRuntime` property to True.

   C. Call the `InvisibleNow` method of the ActiveX Control.

   D. This cannot be done because ActiveX Controls in Visual Basic are always visible.

8. Which of the following statements is true about ActiveX Controls?

   A. ActiveX Controls can be used only from web pages.

   B. ActiveX Controls cannot contain other controls.

   C. ActiveX Controls must be visible at runtime.

   D. An ActiveX Control can read or save its properties from a persistent location.

9. Which statement is the best description of a PropertyBag object?

   A. The Property Bag is a collection of the ActiveX Control properties.

   B. PropertyBag is an object used to read and write properties to a persistent location.

   C. A Property Bag is an array of properties of an ActiveX Control.

   D. PropertyBag is not a valid object type in Visual Basic.

Answers to Review Questions

1. A. The OBJECT tag is used to embed ActiveX Controls in HTML documents. For more information, see the section titled "Adding an ActiveX Control to a Web Page."

2. B. Events can be defined in Visual Basic. However, a Sub or Function statement is not allowed. For more information, see the section titled "Declaring and Raising Events."

3. C. Events can be raised by using the RaiseEvent statement. For more information, see the section titled "Declaring and Raising Events."

4. D. The SelectedControls collection of the Property page will return all the current selected controls. In this case, the first item's caption is set. For more information, see the section titled "Creating and Enabling a Property Page."

5. A. The RaiseEvent statement fires an event in the container. For more information, see the section titled "Declaring and Raising Events."

6. B. The ReadProperties receives a Property Bag from the container used to read the property. For more information, see the section titled "Saving and Loading Persistent Control Properties."

7. B. The `InvisibleAtRuntime` property is used to determine whether the control is hidden at runtime. For more information, see the section titled "Understanding the `UserControl` Module."

8. D. An ActiveX Control can read and write its properties from a persistent location. ActiveX Controls can be used from any container that supports ActiveX Control, such as Visual Basic, Powerbuilder, or Microsoft Internet Explorer. In addition, ActiveX Controls can be visible or invisible at runtime. For more information, see the section titled "Creating the Control."

9. B. The Property Bag is a simple interface that allows the ActiveX Control to read and write its properties. For more information, see the section titled "Saving and Loading Persistent Control Properties."

Answers to Test Yourself Questions at Beginning of Chapter

1. Events are raised by controls by using the `RaiseEvent` statement. The `RaiseEvent` statement allows a control to fire an event that its container may respond to if something of interest occurs. If the user changes the `Text` property of an ActiveX Control, for example, it may fire the `Changed` event to notify its container that the property has changed. See "Declaring and Raising Events."

2. The `UserControl` provides the developer with three events that help in loading or writing properties. These events are the `InitProperties`, `WriteProperties`, and `ReadProperties`. The `ReadProperties` and `WriteProperties` events provide a `PropertyBag` object that is used to read or write property values. See "Saving and Loading Persistent Control Properties."

3. The developer of the ActiveX Control can prevent the control from being visible at runtime by using the `InvisibleAtRuntime` property or by setting the Top or Left properties so that they are outside the visible portion of the screen. See "Understanding the `UserControl` Module."

4. The `PropertyBag` object is used to read and write property from a persistent location provided by the container. The `PropertyBag` object is accessible only when the `ReadProperties` or the `WriteProperties` are fired. See "Saving and Loading Persistent Control Properties."

C h a p t e r

14

Creating and Using ActiveX Documents

This chapter helps you prepare for the exam by covering the following objectives:

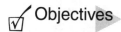 Objectives

▶ Compare ActiveX Documents to embedded objects

▶ Create an ActiveX project with one or more `UserDocument` objects

▶ Persist data for an ActiveX Document

▶ Automate an ActiveX Document

▶ Add an ActiveX Document to a web page

Test Yourself! Before reading this chapter, test yourself to determine how much study time you will need to devote to this section.

1. Describe some of the basic characteristics of ActiveX Documents.

2. What occurs when the displayable area of the ActiveX Document is smaller than the area that the container provides to the ActiveX Document?

3. Briefly describe what objects, methods, or events are read or stored on an ActiveX Document's data from a persistent location.

4. Create a simple HTML page that enables you to open an ActiveX Document called mydoc.vbd.

5. Describe the types of data that can be requested during an Asynchronous Data Request from an ActiveX Document.

Answers are located at the end of the chapter...

Before reviewing this material, you should be very comfortable with creating and using ActiveX components such as Controls and Automation servers. The ActiveX Document provides a document-centric approach to creating applications. The use of ActiveX Documents enables developers to provide a variety of new services previously unavailable. Some of these services are summarized as follows:

▶ You can create applications that can execute within a container application such as Microsoft Internet Explorer or Microsoft Binder.

▶ The ActiveX Document server will execute locally and have all the code needed to carry out its operations.

▶ Designing the GUI portion of ActiveX Documents is easier than using HTML because of Visual Basic's WYSIWIG design environment.

▶ Built-in support of hyperlinks that allow the document to request to be navigated to a specific document or web site.

▶ Support for asynchronous data transfers.

This chapter looks at creating ActiveX Documents. The ActiveX Document consists of two pieces: the ActiveX Document, which contains the data; and the ActiveX Document server. The data in an ActiveX Document cannot be viewed or edited without the ActiveX Document server present on the client machine. If the ActiveX Document server is not on the client, a different document server may view the document contents if it can read the document's data. This chapter covers the following topics:

▶ Understanding the `UserDocument` module

▶ Comparing ActiveX Documents to embedded objects

▶ Creating an ActiveX project with one or more `UserDocument` objects

▶ Persistent data for an ActiveX Document

> ▶ Automating an ActiveX Document

> ▶ Adding an ActiveX Document to a web page

Understanding the UserDocument Module

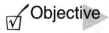 A new module type has been created in Visual Basic 5: the UserDocument. The UserDocument gives you the ability to create your own ActiveX Documents. In prior versions of Visual Basic, you could only use and manipulate ActiveX Documents via Automation or using the OLE Container Control. The UserDocument module is very similar to the form module, in that any control can be placed on UserDocument except an OLE Container Control.

In addition, the UserDocument cannot be displayed without a container. This makes it somewhat of a cross between an ActiveX Control and Form. The UserDocument object has an extension of .DOB.

When an ActiveX Document project is created, a Executable or DLL is created. If an Executable is created, the ActiveX Document will be implemented as an out-of-process server. This means that the ActiveX Document will execute outside the address space of the container. If a DLL is created, the ActiveX Document will be implemented as in-process server. Therefore the ActiveX Document will execute inside the same address space as the container application. In addition, a new file is created as part of the compilation process. This file has a .vbd (Visual Basic Document) extension. This file resides in the same directory as the project file, and has the same name as the project file. To view the ActiveX Document from a container, the .vbd file is used to view the file. If Internet Explorer is used to view file, the following syntax can be used:

> file://c:\chap13\ActiveDocx.vbd

If the ActiveX project is executed from the Visual Basic debugging environment, a temporary .vbd file is created in the directory where Visual Basic is installed. The container that opens the ActiveX Document can use this temporary file.

Several new properties, methods, and events are provided with the UserDocument module. Table 14.1 lists the properties of the UserDocument object.

Table 14.1

UserDocument *Properties*	
Property	Description
ActiveControl	Returns the control that has focus.
Appearance	Sets/returns 3D look for a given UserDocument.
AutoRedraw	If set to True, allows automatic repainting of a control. The graphics are written to screen and a memory area. If the object does not receive paint events, it is painted from the image stored in memory.
BackColor	Returns or sets the BackColor of an ActiveX Document.
ClipControls	Returns or sets a value that denotes that the document should repaint the entire display area as opposed to a specific area.
ContainedControls	Returns a collection of controls contained within the ActiveX Document.
ContinuousScroll	Sets/returns a value that makes scrolling continuous or non-continuous.
Controls	Returns a reference to a collection of all the controls for an ActiveX Control.
Count	Returns the number of controls for an ActiveX Control.
CurrentX	Returns or sets the horizontal positions for the next drawing operation.
CurrentY	Returns or sets the vertical position for the next drawing operation.
DrawMode	Returns or sets the DrawMode used by the ActiveX Document.

continues

Table 14.1 Continued

Property	Description
DrawStyle	Returns or sets the DrawStyle used by the ActiveX Document.
DrawWidth	Returns or sets the DrawWidth used by the ActiveX Control.
FillColor	Returns or sets the FillColor of the ActiveX Control.
FillStyle	Returns or sets the FillStyle of the ActiveX Control.
Font	Returns the standard Font object for the control.
FontBold	Returns True or False indicating that the font is bold face.
FontItalic	Returns True or False indicating that the font is italic face.
FontName	Returns the name of the font.
FontSize	Returns the size of the font.
FontStrikethru	Returns True or False indicating that the font is strikethru face.
FontTransparent	Returns True or False indicating that the font is transparent face.
FontUnderline	Returns True or False indicating that the font is underline face.
ForeColor	Returns or sets the ForeColor for the ActiveX Control.
hDC	Returns the handle to a device context (hDC) for the ActiveX Control.
Height	Sets/returns the height of the ActiveX Document.
HScrollSmallChange	Sets/returns the horizontal distance the UserDocument will scroll when the user selects the scroll arrow.
hWnd	Returns the Windows handle (hWnd) for the ActiveX Control.

Property	Description
Hyperlink	Returns the hyperlink object used to instruct the container to navigate to certain pages.
Image	Returns a handle to a persistent bitmap.
KeyPreview	Determines whether keyboard events for an object are processed by the ActiveX Control before the controls that are a part of the ActiveX Control.
MinHeight	Sets/returns the minimum height of the viewport at which scrollbars will appear on the container.
MinWidth	Sets/returns the minimum width of the Viewport at which scrollbars will appear on the container.
MouseIcon	Sets/returns the MouseIcon for the ActiveX Document.
MousePointer	Returns or sets the MousePointer for the ActiveX Document.
Name	Returns the name of the ActiveX Document.
OLEDropMode	Sets or returns the OLEDropMode for the ActiveX Document.
Palette	Returns or sets an image that contains the palette used when the Palette mode is set to Custom.
PaletteMode	Returns or sets the Palette mode.
Parent	Returns the parent of the ActiveX Document.
Picture	Returns or sets the graphic to be displayed in the control.
ScaleHeight	Returns or sets the number of units used for vertical measurement of an ActiveX Document's interior.
ScaleLeft	Returns or sets the horizontal coordinates for the left edges of an ActiveX Document.

continues

Table 14.1 Continued

Property	Description
ScaleMode	Returns or sets a value that denotes the measurement units for ActiveX Documents. It is used when using graphics methods or when moving objects within the Document.
ScaleTop	Returns or sets the vertical coordinates for the top edges of the ActiveX Document.
ScaleWidth	Return or sets the number of units for horizontal measurement of an ActiveX Document's interior.
ScrollBars	Sets/returns a value that denotes whether the ActiveX Document supports horizontal and/or vertical scrollbars.
Tag	Returns or sets the Tag property of the ActiveX Control.
ViewportHeight	Returns the Viewport height.
ViewportLeft	Returns the Viewport left position.
ViewportTop	Returns the Viewport top position.
ViewportWidth	Returns the Viewport width.
VScrollSmallChange	Sets/returns the vertical distance the UserDocument will scroll when the user selects the scroll arrow.

These properties are discussed in more detail throughout the chapter. The UserDocument also has methods that can be used to modify the behavior of the document. Table 14.2 lists these methods.

Table 14.2

UserDocument *Methods*

Method Name	Description
AsyncRead	Starts the reading of data asychronouusly from a file or an URL.
CancelAsyncRead	Cancels an asynchronous read request.

Method Name	Description
Circle	Draws circles, ellipses, or arcs.
Cls	Clears the graphics and text created at runtime.
Line	Draws lines, squares, and rectangles.
OLEDrag	Starts the OLE Drag/Drop operation.
PaintPicture	Draws a graphics file on an ActiveX Control.
Point	Returns an RGB value for a specific point on an ActiveX Document.
PopupMenu	Displays a popup menu.
PrintForm	Sends a bit image of the document object to the printer.
PropertyChanged	Notifies the UserDocument that a property has been changed.
PSet	Sets the pixel at a given location.
Refresh	Causes a repaint of the document to occur.
Scale	Defines the coordinate system used by the ActiveX Document.
ScaleX	Converts the X unit of measure value to a different unit of measure.
ScaleY	Converts the Y unit of measure value to a different unit of measure.
SetFocus	Moves focus to a control within the ActiveX Document.
SetViewport	Sets the top and left coordinates of the UserDocument that is visible in the Viewport.
TextHeight	Returns the height of the text string as seen on the ActiveX Document for the current font.
TextWidth	Returns the width of the text string as seen on the ActiveX Document for the current font.

The UserDocument object also has a set of events that are used to notify you of changes as they occur (see Table 14.3).

Table 14.3

UserDocument *Events*	
Event	Description
AsyncReadComplete	Fired when the Asynchronous Read operation is completed.
Click	Fired when the user clicks on the control.
DblClick	Fired when the user double-clicks on the control.
DragDrop	Fired when a Drag/Drop operation occurs.
DragOver	Fired when a item is dragged over the control.
EnterFocus	Fired when a control enters focus.
ExitFocus	Fired when a control exits focus.
GotFocus	Fired when a control gets focus.
Hide	Fired when the control's visible property is set to True.
Initialize	Fired when an instance of the control is created.
InitProperties	Fired when the control is created.
KeyDown	Fired when the user presses a key when the control has focus.
KeyPress	Fired when the user presses and releases an ASCII key when the control has focus.
KeyUp	Fired when the user releases a key when the control has focus.
LostFocus	Fired when the control loses focus.
MouseDown	Fired when the user presses the mouse button when the control has focus.
MouseMove	Fired when the user moves the mouse over the control.

Event	Description
MouseUp	Fired when the user releases the mouse button when the control has focus
OLECompleteDrag	Fired at the control when a manual or automatic Drag/Drop is completed or canceled.
OLEDragDrop	Fired when data is dropped on a control via an OLE Drag/Drop operation and the OLEDropMode property is set to Manual.
OLEDragOver	Fired when data is dragged over the control.
OLEGiveFeedback	Fired at the source control to provide mouse and cursor feedback.
OLESetData	Fired at source control when the target requests data that was not provided in the DataObject during the OLEStartDrag event.
OLEStartDrag	Fired when an OLE Drag/Drop operation is initiated.
Paint	Occurs when the control is moved or changed.
ReadProperties	Occurs when the control is asked to read its data from a file.
Resize	Fired when the control is resized.
Scroll	Determines which scrollbars are shown when scrollbars are needed.
Show	Fired when the control's visible property is set to True.
Terminate	Fired when the control has been destroyed.
WriteProperties	Fired when the control is asked to write properties to file.

As shown in the previous tables, there are many properties, methods, and events to contend with when creating ActiveX Documents. As with most Visual Basic components, you will only provide code for the properties, methods, and events of interest and rely on the default implementation provided by Visual Basic. The following sections look at creating and using an ActiveX Document.

Viewport

ActiveX Documents introduce a new concept, known as *Viewports*, to Visual Basic. The ActiveX Document is always viewed inside a container. The area in which the container provides the view of the ActiveX Document is known as a Viewport. In most cases, your ActiveX Document's visible area is smaller that your ActiveX Document's total viewable area. The UserDocument object provides methods and properties that enable the developer to manipulate the Viewport. The following properties are used to set or return the Viewport size:

> ViewportHeight returns the height of the Viewport.
> ViewportLeft returns the left value of the Viewport.
> ViewportTop returns the top value of the Viewport.
> ViewportWidth returns the width value of the Viewport.

The Viewport dimensions are set by the container. Therefore the ActiveX Document can only read the Viewport values and adjust its graphical display accordingly. The Viewport's upper-left corner can be set by the ActiveX Document. The SetViewport method allows the location of the Viewport to be changed. The method is defined as follows:

```
SetViewport left, top
```

The left and top parameters correspond to the upper-left corner of the Viewport location. The Chapter 14 directory on the accompanying CD contains a sample application called ActDocx.vbp. This project file creates a simple ActiveX Document with two buttons. Figure 14.1 shows the UserDocument module at design time.

The UserDocument has two buttons. Each button when pressed will change the Viewport. The following code changes the Viewport:

```
Private Sub Command1_Click()
    ➥SetViewport ViewportWidth * 0.95, ViewportHeight * 0.95
End Sub
```

```
Private Sub Command2_Click()
    SetViewport 0, 0
End Sub
```

Figure 14.1

The BasicDoc UserDocument module at runtime.

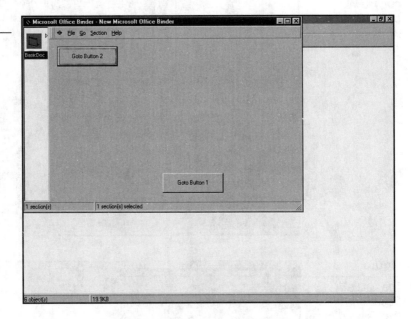

Not very impressive is it? At runtime, however, it provides some interesting results. When the application is executed, nothing happens because an ActiveX Document must be contained within a container application. Within the same directory, you can find a binder document called sample.obd. It contains an ActiveX Document of the type BasicDoc (an instance of the UserDocument module). When the binder is opened, it will try to load the ActiveX Document server component into memory and display the document. This will result in a window as shown in Figure 14.2.

Note   Sample OBD will not work without MS Binder.

Note that errors will occur in the binder document if the Visual Basic project is not running or the executable is not registered.

If the Button display is clicked, the Viewport will change to the other button. Figure 14.3 shows the changed view.

Figure 14.2

The ActiveX Document opened in a binder.

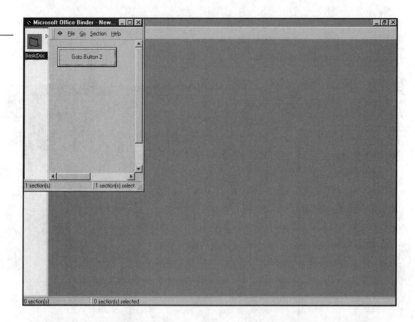

Figure 14.3

The ActiveX Document after the Viewport has been changed.

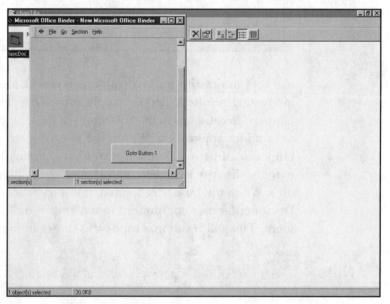

In this example, the Viewport is smaller that the ActiveX Document's displayable area. If the Viewport is larger or equal to the ActiveX Document's displayable area, changing the Viewport does not do anything.

Scrolling and Resizing Issues

As shown earlier, the Viewport can be smaller than the displayable area of the ActiveX Document. In these situations, the developer should be concerned with scrolling and resizing issues.

The UserDocument modules provide methods and properties for managing scrolling issues. The Scroll event is used to notify the ActiveX Document that scrolling is occurring. The document can use this event to move GUI objects that are coordinated with the scrollbar. In addition, the UserDocument has a ContinousScroll property. The property can be set to True or False. If set to True, scrolling is continuous. If set to False, the UserDocument will only be redrawn when the thumb on the scrollbar is released. The default is set to True.

With the HScrollSmallChange and VScrollSmallChange properties, you can control the scrolling amount when the user clicks on the scrollbar. There are no corresponding large change properties provided; this view is determined by the ViewportHeight and ViewportWidth properties.

The point at which the scrollbars and types of scrollbars are supported can be controlled using the MinHeight and MinWidth and Scrollbars properties. The MinHeight and MinWidth properties determine when the scrollbars are visible. The Scrollbars property is used to determine which scrollbars are visible in the Viewport.

Asynchronous Properties

ActiveX Documents, like ActiveX Controls, have the capability to load properties at runtime asynchronously. The use of asynchronous properties will reduce wait times by the end user because the user can use other parts of the ActiveX Document while the property is been downloading. The UserDocument provides notifications via events as the properties are downloaded asynchronously. The UserControl provides the two methods for managing asynchronous property loads. These methods are AsyncRead and

CancelAsyncRead. The AsyncRead method is used to start the property read process. The function is defined as follows:

```
AsyncRead Target, AsyncType [, PropertyName]
```

The Target parameter defines the URL location where the property value is stored. The AsyncType parameter is an integer value that defines the type of AsyncRead being performed. The variables are enumerated as follows:

vbAsyncTypeFile   The data being requested is in a file.

vbAsyncTypeByteArray   The data being requested is in an array of bytes.

vbAsyncTypePicture   The data provided is for a Picture object.

The PropertyName parameter is an optional parameter used to define which property the data requested is for.

If an asynchronous request is made, it can be cancelled by using the CancelAsyncRead method. The CancelAsyncRead method is defined as follows:

```
CancelAsyncRead [PropertyName]
```

The method takes only one optional parameter, the PropertyName. Only the asynchronous request of that property name will be cancelled; all other requests will still be carried out. If the PropertyName is not specified, the request that did not have a property name will be cancelled.

After the data request is completed, the UserDocument object receives an AsyncReadComplete event. This event is used to notify the UserDocument that the read operation is completed. The event is defined as follows:

```
Sub object_AsyncReadComplete(PropertyValue As AsyncProperty)
```

An instance of the `AsyncProperty` object is supplied to the event, which has all the data returned from the asynchronous request. The `AsyncProperty` has the following three properties:

`Value`   A variant value that contains the result of the property read

`PropertyName`   A string property name that was passed to the `AsyncRead` property

`AsyncType`   An integer that specifies the type of data returned—a file, byte array, or picture

Determining the Type of Container

When writing an ActiveX Document, you cannot assume that the only container will be Internet Explorer or Microsoft Binder. In some cases, you may wish to place container-specific code in your ActiveX Documents in order to use some of the features provided by the container. You may wish to notify Internet Explorer to navigate to a specific URL, for example. If this code is used with a Microsoft Binder container, nothing will happen.

The `UserDocument` module provides a `Parent` property that re-turns the object of the container in which the Document is running. Therefore, if you are running in an Internet Explorer container, the `Parent` property is pointing to the object that supports the `IwebBrowserApp` interface. The method and properties of this object can be used in your ActiveX Document to carry out tasks as needed.

If the type of the container must be determined, the `TypeName` function is used to return the name of the interface for the `Parent` object. The following code snippet demonstrates this:

```
Dim strName as string
strName = TypeName(Parent)
```

Depending on the container, the `TypeName` value could be `SECTION`, `IwebBrowserApp`, and so forth. You can write code that restricts the types of containers that your application supports. The following code snippet demonstrates this:

```
Dim strName as string
strName = TypeName(Parent)
select case UCASE(strName)
     case "SECTION"
          'This object is ok
     case else
          msgbox "Using this document in a container other than
          ➡Microsoft Binder, could cause unpredictable results"
end select
```

Comparing ActiveX Documents to Embedded Objects

ActiveX Documents can be used in one of two ways by a container. Documents can be *linked* or *embedded*. When a container has a link to an ActiveX Document, it actually has a reference to the document. The reference points to a file stored on some device. When the document is changed, the link can be updated; it then reflects the changes made to the document. Linked documents cannot be edited in-place. This means that the linked document is always edited from its *host* application. If a Word document has linked an Excel spreadsheet, when the user opens the linked Excel spreadsheet from Word, the Excel application shows the linked document.

An alternative method to linking a document is to use embedding. When embedding occurs, a copy of the document is taken and placed in the container. This means that changes to the source document are not reflected in the embedding document. If embedding is used, the overhead in terms of file size is larger because a full copy of the embedded document is kept inside the container document. ActiveX Documents can behave as either embedded or linked documents—this is largely a function as to how the ActiveX Document is placed in the container.

Creating an ActiveX Project with One or More UserDocument Objects

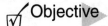 Objective

Many ActiveX Document projects will have more than one type of ActiveX Document. In these cases, you will have two or more UserDocument objects. It may be necessary to pass data between the two documents. This can occur when one document has data that the other document depends on. In addition, with ActiveX Documents, you do not necessarily know in what sequence your ActiveX Document was invoked. You might expect that the normal course of your application is to use document A, for example, and then document B. However, there is no default behavior that prevents the user from going to document B directly. If you have code in document B that depends on data from document A, you could have some problems.

This behavior can be controlled using global variables, to pass between documents. The sample application in the Ex14.2 directory demonstrates this concept. The project is made up of three files, a module, and two UserDocument modules. In the module, a global variable called gobjCurrentDocument is defined as an object. This variable is used to pass the document object references between documents. The two UserDocuments are for the most part identical; they both display each other's data. The code listing for one UserDocument is shown as follows:

```
Public Property Get DocText()
   'Return the current document's code
   DocText = txtDocOne.Text
End Property


Private Sub Command1_Click()
   'Navigate to a new document
   Set gobjCurrentDocument = Me
     Hyperlink.NavigateTo App.Path & "\usrdoc2.vbd"
End Sub
```

```
Private Sub UserDocument_Show()
    'When show is called then get the other documents
    'data using the global variable
    If gobjCurrentDocument Is Nothing Then
        txtOutputFromOtherDoc.Text = "No Older Document"
    Else
        txtOutputFromOtherDoc.Text = gobjCurrentDocument.DocText
        'destroy the object reference
        Set gobjCurrentDocument = Nothing
    End If
End Sub
```

Each module has only the three following procedures:

▶ The `DocText` property is used to return the document's data.

▶ The `Command1_click` event is used to navigate to the other document, and it sets the global variable to itself.

▶ The `Show` event is fired when the document is displayed. The global variable is checked, and the data from the other document or a `No Older Document` message is shown.

When the application is executed from an Internet Explorer container, a window like Figure 14.4 appears.

Figure 14.4

The first document opened.

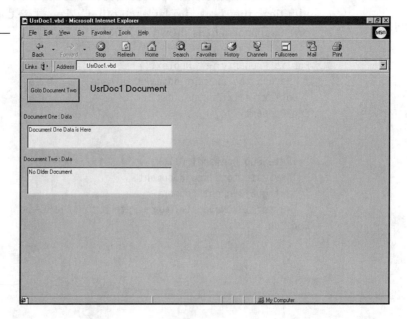

Notice that the Document Two text box is set to No Older Document. This mean that the global variable is set to nothing, and an older instance of Document Two was not running. When the command button is presented, a window as shown in Figure 14.5 appears.

Figure 14.5

The second document opened.

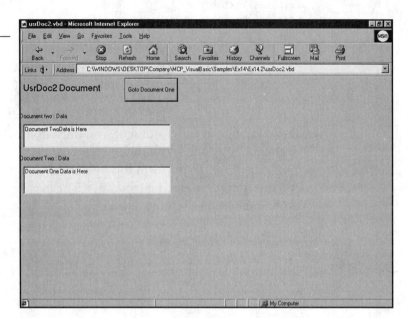

Notice that the second text box now has Document One's data. This method can also be used to enforce the sequence in your ActiveX Documents. If the global variable is not equal to a given value, you could then notify the user and navigate to the appropriate document.

Persistent Data for an ActiveX Document

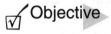 Objective

ActiveX Documents need to have data saved to a persistent location. The UserDocument object provides events to manage the saving of persistent data. The ReadProperties, WriteProperties, and InitProperties events are used to notify the UserDocument to save data out to disk. These events are discussed in detail in Chapter 13, "Creating and Using ActiveX Controls." The ReadProperties and WriteProperties events both receive a PropBag object. The

`PropertyBag` object is used to read and write data from a persistent location. An example of using the `ReadProperties` and `WriteProperties` events is shown as follows:

```
Private Sub UserDocument_ReadProperties(PropBag As PropertyBag)
  txtnotes.Text = _
    PropBag.ReadProperty("UserNotes", _
    "Hello")
End Sub
Private Sub UserDocument_WriteProperties(PropBag As PropertyBag)
    PropBag.WriteProperty " UserNotes ", txtnotes.Text, ""
End Sub
```

As items change in the document, you must notify the container. The container will then call the `WriteProperties` event at some appropriate time. To perform this task, the `PropertyChanged` method is used to notify the container. The `PropertyChanged` syntax of the method is defined as follows:

```
PropertyChanged PropertyName
```

If the optional `PropertyName` parameter is specified, you are notifying the container that a specific property has been changed.

Automating an ActiveX Document

 Objective

Automating an ActiveX Document can be done every easily. All public properties and methods are accessible after an instance of the document is created. Early binding or late binding can be used with the ActiveX Document. For more information on early or late binding, refer to Chapter 11, "Building Microsoft ActiveX Clients." The most important element of automating an ActiveX Document is to determine the `ProgID` (appname.docname). The application name is usually specified in the Project Properties window. The document name is the name of the `UserDocument` module as assigned by the programming. After this information is obtained, you can automate the ActiveX Document as follows:

```
Dim objDoc as object
Set objDoc = CreateObject("MyApp.MyDoc")
'Call methods and properties of the UserDocument objDoc.
```

The properties and methods of this will be unique to each type of ActiveX Document type.

Adding an ActiveX Document to a Web Page

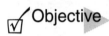

An ActiveX Document can be added to a web page. The HREF tag in HTML can be used to refer to an ActiveX Document. After the user selects the HREF tag, the web browser will try to open the file. If the server for the ActiveX Document is installed on the machine, the document will open.

An example of using the HREF tag is shown as follows:

```
<HTML>
<HEAD>
<META HTTP-EQUIV="Content-Type" CONTENT="text/html;
➥charset=windows-1252">
<META NAME="Generator" CONTENT="Microsoft Word 97">
<TITLE>Sample HTML</TITLE>
<META NAME="Template" CONTENT="C:\PROGRAM FILES\MICROSOFT
➥OFFICE\OFFICE\html.dot">
</HEAD>
<BODY LINK="#0000ff" VLINK="#800080" BGCOLOR="#ffffff">

<P> 
<P>This is a sample HTML that will open up an ActiveX Document
➥when the "Open User Document" hyperlink is clicked
<P ALIGN="CENTER"><IMG SRC="line1.gif" WIDTH=623 HEIGHT=7>
<P ALIGN="CENTER"><A HREF=" UsrDoc1.vbd">Open User Document
➥</A><BR>
</P>
<P ALIGN="CENTER"><IMG SRC="line1.gif" WIDTH=623 HEIGHT=7></P>
</BODY>
</HTML>
```

Note that the HREF tag just refers to the ActiveX Document called UsrDoc1.vbd.

Exercises

Exercise 14.1: Making ActiveX Documents Persistent

In this exercise, you read and write properties from Property Bags. To complete this exercise, follow these steps:

1. Write the code necessary to read the following properties in the `UserDocument_ReadProperties` event:

   ▶ The caption of a button named `btnMain`

   ▶ The `text` property of a text box called `txtUserId`

   ▶ The backcolor of the `UserDocument`

2. Write the code necessary that will write the following properties in the `UserDocument_WriteProperties` event:

   ▶ The caption of a button named `btnMain`

   ▶ The `text` property of a text box called `txtUserId`

   ▶ The backcolor of the `UserDocument`

3. Save the file for the next exercise.

The solution to this exercise is as follows:

```
Private Sub UserDocument_ReadProperties(PropBag As PropertyBag)
   btnMain.Caption = _
   PropBag.ReadProperty("btnMain", _
   "")
   ➥txtUserId.text = _
   PropBag.ReadProperty("txtUserId", _
   "")
   ➥backcolor = _
   PropBag.ReadProperty("backcolor")

End Sub
Private Sub UserDocument_WriteProperties(PropBag As PropertyBag)
   PropBag.WriteProperty "btnMain", _
   ➥btnMain.caption, ""
   PropBag.WriteProperty " txtUserId ", _
   ➥txtUserId.text, ""
```

```
      PropBag.WriteProperty " backcolor", _
    backcolor, ""
End Sub
```

Exercise 14.2:   Adding ActiveX Documents to a Web Page

In this exercise, you need to create an HTML file that enables the user to open the ActiveX Document from the preceding exercise.

The solution to this exercise is as follows:

```html
<HTML>
<HEAD>
<TITLE>Solution to Exercise</TITLE>
<META NAME="Template" CONTENT="C:\PROGRAM FILES\MICROSOFT
OFFICE\OFFICE\html.dot">
</HEAD>
<BODY LINK="#0000ff" VLINK="#800080" BGCOLOR="#ffffff">

<P>This is a sample HTML that will open up an ActiveX Document
when the "Open User Document" hyperlink is clicked
<P ALIGN="CENTER"><IMG SRC="line1.gif" WIDTH=623 HEIGHT=7>
<P ALIGN="CENTER"><A HREF=" UsrDoc1.vbd">Open User Document
</A><BR>
</P>
<P ALIGN="CENTER"><IMG SRC="line1.gif" WIDTH=623 HEIGHT=7></P>
</BODY>
</HTML>
```

Review Questions

1. Your ActiveX Document needs to determine what type of container is siting it. Which of the following commands will provide this functionality?

   A. `TypeName(Parent)`

   B. `GetName(Parent)`

   C. `Parent.Name`

   D. `Parent.Type`

2. Your project file has two documents. You need to pass data between the two documents at runtime. How can this be done?

   A. You cannot pass data between documents at runtime.

   B. Create a public method and use it.

   C. Create a global variable in a module.

   D. This is not necessary.

3. Which of following events is fired when an Asynchronous Data Request is completed?

   A. Asynchronous Data Requests are not available in Visual Basic.

   B. `AsyncReadComplete`.

   C. `ReadComplete`.

   D. `Load`.

4. To start and cancel an Asynchronous Data Request, which of the following commands should be used?

   A. `AsyncRead` and `CancelAsyncRead`.

   B. `StartAsyncRead` and `CancelAsyncRead`.

   C. `Parent.AsyncRead` and `Parent.CancelAsyncRead`.

   D. The Asynchronous Data Request is not supported in Visual Basic.

5. Which of the following statements are false about ActiveX Documents?

    A. ActiveX Documents can only be used in Microsoft Internet Explorer.

    B. ActiveX Documents can be implemented as DLLs or Executables.

    C. ActiveX Documents can run only inside a container.

    D. All are incorrect.

6. The user has changed some items in your ActiveX Document and you must notify the container that data has been changed. Which of the following statements will notify the container?

    A. `Parent.PropertyChanged = True`

    B. `PropertyChanged = TRUE`

    C. `PropertyChanged`

    D. `Container.ChildChanged`

7. Your ActiveX Document has two string properties, named `MyData` and `YourData` respectively. The variables are declared as follows:

    ```
    Friend MyData As String
    Public YourData As String
    ```

    If a client uses automation to create an instance of the ActiveX Document, which of the following is true?

    A. The client does not have access to the variable `YourData` because it is not a container.

    B. The client cannot use automation to create an instance of an ActiveX Document.

    C. The client has access to both variables.

    D. The client has access to the `MyData` variable only.

    E. The client has access to the `YourData` variable only.

8. If the display area that the container provides is smaller than the display area of the ActiveX Document, what happens?

   A. Nothing.

   B. Scrollbars will appear that enable you to see the ActiveX Document.

   C. A new larger window is created that enables you to edit the document.

   D. A runtime error that the ActiveX Document must trap occurs.

9. When an ActiveX Document created in Visual Basic is compiled as a DLL or executable, an additional document file is created. What is the extension of the file, and what is its purpose?

   A. .vbd (Visual Basic document)—the file is used by a container to open the ActiveX Document.

   B. The file has no extension. The file is used by a container to open the ActiveX Document.

   C. .ado (ActiveX Document object)—the file is used by a container to open the ActiveX Document.

   D. This file type does not exist in Visual Basic.

Answers to Review Questions

1. A. TypeName function is used to return the type of object a current object pointer contains. For more information, see the section titled "Determining the Type of Container."

2. C. Global variables defined in a module can be effectively used to pass data between documents. For more information, see the section titled "Creating an ActiveX Project with One or More UserDocument Objects."

3. B. When an Asynchronous Data Request is completed, the `AsyncReadComplete` event is fired to notify the client. For more information, see the section titled "Asynchronous Properties."

4. A. The `AsyncRead` method starts the Asynchronous Data Request, and a `CancelAsyncRead` terminates the request. For more information, see the section titled "Asynchronous Properties."

5. A. ActiveX Documents can be used with any container that supports ActiveX Documents, such as the OLE control or the Microsoft Binder application. For more information, see the section titled "Determining the Type of Container."

6. B. The `PropertyChanged` property is a Boolean used to denote whether the ActiveX Document data has changed. For more information, see the section titled "Persistent Data for an ActiveX Document."

7. E. A client application can use automation to create an instance of ActiveX Documents. The only variables that the client has access to are variables defined as public variables. For more information, see the section titled "Automating an ActiveX Document."

8. B. In this instance, scrollbars would appear around the displayable area that would allow navigation within the displayable area. For more information, see the section titled "Viewport."

9. A. The .vbd file is used by a container to open an ActiveX Document. For more information, see the section titled "Understanding the `UserDocument` Module."

Answers to Test Yourself Questions at Beginning of Chapter

1. ActiveX Documents, like automation components, can be implemented either as Dynamic Linked Libraries or executables. ActiveX Documents can viewed inside any container that supports ActiveX Documents, such as Microsoft Internet Explorer or Microsoft Binder. ActiveX Documents can obtain data asynchronously from an URL or a file. The data in an ActiveX Document can be saved to a persistent location such as a file. See "Understanding the `UserDocument` Module."

2. Scrollbars that enable the user to navigate around the displayable area will appear. See "Scrolling and Resizing Issues."

3. During a `Write` operation, the developer uses the `PropertyChanged` property of the ActiveX Document to notify the container that data has been changed in the ActiveX Document. At some point, the ActiveX container will fire the `WriteProperties` event of the ActiveX Document. The container supplies a `PropertyBag` object when the `WriteProperties` event is fired. This `PropertyBag` object can be used to write data to a persistent location by using the `WriteProperty` method.

   During a read operation, usually when the ActiveX Document is loaded, the `ReadProperties` event is fired by the ActiveX Document container. As with the `WriteProperties` event, a `PropertyBag` object is supplied that allows the object to be read from the persistent location by using the `ReadProperty` method.

   See "Persistent Data for an ActiveX Document."

4. The following HTML code will open an ActiveX Document called mydoc.vbd:

   ```
   <A HREF="mydoc.vbd">Open User Document</A>
   ```

   See "Adding an ActiveX Document to a Web Page."

5. The types of data that can be requested are file, byte array, and picture. See "Asynchronous Properties."

Chapter 15

Creating Applications That Can Access the Internet

This chapter helps you prepare for the exam by covering the following objectives:

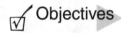

▶ Gain access to the Internet or an intranet by using the Hyperlink object

▶ Create an application that has the capability to browse HTML pages

▶ Create an application that enables connections to the Internet

Test Yourself! Before reading this chapter, test yourself to determine how much study time you will need to devote to this section.

1. What is the difference between TCP and UDP?

2. Name some objects that have a `Hyperlink` object.

3. What are some benefits of asynchronous downloading?

4. Name some protocols that are available using the Internet Transfer Control?

5. You want to create an FTP client in VB5. Which control(s) would enable you to do this?

6. You want to create a WWW browser in VB5. Which control(s) would enable you to do this?

7. What will happen when the following line executes in the code for an ActiveX Control that is hosted by a VB5 form?

```
Hyperlink.Navigate "http://www.mcp.com/"
```

Answers are located at the end of the chapter...

This chapter covers accessing the Internet or an intranet using VB5. The Internet is a large, globally interconnected network of computers; an intranet, on the other hand, is a smaller network. Usually, this is a company-specific network. Both share a common set of communication methods and protocols.

Visual Basic has features for accessing these networks. `UserControls` and `UserDocuments` directly support Internet communication using the `Hyperlink` object and asynchronous download. By adding the appropriate ActiveX Controls to a project, you can allow any program to access this valuable resource.

This chapter covers the creation of programs to access the Internet in the following sections:

▶ What is the Internet?

▶ Communication methods and protocols

▶ `Winsock` control

▶ Internet Transfer Control

▶ `Hyperlink` object

▶ Asynchronous download

▶ `WebBrowser` object

What Is the Internet?

The Internet began its existence to enable communication. American military leaders wanted to ensure that they could communicate in case of nuclear war. Researchers used this need to develop a series of communication protocols. The benefit of these protocols was that they did not just exist on a single company's computers. They were open and extensible. The protocols allow different computer systems to communicate and share information. They have allowed the original network to expand into what is called the Internet.

The Internet has grown into a massive, world-spanning network. However, the core technology has not changed fundamentally. Many of the original protocols remain the same and are available on many types of computers. This allows for the creation of smaller, company-wide or regional networks. These smaller internets have come to be known as intranets.

In reality, any network that supports the protocols that make the Internet are internets in their own right. VB5 can create programs for any of these networks. ActiveX Controls and Documents enable the programmer to reach across one of these internets and pull information back. The core product has become Internet aware. Controls have been added to allow for easy communication on a regional, national, or global scale.

 Note Before you can begin to program for the Internet, you need to be running TCP/IP as a network protocol. For more information on installing TCP/IP, see your operating system manuals.

Communication Methods and Protocols

Any communication on the Internet uses one or more of a variety of communications protocols. In fact, a veritable alphabet soup of protocols has sprouted over the years the Internet has been in existence. They form a hierarchy of protocols, from the higher-level ones such as SMTP (Simple Mail Transfer Protocol) or HTTP (Hypertext Transfer Protocol), down to the lower-level protocols that they make use of to perform their tasks.

The idea of a protocol, however, is very simple. It is the same idea that guides most conversations. Someone says something. That something leads to a reply. The reply leads to further conversation, and onward. The conversation in Table 15.1 represents a protocol in action, for example, and one possible Internet interpretation.

Table 15.1

The Pizza Protocol		
Caller	Pizza Place	Interpretation
Dials pizza outlet		OPEN pizza
	"Hello, you have reached Pizza Heaven."	HELO
"I'd like a large pizza with everything."		GET pizza
	"OK"	ACK
"Goodbye"		CLOSE
	"Goodbye"	ACK

Any conversation that you may think of that follows a regimented or partially regimented flow is really a protocol. Usually it involves a two-way passage of information. Often there are acknowledgments before the conversation can continue. It is the same with Internet protocols.

Sockets

By its very nature, network programming is complex. At the lowest level, a great deal of overhead is needed to manage the conversation. Checksums, for example, ensure that the message received is the same as the message sent. Handshaking is required, and all members of the conversation must be able to identify themselves and the source of any message. To avoid the majority of this overhead, a group of students at the University of California at Berkeley developed *sockets*.

A socket is a communication tool. It is an abstraction of the real conversation allowing two programs to communicate without requiring management of the low-level details of the network (see Figure 15.1). Many programs written to access an Internet use sockets for this reason. In the Win32 environment, the Windows sockets DLL—WINSOCK.DLL—is the implementation of sockets.

Figure 15.1

An example of sockets.

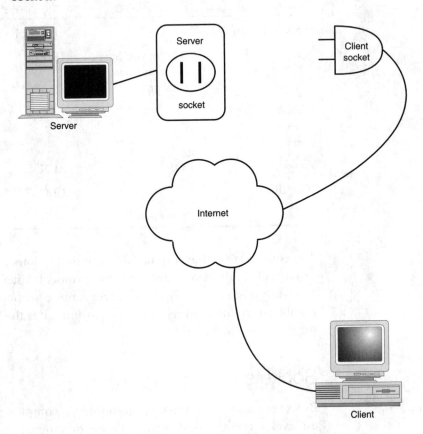

A socket is a combination of address, direction, port, and protocol. First, a machine on the Internet must "serve up" the socket. This supplies the address of the socket. It also identifies the socket as a server, or "listening" socket. When you attempt to connect to `http://www.microsoft.com` with your web browser, you are in fact attempting to connect to a socket made available by the computer at a specific Internet address—in this case, 207.68.158.58 (as of this writing). This computer is running a program that has created a socket "listening" to a specific port.

A port is essentially a subaddress on that machine. It is an unsigned 16-bit value (from 1 to 65536). The purpose of the port is to identify an application on a computer. Each program has a port assigned when created. Many of these ports are common, and have numbers that are well known. Table 15.2 shows some of these.

Table 15.2

Well-Known Port Numbers	
Port	Program
21	FTP (File Transfer Protocol)
23	Telnet
25	SMTP (Simple Mail Transfer Protocol)
80	HTTP (Hypertext Transfer Protocol)
110	POP3 (PostOffice Protocol)
119	NNTP (Network News Transfer Protocol)

These ports, as well as many others, are listed in a document available online. This document is available at `http://ds1.internic.net/rfc/rfc1700.txt`. This document is known as an RFC (Request for Comment). Requests for Comments are suggested standards for the Internet. Most, if not all, of the protocols used on the Internet are described in one or more RFCs.

Any port number not listed in this document can be considered available. To avoid possible conflict with existing assigned port numbers, however, any programs you create should have a port number greater than 1024.

After you know the server that has a socket listening at a specific port, your client program can attempt to connect to it. Do this by having the client program create a socket connecting to the address of the server machine, at that specified port.

The final important part of a socket is its protocol. This is the focus of the next section.

Protocols

Three of the lower-level Internet protocols are TCP (Transmission Control Protocol), UDP (User Datagram Protocol), and IP (Internet Protocol). Most of the higher-level protocols use these three protocols to perform their work.

Internet Protocol (IP)

IP is the protocol responsible for identifying and locating computers on the Internet. Each computer must have a unique IP address. This ensures that a message addressed to one computer will arrive at that computer. (Think of it as the computer's phone number.) When one computer attempts to send a message to another computer, it needs to know the number to dial. An IP address is a 32-bit value, usually displayed in the form of four numbers. These four numbers are the four bytes that make up the 32-bit value. One example of an IP address is 205.200.16.65. If more than one computer had this address, there would be confusion because messages directed at one computer would arrive at both.

Note

> The 4-byte representation of an IP address is really for the benefit of humans. As far as the computers on the Internet are concerned, 205.200.16.65 is the computer at 11001101110010000001000001000001 or 3452440641.

Transmission Control Protocol

TCP is one of the most used of the lower-level protocols. It is a connection-oriented protocol. This means that it guarantees the reliability of the connection. When you attempt to connect to a specific computer across the Internet, either you will connect or you will get an error. If something happens with the connection, an error will occur. For this reason, TCP is a very reliable protocol because you are constantly made aware of the state of the connection.

One excellent comparison of TCP is a phone call. You dial a phone number. If the phone number doesn't exist, the phone company makes you aware. The connection should happen only with the number you called. Similarly, when you say something to the other party, if he or she doesn't understand what you said, that person lets you know immediately. Finally, if something happens to the connection, both parties are aware of it.

TCP also requires a great deal of overhead. At each step in the connection and conversation between two computers using TCP, there will be handshaking and checksums. *Handshaking* occurs when one computer either positively or negatively acknowledges receipt of information. It is like when you ask during a conversation, "Is that okay?" The other person responds, "Yes" or "No." A *checksum* is some calculation that can be performed on the data. The server performs the calculation on the data before sending. It includes the checksum with the data. The client computer then performs the calculation on the data upon receipt. If the checksum that came with the data matches the new checksum, the receiving computer will acknowledge its receipt. This ensures that nothing happened to the data during transit.

The reliability of TCP outweighs any possible performance issues with most computers. For this reason, most high-level Internet protocols use TCP as a transport mechanism.

User Datagram Protocol (UDP)

UDP is a connection less protocol. This means that UDP does not guarantee the reliability of the connection between server and client. It is broadcast, targeted at one recipient computer. However, the message is sent without any form of checking. The sender cannot confirm whether the recipient receives it, as is possible with TCP. The recipient cannot determine whether it missed the message. Finally, one last possible problem with UDP is that each message has a limited amount of space for the message. This limitation is determined by the operating system.

One comparison with UDP is mailing post cards. You can write only so much information on a post card. If you have more information, you must use multiple post cards. You send the post card out. You have no idea whether the recipient has or has not received it, unless the recipient writes back. Finally, the recipient has no knowledge of your sending the message.

With all the limitations of UDP, one might ask, "Why would I ever want to use it?" The answer is those very limitations. UDP is a very "thin" protocol. Very little overhead is required to transmit any information. In addition, with the improvement in network reliability, many of the seemingly unreliable features of UDP are overshadowed. For this reason, many of the protocols originally written to use TCP have UDP versions.

Higher-Level Protocols

Many high-level protocols are used on the Internet. Most of the programs associated with the Internet are wrappers around one or more protocols. Some of these protocols include the following:

▶ FTP
File Transfer Protocol
Protocol used to do basic file management
Uses text messages as commands

▶ SMTP
Simple Mail Transfer Protocol
Protocol used to transfer mail between peers (server to server or client to server)
Uses text messages as commands

▶ LDAP
Lightweight Directory Access Protocol
Protocol used to view "White Page" like directories of information
Uses function calls as commands

Each of these protocols uses either TCP or UDP to perform its functions. TCP and UDP are the transports used to carry the messages for these high-level protocols.

Uniform Resource Locators (URLs)

With all the information available on the Internet, it becomes a problem to uniquely identify anything. URLs were developed to help with this problem. An URL is a globally unique name for a file, program, or other resource.

Most people who have used the World Wide Web have seen an URL. It identifies the protocol used to communicate, the computer making the resource available, and the location on that computer where the resource is located. Figure 15.2 is an example of an URL and Table 15.3 describes the different sections of an URL.

Figure 15.2

An example of a Uniform Resource Locator.

Table 15.3

Sections of an URL		
Section	Purpose	Example
Protocol	Identifies the protocol that will be used to access the resource.	http: ftp: telnet:
Server	Identifies the server supplying the resource. May point to a real server, or a virtual server (an alias for another server).	www.microsoft.com
Port	Identifies the port on the server supplying the resource. If not used, the default port for that protocol will be used.	:80
Path	Identifies the location on the server for the resource. May be an actual path or a virtual path that is actually located somewhere else on the server or another server.	/vbasicdefault.htm

Many of the new features in VB5 that use the Internet use URLs to access the Internet.

Winsock **Control**

The Winsock control is a wrapper around TCP and UDP. It enables the programmer to create almost any type of program that accesses the Internet. The programmer is responsible for implementing any high-level protocol the control will be used for. Simple data transfer is provided by the control, however.

TCP Client

A TCP client is any program that actively connects to a TCP server. It may also be a server in another communication. As the active participant, the most important properties are those that relate to making the connection. They are as follows:

- ▶ Protocol
  Either TCP or UDP
  The communication protocol that will be used for the communication

- ▶ RemoteHost
  The name or IP address that this client will attempt to access

- ▶ RemotePort
  The port number that the client will attempt to access

After setting the preceding properties, the client connects to the server with the Connect method. A sample connection would look similar to this:

```
Private Sub cmdConnect_Click()
    With sckClient
        .RemoteHost = txtHost.Text
        .RemotePort = txtPort.Text
        .Connect
    End With
End Sub
```

If the host responds, the Connect event of the Winsock control will execute. This enables you to notify the user of your program that the connection has been made. In addition, any configuration that needs to be done to prepare for the connection may be done at this time.

To send information to the server, use the SendData method of the Winsock control. This method takes one parameter, the data to transmit:

```
Private Sub cmdSend_Click()
    SckClient.SendData txtOut.Text
End Sub
```

When the server sends data, the DataArrival event is fired. This event allows the program to receive the information sent in. This could be displayed, saved to a file, or used to perform some other operation. To receive the data, use the GetData method of the Winsock control:

```
Private Sub sckClient_DataArrival(ByVal bytesTotal As Long)
    Dim sTemp As String
    sckClient.GetData sTemp, vbString, bytesTotal
    txtData.Text = txtData.Text & sTemp
End Sub
```

The GetData method takes three parameters, although the second and third parameters are optional. The first parameter is a variable that will receive the data. The second parameter is the data type of the data. Finally, the last parameter is the number of bytes to receive. Normally, the bytesTotal argument of the subroutine would be used here. Use a smaller value only if you don't need all the data received.

TCP Server

Many of the operations used to create a TCP client are also used to create a TCP server. Data is also transferred with the SendData method, and received during the DataArrival event. The only difference between the two is that the server does not actively connect to the client. The server waits, listening to a specific port, until a client attempts to connect.

When setting up a TCP server, you must first set the `LocalPort` property. Next, run the `Bind` method to connect to the port and begin listening with the `Listen` method. This creates the server and prepares it for a client to connect.

```
Private Sub Form_Load()
    With sckServer
        .LocalPort = 32000
        .Bind
        .Listen
    End With
End Sub
```

The `LocalPort` is the port the server will respond on. Later clients will connect to this server by connecting to this same port. The `Listen` method starts the server.

The server is notified of a client attempting to access it with the `ConnectionRequest` event. At this point, you can accept the connection request with the `Accept` method, or ignore it by doing nothing, which will refuse the connection attempt. The `ConnectionRequest` receives a single argument, `RequestID`. This value should be saved to identify the client later.

 Note   The `Close` method should be run before accepting the request. This ensures that the `Winsock` control is ready to accept the request. Alternately, you should check the `State` property to see whether an active connection already exists:

```
Private Sub sckServer_ConnectionRequest(ByVal requestID As Long)
    MsgBox "Connection request"
    sckServer.Close
    sckServer.Accept requestID
End Sub
```

After the client connects to the server, you should be able to communicate between the two programs, as can be seen in Figure 15.3.

Tip Each `Winsock` control can accept only a single client. If you need to accept multiple clients with your server, use a control array of `Winsock` controls. Create a new member of the array with each new connection request, and accept the request.

Figure 15.3

The TCP server and client communicating.

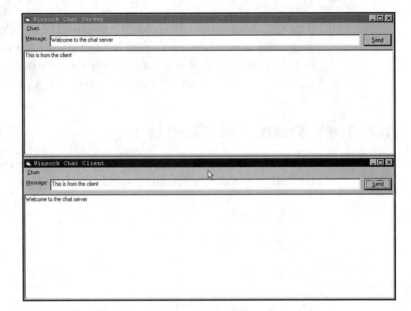

UDP Peer

Creating a program using UDP is easier than creating a program using TCP. Because UDP is a connection-less protocol, there is no need for the `Listen` and `Connect` methods. Instead, a UDP program acts less like a client or a server and more like a peer. Each UDP program is basically equivalent, loosely connected to a port, sending and receiving data.

To prepare the UDP program for sending and receiving information, `Bind` to a local port. This ensures that no other programs are currently using this port. Messages that arrive on this port will be passed to your program:

```
Private Sub Form_Load()
    With sckUDP
        .Protocol = sckUDPProtocol
```

```
            .LocalPort = 32001
            .Bind
        End With
End Sub
```

Later, data is sent and received in the same way as with the TCP protocol.

The Winsock control allows for the creation of a variety of Internet programs by wrapping an ActiveX Control around the two protocols TCP and UDP. It is a rather low-level control that exposes an easy interface for sending and receiving data via TCP/IP.

Internet Transfer Control

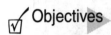 Objectives

The Internet Transfer Control (ITC) is an easy-access method to three of the most significant Internet protocols:

- ▶ Gopher

- ▶ FTP

- ▶ HTTP

The advantage of the ITC over the Winsock control is that it simplifies many of the functions of the supported protocols, which may take a great deal of code to perform with the Winsock control (downloading a file with FTP, for example).

Using the Internet Transfer Control

Much of the functionality of the ITC is in the following two methods:

- ▶ OpenURL

- ▶ Execute

These two methods are used by the three protocols exposed by the ITC to open files or to execute commands for the protocols. Each protocol has its own set of commands that are significant to it. The OpenURL method has this syntax:

```
object.OpenUrl URL [,datatype]
```

The DataType parameter can be one of the following:

- ▶ icString
  Data will be downloaded as a string. It will be converted to
  Unicode if necessary for display.

- ▶ icByteArray
  Data will be downloaded using the 8-bit ASCII character set.
  This is the method that should be used for downloading
  binary files.

The Execute method has this syntax:

```
object.Execute URL, operation, data, requestHeaders
```

The Operation parameter is specific to the protocol. Various values for this parameter will be discussed in the next sections. The
Data and RequestHeaders parameters are used when sending information to the server. This is especially true for HTTP forms.

For both protocols, the URL parameter defines the filename. For
HTTP, this is typically the file that will be displayed. For FTP, this
is the file that will be downloaded.

The other major difference between the two methods is that
OpenURL is synchronous; Execute is asynchronous. This means that
when OpenURL is used, the program will not continue executing
until either the URL has been opened or until an error occurs.
Execute, on the other hand, operates in the background. You
must either poll the control to determine the state of the operation or react to the events fired by the control.

StateChanged

Information on the state of the ITC is provided by the State-
Changed event. This event fires at each step in the communication

between server and client. The event provides a single argument, State. This argument identifies the current state of the communication and can be one of those listed in Table 15.4:

Table 15.4

Values for the State argument

Constant	Value	Description
IcNone	0	No state to report.
IcHostResolvingHost	1	The control is identifying the IP address for the requested computer name.
icHostResolved	2	The control successfully identified the IP address of the requested computer name.
icConnecting	3	The control is connecting to the server.
icConnected	4	The control has connected.
icRequesting	5	The control is sending a request.
icRequestSent	6	The control has sent the request.
IcReceivingResponse	7	The control is beginning to receive information from the remote computer.
IcResponseReceived	8	The control has received information from the remote computer. Data can be retrieved at this point with the GetChunk method.
IcDisconnecting	9	The control is disconnecting from the remote computer.
icDisconnected	10	The control has disconnected from the remote computer.
icError	11	An error has occurred.

Constant	Value	Description
IcResponseCompleted	12	The request has completed. All data has been sent and received. The operation has completed. Data can be retrieved at this point with the GetChunk method.

As described in the preceding list, the GetChunk method is used to retrieve the data sent. The GetChunk method has this syntax:

```
object.GetChunk( size [,datatype] )
```

Size is the number of bytes to accept from the connection. There are two options for setting the size parameter. You can set it to a value much higher than expected. Only the actual data will be returned. Alternatively, you can repeatedly call the GetChunk method with a smaller size until it returns nothing.

File Transfer Protocol

File Transfer Protocol (FTP) is used to transfer files between computers on the Internet. Traditionally, it is a text-based protocol, where simple text messages are sent to the server. The server then replies, either sending or receiving a file, or sending text information.

If all that is required is the download of a file, use the OpenURL method. If you require more control over the transfer, or if you want to use the control to perform file management operations, you must use the Execute method. Many of the possible settings should be familiar to those who remember DOS. Valid settings for the Operation parameter of the Execute method include those listed in Table 15.5.

Table 15.5

Settings for the *Operation* *Method for FTP*		
Operation	Description	Example
CD *DirectoryName*	Change Directory	Execute , "CD pub"
DELETE *FileName*	Delete file	Execute , "DELETE read.me"
DIR [*FileName*]	Same as Dir command in DOS	Execute , "DIR /pub"
GET *Source* [*Destination*]	Copies the file Source to the local hard drive as Destination	Execute , _"GET index.txt C:\index.txt"
MKDIR *DirectoryName*	Creates directory	Execute , "MKDIR /test"
PUT *Source* [*Destination*]	Copies the file Source from the local hard drive as Destination	Execute , _"PUT C:\index.htm /index.html"
QUIT	Close connection	Execute , "QUIT"
RMDIR *DirectoryName*	Removes directory	Execute , "RMDIR test"
SIZE *FileName*	Returns the size of the file	Execute "SIZE /index.html"

To execute one of these commands, use the full command as the second argument to the Execute method:

```
Private Sub cmdGetFile_Click()
    Inet1.Execute "ftp://ftp.microsoft.com", "Get index.txt"
End Sub
```

Hypertext Transfer Protocol

HTTP is the language used between web browsers and servers. Each request you make to a web server is actually an HTTP request for a specific page, graphic, or program. This happens in the background; and what is returned to you is the file, graphic, or result of the program.

If all that is required is the text of an HTML file, use the `OpenURL` method. This returns the full text of the file, as Figure 15.4 shows. If you require more control over the transfer, or if you want to use the control to pass information to a program on the Internet, you must use the `Execute` method. Valid settings for the `Operation` parameter of the `Execute` method include those listed in Table 15.6.

Figure 15.4

Using the HTTP protocol to view an HTML source.

Table 15.6

Settings for the `Operation` Method for HTTP

Operation	Description	Example
GET	Retrieves the file named in the URL parameter Same as `OpenURL`, but asynchronous	Execute "http:/ www.microsoft.com/ vbasic" & _"/ default.htm", "GET"
HEAD	Retrieves the headers of the file named in the URL property	Execute , "HEAD"
POST	Used to post information to a WWW form	Execute , "POST", sExtraInfo

Just as with FTP, acceptance of the data returned is performed with the `GetChunk` method in the `StateChanged` event.

Proxy Servers

Many intranets are located behind proxy servers and firewalls. These are hardware or software that limit the network traffic between the Internet and the local intranet. They do this by acting as an intermediate between the two networks. Any messages from the inside are sent to the proxy. The proxy then sends the information out. Similarly, the proxy must approve any network messages coming in.

The Internet Transfer Control is set up to allow for HTTP, Gopher, or FTP using a proxy. This is configured with the Proxy and AccessType properties. The AccessType property can be set to one of the following three values (see Table 15.7):

Table 15.7

Values for the AccessType Property		
Constant	Value	Descriptions
icUseDefault	0	Causes the ITC to use the information stored in the Registry for its proxy information.
icDirect	1	Causes the ITC to ignore any proxy and communicate directly with the host. This could be useful if the proxy is within the intranet.
icNamedProxy	2	Causes the ITC to use the proxy named in the Proxy property to route messages.

The Proxy property is used only if the AccessType is icNamedProxy.

Note

Internet Explorer 3.x stores its information about any proxy server in the Registry. This is the same information that the ITC will read. Therefore, if you have Internet Explorer configured to use a proxy, no other information is required to use the ITC.

The Internet Transfer Control is a wrapper around three of the most commonly used Internet protocols: FTP, Gopher, and HTTP. It allows a program to access these three protocols with a very simple interface. This interface includes the methods OpenURL and Execute. The ITC can also be made aware of any proxy server available.

Hyperlink **Object**

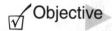 Objective

UserControls and UserDocuments were designed with the Internet in mind. One feature added to extend this is the Hyperlink object. This control is designed to assist in navigation, and has three methods to assist the programmer in creating linked documents. Those methods are as follows:

- ▶ GoForward

- ▶ GoBack

- ▶ Navigate

The Hyperlink object allows a programmer to access the hyperlinking capability of the host of the UserControl or UserDocument. ActiveX Controls and Documents can actually be displayed, or hosted, in many clients. The Hyperlink object is best used with those clients that support hypertext navigation, such as Internet Explorer.

 Tip

If the client does not support hypertext, you can still use the Hyperlink object. When you first attempt to use this object to navigate to a site, a client that supports hyperlinking—normally a web browser—will be started.

Navigation

The function of hyperlinking is to join information. It becomes useful only when you can move between two related chunks of information. With the Hyperlink object, this is done with the

NavigateTo method. This method takes one parameter: the location to navigate to. For example:

```
Private Sub cmdGoVB_Click()
    Hyperlink.NavigateTo "http://www.microsoft.com/vbasic/"
End Sub
```

The location you navigate to could be a location on the Internet or a local file.

The NavigateTo method has two optional parameters. The second parameter is the target within the location to navigate to. The third is the frame to use for the navigation.

Using the History

Part of navigation includes knowing where you were, and the Hyperlink object enables you to make use of this knowledge. Most hypertext clients will track the locations you have navigated to, and offer you the capability to move back to those sites. The Hyperlink object exposes this functionality through two methods: GoBack and GoForward. To move to past locations, run the GoBack method:

```
Private Sub cmdBack_Click()
    HyperLink.GoBack
End Sub
```

This causes the host of the UserControl or UserDocument to attempt to navigate back to the preceding page. Repeatedly calling this method enables the user to navigate to the beginning of the session.

After the GoBack method has been executed at least one time, the GoForward method becomes usable. The GoForward method causes the host to attempt to navigate forward through the history up to the current location.

 Tip There is no way to tell whether the GoForward and GoBack methods are available. That is, there is no way to identify whether any items are in the history list.

Asynchronous Download

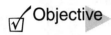 Objective

Asynchronous download is a process that allows `UserControl` or `UserDocument` objects to download information from an Internet. This download occurs in the background, allowing your program to continue to respond to the user. This feature is useful when loading data or pictures off an Internet site for use by the control or document.

One of the main uses for `UserControls` and `UserDocuments` is the display of information downloaded across the Internet. This information could be pictures, a file, or just raw data. The `UserControl` or `UserDocument` then uses this information to display to a user. Instead of waiting for the download to complete, asynchronous download allows the control to begin the download, and then to use the information after the download is complete. The download may be stopped at any point.

Information Available

The following types of information can be downloaded using asynchronous download:

- ▶ Pictures

- ▶ Files

- ▶ Binary data

If the download is of a picture, this picture is typically used to fill a picture box on the `UserControl` or `UserDocument`. The default VB5 picture box has been extended to allow the use of the two most common picture types that can be on the Internet: GIFs and JPGs. After the picture has been downloaded, there is no need to use the `LoadPicture` function. To load the picture, use the `Set` keyword to assign the picture property of the `PictureBox`. Figure 15.5 shows the result of this.

If the download is a file, the value returned will point at the location of the downloaded file, usually in the TEMP directory. It is the program's responsibility to read the file, move it, or perform whatever action is necessary, as Figure 15.6 shows.

Figure 15.5

Asynchronous download of a picture.

Figure 15.6

Asynchronous download of a file.

If the download is of a byte array, the value will be the bytes downloaded, as Figure 15.7 shows. If this information is binary data, it can then be used as is. More work must be done, however, if it is text information.

Figure 15.7

Asynchronous download of a byte array.

Internally, VB5 tracks all string variables as Unicode strings. This means that it uses 2 bytes for each character. A byte array uses 1 byte per character downloaded. Therefore, the byte array must be converted to Unicode before displaying or using it. Convert the byte array to a string with the StrConv function. StrConv performs a variety of string conversions, but the most significant is the capability to convert to and from Unicode. If you view a byte array before and after using StrConv, it will look similar to the following:

Before StrConv:

```
?????4?????????????
```

After StrConv (now Unicode):

```
The easiest way to program for Windows
```

Convert the byte array to a string with the following code:

```
sStringVar = StrConv(bytArray, vbUnicode)
```

Flow of Events

Begin the asynchronous download with the method AsyncRead. This is a method of UserControls and UserDocuments, and has the following form:

```
object.AsyncRead Location, AsyncType, [Property]
```

The location parameter represents the location of the information to download. This can be a path or an URL.

The type parameter represents which of the three types of information the object will be downloading. It can be one of the three values in Table 15.8.

Table 15.8

Legitimate Values for the AsyncType *Parameter*

Type	Value	Constant
Picture	0	vbAsyncTypePicture
File	1	vbAsyncTypeFile
Byte array	2	vbAsyncTypeByteArray

The property parameter is an optional setting. It is used to identify this download. This enables the programmer to start multiple asynchronous downloads for the same object and to deal with each in an independent way. The same value will be returned on completion of the download. Typically, it is used when the asynchronous download will be changing a property of the ActiveX Control or Document.

At any point after the download has begun, it can be cancelled. Canceling an asynchronous download is done with the CancelAsyncRead method. The CancelAsyncRead method takes one parameter to cancel: the property name. This is the same property name used in the call to AsyncRead.

AsyncReadComplete

If the asynchronous download is not interrupted, the AsyncReadComplete event will fire when the information has finished being downloaded.

AsyncProp

The program receives the information downloaded as an object. This object, AsyncProp, is a parameter of the AsyncReadComplete event. It has the following three properties:

- ▶ AsyncType

- ▶ Property

- ▶ Value

AsyncType defines the type of download that has just been completed. This value should match the AsyncType passed in the call to the AsyncRead method.

Property represents the unique identifier used in the call to AsyncRead.

Value represents the information downloaded.

WebBrowser **Object**

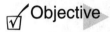 One very popular way of accessing the Internet is through the World Wide Web (WWW). Through the WWW, you can access a great deal of information. That information is bound together via hypertext, enabling you to jump from page to page. One page may be in North America, and the next in Europe.

With the advent of the WWW, and its increasing popularity, many forms of multimedia and extensions to HTML have arisen. Creating a browser to access all the types of information available on the WWW is a huge task. Why bother to create your own Web browser, however, when most users probably have one already? Anyone who is running Windows 95 or Windows NT 4 will already have a web browser: Internet Explorer.

Internet Explorer (3.0 and later) is made up of two main components. The first is the web browser itself; the other is the menu and interface structure. The web browser component of Internet Explorer is implemented as an ActiveX Control. This ActiveX Control can be automated, in place, inside the Internet Explorer application. It can also be used in a standalone application. This gives you all the benefits of your own web browser, without having to write one from scratch. In addition, as new extensions to HTML come out and Microsoft supports them, your application will receive those upgrades as well.

To perform either Automation of Internet Explorer or use of the WebBrowser object within it, your users must have Internet Explorer installed. The license agreement for Internet Explorer does not allow you to distribute the component parts of it individually. Because Internet Explorer is available free for Windows 95 and Windows NT, however, this should not pose a problem.

Note

An excellent tool for testing anything related to HTTP or HTML is Microsoft's Personal Web Server (PWS). This is a version of Internet Information Server that runs on either NT Workstation or Windows 95. There are different versions for these two operating systems. They enable you to test Web connections without having to be constantly online, tallying up an expensive access charge. They also enable you to use many of the IIS features such as Active Server Pages. PWS is available for download from Microsoft.

Automating Internet Explorer

Internet Explorer exposes an object model. This object model can be automated, using the same methods seen in Chapter 12, "Creating an Automation Server That Exposes Objects, Properties, Methods, and Events." The topmost object exposed by Internet Explorer is the `Application` object. This object enables the programmer to access the functionality of Internet Explorer, causing it to navigate to specific sites on the Internet. It also enables you to change the way the Internet Explorer window will appear onscreen.

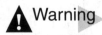

Warning

Internet Explorer 3.x does not support accessing previously created objects with the GetObject function. There is no way in VB5 to perform Automation on an already open copy of Internet Explorer.

To create a new instance of Internet Explorer, you should first load the Internet Explorer type library. This is available as Microsoft Internet Controls in the References list. Selecting this allows VB5 to perform type checking on your variables, and has the additional bonus of speeding up your code as well. A new object variable can then be created and pointed at a newly created instance of Internet Explorer:

```
Dim Ie As Object
Private Sub Form_Load()
    Set Ie = CreateObject("InternetExplorer.Application")
End Sub
```

A number of methods and properties allow the program to navigate using the web browser built into Internet Explorer, as well as to change its appearance. Table 15.9 lists some of these properties and methods.

Table 15.9

Methods and Properties of Internet Explorer

Methods/ Properties	M/P	Purpose
LocationName	P	Title of the current page in the Web browser
LocationURL	P	URL for the current page
Toolbar	P	Determines which toolbar is displayed
StatusBar	P	T/R if the status bar is currently displayed
StatusText	P	Text displayed on the status bar
Navigate	M	Enables you to direct Internet Explorer to another site
GoHome	M	Goes to the defined home page
GoSearch	M	Goes to the defined search page
Quit	M	Ends the Internet Explorer session

Using the `object` variable, you can navigate to a support site or intranet page by using the `Navigate` method:

```
Private Sub cmdNav_Click()
    Ie.Navigate "http://www.mcp.com/newriders/"
End Sub
```

Figure 15.8 shows the result of this.

Figure 15.8

*Automating
Internet Explorer.*

Using the WebBrowser Object

Alternatively, instead of automating the entire Internet Explorer application, you can add the WebBrowser object to your own application. This allows for greater control over the user environment. It also enables you to better integrate web browsing in your applications. Finally, it enables you to continually update the HTML support of your application. As Microsoft upgrades the HTML support in Internet Explorer, your application gets this upgrade for free.

The WebBrowser object is similar in functionality to the Internet Explorer Application object. The main difference is that the properties, methods, and events relating to the user interface of Internet Explorer are not available. It is the visual HTML parser and viewer that is normally associated with Internet Explorer. It is implemented as an ActiveX Control.

To add the WebBrowser object to your tool palette, select the Microsoft Internet Controls from the Components dialog box, as in Figure 15.9. This adds the WebBrowser object to the tool palette. This control is visible at design time, but appears only as a blank box.

Navigating with the WebBrowser object begins with one of the following three methods:

▶ GoHome

▶ GoSearch

▶ Navigate

Figure 15.9

*Selecting the
Microsoft Internet
controls.*

Normally, the `Navigate` method would be called to take the user
to the desired site. From there, the user can then navigate as normal. You could use this control to take a user to a support site for
your product or to a jump-off point of information related to your
program. Figure 15.10 shows an example.

Figure 15.10

*A WebBrowser
control in action.*

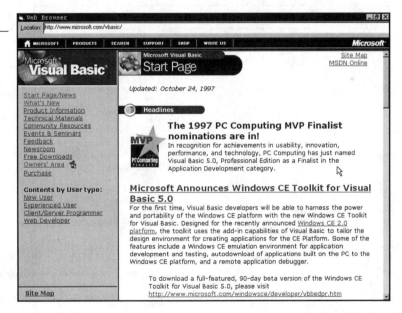

Exercises

Exercise 15.1: Creating a TCP Chat Server

To create a TCP chat server, complete the following steps:

1. Create a new Standard EXE project.

2. Choose Components from the Project menu.

3. Select the Microsoft Winsock Control and click on OK.

4. Add a Label, two TextBoxes, a CommandButton, and a Winsock control to the form.

5. Set the properties of the controls as listed in Table 15.10.

Table 15.10

Controls in the Winsock Server Exercise

Control	Property	Value
Label	Name	lblMsg
	Caption	&Message:
TextBox1	Name	txtMsg
TextBox2	Name	txtHistory
	Multiline	True
CommandButton	Name	cmdSend
	Caption	&Send
Winsock	Name	sckServer

6. Add code to Form_Load to set the LocalPort of the Winsock control (use a value above 1024) and start listening.

```
Private Sub Form_Load()
    With sckServer
        .LocalPort = 32000
        .Listen
    End With
End Sub
```

7. Add code to the `ConnectionRequest` event to accept any connections. The control should close any open connection
   before accepting.

```
Private Sub sckServer_ConnectionRequest
➥(ByVal requestID As Long)
    With sckServer
        If .State <> sckClosed Then
            .Close
            .Accept requestID
        End If
    End With
End Sub
```

8. Add code to the `DataArrival` event to add the arrived text to
   `txtHistory`.

```
Private Sub sckServer_DataArrival(ByVal
➥bytesTotal As Long)
    Dim sTemp As String
    sckServer.GetData sTemp, vbString,
    ➥bytesTotal
    txtHistory.Text = txtHistory.Text &
sTemp
End Sub
```

9. Start the program. Start a copy of Telnet, and connect to the
   server "LocalHost" using the same port you assigned to your
   `Winsock` control. You should be able to type messages back
   and forth.

Exercise 15.2: Creating a TCP Chat Client

To create a TCP chat client, complete the following steps:

1. Create a new Standard EXE project.

2. Choose Components from the Project menu.

3. Select the Microsoft Winsock Control and click on OK.

continues

4. Add a `Label`, two `TextBoxes`, a `CommandButton`, and a `Winsock` control to the form.

5. Set the properties of the controls as listed in Table 15.11.

Table 15.11

Controls in the Winsock Client Exercise

Control	Property	Value
Label	Name	lblMsg
	Caption	&Message:
TextBox1	Name	txtMsg
TextBox2	Name	txtHistory
	Multiline	True
CommandButton1	Name	cmdSend
	Caption	&Send
Winsock	Name	sckClient

6. Add a control to the form that will enable you to connect to the server "LocalHost" at the port used for the server in Exercise 15.1.

```
Private Sub cmdConnect_Click()
    With sckClient
        .RemoteHost = "localhost"
        .RemotePort = 32000
        .Connect
    End With
End Sub
```

7. Add code to the `cmdSend` button to send a message across the open connection. Use the text in `txtMsg`.

```
Private Sub cmdSend_Click()
    If Len(txtMsg.Text) Then
        sckClient.SendData txtMsg.Text
    End If
End Sub
```

8. Add code to the DataArrival event to add the arrived text to txtHistory.

```
Private Sub sckClient_DataArrival(ByVal
➥bytesTotal As Long)
    Dim sTemp As String
    sckClient.GetData sTemp, vbString,
    ➥bytesTotal
    txtHistory.Text = txtHistory.Text &
sTemp
End Sub
```

9. Start the program. Start a copy of the server application created in Exercise 15.1. You should be able to type messages back and forth.

Exercise 15.3: Creating a "View Source" for Web Pages

To use the Internet Transfer Control to view HTML as text, complete the following steps:

1. Create a new Standard EXE project.

2. Choose Components from the Project menu.

3. Select the Microsoft Internet Transfer Control from the list and click on OK.

4. Add a Label, two TextBoxes, a CommandButton, and Internet Transfer Control to the form.

5. Set the properties of the controls as in Table 15.12.

Table 15.12

Controls in the Internet Transfer Control Exercise

Control	Property	Value
Form	Name	frmITC
	Caption	Internet Transfer Control

continues

Exercise 15.3: Continued

Table 15.12 Continued

Controls in the Internet Transfer Control Exercise

Control	Property	Value
Label	Name	lblURL
	Caption	&Location:
TextBox	Name	txtURL
	Text	blank or a valid URL
CommandButton	Name	cmdView
	Caption	&View
TextBox	Name	txtView
	Text	blank
Internet Transfer Control	Name	Inet1

6. Add code to the form to resize the controls at runtime.

```
Private Sub Form_Resize()
    cmdView.Left = ScaleWidth -
    ➡cmdView.Width - 60
    txtURL.Width = cmdView.Left -
    ➡txtURL.Left - 240

    With txtView
        .Move 0, .Top, ScaleWidth,
        ScaleHeight - .Top
    End With
End Sub
```

7. Add code to cmdView to get the information from the re-quested URL. Use the location in the txtURL text box as a location. Display the information in txtView.

```
Private Sub cmdView_Click()
    txtView.Text =
    Inet1.OpenURL(txtURL.Text, icString)
End Sub
```

8. Run the application and view the source of various locations on the Internet.

Exercise 15.4:   Using the `Hyperlink` Object

To use the `Hyperlink` object of a `UserControl`, complete the following steps:

1. Create a new ActiveX Document DLL project.

2. Add a `CommandButton` and `TextBox` to the `UserDocument`.

3. Set the properties of the controls as listed in Table 15.13.

Table 15.13

Controls in the `Hyperlink` Example

Control	Property	Value
UserDocument	Name	DocNav
CommandButton	Name	CmdNav
	Caption	&Navigate
TextBox	Name	txtURL
	Text	blank or valid URL

4. Add an event procedure to the `Click` event of `cmdNav`. This should use the `Hyperlink` object to cause the host to navigate to the page defined in the URL property.

```
Private Sub cmdNav_Click()
    If Len(txtURL.Text) Then
        UserDocument.Hyperlink.NavigateTo
        ➥txtURL.Text
    End If
End Sub
```

5. Compile the project and create a DLL.

6. View the ActiveX Document in Internet Explorer and click the button. It should cause Internet Explorer to navigate to the assigned URL.

Exercise 15.5: Implementing Asynchronous Download

To create and use a UserControl object that uses asynchronous download, complete the following steps:

1. Create a new Standard EXE project.

2. Add a UserControl object to the project.

3. Add a PictureBox control to the new UserControl.

4. Set the properties of the PictureBox and UserControl as listed in Table 15.14.

Table 15.14

Controls in the URLPicture Control

Control	Property	Value
UserControl	Name	ctlURLPicture
PictureBox	Name	picImage

5. Add a Label, TextBox, and copy of the new UserControl to the form. Set the properties as listed in Table 15.15.

Table 15.15

Objects in the Asynchronous Download Example

Control	Property	Value
Form	Name	frmAsync
	Caption	asynchronous download
CommandButton	Name	cmdView
	Caption	&View
TextBox	Name	txtURL
	Text	blank or any value URL or file location for a graphic
URLPicture control	Name	ctlURLPicture1

6. Add code to the `UserControl` resize event procedure to allow the `PictureBox` to expand to fit the available space.

```
Private Sub UserControl_Resize()
    picImage.Move 0, 0, ScaleWidth,
    ➥ScaleHeight
End Sub
```

7. Create a new property called `PictureURL`. When this property is set, start an asynchronous download to attempt to download the picture from the new value.

```
Public Property Let PictureURL(NewURL As
    ➥String)
    AsyncRead NewURL, vbAsyncTypePicture
End Property
```

8. When the download is complete, load the picture into the `PictureBox`.

```
Private Sub
UserControl_AsyncReadComplete(AsyncProp
    ➥As AsyncProperty)
    On Error Resume Next
    Set picImage.Picture =
    ➥AsyncProp.Value
End Sub
```

9. Add code to the `CommandButton` to set the `PictureURL` property of the `UserControl`. Use the value in `txtURL` for the location.

```
Private Sub cmdView_Click()
    ctlURLPicture1.PictureURL =
    ➥txtURL.Text
End Sub
```

10. Run the program and use it to display various pictures local to your hard drive, and on the Internet.

To use Automation with Internet Explorer 3.x, complete the following steps:

1. Create a new Standard EXE project.

2. Choose References from the Project menu.

3. Add a reference to the Microsoft Internet Controls and click on OK.

4. Add an object variable to the General Declarations section of the form. This variable will be used in a number of routines to access Internet Explorer.

5. Add a number of controls to the form, as in Table 15.16.

Table 15.16

Controls in the Internet Explorer Automation Exercise

Control	Property	Value
Form	Name	FrmAuto
	Caption	Automating Internet Explorer
CommandButton	Name	cmdCreate
	Caption	&Create
CommandButton	Name	cmdSet
	Caption	&Set
	Enabled	False
TextBox	Name	txtURL
	Text	blank, or a valid URL
CommandButton	Name	cmdGet
	Caption	&Get
	Enabled	False
CommandButton	Name	cmdEnd
	Caption	&End

6. Set the object variable to point at a newly created Internet Explorer object in the Click event of the cmdCreate button. Use the CreateObject method of creating the object. Make the newly created object visible to view the results. This may look similar to the following:

```
Private Sub cmdCreate_Click()
    If ie Is Nothing Then
        Set ie =
          ➥CreateObject("InternetExplorer
          ➥.Application")
        ie.Visible = True
        cmdCreate.Enabled = False
        cmdGet.Enabled = True
        cmdSet.Enabled = True
    End If
End Sub
```

7. Add code to the cmdEnd button to destroy the object variable if it has been set, and to end the program.

```
Private Sub cmdEnd_Click()
    If Not ie Is Nothing Then
        Set ie = Nothing
    End If
    Unload Me
End Sub
```

8. Add code to the cmdSet button to cause the Internet Explorer object to navigate to a specific site on the Internet.

```
Private Sub cmdSet_Click()
    If Len(txtURL.Text) Then
        ie.Navigate txtURL.Text
    End If
End Sub
```

9. Add code to the cmdGet button to display the current location that Internet Explorer has loaded.

```
Private Sub cmdGet_Click()
    MsgBox ie.LocationURL, vbInformation,
      ➥ie.LocationName
End Sub
```

continues

10. Run the program. Use the `cmdSet` button to navigate to some location on the Internet. View the results of clicking the `cmdGet` button.

Exercise 15.7: Creating a Simple WWW Browser

To create a simple WWW browser, complete the following steps:

1. Start a new Standard EXE project.

2. Choose Components from the Project menu.

3. Select the Microsoft Internet Controls object and click on OK.

4. Add a `Label`, TextBox, and `WebBrowser` control to the form.

5. Set the properties for the controls as in Table 15.17.

Table 15.17

Controls in the WWW Browser Exercise

Control	Property	Value
Form	Name	frmWeb
	Caption	My Web Browser
Label	Name	lblURL
	Caption	&Location:
TextBox	Name	txtURL
	Text	http://www.microsoft.com/vbasic/ (or any other site)
WebBrowser	Name	webView

6. Add the following code to allow the controls to resize at runtime:

```
Private Sub Form_Resize()
    txtURL.Width = ScaleWidth -
    ➡txtURL.Left
    With webView
```

```
            .Move 0, .Top, ScaleWidth,
            ➥ScaleHeight - .Top
        End With
    End Sub
```

7. Add the following code to navigate to the initial site when the program begins:

```
Private Sub Form_Load()
    webView.Navigate txtURL.Text
End Sub
```

8. Add the following code to navigate to selected sites when the Enter key is pressed in the text box:

```
Private Sub txtURL_KeyPress(KeyAscii As
Integer)
    If KeyAscii = vbEnter Then
        If Len(txtURL.Text) Then
            webView.Navigate txtURL.Text
        End If
    End If
End Sub
```

9. Run the program. Try typing in various locations and view the results.

Review Questions

1. What type of application would be a good candidate for using UDP?

   A. File Transfer Program

   B. Program broadcasting the time at regular intervals

   C. Terminal emulation program

   D. Web server

2. Which protocols are made available by the Winsock control? (Select all that are appropriate.)

   A. TCP

   B. Gopher

   C. FTP

   D. UDP

3. Which of the following is not a method of the Hyperlink object?

   A. GoForward

   B. NavigateTo

   C. GoBack

   D. Navigate

4. What method enables you to cancel an asynchronous download?

   A. CancelRead

   B. CancelAsynchronous

   C. CancelAsyncRead

   D. Abort

5. What type of information can you not use asynchronous download to download?

   A. String

   B. File

   C. Picture

   D. Byte array

6. What is the importance of the port for a socket?

   A. Identifies the server's network address

   B. Identifies the program on the server listening or accessing information

   C. Identifies the client program

   D. Identifies the type of access

7. (Fill in the blank) TCP is a connection _____ protocol.

   A. -oriented

   B. -less

Answers to Review Questions

1. B. UDP is a lightweight protocol ideally suited to broadcast small amounts of data to an unknown number of clients, such as the time broadcaster. For more information, see the section titled "Protocols."

2. A and D. The Winsock control is a wrapper around the Internet protocols TCP and UDP. For more information, see the section titled "Winsock Control."

3. B. Only the NavigateTo method is available with the Hyperlink object. The other methods are used with the WebBrowser object. For more information, see the section titled "Hyperlink Object."

4. C. `CancelAsyncRead` enables you to abort an asynchronous download. For more information, see the section titled "Asynchronous Download."

5. A. Asynchronous download can be used to download files, pictures, and byte arrays. It cannot be used to directly download strings. For more information, see the section titled "Asynchronous Download."

6. B. The port of a socket is used to identify the program on the server (or client) that is used to provide or access the information. For more information, see the section titled "Communication Methods and Protocols."

7. A. TCP is a connection-oriented protocol; UDP is a connection-less protocol. For more information, see the section titled "Communication Methods and Protocols."

Answers to Test Yourself Questions at Beginning of Chapter

1. TCP is a connection-oriented protocol. UDP is connectionless. See "Communication Methods and Protocols."

2. The `UserControl` and `UserDocument` objects have the `Hyperlink` object. The `Hyperlink` object is used to allow ActiveX Controls and Documents to access information via URLs. See "`Hyperlink` Object."

3. Allows access to information across the Internet. Does not stop processing in your programs while the download is happening. See "Asynchronous Download."

4. HyperText Transfer Protocol (HTTP), File Transfer Protocol (FTP), and Gopher can all be accessed using the Internet Transfer Control. See "Using the Internet Transfer Control."

5. An FTP client could be created using either the `Winsock` control or the Internet Transfer Control. See "`Winsock` Control" and "Internet Transfer Control."

6. A WWW browser could be created using the `WebBrowser` object. See "`WebBrowser` Object."

7. A new copy of Internet Explorer would start and load the requested page. This is due to the fact that the program is associated with HTTP. See "`WebBrowser` Object."

Chapter 16

Implementing Error-Handling Features in an Application

This chapter helps you prepare for the exam by covering the following objectives:

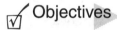

Objectives

▶ Use the appropriate error-trapping options, such as Break on All Errors, Break in Class Module, and Break on Unhandled Errors

▶ Display an error message in a dialog box by using the Err object

▶ Create a common error-handling routine

▶ Raise errors from a server

Test Yourself! Before reading this chapter, test yourself to determine how much study time you will need to devote to this section.

1. What Visual Basic object is used to identify a runtime error that has occurred in an application? What property of that object describes the error?

2. If you are coding a class module, and want to return error information through the Err object, what method of the Err object do you use to do this?

3. You code an application that starts in Sub Main. Main calls subroutine Sub1. A runtime error occurs in Sub1. Neither Main nor Sub1 has error handling. What happens to your application?

4. You are developing a server application in Visual Basic. In the event of a runtime error, you want to pass generate an error that will get passed back to a client application through the Err object. How do you do this?

5. Early in the development stage of an application, you want to run and debug your code interactively. What is the best error option to choose so that execution stops every time a runtime error is generated?

Answers are located at the end of the chapter...

This chapter discusses error handling in Visual Basic applications. Being able to trap, identify, and handle errors is a vital part of developing a user-friendly application. Error trapping and error handling can provide important feedback to the user about why an error occured. The information provided through error handling can also help the developer find, correct, and prevent errors.

Trapping and handling errors in an executable is covered in this chapter, as well as dealing with errors at design time while debugging a project. You will learn different ways to trap errors when they occur, and how you can handle different error situations. In this chapter, recommendations for creating common error-handling procedures are provided, and examples of how error information should be presented to the user are given.

This chapter covers the following objectives:

▶ Setting error-handling options

▶ The Err object

▶ Handling errors in code

▶ The error-handling hierarchy

▶ Common error-handling routines

▶ Raising errors from a server

▶ The Error function

▶ The Error statement

Setting Error-Handling Options

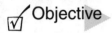

The first time that you will encounter errors in your application is at design time. No matter how careful you are in coding, you will always find something that you did incorrectly—or a condition you did not anticipate—the first time you run your application. *How* you want to handle these errors when you run in the development environment depends on several factors. You might want to stop your application and go into Debug mode every time your application generates a runtime error. You may also want to bypass runtime errors, or allow any error handling which you have already coded to take control.

Visual Basic provides several different options for you to use in the development environment. These choices for handling errors impact your application only while you are in the IDE, and do not affect an executable created with Visual Basic. The choice that you make depends on how complete your code is and the type of application you are developing.

Setting Break on All Errors

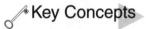

Error-handling options are set in the development environment with the Options dialog box. From the Visual Basic menu, choose Tools and then Options. The Options dialog box appears. The error-handling options are on the General tab, as shown in Figure 16.1.

Figure 16.1

The error-handling options available.

The first option for error handling in the development environment is to Break on All Errors. If this option is selected, and a runtime error occurs in your application, the program will stop immediately. Execution will stop regardless of any error-handling procedures you have in your code (discussed later in the section "Handling Errors in Code"). The program stops regardless of whether the code that caused the error is in a class module, which is part of your Visual Basic environment.

Key Concepts

Remember that these options are in effect only when you are running your code in the Visual Basic development environment, not for executables. Break on All Errors is usually used when you have very little error handling in your procedures and you expect some runtime errors to occur. It enables you to find and correct the errors while you run your project interactively.

Setting Break in Class Modules

Key Concepts

The second option for handling errors at runtime is to Break in Class Modules when there is no error handling present. This option is used for projects that contain class modules, especially for projects that are using ActiveX components created as other Visual Basic projects.

When debugging ActiveX components, it will be important for you to see the code that generates an error in the ActiveX project. With this option, you have to ability to see a line of code that generated an error in a class module. If you did not use this option, errors generated in a class module would return back to the client program instead of breaking in the class module.

Breaking in class modules is different from breaking on all errors when error handling is in place. If Break in Class Modules is selected, and error handling is in place for the code that generated a runtime error, the error handler would be executed, and the continued program execution would depend on that error handler.

Setting Break on Unhandled Errors

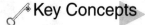

The final option for error handling in the IDE is to Break on Un-handled Errors. For this option, if an error occurs and an error-handling routine is in place, that error handler will be run and execution will continue without entering Break mode. If no error-Handling routine is active (see the section "Using the Error-handling Hierarchy") when a runtime error occurs, the program will go into Break mode.

The difference between breaking in class modules and breaking on unhandled errors comes into play when the code that generated a runtime error is in a class module. In Break in Class Module option, if an unhandled error occurred in a class module, Visual Basic would enter Break mode at that line of code in the class module. In the Break on Unhandled Errors option, if the unhandled error occurs in a class module, Visual Basic enters Break mode at the line of code that referenced the procedure in the class module.

Using the Err Object

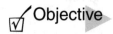

Visual Basic uses the Err object to provide information to your application for error handling. The Err object can be used to retrieve information about the type of runtime error that has occurred. The information contained in the Err object can be used to determine how and whether your application should continue. It can also be used to present information to the user, if either the user can take some action to correct the problem or error information has to get back to the developer.

This section defines and describes the properties and methods of the Err object. You can use the properties to retrieve information about an error that has occurred. They can also be set with other information that can be used by other procedures in an application. The Err object can be manipulated with the methods of the object. In some cases, it is necessary to use these methods to pass information between modules.

Properties of the Err Object

The properties of the Err object identify an error by number, description, and source. These properties are set by whatever generated the error. Usually this is the Visual Basic application or an object used by the Visual Basic application. They can also be set by a Visual Basic developer in class modules to identify errors to external users of those class objects (see the section "Raising Errors from a Server").

After an error occurs, the properties of the Err object can be used to identify the problem and to determine what action, if any, should be taken to correct the error.

Number Property

Key Concepts

The Number property of the Err object identifies an error by number. It is set by Visual Basic when a runtime error occurs. It can also be set in code by a developer to identify a user-defined error. The use of the Err object for user-defined errors are described later in this chapter (see "Raising Errors from a Server").

When a runtime error occurs, the Err.Number property can be used to determine what that error was and how it should be handled. Some error numbers that Windows generates are described later in this chapter in the section "Handling Errors in Code."

The Number property contains a long integer value. Visual Basic error numbers, and user-defined numbers, range from 0 to 65535. If you define any of your own errors in your application, use numbers below the 65535 limit specified by Visual Basic. Also be careful not to use a number already defined by Visual Basic (see "Trappable Errors" later in this chapter).

Caution

Implementing user-defined errors with numbers in the range from 0 to 65535 can cause confusion for other developers working with your projects. If you accidentally use an error number that already has meaning to Visual Basic, another developer will not know whether the error should be treated as a user-defined error or as a standard error. Even if you use a number in the range which is not defined in the current release of Visual Basic, it might be implemented in subsequent releases. To avoid confusion, it is best to implement user-defined error numbers outside the 0 to 65535 range.

`Description` Property

A brief description of an error is available in the `Description` property of the `Err` object. The text corresponds to the error identified by `Err.Number`.

Key Concepts

When a runtime error occurs in a Visual Basic application, such as a division by 0 or an overflow, the `Err.Number` and `Err.Description` properties get set, and can be used to handle the error or display information to the user. The easiest way to display error information is with a message box, as follows:

```
Msgbox Err.Number & "-" & Err.Description
```

Where you code this message box depends on how you have implemented error handling for your application (see the section "Handling Errors in Code").

As with the `Err.Number`, the `Err.Description` can be set in code. If you set the `Err.Number` property in your code, you should also set the `Err.Description` property to provide a description of the error. If you do not set the `Description` property, and you use an error number recognized by Visual Basic, the description will be set for you automatically. If Visual Basic does not recognize the error, it sets the `Description` property to Application-Defined or Object-Defined Error. This is discussed in more detail later in this section, under the section titled "`Raise` Method."

Source Property

The Source property of the Err object is a string expression of the location at which the error occurred in your application. If an unexpected runtime error occurs, Visual Basic sets the Err.Source for you. If the error occurred in a standard module, the source will be set to the project name. If the error occurred in a class module, Visual Basic uses the project name and the class module name for the source. For errors in class modules, the source will have the form project.class.

Like the Number and Description properties, the Source property can be set in code. Even if Visual Basic generates the error and populates the properties of the Err object, you might want to overlay the source with a more descriptive text. Because Visual Basic uses only the project, class, and form names to create the source description, you may want to add to the source to specify a more exact location for the error. You could add the name of the procedure in which the error occurred, for example.

The Err.Source property is typically used in an error-handling routine within a procedure or a common error-handling procedure for the application (see the section "Handling Errors in Code").

HelpFile Property

If you are generating errors within your code, and you want to provide additional help—beyond the Err.Description—for the user, you could have a help file associated with the error information. The HelpFile property is a string expression that contains the path and filename of the help file.

The HelpFile property is used in conjunction with the HelpContext property described in the following section. Together, they can be used to provide the user with optional help when an error message is displayed in a message box.

HelpContext Property

The HelpContext property of the Err object defines a help topic within the file identified by the HelpFile property. Together, the two can be used to add additional help to a message box when an error is displayed to the user. An example of using a help file in conjunction with an error might look like this:

```
Dim Msg As String

Err.Number = 61 'Disk Full
Err.Description = "Your disk is full.  Try another drive."
Err.HelpFile = "project1.hlp"
Err.HelpContext = 32   'context ID for a topic within the help
➥file

Msg = Err.Number & "-" & Err.Description & vbCrLf & _
      "To see more information, press F1."
MsgBox Msg, , "Error in Project1", Err.HelpFile, Err.HelpContext
```

This displays a message box containing the error number, description, and the option to get help from the help file identified by the HelpFile and HelpContext properties, as shown in Figure 16.2.

Figure 16.2

An error message with a Help option.

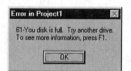

LastDLLError Property

The LastDLLError property is a *read-only* property used by DLLs to return error information to Visual Basic applications. For versions of Visual Basic prior to 5.0, it is important to know that LastDLLError is available only in 32-bit Windows operating systems.

  Caution

Because the LastDLLError property is available only in 32-bit Windows operating systems, you must be cautious when developing code that will be conditionally compiled for both 16-bit and 32-bit environments. Make sure that you do not include references to LastDLLError in code that will be compiled for a 16-bit executable.

If an error occurs in a DLL, the function or subroutine will signify that error through a return value or an argument. Check the documentation for that DLL to determine how errors will be identified. If an error does occur, you can check the LastDLLError property of the Err object to get additional information for that error. When the LastDLLError property is set, an error exception is not raised, and error handling in your Visual Basic application will not be invoked.

Methods of the Err Object

The Err object has two methods that you can invoke in your applications. These methods are also invoked automatically in Visual Basic applications as described in the following sections.

Clear Method

Key Concepts

The Clear method of the Err object reinitializes all the Err properties. You can use the Clear method at any time to explicitly reset the Err object. Visual Basic also invokes Clear automatically in the following three situations:

- When either a Resume or Resume Next statement is encountered

- At an Exit sub, Exit function, or Exit property

- Each time an On Error statement is executed

Raise Method

Key Concepts

The Raise method of the Err object is used to generate errors within code. You can use Raise to create your own runtime errors that will be used elsewhere in your application. The Raise method can also be used to pass error information from a class module to another application that uses objects of that class.

The arguments of the Raise method correspond to the properties of the Err object. They are as follows:

▶ Number   This is a required argument. It is a long integer that contains the error number. Remember that Visual Basic errors fall between 0 and 65535, inclusive. If you are defining any of your own errors, use numbers within that range. Exceptions are noted in the section "Raising Errors from a Server."

▶ Source   An optional argument identifying where an error occurred. Source is a string property that can contain any information that will help point to the exact location of the problem. It may contain the class module name, form name, and procedure. The standard is to set the Source to project.class.

▶ Description   An optional argument describing the error that has occurred. If the description is not set, Visual Basic examines the Number argument to determine whether the error number is recognized (between 0 and 65535). If Number does map to a Visual Basic error, the Description property is set automatically. If Number does not correspond to a Visual Basic error, the Description is set to Application-Defined or Object-Defined Error.

▶ HelpFile   Identifies a help file and a path to the file. This optional argument sets the Err.HelpFile property, which can be used with the HelpContext property, to provide help to the user. If HelpFile is not specified, the path and file-name for the Visual Basic Help file is used.

▶ HelpContext   Used with the HelpFile argument, the optional HelpContext argument identifies a topic within the HelpFile. If the HelpContext is not specified, Visual Basic uses the help topic of the Visual Basic Help file, corresponding to the Number argument (if a topic is available).

The Raise method is usually used within class modules. It allows you to generate your own runtime errors to pass information to another application using your application as a server. The Raise method is discussed further later on in this chapter in the section "Raising Errors from a Server."

Using the `vbObjectError` Constant

When you return error information from a class module, you must be aware that some special handling is required. If you want to generate a certain numbered error in a class module, you should add a constant number (– 2147221504) to your error number before you invoke the `Raise` method. You should do this to differentiate between Visual Basic error numbers and user-defined error numbers.

This constant, `vbObjectError`, is provided for you to use when raising errors. If you wanted to raise error number 500 in your class module, for example, you would invoke the `Err.Raise` method and pass `vbObjectError + 500` as the error number. The program or module interpreting the runtime error generated by the `Raise` method would interpret the error as 500.

Note

Currently, not all the numbers between 0 and 66535 are being used by Visual Basic. Some of the numbers are used; others are being reserved for future use. Using the `vbObjectError` enables you to define your own error numbers. It also prevents rewrite in the future—when later versions of Visual Basic, which use more error numbers, are released.

Handling Errors in Code

Objective

There are several ways to handle errors in your Visual Basic applications. The simplest, but least effective, way is to not do anything. Let the errors occur. Windows will generate error messages to the user, and the application will shut down. A better way to handle errors is to trap the errors with the Visual Basic statement `On Error`. By coding `On Error`, you are handling errors in a more graceful manner. You have the option of trying to correct the problem through code, to bypass the code that caused the error, or to shut down the application if the error is unrecoverable.

This section discusses the On Error statement, and the different means of using it in procedures. The discussion examines inline error handling and error-handling routines found at the end of procedures. Some trappable errors will also be covered, with recommendations on how to use them and what to look for in code.

Using the On Error Statement

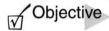 Objective

The On Error statement in Visual Basic identifies how errors will be handled for a particular routine. It can be used to turn on and turn off error handling for a procedure, and in some cases subroutines and functions called from the procedure in which it is coded (see "Using the Error-Handling Hierarchy"). An On Error statement instructs Visual Basic on what should be done if a runtime error occurs.

It is good practice to place error handling in every procedure. Generally, it is especially important in any routine prone to errors. These include routines that process database information, routines that read from and write to files, and procedures that perform calculations. If an application contains code that relies on some outside events—such as a network connection being available, or a disk being ready in a drive—there are always situations that are beyond the control of the developer. For these instances, good error-handling routines are very important.

Different routines require different types of error handling. The syntax of the On Error statement can be coded several ways, depending on each situation.

Goto <line>

The first way to code the On Error statement is as follows:

```
On Error GoTo Main_Error
```

where Main_Error is a line label in a procedure. This is the most common use of the On Error statement, and gives the developer the most control over error handling. A procedure using this format would look something like this:

```
Private Sub Main()
     On Error GoTo Main_Error
     ' … some processing …
     Exit Sub
Main_Error
     ' error handling code
End Sub
```

As in the preceding procedure, it is generally best to put the On Error statement as the first executable statement in a procedure so that any other lines of code will fall under the control of the On Error statement. In this example, when an error occurs anywhere after the On Error statement, execution will continue in the error-handling code.

 **Key Concepts**

Error-handling code can contain any Visual Basic statements that can be coded elsewhere. It is important, however, to keep error-handling code simple to prevent additional errors from occurring. If a runtime error occurs in the error-handling code, a fatal error is generated.

Resume Next

The second way of coding an On Error statement is with a Resume Next clause. With a Resume Next clause, the On Error would look like this:

```
On Error Resume Next
```

Resume Next tells Visual Basic that when a runtime error occurs, ignore the statement that caused the error and continue execution with the next statement.

GoTo 0

The last way to code the On Error statement is with the GoTo 0 clause, as in the following:

```
On Error GoTo 0
```

This is different from the other On Error statements in that it disables rather than enables error handling for the current routine. Even if there is a line labeled "0", error handling will be disabled.

Inline Error Handling

Not all error handling occurs at the end of a procedure, and you are not limited to one On Error statement in each subroutine or function you code. Sometimes the error-handling requirements change from the beginning of a routine to the end. There may be some sections of your code where you expect errors to occur—and don't care—and there are other lines where you do not expect errors, and want to be warned when they occur.

You may have a procedure that reads information from a file, for example, does some processing, and exits. If the file is not found, you want to exit the routine. If any other error occurs, you want to display a message box. Your code could look something like this:

```
Private SubA()
    ' set the initial error handling to go to line SubA_Exit
    On Error Goto SubA_Exit

    Dim sFile as String
    sFile = "filename.dat"

    ' do some additional processing

    ' Reset the error handling to go to line SubA_Exit
    ' for the Open statement.
    On Error Goto SubA_Exit
    Open sFile For Input As #1

    ' Reset to original error handling
    On Error Goto SubA_Error
    ' continue processing…

SubA_Exit
    Exit Sub

SubA_Error
    ' error handling

End Sub
```

In this sample, the On Error statement is used three times. First, at the beginning of the subroutine, the On Error statement is used to tell Visual Basic to go to the error-handling code at SubA_Error when an error occurs. Then, before the Open statement, On Error is used again to say that if any error occurs to go to line SubA_Exit, and then to leave the routine. Finally, the On Error statement is used again to send errors to the SubA_Error line after the Open has run successfully.

The number of On Error statements in a procedure is only constrained by the limit on total lines and bytes of code for Visual Basic procedures. In addition, you can use any of the On Error types in the same procedure. You can use the Resume, Resume Next, Goto <line>, and Goto 0 all in the same procedure, and each can be used several times to toggle between different types of error handling.

Error-Handling Routines

This chapter has already discussed the Err object, and has also examined the options for the On Error statement in Visual Basic. In addition, the error-handling routines within subroutines and functions have been mentioned. This section continues the discussion of error-handling routines in procedures, and recommends some standards for their creation.

Error-handling routines are sections of code that are executed in the event of an error. They can range from being very simple, with only a few lines of code, to being very lengthy. Unlike inline error handling, using an error-handling routine enables you to localize all your exception processing in one place within a procedure.

Key Concepts   Some things to remember when you code error routines within your Visual Basic procedures include the following:

> **Keep your error-handling routines simple.** If another error occurs in your error-handling routine, your application will generate a fatal error and shut down.

▶ **Error-handling routines are generally found at the end of a procedure.** Make sure that you put an `Exit Sub` or `Exit Function` statement before the error-handling routine so that during normal execution, your program does not fall through to the error-handling code.

▶ **Use the `On Error Goto <line>` statement to control program flow in the event of an error.**

▶ **Anticipate the types of errors that are common to the functionality of your code.** This will enable you to handle different errors in different ways. It could also prevent fatal errors from occurring (see "Trappable Errors" later in this section).

▶ **If you need to display error messages to users, provide information useful to them.** A user typically does not understand errors such as `Invalid File Format`. Instead, provide a message that states `The file you selected is not an Excel spreadsheet`.

▶ **When you display error messages to the user, also include information that will help you—as the developer—track down errors.** Include the form, class, or standard module name. Identify the procedure in which the error occurred. Add any other additional information that will help you find and correct problems.

▶ **Whenever possible, give the user the chance to correct problems.** If they try to read a file from a floppy drive and forget to insert a disk, for example, provide an opportunity for them to retry the operation.

No matter how hard you try, conditions beyond your control will sometimes cause errors to occur in your application. Using some or all of the preceding tips will provide a more user-friendly environment for your users. These tips help provide more information to the user when an error occurs, and they will also make it easier to track down and debug problems in an application.

Trappable Errors

In parts of your applications, you can anticipate the types of errors that can occur. If your application is reading and writing to disk files, for example, you know that you may encounter some file errors. Disks can be full, the user may not have placed a disk or CD-ROM in a drive, or a disk could be unformatted or corrupt.

Errors that you can anticipate and code for in your applications can be found in Visual Basic's Help file. If you search Help for "Trappable Errors," you will get a list of errors for which you can trap in your application (see Figure 16.3).

Figure 16.3

Visual Basic's Help for Trappable Errors.

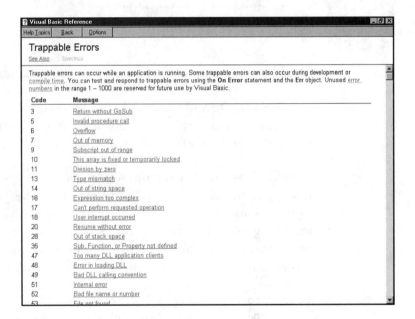

Help will provide you with a description of the error and the number corresponding to that error. These will be the same number and description found in the `Err.Number` and `Err.Description` properties after the runtime error has occurred. If you select an error message from Help—as shown in Figure 16.3—you will get further information for that error, as shown in Figure 16.4.

Figure 16.4

Detailed Help for Visual Basic errors.

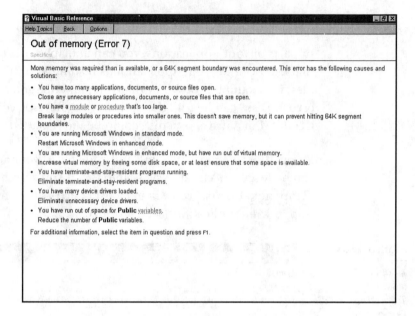

It makes sense to anticipate and code for errors that could occur frequently in your application. If you know where errors may occur, and what those errors are, you can handle them gracefully.

Instead of displaying an error message and ending your application when the user has not placed a disk in a drive, you may want to give the user a chance to use a disk or cancel what he or she was trying to do. You can trap for error number 71, Disk not ready, and prompt the user for his or her input. As part of your error-handling routine, you might include the following:

```
If Err.Number = 71 Then    ' Disk Not Ready
    If Msgbox("Disk not ready.  Retry?", vbYesNo) = vbYes Then
        Resume
    Else
        Exit Sub
    Endif
Endif
```

Now the user has a choice. If he or she places a disk in the drive and clicks on the Yes button, the process can continue. If the No button is clicked, Visual Basic will exit the subroutine.

If a disk has not been formatted, you may want to give the user the option to format that disk. If a disk is full, you can let the user insert a new disk. Always be aware of the problems that can occur, especially because of user interaction, and code accordingly.

Using the Error-Handling Hierarchy

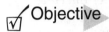 **Objective**

Unless you code error-handling routines in every procedure you write, Visual Basic needs a way of finding that error handler when a runtime error occurs. This section discusses the methods by which Visual Basic finds that error-handling procedure, and what happens if one is not found.

Developers of Visual Basic programs control error handling with the On Error statement. The On Error statement dictates how a runtime error will be handled when encountered. If a procedure in your code is executing, and an error occurs, Visual Basic looks for On Error within that procedure. If the On Error statement is found, the commands following On Error are executed. If error handling does not exist in the procedure in which the error occurred, Visual Basic goes up in the calling chain to the code that called the current procedure to look for an On Error statement. Visual Basic continues going up the calling chain until some kind of error handling is found. If there is no procedure in the calling chain with error handling, the application ends with a fatal error.

The following example shows how errors will be handled in a simple code example:

```
Private Sub Main()
     Call SubroutineA
End Sub
Private Sub SubroutineA()
     Call SubroutineB
End Sub
Private Sub SubroutineB()
     Dim I as Integer
     Dim J as Integer
     I = 0
```

```
        J = 10 / I
End Sub
```

If you have these three procedures in your application, you can see that this code will generate a runtime error in SubroutineB. The statement J = 10 / I will generate a "divide by zero" error. When this application runs, subroutine Main starts, and then it calls SubroutineA, which in turn calls SubroutineB. After the runtime error occurs in SubroutineB, Visual Basic must determine how to handle the error.

In this case, when the error occurs in SubroutineB, Visual Basic looks in SubroutineB for error handling, specified by an On Error statement. Because it is not coded, Visual Basic goes up the calling chain to SubroutineA and checks there for error handling. Again, because none is found, Visual Basic goes up the chain to Main. Because Main does not have any error handling either, a fatal error occurs and the application shuts down.

Now consider the case where subroutine Main is modified to look like this:

```
Private Sub Main()
        On Error GoTo Main_Error

        Call SubroutineA
        Exit Sub

Main_Error:
        Msgbox "An error occurred."
        Resume Next

End Sub
```

When this code runs, a division by 0 still occurs in SubroutineB. Visual Basic still checks for error handling in SubroutineB, and then in SubroutineA. When it is not found, Visual Basic checks Main for an On Error statement. This time it finds one, and does whatever the error-handling statement instructs. In this case, there is a statement instructing that execution continue at the label Main_Error. A message box is displayed, and then a Resume Next is encountered.

You must be aware of the point to which a `Resume Next` or a `Resume` statement will send you after the error occurs. A `Resume Next` statement will not send you back into `SubroutineB`, to the statement after the divide by 0. It sends you instead to the statement in `Sub Main` after the line that made the call to the procedure that generated the error. In this case, the `Exit Sub` statement would be executed next.

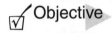

Key Concepts

It is important to remember two important things about the error-handling hierarchy. The first is that Visual Basic will search up the procedure in the calling chain until an error handler is found. As an example, look at a case where there are three procedures in the calling chain: `ProcA`, `ProcB`, and `ProcC`. `ProcA` calls `ProcB`, which in turn calls `ProcC`. If an error occurs in `ProcC`, Visual Basic will look in that procedure for an error handler. If one is not found, Visual Basic will go up the calling chain to `ProcB`, and look for an error handler there. Again, if one is not found, Visual Basic will check `ProcA`. The second thing to remember is that if there is no error handler in the calling chain, a fatal error occurs and the application shuts down.

Common Error-Handling Routines

Objective

Sometimes while you are creating an application with error-handling routines in procedures, you may find yourself writing the same code over and over again. All your error-handling routines may be anticipating the same error numbers. Instead of duplicating the same error-handling code in many procedures, you can create a common error-handling function and call it from the individual error-handling routines within your other procedures.

Assume, for example, that you are developing an application that does extensive file processing. You find that many of your procedures check for errors 53 (`File Not Found`), 58 (`File Already Exists`), and 61 (`Disk Full`). Without a common error-handling routine, you might find yourself coding the following in every procedure that references files:

```
fErrorHandler:

    Dim msg As String
```

```
    Select Case Err.Number
        Case 53  ' file not found
            msg = "File not found.  Do you want to try again?"
            If MsgBox(msg, vbYesNo) = vbYes Then
                Resume
            Else
                Exit Function
            End If
        Case 58  ' file already exists
            msg = "The file already exists.  Do you wish to overlay?"
            If MsgBox(msg, vbYesNo) = vbYes Then
                Resume Next
            Else
                Exit Function
            End If
        Case 61  ' disk full
            MsgBox "The disk you specified is full.  The
            ↪operation cannot continue."
            End
    End Select
```

Your error handlers can be even longer, trapping additional errors that your users might encounter.

Instead of repeating the same code many times in different procedures, you should move your error-handling code to a common error-handling function. You may find yourself not only using the common function many times within a project, you may also find yourself including the common error handling in many projects you write. For this reason, it is best to put your common error-handling function in a separate standard module so it can be easily ported to other projects.

When you create a common error-handling function, consider the following:

▶ **A common error-handling routine needs to know what error occurred.** The easiest way to pass this information is by passing the Err object to the function.

▶ **You need to know the results of the error handling.** Will execution continue? Should the line of code that caused the exception be bypassed or run again? This information can be passed back as the return value or as an argument of the function.

▶ **The error-handling function or module may be used in other projects.** Try not to reference forms or procedures specific to one project. This will prevent rewrites later.

▶ **Code the function to handle as many trappable errors as you can.** The more types of errors you trap for, the more specific and more user friendly your error handling can be. Even if you do not code for all the trappable errors, you can add to the function at a later time.

▶ **Include handling of any errors for which you do not have specific error handling.** For example, your error handler may trap for errors 53, 58, and 61. Include some code to handle any other errors. Unexpected errors always occur in applications. In addition, future releases of Visual Basic may include more trappable errors than the current release.

When you create an error-handling function, you must decide how to tell a calling procedure what should be done after the error handling has completed. Do you want the code to retry (Resume), bypass the code (Resume Next), or shut down the application? One way to do this is to pass back the information through the return code of the function by using constants:

```
Public Const iRESUME = 1
Public Const iRESUME_NEXT = 2
Public Const iEXIT_PROCEDURE = 3
Public Const iEXIT_PROGRAM = 4
```

Remember to include the constant definitions in the BAS module that contains the error-handling function.

The error code that you previously had in many procedures throughout your application can now be combined into one error-handling function:

```
Public Function fErrorHandler(objError As Object) As Integer

    Dim msg As String

    Select Case objError.Number
        Case 53   ' file not found
            msg = "File not found.  Do you want to try again?"
            If MsgBox(msg, vbYesNo) = vbYes Then
                fErrorHandler = iRESUME
            Else
                fErrorHandler = iEXIT_PROCEDURE
            End If
        Case 58   ' file already exists
            msg = "The file already exists.  Do you wish to overlay?"
            If MsgBox(msg, vbYesNo) = vbYes Then
                fErrorHandler = iRESUME_NEXT
            Else
                fErrorHandler = iEXIT_PROCEDURE
            End If
        Case 61   ' disk full
            MsgBox "The disk you specified is full.  The
            ➥operation cannot continue."
            fErrorHandler = iEXIT_PROGRAM
        Case Else   ' covers all other errors
            msg = objError.Number & "=" & objError.Description & _
                    vbCrLf & "Source = " & objError.Source
            MsgBox msg
            fErrorHandler = iEXIT_PROGRAM
    End Select

End Function
```

Now that your error handling has been centralized in a common function, the error handling in individual procedures can be simplified to something that looks like this:

```
sub1_error:

    Select Case fErrorHandler(Err)
        Case iRESUME
            Resume
        Case iRESUME_NEXT
            Resume Next
        Case iEXIT_PROCEDURE
```

```
            Exit Sub
        Case iEXIT_PROGRAM
            End
    End Select
```

For most of your procedures, the preceding code will be sufficient for handling errors. The common error function will be called, and the way of handling any given error will be returned. There are always times, however, where you will customize the error handling in different subroutines and functions to handle unique situations. For these cases, it is best not to alter a common error-handling function.

Raising Errors from a Server

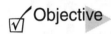 An important use of error handling is providing error information from a server to other projects. If a project, Project1 for example, is using a Visual Basic server, Server1, errors that occur within the server are not visible to Project1. That server must be coded in such a way as to pass that error information back to the calling program.

This chapter has already discussed the means of passing error information between projects, but not always in relation to servers. Returning error information from a server involves error-handling routines, the On Error statement, and the anticipation of trappable errors, as does any other Visual Basic application. The only difference is how the information is passed to a client, and how the information is interpreted by that client.

Errors occur in Visual Basic server applications as well as any other application you may write. These errors can be handled within the server, or can be passed back to the client. Whenever possible, you should handle errors within the server to reduce the amount of duplicated code in client applications. Occasionally, error handling cannot be performed in the server and must be done in the client application.

Servers can return error information by using the Raise method of the Err object (see "Using the Err Object"). The Raise method will generate an `Err` object in the client application and provide details of the error number, description, and source. Server applications can return either Visual Basic errors or custom errors unique to the server. When using custom numbers, you should add the Visual Basic constant `vbObjectError` to the error number to identify the error as a custom error.

It is important that your server application be well documented, especially if you are generating custom error numbers that will be returned to a client through the `Err.Raise` method. Sometimes you will be writing both the client and server application; many times, however, the client and server programs will be created by different developers. These developers will have to understand what to expect from each other's programs.

Based on the documentation provided with a server, the developer of the client application can code for errors returned from the server. Based on the value of `Err.Number`, the programmer will know whether the error is a Visual Basic error (from 0 to 65535) or a custom error (a large negative number, if `vbObjectError` was used). The client developer can trap these errors as any other error generated by Visual Basic.

Using the `Error` Function

A function related to errors and error processing is the `Error` function. The `Error` function has one argument, an error number. It returns a string description of the error corresponding to that number. For example, if you coded the following:

```
Msgbox Error(61)
```

the user would see a message box with the error description `Disk full`, as shown in Figure 16.5.

Figure 16.5

An error message from the Error function.

If the error number is not specified, the description of the most recent runtime error is displayed (the same value as `Err.Description`). If there have been no runtime errors, the result is a 0-length string. If the error number is valid, but has no Visual Basic definition, the return value will be Application-Defined or Object-Defined Error. An error will occur if the error number is not valid.

Using the `Error` Statement

The `Error` statement can be used to simulate, or force errors to occur. The syntax is as follows:

```
Error <error number>
```

For example,

```
Error 51
```

generates an `Internal Error`.

The `Error` statement is available in Visual Basic 5 for compatibility with older versions. With version 5, you should use the `Raise` method of the `Err` object.

Exercises

Exercise 16.1:   The Error-Processing Hierarchy

In this exercise, you create a simple application that illustrates the error-processing hierarchy. You will create a project with multiple layers of subroutine calls to see how Visual Basic finds error-handling routines. You will also code several On Error statements to handle errors instead of allowing Visual Basic to generate fatal errors and shut down your application.

1. Open a new project with a standard module and no forms. Make sure that you set the project options so that execution starts in Sub Main.

2. Create three subroutines: Main, SubA, and SubB. In Main, add a call to SubA. In SubA, add a call to SubB.

3. In SubB, you will want to force a runtime error. Dimension a variable as an integer. Then divide the variable by 0. For example:

```
Dim I as Integer
I = 1 / 0
```

4. Run the application. You should get a dialog box indicating a division by 0 error. It will give you the option to end the application or debug. If this happened in an executable, the application would shut down.

5. Stop the program. Edit subroutine Main, and add error trapping. Create an error-processing routine at the end of the subroutine. Use Main_Error as the line label. Then add a message box that displays "Error trapping in sub Main.". Remember to put an Exit Sub before the Main_Error label. Your Main should look like this:

```
Sub Main()

    On Error GoTo Main_Error
```

```
        Call SubA

        Exit Sub

    Main_Error:

        MsgBox "Error handling in sub Main."
        End

    End Sub
```

6. Run the application again. This time you should get your own error message, not the fatal error displayed last time.

7. Now add error handling to SubA, similar to that of Main.

8. Run the application again. Did you get the error message from SubA or from Main? Because Visual Basic searches up the calling chain for error handling, you will get the error message from SubA.

Exercise 16.2:   Trapping Specific Errors

In this exercise, you build on the code that you created in Exercise 16.1. You will add error handling to trap for specific errors, and code for each accordingly. You will also use message boxes to allow the users to make determinations on how execution will continue.

1. Using the project that you started in Exercise 16.1, edit SubB. Add an error-handling routine at the end of the procedure:

```
Private Sub SubB()

    On Error GoTo SubB_Error

    Dim i As Integer

    i = 1 / 0

    Exit Sub
```

continues

Exercise 16.2: Continued

```
SubB_Error:

    ' error processing for SubB

End Sub
```

2. Now add a `Select Case` statement to the error handling. The first case you will test for is division by zero, error number 11 (see "Trappable Errors" in Visual Basic help).

```
    ' error processing for SubB

Select Case Err.Number
    Case 11
        If MsgBox("Division by zero.
        ➥Continue?", vbYesNo) =
        ➥vbYes Then
            Resume Next
        Else
            End
        End If
End Select
```

3. Run the application again. Was the error trapped correctly?

4. Edit SubB again. Add a statement after the division by zero to move a long integer value (that is, 99999) into the I variable. This will cause an overflow.

5. Add code to the error handler to trap for an overflow error. Use Visual Basic help to find the error number for an overflow.

6. Save and run the application again. When you get the error message for division by zero, make sure that you continue processing to get to the line of code that creates the overflow condition.

Review Questions

1. In your application, procedure SubA calls procedure SubB. A runtime error occurs in SubB, but that procedure does not have any error handling. What does Visual Basic do?

   A. Generates a fatal error and shuts down the application

   B. Checks SubA for an error handler

   C. Displays a Windows error message and continues execution

   D. Adds error handling to SubB

2. An error occurs in your application, and you want to display information in a message box. You will display the description of the error for your user, and you also want to display the error number so that you as the developer can identify the exact error which occurred. What two properties of the Err object do you want to use?

   A. Err.ErrDescription and Err.ErrNumber

   B. Err.Desc and Err.Number

   C. Err.Message and Err.Num

   D. Err.Description and Err.Number

3. What does the statement On Error Goto 0 do?

   A. Disables error handling

   B. Causes a runtime error

   C. Generates a syntax error

   D. Causes execution to continue with the first statement in a procedure when an error occurs

4. Which three are options for handling errors at design time?

   A. Break On All Errors

   B. Break On Fatal Errors

   C. Break On Unhandled Errors

   D. Break In Class Modules

5. What Visual Basic constant should be added to custom error numbers returned from a server application with the `Raise` method?

   A. `vbCustomError`

   B. `vbErrorConstant`

   C. `vbUserError`

   D. `vbObjectError`

6. In Visual Basic 5, what is the best way to generate a runtime error?

   A. The `Error` statement

   B. The `Error` function

   C. `Err.Raise`

   D. Divide by zero

7. What will happen if an error occurs in an application, and Visual Basic does not find an error-handling routine?

   A. A message will be displayed, and execution will continue with the next line of code.

   B. A message will be displayed, and the application will end.

   C. No message will be displayed, and execution will continue with the next line of code.

   D. No message will be displayed, and the application will end.

8. What is the best error-handling option to use when debugging ActiveX components?

    A. Break On All Errors

    B. Break On Unhandled Errors

    C. Break In Class Modules

    D. None of these

9. In which environment can the `LastDLLError` property of the `Err` object be used?

    A. 16-bit only

    B. 32-bit only

    C. 16-bit and 32-bit

    D. Neither 16-bit nor 32-bit

10. Which of the following are valid options for the `On Error` statement?

    A. `Resume`

    B. `Resume Next`

    C. `Goto 0`

    D. `Goto <line number>`

11. If you are raising an error in your code and want to pass the location—such as the procedure name—at which the error occurred, which property would you use?

    A. `Err.Source`

    B. `Err.Context`

    C. `Err.Location`

    D. `Err.Procedure`

Answers to Review Questions

1. B. Visual Basic will search up a calling chain to find an error handler. If SubB does not have error handling, Visual Basic will check SubA for an error handler. If no error handling exists in the calling chain, a fatal error occurs and your application ends. For more information, see the section titled "Using the Error-Handling Hierarchy."

2. D. Err.Description is a brief description of the error. Err.Number is the Visual Basic number corresponding to the error. For more information, see the section titled "Using the Err Object."

3. A. On Error Goto 0 disables error handling. For more information, see the section titled "Handling Errors in Code."

4. A, C, and D. The option that is not valid is Break On Fatal Errors. For more information, see the section titled "Setting Error-Handling Options."

5. D. Use of the vbObjectError differentiates Visual Basic errors from user-defined errors. For more information, see the section titled "Raising Errors from a Server."

6. C. The recommended way to generate runtime errors is with the Err.Raise method. The Error statement can also be used, but it is available in Visual Basic 5 for backward compatibility only. For more information, see the sections titled "Raising Errors from a Server" and "Using the Error Statement."

7. B. The user will see a message corresponding to the error that occurred, and the application will stop executing. For more information, see the section titled "Handling Errors in Code."

8. C. Because most ActiveX components consist of class modules, you usually want to use the Break In Class Modules option in the event that an error does occur. For more information, see the section titled "Setting Error-Handling Options."

9. **B.** The `LastDLLError` property of the Err object is only available in 32-bit environments. For more information, see the section titled "Using the `Err` Object."

10. **B, C, and D.** Only `Resume` is not a valid option for the `On Error` statement, although it can be used within an error-handling routine. For more information, see the section titled "Handling Errors in Code."

11. **A.** The `Err.Source` property is used to identify the location of an error. For more information, see the section titled "Using the `Err` Object."

Answers to Test Yourself Questions at Beginning of Chapter

1. The `Err` object, instantiated by Visual Basic, provides information about runtime errors. The `Description` property gives a brief description of the error. See "Using the `Err` Object."

2. The `Raise` method of the `Err` objects enables you to return error information from a class module. The arguments of the `Raise` method specify the error number, description, source, and help information. See "Using the `Err` Object."

3. A fatal error occurs, and your application shuts down. When an error occurs, Visual Basic searches up through the calling chain for an error handler. If none is found, a fatal error occurs. See "Using the Error-Handling Hierarchy."

4. Passing error information from a server to a client application through the `Err` object requires that you use the `Raise` method of the `Err` object within the server. The arguments of the `Raise` method will specify the error number, description, and source. See "Raising Errors from a Server."

5. The Break On All Errors option will stop execution in the IDE every time an error occurs, regardless of any error handling in place. This option is set on the General tab of the environment's Options dialog box. See "Setting Error-Handling Options."

Chapter

17

Implementing Help
Features in an Application

This chapter helps you prepare for the exam by covering the following objectives:

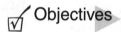 Objectives ▶

▶ Set properties to automatically display help information when a user presses F1

▶ Use the `HelpFile` property to set the default path for Help files in an application

▶ Use the `CommonDialog` control to display the contents of a Help file

Test Yourself! Before reading this chapter, test yourself to determine how much study time you will need to devote to this section.

1. You have an online Help file that you would like to distribute with your application. How do you set a reference to this Help file, through the development environment, so that the application displays help when the user presses the F1 key?

2. An application you have created will be used by people in several departments. Each department will have a different Help file. The name of the Help file will be stored in the System Registry and read by your application at runtime. After your application has read the file name from the Registry, how do you set a reference in code so that online help becomes available when the user presses the F1 key?

3. What property of the CommonDialog control identifies the Help file that will be displayed? What method of the CommonDialog control will display that online Help file?

4. You are developing an application with Visual Basic 5. In other applications, such as Microsoft Office, you have seen little explanations pop up when you leave the mouse pointer over a button on the toolbar. You want to add this functionality to your application for your users when they leave the mouse pointer over a button in the toolbar. How can you implement these little pop-up tips in your Visual Basic applications?

5. If you are going to add context-sensitive help to your Visual Basic application, what important information do you need from the person who is creating the Help file?

Answers are located at the end of the chapter...

This chapter describes the implementation of help in a Visual Basic project. Several different ways of including help in an application are discussed. One way is by using a Help file (*.hlp) created with the Windows Help Compiler, hc.exe, that comes packaged with Visual Basic 5. Help files can be integrated into applications at design time or at runtime and displayed using different means in Visual Basic. Additional information can be provided to the user with the ToolTips feature of Visual Basic.

Integration of Help files has been available to developers since the early releases of Visual Basic. Some of the newer means of providing information to a user, such as ToolTips and WhatsThis help have been added by Microsoft with the releases of the 32-bit development environment. These features enable the developer to create applications that follow the current trends of Windows applications' functionality and appearance. Products such as Microsoft Office have incorporated ToolTips and information in the last several releases. Help files have been available in applications since the early releases of Windows.

This chapter examines the different ways of referencing help in Visual Basic applications, including the following:

- Referencing help through the `HelpFile` property of an application

- Implementing context-sensitive help

- Using the `CommonDialog` control to display help

- Adding ToolTips to an application

- Providing WhatsThis help

Referencing Help Through the `HelpFile` Property of an Application

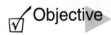 Objective The simplest way to implement help in an application is to tell the application the name and, sometimes, the location of a Help file. The user can then access help by pressing the F1 key.

Visual Basic provides ways for the developer to specify a Help file at either design time or at runtime. For most applications, it is sufficient to identify the Help file during development and to distribute the Help file with the application. Occasionally, the application's Help file cannot be included at development time because the name of the file is unknown, the file doesn't exist, or because different users will have different files. In these cases, the Help file can be specified at runtime. This section describes both ways of identifying the Help file to an application.

Setting Help Files at Design Time

Key Concepts

The easiest way to include help with Visual Basic is to identify the Help file at design time. This is done through the Properties window for that project, as shown in Figure 17.1. To reference the properties for a project, choose <*project name*> Properties from the Project menu in the development environment.

Figure 17.1

The Project Properties dialog box.

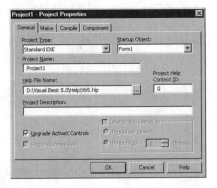

On the General tab of the Project Properties dialog box, the name and path of the Help file will go under Help File Name. If the *.hlp file will be in the same directory as the application, it is not necessary to include the full path to the file. The application will use the same search rules to find the file as other Windows applications. Visual Basic will enable you to specify only one Help file to the application. To use more than one Help file, you will have to use one of the options described later.

Setting Help Files at Runtime

The second way to include help in an application, specifying the file name at runtime, is more flexible than setting the project properties for the file at design time. With this method, different users have the ability to reference different Help files, or a single user can use different Help files depending on how the application is being used.

As an example, imagine that you are creating an accounting system that will be used by both a data entry group and the financial analysis staff of a company. The data entry group will use the windows of the application to enter and change data in the system. The financial analysis group may require only read-only access to the data. You may want to provide customized Help files to each group, describing their own needs within the application. If you were to set the Help file of the application as previously described, you could provide only a single Help file. By setting the Help file at runtime, you are not constrained to a single file.

Key Concepts   The `HelpFile` property of the `App` object is used to set a reference to a Help file at runtime. The `App` object is a global object available to the application. It provides information about the application, as well as the means to change some of the characteristics of the application. The `HelpFile` property identifies the Help file that was entered into the Project Properties dialog box (refer to Figure 17.1). It is a read/write property at runtime, so the Help file can also be set after the application has started.

A Help file is specified in code by the following:

```
App.HelpFile = filename
```

where `filename` is the Help file name, and optionally a path to that file. To set a reference to the Visual Basic Help file, for example, you would use this:

```
App.HelpFile = 'C:\Program Files\Visual Basic 5.0\Help\vb5.hlp'
```

Usually, if an application needs to set the Help file path at run-time, it will get the data it needs from previously stored information in the System Registry. Occasionally, it will be necessary for the user to specify the file name, and sometimes the path to that file. The `HelpFile` property is a text string that describes the path and file. If the path is not defined, the application follows the standard Windows search methods, as it does if the file is identified at design time.

Implementing Context-Sensitive Help

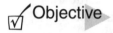
Objective

The preceding section described how to connect a Windows Help file to a Visual Basic application. With the methods previously described, the user would press the F1 key and be presented with the main Contents page of help for that file, as shown in Figure 17.2. The user would then have to search through the Help file, by navigating through the contents or by using the index or the Find feature of the help engine.

Figure 17.2

The main Contents page of the Visual Basic Help 5 file.

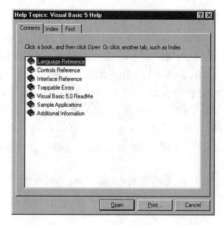

This section describes how your application can display a specific topic within Help, determined by what the user was doing at the time F1 was pressed.

Help files are made up of many different "topics." These topics are created at the time the Help file is written. Each topic will have what is referred to as a *context number* or *context ID* associated with it. This section expands on the ideas of the preceding section, and shows how to provide "context-sensitive" help in a Visual Basic application.

Help File Basics

To be able to use your own Help files and context-sensitive help in an application, you must first understand the basics of creating a Windows Help file. Although the details of creating a Help file are not discussed here, this section does provide some background on the process of building them. When you do create Help files, it will assist you in understanding what is required to make full use of the files in a Visual Basic application.

The Professional and Enterprise versions of Visual Basic, along with Microsoft Word, provide all the tools required to create Windows Help files. Many other software vendors also market their own utilities to create Help files. No matter what means is used to create the Windows Help file, the result of the process is the same to the application developer. The basic steps for creating a Windows Help file (.hlp) are as follows:

1. Create an .rtf file that contains all the codes and text for the Help file. This file also contains information about links and hotspots in Help. It can be created with either Microsoft Word or utilities from other software vendors that create .rtf files.

2. Identify context IDs for topics within the Help file. The process of doing this depends on the tool used to create the .rtf file. The method varies from product to product. These context IDs can be used in a Visual Basic application to bring a user directly to the corresponding Help topic. Typically, there is a *map* file that describes how topics map to context IDs.

3. Create an .hpj file. This file contains references to any data, text, or graphic information that will be included in the Help file.

4. Compile the Help file by using hc.exe provided with Visual Basic. This will create the .hlp file that can be used in an application.

After the Help file has been built, it can be included in a Visual Basic application as previously described. Specific topics within the Help file can also be accessed directly by using the context IDs created with the .rtf file.

Context-Sensitive Help for Forms and Controls

Providing context-sensitive help in an application can save users time when trying to find information by navigating through a Help Contents page or with an index. Context-sensitive Help gets the user to the required information quickly and directly.

Key Concepts

Each control in Visual Basic which has a visible interface, including the menus and forms, has a HelpContextID property. The HelpContextID property is a numeric value corresponding to a context ID in a Help file. The default value for HelpContextID is 0, meaning no context help is provided. The HelpContextID for an object is usually specified at design time, but can be defined at runtime as well.

The HelpContextID property of an object maps to a context ID and topic from a Help file. At runtime, when that object is active and the F1 key is pressed, Windows will open the Help file for the application with a specific topic displayed. Visual Basic applications have a hierarchy, which is followed to determine which topic to display when Help is invoked. When the F1 key is pressed, the application

1. Checks the HelpContextID of the active control on the active form. If that ID is non-zero, it opens the application Help file with the corresponding topic displayed. If the HelpContextID is zero,

2. Visual Basic checks the HelpContextID of the container control for the active object. Usually, this is the active form itself.

It can also be another container control such as a `Frame` or `PictureBox`. If the ID of the container is non-zero, help is opened with the container's corresponding help topic displayed. If the `HelpContextID` for the container is also zero,

3. Visual Basic keeps checking the IDs of containers until it gets to the form. If a non-zero context ID is found, that Help topic is displayed. If all the context IDs up through the form level are all zero,

4. The Help file for the application is opened to the Contents page (refer to Figure 17.2).

The `HelpContextID`s of objects must correspond to the IDs of the Help file specified in the Project Properties window (refer to Figure 17.1), or to a Help file previously identified to the application through the `App.HelpFile` property. If a context ID for an object has been defined, but Help file has not been specified to the application, the user will get no response when the F1 key is pressed. Help is displayed only if the Help file has been set in the application and a context ID has been defined for a control. If the context ID does not exist in the Help file, the Windows Help engine will display an error stating that `The help topic does not exist`.

Using the `CommonDialog` Control to Display Help

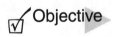
Objective

Help files can be accessed by your application through the use of the `CommonDialog` control. By using the `CommonDialog` control, multiple Help files can be displayed by the same application, and help can be displayed in a variety of ways, including those already described.

The `CommonDialog` control adds additional flexibility for the developer to present help to the user of an application. With the `CommonDialog` control, a Help file can be opened to a Contents page, to the index, to a search window, or to a specific topic identified with a context ID. The `CommonDialog` control is a control that has no visible interface at runtime, but can be manipulated with properties and methods to present the user with a Help interface.

When using the `CommonDialog` control to display Help, it is important that the Visual Basic developer understand the structure of the Help file. Necessary information includes the following:

▶ Whether there is a Contents page and/or an index

▶ The context IDs and the topics to which they map

▶ Keywords used in the file

Setting Up the `CommonDialog` Control

The `CommonDialog` has many different uses in Visual Basic. The only one covered here is the use of the control to display Help files to the user.

To display help by using the `CommonDialog` control in the simplest means possible, follow these steps:

1. Add the `CommonDialog` control to the Toolbox, if is not already present. This is done by opening the Components dialog box (from the Project, Components menu), and selecting Microsoft Common Dialog Control 5.0 from the list of components, as shown in Figure 17.3.

2. Draw a `CommonDialog` control on a form. Because it has no visible interface at runtime, the placement doesn't matter.

3. Set the `HelpFile` property of the control to the filename, and optionally the path, of the Help file.

4. Set the `HelpCommand` property to tell Visual Basic how to display help. To display the Contents page of a Help file, use the constant `cdlHelpContents`. This constant, and the others available, are discussed later in this section under "`CommonDialog` Help Constants."

5. Use the `ShowHelp` method of the `CommonDialog` control to display help to the user.

Figure 17.3

The Components dialog box—selecting the CommonDialog *control.*

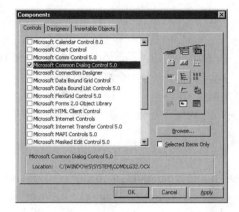

After a CommonDialog control has been added to a form, the following will display the Contents page of a Help file to a user:

```
' Set the name of the Windows help file
CommonDialog1.HelpFile = 'filename.hlp'

' Tell Visual Basic how to present help to the user
CommonDialog1.HelpCommand = cdlHelpContents

' Open the help window
CommonDialog1.ShowHelp
```

The HelpFile property and the HelpCommand property of the CommonDialog control must be set before the ShowHelp method is called. If they are not set correctly, help will not open, and the ShowHelp method either will not function or will generate an error.

Properties of the CommonDialog Control

Key Concepts

The performance of the CommonDialog and the appearance of a Help window are controlled by the Help properties of the CommonDialog control. These properties work in conjunction with the ShopHelp method to display a Help dialog to the user. They determine what Help file will be used, how Help will be presented (Contents page, index, or search), or whether a specific topic from the Help file will be shown.

HelpFile Property

The HelpFile property is used to identify the .hlp file which contains help information. As described previously for the App object, the HelpFile property will use the name of the .hlp file, and can also contain the path to that file, if necessary. The HelpFile property must be set before the ShowHelp method is called.

HelpCommand Property

The HelpCommand property of the CommonDialog control must also be set before the ShowHelp method is invoked. The HelpCommand determines how the Help file will be opened—whether the Contents page, the Find dialog box, or help for a specific topic is displayed. The most common values for the HelpCommand property are described as follows with the constants that are predefined for the developer in Visual Basic.

HelpContextID Property

HelpContextID for a CommonDialog control works in the same way that it does for controls in connection with the App.HelpFile. It must contain a context ID that maps to a valid topic in the specified Help file. For the CommonDialog control, the HelpContextID works in conjunction with a HelpCommand, when that property is set to cdlHelpContext.

HelpKey Property

The HelpKey property defines a keyword that identifies a topic in a Help file, which will be displayed when the ShowHelp method is invoked. HelpKey differs from the context ID in that it is alphanumeric and maps to a keyword in the Help file. In addition, it does not have to be an exact match to those keywords. This property works with a CommonDialog control that has its HelpCommand set to cdlHelpKey.

CommonDialog Help Constants

A CommonDialog control on a form does not function until one of the Show methods (ShowHelp for this discussion) is invoked. When the ShowHelp method is called, the CommonDialog displays a Windows Help dialog box. The appearance of this dialog box is determined by the value of the HelpCommand property of the CommonDialog control. Some of the more common values used for the HelpCommand are described in the following sections.

cdlHelpContents Constant

If the HelpCommand is set to cdlHelpContents when the ShowHelp method is used, the CommonDialog control will display the Contents page of the .hlp file specified by the HelpFile property of the control.

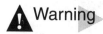 **Warning**

When using the cdlHelpContents constant to display a Contents page, you should be aware that Windows Help files created with newer versions of the Help Compiler might not contain Contents pages. Recent releases of the Windows Help Compiler no longer support Contents pages.

cdlHelpContext Constant

If the HelpCommand property of a CommonDialog control is set to cdlHelpContext when the ShowHelp method is called, the HelpContextID property of the control will be checked to determine the topic within a Help file which will be displayed.

cdlHelpIndex Constant

To display the Index tab of the Help dialog box, set the HelpCommand property to be cdlHelpIndex before invoking the ShowHelp method.

cdlHelpKey Constant

If the HelpCommand property of a CommonDialog control is set to cdlHelpKey when the ShowHelp method is invoked, the Windows help engine will use the value of the HelpKey property to determine which topic in the Help file to display. The value of the HelpKey property must be an exact match with the keyword defined in the Help file for that topic to display.

If the value of the HelpKey property is not found in the Help file, the Help dialog box will still open. In this case, however, it will open to the Index tab with the value of the HelpKey property filled in on the Index Search field.

If you are using the VB5.hlp file, for example, and you want to display Help information for the TextBox control, you might code the following:

```
' Set the help file name
CommonDialog1.HelpFile = 'vb5.hlp'

' Set the keyword
CommonDialog1.HelpKey = 'Textbox'

' Set the help command type
CommonDialog1.HelpCommand = cdlHelpKey

' Show help
CommonDialog1.ShowHelp
```

When the code runs, you might expect to see the Textbox topic appear in the Help window. Instead, what you see is the Help Index with the word "Textbox" prefilled, as shown in Figure 17.4.

Figure 17.4

Index tab of the Help Topics Visual Basic 5 Help dialog box.

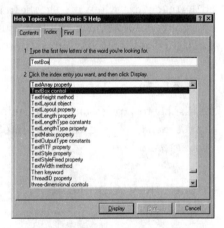

This occurs because the VB5.hlp file does not have a keyword "TextBox." The entire keyword that should be used is "TextBox control." If the following were coded instead, what you would see would be the Help topic for the `TextBox` control, as shown in Figure 17.5.

```
' Set the keyword
CommonDialog1.HelpKey = 'Textbox control'
```

Figure 17.5

The "TextBox Control" Help topic.

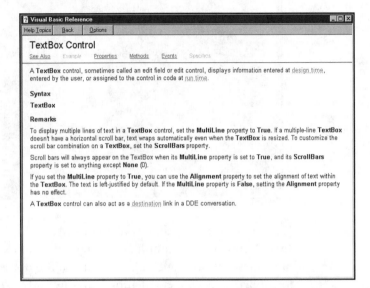

Adding ToolTips to an Application

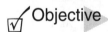

A fast and simple way of adding *help* information to an application without using an .hlp file is by providing ToolTips to the users. *ToolTips*, which are becoming more and more common in Windows applications, are little bits of information that appear when the user rests the mouse pointer over an object in a window.

Visual Basic 5 is a good example of an application that provides ToolTips. If you rest the mouse pointer over a button on the toolbar, or a control in the Toolbox, a message identifying the purpose of the object appears. Figure 17.6 shows an example of this.

Adding ToolTips to an application is easy in Visual Basic. Just set the `ToolTipText` property of each control to the text you want displayed when the mouse pointer is over that control.

Figure 17.6

*An example of
ToolTips in
Visual Basic 5.*

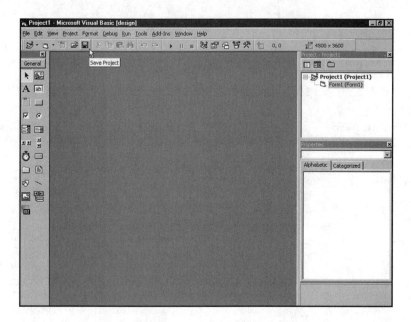

If an application performs calculations and displays results in a
`label` control, for example, you might want to explain to the user
how the result was determined. This can be done by putting the
formula used in the calculation into the `ToolTipText` property of
the `label` control. When the user rests the pointer over the label,
the formula will appear.

You may also want to add ToolTips to command buttons to identify the purpose of each button to the user. Instead of placing large
amounts of descriptive text in the `Caption` of a `CommandButton`, you
can provide additional help to the user through ToolTips, as
shown in Figure 17.7. By doing this, the captions of the buttons
are kept simple, and after the user is familiar with the functionality of a button, that user will no longer need to use the ToolTips.

 Objective

If an application has ToolTips in a `ToolBar` or a `TabStrip` control,
the `ShowTips` property of these controls must be set to `True` for the
tips to appear at runtime. Controls that do not have a visible interface at runtime, such as the `Timer` or `CommonDialog` controls, do
not have a `ToolTipText` property.

Figure 17.7

A Visual Basic application with ToolTips on command buttons.

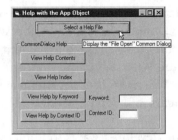

Providing WhatsThis Help in an Application

When ToolTips don't provide enough information, and you don't want to force the user to toggle between a Help file and your application, Visual Basic provides another means of displaying tips to the user. WhatsThis help gives the means to pop up information—from the `App.HelpFile` object, to the user, in the same format used by ToolTips (see Figure 17.8).

Figure 17.8

WhatsThis help as it appears in a Visual Basic application.

Unlike ToolTips, WhatsThis help gets the pop-up information from a topic within a Help file, so more extensive explanations of objects can be provided. Also unlike context-sensitive help discussed earlier in the chapter, the Help file does not open in a separate window. WhatsThis help pops up for the user, and is visible only until the user clicks on the application window again.

WhatsThisHelp Property

WhatsThis help usually functions on the form level in Visual Basic. The user typically invokes WhatsThis help by clicking on a menu item on the form, and by then selecting the object for which help is desired.

A form has a top-level menu of Help, for example, with submenus for Contents, Index, Find, and WhatsThis. To get help for an object on the form, such as a command button, the user would click on the WhatThis menu item and then select the command button. When this is done, the help topic for the command button appears in a pop-up window (see Figure 17.8).

If the developer wants to implement WhatsThis help on a form, the `WhatsThisHelp` property of the form must be set to `True`. This is done by the developer at design time.

The `WhatsThisHelp` property has to be set to `True` for any of the WhatsThis help methods discussed in this section to work.

`WhatsThisMode` Method

After the developer has decided to implement WhatsThis help on a form, a means must be provided for the user to invoke the pop-up information. The `WhatsThisMode` method of a form will start the process of WhatsThis help in an application. In the preceding example, the code to do this would be in the WhatsThis menu item, and would look something like this:

```
Form1.WhatsThisMode
```

where the `WhatsThisHelp` property of `Form1` is set to `True`. Invoking the `WhatsThisHelp` method will automatically change the appearance of the mouse pointer to let the user know that normal actions have been suspended while in the Help mode (see Figure 17.9). The mouse pointer remains like this until the user clicks on an object on the form.

`WhatsThisHelpID` Property

After WhatsThis help has been invoked, and the WhatsThis mouse pointer is showing (refer again to Figure 17.9), the user can select an object on the form to get help for that object. When this happens, Windows uses the WhatsThisHelpID of the object to determine what information will be displayed. The WhatsThisHelpID maps to a topic in a Help file, in the same way that a HelpContextID does. The only difference is that with the WhatsThisHelpID, the help information appears in a pop-up window, and not a separate dialog box. As soon as the user clicks again in the application, the pop-up window goes away.

Figure 17.9

The WhatsThis Help mouse pointer.

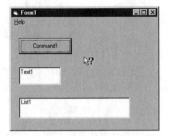

WhatsThisButton Property

A second way of invoking WhatsThis help is from a button on the title bar of a form, as shown in Figure 17.10. The WhatsThisButton property will not require that the WhatsThisMode method be invoked as described earlier with the menu example. Windows controls the transition into Help mode.

WhatsThis button

Figure 17.10

A WhatsThis Button on the title bar of a form.

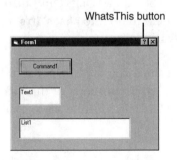

The following conditions must be true for the WhatsThisButton to appear on a title bar:

1. The WhatsThisHelp property of the form must be True, and

2. Either all the following must be set:

   ▶ The ControlBox property of the form must be True.

   ▶ The MinButton and MaxButton properties of the form must be False.

   ▶ The Borderstyle of the form must be either Fixed Single or Sizeable.

3. or the BorderStyle of the form must be Fixed Dialog.

If any of these conditions is not met, the WhatsThisButton will not appear for the form.

ShowWhatsThis Method

The third way of displaying WhatsThis help in an application is by using the ShowWhatsThis method of a control. Code such as

```
Command1.ShowWhatsThis
```

will show help for the topic defined by the property Command1.WhatsThisHelpID. For ShowWhatsThis, the user does not have to click on a WhatsThis button on the title bar, or select a menu item to go into WhatsThis mode. Instead, ShowWhatsThis is usually invoked with a pop-up menu on each control.

As with the other methods of showing WhatsThis help, the WhatsThisHelp property of the form containing the controls with WhatsThis help must be set to True.

Exercises

Exercise 17.1:   Setting the Help File for an Application

This exercise enables you to connect a Help file to an application so that when the application is running, and you press the F1 key, help appears. You will do this two different ways, once at design time, and then once at runtime.

For this exercise, you will be using the Visual Basic 5 Help file, vb5.hlp. The default location of this file is the \help subdirectory of the Visual Basic 5.0 directory on your PC. If it has been moved to another location, you will have to adjust the exercise accordingly.

1. Begin a new Standard Executable.

2. First, you will attach the Help file to your application at design time. You will do this by opening the Project Properties window. From the VB menu, choose Project and then the submenu Project1 Properties. The Project Properties dialog box (similar to that shown in Figure 17.1) should appear.

3. Now set the Help file name. You can do this in one of two ways. You can type the name and path under Help File Name, or you can browse the hard drive for this file. If you choose to type the path, you can use either the relative path from the Visual Basic directory, or you can use the entire path from the root of the hard drive. By default, the relative path is \help\vb5.hlp (without the double quotation marks). The dialog box should look like that shown in Figure 17.11.

4. Click on OK to close the Properties window, and run the application. After it is running, press the F1 key. Help for Visual Basic should appear. Close Help and stop the application.

5. Now you will set the Help file at runtime. Open the project Properties window again, and clear the Help File Name. Click on OK.

continues

Exercise 17.1: Continued

Figure 17.11

The Project Properties with the Visual Basic 5 Help file.

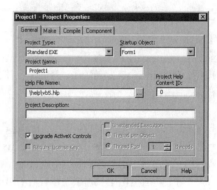

6. Add a command button to your form. Open the code window, and add code to the Click event for the command button to identify the Help file application. Again, you will use vb5.hlp. Use the following code:

```
Private Sub Command1_Click()

    App.HelpFile = '\help\vb5.hlp'

End Sub
```

7. Run the application again. When the application is running, before clicking the command button, press the F1 key. Did help appear? Now click the command button and press F1 again. You should see the Visual Basic 5.0 Help file.

Exercise 17.2: Using the `CommonDialog` Control to Create a Help Menu

In this exercise, you build an application that uses the `CommonDialog` control to display help. You will use the methods and properties of the `CommonDialog` control to display help in several different ways.

1. Open a new project in Visual Basic. Then, through the Components dialog box, select Microsoft's `CommonDialog` control. Draw a `CommonDialog` control on `Form1`.

2. Add a command button to the form. This command button will be used to display a specific topic by referencing the context ID. Set the caption to `Display Help For The Textbox`.

3. Add code to the command button to display context help. For this exercise, you will be using a Help file on the accompanying CD. The file is called sample.hlp.

   ▶ Set the `HelpFile` property of the `CommonDialog` control to this file. Remember to include the path as well as the file name.

   ▶ Set the `HelpContextID`. The context ID for the Textbox topic is 1.

   ▶ Set the `HelpCommand` property to `cdlHelpContext` to indicate that help will open using a context ID.

   ▶ Then use the `ShowHelp` method to invoke help.

The code will look something like this:

```
Private Sub Command1_Click()

    ' Set the help file name
    ' use the appropriate path to your sample.hlp file
    CommonDialog1.HelpFile = 'd:\sample.hlp'

    ' Set the type of help to context
    CommonDialog1.HelpCommand = cdlHelpContext
```

continues

Exercise 17.2: Continued

```
                    ' Set the context ID
                    CommonDialog1.HelpContext = 1

                    ' Display help
                    CommonDialog1.ShowHelp

              End Sub
```

4. Run the application and test the button. The Help dialog box should open to the Textbox topic.

5. Now add a second command button to the form. Label this one `Display Keyword Help`.

6. Next, add code to the new command button to display the keyword `help`.

   ▶ Set the `HelpFile` property of the `CommonDialog` to the Help file. This will be the same file used in Step 3.

   ▶ Set the `HelpKey` property. Use "Text" for the key.

   ▶ Set the `HelpCommand` property to `cdlHelpKey` to indicate that help will open using a keyword.

   ▶ Then use the `ShowHelp` method to invoke help.

   The code will look like this:

```
Private Sub Command2_Click()

              ' Set the help file name
              ' use the appropriate path to your sample.hlp file
              CommonDialog1.HelpFile = 'd:\sample.hlp'

              ' Set the type of help to keyword
              CommonDialog1.HelpCommand = cdlHelpKey

              ' Set the keyword property
              CommonDialog1.HelpKey = 'Text'
```

```
' Display help
CommonDialog1.ShowHelp

End Sub
```

7. Run the application and click on the new button. Does the help topic for Textbox appear or was the index displayed? Why?

8. Stop the application. Change the `HelpKey` property of the `CommonDialog` control to "Textbox" and try it again. This time, the Textbox topic should appear.

Review Questions

1. Which property of the App object identifies the Help file and the path to that file that will be displayed when the user presses the F1 key?

   A. `Help`

   B. `HelpContents`

   C. `HelpFile`

   D. `HelpTopic`

2. What method of the `CommonDialog` control will show a Help file after all the appropriate properties have been set?

   A. `OpenHelp`

   B. `ShowHelp`

   C. `ShowFile`

   D. None of these

3. What two properties of the `CommonDialog` control must be set before it can be used to display a Help file?

   A. `HelpFile`

   B. `HelpContents`

   C. `HelpCommand`

   D. `HelpType`

4. If you are using WhatsThis help on a form in your application, which property of that form must be set to True, regardless of the method used to display WhatsThis information?

   A. `ShowWhatsThis`

   B. `WhatsThisHelpID`

   C. `WhatsThisMode`

   D. `WhatsThisHelp`

5. Where does Visual Basic get the information that is displayed as ToolTips?

   A. From the Help file specified in the Project Properties window

   B. From the Help file specified by `App.HelpFile`

   C. From the Help file specified by the `HelpFile` property of a `CommonDialog` control

   D. None of these

6. What are the two ways that can be used to connect a Help file to an application so that when the user presses the F1 key, the Help file is displayed?

   A. Setting the `HelpFile` property of a `CommonDialog` control

   B. Setting the `HelpFile` property of the `App` object

   C. Identifying the Help file on the Project Properties dialog box

   D. Using the `OpenFile` statement in the `KeyPress` event of an MDI form

7. You have a window, `Form1`, with two controls, a frame, `Frame1`, and a text box, `Text1`. `Text1` is drawn on `Frame1`. If the cursor is in `Text1` when the user presses the F1 key, where will Visual Basic look for a `HelpContextID`?

   A. `Text1.HelpContextID`

   B. `Frame1.HelpContextID`

   C. `Form1.HelpContextID`

   D. None of these

8. Which of the following is not a valid constant to be used with the `CommonDialog` control?

   A. `cdlHelpContents`

   B. `cdlHelpDialog`

   C. `cdlHelpIndex`

   D. `cdlHelpContext`

   E. `cdlHelpKey`

9. If you are using WhatsThis help in your application, how does Visual Basic determine the help topic that will be displayed for an object?

   A. Code must be placed in the `Click` event of the object the user selects when in WhatsThis mode.

   B. Visual Basic uses the `HelpContextID` of the selected object.

   C. Visual Basic uses the `WhatsThisHelpID` of the selected object.

   D. None of these

Answers to Review Questions

1. C. The `App.HelpFile` contains the name, and optionally, the path to a Help file associated with the application. The `HelpFile` property can be set at design time through the Project Properties window, or at runtime by setting the `App.HelpFile` property. For more information, see the section titled "Referencing Help Through the `HelpFile` Property of an Application."

2. B. The `ShowHelp` method of the `CommonDialog` control is used to display a Help file. For more information, see the section titled "Using the `CommonDialog` Control to Display Help."

3. A, C. Before a Help file can be opened with the `CommonDialog` control, both the `HelpFile` and the `HelpCommand` properties must be set. The `HelpFile` identifies the .hlp file that will be used, and the `HelpCommand` property tells the Windows help engine how to display help (that is, by topic, index, contents, and so forth). For more information, see the section titled "Using the `CommonDialog` Control to Display Help."

4. D. `WhatsThisHelp` must be set to True whether you are using `ShowWhatsThis`, `WhatsThisMode`, or a `WhatsThisButton` on your form. For more information, see the section titled "Providing WhatsThis Help in an Application."

5. D. ToolTips don't come from a Help file. They come from the `ToolTipText` property of the control for which the tip is intended. For more information, see the section titled "Adding ToolTips to an Application."

6. B and C. Help will automatically be invoked with the F1 key when the `App.HelpFile` property is set and when the Help file is identified on the Project Properties dialog box. For more information, see the section titled "Referencing Help Through the `HelpFile` Property of an Application."

7. A. Visual Basic will check the active control for a `HelpContextID` first. If one is not found there, the container of the active control will be checked next. For more information, see the section titled "Implementing Context-Sensitive Help."

8. B. `cdlHelpDialog` is not valid. For more information, see the section titled "Using the `CommonDialog` Control to Display Help."

9. C. The `WhatsThisHelpID` identifies the help topic that will be used. For more information, see the section titled "Providing WhatsThis Help in an Application."

Answers to Test Yourself Questions at Beginning of Chapter

1. A reference to a Help file for an application can be set through the Project Properties window. From the Project menu, choose *<project name>* Properties. Either type the Help file name in the Help File Name field, or browse for and select the file. See "Referencing Help Through the `HelpFile` Property of an Application."

2. If the name and/or location or a Help file is not known at design time, a reference to the file can be set at runtime by using the `HelpFile` property of the `App` object. After the file name has been set, pressing F1 in the application will display the online help. See "Referencing Help Through the `HelpFile` Property of an Application."

3. The `HelpFile` property of the `CommonDialog` control can be used to set the name of the Help file that will be displayed. The `ShowHelp` method will use the Windows help engine to display the file identified by the `HelpFile` property. See "Using the `CommonDialog` Control to Display Help."

4. Pop-up tips for controls in Visual Basic applications can be implemented by just putting the desired text in the `ToolTipText` property of controls. For ToolTips to work on `ToolBars` and `TabStrips`, you must also set the `ShowTips` property of these controls to True. See "Adding ToolTips to an Application."

5. To add context-sensitive help to an application, you need to know the mapping between context IDs that will be used in the project and topics in the Help file. The mapping is usually created by the person who writes the Help file. Cooperation between the help author and developer is important to ensure that the correct context IDs are associated with the proper objects in the application. See "Implementing Context-Sensitive Help."

P a r t **3**

Debugging and Testing Issues

Chapter 18

Selecting Appropriate Compiler Options

This chapter helps you prepare for the exam by covering the following objectives:

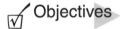 Objectives

> ▶ List and describe options for optimizing when compiling to native code
>
> ▶ List and describe the differences between compiling to p-code and compiling to native code

Test Yourself! Before reading this chapter, test yourself to determine how much study time you will need to devote to this section.

1. What optimization options are available when compiling a VB application to native code?

2. What are the differences among interpreted code, machine code, and pseudocode?

3. What function is performed by the compile-on-demand feature?

Answers are located at the end of the chapter...

One of the most anxiously awaited new features in Microsoft Visual Basic 5 is the inclusion of a true language compiler. Now the compiler can translate the Visual Basic source code that people can read and understand into executable programs consisting of native machine code that computers can read and understand.

Previous versions of Visual Basic also produce executable files, of course, but the code in those executables did not consist of native machine code. Until the 5.0 release became available in March 1997, executable program files produced by Visual Basic consisted of something generally known as *pseudocode*, or *p-code*, rather than native machine code. Native code provides a performance advantage over p-code that VB programmers have wanted for a long time.

As if it weren't enough to include a native code compiler, Microsoft also gave VB5 an optimizing compiler. In addition to the performance advantage inherent in native code compilation, the optimization switches enable discerning VB programmers to tweak their applications for even greater performance.

This chapter considers the ramifications of these new capabilities so that you may use them wisely. Specifically, this chapter covers the following topics:

▶ P-code versus native code

▶ When and how to optimize

▶ Using compile-on-demand

P-Code Versus Native Code

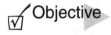 Because VB5 is the very first Visual Basic capable of compiling to native code, you can expect to be asked about this new feature on the certification exam. You should be able to explain the essential differences between p-code and native code. You also need to know the advantages each provides.

Native Code

If you are familiar with other language compilers, such as Microsoft Visual C++, Borland Turbo Pascal, or any of the various assembly language compilers available for a given processor chip, you know that a language compiler turns a programmer's source code into native machine code that is linked into an executable program file. Until now, however, a Visual Basic program couldn't be created that way.

The missing ingredient was *machine code*. Prior to version 5.0, the Visual Basic compiler did not generate the machine code common to other compilers. Instead, it could only create something usually called pseudocode, commonly abbreviated to p-code.

To understand how p-code differs from machine code, take a look at the difference between programs based on interpreted languages and programs based on compiled languages.

At some level, every computer program can be said to consist of nothing but the source code used to write it. Programmers write statements in a high-level language (such as Visual Basic, COBOL, or C++). If you assemble a series of these statements that collectively are supposed to do something useful, you have a computer program. Before the computer can do anything with a program, however, these high-level language statements must be translated into something the computer can understand: machine code.

Machine code instructions govern the most fundamental tasks performed by a CPU. For Intel chips, those basic operations include things such as data transfer, arithmetic, bit manipulation, string manipulation, control transfer, and flag control. The format of an instruction falls into two parts: One part identifies the operation code; the other identifies the address in the computer's memory at which the data to be used in the operation is stored.

Machine code varies with each processor, however. The Motorola chips used in Apple computers, for example, don't respond to same set of instructions used by the Intel chips used in computers that run Microsoft Windows. For a given program to run on a computer, it must be converted into the machine code appropriate for that computer. The code used by a particular processor chip is also known as its *native machine code.*

Until a program is translated from the language used by the programmer into native code, the computer can't do anything with the program. The difference between an interpreted program and a compiled program is the point at which this translation occurs.

With a compiled program, the process of producing an executable file from your source code takes two basic steps. The first step is the *compile step.* If you choose to compile to native code, the compiler produces a series of intermediate files from your source code. These intermediate files are commonly called *object files,* and many compilers (including the VB compiler) give these intermediate files an extension of OBJ.

 Note

Ordinarily, you won't find .OBJ files in your Visual Basic project directories. That's because VB cleans itself up after it produces your executable file, .DLL, or custom control. It still creates object files, but it deletes them after the link step. If you find an .OBJ file in a VB project directory, it may be left over from an earlier attempt to compile the project that was disrupted.

If you are curious to see what usually happens to these object files, run Explorer in a window behind VB. Make sure that you have your project directory displayed in Explorer, and then compile a VB project. You can watch as the object files are created and destroyed just before the end product of your project is produced.

Even though they consist of machine code, the object files themselves can't be used directly by your computer. Because your computer relies on an operating system (for example, Microsoft Windows 95 or Windows NT), another step—called the *link step*—is necessary to produce an .EXE file. During the link step, the object files produced by the compiler are linked together with some *startup code* that tells your operating system where to load your program into memory. The result is written to disk in a form that your computer can use.

Interpreted Code

In an interpreted language, each individual language statement is converted to machine code on a line-by-line basis. A line is read and translated into machine code. The computer then reads the machine code for that line and executes its instructions. Then the next line is read, translated, and executed, and so on for every line in the source code. Because this process must be repeated every time the program runs, interpreted languages are generally rather slow. The source code can be saved for re-use, but it must be re-interpreted every time the program runs.

If you have an old version of MS-DOS or PC-DOS, you probably have an example of an interpreted language. The GW-BASIC and BASICA implementations of BASIC that were included with DOS each provided an interpreted environment for running BASIC commands and programs. You could type a line of code and see just what effect it would produce before typing the next line. Despite the slow speed of execution, one real strength of an interpreted language is this capability to interactively test and debug portions of code within the development environment at any time.

A compiled program is executed differently than an interpreted program. When a program is compiled, the entire program is read and translated into machine code prior to execution. The translation from high-level language into machine code occurs just once, and the translation is saved for re-use. Because there is no overhead for the concurrent translation that occurs with an interpreter, programs produced in compiled languages generally execute faster than those produced in interpreted languages.

The speed at which one's code executes isn't always the defining characteristic of an application's speed at runtime, however. If an application is internally responsible for a lot of processing—for instance, if it performs complex mathematical calculations, or processes lengthy loops or large arrays—it certainly will benefit from compilation.

If an application depends on external resources—say, the speed at which a remote database searches and sorts its records—the benefits of compilation will be less apparent, as its internal code execution is less of a factor in the performance of the application as a whole. If it takes several seconds to return records from a remote database in Cleveland, it doesn't matter so much to the person running your program in Cincinnati that compilation to native code cut the time required to build the SQL statement by a few hundredths of a second.

Until the release of version 5.0, Visual Basic did not compile to native code, but it didn't depend on an interpreter, either. Instead, it produced p-code, which stood somewhere in between.

Understanding Early Pseudocode

Even though programmers commonly refer to the code produced by VB as pseudocode, this term actually has another meaning that predates VB.

Pseudocode is a technique for expressing the operations of a computer program or an algorithm in a natural language, such as English. It was developed as an alternative to flowcharting.

A pseudocode representation of a program generally retains the flow control directives of the computer language actually being used to develop the program, but it replaces the rest of the program with high-level, natural language descriptions of the processes.

Because Visual Basic flow control uses reserved words such as DO, LOOP, WHILE, IF, and so on, here's the pseudocode for a program to read a book:

```
open book to first page
DO
     read page
     turn to next page
UNTIL end of book
```

The implementation details of reading a page and turning pages are not provided, but there is enough information to determine whether any tasks are omitted or out of sequence. It is easy to see that the read page step needs to occur before the turn page step. If these were reversed, the first page of the book would never be read.

This is called pseudocode because it looks sort of like programming code, but it really isn't (the prefix *pseudo* comes from the Greek word for *false*). This kind of pseudocode is much different than Visual Basic p-code, which bears some resemblance to native machine code, but isn't fully translated.

In any case, the term is commonly used to refer to the pseudo–machine-code produced by VB, so you are stuck with it. If you talk to other programmers who don't work with VB, you may find that their notion of pseudocode differs from yours.

P-Code

As already mentioned, the executable files produced by earlier versions of VB don't consist of native code. For computers to run these programs, it is clear that they must entail some extra overhead for the computer to understand them. Because you have just taken a brief look at how interpreters work, you might fairly expect to discover that there is an interpreter at the heart of VB. However, VB does not rely only on an interpretive mechanism to perform this decoding at runtime.

Every time you type a new line of code in the VB code editor, VB *tokenizes* it as a symbol that represents a series of machine instructions. That is, VB doesn't compile directly to machine code, but it produces a series of tokens that are a sort of shorthand for particular operations.

The process of tokenization occurs when an object is regularly represented by a particular set of signs or symbols. The most familiar form of tokenization is language. Words are not identical with the things for which they stand—for instance, the word *apple* isn't the same thing as an actual apple—but words are understood to be tokens for the things they represent.

A programming language such as Visual Basic is a special form of language. Unlike natural languages, the expressions formed by a programming language literally can be transformed into the things that they represent. Even though the computer can't understand words, programs can be thought of as instructions for a computer, and certain tools (compilers and linkers) turn words into actual computer instructions. Think about turning the word *apple* into an actual apple, and you begin to see how a programming language is distinct from a natural language such as English.

When you compile your program, the source code compiles to p-code, which consists of a series of these symbols. When you turn your program into an .EXE file, VB builds an executable file that contains the p-code and the necessary executable header and startup code.

When VB code is compiled, however, you don't immediately get actual computer instructions. P-code itself isn't executable. If a computer were told to take the contents of the p-code literally, it wouldn't know what to do. In this way, p-code is analogous to the function of idioms in natural language.

Taken literally, idioms don't make sense. If you say that someone is "running off at the mouth," you don't mean that he has developed an extra set of legs under his nose; those words just mean that someone is talking too much. Idiomatic expressions such as these take on special, non-literal meanings in a culture, and native speakers of the language learn how to understand the expression in the correct, non-literal way.

Because they don't translate exactly into other languages, idioms are often very difficult for non-native speakers to understand. Literal meanings of a language's vocabulary are easier to commit to memory than idioms, which may still have to be looked up in a translation manual.

Think of p-code as idiomatic machine language, and the VB runtime module as the translation manual. Because the p-code symbols are not pure machine code, your VB program must look up these symbols at runtime to figure out what machine code corresponds to each symbol. That's the reason VB programmers have historically needed to distribute VB programs with a runtime DLL file (for example, VB 3.0 programs relied on a file named VBRUN300.DLL).

When a p-code .EXE file produced by VB runs, the runtime DLL loads to translate the program's p-code into instructions a computer can understand. Because the Visual Basic language statements have been precompiled to p-code, VB programs are faster than if they relied on pure interpretation. It still takes longer to translate p-code into machine code, however, than it does to run native machine code in the first place.

Although p-code has many advantages over interpreted code, native code offers yet another advantage: It can be optimized. You will need to compile to native code if you want to take advantage of VB's new optimization features. The following section discusses code optimization.

Understanding When and How to Optimize

Executable files are still produced in the same way as in previous VB releases: Select the VB File menu and choose Make. However, VB5 gives you several new choices when you are ready to produce an .EXE. These choices depend on whether you care to take advantage of the new native code compiler.

In the following examples, you will use one of the sample projects included with VB. The project file is Optimize.VBP. Assuming that you installed the sample files and that you used the default directory structure when you installed VB, you will find the Optimize project in the \VB\Samples\Pguide\Optimize directory.

You can follow along with any project you like, of course, but this particular project also illustrates some of the optimization issues explored during the rest of this chapter. Therefore, it may be helpful to install it if you haven't already done so.

Compiling to P-Code

Yes, p-code is still a compiler option. After you have loaded a project and are ready to produce an .EXE, your File menu might look like Figure 18.1.

Figure 18.1

The menu command to produce your .EXE file.

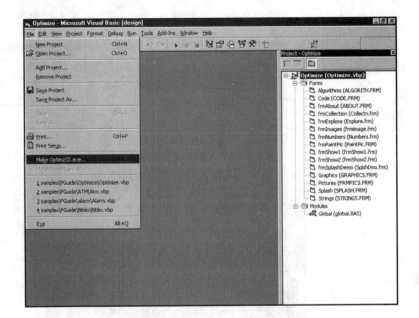

When you choose Make, you will see another dialog box that enables you to set various compiler options. To instruct the compiler to produce a p-code .EXE, all you need to do is select the p-code option from the dialog box, as shown in Figure 18.2.

If you want to set your compiler options, but you aren't yet ready to compile to an .EXE, you can also reach the compiler properties by pulling down the Project menu and choosing Optimize Properties. It looks like Figure 18.3.

Figure 18.2

The Project Properties dialog box enables you to set project options from either of two tabs.

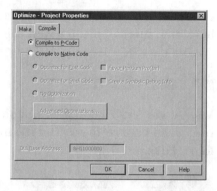

Figure 18.3

Setting optimization preferences from the Project menu.

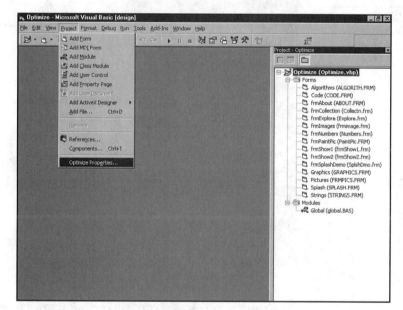

You will work from the Project menu for the rest of this chapter. Notice that the Project Properties window, as shown in Figure 18.4, has two additional tabs that don't appear on the dialog box you get when you choose Make from the File menu. Because you are only concerned about setting compiler options now, the extra tabs don't matter.

Figure 18.4

The Project Properties dialog box uses four tabs to set project options.

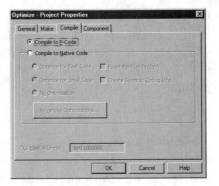

When you select the Compile to P-Code option button, the other controls on the dialog box are disabled. That's because the other controls set optimization preferences, and p-code still doesn't get optimized in VB5. The .EXE generated on compilation behaves just like the p-code .EXEs from earlier versions of VB.

If the capability to compile to native machine code is such a big deal, why does Visual Basic 5 enable you to choose not to take advantage of this great new feature? After all, if native code always executes faster, why would you ever want to bother with p-code any more? Three reasons come to mind.

First, speed isn't everything. Because it doesn't have to bundle in all the native machine code into the .EXE (remember: with a p-code .EXE, the runtime file contains the native routines), compiling to p-code produces smaller .EXE files. The advantage of this smaller footprint increases as multiple VB applications are deployed on a single computer.

Theoretically, this can be a compelling factor in favor of p-code, especially on a computer with a relatively small hard drive. In practice, however, this was more of an advantage for Visual Basic versions 3.0 and earlier, when the runtime files weren't nearly so big as they are now. The VB3 runtime file (VBRUN300.DLL) is about 390K. The VB4 runtime files take up about 700K. With VB5, the least you can get away with is about 1.3MB.

With the growth of the runtime files, the size of the .EXE itself has become proportionately less significant a factor in distributing applications. Still, the runtime files need to be installed just once to support any number of applications. Therefore generating a smaller p-code .EXE may still be important to those running short of disk space.

A second reason why p-code is still an option may be because the native code speed advantage isn't always a huge factor. The degree to which p-code incurs a performance hit depends on the granularity of the interpreted routines. If even the slightest action entails a call to the interpreter, the slowdown could be immense.

Fortunately, however, the VB p-code system has evolved to the point that it uses many fairly large-scale instructions, each of which is executed by a big compiled subroutine. VB's built-in functions fall into this category, for instance. (Although some, such as IIF(), are still notoriously slow. Given the speed of the C/C++ ternary operator that IIF() emulates, this is surprising.) After they have been passed to the runtime files, these subroutines run at native speed, so the p-code overhead need not be substantial.

Third and finally, a p-code engine certainly simplifies the distribution of common features among multiple programs. Why do you suppose Microsoft settled on this mechanism for building macro and programming capabilities into so many of its applications via Visual Basic for Applications? A native compiler for VBA would certainly have been interesting, but the convenience of the p-code engine is compelling, especially when you consider that Microsoft applications such as Word and Excel need to run on Apple platforms in addition to Windows.

Compiling to Native Code

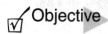 Objective

Although p-code has its advantages, the capability to compile to native code is an advantage that most VB5 programmers are likely to put to good use, especially because it permits additional optimizations. This discussion focuses on the basic compiler options for native code next.

With the release of Visual Basic 5, VB gained the capability to compile native machine code into the .EXE files it produces. Like the applications normally produced with other language compilers that produce Windows programs (for example, Visual C++), VB programs require library files. The difference is that a compiler such as Visual C++ can create completely independent .EXEs— if the programmer is willing to write all the program's interface code from the ground up. VB can't do that.

Why is native code important? You already know the answer: speed. As hardware has gotten faster and operating systems have grown more sophisticated, programmers feel the need to produce applications that can keep pace. In a world where desktop computers featuring 200+ MHz Pentium processor chips and 32MB+ RAM are becoming commonplace, and developers routinely produce Internet-enabled programs, your applications absolutely *must* be fast if they are to be taken seriously. Now that VB5 generates native code, it may be as much of a boon to those who develop distributed applications as earlier versions have been for building desktop applications.

To compile to native code, open the Project Properties dialog box and select the Compile To Native Code option button. When you do, additional choices on the dialog box become available. The following sections look at these choices.

Basic Optimizations

Two sets of optimizations are available. The basic optimization choices are all accessible from the Compile tab of the Project Properties dialog box as depicted here (see Figure 18.5). A set of advanced optimizations is also available if you click on the Advanced Optimizations button.

Figure 18.5

Compiling to native code basic optimizations.

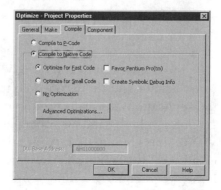

Take a look at the basic optimization choices first. By selecting the appropriate option button, you can optimize for fast code, small code, or use no optimizations at all. It is also important to consider the impact these optimization choices have on a sample project.

Optimizing for Fast Code

After you have selected Compile To Native Code, select the first option button underneath it to generate the fastest code possible (the Optimize For Fast Code option). Even if the compiler decides that it needs to produce more machine instruction code to handle certain portions of your application, thereby resulting in a bigger .EXE file, the end result ought to be faster than the smaller alternatives.

You may wonder how one set of instructions can be faster than another if each accomplishes the same end result. Well, you can get to your next-door neighbor's house by walking about 25,000 miles around the earth or by walking a few steps the other direction and knocking on the door. You get the same result either way. A compiler that can optimize for speed just knows how to take those shorter routes.

Some kinds of optimizations can be performed by the VB programmer. VB doesn't short-circuit expressions like C or C++, for example. That is, in a conditional expression such as the following:

```
If iConditionOne < 1 and iConditionTwo < 10 then
    ' do something
End If
```

VB evaluates both parts of the conditional every time. Even if the value of `iConditionOne` were 5, so that the overall expression must evaluate to `False`, VB would still evaluate the value of `iConditionTwo`. If a C or C++ compiler evaluated this conditional, it would know that the overall expression must evaluate to `False` as soon as it evaluated the first expression. This is called *short-circuiting*.

If a programmer knows that VB doesn't short-circuit logical expressions, it is simple to develop the more efficient habit of coding like this:

```
If iConditionOne < 1 then
    If iConditionTwo < 10 then
        ' do something
    End If
End If
```

It takes two extra lines of code, but the second fragment executes more quickly than the first when the first condition is false. In this case, knowing how the language behaves makes it possible for you to write smarter code.

Optimization for performance generally occurs in two ways: globally and at the register level. If a compiler employs *global* optimization methods, that means that it tries to change the order in which your program's instructions are executed. This can save time if an action is being repeated unnecessarily, as in a loop such as this:

```
Do
iBadlyPlacedVariable = 1
    ' more processing occurs here, but
    'doesn't change the value of the variable
Loop
```

In this case, the variable is assigned a value of 1 every time this loop repeats. If the loop iterates several thousand times, that's several thousand unnecessary assignments. Clearly, the assignment should have been done outside the loop, but the programmer made a mistake. If it uses global methods, an optimizing compiler can correct this mistake.

Register-level optimization tries to save time by putting data where it can be reached most quickly. Generally speaking, the data your computer needs can be found in one of just three places. In order of increasing speed, these are as follows:

▶ Physical storage

▶ Random Access Memory

▶ A CPU register

When possible, register optimization tries to put data into a register for quick access.

It takes a relatively long time to find data on a physical storage device such as a hard disk. Even fast hard disks have average seek times measuring in the millisecond range, which is an awfully long time compared to the nanoseconds used to measure RAM chips. Given a choice, it is always better to search RAM than to search a hard disk. (That's why disk caching programs are useful: They store recently accessed data from the hard drive in memory for faster access.)

Because they are part of the CPU itself, registers are even faster than RAM. If data or an instruction is in RAM, the CPU has to wait for it to be copied into a register to do anything with it. If it is already in a register, the CPU obviously doesn't have to wait on the RAM access operation. Register optimization occurs when a compiler is able to reduce the amount of register manipulation necessary to give the CPU what it needs to run the program.

You will see how well the basic speed optimizations work shortly, but first, this section looks at the other basic optimization choices. The explanations of the remaining basic optimizations will be brief; they're quite simple.

Optimizing for Small Code

Selecting the second button causes the compiler to minimize the size of the code it produces. You can easily guess the trade-off between the speed and size optimizations. If selecting fast code produces speed at the expense of a larger .EXE, selecting small code may generate a more compact file at the expense of performance. As you have already seen, a shorter list of instructions doesn't necessarily correlate with greater performance.

No Optimization

If you select the third button, the compiler still generates native code, but it will no longer be optimized. Before you decide that Microsoft was asleep at the switch when this option was released, think about what it takes to develop an optimizing compiler. It isn't easy to determine precisely how to handle every conceivable combination of factors governing the use of an optimization. Detecting when it is safe to move an instruction out of a loop or when a particular register value ought to be retained is no mean feat, and it is possible that the optimizer may make a mistake.

In other words, the opportunity to optimize one's code is also another opportunity to introduce a bug. As of this writing (mid-January 1998), no VB5 optimization bugs have surfaced. Generally speaking, however, it is certainly possible to introduce a bug via an optimization switch. The initial release of Visual C++ 5.0 had some problems with its speed optimizations, for example. (The problem was quickly identified and remedied with a Service Pack.)

Optimized or not, native code still ought to execute faster than p-code. If you find that your program doesn't run properly when you compile it with optimization features activated, you should try compiling with no optimization. If your program still misbehaves, it is probably not the fault of the compiler—this bug belongs to you! If the program behaves properly after being compiled with no optimization, however, it is just possible that you have found a bug in the VB5 optimization routines.

Favoring Pentium Pro

Whereas the speed/size/no optimization switches are mutually exclusive, the remaining choices on the Project Properties dialog box can be selected for either the speed or size optimization. If you select Favor Pentium Pro, your code will run a little faster on computers with Pentium Pro processors. (Presumably this extends to the Pentium II processor as well, but the Pentium II wasn't commercially available when VB5 was in development.)

It probably doesn't need to be said, but you shouldn't use this option unless you know that your program is likely to be deployed on a machine equipped with a Pentium Pro. Don't worry about breaking anything if you run the program on a computer with a slower CPU. The program will still run on a standard Pentium, or even a 486 or 386. As long as the computer can run a 32-bit Windows program, your program will still run—it just won't perform as well. If you aren't sure where your program will be deployed, don't use Favor Pentium Pro.

Creating Symbolic Debug Info

The last of the choices you can make on the basic optimization dialog box isn't really an optimization at all. If you check the Create Symbolic Debug Info box, the compiler will generate symbolic debug information for your project. This doesn't change the size or performance of your .EXE file, but it does generate a .PDB file containing the symbol information for the .EXE. Bear in mind that the .PDB file is of no value to you unless you have a debugger that can use CodeView-style debug information. That rules out the built-in VB debugger. If you want to use the Visual C++ debugger, however, you can.

Results of Basic Optimization

Use the sample Optimize project included with VB. The project file is "Optimize.VBP." Assuming that you installed the sample files and used the default directory structure when you installed VB, you will find the Optimize project in the \VB\Samples\Pguide\Optimize directory.

The Optimize project is particularly appropriate here because it assesses the speed at which certain VB operations run. The point of the "Real Speed" portion of the project is to show how to write more efficient routines for string and file manipulation, variable access, and numeric data processing.

You will use the Real Speed tests from the Optimize project to assess the relative impact of VB5's basic optimization scheme in these areas. All you need to do is to compile the project four times, producing a separate .EXE corresponding to each of the basic options: one .EXE each for p-code, native code optimized for speed, native code optimized for size, and native code with no optimization.

Before you measure performance, take a look at the size of the .EXE produced by each option, as shown in Figure 18.6.

Figure 18.6

Comparative sizes of the Optimize project .EXE.

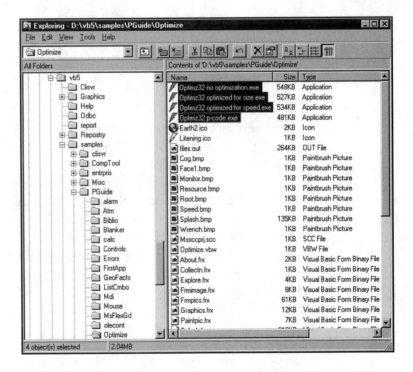

The p-code .EXE is smallest, and native code with no optimization is largest. Optimizing for speed doesn't produce a file much larger than optimizing for size. Considering the total size of the files necessary to distribute the application, there isn't really a great size difference among the four files. This suggests that compiling for fast performance may be worthwhile as a matter of course. In any case, the price of speed doesn't seem to result in a large enough size penalty to worry about unless you are extremely pressed for disk space.

When you run the Optimize project, its main form looks something like Figure 18.7.

Figure 18.7

The Optimize application with all nodes closed except for the tests of Real Speed.

The first test shows how to improve the performance of string manipulation and file I/O. (Strings are built more efficiently outside a loop, and binary file access is faster than random file access.) You shouldn't see any deviation from these general conclusions in your comparison of the four .EXE files, but you ought to learn something about the effect of the basic optimizations on string manipulation and file I/O. Because you are working from the same code base and running the tests on a single machine (in the author's case, a Dell P-133 with 32MB RAM running Windows NT Workstation 4), any significant differences in the timings assessed by the Optimize project can be attributed to the optimizations introduced by the VB5 compiler.

Figures 18.8, 18.9, 18.10, and 18.11 show the results of the string manipulation and file I/O tests.

Figure 18.8

Results of the string manipu- lation and file I/O test when compiling to p-code.

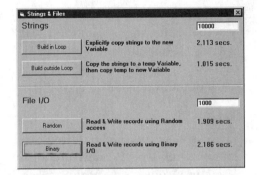

Figure 18.9

Results of the string manipu- lation and file I/O test when compiling to native code optimized for speed.

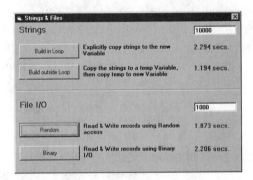

Figure 18.10

Results of the string manipu- lation and file I/O test when compiling to native code optimized for size.

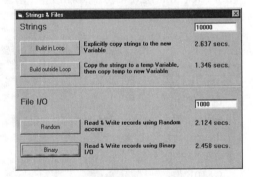

Figure 18.11

Results of the string manipu- lation and file I/O test when compiling native code with no optimi- zations.

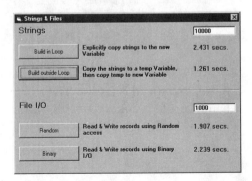

Depending on your machine, you may want to specify a different number of iterations than the 100,000 string operations and 10,000 file operations used here. The goal is to run enough iterations to discern measurable differences among the behaviors of each optimization choice.

What conclusions can you draw here? In these tests, it looks as if there isn't a great deal of difference between the results for each optimization type. Because the measurements are all fairly close, even for p-code, perhaps this merely indicates that the string manipulation code in the VB runtime is already pretty well optimized. The close timings on the file I/O tests are a reminder that other factors besides native code influence performance: No matter how fast the code executes in memory, you still depend on a relatively slow hard drive for accessing data files.

The second test should be more instructive (see Figures 18.12, 18.13, 18.14, 18.15). As its name implies, the code optimization test is more a measure of how VB handles its own code. It is a test of internal factors that shouldn't be influenced either by runtime libraries that have been optimized in advance or by the speed of a physical device.

Figure 18.12

Results of the code optimizations test when compiling to p-code.

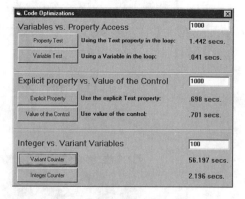

In every test here, you clearly see that p-code is slowest and optimizing for speed is fastest. The single biggest difference is in the handling of Variant data types, which native code does much more efficiently than p-code. On the whole, it looks as if optimizing certainly makes a difference, although it doesn't make much difference whether one optimizes for speed or size; both are generally faster than p-code or unoptimized native code.

Figure 18.13

Results of the code optimizations test when compiling to native code optimized for speed.

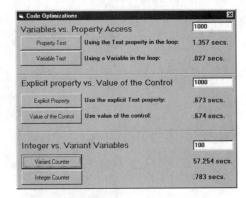

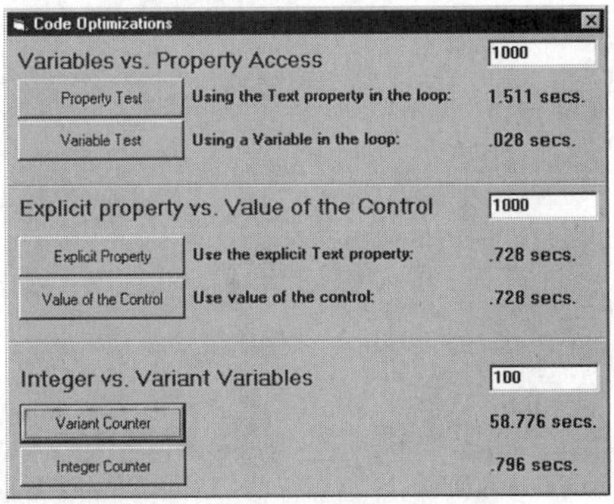

Figure 18.14

Results of the code optimizations test when compiling to native code optimized for size.

Figure 18.15

Results of the code optimizations test when compiling to native code with no optimizations.

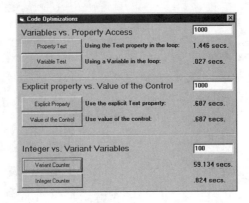

The final test you will explore from the Optimize project tests performance with numeric data types. The differences here are striking even over a small number of iterations, as shown in Figures 18.16, 18.17, 18.18, and 18.19.

Figure 18.16

Results of the numeric data type test when compiling to p-code.

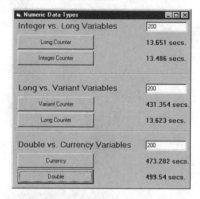

Figure 18.17

Results of the numeric data type test when compiling to native code optimized for speed.

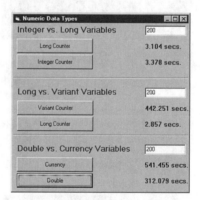

Figure 18.18

Results of the numeric data type test when compiling to native code optimized for size.

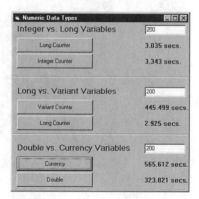

Figure 18.19

Results of the numeric data type test when compiling to native code with no optimizations.

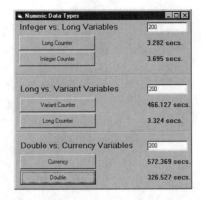

Again, p-code is slowest by a big margin in every test. Either optimization is an improvement on unoptimized native code. But once again there doesn't seem to be a great deal to recommend optimizing for speed over optimizing for size; both seem to execute at fairly similar speeds.

On the whole, it looks as if some real performance benefits are available through the basic optimizations. Take a look at the advanced optimizations next.

Advanced Optimizations

These advanced optimization choices appear if you click on the Advanced Optimizations button on the Compile Properties tab, as shown in Figure 18.20.

Figure 18.20

Options for advanced optimization.

Next you will see what these optimizations are intended to do.

Activating any advanced optimization turns off a built-in VB safety check. Although removing these checks will speed program execution, the extra speed certainly isn't worth it if your programs crash. The basic optimizations are probably safe enough, but you may want to heed the voice of conservatism when using the advanced optimizations:

▶ Don't use them unless you absolutely must. Any optimization that turns off a built-in safety check is another opportunity to ship a bug.

▶ You must remember to apply any necessary safety checks yourself. If you don't have time to conduct your own safety checks, refer to the punch line of the first rule.

Assuming No Aliasing

A programming *alias* is much the same as an alias used for a person's identity. Consider how you can declare a sub from a C++ .DLL in your program. If necessary or desirable, you can give it an alias too:

```
Declare Sub MySub Lib "z:\MyLibrary.DLL" Alias "_MySub" (Arg1 as
➥string, Arg2 as string)
```

In this case, the alias was necessary because the function name in the library begins with a leading underscore, which isn't legal in VB. The declaration enables you to call the _MyFunction routine in the library by the name MyFunction, which VB will accept. Even though you have two different names for the function, both names refer to the same function.

This optimization is concerned about the kind of aliasing that occurs when the same object in memory is referred to by more than one name. Assume, for example, you use the MySub routine (previously sketched) like this:

```
Dim szName as string
MySub szName, szName
```

According to the declaration statement, MySub receives two string variables as arguments. This example meets that requirement, even though the two variables happen to be the same. When MySub is called, the arguments are passed and MySub does whatever it needs to do with the argument variables. There is nothing special about that, is there?

Ordinarily, no. But recall that, by default, VB passes arguments by reference. Instead of passing by value, in which a routine receives copies of the arguments passed on the stack, the two arguments passed to MySub are actually the memory locations of the string variables. Because it no longer is working with a copy of the argument variable, a routine that receives an argument by reference has the power to change the original variable by modifying the value stored at its location in memory.

The MySub example is a special case. The same variable is used for both of its arguments, and both arguments are passed by reference. This means that MySub receives the same memory location for each argument. Therefore if MySub modifies the value of one of its arguments, it will unknowingly also modify the other argument as well.

From the perspective of an optimizing compiler, this poses a problem. One of the general forms of optimization mentioned earlier is register optimization, in which values are kept as easily accessible to the CPU as possible. When multiple variables refer to the same memory location, only one instance of the variable needs to be copied to a CPU register. That is, if the address of the first instance of szName is already in a register, copying the address of the second instance of szName is redundant. But how is the compiler supposed to know that the two arguments are really identical?

Register optimization can be confusing when two arguments actually refer to the same thing, so VB ordinarily avoids this problem by not doing this kind of optimization. If you use Assume No Aliasing as an optimization, you are telling the compiler that each variable name you use refers to a value held in a memory location separate and distinct from the values referred to by every other variable name. This opens up the prospect of successful register optimization. If you inadvertently slip in a dual reference, however, you may actually slow your program down.

Removing Array Bounds Checks

Whenever you access or modify an element in an array, VB validates the index values of the array to make sure that you aren't trying to overwrite its bounds. If you have 10 items in an array, you don't want to inadvertently refer to a non-existent eleventh item, as for instance:

```
Dim aiMyArray (9) as Integer
```

This ordinarily gives you 10 items in the array, as Option Base 0 is the VB default. Because there are 10 items, attempting to access the item at index 10 is a common mistake:

```
Dim iIndex as integer
Do While iIndex <= 10
   iIndex = iIndex + 1
   aiMyArray(iIndex) = iIndex
Loop
```

Because the index is zero-based, this loop never assigns a value to the item at index 0, and the last pass through the loop attempts to assign a value to a non-existent eleventh item in the array. By default, VB saves you from attempts like this to overstep the bounds of an array. (It doesn't help you with the overlooked item 0, however). Naturally, this takes some processing time. You can eliminate this checking by using this optimization option.

To make sure nothing goes wrong, you will want to use the Ubound() and Lbound() functions to ensure that you aren't doing anything illegal. The real savings will occur if you process arrays in loops. Instead of having VB's automatic checking occur with every access, you can conduct your tests outside the loop. This way, you can still be assured that your program is safe and cut down on the array processing overhead.

The preceding example, for instance, could be rewritten this way:

```
Dim aiMyArray (9) as Integer
Dim iIndex as Integer, iLimit as Integer
iIndex = LBound(aiMyArray) ' assure start at first item
iLimit = UBound(aiMyArray)
Do While iIndex <= iLimit
    iIndex = iIndex + 1
    aiMyArray(iIndex) = iIndex
Loop
```

Now that the necessary checks are in place, you can take advantage of this optimization without fear of writing beyond the bounds of the array.

Removing Integer Overflow Checks

This is conceptually similar to array bounds checking. Whereas the programmer determines the upper and lower bounds of arrays, the ranges of the basic data types are set in stone. Whenever you perform any calculations on integer types, VB automatically checks to make sure that the resulting values can still be stored in an integer variable. VB will raise an error code if you try to *overstuff* an integer variable with a value that it can't hold.

Just like all the other built-in checks, testing for overflow takes some processing time. If you don't want to spend time on these checks, you can turn off overflow checking.

Removing Floating-Point Error Checks

This is similar to integer overflow, but applies to the non-integral data types (that is, singles and doubles). VB's automatic tests also check for division by zero. If you test your code and are confident that you aren't performing any disallowed arithmetic actions, you can save the overhead of these tests by deactivating them with this optimization.

Allowing Unrounded Floating-Point Operations

This is another floating-point optimization. It applies when a VB program compares the values of floating-point variables in the evaluation of conditional expressions. Because the variables being compared may not be of the same type, the compiler performs a rounding operation prior to the actual comparison. This enables it to compare like types to one another. For example:

```
Dim singleValue as Single, doubleValue as Double
singleValue = 1
doubleValue = 1
If singleValue = doubleValue Then
    ' do something
End If
```

Before comparing the values, singleValue is rounded up to the same precision as doubleValue. Otherwise, the compiler might decide that 1.000000 doesn't equal 1.00000000000000, which would be confusing.

The rounding process takes some extra time, so this optimization enables you to turn it off. You can avoid any problems this may cause by making sure that you compare variables that are already the same type as one another.

Removing Safe Pentium FDIV Checks

This is yet another floating-point optimization. Some of Intel's early Pentium chips had a bug that affected certain floating-point division calculations. By default, VB's mathematical routines guard against the Pentium bug, but doing the math in VB code is slower than letting the processor chip do it for you. If you are confident that your programs won't run on a machine with the Pentium FDIV bug, you may want to activate this optimization.

Using Compile-on-Demand

Compile-on-demand doesn't really make your code execute any faster, but it may save you time just the same. The time savings comes from quicker loading of your application when you run it in Debug mode. To use it, pull down the Tools, Options menu and choose the General tab. Figure 18.21 shows this tab.

Figure 18.21

The Compile On Demand option on the General tab.

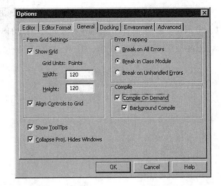

The two check boxes in the Compiler group determine how this feature operates. If you check the Compile On Demand box, VB no longer will perform a full compilation of your project before running it in Debug mode. Instead, VB will compile only as much as it needs to start your project. After the application is running, it will then compile your code on an as-needed basis.

If you have two command buttons on a form, for example, the code behind each button won't be compiled unless you click on the button while the application is running. Because you've asked to execute the code for the button's Click event, that portion of your code will be compiled. If there are no errors, the code executes at once. If there are compiler errors, however, a message box informs you of the problem and gives you a chance to fix your code.

The main advantage of compile-on-demand is that you don't have to get every bug out of your project to test one particular part of it. You may discover that some of your code for a list box won't compile, for instance, but now you don't have to remove that code (or comment it out) just to test the code for a set of command buttons. If compile-on-demand is activated, you can test each portion of your project independently.

The Background Compilation switch is available only if you also select compile-on-demand. With this switch activated, VB will try to compile additional portions of your application even if you haven't tried to use them yet. The compiler accomplishes this by waiting for idle time while you test the project. It won't notify you of compilation errors unless you've specifically tried to use a feature, but any successful compilations will be available instantly when you are ready to use them.

Exercises

Exercise 18.1: Measuring the Benefits of Basic Optimizations

VB5 includes a sample Optimize project. As you have already seen, the project shows the relative merits of various approaches to coding so that you can write more efficient programs.

The time measurements used in the Optimize project all depend on the VB Timer() function. Timer() isn't really as accurate as the Optimize project would have us believe. The text boxes used to display elapsed time are formatted to display hundredths of a second, but Timer() only purports to return time values in whole seconds. Because the speed comparisons among the basic optimization choices were so close in certain cases, some advantages may merely have been apparent due to the inaccuracy of Timer().

The goal of this exercise is to modify the optimization project to apply a finer measure of performance differences among the basic optimizations by substituting another function for Timer(). Hint: The Win32 API includes several functions that return elapsed time in milliseconds.

To create this exercise, follow these steps:

1. Open the Optimize project. Its default location is in the \VB\Samples\Pguide\Optimize directory.

2. Add a function declaration in a global module. Use the Windows API Viewer if you like, or type in the following:

   ```
   Declare Function GetTickCount Lib "kernel32" () As Long
   ```

3. Add a new function in the global module:

   ```
   Public Function ElapsedTime(ByVal timeStart As Single, ByVal
   ➥timeEnd As Single) As String
   ElapsedTime = Format$((timeEnd—timeStart) / 1000, "##.###")
   ➥& " secs."
   End Function
   ```

continues

Exercise 18.1: Continued

4. In each of the forms used in the Real Speed tests, change the calls to the `Timer()` function so that they call `GetTickCount()` instead.

5. In each of the forms used in the Real Speed tests, change the string assigned to the `Label` controls used to display elapsed time so that they receive their values from the new `ElapsedTime()` function.

6. Conduct your own tests of .EXE files built to p-code, fast native code, small native code, and unoptimized native code to see where the benefits are most apparent.

Exercise 18.2: Measuring the Benefits of Advanced Optimizations

The tests discussed so far apply only to the basic optimizations. Next you will create some tests to measure the benefits of the advanced optimization features. The instructions assume that you have already completed the first exercise.

To create this exercise, follow these steps:

1. Again, you use the Optimize project. Its default location is in the \VB\Samples\Pguide\Optimize directory.

2. Create five native code .EXEs optimized for speed. Use the Advanced Optimizations features to create one executable for each of the five optimization features. Each .EXE should have just one advanced feature activated. That is, one option will use Assume No Aliasing, but no other switches; one will use Remove Array Bounds Checks, but no others; and so on. Choose a meaningful name for each .EXE to make it easier to remember which optimization is used in each of them.

3. Run the tests again. Compare your results to the previous tests conducted with the fast native code .EXE to see how much difference the advanced optimizations make.

Optional Exercise 18.3: More Accurate Measurements

Although it is more accurate than `Timer()`, the `GetTickCount()` function still isn't a perfect measure of optimizations. Like `Timer()`, it measures the total time elapsed between a starting and ending time. Because other processes run concurrently on a Windows computer besides the one that you want to time, the time between two measures of `GetTickCount()` includes time used by processes irrelevant to your measurement.

The Win32 API also has a `GetProcessTimes()` function, however, which measures the elapsed time within a single process. Its declaration, and that of a user-defined type that it requires, are as follows:

```
Type FILETIME
    dwLowDateTime As Long
    dwHighDateTime As Long
End Type

Declare Function GetProcessTimes Lib "kernel32" ( _
    ByVal hProcess As Long, _
    lpCreationTime As FILETIME, _
    lpExitTime As FILETIME, _
    lpKernelTime As FILETIME, _
    lpUserTime As FILETIME) _
    As Long
```

If you want to get an even more accurate view of the relative merits of VB5's compiler optimizations, replace the measurements of elapsed time derived from `GetTickCount()` with `GetProcessTimes()`.

Review Questions

1. Pseudocode is _____.

    A. A natural language description of the operations of a computer program

    B. A partial compilation of source code into machine code

    C. A portable code format capable of running on multiple platforms without modification

    D. A formal means of expressing an algorithm

2. The total size of the files necessary to distribute an application will be _____ when the program is compiled to optimize for size than when compiled to optimize for speed.

    A. Much smaller

    B. Slightly smaller

    C. Slightly larger

    D. Much larger

3. Native code executes _____ than p-code.

    A. Much faster

    B. A little faster

    C. No more quickly

    D. A little slower

4. A program which has been optimized to run on a Pentium Pro on a 386 or 486 _____.

    A. Will not load into memory

    B. Loads into memory but produces a GPF on execution

    C. Runs more slowly

    D. Runs just as well

5. The optional symbolic debug information that can be created when compiling to native code _____.

    A. Significantly increases the size of the executable file

    B. Slows down the execution of the executable file

    C. Makes it possible to reverse a program's execution during a trace

    D. Is useful only with an external debugger

6. Compile-on-demand makes it possible to _____ .

    A. Distribute applications that build their .EXE on-the-fly when the user is ready to install a program

    B. Create application components that are responsible for compiling themselves

    C. Test portions of an application without fully compiling the entire program first

    D. View the values of variables without explicitly setting a Watch window

Answers to Review Questions

1. B. Microsoft's implementation of pseudocode in VB partially compiles your program code, which still must be interpreted by a runtime DLL as it executes. For more information, see the section titled "P-Code."

2. B. The total size is only slightly smaller because the executable file is a relatively small portion of the files necessary to distribute an application. The runtime files and custom control files consume a proportionately greater amount of space. For more information, see the section titled "Compiling to P-Code."

3. A. Native code is generally much faster than p-code. For more information, see the section titled "P-Code."

4. C. The program will run, but not as quickly. For more information, see the section titled "Favoring Pentium Pro."

5. D. You need an external debugger to use the symbolic debug information. For more information, see the section titled "Creating Symbolic Debug Info."

6. C. Using compile-on-demand, an application need not be fully compiled to test it. For more information, see the section titled "Using Compile-on-Demand."

Answers to Test Yourself Questions at Beginning of Chapter

1. Basic optimizations choices include: optimizing for fast code, optimizing for small code, and no optimization. You also may choose to favor the Pentium Pro. Advanced optimization choices are: assume no aliasing, remove array bounds checks, remove integer overflow checks, remove floating point error checks, allow unrounded floating point operations, and removing Pentium FDIV checks. See the individual sections for each of these under "Basic Optimizations" and "Advanced Optimizations."

2. When a program is interpreted, each line of source code is converted into machine instructions whenever it is encountered at runtime. When a program has been compiled to machine code, this conversion has already been done, so the program executes more quickly. Pseudocode stands midway between interpreted code and machine code. Your source code isn't compiled directly to machine code, but instead is turned into a series of tokens that represent particular operations. These tokens are passed to the runtime files, which contain the actual executable code. See "P-Code Versus Native Code."

3. Instead of fully compiling your application prior to testing it, compile-on-demand compiles code on an as-needed basis during testing. See "Using Compile-on-Demand."

Chapter 19

Compiling an Application Conditionally

This chapter helps you prepare for the exam by covering the following objectives:

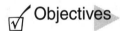 Objectives

▶ Use the #If...#End If and #Const directives to conditionally compile statements

▶ Set the appropriate conditional compiler flags

Test Yourself! Before reading this chapter, test yourself to determine how much study time you will need to devote to this section.

1. A compiler constant verDEBUG is defined in code module MOD1.BAS and assigned a value of 1. On the command line, verDEBUG is assigned a value of 2. What value will be used when the constant is encountered in MOD1.BAS?

2. You need to maintain a single code base for two versions (16-bit and 32-bit) of an application. Using conditional compilation, what directives must be used to keep the version-specific elements of your code separated?

3. Explain how to create a single executable file for both 16-bit and 32-bit platforms. The application should detect the CPU type and use conditional compilation to intelligently run 16-bit or 32-bit code as needed.

Answers are located at the end of the chapter...

Source code does not directly put you in control of a computer. The programs that you write don't enable you to directly communicate with a computer because the CPU can't use your raw source code until it has been translated into machine code.

Direct or not, the process by which you communicate with a computer is simple enough to understand: You use another piece of software to serve as an intermediary between your source code and the CPU. If you know how to express your wishes properly, a reliable interpreter or compiler enables you to make the computer do what you want by translating your source code into machine code.

Even though the primary purpose of source code is to provide clear instructions for the CPU, it is occasionally useful to be able to talk to the compiler, too. When necessary, this permits you to give the compiler special instructions about how it should produce the code that finally gets sent to the CPU.

Visual Basic permits the programmer to talk directly to the compiler itself by embedding instructions directed to the compiler in VB source code. This chapter explores the use of these special preprocessor directives. Specifically, this chapter examines these topics:

▶ Conditional compilation defined

▶ Preprocessor directives

▶ Preprocessor constants

▶ Applications and styles

Understanding Conditional Compilation

Ordinarily, the VB compiler reads all the source code in a project and translates it into either p-code or native code that can be used by a computer. It doesn't omit a single line of executable code (naturally, comments aren't compiled), so every instruction that was in the source code also winds up in the compiled .EXE, .DLL, or custom control.

Note

> VB can produce custom controls, .DLLs, or .EXEs consisting of either p-code or native code. Rather than unnecessarily complicating the explanation of the compilation process by referring to all options every time, the rest of this chapter assumes that the programmer is compiling an .EXE to native code. None of the conditional compilation concepts change if you change your project options, but the rest of the explanations in this chapter will be more readable if the discussion addresses just one case.

With conditional compilation, this no longer is the case. Using conditional compilation, it is possible for the programmer to tell the compiler whether to skip or include a portion of code or to compile one section rather than another. (Reasons for doing these things are discussed later in the section titled "Applications and Styles.") This means that there may be code in the source files that does not get compiled into the .EXE for a project.

To understand how this works, it may help to think about the compilation process as consisting of two phases. During the first phase, the source code is scanned to determine what parts of the source are actually supposed to be translated into machine code. The code that fails the test is ignored; the code that passes is written to temporary storage for use in phase two. During the second phase, the code in the temporary storage is compiled into an executable program file.

Because the determination of which code is included and which code is omitted occurs before the compiler actually processes the code, this phase is often called *preprocessing*. Although it was not introduced into VB until version 4.0, other languages have had access to a preprocessor for a long time.

The C and C++ preprocessor, for instance, makes it possible for the contents of one file to be inserted into another (the #include directive), to expand a token into another series of characters as a macro (the #define directive), and even to change the rules of the language temporarily (the #pragma directive). Remember that all these actions occur *before* the code is presented to the compiler. The compiler never sees the original state of your source code; it operates only on the code that has passed the conditional tests put in place by the programmer.

The Visual Basic preprocessor is not as powerful as that found in C or C++—VB can't do the tricks mentioned in the preceding paragraph (not yet, anyway)—but it is still quite useful. The following section takes a look at VB's preprocessor directives.

Preprocessor Directives

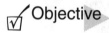 Objective ▶

A preprocessor gets its name precisely because it operates on source code before the compiler processes the code. The only function of the VB preprocessor is to conditionally evaluate code to determine what parts of it should be processed by the compiler.

The preprocessor uses just the following four conditional flow control directives:

- ▶ #If
- ▶ #ElseIf
- ▶ #Else
- ▶ #End If

Aside from the "#" prefix, the preprocessor syntax is just like that of the If, ElseIf, Else, and End If flow control directives in the Visual Basic programming language. The only difference is that

If/Then/Else/End If conditional tests used in a program determine the path of execution taken by the code, whereas the #If/#Then/#Else/#End If preprocessor conditional tests determine what code will be included when a project is compiled.

Because any code that the preprocessor screens out is completely absent from the final compiled product, its presence in the source code does not influence the executable program in any way. No size or performance penalty accrues.

The formal syntax for the preprocessor directives is represented like this in the VB Help system (blocks enclosed in brackets are optional):

```
#If expression Then
   statements
[ #ElseIf expression-n Then
   [ elseifstatements ] ]
[ #Else
   [ elsestatements ] ]
#End If
```

At minimum, a preprocessor block must consist of #If/Then/ #End If. Optionally, any number of #ElseIf blocks can be included with additional expressions to be evaluated should the expression in the main #If be False. A single #Else block can be included, but is not required. The #Else block has no expressions to evaluate because it is the default block. It is reached only if all the #If and #ElseIf expressions evaluated as False.

The sections marked statements, elseifstatements, and elsestatements represent lines of VB code that are subject to conditional compilation. After the conditional expressions are evaluated, only those lines found in the active conditional block (that is, the lines in an #If or #ElseIf block that evaluates as True, or, if no expression is True, the lines in an #Else block) will be passed to the VB compiler. Besides containing lines of VB code, these sections also can hold additional preprocessor blocks.

If you know how VB evaluates a programming If block, you already know how to evaluate a preprocessor #If block. A conditional expression is evaluated on the #If line. Should the conditional expression be evaluated as True (that is, any non-zero value), the set of statements immediately following the #If line will be included in the compiled form of the program, until an #End If (or, optionally, an #ElseIf or #Else) is encountered. If the conditional expression is not True, the code in the #If branch of the conditional block is excluded from the compiled form of the program.

Should the preprocessor find an #ElseIf after an #If expression evaluates as False, the preprocessor evaluates the #ElseIf expression, applying to it the same guidelines as previously described for the #If block. This process continues until the preprocessor finds an expression that evaluates to True, whereupon the code wrapped in that branch will be sent to the compiler.

When no #If or #ElseIf condition evaluates to True, those branches are excluded from the compiled form of the program. The preprocessor then tries to find an #Else branch. If one is present, any code wrapped in it will be included by default in the compiled form of the program.

Again, if you understand VB flow control with an If block, you shouldn't have any difficulty with the logic used in the VB preprocessor. They follow the same rules, with just one exception: A conditional expression and a single action are allowed to appear on a single line in a VB program, such as this:

```
If TestCondition = True Then DoSomething()
```

When a single action is involved, the usual closing End If is unnecessary. (Of course, if more than one action should be taken as a result of a conditional test, this form can't be used; all the actions must appear on separate lines, and the terminating End If is required.)

With the preprocessor, however, the conditional test must be on a different line from any actions, even if there is just one action to perform. To work with the preprocessor, the preceding code would have to be written like this:

```
#If TestCondition = True Then
    DoSomething()
#End If
```

Keeping preprocessor commands on lines separate from other VB actions is necessary due to the way the preprocessor does its job. When it determines what portions of the source code to pass on to the compiler, it does more than just remove the code blocks that didn't satisfy its conditional tests: It also strips out the tests themselves, as well as every other line that begins with a preprocessor directive. After all, the preprocessor commands are not part of your program. (Think about it—they aren't in the Visual Basic programming language, so the VB compiler doesn't know how to compile them.) If a programming command were to appear on the same line as a preprocessor directive—as is the case with the single-line version of the conditional test shown previously—it would be stripped out of the program, too.

It may help to think of the preprocessor and the VB compiler as two separate compilers that don't speak each other's language. To not confuse them, you must keep the commands for one separated from the commands for the other.

Types of Expressions

So far, this discussion has focused on how the process of evaluating conditional compiler expressions works. You still need to know more about the kinds of expressions that the preprocessor can handle. Just like any other conditional statement, the preprocessor requires the expressions it evaluates to have a truth value—that is, they must evaluate to True or False, where True is defined as any non-zero value and False is zero. These expressions may consist of the following three components, two of which are probably already familiar:

▶ Operators

▶ Literals

▶ Compiler constants

You probably understand operators already. The same arithmetic and logical operators used in any other conditional statement are available for use in preprocessor conditional statements, with one exception: You can use any arithmetic or logical operator except Is. That's because Is is a special operator used to compare VB object variables, and the preprocessor doesn't understand VB variables.

Literals are probably familiar by now, too. A literal can be a numeric value, such as 1 or 256, or a text string, such as "Hello, world." When comparing values, the Option Compare statement has no effect upon expressions in #If and #ElseIf statements. Conditional compiler statements are always evaluated with Option Compare Text.

Because these tests use only operators and literals, both tests are valid:

```
#If  1 < 2 Then
   ' do something
#ElseIf "MyString" = "MyString" Then
    ' do something else
#End If
```

Not only are both of the tests valid, but it so happens that both are also True. However, only the do something code will be compiled into the executable because the conditional statement upon which it depends, 1 < 2, is evaluated first. The do something else conditional, "MyString" = "MyString", is True, but because it is part of an #ElseIf test, it is skipped when any previous #If or #ElseIf at its level in the block evaluates to True.

However, this test is not valid:

```
Dim db1 as Database, db2 as Database
Set db1 = DBEngine(0)(0)
Set db2 = db1
iCounter = 100
#If db1 Is db2 Then
    ' try this
#ElseIf iCounter > 0 Then
```

```
    ' try this instead
#End If
```

There are two problems here. The first should be obvious from the rule for operators stated earlier: The #If statement uses the Is operator, which is explicitly disallowed.

What's wrong with the second conditional? Because it is True that iCounter is greater than zero, it may seem that nothing is wrong here. The problem is that the preprocessor can't use VB variables, so it has no idea what to do with iCounter. (In fact, that's also a problem with the #If statement's use of the db1 and db2 variables.)

Although these variables make perfectly good sense in the context of a VB program, remember that the preprocessor doesn't speak the same language as the compiler. The preprocessor may be responsible for deciding what code gets sent to the compiler, but it doesn't have to know anything about VB code to accomplish that task.

If you could use only literals in your tests, the preprocessor wouldn't make for a very interesting tool. You could construct only tautologies (statements that are always true) or contradictions (statements that are always false). You could move such statements from place to place in your code—explicitly selecting the lines you want to include by wrapping them with tautologies, and screening the lines you want to exclude with contradictions—but that's a lot of manual labor. It would almost be as easy to wade through each project's code, manually commenting out any undesired lines on a build-by-build basis.

Fortunately, an easier way exists. Besides operators and literals, you will recall that a third component is allowed in conditional compiler tests: compiler constants. Compiler constants are the key to doing tricks with the VB preprocessor.

Compiler Constants

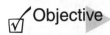

Compiler constants have two sources. Some are predefined by VB, and others are created by the programmer. Each is looked at in turn in this section.

Predefined Compiler Constants

Visual Basic for Applications predefines two constants for use with the preprocessor: Win16 and Win32. These values are automatically available everywhere in a project (that is, they are global constants). These constants exist to make it easier to develop projects for both 16-bit and 32-bit Windows from the same source code.

The values of Win16 and Win32 depend on whether you are compiling on a 16-bit or 32-bit Windows platform. If you are compiling under a 16-bit platform (for example, Windows 3.1), the value of Win16 is defined as True, and the value of Win32 is defined as False. On a 32-bit platform (for example, Windows 95 or Windows NT), the values are reversed: Win16 is False and Win32 is True. You will see what this scheme does for you shortly.

Declaring Compiler Constants

Besides the predefined constants, you can also define preprocessor constants for yourself to automate your preprocessing requirements. You can declare a compiler constant in the following three ways:

- ▶ In code

- ▶ In the Project Properties dialog box

- ▶ From the command line

Each method produces slightly different results from the other two. First, it is important to understand the mechanics of declaration for each case. After that's clear, the discussion examines how each method behaves.

Declaring in Code

There is one more preprocessor directive to remember in addition to the #If, #Else, #ElseIf, and #End If talked about earlier: #Const. Not surprisingly, the #Const preprocessor directive is similar to the VB keyword Const. Const enables you to define a name to use in place of a constant value in your VB code, such as this:

```
Const MAX_LINES as Integer = 60
```

Then, whenever you need to use this value, you can type **MAX_LINES** rather than **60**. This makes your code easier to understand because your code can use a meaningful name rather than a magic number. For instance,

```
Do While iCount <= 60
```

is harder to understand and more difficult to maintain than the following:

```
Do While iCount <= MAX_LINES
```

In the first case, it is not clear what makes 60 a special value, and if the value ever needs to be changed, every conditional that uses it must be changed manually. In the second case, the use of a meaningful constant name clarifies the meaning of the value, and if it ever needs to be changed, a single change to the constant definition propagates the change to all instances of its use.

#Const works in much the same way for the preprocessor. For instance:

```
#Const TESTING = 1
```

Just like a programming constant, a compiler constant must be defined only once. The syntax for compiler constants is slightly different, however, than for programming constants. Although you can optionally specify a data type with a programming constant (if you don't, the constant defaults to a Variant, or whatever the programmer has specified as a default type via the family of Def statements—for example, DefInt, DefLng, and so on), it is not possible to specify a data type for a preprocessor constant. All preprocessor constants are treated as if they are Variants of type string.

You may notice something slightly odd about this chapter's treatment of compiler constants: Even though you generally use them as Booleans, the sample constants you will see in this chapter have all been assigned numeric values. In fact, the values True and False can be used for compiler constants, too. The reason this chapter avoids doing so is that the value for True is explicitly defined as –1, which can lead to some puzzling results with the preprocessor:

```
#Const VexingVariable = True
#If VexingVariable = 1
    MsgBox "You Won't See Me"
#End If
```

The message box won't appear because the preprocessor sees the test as -1 = 1, which it concludes is False. If you are accustomed to thinking of any non-zero value as True, this can be confusing. That is why this chapter assigns unambiguous literal values to compiler constants rather than Boolean values.

Once again, remember that the preprocessor and the compiler don't speak the same language. (In this case, perhaps it is more appropriate to say that they don't share the same name space.) Just as the preprocessor can't use a variable you have declared in your code, your code can't use compiler constants anywhere but in a preprocessor directive. This is illegal:

```
Dim ProgramVariable as Integer
#Const NothingButACompilerConstant = 1
If ProgramVariable = NothingButACompilerConstant Then
➥DoSomething()
```

When you try to compile code like this with Option Explicit, VB will tell you that you haven't declared NothingButACompilerConstant. By now, you have certainly noticed the pattern. As long as you don't mix the stuff you do on lines beginning with pound signs with any of your other code, you shouldn't have any trouble. Just keep track of those pound signs.

Declaring in the Project Properties Dialog Box

If you pull down the Project menu and choose Properties at the bottom of the menu list, the Project Properties dialog box appears, as shown in Figure 19.1. If you select the Make tab on the dialog box, you will see a field for Conditional Compilation Arguments.

Figure 19.1

The Project Properties dialog box.

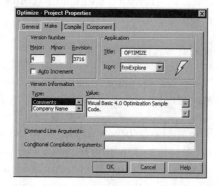

To define a preprocessor constant here, you don't use #Const, but the syntax is otherwise the same as for doing so in code: Type a name for the constant, an equals sign, and the value you wish to assign to the constant. As the illustration shows, you can define more than one constant in the Project Properties dialog box by separating them with colons. (When you realize that the colon also acts as a line separator in VB code, this makes pretty good sense.)

Declaring in the Command Line

You can also use the VB command line to set up preprocessor constants. If you want to compile a project from outside the development environment, you can start the compilation process from a command line with the /make switch, adding the /d switch to enter compiler constants. For example:

```
vb.exe /make ProjectName.vbp /d VERSION=2:CLIENT="Pointy-haired
➥boss"
```

You don't need to leave a space between the /d switch and the constant, but it makes the example easier to read. Notice how the example defines multiple constants by separating them with colons.

Scope and Persistence

The scope and persistence of a compiler constant depends on where it is declared.

If the #Const directive is used to define a compiler constant in code, that constant is Private to the module in which it is defined. This means that if you want to use the same constant in multiple modules, it must be defined in each module; you can't use #Const to create Public compiler constants. Naturally, compiler constants defined in code persist between sessions. That is, they won't go away unless you explicitly remove them from your source files.

If you need to use a Public compiler constant, you can define it either in the Project Properties dialog box or on the command line. Constants defined in either way are Public to all modules in a project. If you need to use the same constant throughout an entire project, this is obviously more convenient than manually entering it into every module and form.

Why are there two ways to define Public compiler constants? The scope is the same using either method, but the persistence differs. If you use the Project Properties dialog box to define a constant, it is saved with your project. If you close the project, any compiler constant you have defined as a property of the project will still be there the next time you open the project.

When you specify a compiler constant on the command line, it applies only to the instance of the project that you are running at that very moment. The primary reason for this is to enable you to use a different value for a `Public` compiler constant that you have already defined in the Project Properties dialog box. The value you use on the command line temporarily overrides the stored value but doesn't erase it.

Consider that a `Public` compiler constant is defined under Project Properties such that USER="Wally" and that the following is entered on the command line:

```
vb.exe /make ProjectName.vbp /d USER="Alice"
```

Any conditional compiler tests will substitute the value "Alice" for the USER constant during the current debug session. The next time the project is run, however, USER will still be defined as "Wally" (unless it is overridden on the command line again, of course). Values set on the command line don't persist between sessions.

What happens if you use the same name for a constant both in your code and in the Project Properties dialog box? The same thing that happens when a local variable has the same name as a global variable: The local variable overrides the global variable. The value of the compiler constant set in your code will override the `Public` constant set in the dialog box.

If BUDDYLIKESSOCKS = 0 is specified in the dialog box, for example, and #Const BUDDYLIKESSOCKS = 1 is specified in a code module, the value of BUDDYLIKESSOCKS will be 1 in the code module and 0 will be everywhere else. This enables you to override `Public` compiler constants on a module-by-module basis.

Applications and Styles

The discussion to this point has focused on the mechanics of how conditional compilation enables you to selectively include and exclude parts of your code from the compiled version of a project. Now the focus changes to some applications of these concepts. What follows is hardly an exhaustive list of all the possibilities, but it should at least suggest some ways to use the preprocessor to your advantage.

16-bit Versus 32-bit Code

If you develop applications for both 16-bit systems (Windows 3.1) and 32-bit systems (Windows 95 and Windows NT), you will appreciate the predefined Win32 and Win16 constants. By wrapping code that is intended exclusively for a particular platform in the appropriate conditional blocks, you can maintain a single body of code instead of working with separate projects for each platform.

Because VB5 is exclusively a 32-bit development platform, you will need a separate 16-bit VB compiler (for example, VB 4.0 16-bit, or VB 3.0) for this to be useful.

Maintaining Separate .EXEs for Each Platform

Once introduced to the concept of conditional compilation, some programmers automatically assume that the conditional compiler code allows VB to generate a single .EXE smart enough to selectively run 16-bit or 32-bit code by detecting the processor under which it runs. That is incorrect.

Remember that the preprocessor instructions are processed at compile time, not at runtime. This isn't like a programming conditional test that just determines which path of execution to take—these tests determine what code gets compiled into the .EXE in the first place. Only the first branch of a conditional compile block whose conditions evaluate to True is compiled, and the code in the other branches is ignored.

If you use the test for the Win32 and Win16 compiler constants in the sample declarations fragment (see the following section, "Declaring Windows API Functions"), for example, only one set of the

API declarations will be compiled. The preprocessor strips out the code in the "false" branch before sending the code to the compiler. The compiler never even sees the code in the Win16 branches when compiling in a 32-bit environment, and vice versa.

It is impossible to create an .EXE that uses both sets of declarations simultaneously, automatically selecting either the 16-bit or 32-bit version calls depending on the environment it detects. The only way to produce an .EXE that will run on both 16-bit and 32-bit Windows systems is to compile your project twice—once under the 16-bit operating system, and once under the 32-bit operating system—to get two separate .EXE files.

This principle applies to all cases of conditional compilation, not just those involving the Win32 and Win16 constants. You can't produce a single .EXE that contains the code from all branches of a conditional test. In every case, the compiler will see only the code from the first branch of the test that evaluates to True.

Declaring Windows API Functions

A common reason to divide 16-bit code from 32-bit code is to ensure that Windows API functions are declared from the appropriate libraries. Portions of the 32-bit Windows API are very similar, but not precisely identical, to the 16-bit API.

Among other things, the names of the primary libraries are generally different. Many of the 32-bit libraries have a "32" suffix that the 16-bit libraries don't use. The three primary 32-bit libraries, for example, are named "kernel32," "GDI32," and "user32." The 16-bit versions of these libraries are named "kernel," "GDI," and "user," so a single set of declarations won't work if you need to build both a 16-bit and a 32-bit version of a program.

If not for conditional compilation, you would need to maintain two parallel sets of code. By using conditional compilation, however, you can maintain a single body of code by wrapping the different declarations in the appropriate preprocessor blocks. The following example shows the declarations for reading and writing Windows initialization files:

```
#If Win32 Then
    Private Declare Function WritePrivateProfileSection Lib
    ➥"kernel32" Alias "WritePrivateProfileSectionA" (ByVal
    ➥lpAppName As String, ByVal lpString As String, ByVal
    ➥lpFileName As String)as Long
    Private Declare Function WritePrivateProfileString Lib
    ➥"kernel32" Alias "WritePrivateProfileStringA" (ByVal
    ➥lpApplicationName As String, ByVal lpKeyName As String, ByVal
    ➥lpString As Any, ByVal lpFileName As String) as Long
    Private Declare Function GetPrivateProfileSection Lib
    ➥"kernel32" Alias "GetPrivateProfileSectionA" (ByVal lpAppName
    ➥As String, ByVal lpReturnedString As String, ByVal nSize As
    ➥Long, ByVal lpFileName As String) as Long
    Private Declare Function GetPrivateProfileString Lib
    ➥"kernel32" Alias "GetPrivateProfileStringA" (ByVal
    ➥lpApplicationName As String, ByVal lpKeyName As String, ByVal
    ➥lpDefault As String, ByVal lpReturnedString As String, ByVal
    ➥nSize As Long, ByVal lpFileName As String) as Long
    Private Declare Function GetPrivateProfileInt Lib "kernel32"
    ➥Alias "GetPrivateProfileIntA" (ByVal lpApplicationName As
    ➥String, ByVal lpKeyName As String, ByVal nDefault As Long,
    ➥ByVal lpFileName As String) as Long
    ➥#Else ' Win16
    'Function WritePrivateProfileSection is not available in the
    ➥WIN16 API.
    Private Declare Function WritePrivateProfileString Lib
    ➥"kernel" (ByVal lpApplicationName As String, ByVal lpKeyName
    ➥As String, ByVal lpString As String, ByVal lplFileName As
    ➥String) as Integer
    'Function GetPrivateProfileSection is not available in the
    ➥WIN16 API.
    Private Declare Function GetPrivateProfileString Lib "kernel"
    ➥(ByVal lpApplicationName As String, ByVal lpKeyName As Any,
    ➥ByVal lpDefault As String, ByVal lpReturnedString As String,
    ➥ByVal nSize As Integer, ByVal lpFileName As String) as Integer
    Private Declare Function GetPrivateProfileInt Lib "kernel"
    ➥(ByVal lpApplicationName As String, ByVal lpKeyName As
    ➥String, ByVal nDefault As Integer, ByVal lpFileName As
    ➥String) as Integer
#End If
```

If you compare the 32-bit and 16-bit APIs, you will find that many of the functions are almost identical. They have the same names and take the same arguments, but the numeric types of arguments or return values may be slightly different. Take another look at the `GetPrivateProfileString` declarations in the preceding example, for instance. Besides being declared from different libraries, the 16-bit version returns an `Integer`, whereas the 32-bit version returns a `Long`.

This is a common pattern among many API calls. Its origin lies in the fact that the Windows API is predominantly a creation of the C programming language. Whereas the rules of VB dictate that the size of an `Integer` is always 2 bytes, the rules of C dictate that the size of its integer type is variable. The size of a C integer depends on the natural size of a machine word for the CPU used to compile a program. (In this context, a word is the number of bytes of instructions the CPU can process simultaneously.) The natural size of a word for a 286 machine is 16 bits, for example, or 2 bytes. The natural size of a word for a 386 machine is 32 bits, or 4 bytes.

Windows 3.1 runs on machines that process 16-bit instructions, so it is not surprising that the return value of many 16-bit Windows API calls fits into 16 bits, or the size of a VB `Integer`. Windows NT and Windows 95 are 32-bit operating systems, and many of the 32-bit counterparts to the 16-bit API functions return 32-bit values, which is the size of a VB `Long`.

As far as a C programmer is concerned, these functions return the same C `"int"` data type in any version of Windows—`GetPrivateProfileString`, for example, just returns an `int`, regardless of the platform. C programmers can port an `"int"` to any platform without much fuss. (That is the point to allowing the integer type to have a size that varies.)

VB programmers must cope with the legacy of Windows's C heritage, however, by explicitly specifying either an `Integer` or a `Long` when dealing with functions written using C's integer type. Therefore, even if you didn't have to worry about the different naming conventions used for the core libraries, you still would need to use conditional compilation to specify the appropriate data types in your function declarations.

Calling Windows API Functions

Getting the Windows API declarations right is really only half the battle. You must also see to it that only those functions that you have actually declared are called in your code, and that they always use the proper data types. What happens, for example, if you want to use GetPrivateProfileString after you have declared it? Relying on the preceding declarations, you need to write your code as follows:

```
Sub Form_Load ()
   Dim strTitle as String * 15
   Dim strKeyValue as String, strKeyDefault as String, strKeyName
   ➥as String
   Dim strSection as String, strFileName as String
   strKeyValue = String$(16,0)
   strKeyDefault = "Sample Key"
   strKeyName = "Title"
   strSection = "Sample Section"
   strFileName = "Sample.Ini"
   #If Win32 Then
      Dim rc as Integer
      rc = GetPrivateProfileString (strSection, strKeyName,
      ➥strKeyDefault, strKeyValue, Len(strKeyValue), strFileName)
   #Else ' Win16
   Dim rc as Long
      rc = GetPrivateProfileString (strSection, strKeyName,
      ➥strKeyDefault, strKeyValue, Len(strKeyValue),
      ➥strFileName)
   #End If
   Me.Caption = strKeyValue
End Sub
```

Because the return type of the function is the only significant difference between the two versions of GetPrivateProfileString, you actually needed to use conditional compilation solely to create the right type of variable to accept the return value. That is, the conditional test and the function call could have been written as follows:

```
#If Win32 Then
   Dim rc as Integer
#Else ' Win16
   Dim rc as Long
```

```
#End If
    rc = GetPrivateProfileString (strSection, strKeyName,
    ↪strKeyDefault, strKeyValue, Len(strKeyValue), strFileName)
```

This works because the second argument, `lpKeyName`, is declared as `Any` for the 16-bit version and as a `String` for the 32-bit version. You pass it the `strKeyName` string in either case, so the same call works under both APIs. The value of the fifth argument, `nSizefor`, is declared as a `Long` for the 32-bit version and as an `Integer` for the 16-bit version. This does not pose a problem, however, because you don't need to create a variable of either type to pass the value. Instead, you pass the return value of `Len(strKeyValue)`, which is acceptable to both versions of the function.

The shortcut cuts down on the amount of code you actually need to type, but there is yet another even more efficient way to handle API calls.

Setting Platform Defaults

The need to specifically use either an `Integer` or a `Long` when working with the Windows API is because of that quirk in C that lets a single data type take on different sizes. VB can accomplish the same thing—well, nearly enough that it makes no difference, anyway.

Normally, the default data type in VB is a `Variant`. It is possible, however, to change the default type by using the VB family of `Def` functions. Combining these functions with conditional compilation enables you to use a different default type depending on your platform. If the following code appears in the declarations section of a module, your default type for that module will be `Long` in the 32-bit world and `Integer` in the 16-bit world:

```
#If Win32 Then
    DefLng A-Z
#Else ' Win16
    DefInt A-Z
#End If
```

This doesn't exactly produce a data type with a variable size like the int in C, but you can rely on the default type in much the same way. This technique means that you no longer have to write conditional code blocks to create separate variables for use with API calls that differ only by data types. The call to GetPrivateProfileString that you have been using as an example could be written as follows:

```
Dim rc
rc = GetPrivateProfileString (strSection, strKeyName,
➥strKeyDefault, strKeyValue, Len(strKeyValue), strFileName)
```

Because rc is not explicitly coded as a particular type, it becomes the system default type, which you have redefined to be an Integer on a 16-bit platform and a Long on a 32-bit platform. This coincides perfectly with the return type of GetPrivateProfileString, so you no longer need to use conditional compilation in the Form_Load function used in the example.

Naturally, this approach also works when the arguments passed to API functions parallel the 32-bit API=Long, 16-bit API=Integer pattern that you have observed for return types. The nSize argument passed to GetPrivateProfileString is a good example. The sample code you have seen so far has passed the nSize value by calling the VB Len function directly inside the call to GetPrivateProfileString. If you decided to create a variable to pass to nSize, you could do it like this:

```
Dim rc, cBuffer
CBuffer = Len(strKeyvalue)
rc = GetPrivateProfileString (strSection, strKeyName,
➥strKeyDefault, strKeyValue, cBuffer, strFileName)
```

Both rc and cBuffer will be the system default type. As long as the conditional compiler block with DefInt and DefLng appears in the declaration section of the module where this code fragment appears, they will be the right types.

Many VB programmers have trained themselves to avoid using the standard default Variant type by explicitly declaring variable types. Consequently, a maintenance programmer may not immediately understand code like this that relies on changing the default types. If these variables are given an explicit type, however, it breaks the code on at least one platform. To prevent problems later in the life of your program, it may be worthwhile to comment your code so that subsequent programmers understand your rationale for relying on default behavior.

Using Debug Mode

Conditional compilation makes it easier to remove debugging tests from your code prior to building a release version of a project. Rather than having to manually search and remove (or comment out) tests that may be scattered in multiple modules, you can place your debug code in conditional compiler blocks:

```
    Dim BuggyVariable as String
    ' ... processing occurs
#If TESTING = 1 Then
    ' see if THIS is where BuggyVariable blew up
    MsgBox "Current value of BuggyVariable" " & BuggyVariable
#End If
```

Naturally, you don't want this to appear in a released product. The key is to define a constant that will be True only when you are debugging and False otherwise. Visual C++ includes a predefined compiler constant that serves just such a purpose, but Visual Basic requires you to create your own "Debug mode" constant. Recall that there are three ways to define a compiler constant. You could define:

```
#Const TESTING = 1
```

in every module with debug code and then wrap your tests in the following:

```
#If TESTING Then
#End If
```

Of course, this requires you to manually alter each module so that TESTING is no longer defined as 1 when it is time to build a release. One of the reasons to use conditional compilation in the first place is to cut down on that kind of drudgery. Therefore, defining the constant via #Const probably isn't the best choice unless your debugging tests are confined to a single module.

Defining a Public compiler constant, either via the Project Properties dialog box or on the command line, defines a constant for the entire project. Of course, if you use the Project Properties dialog box, you must remember to change the value of TESTING (for example, TESTING = 0) before building your release. This approach has the advantage of leaving you with only one place to make the change. Still, it is possible to forget, especially if you don't visit the Project Properties dialog box regularly. This approach is less risky than having to track down #Const in multiple source files, but there is still a chance that you will release a project that includes your debug code.

What about the command line? Because you have to explicitly define your Public compiler constant with the /d switch before beginning each debug session, this is less convenient than setting the constant with the Project Properties dialog box. However, it also means that you're extremely unlikely ever to ship a version of a project with your debug tests accidentally enabled.

This raises another issue, however: What happens to a conditional compiler test when a compiler constant is undefined?

If you leave the conditional tests in place after eliminating the definition of a constant, you might expect to see some kind of preprocessor error message or warning. In fact, you won't get one. Recall that preprocessor constants are treated as Variants. If a Variant hasn't been initialized, it has the value Empty. Now, assume that the RELEASEMODE constant in this example has not yet been defined:

```
#If Not RELEASEMODE Then
    MsgBox "But I thought this code wouldn't be compiled!"
#End If
```

In this case, the message box will appear. A Variant containing Empty is treated as 0, and Not 0 evaluates to True. This means that the message box pops up even if you haven't assigned a value to RELEASEMODE.

Because you can't rely on a compiler warning or preprocessor error message to inform you of your mistake (there is no Option Explicit for compiler constants), it is a good idea to take this default behavior into account when you code your tests to avoid surprises. Always test the compiler constant used to wrap your debug code for a non-zero value. (That is, never rely on a test that reduces to "MYCONSTANT = 0".) If you use the command line switch to define your debug compiler constant, this will make it impossible to accidentally compile your debug tests into a release.

From a mechanical standpoint, there is nothing more to know about the process of conditional compilation. After you understand the rules for defining and testing constants, all that is left is to dream up new ways to apply them. The rest of this chapter suggests a few ideas to get you started.

Comparing Algorithms

If you are not sure what algorithm is best-suited to a procedure, implement the ones you want to compare in a conditional block. For example:

```
#Const SortMethod = 1
#If SortMethod = 1
' Insertion Sort
#Else If SortMethod = 2
' Bubble Sort
#Else If SortMethod = 3
' QuickSort
' #Else If etc.
#End If
```

The quantity and state of the data it manipulates may affect the performance of an algorithm. Insertion sorts are fast with small lists, for example, but performance deteriorates as the size of the list increases. If a list is already nearly sorted, a bubble sort can be quite fast.

Conditional compilation to support different algorithms makes it easier for you to test different approaches to programming problems. Depending on the completeness of your implementation, you may also find it useful to be able to adapt your program to the demands of different data sets just by changing the value of a compiler constant and recompiling.

Feature Sets

The same body of code can support different combinations of features. You may want to use the same interface for a database program, for example, but employ it with different data engines. Using conditional compilation, you could produce separate versions of your program for DAO, RDO, and ODBC.

Unlike the database scenario, which requires selecting one approach from among competing alternatives, you can also take an additive approach. If you add fax support to your program, but you want it to be included only in releases 2.0 and later, you can still produce a 1.0 .EXE from your source, as shown here:

```
#If ReleaseNumber >= 2 Then
' fax support
#End If
```

Just make sure that you specify #Const ReleaseNumber = 1 when you need to generate a 1.0 copy of your program. It is no match for a full-blown version control system, but conditional compilation can serve as a limited VCS.

Client Specific

If you provide the same program to multiple clients who require slightly different features, you can implement these features in a common body of code by wrapping the client-specific features in conditional compiler blocks that compare a constant to the client name:

```
#If ClientName = "Clinton" Then
' ingenious code that cripples the Republican party,
' except for that pesky Whitewater bug
#End If
#If ClientName = "Dole"
' ingenious code that cripples the Democratic party,
' except for that annoying 1996 bug
#End If
```

Looking at Style

Code maintenance is difficult enough without compounding the problem by maintaining parallel code. When you begin to keep multiple versions of a program in a single body of code, anything that eases your maintenance tasks may be worth considering. This example comes from the Windows API, but the issue arises anytime your code takes parallel paths. It might be for versioning, different client needs, or any other reason you can think of.

Hundreds of functions can be declared from the Window API. Some aren't available in both 16-bit and 32-bit Windows. When declarations are grouped solely because they all apply to the same platform, it is easy to lose track of how the platforms actually parallel one another on a feature-by-feature basis.

If you take a close look at the initialization file declarations used earlier in this chapter, for example, you will notice that a few functions available in 32-bit Windows don't exist for 16-bit Windows (for example, `WritePrivateProfileSection`). Because the example has only five declarations, it is not terribly difficult to spot the "holes" in the 16-bit declarations. If the code included declarations for several dozen API calls, however, these differences might easily be overlooked.

To ensure uniformity among the paths of a parallel implementation, it may be useful to break down your conditional compilation tests by function rather than platform. Here are the declarations of two API calls to illustrate:

```
'WritePrivateProfileSection
#If Win32 Then
   Private Declare Function WritePrivateProfileSection Lib
   ➥"kernel32" Alias "WritePrivateProfileSectionA" (ByVal only
   ➥lpAppName As String, ByVal lpString As String, ByVal
   ➥lpFileName As String) as Long
#Else ' Win16
   'Function WritePrivateProfileSection is not available in the
   ➥WIN16 API.
#End If
' WritePrivateProfileString
#If Win32 Then
   Private Declare Function WritePrivateProfileString Lib
   ➥"kernel32" Alias "WritePrivateProfileStringA" (ByVal
   ➥lpApplicationName As String, ByVal lpKeyName As String, ByVal
   ➥lpString As Any, ByVal lpFileName As String) as Long
#Else ' Win16
   Private Declare Function WritePrivateProfileString Lib
   ➥"kernel" (ByVal lpApplicationName As String, ByVal lpKeyName
   ➥As String, ByVal lpString As String, ByVal lplFileName As
   ➥String) as Integer
#End If
' etc.
```

A functional approach requires additional typing due to the increased number of tests, of course. (Remember, these tests won't affect your program's performance because they don't get compiled into the program.) By some standards, it may even be less readable, but that really depends on what you're looking for when you read. (If you use a comment header for each function and a conspicuous color code for your comments, it is surprisingly easy to navigate code like this.)

It is all the same to the compiler. If this approach makes it easier to find holes in otherwise parallel code sets, it is worthwhile.

Exercises

Exercise 19.1:　Windows API Calls

Create a program that will conditionally run under either a 16-bit version or a 32-bit version of Windows. The program will use the Windows API to locate another application by its window name or the class name of the application. To create this exercise, follow these steps:

1. Create a new project.

2. Use the API Viewer included with VB5 to insert the 32-bit declaration for the FindWindow function into your code. You will also need to insert the 16-bit version of the declaration. In case you don't have access to a source for the 16-bit API declaration, here it is:

   ```
   Declare Function FindWindow Lib "User"
   ➥(ByVal lpClassname as Any, ByVal
   ➥lpCaption as Any) as Integer
   ```

3. Wrap the two function declarations in a conditional compiler block so that the appropriate function is called for the environment in which the application is compiled.

4. Place a command button on a form. The button's Click event code for the 16-bit API call should be as follows:

   ```
   strClassName = "Calculator"
   If FindWindow(0&, strClassName) Then
       MsgBox "Calculator is active"
   Else
       MsgBox "Calculator is not active"
   End If
   ```

5. If any conditional tests need to be made to use the correct version of the function, apply them here.

6. If you have access to a 16-bit VB environment (for example, VB 3.0 or VB 4.0 16-bit), try compiling and running the project there.

Exercise 19.2: Compiler Constants

In this exercise, you create a program that uses a compiler constant to compile code to generate different messages. To create this exercise, follow these steps:

1. Create a new project.

2. In the General Declarations section of a form, write code to create a compiler constant. Call the constant ZIPPY and assign it a value of 1.

3. Create a command button on the same form. In the button's Click event code, enter the following:

```
#If ZIPPY = 1 Then
    MsgBox "Zippy = 1.  What a surprise."
#Else If ZIPPY = 2
    MsgBox "Zippy = 2.  Alert the media."
#Else
    MsgBox "Zippy = a value wholly unlike
    ➥1 or 2.  Yow!"
#End If
```

4. Compile and run the project.

5. Now open the Project Properties dialog box to give ZIPPY a value of 2. Compile and run the project again.

6. Finally, use the command line to set the value of ZIPPY to 3. Compile and run the project again. If you wish to attain a truly Zippy-like state of Zen (and honorary lifetime status as a true Pinhead), continue the tests, incrementing the value of ZIPPY by 1 each time, to see whether you ever produce a different result.

Review Questions

1. A compiler constant gDEBUG is defined and assigned a value of 1 in a global module. The following code is placed in the load event of form frmStartUp:

```
#If gDEBUG Then
  MsgBox "Debugging"
#End If
```

If compile-on-demand is active, what happens when frmStartUp loads?

   A. The form's Load event code generates a compiler error.

   B. A message box displays with the message "Debugging".

   C. The program enters Break mode.

   D. The form loads normally, but no message box displays.

2. A compiler constant verDEBUG has been defined and assigned a value of 1. Several code blocks are enclosed by #If verDEBUG / #End If pairs. The program is compiled by typing:

```
vb.exe /make ProjectName.vbp /d verDEBUG=0
```

Which of the following is true?

   A. The value of verDEBUG set in code takes precedence.

   B. The value of verDEBUG set on the command line takes precedence.

   C. A VB runtime error occurs due to an invalid command line parameter.

   D. The compiled program permits a user to specify the value of verDEBUG on the command line.

3. A compiler constant is defined #Const Bumble = 1 in the General Declarations section of a form. The same form has a command button with a compiler constant defined in its Click event code as #Const Bumble = 0. The rest of the Click event code looks like this:

```
#If Bumble Then
    MsgBox "Lookie what Bumble can do!"
#End If
```

What happens when the project is run and the command button is clicked?

A. The project will not run due to a compiler error.

B. The form-level constant takes precedence over the local constant, so the message box displays.

C. The form-level constant takes precedence over the local constant, so nothing happens.

D. The local constant takes precedence over the form-level constant, so nothing happens.

4. A compiler constant verDEBUG has been defined and assigned a value of 1. Select the combination of commands to begin and end each code block that will cause the compiler to ignore a code block when building a verDEBUG version of a program:

A. #Ifdef verDEBUG

   #Endif

B. #If verDEBUG = TRUE Then

   #Endif

C. #If verDEBUG = TRUE

   #End If

D. #If verDEBUG Then

   #End If

5. Projects using conditional compilation require extra lines of code for the preprocessor directives and for the alternate versions of the project. Consequently, the size of the executable program is _____ than if separate versions of the project were maintained with no use of the preprocessor.

    A. Larger (by the size required by the extra lines of code only)

    B. Larger (by the size required by the preprocessor code only)

    C. Larger (by the size required by both the extra lines of code and the preprocessor code)

    D. No larger

Answers to Review Questions

1. D. With compile-on-demand activated, the global module in which gDEBUG is defined will not have been compiled. For more information, see the section titled "Using Debug Mode" in this chapter and also refer to the section "Using Compile-on-Demand" in Chapter 18.

2. B. The value set on the command line overrides the value set in code. For more information, see the sections titled "Declaring in the Command Line" and "Scope and Persistence."

3. A. A constant can be defined to have only a single value, so the second attempt to define the constant with a new value generates a duplicate definition error. For more information, see the section titled "Declaring in the Command Line."

4. D. The first choice uses the wrong syntax ("#Ifdef" isn't part of VB). The second choice fails because True is defined as -1. The third choice omits "Then". For more information, see the section titled "Using Debug Mode."

5. D. The extra lines aren't compiled, so they make no difference to the size of an .EXE file. For more information, see the section titled "Preprocessor Directives."

Answers to Test Yourself Questions at Beginning of Chapter

1. The value of verDEBUG will be 2. The command line overrides the assignment in code. See "Scope and Persistence."
2. Here is one approach: Begin your 32-bit code with #If WIN32 followed by an #Else, and then enter your 16-bit code. End the block with #End If. See "Predefined Compiler Constants."
3. Although this might be accomplished via API calls, conditional compilation does not permit this to be done. See "Maintain Separate .EXEs for Each Platform."

Chapter 20

Setting Watch Expressions During Program Execution

This chapter helps you prepare for the exam by covering the following objective:

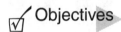 Objectives

▶ Set watch expressions during program execution

Test Yourself! Before reading this chapter, test yourself to determine how much study time you will need to devote to this section.

1. Identify the various kinds of watches available in VB5.

2. How are arrays and user-defined types displayed in a Watch window?

3. What is "Break mode"?

Answers are located at the end of the chapter...

Bugs are a fact of life. Even the most finely honed programming discipline can't guarantee error-free code. Because you can't absolutely prevent bugs from being written in the first place, you have to settle for second best by trying to stamp them out before they inadvertently get released into a product.

Fortunately, VB gives you a lot of opportunities to find your bugs before you put your software into the hands of your users. The primary debugging tools in the Visual Basic programming environment are the following three debugging windows:

- ▶ The Watch window

- ▶ The Immediate window

- ▶ The Locals window

The next chapter examines the Immediate window and the Locals window. This chapter focuses on the Watch window. Specifically, this chapter covers the following topics:

- ▶ Bug prevention

- ▶ Watch expressions and contexts

- ▶ Break mode

Preventing Bugs

This discussion starts by testing your debugging skills by looking at a simple problem in a loop that assigns values to an array of string variables. The array is defined in a module as follows:

```
Public astrName(9) as String
```

Because arrays are zero-based by default, this creates an array of 10 variables in the astrName array. Assume that each of the variables is properly assigned a value, but that you later try to display the names in the array using this code:

```
Dim i as Integer
For i = 1 to 10
    MsgBox "Name #" & i  & " is " & astrName(i)
Next
```

As this loop executes, you begin to see a series of message boxes for Name #1, Name #2, and so on. However, when you reach Name #10, a subscript out of range error message appears (assuming, that is, that you haven't used an advanced optimization feature to disable array bounds checking). Obviously, something is wrong, but what is it? After all, you know there are supposed to be 10 variables in that array, and you are only asking to see items 1 to 10. This hardly seems like it should give you any trouble.

This is a simple example, and if you already understand arrays, you can spot the problem without bothering with a watch. The array does have 10 elements, but because it is zero-based, the index values range from 0 to 9, not 1 to 10. When the loop tried to display the value of astrName(10), it was outside the bounds of the array.

The same person who wrote the buggy display loop might also make this mistake in assigning values to the array:

```
For i = 1 to 9
    astrName(i) = "Some name value"
Next
```

This is a little more insidious than the display loop. This assignment loop doesn't generate any error messages, but it is wrong nonetheless. If the default Option Base 0 has not been changed, the first element of the array is astrName(0), to which this loop never assigns a value.

A programmer with some VB experience will understand these problems almost at once, but that doesn't help the beginner who wrote the buggy code in these loops. You can use certain techniques to help prevent these problems by making your intent clearer to others who may later need to maintain your code. Even if no one else but you will ever touch your code, you may benefit from these techniques yourself if you ever have to resume a project that you haven't touched in a long while.

First, the array might have been defined by explicitly specifying its upper and lower bounds:

```
Public astrName(0 to 9) as String
```

This makes it clear that the range of values begins with 0 and ends with 9, so it should be less likely that the flawed assignment loop above will be repeated. It also ensures that there will still be 10 elements in the array even if someone later adds Option Base 1 to the code to change the default lower boundary of an array.

Second, additional care could be taken in the display loop by finding out both the upper and lower boundaries of the array before trying to access its elements:

```
Dim iLower as Integer, iUpper as Integer
iLower = LBound(astrName)
iUpper = UBound(astrName)
For i = iLower to iUpper
    MsgBox "Name #" & i & " is " & astrName(i)
Next
```

This code is guaranteed to access each element of the array from beginning to end. Nothing gets skipped, and the code can't step outside the bounds of the array. Remember that you will need to use this technique for safety's sake if you use the advanced optimization switch that disables automatic array checking (see Chapter 18, "Selecting Appropriate Compiler Options").

You can (and you should!) take preventive measures like these to guard against potential bugs. Even simple safeguards have great value. For instance, I can't imagine coding without being forced to declare variables via Option Explicit, for example, and On Error Resume Next is reserved only for extremely brief routines with their own internal error checks. When you run into a new problem that isn't so obvious, and you can't understand what's wrong just by reading the code, you will develop an instant appreciation of VB's debugging aids. The first type you will examine is the watch expression.

Using Watch Expressions and Contexts

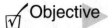 Objective ▶

A watch expression is essentially what its name implies: It is an expression whose value you want to watch change while your program runs. The expression may be simple or complex. A simple expression might consist of a single variable. A complex expression might perform calculations on multiple variables, or even call functions. The only requirement is that a watch expression must be a legal VB expression. In other words, if you can't use an expression in a line of code without generating a compiler error, you can't use it as a watch expression either.

Creating a Watch Expression

A watch enables you to observe the value of an expression while your code executes. To create a watch expression, open a project and pull down the Debug menu to choose Add Watch, as shown in Figure 20.1.

Figure 20.1

Use the Debug menu to create a watch expression.

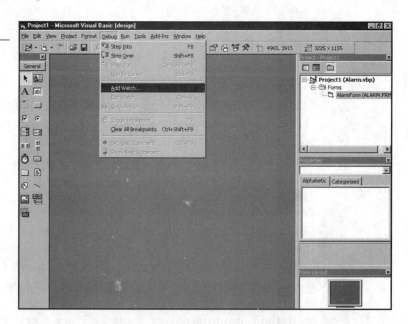

After you click on the Add Watch option, you will see the dialog box shown in Figure 20.2.

Figure 20.2

The Add Watch dialog box.

When you create a watch, you can specify any valid VB expression. The expression may range in complexity from the name of a single variable to a calculation involving a series of nested function calls. As long as it is a legal VB expression, you can monitor its value while your code executes.

However, if you make a mistake when you type the expression, VB won't tell you about it. There is no watch expression equivalent of the VB syntax checker to tell you that you have made a mistake after you enter a line. Consequently, it is up to you to pay close attention to ensure that you type what you intended. If you type nonsense that VB can't evaluate at runtime, the Watch window will cheerfully display it for you in the Watch window without complaint, as shown in Figure 20.3.

Figure 20.3

If your expression can't be evaluated, the Watch window will say so.

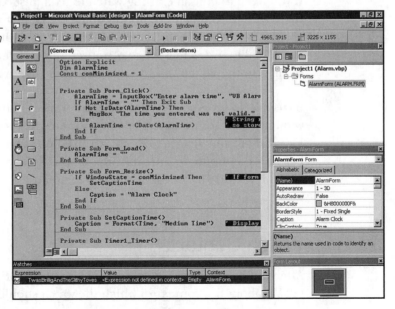

The closest thing you will get to an error message is the text in the Value column of the Watch window that says `Expression not defined in context`, but you will see that message under normal circumstances anyway. That is because the mechanism that enables you to set watches isn't omniscient. The same rules that apply to standard VB code also govern the evaluation of a watch expression. That means that the expression being watched must be in the scope of the currently executing code for the Watch window to report its value.

That is why you don't get an error message in the Watch window even if you try to set a watch for nonsense. The watch expression is evaluated only during runtime when VB is in Debug mode. You can, however, enter watch expressions when VB is in Design mode.

You don't need to type the expression you want to watch. You can double-click on a variable name to select it, and then drag it to the Watch window. Likewise, if you highlight an expression, the expression can be dragged to the Watch window. Whatever you drag into the Watch window is automatically used to create a new watch expression.

If you need to edit an existing watch to fix a mistake, select it in the Watch window, and then pull down the Debug menu to choose Edit Watch. You can also right-click the Watch window to add, edit, or delete a watch. Another way to delete a watch is to select it in the Watch window and press the Delete key.

As usual, VB gives you a lot of different ways to manage the Watch window itself. You can let the Watch window float or drag it to a location on your screen to dock in a fixed position. Grab its title bar with the mouse to drag it from one place to another. Double-clicking the title bar toggles its status between docked and floating.

Watch Contexts

After you have entered an expression to watch, you need to tell VB about the context in which the watch should be active.

Remember that the watch expression must be in the scope of the currently executing code for VB to tell you its value. If you specify a context in which the expression isn't valid, you will see the `Expression not defined in context` message. Again, that message doesn't necessarily mean that you've entered a bad expression. It does pay, however, to check the entry just in case.

If you don't have a form or module open when you create your watch, the context options for your watch defaults to all procedures and all modules.

If you accept the default context options, the expression is evaluated constantly throughout the entire project. Such a broad setting may sometimes make sense (as for a global variable, for instance), but you will make VB work harder if you monitor watch expressions in every possible context. The narrower the scope, the faster you see the results.

Bear in mind that the goal of a watch is to locate a problem in your code, such as a failure to modify a variable or assigning it a bad value. If you have some idea of where the problem is, it makes sense to limit the watch to a more appropriate context. When you set a watch, VB will change the module context setting for you to default to the form or module you are current viewing, as shown in Figure 20.4.

Figure 20.4

You can limit the scope of your watch expression to a single module.

The default procedure selection is also context sensitive. If the cursor is in a particular procedure, it will be used as the default scope, as shown in Figure 20.5.

Figure 20.5

You can also limit the scope of a watch expression to a particular procedure.

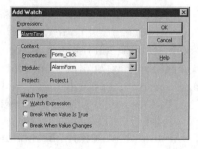

If you have an expression selected in a code window, the value of the watch expression defaults to it, too. If you want to watch a variable, you don't need to highlight its entire name—the word in which the cursor appears will be used by default. Of course, you aren't locked into the defaults. You can type a different expression for the watch if the default isn't what you want. If you need to select a different scope, you can select from a list of the modules and procedures in the current project, as shown in Figure 20.6.

Figure 20.6

Use the combo boxes to change the module or procedure scope of a watch expression.

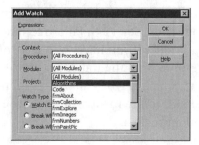

Using Break Mode

You can't actually use the Watch window until you are in Break mode. Break mode is sort of a programmatic limbo: Your program is still active, but its execution is temporarily suspended while the programmer pokes around. All your variables retain their values, as do the properties of any objects in your project. During Break mode, you can inspect any of these values. Remember, however, that only those variables within the scope of the currently executing code are available at any given moment.

Entering Break Mode Manually

You can manually enter Break mode in several ways:

▶ Press Ctrl+Break

▶ Choose Break from the Run menu

▶ Click on the Break button on the toolbar

If you aren't sure what part of your code may be responsible for a problem, but you see it when it happens, the ability to manually enter Break mode can be handy. It is possible for so many Windows events to occur in rapid succession, however, that the few hundred milliseconds it takes for you to click your mouse or press a key after you spot the problem may put you into a part of your code that has nothing to do with the problem.

If you can localize your problem to some extent, you can also specify places in your code at which to enter Break mode automatically:

▶ Set a breakpoint

▶ Use the Stop command

You can toggle a breakpoint either from the Debug menu, as shown in Figure 20.7, or by pressing the F9 key. If the current line has no breakpoint set, F9 sets one; if the line already has a breakpoint, F9 turns it off. If you want to remove all breakpoints from your project, you can either use the Debug menu to do so or press Ctrl+Shift+F9. The color of the line in the VB code editor reflects the status of any line with a breakpoint. Once set, your program will enter Break mode the moment at which it reaches the line of code with the breakpoint. The program's execution is suspended just before that line of code executes.

One problem with breakpoints is that they are not preserved between programming sessions. That is, if you close a project after setting a breakpoint and then reopen the project, your breakpoints will be gone. If you want to set a breakpoint that persists between sessions, use the Stop command. The moment the Stop line is reached in your code, the program enters Break mode.

Figure 20.7

Setting a breakpoint from the Debug menu.

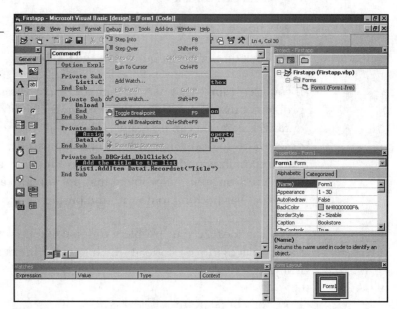

 Caution

If you're worried about inadvertently leaving a Stop command in a project before you deliver it to a client, remember that you can use a conditional compiler switch:

```
#Const DEBUGMODE = 1
#If DEBUGMODE Then
    Stop
#End If
```

To be extra safe, set the value of DEBUGMODE on the command line. Then you won't have to worry about forgetting to remove the definition of the compiler constant from your code either.

Stepping Through Your Code

Setting breakpoints usually isn't an exact science. While tracking down a bug, you may observe that problems occur after clicking on a certain command button. That doesn't necessarily mean that the `Click` event code in the command button is at fault, of course. You don't have to wait to pin down the problem more closely before setting a breakpoint, however. Because you know that the problem occurs at some point after that procedure executes, go ahead and set a breakpoint there so that you are at least that much closer to the problem when you are in Break mode.

Because program execution is suspended during Break mode, you may wonder how this helps you get closer to the bug. After all, you haven't reached the bug yet, and the program has stopped. How do you get to the problem?

Besides enabling you to watch variable and property values during Break mode, VB also enables you to continue to execute the program on an incremental basis. The process is typically called *stepping through* your code, and it enables you to execute a program a line at a time. You may not be right at the point at which a problem occurs, but you can step through your code to sneak up on the bug and catch it in the act.

The following four stepping commands are available in Break mode:

▶ `Step Into`

▶ `Step Over`

▶ `Step Out`

▶ `Step to Cursor`

The stepping commands are available in several ways: from the Debug menu, from the keyboard via the F8 key (by itself, or in conjunction with the Shift, Ctrl, and Alt keys), or from the Debug toolbar—as shown in Figure 20.8. If the Debug toolbar is not already visible, you can pull down the View menu and choose Toolbars, where you can toggle it off and on. The Debug toolbar can be docked or permitted to float.

Figure 20.8

The Debug tool-bar.

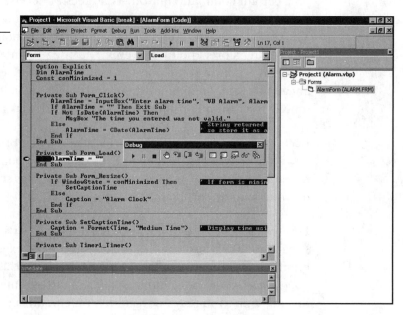

Here is a simple example to illustrate how the step commands behave after a program is in Break mode. Consider a project containing one form with a single command button. The code looks like this:

```
Sub cmdCommand_Click()
   Dim strName as String
   Msgbox "After this message, break mode begins."
   Stop
   strName = MyFunction()
End Sub
Function MyFunction() as String
   Dim strPrompt as String
   strPrompt = "Please enter your name"
   MyFunction = InputBox (strPrompt)
End Function
```

After you run this project and click on the command button, the program enters Break mode when it reaches the Stop command. The code editor will appear with the Stop command highlighted in the `cmdCommand_Click` function. Program execution is suspended, and nothing else happens until you issue a step command.

Step Into

If you select `Step Into`, the highlight moves to the next line of code, where `strName` is assigned the value returned by `MyFunction`. If you select `Step Into` again, the code editor will display the code for `MyFunction` with the highlight in its first line (recall that the highlighted line hasn't executed yet; it runs after you perform the next stepping action). If you continue to select `Step Into`, you will see where the command gets its name: `Step Into` enables you to step into any code that is called in your project, executing every procedure a line at a time.

Step Over

`Step Over` is similar to `Step Into`. Within the current procedure, `Step Over` continues to execute the code one line at a time. The difference is how it handles calls to other procedures. If you run this project again and select `Step Over` when you reach the `strName = MyFunction()` line in the `Click` event, you won't step into the `MyFunction` code. Instead, it runs all at once and you are returned to the function which called it. When you aren't interested in observing the behavior of another procedure called from within the one you are debugging, choose `Step Over`.

Step Out

What if you selected `Step Into`, only to realize that you really don't need to watch the execution of every step of the procedure you just stepped into? No, you don't have to lean on the F8 key to force the execution of every line. That's what `Step Out` is for: It causes the rest of the current procedure to run and returns to the calling procedure. That is, you could select `Step Out` as soon as you entered `MyFunction`, and you would find yourself back in the `Click` event just after `MyFunction` had completed its work.

Step to Cursor

You may step into a procedure that has only a few lines that you want to watch execute. If that happens, and there are a lot of lines from your point of entry to the lines that interest you, you don't need to wade through the boring parts with Step Into or Step Over. Instead, move the cursor to the first line you want to watch, and then select Step to Cursor. All the code will execute between the line at which you originally entered Break mode and the line where you placed the cursor, and then you can begin to step through the interesting parts again.

Setting Stepping Options

You will also notice a couple of other options at the bottom of the Debug menu. If you want to prevent a few lines of code from executing, but otherwise let your program continue normally, use Set Next Statement. While in break mode, this enables you to move the cursor to the next line that you want your program to execute. Because this skips the intervening lines, use this feature carefully. If you inadvertently skip some lines that modify values in your program, you may not catch the bug you are after. If you aren't sure what line is supposed to execute next, use Show Next Statement.

To exit Break mode and resume the normal operation of your program, choose Continue from the Debug menu or toolbar. (Its keyboard equivalent is F5.) If you have seen all that you need to see, you can also halt the program by choosing End, which is available on the Debug menu or on the toolbar.

Using the Watch Window

While you are busy stepping through your code, you can watch the values of your watch expressions in the Watch window. For instance, consider a loop such as this:

```
Dim i as Integer, j as Integer, k as Integer
Dim astrAlphabet(0 to 25) as String
j = LBound(astrAlphabet)
k = UBound(astrAlphabet)
```

```
For i = j to k
    astrAlphabet (i) = Chr$( i + 65)
Next
```

This loop populates a 26-element array with the letters of the alphabet. If you set a breakpoint and create a watch on the `astrAlphabet` array, you can watch the values of each element of the array as they are assigned values in the loop. However, you won't see the array build a string such as `"ABCDEFGHIJKLM-NOPQRSTUVWXYZ"`. In fact, if you watch only the single line containing the name of the array, you won't see much of anything useful except for the range of the array index values (in this case, 0 to 25). That's because an array is a data structure that contains more than one value, and each line in the Watch window can display only an individual value.

Watching Arrays

Don't worry. You don't need to set a separate watch for each element of the array. When dealing with a data structure such as an array, the Watch window will display the name of the array with a boxed plus sign next to it, as shown in Figure 20.9. It works in the same way that Windows Explorer displays a disk drive's directory structure in a tree control. Just as Windows Explorer uses plus signs to indicate that nested subdirectories remain to be displayed, the VB Watch window uses plus signs to indicate that more data elements are nested within the selected structure.

If you click the plus sign, the structure unfolds to display each individual data element, as shown in Figure 20.10. The plus sign changes to a minus sign, which you can click on to hide the elements contained in the structure again.

Watching User-Defined Types

The same nesting principle applies to user-defined types. If you create a type to store an employee's name, ID number, and Social Security number, it might look like this:

```
Type tEmployee
    strName as String
```

```
        iIDNumber as Integer
        lSocSecNum as Long
   End Type
```

Figure 20.9

When a watch is set on an array, you will see a boxed plus sign next to it.

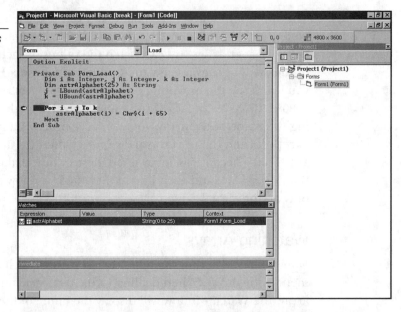

Figure 20.10

Click on the plus sign to monitor the values of the elements contained in the array.

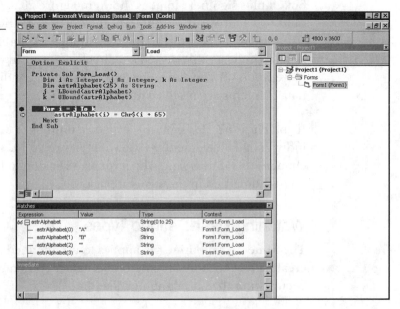

If you create a variable of type `tEmployee`, and then set a watch on that variable, the Watch window will display the name of your variable and a plus sign. As with the array, you need to click on the plus sign to unfold the `strName`, `iIDNumber`, and `lSocSecNum` elements of the data structure.

It is also possible to have multiple levels of nested structures in the Watch window. If you were to create an array of `tEmployee` variables called `atMyEmployees`, for example, you would need to click on the plus sign associated with the `atMyEmployees` array to display the `tEmployee` elements. To see the values contained for each `tEmployee`, you would in turn have to click on the plus sign associated with each element in the array.

Entering Break Mode Dynamically

If you're waiting to see where a watch value changes, the process of manually executing each individual line of your code can get to be awfully tedious, particularly if you're executing a lengthy loop. Waiting for the 26 letters of the alphabet to be assigned is no big deal, but what if you're processing hundreds or thousands of records? Rather than forcing you to manually execute the code until the change occurs (or until the F8 key on your keyboard wears out), VB gives you a couple of more convenient options.

Breaking on True

One of your options is to set a watch that causes your program to enter Break mode only when the value of the watch is True. This kind of watch spares you the bother of manually stepping through each individual line of code, taking you directly to Break mode when the program gets to a point that is really interesting.

Here's a simple procedure to illustrate the point:

```
Private Sub Form_Click()
    Dim iCounter As Integer, iTotal As Integer
    Dim fIncrementTotal As Boolean
    Print "From 1 to 100, the even multiples of 7 are:"
    For iCounter = 1 To 100
```

```
        ' set flag if value is an even multiple of 7
        fIncrementTotal = Not CBool(iCounter Mod 7)
        If fIncrementTotal Then
            Print iCounter
            ' sum even multiples of 7
            iTotal = iTotal + iCounter
        End If
    Next
    Print "The sum of these values is " & iTotal
End Sub
```

If you set a simple watch on the iTotal variable, you would have to set a breakpoint and then manually execute every subsequent line to observe changes in iTotal's value. However, if you instead set a watch that causes the program to enter Break mode only when fIncrementTotal is True, you will save yourself some drudgery. To set this kind of watch, just select the appropriate option in the Watch dialog box, as shown in Figure 20.11.

Figure 20.11

Select Break When Value Is True to enter Break mode automatically when a value is True.

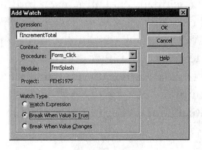

When you hit the first breakpoint, you can inspect the values of the program to make sure your calculations are correct. Instead of stepping through each individual line, you can select Continue and the program will run normally until the watch expression evaluates to True again, at which point you are back in Break mode.

Breaking on Change

Another way to evaluate this procedure is to set a watch so that the program enters Break mode only when the value of a watch expression changes, as shown in Figure 20.12. In this case, you could set this type of watch on the iTotal variable. The program would enter Break mode only when iTotal changes. This accomplishes the same thing as the previous example, of course, because iTotal is incremented only when fIncrementTotal is True.

Figure 20.12

Select Break When Value Changes to enter Break mode automatically when a value changes.

When you are working with different kinds of watches simultaneously, VB makes it easy to see what kind of watches are in play by displaying a different icon for each type in the Watch window, as shown in Figure 20.13. An eyeglasses icon denotes a simple watch expression.

Break When Value Is True and Break When Value Changes both use an open palm to indicate that these watches use VB's internal breakpoint traffic cop to force your program into Break mode. The Break on Change icon also includes a small triangle, which you may also recognize as the Greek letter "delta," which is often used to indicate changes in a value. Break on True displays a small blue rectangle in addition to the open palm, which is perhaps meant to call the expression "true blue" to mind.

If you find that setting a watch that enters Break mode is more convenient than using the simple watch expression you have already entered, remember that you can always change a watch from one type to another via the Debug menu's Edit Watch selection. A right-click of the mouse in the Watch window also displays this option on the pop-up menu.

Figure 20.13

Each type of watch is associated with its own icon in the Watch window.

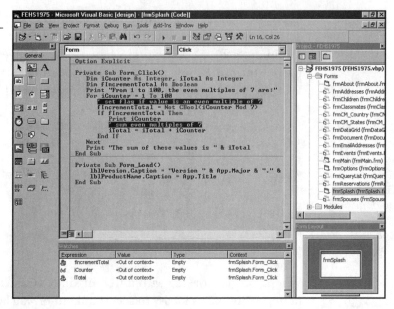

Using Quick Watch

When you are in Break mode, you may want to determine the value of an expression in your code for which a watch has not already been set. You can use the Quick Watch feature to display the value of any expression, as shown in Figure 20.14. Select the expression, and then pull down the Debug menu and choose Quick Watch. This displays the value of the selected expression in a Quick Watch dialog box. The dialog box also gives you a chance to add the expression to the Watch window.

Figure 20.14

The Quick Watch dialog box.

Watching on Demand

Finally, you can also evaluate any expression in Break mode by selecting it and positioning the mouse cursor over the expression for a moment. The expression and its value are displayed like the ToolTips that appear when you momentarily hold the mouse pointer over a toolbar button. You don't get a chance to add the expression to the Watch window this way, but you can take advantage of this technique to minimize clutter in your Watch window. If you don't need to constantly monitor a variable, just point at it when you need to know its current value.

Exercises

Exercise 20.1:   Using the Call Stack

Most programs will have procedures that call other procedures, which in turn call still other procedures. VB has a tool to show the call stack to help you keep track of the calling chain. You can use the Call Stack window anytime you need to trace the interactions of procedures in a program. This exercise demonstrates its use.

To create this exercise, follow these steps:

1. Create an application consisting of a single form with a command button. The form should resemble that shown in Figure 20.15.

Figure 20.15

The call stack demonstration form.

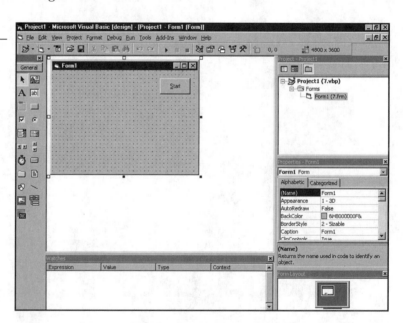

2. Enter the following code for the Click event of the command button:

```
Private Sub cmdStart_Click()
Cls
    Print "Beginning Start button code."
    Print "Calling Procedure A"
```

```
ProcedureA
Print "Ending Start button code."
End Sub
```

3. Create three additional procedures in the form, as follows:

```
Private Sub ProcedureA()
Print Tab(5); "Beginning Procedure A."
   Print Tab(5); "Calling Procedure B"
   ProcedureB
   Print Tab(5); "Ending Procedure A."
End Sub

Private Sub ProcedureB()
   Print Tab(10); "Beginning Procedure B."
   Print Tab(10); "Calling Procedure C"
   ProcedureC
   Print Tab(10); "Ending Procedure B."
End Sub

Private Sub ProcedureC()
   Print Tab(15); "Beginning Procedure C."
   ' Stop
   ' Print "Entering break mode"
   Print Tab(15); "Ending Procedure C."

End Sub
```

4. Run the exercise program and click on the command button. The form will display text in the form indicating the sequence in which the program's procedures have been called.

5. Close the form. Open the form's code module and remove the comment characters from the ProcedureC code. ProcedureC should now look like this:

```
Private Sub ProcedureC()
   Print Tab(15); "Beginning Procedure C."
   Stop
   Print "Entering break mode"
   Print Tab(15); "Ending Procedure C."
End Sub
```

continues

Exercise 20.1: Continued

6. Run the application again. When the program enters Break mode, pull down the VB View menu and select the menu option titled Call Stack (notice that Ctrl+L is a keyboard shortcut for the call stack).

7. Experiment with the Call Stack window. Notice how you can use it to view the point in any active procedure at which a subsequent procedure call was issued. You can use information about the call stack to guide your decisions about how to use the Debug menu's stepping commands to step into, out of, or to a particular line via step to cursor.

Review Questions

1. A _____ cannot be changed in the Watch window.

   A. Watch expression

   B. Watch on demand

   C. Watch, break on change

   D. Watch, break on true

2. If you no longer need to monitor the values in the current procedure, but you want to remain in Break mode, which options can you select to continue execution in another procedure?

   A. `Step Into`

   B. `Step Over`

   C. `Step Out Of`

   D. `Step to Cursor`

3. You entered Break mode in the current debugging session by pressing Ctrl+Break. To resume program execution, you should _____.

   A. Select Continue

   B. Toggle the current breakpoint from on to off

   C. Select Stop to exit Break mode

   D. Press Ctrl+Break again

4. Your program enters Break mode when the value of an integer (`iVariable`) watch variable is assigned a value of 25. As the program continues, `iVariable` is later assigned a value of 0, but the program does not enter Break mode this time. The type of watch set on the variable is _____.

   A. A simple watch expression, `iVariable` >= 25

   B. Watch, break when expression changes

    C. Watch, break when expression is `True`

    D. A quick watch

5. If a plus sign appears next to a watch variable used in a loop, you can click on the plus sign to ____.

    A. Increment the loop counter by one and process the next iteration of the loop

    B. Increment the value of the watch variable

    C. Toggle the status of the watchpoint from active to inactive

    D. Display the elements contained in the user-defined type or array being watched

6. If you type an invalid expression for use as a watch expression, VB will _____.

    A. Display a compiler error

    B. Immediately display a watch error

    C. Display a watch error the first time it evaluates the expression in Break mode

    D. Do nothing

Answers to Review Questions

1. B. The watch on demand isn't available in the Watch window; it appears like a ToolTip when the mouse pointer lingers over an expression. For more information, see the section titled "Watching on Demand."

2. A, C. Both will continue execution in Break mode, either in a procedure called from the current code (`Step Into`) or in the procedure which called the current code (`Step Out`). `Step Over` executes a called procedure in its entirety, but Break mode remains in the current code. `Step to Cursor` works only within the current procedure. For more information, see the section titled "Stepping Through Your Code."

3. A. Continue is the only way to resume execution. Deactivating a breakpoint in code doesn't automatically resume program execution. The other means of entering Break mode are one way; they don't toggle it on and off. For more information, see the section titled "Setting Stepping Options."

4. C. It isn't A or D, because neither a simple watch expression nor a quick watch affects break mode. It isn't B because then the program would enter Break mode on any change to the variable. Remember that 0 is equivalent to `False`. For more information, see the section titled "Breaking on True."

5. D. The plus sign can be used to expand or collapse the variable being watched. For more information, see the sections titled "Watching Arrays" and "Watching User-Defined Types."

6. D. If an expression can't be evaluated, it is just as if it were out of scope. No error occurs. For more information, see the section titled "Creating a Watch Expression."

Answers to Test Yourself Questions at Beginning of Chapter

1. Simple watch, watch (break when expression changes), watch (break when expression is true), quick watch, and watch on demand. See "Using Quick Watch," "Watching on Demand," and "Entering Break Mode Dynamically."

2. Arrays and user-defined types appear in Watch windows with a boxed plus sign to the left of their name. Their data elements can be selectively displayed or hidden by toggling the boxed symbol between "+" and "-". See "Using the Watch Window."

3. In Break mode, a program is temporarily suspended during execution so that the programmer can inspect the program state. See "Using Break Mode."

Chapter 21

Monitoring the Values of Expressions and Variables by Using the Debugging Windows

This chapter helps you prepare for the exam by covering the following objectives:

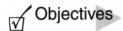 Objectives

▶ Use the Immediate window to check or change values

▶ Explain the purpose and usage for the Locals window

Test Yourself! Before reading this chapter, test yourself to determine how much study time you will need to devote to this section.

1. What method of the Debug object can be used to display a value in the Immediate window during a debugging session?

2. A boxed plus sign appears in the Locals window next to the name of a variable being processed in a loop. What does this mean?

3. What happens when a procedure name is entered into the Immediate window?

Answers are located at the end of the chapter...

As you observed in the preceding chapter, bugs are a fact of life. Anyone who ever writes a program for a computer is bound to commit a coding error sometime. Naturally, you want to develop good habits that make you less likely to introduce problems into your programs, but you can't guarantee that every bug gets stamped out. Realistically speaking, it is very likely that you will ship a product to a client before you have eliminated all of its bugs. After all, even world-class software companies ship flawed products that require post-release patches to fix bugs that eluded their Quality Assurance practices. Many software design experts even claim that shipping absolutely bug-free software ought not to be a production goal.

Acknowledging that you are bound to create (and even ship) bugs is one thing; tolerating them is another matter. Just because bugs are bound to occur, you ought not to become complacent about them. The initial introduction of a bug is forgivable. If it slips by because you failed to exercise due diligence in your testing procedures, however, you have no excuse.

Due diligence doesn't mean you have to painstakingly verify that your code is 100% bug-free. At the very least, however, isn't it reasonable for your clients to assume that you use the VB's built-in debugging tools? Your primary debugging equipment consists of the three debugging windows: the Watch window, the Immediate window, and the Locals window. If you don't know how to use them, you fail the due diligence test.

Because you have already covered the Watch window, this chapter examines the Immediate window and the Locals window. Specifically, this chapter covers the following topics:

- ▶ The Immediate window and the Debug object

- ▶ Interacting with the Immediate window

- ▶ Locals

- ▶ When to use the Immediate window in place of breakpoints

Immediate Window and the Debug Object

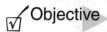
Objective

The Immediate window is so called because it gives the VB developer an opportunity to interact with a program during Break mode. By displaying almost instantaneous responses to your questions, you get a degree of immediate gratification that isn't available in many contemporary Windows development environments.

Displaying the Debug Window

To open the Immediate window, pull down the VB View menu and choose Immediate Window. The Immediate window will appear.

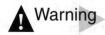
Warning

Unlike some options that can be turned on and off via the same command, be aware that neither the menu option nor the shortcut serve as a toggle for the Immediate window; they can only be used to display the Immediate window when it is not currently displayed.

The Immediate window enables programmers to do the following three things:

▶ Display messages programmatically with the Debug object

▶ Query or modify data values *on-the-fly*

▶ Test and execute VB procedures

The first two capabilities are only available when a program is in Break mode. Messages can be programmatically displayed in the Immediate window by embedding certain statements in a program. This entails use of a built-in VB object called the Debug object.

Unlike the fixed response in the other windows that can be used to monitor the state of variables and properties, the Immediate window also permits programmers to interactively inquire about these values, or even to change a value at will.

The last capability doesn't require that a program be running in Break mode, or even that a VB program be running at all. At design time, the Immediate window can be used to test code or execute commands without actually running the application under development. If you want to find out what value a function returns, for example, you can enter and run the function in the Immediate window.

The following sections take a closer look at each of these capabilities.

Displaying Messages Programmatically with the Debug Object

If you want to display messages about the status of your program during a debug session, but you don't want to enter Break mode, you can do so by calling the Debug object and its methods in your code. The Debug object is built into VB itself, so you don't need to declare an object variable or do anything special to use it.

The Debug object has two methods: Print and Assert. Each displays information in the Immediate window, but the methods have different applications.

Using the Print Method

Like any other VB method, you must use the dot operator syntax to call the method from its object. Because you don't need to declare an object variable to use the Debug object, you just invoke the method from the object itself, like this:

```
Debug.Print "Eat at Joe's."
```

If this statement were in your code, the message "Eat at Joe's." would appear in the Immediate window when this line executed in your code. More useful messages might tell you that a particular function has been entered, or into which branch of a conditional test your code has entered. For instance:

```
Select Case iConditionTest
    Case 1
        Debug.Print "Branched into Case 1"
        ' real case 1 code follows
        Case 2
        Debug.Print "Branched into Case 2"
        ' real case 2 code follows
    ' Case etc.
End Select
```

Although you could also find out this kind of information by single-stepping through your code in Break mode and observing the path of execution, using the Immediate window to display *signpost* messages saves you the bother of manually stepping through the code. It is especially handy when all you wanted to know was the information displayed in the signpost itself. If you just want to know whether your code branches into condition A rather than condition B, and the details of execution are otherwise unimportant, a message in the Immediate window is much more convenient than single-stepping.

Because this is a debugging technique, you may recall a lesson from the chapter on conditional compilation that explains how to keep your debug code from inadvertently making its way into a product release. One way to prevent your Debug.Print statements from appearing in the release version of your programs might be to wrap in a conditional compiler block like this:

```
#CONST DebugConstant = 1
#If DebugConstant Then
    Debug.Print "This message only appears when DebugConstant is
    ➥True"
    #End If
```

Fortunately, Microsoft did everyone a favor that saves the bother of writing a conditional compiler block every time you want to use Debug.Print. Statements involving the Debug object are effectively stripped out of your program when it is compiled.

Note The Debug.Print message appears only when testing an application in the debugging environment. When a user runs an application, it is not running in the debugging environment, so there is no Immediate window to display the message.

Formatting Debug.Print Messages

The Debug.Print examples so far have been quite simple—Debug.Print followed by a message statement—but the syntax of the message can be somewhat more elaborate than simple text.

For one thing, the position in which the message appears in the Immediate window can be specified by preceding the message text with VB's Spc() or Tab() functions. If you want to indent a message by 10 spaces, you could do so in either of two ways:

```
Debug.Print Spc(10) "This message is preceded by ten spaces."
```

or:

```
Debug.Print Tab(11) "This message begins on column eleven, which
➥is functionally identical."
```

Obviously, Spc() inserts spaces in the output, and Tab() sets the position at which the next message will appear.

It is also possible to use more than one text expression on the same line:

```
Dim sDebugMsg as String
sDebugMsg = " will self-destruct in five seconds, Mr. Phelps."
Debug.Print "This message" & sDebugMsg
```

When you need to combine multiple text expressions for use with a single Debug.Print statement, the syntax starts to get a bit cluttered. After each text expression, you can tell VB where to put the next expression. There are three ways to do this.

First, you can place a semicolon after a text expression. This puts the insertion point immediately after the last character displayed. That is, the first character in the next expression that prints will appear immediately after the last character in the expression preceding the semicolon. For all practical purposes, this behavior makes the semicolon act just like the "&" concatenation operator. In fact, the last line of the preceding example could have been written like this:

```
Debug.Print "This message"; sDebugMsg
```

 Note

If you try to place two `Debug.Print` text expressions immediately after one another, VB will insert a semicolon between them for you. In other words, if you type:

```
Debug.Print "Message #1" "Message #2"
```

As soon as you press Enter to move to the next line, VB will automatically change your debugging message into this:

```
Debug.Print "Message #1"; "Message #2"
```

Second, you can use the `Tab()` function to move the insertion point to a specific column. If you want some space between your messages, you might try something like this (if you have an exceptionally wide screen):

```
Debug.Print "That's one small step for man"; Tab(100); ";one
➥mighty leap for VB"
```

What happens if you specify a Tab position that would cause part of the previous text expression to be overwritten? The first text expression in the preceding example is 29 characters long, for example. What happens if you enter this?

```
Debug.Print "That's one small step for man"; Tab(11); ";one
➥mighty leap to the next line for VB"
```

You might expect the output in the Immediate window to look like "That's one;one mighty leap to the next line for VB", starting the second text expression in column 11 of the same line.

In fact, however, VB saves you from such mistakes by moving the second expression to column 11 of the next line.

Finally, you can use Tab with no argument (remember to omit the parentheses too, or VB will generate a syntax error) to position the insertion point at the beginning of the next print zone. (On average, a print zone occurs about every 14 columns.)

Remember that all the semicolons and Tabs are optional. If you don't specify where to place the next character, it will print on the next line. You can use these formatting rules to produce output in a variety of ways. However, this example should give you some idea of how to combine them. Figure 21.1 shows the result:

```
Private Sub cmdOK_Click()
    Dim sRef As String, sMsg1 As String, sMsg2 As String
    sRef = "1234567890123456789012345678901234567890"
    sMsg1 = "I am a string exactly 40 characters long"
    sMsg2 = "followed by more text at column 46."
    Debug.Print sRef
    Debug.Print sMsg1; Spc(5); sMsg2
    Debug.Print sMsg1; Tab(46); sMsg2
    Debug.Print sMsg1; Tab(Len(sMsg1) + 6); sMsg2; vbCr
    Debug.Print "The End!"
End Sub
```

Figure 21.1

The output of the **Debug.Print** *formatting example looks like this.*

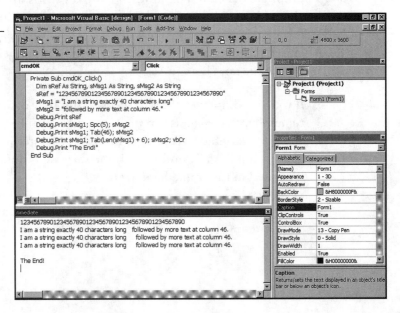

Among other things, notice how it is legal to use a function call and calculations in the Debug.Print line. The Len() function determines how long the sMsg1 string is, and then you add another 6 columns to that to duplicate the output of the other lines. Why is there an empty line just before "The End!"? That's because there isn't a position specifier after the vbCr constant (yes, built-in constants are available, too). You didn't specify where to place the next character, so it printed on the next line following vbCr.

Displaying Data Values

So far, you have only been using Debug.Print to print simple text messages to yourself, but you can also use it to display data values. (Because some of your text messages have used string variables, perhaps that is obvious.) A few rules apply to data variables when they are displayed via Debug.Print. Most of these rules apply equally well to every other aspect of VB, so they are pretty straightforward and should not cause you any difficulty even if you don't remember them.

The Immediate window is aware of any locale settings you have established for your system. Consequently, if you use Debug.Print to display numeric data, the values will be displayed with the appropriate decimal separator, and any keywords will appear in your chosen language. Date variables will be displayed in the short date format recognized by your system. Boolean values are displayed as either True or False. These are the same default behaviors you should see anywhere in VB.

If you are testing variables to see whether they contain values, remember that *empty* is not the same state as null. If the value of an empty variable is displayed, nothing is printed (not the word *nothing*, but literally nothing). If the variable is null, the word *Null* is printed in the Immediate window.

Here are some examples of how data may be output to the Immediate window:

```
Sub DebugPrintExamples()
    ' Display a decimal value
    Dim s As Single
    s = 3.14159
    Debug.Print "The value of s is"; s
    ' Display a Boolean
    Dim fMakesSenseToMe As Boolean
    Debug.Print "The default value of a Boolean is ";
    ➥fMakesSenseToMe
    ' Display a date
    Dim d As Date
    d = Date
    Debug.Print "Today is "; d
    ' Empty vs. Null
    Dim var1 As Variant, var2 As Variant
    Debug.Print "Before any assignment, a Variant is "; var1
    Debug.Print "Can't see that?  Of course not; it really IS
    ➥empty!"
    Debug.Print "OK, True or False.  The statement 'var1 is Empty'
    ➥is "; IsEmpty(var1)
    Debug.Print "and the statement 'var1 is Null' is ";
    ➥IsNull(var1)
    ' After an assignment, can var be reassigned a value of Empty?
    var1 = 1: var1 = Null
    Debug.Print "Now, var1 is "; var1;
    Debug.Print ", so the value of IsEmpty(var1) is ";
    ➥IsEmpty(var1)
    Debug.Print "Not surprisingly, the statement 'var1 is Null' is
    ➥"; IsNull(var1)
    var1 = Empty
    Debug.Print "A Variant can become Empty again by assignment:
    ➥"; IsEmpty(var1)
    var1 = 1: var1 = var2
    Debug.Print "or by being assigned the value of another empty
Variant: "; IsEmpty(var1)
End Sub
```

It used to be that after a Variant had been assigned a value, it could become empty again only by being assigned the value of another empty Variant. Now you can just reassign the value *empty* to the variable.

Using the `Assert` Method

The `Debug` object's `Assert` method is derived from the C programming language's *assert* facility. An assertion enables a programmer to test the validity of an assumption. If the assumption is true, the program continues to execute normally. If the assumption is false, an appropriate message is displayed and the program halts.

The `assert` macro is a great debugging tool. Used appropriately, it helps programmers to automatically alert themselves to problems in their code. A C programmer might want to verify that the value of a key variable is appropriate for an operation, for example, like this (this is a very short example, so please forgive the use of C):

```
void main()
    {
        int i, aszReasons[10];
        /* many lines pass, during which i is modified and the
        ↪string array is filled */
        ↪assert (10 == i);
        ↪for ( ; i > 0; i--)
        {
            printf("Reason number %u for assertions is: %s", i,
            ↪aszReasons[i-1]);
            }
    }
```

In this example, an integer variable (`i`) is used as a loop counter, and a string array (`aszReasons`) is displayed during the loop. Due to the special nature of the application, the programmer wants to be absolutely certain that the value of i winds up as exactly 10. The use of the `assert` macro guarantees that the value of *i* must be 10 for the program to continue. If i were anything but 10, the program would display a message and then abort execution.

C (and C++) permits the ISO C standard library's assertion macro to be redefined, but it is normal for it to be written so that it is only active in the debug version of a program, not the release version. This enables the programmer to use the same body of code without having to worry about a program aborting due to an assertion failure after it is in a client's hands.

Consequently, it is important to realize that the point of an assertion is not to serve as a general-purpose error handler. An assertion is only active during a debugging session. Its purpose is to cue the programmer that an assumption behind the previous code is flawed and that greater care need be taken before the subsequent code should execute.

Writing a VB Assertion Procedure

The VB preprocessor facility only extends to conditional compilation. There is no such thing as a preprocessor macro in VB, so naturally there is no VB assertion macro. However, it is pretty easy to write a general-purpose procedure that essentially serves the same purpose. Here's a very simple example of a VB assertion procedure:

```
Sub vbAssert ( ByVal vTestThis as Variant, ByVal sAssertText as
➡String)
    #If DebugMode Then
    If vTestThis Then
       ' no problem - return to calling procedure
    Exit Sub
    Else
       ' problem -alert the programmer
       MsgBox sAssertText & " is False"
       Stop
    End If
    #End If
End Sub
```

The vbAssert procedure accepts two arguments: vTestThis and sAssertText. Both arguments are passed by value because you don't want to run the risk of a debugging tool inadvertently modifying a value elsewhere in a program. vTestThis is a Variant because you want to maximize the applicability of the vbAssert procedure. Rather than having separate procedures for each data type, this enables you to use a single procedure to address every case.

sAssertText is used to display the actual content of the vTestThis expression triggering the assertion failure in case vTestThis turns out to be False. The sAssertText argument is needed to do this because the expression can't be derived from vTestThis, which is passed by value. That is, vbAssert never sees the expression passed as vTestThis; it sees either the value True or False, and that is all it gets for its first argument.

Notice that the body of vbAssert is wrapped in a conditional compiler block. Assuming that the DebugMode compiler constant is defined so that it is only True during Debug mode, the call to vbAssert will have no effect on a release version of a program. The procedure still will be called, but it becomes a *do-nothing* procedure—its body will be empty because the preprocessor prevents the code from being compiled into your release version executable file.

If you are in Debug mode, however, the procedure evaluates TestExpression. If it is True, vbAssert exits and the rest of the program proceeds just as it normally would. If TestExpression is False, however, a message box appears to tell you so. After you respond to the message box, the program stops. The Stop command doesn't actually unload your program, but it is thrown into Break mode, giving you a chance to inspect your code and track down the problem.

Consider a rewrite of the C example in VB. This rewrite enables you to see what happens if you replace the assert macro with this vbAssert procedure:

```
Sub Main()
    Dim i as Integer, aszReasons(9) as String
    ' many lines pass, during which i is modified and the string
    ➥array is filled
    vbAssert i = 10, "i = 10"
    For i = i to 1 Step -1
        Print "Reason number " & i & " for assertions is: " &
        ➥aszReasons(i - 1)
    Next i
End Sub
```

This VB program effectively replaces the C program, even including your equivalent of the C assertion macro. VB programmers have had to go to relatively great lengths to enjoy the benefits of an assertion procedure, but the process is greatly simplified in VB5 with the addition of the Assert method to the Debug object.

Using the Assert Method

The syntax of the new Assert method is similar to the other assertion procedures you have been examining. It accepts one argument, which is evaluated as a Boolean expression. Because Assert is a method of the Debug object, the dot operator must be used with the Debug object to make the assertion. Here is how the preceding code looks when the vbAssert call is replaced by Debug.Assert:

```
Sub Main()
   Dim i as Integer, aszReasons(9) as String
   ' many lines pass, during which i is modified and the string
   ➥array is filled
   Debug.Assert ( i = 10 )
   For i = i to 1 Step -1
      Print "Reason number " & i & " for assertions is: " &
   ➥aszReasons(i - 1)
   Next i
End Sub
```

As you can see, there is scarcely any difference. Other than taking one argument rather than two, Debug.Assert is a direct substitution for the call to vbAssert. Of course, you can still use your own assertion routines if you prefer, but the convenience of calling a built-in method is nice.

Like the other assertion procedures, Debug.Assert is active only during a debug session; it isn't compiled into the release version of a program. If the Boolean expression evaluated by the assertion is determined to be False, the program enters Break mode and the line containing the assertion is highlighted. This gives you an opportunity to use the other debugging tools to determine the likely source of the problem.

Figure 21.2 is what the result of an assertion failure looks like in the debugging environment.

Figure 21.2

An assertion failure.

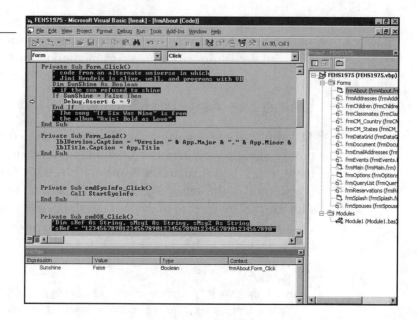

Notice how the code executed normally until it reached the Debug.Assert line. The expression "SunShine = False" evaluates as True because the SunShine variable is a Boolean, and VB initializes Boolean variables to False by default. The code then branches into the conditional block with the assertion, where the expression "6=9" is evaluated. Because this expression is False, the Debug.Assert on this line caused the application to enter Break mode. The line with the assertion is highlighted, and an arrow immediately to the left of the assertion indicates the program is still running, but execution is suspended at the indicated line.

So far, this discussion has focused on the mechanics of assertion procedures, but has not said much about when to use them. Consider using an assertion whenever your code depends on an expression satisfying certain criteria.

If you have already gone to great lengths to ensure that your code is trouble-free, why not take an extra step to verify that you haven't let something slip through the cracks? Even after you have applied every reasonable test that you can imagine, an assertion may lead you to some things you had not imagined. If you plug the expression into an assertion only to trigger an assertion failure, maybe your original tests weren't as good as you thought.

By alerting you to conditions that are contrary to your expectations, assertions help you to create tests that more completely reflect the actual conditions under which your code must perform. When you trigger an assertion failure, you know at once that your assumption is wrong, meaning that you must either do something to ensure that it continues to be valid or reframe the assumption.

Here is some code that might have been ported from a VB3 project, for example. It is predicated on an assumption that was true under Windows 3.1, but is no longer true under Windows 95 or Windows NT:

```
Sub Main()
    Dim strFileFullName As String, strFileName As String,
    ➥strFileExtension As String, strPath as String
    Dim iDotPos As Integer
    strPath = Trim$(InputBox$ ("Enter a directory path below:",
    ➥"Directory prompt", "C:\*.*" ))
    strFileFullName = Dir(strPath)
    Do While strFileFullName <> ""
        iDotPos = InStr(strFileFullName, ".")
        If iDotPos Then
            ' iDotPos will be 0 (False) if period is not found
            strFileName = Trim$(Left$(strFileFullName, iDotPos - 1))
            strFileExtension = Trim$(Right$(strFileFullName,
            ➥Len(strFileFullName) - iDotPos))
        Else
            strFileName = Trim$(strFileFullName)
            strFileExtension = ""
        End If
        Debug.Print strFileName; Tab(9); "."; strFileExtension
        strFileFullName = Dir
    Loop
End Sub
```

This code uses the Immediate window to print a nicely formatted list of all filenames found in a given directory. Notice, however, that it assumes that filenames follow the old 16-bit 8.3 convention (that is, no more than 8 characters in a filename, and no more than 3 characters in a file extension). The introduction of long filenames in Windows 95 and Windows NT will cause the

Debug.Print code to fail when Dir returns a filename longer than 12 characters (8-character filename + 3-character extension + dot = 12-character maximum before long filenames).

This problem is particularly annoying because it doesn't generate a compiler error, nor does it cause a runtime error. The old assumptions are no longer true, but this won't be evident when you compile the code; it compiles cleanly. When the strings are populated at runtime, there will be no runtime error in the code either.

In fact, however, there is a problem at runtime. The Tab(9) in the Debug.Print statement may not leave enough room for the filenames to print properly. Long filenames in Windows 95 or NT can be up to 255 characters. What happens if strFileName is more than eight characters? It won't backtrack to overwrite the strFileName text, but it will break to a new line and print the rest of the output at the specified tab location on the new line. That is not the nicely formatted output that you had back in the 16-bit world.

Because the code originated under 16-bit Windows, it is no surprise that no precautions were taken to avoid this problem. 8.3 was the law, and who knew it was going to change? Still, had the programmer been extremely thoughtful and forward thinking, an assertion could have been used here. Then on the odd chance that the rules governing filenames were to change, you would find out about it pretty quickly. What if this line were inserted at the very beginning of the loop, just before the line that sets the value of iDotPos?

```
Debug.Assert (Len(strFileFullName) <= 12)
```

Of course, the Debug.Assert method would not have been available to the VB3 programmer with whom this code originated, but an equivalent assertion routine (for example, the vbAssert procedure you looked at earlier) could have been used in its place.

Now, it will be instantly evident that the code needs to be modified to account for long filenames because the first one you bump into will trigger an assertion failure.

Because this problem doesn't generate a runtime error, it might have gone unnoticed before the program was released. By announcing itself on the assertion failure, this assertion makes it much more likely that you will catch the problem before the program reaches your clients. That is the whole point to assertions. Even when the item in question seems entirely innocuous, it doesn't cost you much extra effort to test it in an assertion.

Generally speaking, it is a good idea to get into the habit of using assertions. Remember, however, that an assertion is not a substitute for an error handler. It can show you where there may be a problem, but an assertion can't resolve any problems in your code at runtime because it isn't part of the compiled program.

Interacting with the Immediate Window

So far, you have been using the Immediate window as a sort of global message box. Although `Debug.Print` sends useful messages during program execution, it is also possible to type directly into the Immediate window. What can you type? For starters, you can use the same `Debug.Print` commands that you have been using so far in code. Figure 21.3 shows an example. The syntax is as follows:

```
Debug.Print "Insert Your Message Here"
```

Because the `Debug` object is the default object for the Immediate window, you can take advantage of some shortcuts. As this example shows, `Debug.Print` can be abbreviated either to `Print` or just `?`. The method is invoked just as if you typed it completely, so you may as well save yourself that extra typing.

Besides printing messages, the Immediate window can perform a few other useful tricks when you use it interactively. You will look at those next.

Figure 21.3

Debug.Print commands can be entered directly into the Immediate window.

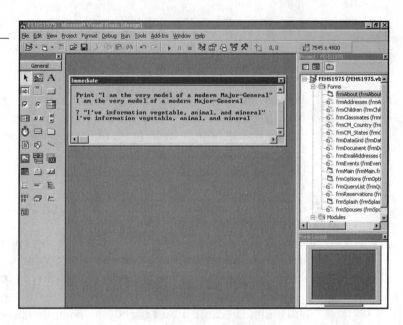

Querying or Modifying Data Values

Besides printing text messages, you can use the Print method to display the value of a variable. It is also possible to change the value of a variable inside the Immediate window. The only catch is that the program must be in Break mode to perform either of these actions.

If you think about it, one reason for this constraint is simple: A local variable exists only in the context of the function in which it occurs. If the function has already finished, the variable no longer exists. Forcing the program to enter Break mode during the execution of a routine ensures that the variables in that routine still exist for you to view or modify. Global variables and form-level variables persist beyond particular functions, of course, but the rules apply to all interactive uses of the Immediate window during program execution: Your program must be in Break mode. Figure 21.4 provides an example.

In this case, the variable i is incremented in a For loop. When the loop finishes, the Debug.Print statement in the code displays the current value of the variable in the Immediate window, and then the embedded Stop command throws the program into Break mode. At this point, the programmer changes the value of i interactively, and then the value change is confirmed via the `Debug.Print` method (which is invoked via the question mark). Sure enough, the value has been changed from 101 to 10.

Figure 21.4

Querying and changing a variable in the Immediate window.

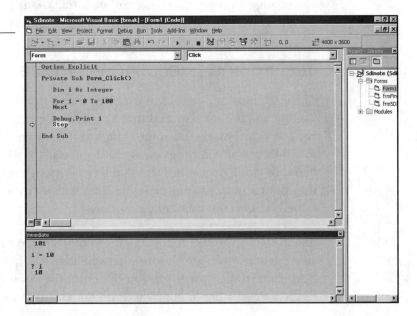

Note

In the example in Figure 21.4, did you expect i to be 100 at the end of the loop? Remember that 100 is the last legal value for the loop. When i equals 100, it is incremented one last time by the `Next` statement in the final iteration. Thus, when the loop exits, i equals 101.

Besides modifying variables interactively, you can also change the values of properties. If you want to hide the form whose code is currently running, for example, you can type "me.Visible = False" in the Immediate window. The form will vanish as soon as you press Enter. To restore the form's visibility, of course, you can type "me.Visible = True". Again, your program must be in Break mode for this to work.

The capability to modify variables and properties in the Immediate window gives you a chance to test a variety of conditions in your debugging sessions that your program will face when it is released. Want to see what happens if a variable value is (pick one) a specific value/very small/very large/empty/null? Modify the variable and see what happens. Want to see what happens if you change a property of a control or form? Go ahead. If you can do it in code, you can do it in the Immediate window.

Testing and Executing VB Procedures

Although most of the uses to which you have put the Immediate window so far have required that a program be suspended in Break mode, you can do some things with the Immediate window that don't require a program at all. If you want to execute a command or run a procedure that you have written, you can just type the command or procedure name (along with any necessary parameters) into the Immediate window.

Assume, for example, that you want to delete a file using the Kill statement, but you aren't sure what will happen if you put the command in your program. You can enter the command in the Immediate window to see what it will do, as shown in Figure 21.5.

Figure 21.5

Deleting a file with the Kill statement.

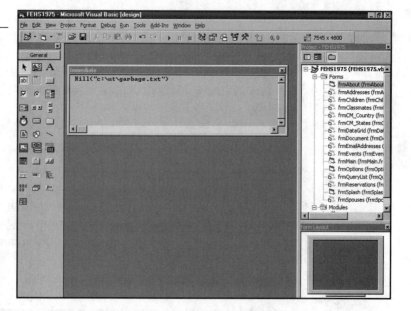

As you can see, nothing special happens in the Immediate window to indicate that the command succeeded. If you try to execute the Kill command again, however, you will generate a runtime error (#53: File not found) because the file was successfully deleted the first time.

Perhaps it would be nice to have a more informative way to delete a file. There is no way to modify the built-in Kill statement to provide extra information, but you can write your own file deletion function that does. Here is one that uses the Kill command to do its dirty work, but that uses the Immediate window to display its status along the way. Most important, the new function also provides a return value to indicate whether it succeeded:

```
Function Delete(sFilename As String) As Boolean
    ' use the return value in the calling function rather than
    ➥trap the error here
    On Error Resume Next
    Dim fReturn As Boolean
    #Const DEBUGGING = True
    ' see if the file exists to delete
    If Dir(sFilename) <> "" Then fReturn = True
    #If DEBUGGING Then
        Debug.Print "File exists = "; fReturn
    #End If
    If fReturn Then
        ' file exists, so kill it
        Kill sFilename
        ' if couldn't delete, set return value
        If Dir(sFilename) <> "" Then fReturn = False
        #If DEBUGGING Then
            Debug.Print "File deleted = "; fReturn
        #End If
    End If
    Delete = fReturn
End Function
```

If you run this function twice in succession, the Immediate window looks like Figure 21.6.

Figure 21.6

Results of the Delete function displayed in the Immediate window.

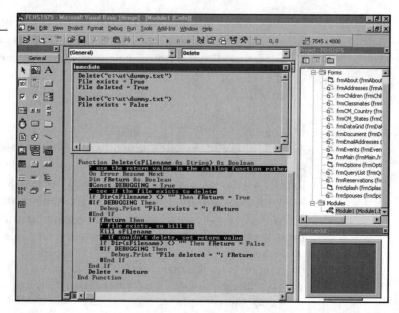

The Delete function is more informative than the Kill statement at debug time because it uses Debug.Print to keep you posted about its progress. Aside from the debugging output, Delete also gives you more to work with in your program. Because it provides a Boolean return value, you can test for the success of the file deletion and take appropriate measures in your program.

Because Delete is a function, it also enables you to display useful output in the Immediate window without sprinkling Debug.Print statements throughout its body. If you remove the "#Const DEBUGGING = True" line and run Delete from the Immediate window, you can use the Debug.Print statement to display its return value, as shown in Figure 21.7.

This gives you two ways to run a procedure from the Immediate window: with or without prefacing it with Debug.Print. If you just want to execute a procedure and disregard its return value (if it has one), don't use the Print method. If you want to display the return value of a function, preface it with a leading question mark to invoke Debug.Print.

Figure 21.7

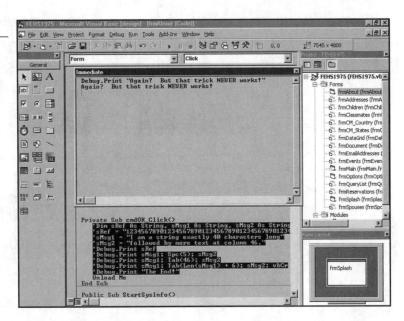

Results of the **Delete** *function displayed in the Immediate window with the* **Debug.Print** *method.*

Note

You can treat a function like a sub in the Immediate window, but you can't treat a sub like a function. If you inadvertently put a leading question mark in front of a sub that you try to run in the Immediate window, you will get this error message: `Compile error: expected function or variable`.

Using the Locals Window

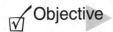Objective

One of VB's debugging windows can save you from endlessly embedding `Debug.Print` statements in code to examine the value of variables. That is the Locals window, which displays the current value of variables within the scope of the currently executing procedure. Because what it displays depends on the current scope, the contents of the Locals window changes whenever a different procedure executes. To display the Locals window, pull down the View menu and choose Locals window. Figure 24.8 shows the Locals window.

Figure 21.8

The Locals window.

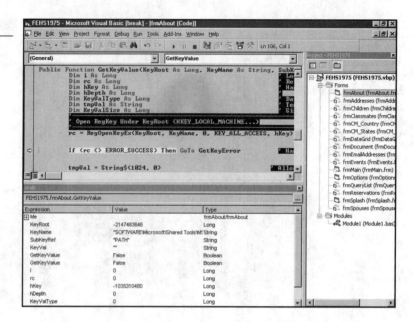

Calling it a "Locals" window is somewhat misleading, as it isn't limited to viewing only those variables that are local in scope. You will see all the local variables, of course, but form-level variables are also visible in the Locals window. (Remember that you will only see the form-level variables for the current form.) For module-level variables, you have to use the other methods covered in this chapter (for example, the Watch window and Debug.Print). The Locals window can't display module-level variables.

Here is an example. Module_1 contains nothing but a global variable, declared like this:

```
Public g_Test As Integer
```

In Form_1, a form-level variable is declared in the General Declarations section:

```
Public f_Test As Long
```

Here is the rest of the Form_1 code:

```
Private Sub Form_Initialize()
    Dim i as integer
```

```
    i = 1
    g_Test = 10
    f_Test = 1000
End Sub
Private Sub Form_Click()
    Dim k as integer
    k = 5
    Stop
End Sub
```

Values are assigned to the form-level variable and the module-level variable in the form's `Initialize` event. When the form is clicked, the program enters Break mode. This is necessary because the contents of the Locals window depends on a specific local scope. After the program enters Break mode, you can use the Locals window to examine the status of the variables.

When the program enters Break mode, the Locals window looks like Figure 21.9.

Figure 21.9

The **local** *variable and* **ME** *are available in the Locals window.*

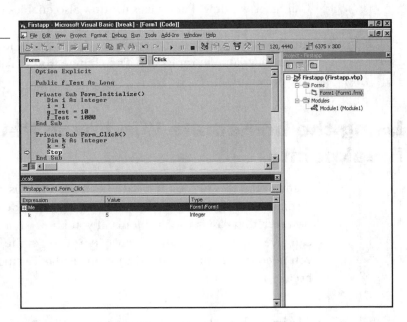

Because program execution was broken in the form's `Click` event, the value of k is available because it is local to that event. Notice what isn't available: You can't see the value of the i variable from the `Initialized` event because it isn't local to the current procedure. You also can't see the form-level variable `f_Test` or the module-level variable `g_Test`. You do see something called `ME`, however, which has a boxed plus sign immediately to its left.

You may recall that `ME` is VB shorthand for the form in which code is currently executing. If you click on the plus sign, the `ME` object will unfold, displaying all the current form's properties in alphabetic order. Look toward the bottom of the window displayed here and you will see that `f_Test` is displayed, but `g_Test` is not. A form-level variable is essentially a property of a form, and so it is available here. The module-level variable, however, is not. What happened to `k`? It is still there, but when you clicked on `ME` to display its contents, it scrolled to the very bottom of the window.

At the top of the Locals window, notice that the name of the currently executing procedure is identified. To the right of the procedure name, the button with the ellipsis can be used to display the Call Stack window. The Locals window also enables you to do one more trick: You can use it to change the value of a property or a variable. If you click on the value displayed for an item, you can type a new value to replace it. The change won't take effect until you press Enter.

Using the Immediate Window in Place of Breakpoints

Many of the techniques that have been used in this chapter to display data require a program to be in Break mode. Sometimes, however, that can cause problems. If you know when Break mode can give you fits, you can use `Debug.Print` to get the information you need in the Immediate window instead of setting watches or breakpoints.

Using the `MouseDown` and `KeyDown` Events

The first potential problem occurs in association with key events and mouse events. If you enter Break mode during a `MouseDown` or `KeyDown` event, you are probably going to release the key or mouse button while you are still in Break mode. After all, you need to use the keyboard and the mouse yourself to carry out your debugging tasks. If you break execution during either of these events and then resume program execution, your application doesn't know enough to trigger a MouseUp or KeyUp event for you. After all, when it went to sleep the button or key was down, and now that it is awake, it thinks that's still the case.

To get the MouseUp or KeyUp event, you need to press the button or key again and release it. But that's where the program goes into Break mode again (a veritable "Catch-22"), so you never really get to the MouseUp or KeyUp events.

Solution: Don't enter Break mode in these events. Instead, use Debug.Print to display the necessary data in the Immediate window.

Using the GotFocus and LostFocus Events

The problem here doesn't pose the same logical difficulty presented by the MouseDown and KeyDown events. Instead, a breakpoint in GotFocus or LostFocus can just throw off the timing of system messages as they are sent. Windows is so sensitive to the timing of system messages that the API even includes several different ways to dispatch them.

SendMessage will send a message to the target object, for example, waiting until the message has been successfully sent before returning a value. PostMessage, on the other hand, returns at once after adding its message to the queue; it doesn't wait for the results. Function calls seem to occur so quickly that it may seem strange to think that the difference would be so important as to require a different function. Remember that a computer's memory access is measured in nanoseconds, however, and perhaps it will make more sense.

Timing is critical, and a breakpoint in the focus events can mess things up. If you need to display values during a GotFocus or LostFocus event, use Debug.Print to send the data to the Immediate window.

Exercises

Exercise 21.1: Using the `Debug.Print` Command

In this exercise, you practice using the `Debug.Print` command to display formatted output in the Immediate window. To create this exercise, follow these steps:

1. Create a new VB application containing a single form.

2. Code the form's `Initialize`, `Load`, `Resize`, `Activate`, `GotFocus`, `Paint`, `Unload`, and `Terminate` events to display a message in the Immediate window notifying you of the current event. Progressively indent the messages in the order of their occurrence until the form paints, and then unindent them as the form exits.

3. Experiment by inserting similar messages into the form's other events. Interact with the form—change its size, obscure it with another program's window, and so on. Which events occur only once? Which ones continue to occur?

Exercise 21.2: Modifying Values in the Immediate Window

In this exercise, you use the debugging tools to modify program values at runtime. To create this exercise, follow these steps:

1. Create an application that contains at least one module and one form. Create public integer variables both in the form and the module.

2. Add code to the form's `Click` event that increments the value of the variables and displays them on the form with the form's `Print` method. (Hint: You also may want to use the `Cls` method when the form's `CurrentY` property approaches its height.) Be sure to set a breakpoint so that you can use the debugging windows.

3. Set the form's `AutoRedraw` property to True so that its contents will be preserved when you return to it from the debugging windows.

4. Click on the form a few times to confirm that the variables are incrementing and displaying properly. After you have displayed a few values, use the Immediate window to change the form's Forecolor property. (Unless you have specific hexadecimal values memorized, this may be most easily accomplished via the QBColor function.) Clear your breakpoint and click on the form again to confirm that the printed output has changed color.

5. Reset the breakpoint and try changing the form's Forecolor property again using the Locals window. If you have trouble selecting a particular value, try using the QBColor function again. Notice how the property value changes to reflect the return value of the function. Continue to experiment with changes in other properties by using both the Immediate window and the Locals window.

6. When you are finished experimenting with properties, try modifying the variables by using both windows. Which way do you prefer? Does either window permit you to do anything that the other window can't do?

Review Questions

1. You have distributed your application to a client in the form of an .EXE file. How can the client recover from a `Debug.Assert` failure that occurs when he runs the program?

    A. Press the F9 key to deactivate the breakpoint, and then press F5 to continue.

    B. Use the Locals window or the Immediate window to modify the bad value that triggered the failure.

    C. Nothing can be done. The client must exit and restart the program.

    D. This scenario cannot occur.

2. Using the Immediate window, you assign an integer variable a value of 32768. What happens?

    A. The program continues to execute normally.

    B. The Immediate window closes and the program shuts down.

    C. A runtime overflow error occurs.

    D. The variable's value wraps to the first legal value, –32768.

3. An application has two forms: `Form1` and `Form2`. `Form2` is displayed only when a command button on `Form1` is clicked. While `Form2` is displayed, you use the Immediate window to change its `Visible` property to False and type **Unload Me**. What happens when you click on the button on `Form1` that should display `Form2`?

    A. The program crashes.

    B. `Form2` cannot be displayed because it is invisible.

    C. `Form2` is displayed and its code is active, but the form is invisible.

    D. `Form2` is displayed normally.

4. To place the insertion point immediately after the last character in an expression displayed in the Immediate window by `Debug.Print`, place a(n) _____ after the expression.

    A. Colon

    B. Semicolon

    C. Ampersand

    D. Concatenator

5. The Immediate window can be used interactively to debug a program _____.

    A. Whenever a call is made to `Debug.Assert` or `Debug.Print`

    B. When a program is waiting for an event to occur

    C. When a program is in Break mode

    D. At any time

6. `Debug.Print` can be represented by _____ when typed directly into the Immediate window.

    A. `?`

    B. `Print`

    C. `>>`

    D. `D.P`

Answers to Review Questions

1. D. Assertions are not compiled into an executable program; they are only available in the debug environment. For more information, see the section titled "Using the `Assert` Method."

2. C. The value 32768 exceeds the bounds of an integer, so the assignment generates a runtime error. For more information, see the section titled "Querying or Modifying Data Values."

3. D. Setting "Form2.Visible = False" applied only to the current instance of the form. The next time the Form2 is loaded and displayed, the original defaults are used, so the form displays normally. For more information, see the section titled "Querying or Modifying Data Values."

4. B. The semicolon puts the insertion point immediately after the prior text. For more information, see the section titled "Formatting Debug.Print Messages."

5. C. A program must be in Break mode to use the Immediate window. For more information, see the section titled "Querying or Modifying Data Values."

6. A and B. Either ? or Print is shorthand for Debug.Print when entered into the Immediate window. For more information, see the section titled "Interacting with the Immediate Window."

Answers to Test Yourself Questions at Beginning of Chapter

1. The Debug object's Print method displays values in the Immediate window. See "Using the Print Method."

2. A boxed plus sign indicates that a variable contains subelements not currently displayed. See "Using the Locals Window."

3. Procedures can be executed by typing them into the Immediate window. See "Testing and Executing VB Procedures."

Implementing Project Groups to Support the Development and Debugging Process

This chapter helps you prepare for the Visual Basic 5 exam by covering the following objectives:

 Objectives

- ▶ Debug DLLs in process

- ▶ Test and debug controls in process

Test Yourself! Before reading this chapter, test yourself to determine how much study time you will need to devote to this section.

1. You are building an ActiveX Control for use in an existing Visual Basic system, and you've added the control's project to the same group as your existing program. Do you need to add a reference to the control before you can use it in your existing program?

2. You have a project group containing three projects, the main program (a standard EXE project), and two ActiveX DLLs. Is it possible to set up Visual Basic to break on errors in your main project, but not on errors in the DLLs?

3. In the project group described in question 2, what project begins to execute first if you choose Start from the Run menu?

4. You have a main project that creates two instances of the same ActiveX DLL while it runs. How many copies of the ActiveX DLL project do you need to have in your project group so that you can use breakpoints?

Answers are located at the end of the chapter...

Visual Basic 5 includes many new features in its development environment, taking some of the headaches out of creating applications. One of the most interesting, and useful, of these additions is the concept of project groups, enabling you to work with multiple projects open simultaneously. In previous versions, you could accomplish this only by using multiple instances of Visual Basic, making it difficult to work with the projects as one complete system. As many of the systems built with Visual Basic 5 will be component-based, using multiple ActiveX projects, the capability to work with all those pieces together in one development environment is really a necessity. This will quickly become one of the most common things you do in Visual Basic, and you will wonder how you ever worked without it.

This chapter covers the following topics:

▶ What exactly are project groups, and how they can be used

▶ How project groups can be used in component-based development

▶ How to debug multiple project applications through the use of project groups

Understanding Project Groups

It is common for a developer to be working with multiple projects at one time, whether they are dependent on each other (such as an application and an ActiveX Control that it uses) or just multiple, independent parts of a large development project (such as an order entry system and an HR application both being built for the same company). Project groups exist because of the fact that Visual Basic projects do not exist in a vacuum; most development consists of many separate projects. As component-based development—using ActiveX Controls, DLL, and Servers—becomes common, single-project systems will be even more unusual.

Project groups give several benefits over the single-project model of Visual Basic 4. All the individual projects you have placed into a group are opened and closed together, reducing the time spent getting ready to work and the time getting ready to quit. Having all the projects opened together also enables you to work with them inside one instance of Visual Basic. If the projects are directly related (through references), you can also execute and debug them together (as discussed in more detail in "Using Project Groups to Debug an ActiveX DLL").

The individual projects are not modified just by being part of a project group. They are still stored individually on disk. The group file (*.vbg) merely contains links (using relative paths) to each member project (*.vbp). The contents of a sample group file are shown here:

```
VBGROUP 5.0
Project=VB MCSD Study Guide\Chapter 23\DateTime.vbp
StartupProject=VB MCSD Study Guide\Chapter 23\Sample.vbp
Project=VB MCSD Study Guide\Chapter 23\ctrlDateTime.vbp
```

Each project can belong to a number of groups, in combination with other projects, and can still be opened directly, as an individual project, at any time. The only limit on combining projects is that a project can be in a project group only once; multiple copies of the same project are not possible.

Creating Project Groups

Project groups cannot be created on their own, you must start with a standard Visual Basic project, and then add other projects into it. By adding a second project, a new group is implicitly created. Adding and removing projects is done through the File menu's Add Project and Remove Project commands, as shown in Figure 22.1.

Figure 22.1

Visual Basic 5 includes Add and Remove Project commands for working with project groups.

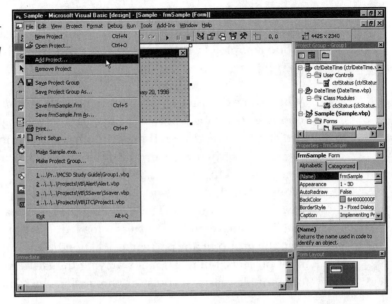

Selecting the Add Project command brings up the same style of dialog box as Visual Basic 5 shows at startup, enabling you to create a new project. Select one from a list of recently opened projects or select any other existing project through a standard directory browser, as shown in Figure 22.2.

Figure 22.2

Using a standard directory browsing dialog box to open an existing project.

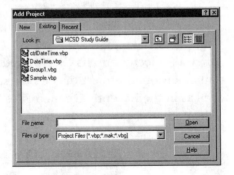

The Remove Project command disassociates the currently selected project with the project group, and is also available through the right-click Context menu in the Project Explorer. Even if you remove projects until only one project remains, it is still contained within a project group. If, on the other hand, you remove all the projects in a project group, it is the equivalent of closing the group completely. Exercise 22.1 takes you through creating a simple project group containing two new projects.

When you exit Visual Basic or attempt to load another project (as opposed to adding a project), the current group and its associated projects must be closed. If the group has not previously been saved, this is when you can specify a name and location for the file, as shown in Figure 22.3. You can also save the entire project group through the two menu options, Save Project Group and Save Project Group As. These commands are not available when you do not have multiple projects loaded. It is not necessary to save the group in any particular location, relative to its component projects, but it can make moving the entire set of your development files easier if you store them all in the same area.

Figure 22.3

Saving a Project Group File (.vbg).*

After a project group has been saved, it will appear in the Recent tab in any open project dialog boxes, as shown in Figure 22.4, as well as in the Recently Opened Files list near the bottom of the File menu.

Figure 22.4

Group Files appear in Visual Basic's Recent List.

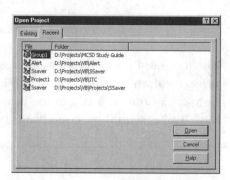

Building Multiple Projects

Visual Basic makes one other important modification to its menus when a project group is loaded: the addition of the Make Project Group command under the File menu. This will perform a build of every project contained within the current project group, which is sometimes more convenient than selecting and building each project individually. Selecting the Make Project Group option brings up a dialog box, as shown in Figure 22.5, where you can select which projects you would like to build.

Figure 22.5

The Make Project Group dialog box enables you to select which projects to build.

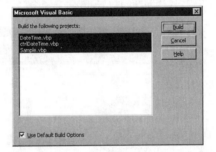

The option at the bottom of this dialog box, Use Default Build Options, is very important. If it is selected, Visual Basic will just go ahead and build each of the selected projects using whatever settings you used last, without displaying any dialog boxes to enable you to change these build settings. If you have never built a project before, and this option is selected, the system will use the standard defaults shown for a first build (save in current folder, name is same as project name, and so on). If you do not have this option checked, the standard build dialog box will come up for each project in turn, prompting you to either accept or change the current settings. If you are using the Make Project Group command with the intention of starting all your projects compiling while you go away and do something else, you should ensure that this option is checked.

Another important difference when you have multiple projects loaded is that Visual Basic needs to know which one is the main, or *startup* project. This project is the one that is run when you press F5 or choose Start from the Run menu. All other projects are only run if they are *instantiated* by that main project. A project is considered instantiated by another project if it is started through some form of ActiveX call, such as `CreateObject`.

The first project placed in a group is, by default, the startup project, but this can be changed through the Project Explorer. If you right-click within any of the projects in the Project Explorer window, you will see the menu option Set As Start Up (see Figure 22.6). If you select that option, the project that was currently selected is now designated the startup project. To indicate its status, the startup project's name is shown in bold in the Project Explorer.

Figure 22.6

Set this project to be the startup project.

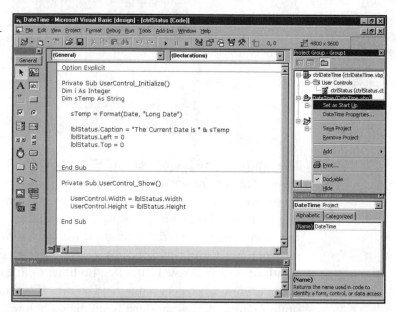

Note

Always ensure that your startup group is set correctly when dealing with ActiveX Objects. ActiveX DLLs in particular, when accidentally set to be the startup group, can cause some puzzling results. Usually, because the DLL probably doesn't have any code that runs without a client application calling it, there are no visible results of starting the project group. This results in Visual Basic being in Execution mode, but nothing else happens—which can cause you to frantically look for errors in your main project (the one you intended to be the startup), without finding anything. Remember to always look for the bold project name as proof of the current startup project.

Generally, the choice of which project should be the main project is obvious to the developer. It is the one that calls or references all the others. It is sometimes necessary, however, to change the startup project while testing. Any project that can be run on its own can be a startup project, which means any type of project other than an ActiveX Control (refer to Figure 22.6). Exercise 22.2 demonstrates the effect of changing the startup project, using the simple project group you created in Exercise 22.1.

Note

Other than the previously mentioned options, the Project Explorer behaves the same when dealing with a project group as it does for a single project. The project affected by the various Add commands, such as for forms and modules, is always the currently selected one.

Using Project Groups to Debug an ActiveX DLL

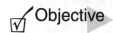Objective

In real development, project groups will usually be used with some form of components. When you are creating a system that uses one or more components, especially components that are still in development, a project group can greatly simplify your work. After a component is stable, or when using third-party components, there should be no need to have their code available and a simple reference to the component should suffice. To illustrate the use of project groups when developing with components, this section walks you through the creation and debugging of an ActiveX DLL.

Setting Up a Sample Group

For the purposes of this demonstration, you will set up two projects: one Standard EXE that consists of a simple form with one command button, and one ActiveX DLL project.

To create the sample projects, follow these steps:

1. Start Visual Basic. The Startup dialog box appears, as shown in Figure 22.7.

2. From the dialog box, select the Standard EXE icon.

Figure 22.7

Selecting a new Standard EXE project through the Visual Basic 5 Startup dialog box.

Note

If the dialog box shown in Figure 22.7 does not appear when you start Visual Basic 5, you have most likely chosen to turn it off, and a default, empty, project is created instead. For the purposes of this example, the project created by default will work just fine. If you want to have the Startup dialog box appear when you start Visual Basic in the future, however, you can turn it back on by selecting Prompt for project under the Environment tab in the Visual Basic Options dialog box, as shown in Figure 22.8.

Figure 22.8

Control whether the Startup dialog box appears through this Option dialog box.

3. This project will include a single form, named Form 1. Change the following properties of Form 1 to the indicated values:

   ▶ Change Name from Form 1 to frmSample.

   ▶ Change Border Style to 3 - Fixed Dialog.

4. On the form, create a new button. Change the button's name to cmdGetStatus, and its caption to "Get Status".

5. Place the following code into the form, replacing anything else that may be there:

```
Option Explicit

Private Sub cmdGetStatus_Click()
    Dim sTemp As String
    Dim objStatus As New clsStatus

    sTemp = objStatus.Status

    MsgBox sTemp, vbOKOnly, "Status"

End Sub
```

   The code itself is very straightforward: It takes a string value from the objStatus object and displays it in a standard Visual Basic Message Box.

6. Change the name of the project to "Sample".

7. Add a second project by selecting Add Project from the File menu. Select ActiveX DLL from the dialog box that appears, as shown in Figure 22.9.

Figure 22.9

Adding a new project to a project group.

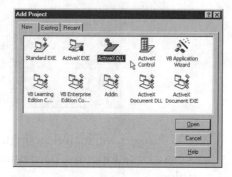

8. The new project already contains one class module, Class 1, so you won't need to add anything. Change the class's name to `clsStatus` in its Property sheet; it is referred to it by that name in the `cmdGetStatus_Click` routine in step 5.

9. Change the new project's name to `DateTime`.

10. Place the following code into `clsStatus`, once again replacing any other code that may already be there:

```
Option Explicit

Public Property Get Status() As String
Dim sTemp As String

    sTemp = Format(Date, "Long Date")
    Status = "The Current Date is " & sTemp

End Property
```

This property procedure, like the preceding code sample, is simple. It puts together a simple string and returns it to the calling program.

After you have completed all the preceding steps, the group is almost complete. The code in your Get Status button won't work, however, if you stop now. (Try it, a `User-Defined type not defined` error will appear when you click on the button.) You still need to add a reference to the DLL to your main project so that you can create instances of your new class.

Adding a reference to a project that is in the same project group is not much different than adding any other reference. It is, in fact, a little easier. If you select the main project in the Project Explorer and then choose the References command from under the Project menu, the standard Visual Basic References dialog box will appear, as shown in Figure 22.10.

Figure 22.10

ActiveX Objects in the same project group appear at the top of the unselected references list.

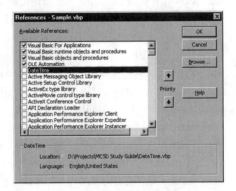

Note that the entry for your new project, `DateTime`, appears directly under the existing, selected references and not in regular alphabetic order. This is not a mistake. Microsoft expects you to commonly be making references to other projects in the same project group. Because this is the main reason why this feature exists, Microsoft has made it a little easier. Another important fact here is that the `DateTime` DLL was never compiled, but still appears in the list. This would not occur if you didn't have the projects in a group. After you check off the `DateTime` reference and close the dialog box, the main project will be ready to run.

Debugging Features in Project Groups

With the project group properly set up, you are now ready to explore some of the debugging features you can take advantage of when using project groups. When working with multiple components, it is possible to treat them all as independent projects and completely finish one before ever working on another. In such a scenario, you would test and debug each of your components separately. Then, after you have built all the components into actual DLLs and EXEs, you would combine them with your main application and begin integration testing. If you were always able to do things this way, and there were never any bugs missed, there would be no need to test or debug in project groups. However, that doesn't happen often.

Debugging within a project group is not any different than regular debugging. The same techniques are used—breakpoints, error-trapping, and stepping through code—but they apply across all the projects in the group. You can set breakpoints in any of the projects, not just the startup. If that line is about to be executed, it will pause at that point, just as you would expect. This can be useful in determining exactly when an object is created, initialized, and terminated, and will even work across multiple instances of one project. The Debugging Error-Trapping setting, which can be set to Break on All Errors, Break in Class Module, or Break on Unhandled Errors, behaves as it does with a normal project, but applies across all the projects in a group. It is not possible to set different debugging options for individual projects because these options are really environment-level options, not project-level ones.

 Caution

In general, when dealing with project groups, it is important to realize whether a setting applies to only the current project or to the entire Visual Basic environment. Settings found in the Options dialog box (under the Tools menu), including the Error-Trapping setting, apply to Visual Basic. Those found in the Project Properties and Compile Options dialog boxes are stored with each individual project.

Stepping through the executing code is where the true power of project groups becomes clear. It is possible to step, line-by-line, through the code of one project, into the code of another. When dealing with ActiveX components, this could mean hitting an object call in one project, which takes you immediately to the code of that object's property or method, possibly passing through some initialization code on the way.

Exercise 22.3 takes you through all three of the debugging options discussed so far, using the sample projects you created in the section titled "Setting Up a Sample Group."

Using Project Groups to Debug an ActiveX Control

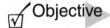

Another new feature of Visual Basic 5, the capability to develop your own ActiveX Controls, naturally works well with the concept of project groups. An ActiveX Control is not designed to ever run on its own, and will even generate an error if you try to do so. As Figure 22.11 shows, it always requires a host project. Whenever you develop a control, you need to add some other project to your project group—before you can run, test, or debug your control. For testing purposes, there doesn't need to be anything more than a single form in the other project, but it always requires the use of a group because it has to be separate from the ActiveX Control's project.

Figure 22.11

ActiveX Control projects cannot be run without another project acting as their host.

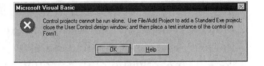

As in the previous DLL examples, you can use all the debugging features of Visual Basic when working with your ActiveX Control in a project group. Using breakpoints, you can cause Visual Basic to pause execution at any point in your control, or in the code of the host project. When stepping through code, the entire project group is treated as one complete, uninterrupted collection of code. You can step directly from a line of code in the host project to a line in your control, transparently. The Error-Trapping settings also function as in the DLL examples: The settings always affect all projects in the group. Exercise 22.4 builds on the sample project from the previous exercises and illustrates the various debugging methods with an ActiveX Control.

Overall, there are only a few important differences about working with ActiveX Controls rather than DLLs in project groups:

▶ You do not need to create a reference to the control in your other projects (in that group). It is always available on the toolbox, and a reference is automatically created for you when you place the control onto any of your forms.

▶ Breakpoints placed in key startup code (such as the UserControl's Initialize event) can prevent proper display or functioning of the control during design time.

The first difference is not a problem; it is merely a convenience not provided for ActiveX DLLs, and saves you a few seconds of effort. Because you have to load the control into another project before you can run it, every project in the group references the control by default.

The second point is a bit more of an issue, and exists because of the differences between DLLs and controls. ActiveX Controls have a visual interface at design time, so their code is loaded into memory and executed even when you are not running the project. Visual Basic is not really in Execution mode at this point, however, so it is not possible to debug what happens when the code is run at this point. If you attempt to open a form containing your control, and the control has an error, you will receive a generic error message, as shown in Figure 22.12, and the form will not be opened. Fortunately, you are given the option to enter Debug mode at this point, enabling you to fix the problem. Exercise 22.5 takes you through a series of steps to demonstrate the design-time effects of breakpoints and errors in a control project.

Project groups are not the biggest new feature in Visual Basic 5, but they are easily the one you will notice the most and use day after day. Because of their obvious benefits in working with any ActiveX Object and necessity for working with ActiveX Controls, it is important to understand and begin using them as soon as you can. As such a common feature, project groups are almost guaranteed to appear on the certification exam in some format. The exercises in this chapter will help prepare you for those questions.

Figure 22.12

Errors in your ActiveX Control project can cause "Errors during load" when opening a form containing the control.

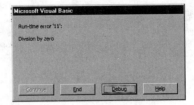

Exercises

Exercise 22.1: Creating a Simple Project Group

In this exercise, you create a project group consisting of two new Standard EXE projects. To create this exercise, follow these steps:

1. Start Visual Basic. The Startup dialog box displays.

2. From this dialog box, select Standard EXE, double-click on the icon, or click on the OK button.

3. You should now have one project one, named Project 1, with a sample form displayed. Choose Add Project from the File menu.

4. The Add Project dialog box appears, as shown in Figure 22.9, enabling you to choose between a new project, an existing project, or a recent project. Select the New Project tab.

5. Select the Standard EXE icon. Double-click on that icon or click the OK button.

The exercise is complete. You now have a project group consisting of two projects. Remember that in this case, because the two projects do not reference each other in any way, running this project group is really no different than running the projects on their own. Keep this project group open if you do not want to re-create it before running the next exercise.

Exercise 22.2: Demonstrating the Effects of Changing the Startup Project

For this exercise, you will be starting with the project group created in Exercise 22.1. If you didn't complete that exercise previously, please do so before beginning this one.

To create this exercise, follow these steps:

1. Start with the sample project group (containing two new Standard EXE projects) from Exercise 22.1.

2. Select only the form contained in Project 1.

3. Change the form's caption from "Form 1" to "First Project".

4. Select the form in Project 2.

5. Change its caption to "Second Project".

6. At this point, Project 1 should be displayed in bold (in the Project Explorer) to indicate that it is the startup project. If it is not, make it the startup project by right-clicking on it and choosing Set as Start Up from the context menu that appears.

7. Run the project group by choosing Start from the Run menu, clicking on the Play icon on the toolbar, or pressing the F5 key.

8. A Visual Basic form appears onscreen, with a caption of "First Project". This is because Project 1 is the startup project. No matter what you do, the form with the caption "Second Project" will not appear during this run because it is not referenced in any way from the first project.

9. Stop the execution by closing the visible form.

10. Make Project 2 the startup group. Right-click on the second project in the Project Explorer and choose Set As Start Up in the Context menu. Project 2 should be displayed in bold.

11. Run the project group again. This time, the form that appears has "Second Project" because it is Project 2 running.

Exercise 22.3: Debugging an Active X DLL (in a Project Group)

This exercise requires the use of the sample projects created in the section titled, "Setting Up a Sample Group." After you have this project group created and open, you can follow these steps to experiment with various debugging techniques.

First you step through a project group, as follows:

1. With your sample project group open, ensure that the project Sample is set as the startup.

continues

2. From the Debug menu, choose Step Into, or press the F8 key.

3. The Visual Basic form "frmSample" appears. Click on the button labeled Get Status on this form.

4. At this point, you will enter Break mode as Visual Basic encounters the first executable line of code in this project.

5. Using the Debug menu command Step Into again, step through the lines in the button's Click procedure. When you reach the objStatus.Status call, the next step will take you into the property procedure of your ActiveX DLL.

6. If you continue to step through the code, you will reach the end of the Get Status procedure and return back to the first project.

7. When you have completed stepping through the cmdGetStatus_Click procedure, and dismissed the message box that is displayed, stop the project execution by closing the form.

Add some code into the Class_Initialize() and Class_Terminate() procedures of clsStatus. It doesn't matter what code, so put something simple such as a debug.print command. Step through the project group again and watch what happens. The class's initialization code doesn't fire until you first attempt to actually use the object (by calling its Status property), not when the object is declared (in the Dim objStatus as line).

This happens because Visual Basic is always attempting to conserve memory and other system resources, so it doesn't even create an instance of your DLL until it is referenced. This fact can become extremely important if you place code into the Initialization event of any class. The termination of the object happens later, when objStatus goes out of scope at the end of the cmdGetStatus_Click procedure.

To experiment with the Termination event, try playing with it when the DLL reference is lost. If you move the line declaring objStatus into the global declarations area of the form's code, the initialization will occur at the same time but the termination will not happen until the entire form is closed because the object has broader scope. You can explicitly cause the object reference to be destroyed by inserting a `Set objStatus = Nothing` line at the end of the button's `Click` event; clicking the button more than once will result in an error.

Next you use breakpoints, as follows:

1. With your sample project group open, ensure that the project `Sample` is set as the startup, and that it is not current-ly executing.

2. Open `clsStatus` by double-clicking on it in the Project Explorer. Find and select the line `sTemp = Format(Date, "Long Date")`. Right-click on this line, select the Toggle submenu, and click on the `Breakpoint` command. The line should be highlighted in red, indicating a breakpoint is on.

3. Run the project group (do not step through it, just run it normally). Once again, the main project's form will appear onscreen.

4. Click on the Get Status button. Almost immediately, Visual Basic will enter Break mode and the code from `clsStatus` will be displayed.

5. Stop the execution of the project.

Breakpoints are very powerful in testing ActiveX components. It is not unusual, in a large system of DLLs and other objects, to be interested in a procedure buried deep inside a program. Stepping through all the code up until that point would work, but would take much longer than it needs to. Setting a breakpoint right where you need to check some values or pay special attention to the flow of execution can save you a great deal of time.

Now use the Break on Errors settings, as follows:

1. With your sample project group open, ensure that the project `Sample` is set as the startup, and that it is not current-ly executing.

continues

Exercise 22.3:   Continued

2. Open clsStatus by double-clicking on it in the Project Explorer. Find and select the Class_Initialize procedure. Put code into this event that will cause an error, and an On Error Resume Next statement at the beginning of the procedure, as shown in the following example:

```
Private Sub Class_Initialize()
On Error Resume Next
Dim j as Integer

    j = 1/0

End Sub
```

3. Remove the breakpoint added in the last portion of the exercise, if you haven't already done so.

4. Right-click anywhere in your code and select the Toggle submenu. Select the Break on All Errors setting.

5. Run the project. Visual Basic will break on the line j = 1/0, with a "Division by Zero" error, despite the On Error Resume Next statement. Try the other two settings in the Toggle submenu, restart the project, and note what happens.

The important point to remember, when changing the error-trapping settings in Visual Basic, is that they affect all projects equally.

Exercise 22.4:   Debugging an ActiveX Control

In this exercise, you create a project group containing an ActiveX Control, and then demonstrate various debugging techniques on that control. First, create a test project. This exercise builds on the sample projects created in the section titled "Setting Up a Sample Group." After you have this project group created and open, you can follow these steps to add an ActiveX Control to that project group.

To create this exercise, follow these steps:

1. Choose Add Project from the File menu. A dialog box displays asking you to choose what type of new project to create. Select the ActiveX Control icon by double-clicking on it.

2. A new blank control project has now been added to your project group.

3. Change the new project's name to be "ctrlDateTime", and the Usercontrol's to "ctrlStatus".

4. Place a Label control onto the control. Position and size do not matter.

5. Rename this label to "lblStatus".

6. Add the following code to the control, replacing any other code that may already be there:

```
Option Explicit

Private Sub UserControl_Initialize()
Dim sTemp As String


    sTemp = Format(Date, "Long Date")

    lblStatus.Caption = "The Current Date is " & sTemp
    lblStatus.Left = 0
    lblStatus.Top = 0


End Sub

Private Sub UserControl_Show()

    UserControl.Width = lblStatus.Width
    UserControl.Height = lblStatus.Height

End Sub
```

7. Close the UserControl window. Switch to the main project in your group (Sample) and open its single form.

continues

Exercise 22.4: Continued

 Caution Always close the control's Design window before switching to other projects. If it is left open, you cannot place the control anywhere else, and the toolbox icon will be disabled.

8. Select the new icon from your toolbox, as shown in Figure 22.13. It will be the very last icon, so you may need to expand the toolbox to see it. This is your new control, all ready to place onto this form.

Figure 22.13

Selecting your new User Control item from the form toolbox.

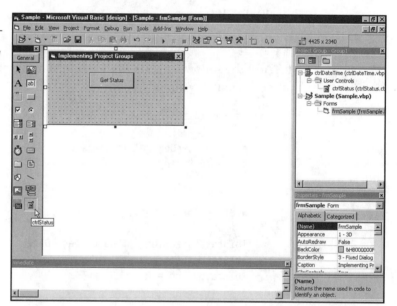

9. Place the control onto your form, just under the command button that is already there. Notice that it is already displaying your status string, meaning your control is working.

10. Ensure that the main project, Sample, is set as the startup, and then step into the project group by choosing Step Into from the Debug menu.

11. Almost immediately (before `frmSample` appears), Visual Basic will break at the `UserControl`'s `Initialize` procedure. From this point, you can step through the control, moving back and forth between it and the main project.

12. Continue to experiment with the control in Debug mode.

Exercise 22.5: Errors in User Controls During Design Time

In this exercise, you continue using the project group created for the preceding exercise:

1. Ensure that the project group is not running by choosing Stop from the Run menu.

2. Open the code for `ctrlStatus`. Add a breakpoint inside the `UserControl_Initialize()` event procedure, at any point.

3. Double-click on `frmSample` (from the main project) in the Project Explorer.

4. Notice how you immediately switch into Debug mode at this point, even though you were not really ever running your project. Continue the execution (F5).

5. Remove the breakpoint and open the form again to see how it should work.

6. Return to the control's initialization routine and add the following lines of code (anywhere):

```
Dim j as integer
j = 1/0 'will cause a division by zero error
```

7. Open `frmSample` again, noticing that an error message is displayed. You are given the option to debug your code.

In both cases, the problem is the same: Visual Basic hits a breakpoint or an error and cannot continue executing the control's code. This causes it not to reach the `Show` event procedure and not to display the status information.

Review Questions

1. What type(s) of projects can be startup projects? (Select all that apply.)

   A. Standard EXE

   B. ActiveX DLLs

   C. ActiveX EXEs

   D. ActiveX Controls

   E. ActiveX Documents

2. When attempting to debug a project group containing project groups, which projects are affected by the Break on All Errors setting?

   A. All non-ActiveX projects

   B. The startup project

   C. Whichever project was selected when the option was set

   D. Any project except ActiveX Controls

   E. All projects

3. Before you can make calls to an ActiveX DLL project in the same project group, what must you do? (Select all that apply.)

   A. Compile the DLL

   B. Check the DLL off in your project's reference list

   C. Make sure the DLL is the startup project

   D. Nothing

4. If you lose or delete your project group file (*.vbg), what information have you lost? (Select all that apply.)

   A. What projects belonged to that group

   B. Compile information for each project

   C. Which project was the current startup project

   D. Any references to projects in the same group

5. If there is an error in the `Initialize` event of your ActiveX Control (part of your project group), when will you receive the error message? (Select all that apply.)

   A. When you run the project and a form is displayed with your control on it.

   B. When you open the ActiveX Control's project.

   C. When you open (in Design mode) a form containing the control.

   D. Never. ActiveX Controls cannot raise error messages.

6. When creating, testing, or debugging an ActiveX Control, when would you need to use a project group? (Select the best answer.)

   A. Only if you are building the control for one of your own projects.

   B. Only if the control has a visual interface.

   C. Any time you need to run the control in a design environment.

   D. All the time. You cannot open an ActiveX Control project on its own.

Answers to Review Questions

1. A, B, C, and E. Any type of project can be a startup project, with the sole exception of ActiveX Controls. ActiveX Controls always need another project to host them before they can be executed. For more information, see the section titled "Understanding Project Groups."

2. E. The Break on All Errors setting is a Visual Basic environment setting and has no connection to any individual project. For more information, see the section titled "Debugging Features in Project Groups."

3. B. (Check the DLL off in your project's reference list.) When running in the Visual Basic environment, you do not need to compile any of your ActiveX projects before you can run them. The calling project has to be the startup project, not the DLL itself. When working with ActiveX Controls, you do not have to do anything (except place the control on your form), but ActiveX DLLs and EXEs need to have a reference set. For more information, see the sections titled "Understanding Project Groups," "Using Project Groups to Debug an ActiveX DLL," and "Using Project Groups to Debug an ActiveX Control."

4. A, C. Reference and compile information are all stored with each individual project and stay intact when the project(s) are opened outside of the project group. For more information, see the section titled "Understanding Project Groups."

5. A, C. ActiveX Controls are executed when they are displayed, both in Design and Execution modes. For more information, see the section titled "Using Project Groups to Debug an ActiveX Control."

6. C. You cannot run an ActiveX Control inside Visual Basic unless it is part of a project group, although you can open, edit, and build the project on its own. For more information, see the section titled "Using Project Groups to Debug an ActiveX Control."

Answers to Test Yourself Questions at Beginning of Chapter

1. No. References to ActiveX Controls in the same project group are created automatically for all projects in the group. See "Using Project Groups to Debug an ActiveX Control."

2. No. Visual Basic's error-trapping settings apply to all projects. See "Debugging Features in Project Groups."

3. Trick Question. You can't tell which project executes first; it will be whichever project was set to be the *startup* project. See "Understanding Project Groups."

4. One. You can create as many instances of your ActiveX components as you want, but you can ever have only one copy of a project included in a project group. See "Understanding Project Groups."

Chapter 23

Defining the
Scope of a Watch Variable

Microsoft's VB5 exam guide doesn't mention any specific objectives regarding this topic, but defining the scope of a watch is one of the subjects included in the exam. This chapter helps you prepare for the exam by covering the following objectives:

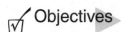
Objectives

▶ Understand the three levels of scope

▶ Choose the appropriate level of scope

Test Yourself! Before reading this chapter, test yourself to determine how much study time you will need to devote to this section.

1. At what three levels may the scope of a watch be set?

2. How does the scope of a watch affect its calculation time?

3. What choices must be selected in the Context group for a watch to have global scope?

Answers are located at the end of the chapter...

A watch makes it possible to observe the value of a variable or an expression at runtime in Debug mode. Chapter 20, "Setting Watch Expressions During Program Execution," discussed how to set watch expressions during execution. This chapter looks more closely at watch behavior by focusing on the scope of a watch.

Just as the scope of a variable depends on where and how it is declared, the scope of a watch depends on the manner of its definition. Specifying the scope of a watch determines the context in which its behavior is observed. If you know where in your program the observation of a variable is significant, you can make more efficient use of your debugging time by specifying the appropriate watch context.

Specifically, this chapter covers the following topics:

▶ Levels of scope

▶ Scope considerations

Levels of Scope

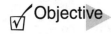

You are already familiar with the issue of scope as it pertains to data variables. In a block-structured programming language such as Visual Basic, the visibility of a variable depends on where it is declared. A variable may exist at any one of the following three levels of scope:

▶ Local

▶ Module

▶ Global

A variable declared in the context of a particular procedure is visible only in the context of that procedure. It is said to be local in its scope, which means that it is invisible to all other procedures in the program. Consider the following subprocedures, for instance:

```
Sub MyProcedure
    Dim iCount as Integer, sName as String
    ' pretend that something useful happens later in the
    ➥procedure
End Sub

Sub YourProcedure
    Dim iCount as Integer
    ' pretend that something else useful happens here, too
End Sub
```

The variables declared in these routines are all local in scope. The variable sName declared in MyProcedure can be accessed only by the code in MyProcedure. It is not visible to YourProcedure, nor is it visible to any other routine in the program. The two iCount variables are each local to the procedures in which they are declared. They are permitted to have the same name because each is unique in the context of the procedure in which it is declared.

A variable may also have module scope if it is declared in the General Declaration section of its code module using the keyword Private. In this case, the variable is visible to all procedures contained in the module, but it is invisible to all other procedures in the program.

Finally, a variable is global in scope if it is declared in the General Declaration section of its code module using the keyword Public. Such a variable is visible to all procedures contained throughout the program.

If you already understand how variables may have their scope defined at these different levels, you will find the scope of a watch fairly easy to understand. Just as a variable's scope may be at the local, module, or global level, the scope of a watch may be defined at these levels, too.

Local Scope

Although the scope of a variable depends on where it is declared in the source code, watches are all created using the same Add Watch dialog box, and edited using the same Edit Watch dialog box. The key to differentiating among the various levels of scope lies in the controls contained in the Context group of the Watch dialog boxes.

The Context group contains three controls: Procedure, Module, and Project. The control pertaining to Project is a simple label that displays the name of the current project. Because it is a label, it can't be edited. It serves as a reminder that only those procedures and modules will be displayed by the other controls in the group.

The real work of determining the scope of a watch is done by the other two controls. If you want to define a watch at the procedure level, that means that you want to assess only the value of the watch expression in the context of a particular procedure. To do this, use the Module combo box to select the appropriate module. The Module combo box displays the names of all modules contained in the current project.

After a module name is selected, use the Procedure combo box to choose the procedure for which the watch should be active. The Procedure combo box displays only those procedures contained in the currently selected module. If the procedure you want isn't in the list, check the Module combo box again. You probably selected the wrong module by mistake.

Figure 23.1 shows how to use the Add Watch dialog box to create a procedure-level watch.

Remember that if you need to modify the settings for a watch, you can use the Edit Watch dialog box to do so. The following section shows you an example of this.

Figure 23.1

A procedure-level watch.

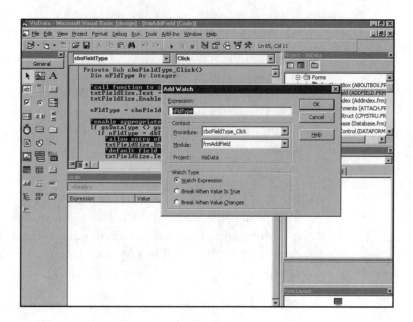

Module Scope

If you want to monitor an expression as it changes throughout an entire module, you don't need to create individual procedure-level watches for each routine contained in the module. Instead, you can set a single watch that applies to an entire module.

To define a watch at the module level, use either the Add Watch dialog box (to create a new watch) or the Edit Watch dialog box (to modify an existing watch). Just as with a procedure-level watch, you still need to select the appropriate module from the Module combo box.

As before, the next step is to select an item from the Procedure combo box's drop-down list. Instead of selecting a particular procedure name, however, select the item that says (All Procedures). (All Procedures) is the first item contained in the drop-down list. By selecting (All Procedures), your watch is automatically activated for every procedure contained in the currently selected module.

Figure 23.2 shows how to use the Edit Watch dialog box to change the local watch you set in the preceding section into a module-level watch.

Figure 23.2

*A module-level
watch.*

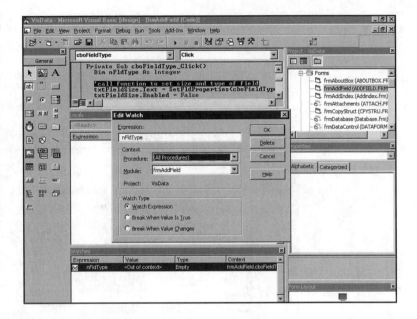

Global Scope

What if you want to monitor an expression throughout your entire program? Just as you can set a single watch pertaining to an individual module, you can also set a single watch that applies to an entire program.

To define a global watch, you once again can use either the Add Watch dialog box or Edit Watch dialog box. First, select (All Modules) from the Module combo box. (As with the Procedure combo box, the All selection is the first item in the drop-down list.) Next, select (All Procedures) from the Procedure combo box. Figure 23.3 shows an example of this.

The watch expression in Figure 23.3 will be evaluated in all procedures in all modules as the program executes, making it global in scope.

As you set watches at various levels of scope, you will notice that the Watches dialog box displays the context of each expression. As shown in Figure 23.4, a procedure-level watch is indicated to apply to a particular procedure by the ModuleName.ProcedureName syntax in the Context column of the Watches dialog box. A module-level watch has the name of its module displayed in this column. A global watch is indicated when the entry is blank, denoting that there is no contextual limitation on the watch.

Figure 23.3

A global watch.

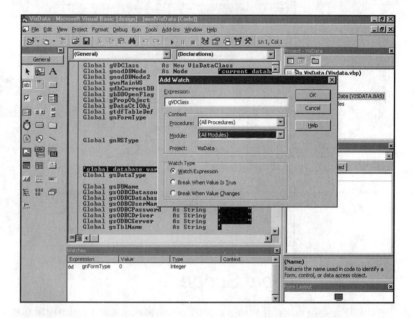

Figure 23.4

The Watches dialog box indicates the level of scope for each watch expression.

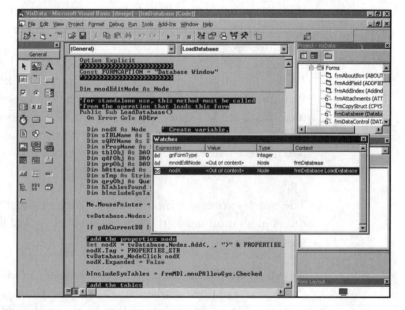

Scope Considerations

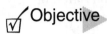

As you have seen, a watch may be set at any of three levels of scope. This section considers how to decide which level of scope is best suited to solve a given problem.

Striving to Narrow the Scope

The rules governing intelligent declaration of variables largely apply to watches, too. It generally makes sense to limit the scope of a variable, for instance. If a variable must be used in just one procedure, it should be declared locally within that procedure; declaring it at a higher level is a needless complication. In particular, global variables should be used sparingly. Because they can be modified anywhere in a program, bugs involving global variables are harder to track down.

In essence, the task of debugging is vastly simplified as the number of places in which data can be modified diminishes. This rule also applies to watches. Limiting the number of places in which a watch expression is evaluated cuts down on distractions during the debugging process. After all, if you monitor a variable in 100 procedures when you need to monitor it in only 10, you expend about 10 times more effort on it than it is worth.

You will recall from the previous chapter on watch expressions (Chapter 20, "Setting Watch Expressions During Program Execution") that you can do three things with a watch:

▶ Monitor the value of the watch expression

▶ Break when the watch expression is True

▶ Break when the value of the watch expression changes

Bear these options in mind as this discussion begins to focus on some strategies and constraints regarding watches set on different kinds of variables.

Global Variables

A global variable can be evaluated in a watch at any level of scope. Because it is available throughout the program, its value can be detected in a watch of module-level or procedure-level scope as easily as in a global watch.

If you suspect that a global variable is being incorrectly modified, you will probably want to begin with a global watch. The value of the variable can be changed anywhere in your program. However, if you set the watch to break on change or when the watch expression is true, you will be able to tell which procedure has modified the value. As you find likely suspects for the bug in question, you may want to narrow the scope of your watch, or to set additional watches of more limited scope.

Module-Level Variables

A module-level variable can be evaluated in a watch at either of two levels: module-level or procedure-level. Naturally, a procedure-level watch makes sense only for procedures found in the same module in which the variable is defined.

The same search pattern suggested for global variables makes sense for module-level variables. Until you have reason to focus the search on a particular procedure or set of procedures, you will initially want to set the watch at the highest scope available. Use watches to trigger a program break to determine which procedure(s) are the source of your problem.

Local Variables

Obviously, only a procedure-level watch is sensible for local variables. Its value can be evaluated only in the context of the procedure in which it is defined. It literally does not exist anywhere else, so there's no point in looking for it elsewhere.

The point to limiting the number of places in which your watches are active is so that you can spend less time looking at meaningless changes. After you have pinned down the likely sources of a bug, it is only logical to limit the search to the likely problem areas.

Performance Concerns

Aside from the logical issue, performance concerns are also a motivation to limit the scope of a watch. Broader watches cause VB to devote more resources evaluating watch expressions than do watches of more limited scope.

Does the performance degradation produced by a watch that is broader in scope than necessary really matter? Most of the time, probably not. However, if you are working with anything particularly time sensitive, the time you may save by limiting the scope of your watch may make a difference. Even a few milliseconds may be important to a real-time system, a callback function, or a program relying on the sequence in which a series of Windows messages are processed.

If you encounter problems along these lines during a debug session in which you are using watches, try deactivating the watches or limiting their scope before you decide that you have found more bugs in your program. If the problems go away after you have changed the watches, it is likely that the watches slowed execution just enough to cause problems.

Exercises

Exercise 23.1: Setting the Scope of a Watch

This exercise shows how to use the Edit Watch dialog box to create watches at different levels of scope. To create this exercise, follow these steps:

1. Create a new project.

2. Add a code module to the project. Enter the following code into the General Declarations section of the module:

   ```
   Public g_iCounter as Integer
   Private m_strModuleString as String
   ```

3. Create a new procedure in the code module as follows:

   ```
   Public Sub MyProcedure
       Dim iAlphaCode as Integer
       m_strModuleString = ""
       For iAlphaCode = 65 To 96
           m_strModuleString =
         ➥m_strModuleString & Chr(iAlphaCode)
       Next
       ' count the number of times this
       ➥procedure runs
       g_iCounter = g_iCounter + 1
   End Sub
   ```

4. Enter the following code for the Click event of the default form VB provides:

   ```
   Call MyProcedure
   ```

5. Set watches for each of the variables declared in the code module (g_iCounter, m_strModuleString, and iAlphaCode). Use the Context controls in the Watches dialog box to experiment with different scopes as described in this chapter.

6. The test code gives you one sample each of a global variable, module-level variable, and local variable. What difference does the scope make in the evaluation of each variable type?

Exercise 23.2: Changing the Scope of a Watch

This exercise shows how to use the Edit Watch dialog box to modify the scope of a watch. To create this exercise, follow these steps:

1. Create a new project.

2. Add a code module to the project. Enter the following code into the General Declarations section of the module:

   ```
   Public g_iTestVariable as Integer
   ```

3. Create a new procedure in the code module as follows:

   ```
   Public Sub TestProcedure
       On Error Resume Next
       ' count the number of times this
       ➡procedure runs
       g_iTestVariable = g_iTestVariable + 1
       If g_iTestVariable > 32767 Then
           g_iTestVariable = 0
       End If
   End Sub
   ```

4. Enter the following code for the `Click` event of the default form VB provides:

   ```
   Call TestProcedure
   ```

5. Set a global watch that will break when the value of `g_iTestVariable` changes. Run the application and notice in which module the break occurs. Change the scope of the watch so that it is active only in that module. Run the application again. This time, notice in which procedure the break occurs. Change the scope of the watch again so that it is active only in that procedure.

Using this general approach, you can narrow the scope of a watch so that it encompasses only that scope that is relevant to the variable being watched. In a live application, of course, you will want to exercise the program more to see whether the variable changes anywhere else before jumping to the conclusion that it needs to be watched only in a single module or procedure.

Review Questions

1. The scope of a watch should be narrowed when _____.

   A. The program is time-sensitive.

   B. The variable is static.

   C. The maximum number of watches of that scope is exceeded.

   D. The expression doesn't need to be evaluated in certain contexts.

2. The scope of a watch expression is determined by _____.

   A. The scope of the variable(s) used in the expression

   B. The watch class module

   C. The watch type library

   D. The watch dialog settings

3. A global variable is visible to a watch of _____ scope.

   A. Global

   B. Module-level

   C. Procedure-level

   D. Unbound

4. A module-level variable is visible to a watch of _____ scope.

   A. Global

   B. Module-level

   C. Procedure-level

   D. Unbound

5. The highest watch scope meaningful to a variable declared in a form using the `Public` keyword is _____.

    A. Global

    B. Module-level

    C. Procedure-level

    D. Unbound

6. The highest watch scope meaningful to a variable declared in a module using the `Private` keyword is _____.

    A. Global

    B. Module-level

    C. Procedure-level

    D. Indeterminate

Answers to Review Questions

1. A, D. Performance considerations may necessitate narrowing the scope of a watch so that it may be calculated more quickly. If a variable need not be observed in certain contexts, it is safe to exclude it from the watch. For more information, see the section titled "Scope Considerations."

2. D. The Context group of controls on the Watches dialog box determines the scope of the watch. For more information, see the section titled "Local Scope."

3. A, B, and C. Global variables are visible to watches of all scope levels. For more information, see the section titled "Global Variables."

4. B and C. Module-level variables are visible to watches set at either the module level or procedure level, assuming that the module is the same one in which the variable is defined and that the procedure is contained in that module. For more information, see the section titled "Module-Level Variables."

5. A. A `Public` form variable is essentially a property of the form, making it globally accessible throughout the program. For more information, see the section titled "Global Variables."

6. B. `Private` makes it a module-level variable. For more information, see the section titled "Module Scope."

Answers to Test Yourself Questions at Beginning of Chapter

1. A watch may be set at three different levels: the procedure level, module level, or globally. See "Levels of Scope."

2. The greater the scope of a watch, the slower it can be calculated. A watch set at the procedure level executes more quickly than a watch set at the global level. See "Scope Considerations."

3. The Context group enables you to select from among the modules and procedures in the current project. Global scope is specified by selecting All Modules and All Procedures in the Module and Procedure combo boxes. See "Global Scope."

P a r t **4**

Distribution Issues

Using the Setup Wizard to Create an Effective Setup Program

This chapter helps you prepare for the exam by covering the following objectives:

 Objectives

▶ Edit the SETUP.LST file

▶ Edit the VB5DEP.INI file

Test Yourself! Before reading this chapter, test yourself to determine how much study time you will need to devote to this section.

1. What utility is provided with Visual Basic 5 that creates a setup program used to distribute an application?

2. What type of Visual Basic project can be used to create a setup program with the Application Setup Wizard?

3. The Setup Wizard can automatically determine files to be included for distribution with the application. What is the main file that is parsed by the Setup Wizard?

4. What is the very first step that must be completed when using the Application Setup Wizard?

5. After the Setup Wizard has completed the creation of a custom setup program, what file can be edited to alter the files being distributed to the target machine?

6. Which section of the text file used by SETUP1.EXE can be used to change the title displayed by the setup program?

7. What are the three default sections found in the SETUP.LST file?

8. Visual Basic 5 provides the VB5DEP.INI file for use by the Application Setup Wizard. What is the purpose of this file?

9. The Setup Wizard uses the VB5DEP.INI file when creating a custom setup program. In what directory can this file be found?

10. What options are available if the VB5DEP.INI file does not contain the required dependency information for a component?

Answers are located at the end of the chapter...

Visual Basic provides the Application Setup Wizard to assist in creating an effective setup program. The Setup Wizard can be used to determine the components of an application, required support files, destination directories, and more.

The setup program for your application is the "first impression" of your application. If the installation of your program is not done correctly, the application will not function correctly. This seemingly simple process can have very detrimental effects on both your program and the users.

After the setup program has been created, the SETUP.LST file lists all the files to be installed to the destination machine. This file can be further modified if required, after the Setup Wizard has generated it.

Another file that can be modified is the VB5DEP.INI file. This file is used to assist the Application Setup Wizard. It provides the Setup Wizard with a comprehensive list of the component dependencies and file references used by Visual Basic.

This chapter examines using the Application Setup Wizard, customizing the VB setup program project, and advanced installation issues.

This chapter covers the following topics:

- ▶ Using the Application Setup Wizard

- ▶ Editing the SETUP.LST file

- ▶ Editing the VB5DEP.INI file

- ▶ Using the Setup Toolkit

- ▶ Modifying the default setup program project (SETUP1.VBP)

- ▶ Uninstalling your application

- ▶ ODBC distribution

Using the Application Setup Wizard

This section reviews the basics of using the Setup Wizard to create a custom setup program for any type of Visual Basic project.

The Application Setup Wizard is a separate application from Visual Basic and can be found in your Visual Basic Start menu program group. The default location for the wizard's application EXE is:

```
C:\Program Files\DevStudio\VB\setupkit\kitfil32\SETUPWIZ.EXE
```

As with all wizards, it is designed to guide you through the process of creating your setup program as easily as possible. Prompts are provided to simplify selection of required information and components.

To get a better understanding of the Setup Wizard, take a high-level look at the basics of how the wizard operates. The points are discussed in more detail as you progress through the chapter.

First, Setup Wizard parses the project file (VBP) you specify, optionally compiles your program executable, and prompts you for the following information:

▶ Whether to create disks, to write the setup to a single directory, or to create disk images on a hard drive

▶ Confirm dependencies/references in your project

▶ Add any ActiveX components/servers required by your application that are not embedded in the application

▶ What files need to be distributed as part of your application

▶ Data access drivers for your application

▶ If applicable, whether the application should be installed as one of the following: an executable, an ActiveX Document, an ActiveX component, or an ActiveX Control

After the required information has been obtained in the preceding step, the Setup Wizard then performs the following actions:

- ▶ Automatically generates a SETUP.LST file. This file will act as a driver for the setup program.

- ▶ Generates a dependency file (DEP), if selected earlier.

- ▶ Compresses the required files and calculates the space/disk layout required for the distribution media.

To collect all the required information, the Setup Wizard provides a total of eight steps. The steps displayed can vary depending on the selected project. Each step is described in the following sections.

Project Selection—Step One

Step One of the Wizard allows for the selection of the Visual Basic project that will be used to create the setup program. Figure 24.1 shows the Project Selection step.

Figure 24.1

Select Project and Options— Step One.

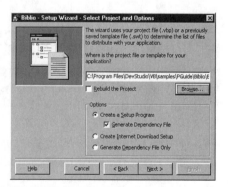

After the desired project has been selected, the Setup Wizard provides a check box to rebuild the project. This can be used to ensure that the project being distributed is correctly built and up to date. Check this box as desired.

The Options section of the Step One dialog box can be used to determine what the final output will be from the Wizard. Valid options include the following:

▶ *Create a Setup Program.* Used to generate a valid installation program with all the required components for your application.

▶ *Generate Dependency File (Check Box).* After the Setup Wizard has examined the VBP project file, a DEP text file will be created that contains a listing of all component and file dependencies for the selected project.

▶ *Create Internet Download Setup.* Used to generate an Internet setup for ActiveX Controls, EXEs, DLLs, and Documents. This special setup will generate a CAB file and HTML code containing object references for web pages.

▶ *Generate Dependency File Only.* The Setup Wizard will examine the VBP project file and create only the DEP text file, which lists all the component and file dependencies for that project.

Distribution Method—Step Two

Step Two of the wizard provides three options for distribution media. The media type selected is used by the Setup Wizard to determine the dialog options shown for Step Three.

Figure 24.2 shows the Distribution Media Options of the Setup Wizard.

Figure 24.2

Distribution Method—Step Two.

▶ *Floppy Disk.* Used to create setup disks for the application. Setup Wizard will determine the amount and layout of the disks.

▶ *Single Directory.* This option allows selection of a single directory to hold all the contents generated by the Setup Wizard.

▶ *Disk Directories.* This option combines the other two previous selections. Instead of directly creating setup disks, this allows a directory to hold subdirectories representing distribution disks.

Distribution Location—Step Three

Step Three of the Setup Wizard is directly controlled by the selection of Distribution Media in Step Two. One of three different dialog boxes will be displayed.

Figure 24.3 shows the result of selecting Floppy Disk as the media choice. It allows further selection of the drive letter to be used and the capacity of the disk.

Figure 24.3

Floppy Disk selection— Step Three.

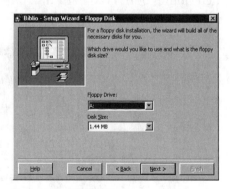

If the Floppy Disk media is selected, disks will not be required until the final Step of the Setup Wizard. The Wizard will present a dialog box prompting for Disk 1 of *x*, based on the required disk space needed for the distribution files.

Figure 24.4 shows the result of selecting Single Directory as the media choice. It allows further selection of the drive to be used, the directory, and subdirectory for placing the setup program generated by the Setup Wizard.

Figure 24.4

Single Directory selection—Step Three.

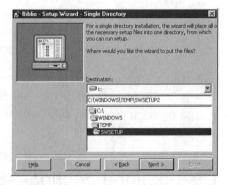

Figure 24.5 shows the result of selecting Disk Directories as the media choice in Step Two. This is a combination of both the Floppy Disk and Single Directory choices.

The Multiple Directories dialog box enables you to select the drive, directory, and subdirectory to be used. The drop-down combo box can be used to specify the Disk Size. The Disk Size determines both how many disk directories will be created, and their individual capacities.

Figure 24.5

Multiple Directories selection—Step Three.

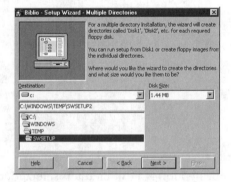

Data Access—Step Four

Step Four of the Setup Wizard is Data Access. The Setup Wizard does not always display this dialog box. After the project selection has been completed, the Setup Wizard determines whether the project contains either a data control or any database references and displays the Data Access dialog box as required.

If presented with this dialog box, the application utilizes some form of data access. This dialog box presents a listing of the various ISAM database engines that can be distributed with the application.

> This dialog box displays a label indicating that if ODBC is used by the application, the separate ODBC setup program must also be distributed. The ODBC setup can be found in the ODBC directory under the VB directory.

Figure 24.6 shows the Data Access dialog box from the Setup Wizard. Notice the two check boxes at the bottom of the dialog box. They determine whether the Jet engine is distributed or the RDO files—two different types of data access supported by Visual Basic 5.

Figure 24.6

Data Access—Step Four.

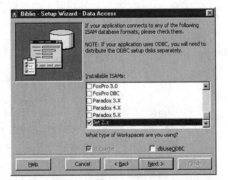

ActiveX Components—Step Five

Step Five of the Setup Wizard, shown in Figure 24.7, provides the opportunity to select any ActiveX Servers required by the application.

The Setup Wizard will automatically include any ActiveX components that it can find. If no components are found, the wizard presents a label message indicating that no ActiveX components were found.

This dialog box will still be displayed regardless of whether the Setup Wizard finds any ActiveX component references. This enables you to include any components that might be required by your application, but that are not directly referenced by the application.

Figure 24.7

ActiveX Server Components— Step Five.

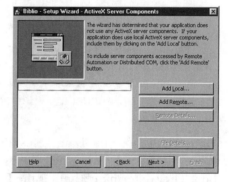

Dependencies—Step Six

Step Six of the Setup Wizard presents a checklist of additional file dependencies determined by the wizard. These files should be distributed with the application, but you can choose to not include them for distribution.

Note

Some files might not be included for distribution because they are common to all machines. If the application requires them, however, they may already be installed on the target system. By not including certain files you are sure will be on the target system, you can reduce the size of the distribution media requirements.

Figure 24.8 shows the Confirm Dependencies dialog box. This dialog box is displayed only if the Setup Wizard has found additional file dependencies.

File Summary—Step Seven

Step Seven of the Setup Wizard is the File Summary. This step presents a list of the files that the Setup Wizard has determined are required for distribution. Although the Wizard is a very good utility, it does not have the capability to determine all the files that you might want to distribute. Figure 24.9 shows the File Summary dialog box.

Figure 24.8

Confirm De-pendencies—Step Six.

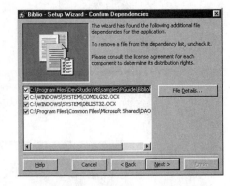

Figure 24.9

File Sum-mary—Step Seven.

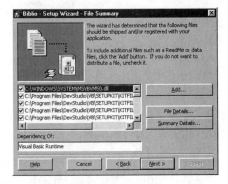

This step enables you to check off files to be included or excluded, as well as specifying additional files to be added. Each individual file can be selected and the File Details reveal both Installation Information and Version Information. Only the final Destination Directory for the selected file can be altered through the File Details dialog box, as shown in Figure 24.10.

This step also enables you to select individual files and will display the file they are a Dependency Of. There is also the Summary Details command button, which gives the overall file count, sizes, compressed sizes, and target directory for creating the setup program. Figure 24.11 shows the Summary Details of the File Summary dialog box.

Figure 24.10

*File Details, a
dialog box of
the File Sum-
mary step.*

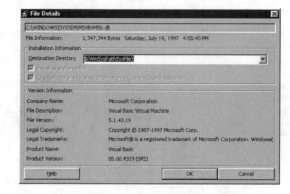

Figure 24.11

*Summary De-
tails, a dialog of
the File Sum-
mary step.*

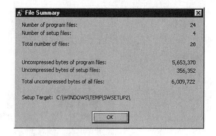

Finished!—Step Eight

Step Eight of the Setup Wizard is the last dialog box displayed.
The only option left is to save the current wizard settings into a
Setup Wizard Template (SWT) file. This allows for the same setup
to be reproduced at a later date and modified as required. Figure
24.12 shows the Finished! dialog box.

Figure 24.12

*Finished!—
Step Eight.*

After the Finish button is selected, the Setup Wizard will compress all selected files and place them into the indicated destination directory. If disks are required, a prompt will be displayed for the disk.

Editing the SETUP.LST File

The SETUP.LST text file is made up of three different sections used by different components of the custom setup program. The following list describes the three different sections:

- ▶ **[BootStrap]**   The SETUP.EXE program uses this section to install Visual Basic support files required by the SETUP1.EXE. Then the SETUP1.EXE program can be invoked.

- ▶ **[Files]**   The SETUP1.EXE program uses this section to install the files required by the application.

- ▶ **[Setup]**   The SETUP1.EXE program uses this section to provide default information for the custom setup program. This section can be easily customized with a text editor, without re-running the Application Setup Wizard.

The following sample [BootStrap] section is taken from the SETUP.LST file generated from the CALC VB sample application in Exercise 24.1.

```
[BootStrap]
File1=1,,setup1.ex_,setup1.exe,$(WinPath),,,2/1/1998
23:39:52,165376,5.0.0.3716,"","",""
File2=1,,VB5StKit.dl_,VB5StKit.dll,$(WinSysPath),,$(Shared),1/
16/1997 0:00:00,29696,5.0.37.16,"","",""
File3=1,,MSVBVM50.dl_,MSVBVM50.dll,$(WinSysPathSysFile),
$(DLLSelfRegister),,7/19/1997 16:55:40,1347344,5.1.43.19,
"","",""
File4=1,,StdOle2.tl_,StdOle2.tlb,$(WinSysPathSysFile),
$(TLBRegister),,5/19/19979:08:12,16896,2.20.4118.1,"","",""
File5=1,,OleAut32.dl_,OleAut32.dll,$(WinSysPathSysFile),
$(DLLSelfRegister),,5/19/1997 9:08:12,492304,2.20.4118.1,
"","",""
File6=1,,OlePro32.dl_,OlePro32.dll,$(WinSysPathSysFile),
$(DLLSelfRegister),,5/19/1997 9:08:12,114960,5.0.4118.1,"",
"",""
```

```
File7=1,,AsycFilt.dl_,AsycFilt.dll,$(WinSysPathSysFile),,,,5/
19/1997 9:08:10,118544,2.20.4118.1,"","",""
File8=1,,Ctl3d32.dl_,Ctl3d32.dll,$(WinSysPathSysFile),,,,8/
21/1996 0:00:00,27136,2.31.0.0,"","",""
File9=1,,ComCat.dl_,ComCat.dll,$(WinSysPathSysFile),
$(DLLSelfRegister),,10/31/1996 0:00:00,22288,4.71.1441.1,
"","",""
```

The following sample [Files] section is taken from the SETUP.LST file generated from the CALC VB sample application in Exercise 24.1.

```
[Files]
File1=1,,Calc.EX_,Calc.EXE,$(AppPath),,,,2/1/1998
➥18:15:02,12288,1.0.0.0,"","CALC","$(AppPath)\Calc.EXE"
```

When examining [BootStrap] and [Files] section entries, notice that required support files appear in only one section. If a file is found in the [BootStrap] section, it is not included in the [Files] section because it has already been installed. This helps to reduce the size requirements of the distribution media.

The files listed in the [BootStrap] and [Files] sections of SETUP.LST use the following format:

```
Filex=y,[SPLIT],file,install,path,register,shared,date,size[,version]
```

where*

File is the keyword that must start each file description line.

x is the sequence number, starting at 1 in each section. The numbering must be sequential, and not skip any values.

y is the disk number on which this file resides on the distribution media. If your distribution media is via network server or compact disc, this number will always be 1.

SPLIT is the flag indicating that this file spans disks and is not the last part of a segmented file. For subsequent file names that are part of this same file, you should not repeat the fields following install. The last piece of the same file will not have the SPLIT keyword. A segmented file that spans two disks can be represented as follows:

```
File16=3,SPLIT,SAMPDB.MB1,
SAMPDB.MDB,$(AppPath),,,11/2/1997
➧10:13:16,3440640,,"","",""
File17=4,, SAMPDB.MD2, SAMPDB.MDB
```

`file` is the name of the file to be distributed.

`install` is the name of the file as it exists on the distribution media, usually in compressed format. However, it can be the same as file.

`path` is either an actual destination path, a symbolic variable indicating a path specified by the user, or a combination of a macro and additional subdirectory names separated by back-slashes. Table 24.1 lists the macros that can be used in the installation.

`Register` is a key that indicates how the file is to be included in the user's system Registry. Table 24.2 lists the four possible keys.

`$(Shared)` is a keyword automatically added to the list entry of any file installed to \Windows, \Windows\System, or $(CommonFiles), the Common Files directory (\Windows or any subdirectory of \Windows with Windows NT 3.51, \Pro-gram Files\Common Files with Windows 95 and Windows NT 4.0). This keyword can be either `$(Shared)`, indicating that it is a shared file and is registered in the Registry, or blank, indicating that it is a private file.

`date` and `size` are the last date modified and file size. This information helps to verify that the correct versions of the files are on the setup disks. Also, `size` is used by SETUP1.EXE to calculate how much disk space your applica-tion requires on the user's machine.

`version` is an optional internal version number of the file.

*Source: Microsoft Visual Basic Books Online.

Table 24.1

*Macros**

Macro	Description
$(WinSysPath)	Installs the file into \Windows\System (Windows 95) or \Windows\System32 (Windows NT) subdirectory.
$(WinSysPathSysFile)	Installs a system file in the \Windows\System subdirectory under Windows 95 or the \Windows\System32 subdirectory under Windows NT. Note that the file is not removed when the application is removed.
$(WinPath)	Installs the file into the \Windows directory.
$(AppPath)	Installs the file into the application directory specified by the user, or the *DefaultDir* value specified in the [Setup] section.
$(AppPath)\Temp	Installs the file into the \Temp subdirectory below the application directory.
C:*path*	Installs the file directly into the directory identified by `path` (hard-coded and not recommended).
$(CommonFiles)	The common directory to which shared application files can be installed: C:\Program Files\ Common Files\ for both Windows 95 and Windows NT 4. This macro is generally combined with a subdirectory, such as $(CommonFiles)\MyApp.
$(CommonFilesSys)	The same as $(CommonFiles)\System under Windows 95 and Windows NT 4.
$(ProgramFiles)	The default root directory where applications are installed: C:\Program Files for both Windows 95 and Windows NT 4. C:\ (Windows NT 3.51).

Macro	Description
$(MSDAOPath)	Location that is stored in the Registry for Data Access Objects (DAO) components. You should not use this for your files.

*Source: Microsoft Visual Basic Books Online.

Note   The $(WinPath) and $(WinSysPath) macros found in Table 24.1 are the only two macros that can be used in the `Path` argument of the [BootStrap] section of the SETUP.LST file.

Table 24.2

*Register Key Values**	
Key	**Use**
(no key)	File does not contain linked or embedded objects and does not need to be registered on the user's machine.
$(DLLSelfRegister)	Self-registering .DLL, .OCX, or any other .DLL file with self-registering information (exports `DllRegisterServer` and `DllUnregisterServer` functions).
$(EXESelfRegister)	ActiveX .EXE component created in Visual Basic, or any other .EXE file that supports the /RegServer and /UnReg-Server command-line switches.
$(TLBRegister)	Type Library file.
$(Remote)	Remote Support file (.VBR).
appname.reg	Any component you distribute that needs to be registered but does not provide self-registration. This key indicates a .REG file (that must also be installed) that contains information that updates the system Registry. The .REG file should be compatible with Windows NT 3.51, or the setup will fail when run on this platform.

*Source: Microsoft Visual Basic Books Online.

Note

REG files—for example, <appname>.reg—contain Registry key information. They are manually merged with the Registry found on the target machine. When a Registry entry is made through the REG file method, no ST5UNST.LOG entry is recorded for this action.

The ST5UNST.LOG text file contains the setup program actions and is used by the ST5UNST.EXE application removal utility when uninstalling the application.

If Registry entries are required by your application, customize the SETUP1.VBP project and use the REG functions to create the Registry entries.

The following sample [Setup] section is taken from the SETUP.LST file generated from the CALC VB sample application in Exercise 24.1. This section can be used to customize some of the default settings used by SETUP1.EXE.

```
[Setup]
Title=CALC
DefProgramGroup=CALC
DefaultDir=$(ProgramFiles)\CALC
Setup=setup1.exe
AppExe=Calc.EXE
AppToUninstall=Calc.EXE
AppPath=
```

where*

Title is the name of your application that will appear on the background windows during installation. This name will also be used for the Program Manager or Explorer icon group and icon name. By default, it is the .EXE name of your application.

DefProgramGroup is the default name of the folder in Windows 95 or Windows NT 4. Special Note: No folder is created for your application under Windows 95 or Windows NT 4; by default, your shortcuts are created directly in the Programs menu of the Start menu.

`DefaultDir` is the default directory into which the application will be installed, unless the user specifies an alternate folder in your Setup program.

`Setup` is the name of the Setup program file. The default is SETUP1.EXE.

`ForceUseDefDir`. If left blank, the user is prompted for an installation directory. If this is set to 1, the application will be installed to the folder specified by "DefaultDir" in SETUP.LST.

`AppPath` is an application-specific `PATH` variable used by Windows 95 and Windows NT 4 to find any additional files needed by your application.

`AppExe` should be set to the name of your application.

*Source: Microsoft Visual Basic Books Online.

Editing the VB5DEP.INI File

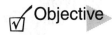 Objective

The VB5DEP.INI file in VB5 is a replacement for the SWDEPEND.INI file used in earlier versions of Visual Basic; yet, its function remains the same. This function is to provide the Setup Wizard with a comprehensive list of dependencies and references used by Visual Basic. This list is created when you install Visual Basic and resides in the \SetupKit\Kitfil32 subdirectory of the main Visual Basic directory.

The following example is a fragment from a typical VB5DEP.INI file:

```
[SetupWiz]
Uses1=E:\DEVSTUDIO\VB\SETUPKIT\KITFIL32\VB5StKit.dll
Drive1=1.44 MB,1457664,512
Drive2=2.88 MB,2915328,1024
Drive3=1.2 MB,1213952,512
Drive4=720 KB,730112,1024
Drive5=360 KB,362496,1024
BootStrap=E:\DevStudio\vb\SETUPKIT\KITFIL32\SETUP.EXE
```

```
VBExe=E:\DevStudio\vb\VB5.EXE
RemoveInstallEXE=E:\DevStudio\vb\SETUPKIT\KITFIL32\ST5UNST.EXE

[DAO2535.tlb]
Dest=$(MSDAOPath)
Uses1=DAO350.dll
CABFileName=MSDAO350.cab
CABDefaultURL=http://activex.microsoft.com/controls/vb5
CABRunFile=MSDAO350.exe -Q
```

It may be helpful to think of DEP files as providing a list of dependencies for individual components or applications, and the VB5DEP.INI file as providing a list of dependencies for your entire Visual Basic development environment.

The VB5DEP.INI is very similar to a DEP file. When you run the Setup Wizard, it first checks the VB5DEP.INI file to locate dependency information. If it is not available, and if a particular component does not have its own DEP file, the Setup Wizard notifies you of the missing dependency and enables you to either ignore this omission or correct the problem.

If you ignore the omission, your program may not function properly after being installed on the user's machine. If you are certain that a particular dependency is already loaded on the user's machine, however, you may safely proceed.

If needed, you can manually insert an entry for a particular component's dependency information by editing the VB5DEP.INI file directly. Or you can create a DEP file for the component with the Setup Wizard. It may come down to contacting the component vendor, however, and requesting a DEP file for that particular component.

As has been noted, the Setup Wizard combines component DEP files with the Visual Basic project and the VB5DEP.INI file to create a setup program, a SETUP.LST, and a project DEP file.

Using the Setup Toolkit

The core of the Setup Wizard is the main Setup program (SETUP1.EXE). SETUP1.EXE can also be manipulated outside the Setup Wizard. The Setup Wizard compiles the Setup Toolkit project into an executable file called SETUP1.EXE.

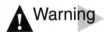 **Warning**

A word of caution: These files are the same files used by the Setup Wizard. Consequently, if a file in the Setup Toolkit is altered, the modified version will be used in later setup programs created by the Setup Wizard. Therefore, it is strongly advised that before you modify the SETUP1 project, save a *clean* copy of SETUP1.VBP to another folder, and make your changes in that other folder.

Because you will be modifying the SETUP1 project, if you make any changes other than cosmetic, you may be required to manually process the steps that the Setup Wizard would otherwise do for you in creating the SETUP.LST file.

Table 24.3 lists the files that comprise the Setup Toolkit.

Table 24.3

Setup Toolkit Files

File name	Description
SETUP.EXE	Program that the user runs to initiate your setup program.
SETUP1.VBP	The source code project for SETUP1.EXE. This file can be renamed, as long as the new file name is reflected in the SETUP.LST file when the installation is run.
SETUP.LST	Text file that lists all the files to be installed on the user's machine. This file is in (.INI) private profile format.
VB5STKIT.DLL	Visual Basic Library containing various functions used in SETUP1.BAS, including

continues

Table 24.3 Continued

Setup Toolkit Files

File name	Description
	routines for expanding files that were compressed with COMPRESS.EXE.
ST5UNST.EXE	Application removal utility that processes ST5UNST.LOG. The application removal log file is generated in the application's installation folder.
COMPRESS.EXE	The file compression utility.
VB5DEP.INI	The Visual Basic 5 dependency file.
MAKECAB.EXE	Cabinet file compression utility—primarily used for creating an Internet-based setup.

Working with the SETUP1 Project

The SETUP1.VBP project is located in the \SETUPKIT\SETUP1 folder under the main Visual Basic folder.

To customize your setup, to add other user prompts and other events to the setup sequence, you can modify SETUP1.VBP. You can write code in the setup program just as you would in any other Visual Basic program. Furthermore, a number of function calls are available in this project that are especially useful in setup routines.

Some examples of when you might use the Setup Toolkit are as follows:

▶ To display billboards and graphics, or to play sound files during the installation process. This is a terrific way to keep the user's attention and display information about your product such as features, service and support, and so on.

▶ To give your setup programs a custom appearance, such as custom dialog boxes, background, sounds, and so forth.

▶ To add special user prompts during installation for additional components to be included in your application, such as prompting to copy help or sample files to the hard drive.

▶ To use your own compression utility to copy the setup files to the distribution media.

Note

The SETUP1 project has many valuable functions for creating setup programs as well as localization settings. Therefore, be sure to take the resource file into account when making any changes.

Customizing the Installation Sequence

In this section, you take a look at customizing the installation sequence that the user must follow. You can simplify your work by using the Setup Wizard with the Setup Toolkit project (SETUP1.VBP).

You could use the Setup Toolkit and the Setup Wizard together to add dialog boxes to your setup program, for example, giving the user options to install additional components in your application. You can use the Setup Wizard to analyze your project and find the associated references and files, and you can manually add selection options to prompt the user to add additional components to your application via the SETUP1.VBP project—the Setup Toolkit. You might have a very large sample database that you offer as a training option, for instance. You can add as many installation options as you want.

Before proceeding, be sure to make a copy of the SETUP1 project to preserve the original setup program, and then complete the following steps:

1. Edit the SETUP1.FRM (frmSetup1) code in the Form_Load event immediately after the code block calls the ShowBeginForm function and comment:

```
' This would be a good place to display
➥an option dialog, allowing the user
' a chance to select installation
➥options: samples, docs, help files, etc.
```

The sample code fragment is as follows:

```
Dim miLoadSampleDB As Integer
➥'--Tobe used as a flag

If vbYes = MsgBox ("Do you want to
➥install the sample database?
➥",vbQuestion + vbYesNo) Then
  miLoadSampleDB = True
Else
  miLoadSampleDB = True
End If

If miLoadSampleDB Then
  CalcDiskSpace "SampleDB"
End If

'---Following cIcons =
CountIcons(strINI FILES) Statement
  If miLoadSampleDB Then
    cIcons = CountIcons("SampleDB")
  End If

'--Following the CopySection
strINI_FILES Statement
  If miLoadSampleDB Then
    CopySection "SampleDB"
  End If
```

2. Save SETUP1.FRM and SETUP1.VBP, and then create an .EXE file (make SETUP1.EXE from the File menu).

3. Run the Application Setup Wizard. On the File Summary panel of the Setup Wizard, add the files you want to install if the user answers Yes to installing the Sample Database dialog box created in SETUP1.VBP.

4. After you are done with the Setup Wizard, generate the appropriate distribution media.

5. From the distribution media, open the SETUP.LST file. Find the files you added on the File Summary panel and cut and paste the optional file(s) from the [Files] section to a new section. This new section will be placed below the [Files] section and have a new section title that matches the string argument used in the `CopySection` statement (in this example, `CopySection "SampleDB"`). Also, as you cut and paste, be sure to renumber the File*number* in the copied lines to be incremented sequentially:

```
[SampleDB]
File1=1,SPLIT,SampApp.DB1,
➡SampApp.DB,$(AppPath),,,11/12/
➡97,23956967
File2=1,SPLIT, SampApp.DB2,
➡SampApp.DB
File3=1,, SampApp.DB3, SampApp.DB
```

In short, when the user executes your setup program, the setup program copies all the [BootStrap] files to the user's machine and then it prompts the user to indicate whether to install the sample database files. If the user selects Yes, the `CalcDiskSpace` statement determines whether there is sufficient disk space, in the proper location, on the user's machine for the database files. The program then installs all the files listed with the [Files] section in SETUP.LST.

Next, the setup program interrogates the `miLoadSampDB` flag again. If the user selected Yes to install the sample database files, SETUP1.EXE then executes the `CopySection` statement for the database files listed in the [SampleDB] section of SETUP.LST and installs the appropriate files.

If you have changed the name of the SETUP1.VBP project when making alterations, you can reference the program by its new name in the SETUP.LST file. Under the [SETUP] section, locate the `Setup=` line. By default it will be `Setup=setup1.exe`. You can edit this line to reflect the new name of your custom setup program.

Advanced Installation Issues

When an application is to be distributed, many issues can arise that prevent it from functioning as required. Users have come to expect software that is simple, intuitive, and yet full of functionality. This section deals with three issues that can prevent the successful deployment of an application.

Most 32-bit applications provide a removal process for cleaning up files, Registry entries, and other components used by the program. Providing a solid removal process helps to ensure that users will install future versions of your application, or other products, without worrying about the effects on their systems.

Another advanced issue that can prevent successful deployment is determining the files to be redistributed. The Application Setup Wizard can usually determine all the files required for distribution, but some files need to be added manually to either the Setup Wizard or the SETUP.LST file. The section on Files to Distribute describes the basic files used by both the Setup Wizard and advanced components. Knowing the correct files to be distributed helps to reduce issues that will arise if these files are not located on the target machine.

A large percentage of Visual Basic applications provide some level of database functionality. ODBC (Open Database Connectivity) allows an application to take advantage of various database platforms. Correctly installing and configuring ODBC ensures that your application can communicate with required databases. The section "ODBC Considerations" examines where ODBC can be found and how to distribute it for your application.

Uninstall Issues

Each time your setup program is run to install your application, an application removal log file (ST5UNST.LOG) is generated in the installation folder that contains entries indicating the following:

▶ Folders created during the installation.

▶ Files that were installed, and the location where they were installed. This list contains all the files in the setup program, including those that were not installed on the user's machine because a newer version of the same file already existed on the user's machine. The .LOG file indicates whether the file is a shared file and if so, whether it replaced the existing shared file.

▶ Registry entries created or modified during the installation.

▶ Start menu entries and links with Windows 95 and Windows NT 4, or Program Manager icons and groups created with Windows NT 3.51.

▶ What DLLs, EXEs, or OCXs were self-registered.

In the Windows 95 and Windows NT operating systems, shared files are reference counted in the system Registry. When the Uninstall utility is used to remove the installation, the reference count for that item will decrement until the count equals zero—at which time the user will be prompted to remove the file, indicating that the file has a shared reference.

In a Windows 95 or Windows NT 4 setup, the application will be added to the list of registered applications displayed by the Add/Remove Programs applet in the Control Panel. To uninstall and remove the application, you use the Add/Remove Programs applet in the Control Panel. Similarly, in Windows NT 3.51, an application removal utility icon will be included in the Program Manager icon group for the application; the corresponding command-line properties are set to the appropriate LOG file.

If a failed or canceled installation should occur, the application removal utility will remove all the folders, files, and registration entries that SETUP1.EXE created during the installation. For a user-initiated uninstall, the LOG file (ST5UNST.LOG) and Registry entries created by your setup program must remain unchanged and accurate. Some actions performed by the user may have an adverse effect on the successful uninstall of the application, including the following:

▶ The user manually copies shared files; therefore, the integrity of the reference counting is not preserved in the Registry.

▶ The user deletes installed files or an application folder instead of using the removal utility. This can create several issues. The setup .LOG file (ST5UNST.LOG) is deleted, rendering removal utility inoperable or making it impossible to remove system Registry entries from program files, DLLs, or OCXs in the application directory—which corrupts their system Registry entries.

▶ The user deletes the application setup log (ST5UNST.LOG). Without the application setup log file, the application-removal utility will fail because it does not have the required installation information.

▶ A setup program for a non-Windows 95–compliant application installs the same shared files that are also installed by your Windows 95–compliant application—thus corrupting their system Registry entries.

▶ A shared file is installed into a folder other than the one in which it already exists on the hard drive, thereby corrupting the Registry entries.

▶ Your setup program has its deployment model set for "Install as standalone application," and the user runs the setup program to install the application on his or her machine. In the meantime, another setup program is created for a different Visual Basic application, and the first application is included in this setup program as a component. If the scenario can exist where the user might install a particular Visual Basic Remote Automation Server as a component in the setup program of another application, you must set its deployment model to "Install as shared component".

▶ The user installs the same Visual Basic application in two different folders. Not only will the first installation no longer work, but the application removal utility's .LOG files will also conflict. You should create your setup program to check for previous installations, or instruct the user to remove the first installation before installing the application to a different folder.

As has been noted, Windows 95 and Windows NT shared files are reference counted in the system Registry. Some of the previous scenarios could adversely affect the installed file reference counts in the Registry, causing the application removal utility to prematurely reach a zero-reference count for a particular file, asking the user whether this file could be deleted. If a file is prematurely deleted, it could cause detrimental effects on other applications—rendering them inoperable or causing them to function incorrectly due to missing file dependencies, missing components, and the like. Therefore it is recommended that you use extreme caution when deleting shared components from the machine and that you always use the Uninstall utility to remove applications.

Files to Distribute

The custom setup program created by the Application Setup Wizard will always distribute the same "core" files. Table 24.4 shows a listing of these standard files that provide the setup program functionality.

Table 24.4

Distribution Files*

Filename	Description
SETUP.EXE	Program that the user runs to initiate your setup program.
SETUP1.EXE	The executable file generated by SETUP1.VBP. This file can be renamed, as long as the new file name is reflected in SETUP.LST.
SETUP.LST	Text file that lists all the files to be installed on the user's machine.

continues

Table 24.4 Continued

Distribution Files

Filename	Description
VB5STKIT.DLL	Visual Basic Library containing various functions used in SETUP1.BAS.
ST5UNST.EXE	Application removal utility for use with the Visual Basic Setup Toolkit. (ST5UNST.LOG, the application removal log file, is generated in the application's installation folder.)

*Source: Microsoft Visual Basic Books Online.

When using the Visual Basic Enterprise edition, the files in Table 24.5 are added to the SETUP.LST file and are installed if your project contains Remote Automation server components.

Table 24.5

*Files Added to the SETUP.LST File**

Filename	Description
CLIREG32.EXE	Remote Automation client registration utility. Included if your project is a Remote Automation server, or if the server also acts as a client.
RACMGR32.EXE	Remote Automation Client Manager. Included if your project is a Remote Automation server.
RACREG32.DLL	Remote Automation Registry. Included if your project is a Remote Automation server.
AUTMGR32.EXE	Automation Manager. Included if your project is a Remote Automation server.
AUTPRX32.DLL	Automation Proxy. Included if your project is a Remote Automation server.

*Source: Microsoft Visual Basic Books Online.

In addition to these files, you must also determine whether your application requires any other files. The most common files are databases, INI files, graphics, sounds, and so forth. These files can be added manually when using the Setup Wizard. During the File Summary (Step Seven), the Setup Wizard provides the ADD File command button for this purpose.

You have seen that the setup program for your application is the first exposure your users will have with your application. If it doesn't function properly, you are setting the tone for the use of your application. The Application Setup Wizard provides you with a step-by-step approach to building high-quality, effective setup programs for your application. In addition, the Setup Toolkit enables you to modify the setup program, customizing it to meet your particular needs.

ODBC Considerations

If you are creating an application that relies on ODBC, you must create and distribute a separate installation disk for ODBC or run the ODBC SETUP.EXE from within your setup program by using the `Shell` function. These files are freely distributable if you have purchased the Professional or Enterprise Edition of Visual Basic.

If you choose to distribute a separate ODBC disk, you should instruct the user to install the ODBC drivers before installing your application. If the ODBC drivers are not installed first, the RDO components in your setup program will not be registered correctly.

To install ODBC on a user's machine, you must use the setup program provided in the \ODBC folder of the main Visual Basic folder. Some of the ODBC files are compressed, and the setup program must decompress them to install them correctly. You should then create the disk and label the ODBC setup disk with a title such as "ODBC Setup Program: Run SETUP.EXE before installing *application.*"

To create an ODBC setup disk, copy all the files in \ODBC subfolder of the main Visual Basic folder to a disk or network directory. As with all setup applications, after you have created the ODBC disk, test the ODBC setup disk on a machine that does not have ODBC files.

Exercises

Exercise 24.1:   Creating a Simple Sample Setup Program

In this exercise, you use a VB sample project to create a custom setup routine by using the Application Setup Wizard. The CALC.VBP sample project will be used. This project is part of the VB samples and you may have removed it to save disk space. Another simple project with no database controls or references could be used.

To create this exercise, follow these steps:

1. Start the Application Setup Wizard.

2. If the Introduction screen appears, click on the Next command button.

3. In the Select Project and Options dialog box, click on the Browse button.

4. Locate the CALC sample project and open it. The default location for this sample is \VB\SAMPLES\PGUIDE\CALC\CALC.VBP.

5. In the Options section, select Create a Setup Program, and check off the Generate Dependency File check box. Click on Next.

6. In the Distribution Method dialog box, click on Single Directory. This will directly determine the next dialog box displayed.

7. In the Single Directory dialog box, select the drive and directory where the Setup Wizard will place all the files generated when the custom setup program is created. Ensure that a clean directory is used or create a new one, such as C:\WINDOWS\TEMP\SWSETUP2.

8. Click on Next when the directory has been selected. If the directory does not exist, a prompt will ask whether it should be created. Answer Yes. If the selected directory contains

files, the Setup Wizard will indicate that the files will not be deleted and ask whether to continue.

9. In the ActiveX Server dialog box, there should be no entries listed by this "Simple" CALC project. If you have used a different project with ActiveX Servers, continue as desired.

10. When the Next button has been clicked after the ActiveX Server dialog box, the Wizard will process all required files to determine the distribution needs.

11. The next dialog box displayed should be the File Summary. Review the files listed by the Setup Wizard. Select individual files to determine what they are a Dependency Of. Also, select individual files and choose File Details to determine the Installation Information and Version Information. The Summary Details can also be viewed at this point.

12. After all the files have been reviewed, click on Next.

13. In the Finished dialog box, click on Finished. The wizard will start the compression of the files and determine disk space and layout requirements. Click on OK when the final message box is displayed.

14. Go to the Installation Directory selected in the Single Directory dialog box. Locate the SETUP.LST file and open it with NotePad.

15. The SETUP.LST file is automatically generated by the Setup Wizard and contains the three sections—[BootStrap], [Files], and [Setup]. Review these three sections and change *no* entries.

16. When finished reviewing the SETUP.LST file, close it.

17. Run the SETUP.EXE file located in the same directory. This will launch the custom setup routine.

18. Proceed as prompted. Notice the titles used and default directory names.

19. Install and remove the sample CALC application if desired.

Exercise 24.2:   Customizing the SETUP.LST file

In this exercise, you customize the SETUP.LST file generated in Exercise 24.1. The [Setup] section of the text file will be changed to alter the defaults used by the SETUP1.EXE program.

1. Open the directory where the custom setup program was located. In Exercise 24.1 the suggested directory was C:\WINDOWS\TEMP\SWSETUP2.

2. Open the SETUP.LST file with a text editor, such as NOTEPAD.EXE.

3. Move to the [Setup] section of the file.

4. When the setup program is run, the background window will display the text value of the `Title=` line.

5. Change the value of `Title=` from `'CALC'` to `'Calculator for Windows 95'`.

6. Save the SETUP.LST file.

7. Run the SETUP.EXE file located in the same directory as the SETUP.LST file. This launches the custom setup routine.

8. Proceed as prompted. Notice the change in the background title used.

9. Install the Calculator application.

10. After CALC has been installed, open the Control Panel, Add/Remove Programs applet.

11. Notice the Uninstall Display Name for the CALC application. This should be the title that was changed in the SETUP.LST file.

12. Uninstall Calculator for Windows 95. Proceed as prompted.

13. When complete, try changing the `Title` value in the SETUP.LST file as desired. Also, try changing the `DefaultDir` value to change the default installation directory.

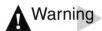 **Warning**

Although the other sections of the SETUP.LST file can be altered, this will be dependent on each individual file and how it is to be installed. Caution should be exercised when changing the [BootStrap] and [Files] section of the SETUP.LST file. If any problems are encountered after customizing the SETUP.LST file, use the Application Setup Wizard to generate another custom setup program.

Review Questions

1. The Application Setup Wizard is provided to create a custom setup program for distributing applications. What is the name of the .EXE file for this utility?

   A. APPWIZ.EXE

   B. ASW.EXE

   C. SWAPP.EXE

   D. SETUPWIZ.EXE

   E. SETUP.EXE

2. The Visual Basic Application Setup Wizard can be used to automatically determine the files required for distribution. What is the VB file used by the Setup Wizard to determine the required custom controls, references, and components used by the application?

   A. <project>.EXE

   B. <project>.VBP

   C. <project>.DEP

   D. <project>.INI

   E. <project>.INF

3. The Application Setup Wizard creates a custom setup program for distributing an application. Which actions does the Setup Wizard perform?

   A. Compresses files for distribution

   B. Creates a SETUP.INF

   C. Creates a SETUP.LST

   D. Creates a SETUP.EXE

   E. Creates a SETUP1.EXE

4. After the Application Setup Wizard has collected all the necessary information about a project, what are the three types of results that can be generated?

   A. A custom setup program

   B. A dependency file

   C. A self-extracting EXE

   D. A ZIP file

   E. A CAB file

5. The Application Setup Wizard provides eight different dialog boxes to specify information about an application. When creating a custom setup program, which dialog box does *not* always appear?

   A. Select Project and Options

   B. Data Access

   C. ActiveX Server Components

   D. File Summary

   E. None of these

6. When creating a custom setup program with the Setup Wizard, how is the destination directory of a file changed?

   A. Through the SETUP.INF file.

   B. Through the Dependencies dialog box.

   C. Through the File Details command button.

   D. Through the Summary Details command button.

   E. The destination directory cannot be specified through the Setup Wizard.

7. The Application Setup Wizard automatically creates a text file that can be used to further customize the setup program created for an application. What is the name of this text file?

    A. SETUP.INF

    B. SETUPLST.TXT

    C. SETUP1.TXT

    D. VB5SETUP.INI

    E. SETUP.LST

8. Which section of the text file used by SETUP1.EXE can be used to customize the destination directory for the application file?

    A. [BootStrap]

    B. [FileList]

    C. [Files]

    D. [Setup]

    E. [Destination]

9. The SETUP.LST file contains information about files to be distributed. Which are valid arguments of the FILEx statement?

    A. Version

    B. DepLocal

    C. Installation

    D. Path

    E. DestDir

10. What section of the SETUP.LST file can be used to customize the name of the program group the application will be installed to?

    A. [BootStrap]

    B. [FileList]

    C. [Files]

    D. [Setup]

    E. [Destination]

11. The Visual Basic Application Setup Wizard can be used to determine the file dependencies of most components. What file is used by the Setup Wizard to determine the files required for a specific component?

    A. SETUP.INF

    B. VB5SETUP.INF

    C. VB5DEP.INI

    D. VB5DEP.INF

    E. SETUP.LST

12. What is the primary type of information contained in the individual sections of the main dependency file used by the Setup Wizard?

    A. Destination directory

    B. Version

    C. Registry entries

    D. File name

    E. Date and time stamp

13. You create a simple application, and are now ready to distribute it. You run the Application Setup Wizard and notice that there several controls listed in the Confirm Dependencies and File Summary panels that you are not actively using in your application. How can you successfully remove these entries to reduce your distribution requirements and to prevent your application from failing when it is run?

A. Uncheck the entries in the Confirm Dependencies and File Summary panels so that Setup Wizard will not process them.

B. Don't do anything at this point. Then when Setup Wizard completes, edit the SETUP.LST file to remove the unwanted files or references.

C. Cancel the Setup Wizard and launch Visual Basic, and then remove the unused controls and references from the Project, Components, Controls tab.

D. Edit the VBSETUP.INF file and delete all entries marked with the DEPINFO tag that are not required for distribution.

E. Remove unneeded dependencies in the VB5DEP.INI file and rerun the Setup Wizard. This prevents the unneeded dependencies from being included.

14. Your application, Loan Calculator, has a project file named LC25.VBP. You create a setup program with Setup Wizard, adding your reference table files, and save the your setup template as LC25.SWT. When you test your setup program, you notice that the title presented in the setup window is "LC25 Setup." What is the easiest way to change the title to be more meaningful, such as "Loan Calculator V2.5"?

A. In the SETUP.LST file, edit the `Title=LC25` line under the [SETUP] section to read `Title=Loan Calculator V2.5`.

B. Rename your project file to Loan Calculator V2.5.VBP.

C. Edit the LC25.SWT file, changing the `AppTitle=LC25` line under the [Flags] section to read `AppTitle=Loan Calculator V2.5` and rerun Setup Wizard using the template file.

D. Make a copy of the SETUP1 project and hard-code the title on the form.

E. Rerun the Setup Wizard and in Step One, use the Application Title text box to change the setup program title displayed.

Answers to Review Questions

1. D. The name of the EXE for the Application Setup Wizard is SETUPWIZ.EXE. It can be found in the Visual Basic Setupkit\kitfil32 directory. The SETUP.EXE, also found in the same directory, is used as part of the custom setup program created by the Setup Wizard. For more information, see the section titled "Using the Application Setup Wizard."

2. B. The file used by the Setup Wizard to determine custom controls, references, and components is the Visual Basic Project (VBP) file. For more information, see the section titled "Using the Application Setup Wizard."

3. A, C. The Setup Wizard compresses files for distribution and creates a SETUP.LST text file. Both the SETUP.EXE and SETUP1.EXE must already be compiled; the Setup Wizard does not create them. For more information, see the section titled "Using the Application Setup Wizard."

4. A, B, E. The results generated by the Setup Wizard include a custom setup program, a dependency file, and a CAB file used for Internet distribution. For more information, see the section titled "Project Selection—Step One."

5. B. The Application Setup Wizard does not always display the Data Access dialog box. This dialog box is displayed only if a Data Control or a Data Access reference has been set in the project. For more information, see the section titled "Data Access—Step Four."

6. C. The destination directory for an individual file can be determined by using the File Details command button provided in File Summary. For more information, see the section titled "File Summary—Step Seven."

7. E. The SETUP.LST file is automatically created by the Setup Wizard. This text file can be edited to further customize the setup program and files to be distributed. For more information, see the section titled "Editing the SETUP.LST File."

8. C. The [Files] section of the SETUP.LST file can be used to customize the destination directory for the application file. The [BootStrap] location is for installing supporting components. For more information, see the section titled "Editing the SETUP.LST File."

9. A, D. `Version` and `Path` are valid arguments from the `FILEx` statement found in the SETUP.LST file. For more information, see the section titled "Editing the SETUP.LST File."

10. D. The [Setup] section of the SETUP.LST file can be used to customize the program group that will be used when installing the application. For more information, see the section titled "Editing the SETUP.LST File."

11. C. The VB5DEP.INI file is used by the Setup Wizard to determine the files required for individual components. This file holds the majority of dependency information used by the Setup Wizard. For more information, see the section titled "Editing the VB5DEP.INI File."

12. A, D. Destination directory and filename information can be found in the individual sections of the VB5DEP.INI file. Components that are listed do not indicate their version or

Registry entries. The date and time stamp is also not located in this file. For more information, see the section titled "Editing the VB5DEP.INI File."

13. C. When you compile your application, it stores all custom controls and references in the project file. If you merely uncheck a component, removing it from the distribution list in SETUP.LST, when your application runs it will look for that component and if it is not found will cause an error condition. It is recommended that you remove the reference from your project before running the Setup Wizard to avoid that condition. For more information, see the section titled "Using the Application Setup Wizard."

14. C. Because you added additional files to the setup, and saved it to a template, this implies that you will be generating the same setup again in the future. The easiest modification would be to change the `AppTitle=` line in the template file under the [Flags] section ensuring the title will be preserved for future runs of the Setup Wizard for this application. This would require one change and a rerun of the Setup Wizard. On the other hand, if this had been a "one time" setup, it may be easier to just modify the SETUP.LST file to make the change to the `Title=` line under the [SETUP] section. For more information, see the section titled "Editing the SETUP.LST File."

Answers to Test Yourself Questions at Beginning of Chapter

1. The Application Setup Wizard is the utility provided with Visual Basic 5 that creates a setup program for distributing applications. See "Using the Application Setup Wizard."

2. Any type of Visual Basic project can be used with the Application Setup Wizard. Standard EXE, ActiveX EXE, ActiveX DLL, ActiveX Control, and ActiveX Documents can all be used. See "Using the Application Setup Wizard."

3. The main file parsed by the Setup Wizard is the Visual Basic Project (VBP) file. This file is selected as the first step of the wizard. See "Using the Application Setup Wizard."

4. The very first step to be completed when using the Application Setup Wizard is the selection of the project. A Browse button allows the selection of the Visual Basic Project (VBP) file to be used for creating the setup program. See "Project Selection—Step One."

5. The file that can be customized to alter the files being distributed is the SETUP.LST file. This file provides various sections and file entries that are installed on the target machine. See "Editing the SETUP.LST File."

6. The section that can be used to change the title of the setup program is [Setup]. This section provides the title of the setup program. See "Editing the SETUP.LST File."

7. The three default sections of the SETUP.LST file are [BootStrap], [Files], and [Setup]. These sections are created automatically by the Setup Wizard when the custom setup program is generated. See "Editing the SETUP.LST File."

8. The purpose of the VB5DEP.INI file is to provide the Setup Wizard with a comprehensive list of dependencies and references used by Visual Basic. This information is used by the wizard to ensure that all required files are included for distribution. See "Editing the VB5DEP.INI File."

9. The VB5DEP.INI file can be found in the \VB\SETUPKIT\KITFIL32 directory. The SETUPWIZ.EXE can also be found in this location. See "Editing the VB5DEP.INI File."

10. If the VB5DEP.INI file does not contain the dependency information required for a component, this file can be manually edited. The Setup Wizard can also be used to generate a DEP file for a custom component. This information can be kept in its own file or appended to the VB5DEP.INI. See "Editing the VB5DEP.INI File."

Chapter **25**

Creating a Setup
Program That Installs and
Registers ActiveX Controls

This chapter helps you prepare for the exam by covering the following objectives:

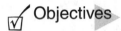 Objectives ▶

▶ Create an installation program for ActiveX Controls

Test Yourself! Before reading this chapter, test yourself to determine how much study time you will need to devote to this section.

1. Visual Basic 5 provides what utility to create a distribution program for ActiveX Controls?

2. Name at least three steps that a setup routine would have to perform when installing ActiveX Controls.

3. When using the Application Setup Wizard, a file with the DEP extension is generated. What is the purpose of this file?

4. The Application Setup Wizard is used to create a setup routine for distributing an application. What is the primary difference between a setup routine for a regular application and an ActiveX Control?

5. When an ActiveX setup routine is going to be distributing a VB License file, what is the destination directory for that file?

6. When distributing an ActiveX Control created with Visual Basic 5, is the VB License file required for distribution?

7. VB5 supports version control. What is the use of version control when developing an ActiveX Control?

8. Where in the Visual Basic 5 IDE are the version control options set?

9. When developing ActiveX DLLs and Controls, a special setting can be specified in the Compile tab of the Project Properties dialog box. What is the base memory address used for when creating these two project types?

10. When two ActiveX DLLs are loaded into an application's memory space, what happens if both components have specified the same base memory address?

Answers are located at the end of the chapter...

Visual Basic 5 enables developers to create ActiveX Controls, which can be used within a VB application or other development environments such as Microsoft Excel.

As part of the distribution strategy for an application, controls used by the application can be distributed either as a part of that application's setup program or as a separate installation routine. Distributing an ActiveX Control with its own setup program provides additional reuse of that component.

An ActiveX Control that provides its own setup routine allows the control to be installed and registered on other computers. Additional benefits include reducing the distribution media size requirements and how many times the control is set up on the same system. With Visual Basic 5's Application Setup Wizard, the control can also be prepared for use in Internet Explorer web pages.

This chapter examines creating a setup program for the distribution of ActiveX Controls. This chapter also covers issues related to the distribution of ActiveX Controls, such as control licensing, version control, and setting a component's Base Memory Address.

This chapter covers the following topics:

- ► Distributing controls
- ► Licensing ActiveX Controls
- ► Versioning of ActiveX Controls
- ► The base memory address of a component

Distributing Controls

After an ActiveX Control has been created with Visual Basic 5, the Application Setup Wizard can be used to create an independent setup program for that control. This enables the developer of the control to effectively distribute the control as part of multiple applications or as a product by itself.

Chapter 24, "Using the Setup Wizard to Create an Effective Setup Program," examined the process and details of creating a setup program. This section details using the Application Setup Wizard to create an installation routine specifically for ActiveX Controls.

Creating a Setup Program

To distribute any type of project, the developer requires an effective installation routine for the application. The setup routine for an ActiveX Control performs the following duties:

▶ Determines whether the installation system meets disk space requirements

▶ Installs ActiveX Control files

▶ Installs ActiveX Control support files

▶ Makes correct Registry entries for all files

▶ Provides an Uninstall routine for removing all installed components

The Application Setup Wizard can be used to assist the developer in creating a program that will identify the requirements for disk space, the control's files, supporting files, and Registry entries. The Setup Wizard also installs an Uninstall program and creates an Installation log for use in removing all installed components.

The Setup Wizard uses a Visual Basic project as the template for creating the setup program. This can be further customized if so desired.

Another very useful function of the Application Setup Wizard is the generation of the dependency file. The wizard will examine the VBP project file created by Visual Basic and will determine all the project references and custom controls that are used. It will also determine the support files required by the selected references and custom controls.

Note

For more information regarding creating a setup program, refer to the following:

► Chapter 24, "Using the Setup Wizard to Create an Effective Setup Program"

► Visual Basic Books Online; using Find, search for "distribution"

► Visual Basic Books Online; using Contents, look under the Programmer's Guide (All Editions), Part 2: What can you do with Visual Basic?, Distributing Your Applications

Creating a Setup Program for ActiveX Controls

Objective

When an ActiveX Control is to be distributed as an independent component, the Application Wizard can be used to create the setup program. The steps are very much the same as for creating a regular setup program. The main difference in the setup program is the registration of a License file, if desired, for using the ActiveX Control in a design environment.

The application developer can enable ActiveX Control licensing in the project. For more information on enabling this feature, see the section "Licensing ActiveX Controls."

During Step Five—Processing, the wizard will generate a message box if a VB License file is found with the ActiveX Control project, as shown in Figure 25.1. This VBL file is generated if licensing support was enabled when the project was compiled.

Figure 25.1

The message box generated by the Application Setup Wizard when a VB License file for an ActiveX Control has been found.

The choice is given to distribute the license and register it on the target system, or to disregard the file. If it is to be distributed, a destination directory must be specified for the License file during the File Summary step, as shown in Figure 25.2. The wizard will then handle making the Registry entry for the ActiveX Control based on the information found in the VBL file. These entries will enable the ActiveX Control to be used within a design environment.

Figure 25.2

Specifying the destination directory for a Visual Basic License file.

If no License file is found, the Setup Wizard will continue as expected for a regular application setup procedure.

When using the Setup Wizard for creating an application, experiment with the options that are available. Many developers rush the distribution program stage of development. Try creating a setup program with licensing support, and without. Take the time to *learn* what options are available with the Setup Wizard. You will have more distribution options available to you for future projects.

In the exercise section of this chapter, an ActiveX Control is created that has licensing support enabled (see Exercise 25.3). Two different setup programs are then created for the ActiveX Control. The first setup routine does not use the License file; the second one does. The CLSID and License sections of the Registry are also examined.

Licensing ActiveX Controls

When an ActiveX Control is installed on a system, you can utilize controls in two different ways. The first use of an ActiveX Control is by an application. The application requests the control and uses the system Registry to determine how to create the control and from which files. The second use of an ActiveX Control is by a developer. The developer can use an ActiveX Control in his or her applications.

Visual Basic 5 provides the capability to take advantage of both types of control use. Licensing support for ActiveX Controls enables developers to have the option of how their controls will be used after they are distributed.

Controls can be distributed without licensing support, which allows the use of the control by both applications and application developers. With licensing support enabled, only applications can use the controls. If an ActiveX Control does not have the correct license entry in the Registry, the control will not be usable in a design environment.

Setting the Licensing Option

Visual Basic provides licensing support for ActiveX Control projects only. The Project Properties dialog box provides the check box Require License Key, as shown in Figure 25.3. A check mark in this box enables licensing support for the control being developed.

Figure 25.3

The General tab of the Project Properties dialog box for an ActiveX Control project, where you can enable licensing support.

After licensing has been enabled, when the ActiveX Control is compiled, a VBL file will be generated in the directory with the

OCX file. The VBL file is a text-based file that contains the Registry entries to be made for the ActiveX Control. The setup routine uses this file to register the license information in the Registry if the ActiveX Control is to be used in a development environment on the target machine.

Applications that use a licensed ActiveX Control have that license compiled internally. This allows the control to be created based on the CLSID found in the system Registry, as shown in Figure 25.4.

 Caution

The REGEDIT utility is a very powerful and dangerous utility for examining and modifying the operating system's Registry. The Registry is a database of support information that is *critical* to applications. Always use REGEDIT with caution. Also, create a backup of the Registry *before* working with it. Both Windows NT and Windows 95 provide utilities for creating backups of the Registry.

Figure 25.4

The CLSID Registry entry for an ActiveX Control.

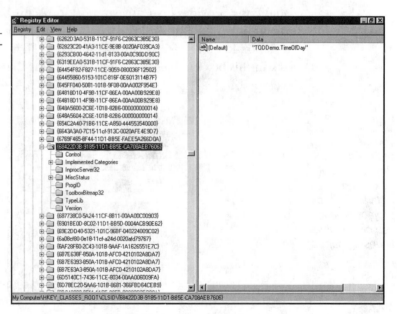

If a licensed ActiveX Control is to be used in a development environment, a reference to the control must be set. This is based on the CLSID information found in the system Registry. When an instance of the control is to be placed on a design object, the License section of the Registry is used to create the control, as shown in Figure 25.5. If no entry exists for the licensed control, a message box indicates that the control cannot be used in the design environment.

Figure 25.5

*The License
Registry entry for
an ActiveX
Control.*

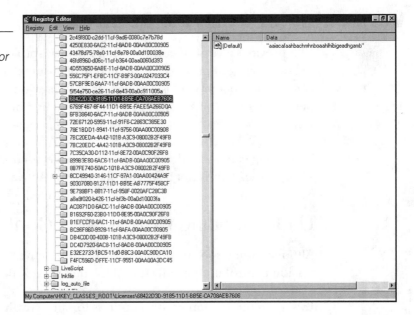

Distributing a License

When an ActiveX Control is to be distributed for use in the development environment, the control license must also be distributed. The Application Setup Wizard will prompt for the action to be taken for distributing the license file after the file dependencies are determined.

If the VB License file is to be distributed by the setup routine, a destination directory must be specified during the File Summary step (refer back to Figure 25.2). The setup program will then register the information in the license section of the Registry. This enables the design-time creation of the distributed ActiveX Control.

Note

When creating ActiveX Controls that utilize licensing, it is best to test the setup routine on two different computers. Ensure that one computer has a development environment that will use the control. Ensure that a different computer has an application that will use the control. This helps to ensure that the ActiveX Control setup program has been properly designed.

Versioning of ActiveX Controls

VB5 provides a version control system to assist programmers with the development process. Version control ensures that new source code added to a project is compatible with previous releases. This helps to reduce the amount of issues that redistribution can cause.

Versioning can be used with all types of projects created with Visual Basic. This is not a specific feature for ActiveX Controls.

Understanding How Version Control Works

Although not a specific feature for creating ActiveX Controls, version control is especially useful for the ActiveX developer.

By setting the version control options for an ActiveX project, compatibility with previously released controls can be ensured. This assists in reducing the amount of recoding required when a new version of the control is released to other applications and developers.

Version control is maintained by having Visual Basic compare the events, methods, and properties supported by the previous control and the one in development. The Binary Compatibility option ensures that any CLSIDs or interface IDs are not changed when the new version of the control is compiled. If new IDs are required, they will then be generated.

Version control also restricts the programmer by limiting the changes that can be made to the previously declared events, methods, and properties. Source code within routines can be modified. However, the arguments and return values they supply cannot be modified. These declarations are considered the interface. If the interface of the control changes, previous applications and source code may not function correctly.

Setting Version Control Options

The version control options of a Visual Basic project can be set through the Project Properties dialog box. The Version Compatibility options can be set under the Component tab, as shown in Figure 25.6. The three options are as follows:

▶ **No Compatibility.** Compatibility will not be enforced for the project. This option is used to create new type library information, class IDs, and interface IDs every time the project is compiled. Other programs that previously used the project cannot use the new version because of the changed references.

▶ **Project Compatibility.** Compatibility will be maintained by keeping only the type library identifier when the component is compiled. This option is useful only in the design environment for testing.

▶ **Binary Compatibility.** Compatibility will be maintained by indicating a compiled component and generating new class IDs and interface IDs as required. Used for "true" compatibility at the distribution level.

Figure 25.6

The Component tab of the Project Properties dialog box for a VB project, where you select the Version Compatibility.

Tip

Setting the version control options while creating a component also reduces any "lost reference" in the test project. When creating an ActiveX DLL, for example, the project that uses the ActiveX DLL must set a reference in the Project, References dialog box. If No Compatibility has been selected, when the ActiveX DLL is recompiled, the reference will change. This is due to the generation of new class IDs and interface IDs created by Visual Basic when this option is used. By using Project or Binary Compatibility, the project with the reference to the ActiveX DLL will not need to have the reference changed.

Base Memory Address of a Component

When ActiveX components are created, including ActiveX Controls, there is a *base memory address* that can be set to further optimize the component. The base memory address is the default address used for loading the component into shared memory.

Understanding How the Base Memory Address Works

When an ActiveX DLL or Control component is loaded into an application's memory space, the base address is used. If this address conflicts with another component that has already been loaded at that location, the new component must be relocated to a different segment of memory. This memory relocation is known as *rebasing* and requires the operating system to slow down the process and perform the calculations required.

After a component has been relocated, or rebased, to another memory address, it is not always accessible to other executables, or processes. Ensuring a unique base memory address for the components you create ensures that your own components will not conflict with one another.

Although an application developer can select a different base memory location in multiples of 64K, this does not ensure that the component will not conflict with another developer's work. This situation can be handled only by dynamic relocation, or re-basing.

Note

One common method of generating a base memory address is to use a random number generator to determine the very first base address to be used. Components developed later are incremented accordingly to the next base address multiple. This helps to ensure uniqueness in your components.

Setting the Base Memory Address

The base memory address of an ActiveX DLL or ActiveX Control project is set in the Project Properties dialog box. The DLL base address is set under the Compile tab, as shown in Figure 25.7.

Figure 25.7

The Compile tab of the Project Properties dialog box for an ActiveX DLL or ActiveX Control project, where you can set the base memory address.

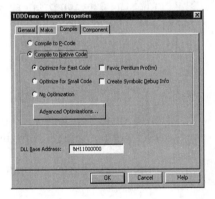

When selecting an address to be used as the base, it must be a multiple of 64K and reside between 16MB and 2GB. The suggested number range is specified using hexadecimal notation. The following is the low address &H1000000 and high address &H80000000. The default project address is &H11000000 (refer to Figure 25.7).

Exercises

Exercise 25.1:   Creating a Simple ActiveX Control with Licensing Support

In this exercise, you create a simple ActiveX Control that displays the current time. The project properties will be set to include licensing support. The control will then be tested in another VB project.

To create this exercise, follow these steps:

1. Create an ActiveX Control project.

2. Change the `Name` property of `UserControl1` to `TimeOfDay`.

3. Add one `Label` control to the form. Place the label in the top-left corner of the `UserControl`.

4. Change the `Name` property of `Label1` to `lblTimeOfDay`.

5. Change the `Caption` property of `lblTimeOfDay` to `99:99:99 PM`. This caption helps to determine the maximum width and height of the `Label` control.

6. Change the `Font` property of `lblTimeOfDay` to `Times New Roman 24 pts`.

7. After the `Font` property has been set, adjust the label to the correct width and height to display the caption.

8. Change the `Alignment` property of `lblTimeOfDay` to `2-Center`.

9. Add one `Timer` control to the form. Place the `Timer` on the right side of `lblTimeOfDay`. It will be invisible at runtime.

10. Change the `Interval` property of `Timer1` to `1000`.

11. Resize the `UserControl` object to remove extra space around the `lblTimeOfDay` label.

12. Open the code window for the `UserControl_Initialize` event procedure and enter the following code:

```
Private Sub UserControl_Initialize()
    lblTimeOfDay.Caption = Format(Time, "Long Time")
End Sub
```

13. Open the code window for the `UserControl_Resize` event procedure and enter the following code:

```
Private Sub UserControl_Resize()
    lblTimeOfDay.Width = UserControl.ScaleWidth
    lblTimeOfDay.Top = (UserControl.ScaleHeight -
    ➥lblTimeOfDay.Height) / 2
End Sub
```

14. Open the code window for the `Timer1_Timer` event procedure and enter the following code:

```
Private Sub Timer1_Timer()
    lblTimeOfDay.Caption = Format(Time, "Long Time")
End Sub
```

15. From the Project menu, choose Project Properties. Options will be set on the General tab.

16. In the Project Name text box, enter `TODDemo`.

17. Enable the check mark for Require License Key, found in the lower-right corner of the General tab.

18. After the Options have been set, close the Project Properties dialog box.

19. Close the UserControl design window and any code windows for the `TODDemo` project. If the design window is not closed, you may encounter errors when trying to test the control in another project.

20. From the File menu, choose Add Project. This will bring up the Add Project dialog box.

continues

Exercise 25.1: Continued

21. Add a Standard EXE project to the Visual Basic environment. You should now have both the TODDemo project and a default Project1.

22. Once added, the new Standard EXE project should be automatically set to the startup project.

23. The toolbox for the new Standard EXE project should have one additional control located at the bottom of the toolbox. The ToolTip will indicate the name of the new control is TimeOfDay.

24. Add one TimeOfDay control to Form1 of Project1.

25. Once on Form1, the TimeOfDay control should be displaying the current time in the center of the control.

26. Resize the control as desired. Notice that the label stays centered as the control is resized in the design environment.

27. If the TimeOfDay control is not functioning correctly, return to the previous steps and ensure the source code is in the correct events. Also double-check property settings and ensure that the ActiveX Control project windows are all closed, but still in the Project Explorer window.

28. Open the TimeOfDay control from the TODDemo project.

29. Save the project in a folder called TODDemo control.

30. Check the contents of the folder TODDemo. Notice that only two files have been saved so far, TimeOfDay.CTL and TODDemo.VBP.

31. From the File menu, choose Make TODDemo.OCX. This will compile the ActiveX Control.

32. Check the contents of the folder TODDemo. Notice the additional files created from compiling: TODDemo.EXP, TODDemo.LIB, TODDemo.OCA, TODDemo.OCX, and TODDemo.VBL.

33. The VBL file is the License file generated when the Require License Key option of the Project Properties has been enabled.

34. Using a text editor, such as NotePad, open the TODDemo.VBL file and exam the entries. These are the samples generated during the creation of this exercise. Yours should differ:

```
REGEDIT
HKEY_CLASSES_ROOT\Licenses = Licensing: Copying the keys may
➥be a violation of established copyrights.
HKEY_CLASSES_ROOT\Licenses\68422D3D-9185-11D1-BB5E-
➥CA708AEB7606 = aaiacafaahbachmhnboaahlhibigeadhgamb
```

35. These are the License Registry entries that will be made for the control if it is to be used in a design environment. Close the text editor when finished.

36. Remove the TODDemo project from the VB environment. When removed, a message box will mention that the project is referenced by another project and ask whether you are sure you want to remove it. Click on Yes.

37. Save Project1 in a folder called Test Project for TODDemo control.

38. From the File menu, choose Make Project1.EXE. This will compile the Standard EXE.

39. Close down the VB environment.

40. Open REGEDIT. Use *caution* when performing the next steps in this exercise. If you are unsure of using the Registry Editor, proceed to the next exercise.

41. From the Edit menu, choose Find. Enter **TODDemo.TimeOfDay**. This will find the Registry entry for the CLSID of the ActiveX Control. This is the sample generated during the making of this exercise. Yours should differ:

continues

Exercise 25.1:   Continued

```
\HKEY_CLASSES_ROOT\CLSID\{68422D3B-9185-11D1-BB5E-
➥CA708AEB7606}
```

42. Open the CLSID by using the plus sign on the left TreeView pane. Select the TypeLib entry for the control. Notice the default value found in the right pane. Write down this value for finding in the next steps. This is the sample generated during the making of this exercise. Yours should differ:

```
(Default)     "{68422D3D-9185-11D1-BB5E-CA708AEB7606}"
```

This is the GUID that is used as part of the License Registry entry for the control.

43. Using the left pane TreeView control, find the License section of the Registry, under HKEY_CLASSES_ROOT\LICENSES and find the TypeLib entry for your control. This is the sample generated during the making of this exercise. Yours should differ:

```
\HKEY_CLASSES_ROOT\Licenses\68422D3D-9185-11D1-BB5E-
➥CA708AEB7606
```

44. Examine the default entry in the right pane. This string value is the second part of the license generated for the control. This value must be present for the control to be generated in a design environment. This is the sample generated during the making of this exercise. Yours should differ:

```
aaiacafaahbachmhnboaahlhibigeadhgamb
```

45. Select the Root of the License key in the left pane. Notice the default value found there. This is usually the same on all systems. These keys are copyright information and should not be manipulated. Changing these values could prevent the use of a control or component.

```
Licensing: Copying the keys may be a violation of
➥established copyrights.
```

46. When finished, close the Registry.

47. If you have another design environment, such as Microsoft Excel, you could try adding the TODDemo control to the design environment. The control should function the same as in the VB environment.

48. With extreme caution, you could also rename the License entry for the control. When you attempt to use it in the design environment, an error message will be generated.

This exercise demonstrated the creation of an ActiveX Control with licensing support enabled. The ActiveX Control was used in another VB project and the system Registry was searched for the control's licensing information.

Exercise 25.2: Creating a Setup Program for Installing and Registering an ActiveX Control

In this exercise, you create a setup program for distributing the ActiveX Control developed in Exercise 25.1. The setup program will install the control for use by applications, but not for design environments. This restriction is enforced by not distributing the control's License file.

To create this exercise, follow these steps:

1. Start the Application Setup Wizard.

2. If the Introduction screen is displayed, press the Next button.

3. Step One—Select Project and Options. Use the Browse button and locate the TODDemo ActiveX Control project created in Exercise 25.1.

4. Still on Step One, under Options select Create a Setup Program and check off Generate Dependency File. Then press the Next button.

5. Step Two—Distribution Method. Select Single Directory.

continues

6. Step Three—Single Directory. Specify the location to place the directory. You can use the C:\WINDOWS\TEMP\SWSETUP default or change the location if desired. Press Next when done.

7. Step Four—ActiveX Server Components. The Setup Wizard should determine that none is used. Press Next to continue.

8. Step Five—Processing. Before this step has completed, a message box should be generated indicating that a License file has been found. You can choose whether the License file should be registered on the end user's machine. For this setup program, select No.

9. Another message box may appear indicating that a Property Page DLL must also be distributed for use of the component in other design environments. For this setup program, you will not distribute that DLL, so select No.

10. Step Six—File Summary. Review all files that have been selected for distribution by the Application Setup Wizard. Notice that the TODDemo.VBL file has not been included in the file listings.

11. Additional support files are indicated in this list. Remember to deselect all references and controls that are not used when you are creating any Visual Basic project. Press Next to continue.

12. Step Seven—Finished. The Setup Wizard settings can be saved as a template at this point, if you desire. Click on Finish to have all files compressed and the wizard will complete.

13. At this point, the setup program for an ActiveX Control has been created. To test the routine, another computer is the best test platform. That system should also have a development environment to test the ActiveX Control.

14. Step One on the other machine would be to run setup and install the ActiveX Control.

15. Step Two would be to test an application, such as `Project1`, that uses the ActiveX Control. This should be a successful use of the control.

16. Step Three would be to test the ActiveX Control in a design environment to ensure that it cannot be used.

This exercise demonstrated using the Application Setup Wizard to create a setup program for an ActiveX Control. The only step that is different for ActiveX Controls is when the wizard determines the files to be processed. A message box will indicate that a VB License file was found and give the option of whether it should be installed on the end user's machine.

Exercise 25.3:   Creating a Setup Program for Installing and Registering an ActiveX Control and Its License

In this exercise, you create a setup program for distributing the ActiveX Control developed in Exercise 25.1. This setup program will install both the control and the license for the control. This will allow the ActiveX Control to be used by both applications and development environments.

To create this exercise, follow these steps:

1. Start the Application Setup Wizard.

2. If the Introduction screen is displayed, press the Next button.

3. Step One—Select Project and Options. Use the Browse button and locate the TODDemo ActiveX Control project created in Exercise 25.1.

4. Still on Step One, under Options select Create a Setup Program and check off Generate Dependency File. Then press the Next button.

continues

Exercise 25.3: Continued

5. Step Two—Distribution Method. Select Single Directory.

6. Step Three—Single Directory. Specify the location to place the directory. You can use the C:\WINDOWS\TEMP\SWSETUP default or change the location if desired. Press Next when done.

7. Step Four—ActiveX Server Components. The Setup Wizard should determine that none is used. Press Next to continue.

8. Step Five—Processing. Before this step has completed, a message box should be generated indicating that a License file has been found. You can choose whether the License file should be registered on the end user's machine.

9. Read the notice at the bottom of the message box. To distribute the VB License file, the File Details button must be used to indicate the destination directory for the License file. For this setup program, select Yes.

10. Step Six—File Summary. Review all files that have been selected for distribution by the Application Setup Wizard. Notice that the TODDemo.VBL file has been included in the file listings for distribution.

11. Select the TODDemo.VBL file and click on the File Details command button.

12. The Default Destination Directory for the License file is (Do Not Install This File). Using the drop-down combo box, select the $(AppPath). This will install the ActiveX Control in the application directory specified by the user.

13. Also notice that the check mark is enabled for the option to Register Contained License Information on the End User's Machine. Click on OK when complete.

14. You should still be at Step Six—File Summary. Additional support files are indicated in this list. Notice the additional file, MsStkPrp.DLL. This is the Property Page DLL support file for ActiveX Controls. This allows the control to be used in design environments other than Visual Basic.

15. Remember to deselect all references and controls that are not used when you are creating any Visual Basic project. Press Next to continue.

16. Step Seven—Finished. The Setup Wizard settings can be saved as a template at this point, if you desire. Click on Finish to have all files compressed and the wizard will complete.

17. At this point, the setup program for an ActiveX Control has been created. To test the routine, another computer is the best test platform. That system should also have a development environment to test the ActiveX Control.

18. Step One on the other machine would be to run setup and install the ActiveX Control.

19. Step Two would be to test an application, such as `Project1`, that uses the ActiveX Control. This should be a successful use of the control.

20. Step Three would be to test the ActiveX Control in a design environment to ensure that it can also be used. This ensures that the license information has been correctly entered into the system Registry.

This exercise demonstrated using the Application Setup Wizard for creating an independent setup program for distribution of ActiveX Controls. This setup program will install not only the ActiveX Control's files and support files, but also will register a license for the control. This license will be in the Registry and allow the ActiveX Control to be used in the design environment.

Review Questions

1. Visual Basic enables developers to create custom ActiveX Controls for use in applications or other design environments. What application is used to create a distribution program for ActiveX Controls?

   A. Application Performance Explorer

   B. Automation Manager

   C. Image Editor

   D. Application Setup Wizard

   E. REGOCX32

2. The Application Setup Wizard is used to create a distribution program for licensed ActiveX Controls. At what point in the wizard do you specify the installation location of the VBL file?

   A. Step One—Select Project and Options

   B. Step Two—Distribution Method

   C. Step Three—Directory Location

   D. Step Five—Processing

   E. Step Six—File Summary

3. The Application Setup Wizard automatically detects a Visual Basic License file. What happens during the creation of a setup routine for an ActiveX Control if no VB License file is found?

   A. You are prompted for the location of the license file.

   B. The Setup Wizard will have to be aborted.

   C. The Setup Wizard will automatically recompile the ActiveX Control and generate a new VB License file.

    D. The Setup Wizard will generate a new VB License file for the ActiveX Control.

    E. Nothing.

4. During the installation of an ActiveX Control, what does the setup program use to register the ActiveX Control for use in a development environment?

    A. The Registry entries in the VBL file

    B. Embedded Registry entries in the ActiveX Control

    C. Registry entries from your development machine

    D. A special REG file generated by the Application Setup Wizard

    E. None of these

5. Visual Basic creates a VBL file when an ActiveX Control is created. What information is contained within the VBL file?

    A. Binary information for the control

    B. Binary information collected from the Registry

    C. Text-based Registry entries for the control

    D. Text-based Registry entries you have entered

    E. Text-based information indicating the installation location for the licensed control

6. Version control can be used to ensure that new distributed applications are compatible with previously distributed applications. What are the three types of version control that can be used when creating an ActiveX Control?

    A. Interface

    B. None

    C. External

    D. Project

    E. Binary

7. Visual Basic provides version control options. Which is the best option to use when ensuring compatibility with previously released controls?

   A. Interface

   B. None

   C. External

   D. Project

   E. Binary

8. What is the purpose of providing the base memory address for a component?

   A. Base memory is the amount of memory required by a component.

   B. To provide the application with the memory location to retrieve the object from another machine.

   C. To provide Internet Explorer with the memory location on the server.

   D. Used as the default address that is used to load a component into shared memory.

   E. None of these.

9. When two components use the same base address, who handles the loading conflict by providing rebasing?

   A. Visual Basic

   B. The operating system

   C. VMM32.OCX

   D. The loading application

   E. The component

10. When setting the base memory address of a component, what is the memory multiple to be used for calculating the new address?

    A. 1GB

    B. 256K

    C. 16K

    D. 64K

    E. 32K

Answers to Review Questions

1. D. The Application Setup Wizard is used for creating a setup program for the distribution of all types of projects created with VB5. For more information, see the section titled "Distributing Controls."

2. E. Step Six—File Summary. This step enables you to select the individual files indicated for distribution. After the VBL file is selected, use the File Details command button to specify the installation location. For more information, see the section titled "Creating a Setup Program for ActiveX Controls."

3. E. Nothing. If the Application Setup Wizard does not detect a VB License file, the wizard will continue with specifying options and creating the distribution program. For more information, see the section titled "Creating a Setup Program for ActiveX Controls."

4. A. The Registry entries in the VBL file. The application setup routine will use the entries in the VBL file created when the control is compiled. The entries will be made only if the license file is distributed with the application, and the option to register license files is selected in the File Details section of the Setup Wizard. For more information, see the section titled "Creating a Setup Program for ActiveX Controls."

5. C. Text-based Registry entries for the control. This text-based file is generated when the control is compiled. The entries are for the system Registry of the target machine. They are used to indicate that the ActiveX Control can be used in a design environment. For more information, see the section titled "Setting the Licensing Option."

6. B, D, E. None, Project, and Binary. All three types of version control can be used when developing ActiveX Controls. For more information, see the section titled "Setting Version Control Options."

7. E. Binary. The binary version control option ensures that the current control is compatible by using the same CLSIDs and interface IDs for the control. If new IDs are required, they will be generated. For more information, see the section titled "Setting Version Control Options."

8. D. Used as the default address that is used to load a component into shared memory. Each component can specify a different base address, which can prevent loading conflicts. For more information, see the section titled "Base Memory Address of a Component."

9. B. The operating system. The rebasing of components whose base memory address conflicts is handled by the operating system. For more information, see the section titled "Understanding How the Base Memory Address Works."

10. D. 64K. When setting the base memory address for a component, multiples of 64K should be used to determine the next loadable address. For more information, see the section titled "Understanding How the Base Memory Address Works."

Answers to Test Yourself Questions at Beginning of Chapter.

1. The utility provided by Visual Basic that creates a distribution program for ActiveX Controls is the Application Setup Wizard. This utility can be used to create an installation routine for all types of projects created with Visual Basic 5. See "Distributing Controls."

2. The most basic steps involved in the installation of an ActiveX Control are to install ActiveX Control files, install ActiveX Control support files, and make correct Registry entries for all files. See "Creating a Setup Program."

3. The DEP file generated by the Application Setup Wizard is known as the project dependency file. This file is used to determine what support files the project references and custom control selections require. This file will list the files to be distributed and which file uses which support file. See "Creating a Setup Program."

4. The main difference between a setup routine created for a regular application and an ActiveX Control is the registration of a VB License file. This registration process creates a special Registry entry in the License section, which enables an ActiveX Control to be used in a design environment. See "Creating a Setup Program for ActiveX Controls."

5. The destination directory for a Visual Basic License file is not specified by default. If the License file will be distributed and registered on the target systems, a destination directory must be explicitly specified. See "Creating a Setup Program for ActiveX Controls."

6. The VB License file is not required when distributing an ActiveX Control. The only time the file is required is if licensing has been enabled and the ActiveX Control is to be used within a development environment. See "Licensing ActiveX Controls."

7. Versioning can be used in the development of ActiveX Controls to ensure that the current control is compatible with previously released controls. See "Versioning of ActiveX Controls."

8. Version control options are set in the Project Properties dialog box, under the Component tab. See "Setting Version Control Options."

9. The Base Memory Address option is used to specify the default memory address that the component is loaded into when called by an application. See "Base Memory Address of a Component."

10. The result of loading two ActiveX DLLs into the same base memory address is known as rebasing. Rebasing is a dynamic relocation of the component into another memory address location. This reduces the performance of the application while the component is being rebased by the operating system. See "Understanding How the Base Memory Address Works."

Chapter
26
Managing the
Windows System Registry

This chapter helps you prepare for the exam by covering the following objectives:

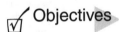
Objectives

- ▶ Use the `GetSetting` function and the `SaveSetting` statement to save application-specific information in the Registry

- ▶ Register components by using the Regsvr32.exe utility

- ▶ Register components by using the Remote Automation Connection Manager.

- ▶ Edit the Registry manually

- ▶ Register a component automatically

Test Yourself! Before reading this chapter, test yourself to determine how much study time you will need to devote to this section.

1. What is the difference between a ProgID and a CLSID?

2. Which executables can be used to register a remote automation component?

3. Name some valid sub-keys of an ActiveX component's CLSID in HKEY_CLASSES_ROOT?

4. What is the purpose of the VBR file?

5. What is the purpose of a GUID?

6. Another developer has asked you for help with an installation problem. He has just installed a program for a user by copying all the files for the program off the user's hard drive on to the user's disc. They receive an error, `ActiveX component can't create object`, when they run it. What is the problem, and how can you fix it?

7. You need to get a large quantity of information out of the Registry in one call. Which function will help you do this?

8. You see a large number of duplicate entries for your ActiveX Objects in the Registry. What could have caused this?

Answers are located at the end of the chapter...

This chapter examines the use of the Registry in Visual Basic. The Registry is an important collection of information about the computer, the software installed on it, and the active user. It consists of a number of files that act as a single logical database of information. The System Registry stores machine-specific information, such as the names and locations of all installed ActiveX Objects on a computer. It also stores user-specific information, such as preferred background colors and window positions. Creation of ActiveX Objects makes changes in the Registry to allow programs to create those objects. VB programs can also read and write information to the Registry to track user preferences or application-specific information.

This chapter covers management of the System Registry in the following sections:

▶ What is the System Registry?

▶ Class information stored in the System Registry

▶ Registering controls—automatically

▶ Registering controls—manually

▶ Storing information in the System Registry

Understanding the System Registry

Any operating system must keep track of information about the computer, the programs available, and (ideally) user preferences. In older versions of DOS and Windows, this information was stored in a variety of files. Some of these files were AUTOEXEC.BAT, CONFIG.SYS, and various INI files. This served the purpose of allowing for configuration and some user preferences. However, the following were some problems with using these files:

> ▶ **Accessibility.** The files are plain ASCII files. They could be viewed or edited with any text editor, such as Notepad. This meant that users could corrupt them with invalid information.

- ► **Security.** There was no way to limit access of users to confidential information.

- ► **Information.** Only textual information could be stored in these files; binary information could not be stored. In addition, only one value could be stored per item.

- ► **Centralization.** The information was scattered throughout the hard drive.

- ► **Individualization.** There was no easy way to have many users sharing a computer, all having different settings.

The System Registry was developed to solve many of these problems. Before looking at how those problems have been solved, it is important to look at what the Registry is. Depending on what version of Windows you are running, the System Registry may be viewed with one of two programs. Under Windows 95, this program is Regedit.exe; under Windows NT 4, there are Regedit.exe and Regedt32.exe. Previous versions of Windows NT only had Regedt32.exe. The two programs display the same information, but in slightly different ways, as shown in Figures 26.1 and 26.2.

Note

Under Windows NT, it is actually useful to use both Regedit.exe and Regedt32.exe. Regedit.exe enables you to do full text searches through the Registry, enabling you to find information that might otherwise elude you. Regedt32.exe is better at connecting to network registries. It is also the only way to access the security applied to the various values in the Registry and to create certain types of Registry keys.

Caution

Always use extreme caution when working in the System Registry. Changes to the Registry can cause software to fail or prevent Windows from initializing properly. Only make changes to the Registry when directed by a service professional, after first making a complete backup of all information in the Registry.

Figure 26.1

An example of the Regedit.exe file.

Figure 26.2

An example of the Regedt32.exe file.

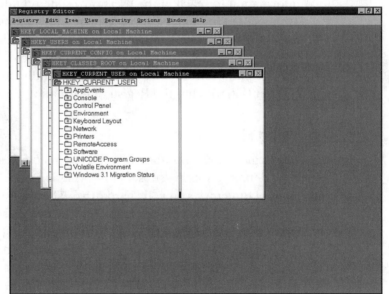

Ways of Storing Information

Windows NT and Windows 95 store the Registry information in slightly different ways. Under Windows 95, this information is stored in two files: USER.DAT (user information, including

HKEY_CURRENT_USER) and SYSTEM.DAT (system information, including HKEY_LOCAL_MACHINE). These files are normally stored in \Windows; however, this can be changed. Windows NT stores the files for the Registry in the \winnt\system32\config directory. The files at this location include the following:

▶ **SAM.** Short for Security Account Manager. This is the listing of valid user and group accounts on this system.

▶ **SECURITY.** The security database for the computer, storing the permission and user rights for any files or resources on this computer.

▶ **SOFTWARE.** Configuration information for the software installed on the computer.

▶ **SYSTEM.** Device driver and hardware information.

Information for each of the users on a system under Windows NT 4 is actually stored in a directory named for that user. This directory is located under the \winnt\profiles subdirectory. For a user, "John Doe" with a UserID of "jdoe", for example, there will be a directory at \winnt\profiles\jdoe. Inside that directory is a file, NTUser.Dat, which is the Registry information for that user.

Using Hives

The Registry has a number of sections, called hives. Each of these hives defines a specific subset of information, much like the highest level directories on your hard drive. The hives have names beginning with the characters HKEY. The two most important of these hives are HKEY_LOCAL_MACHINE and HKEY_CURRENT_USER. The information stored in HKEY_LOCAL_MACHINE describes the computer, operating system, and installed software. The information in HKEY_CURRENT_USER describes the user-specific settings.

Each hive is divided into many sets of keys. These keys are divisions of information in the hive, just as directories are divisions of information on a hard drive. In addition, like directories, keys are further divided into sub-keys. Finally, at the base of each of the trees of sub-keys, are the values stored in the Registry. Each value has three parts. The value has a name that uniquely identifies it in that sub-key. The value has a type that defines the type of information it can store. Finally, there is the value itself.

Information Types

The Registry can store a variety of information other than simple text. Some of the information types available include the following:

► **REG_SZ.** An ordinary string value. The name is due to the origin of the Registry in C programming. The "REGISTRY" part of the name defines it as a Registry type. The "SZ" means: "String, Zero terminated," the default string type in the C programming language.

► **REG_MULTI_SZ.** A set of string values. This is useful when a single key may be associated with many entries (for example, a list of programs to run on startup). This datatype is only available under Windows NT when using Regedt32.

► **REG_EXPAND_SZ.** A normal string value that also allows for replacement of variables with values specific to the machine. These are usually used with the %SystemRoot% and %WindowsRoot% variables. When the value is read, it is replaced with the actual values for the Windows root directory or the Windows\System root directory. This datatype is only available under Windows NT when using Regedt32.

► **REG_DWORD.** A 32-bit unsigned integer. The name is derived from the fact that it is a "Double word," a word being two bytes, or a 16-bit unsigned integer. These are useful for storing any numeric data (for example, a bitmask that may hold a variety of configuration information in compressed format).

► **REG_BINARY.** An arbitrary string of bytes. This is useful for any information (for example, a license key that is important to store in its original non-readable format).

As stated earlier, HKEY_LOCAL_MACHINE stores information about your computer and the software installed on it. Under HKEY_LOCAL_MACHINE is the information about the drivers that need to be loaded, services that should be run (under NT), and program-specific settings. All the users on a system share this information.

HKEY_CURRENT_USER stores information about the user preferences. Typically, any time you change a setting for a program in an Options dialog box, this information is stored in the Registry. Under Windows NT, and under Windows 95 when user profiles have been turned on, each user has an individual set of preferences.

Solving INI File Problems

As described earlier, a number of problems exist with the older INI file configuration style. The Registry solves these problems in the following ways:

▶ **Access.** Registry information is stored in binary format in the Registry files. This prevents users from casually editing the information.

▶ **Security.** The information in the Registry is secure in two ways. In both Windows 95 and NT, the information is secured by the fact that it is stored in a binary file, and that the editors for these files (Regedit.exe and Regedt32.exe) are not apparent to the users. Under Windows NT, this security can be enhanced by applying restrictions to specific keys or values, defining who has the rights to view or change any setting in the Registry.

▶ **Information.** As shown previously, the Registry can now store a variety of string, numeric, or binary data.

▶ **Centralization.** The information about the computer is now stored in a limited number of files. All this information is contained in a single logical format, editable by one program: Regedit.exe (or Regedt32.exe in Windows NT).

▶ **Individualization.** Each user can have his or her own set of configuration settings for all programs. Thus, a number of users can share the same computer without having to reconfigure the system for their preferences each time they log on.

The System Registry is a vital storehouse of information. Windows NT and Windows 95 store and read information from the Registry to find out information about the devices installed, programs loaded, and user preferences. It is also of extreme importance for performing any OLE programming because all class information is stored in the System Registry.

Storing Class Information in the System Registry

One of the most important (and oldest) uses for the Registry is the storage and tracking of information about the installed objects on the computer. This allows for the creation of objects as you have seen in earlier chapters. This information is stored in HKEY_LOCAL_MACHINE\SOFTWARE\Classes. Because it is an important set of information, another hive points directly to this key. This is the HKEY_CLASSES_ROOT hive. This acts as a shortcut when accessing this information. All information required to locate and execute the objects installed on a computer is located under HKEY_CLASSES_ROOT (see Figure 26.3) or HKEY_LOCAL_MACHINE\SOFTWARE\Classes.

HKEY_CLASSES_ROOT contains the same types of information that was associated with the Registry in Windows 3.1. Three main types of entries are found under HKEY_CLASSES_ROOT. The first is file extension associations. After the file extension associations, there are a number of named objects. Finally, an important set of entries falls under the CLSID key.

ProgID

The named objects are the ProgIDs of the objects installed on the computer. A ProgID is a Programmatic Identifier. This ProgID is a friendly name for the object. Figure 26.4 shows the ProdID for the

Microsoft Common Dialog Control. This is the name usually used when creating a copy of an object in a program. If you create a Public class (`clsMyClass`) in an ActiveX DLL called `TestObject`, for example, the ProgID will be `TestObject.clsMyClass`. Under each ProgID key is a sub-key that identifies the object to the operating system. This is the CLSID, or CLASS Identifier.

Figure 26.3

*The HKEY_
CLASSES_ROOT
hive of the
Registry.*

Figure 26.4

*ProgID entry for
Microsoft Com-
mon Dialog
Control.*

CLSID

The CLSID is an example of a value known as a GUID, or Globally Unique IDentifier. It is called a globally unique identifier because no two ActiveX Objects should ever be given the same GUID. A GUID is a unique 128-bit value assigned to that object on creation. This value is normally written as a 32-byte hexadecimal string. The Microsoft Common Dialog control is assigned the GUID F9043C85-F6F2-101A-A3C9-08002B2F49FB, for example, as shown in Figure 26.5.

Figure 26.5

CLSID entry for Microsoft Common Dialog Control.

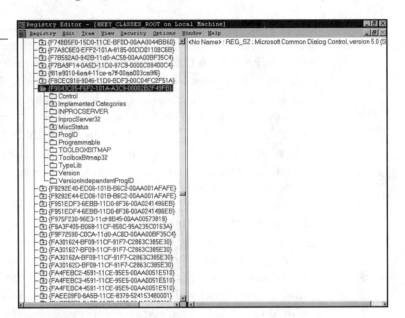

The CLSID allows the operating system to locate the EXE or DLL file that actually contains the code for the object. This information, along with much more, is stored in the various keys and values under the CLSID. The sub-keys normally found under the CLSID include the following:

▶ `InprocServer32` (for ActiveX DLLs)

▶ `LocalServer32` (for ActiveX EXEs)

▶ `Control` (for ActiveX Controls)

▶ `Programmable`

▶ ToolboxBitmap32 (for ActiveX Controls)

▶ TypeLib

▶ InprocHandler32

▶ ProgID

▶ Version

▶ AppID

The most important of these entries are the LocalServer32 and the InprocServer32. The value associated with these keys identifies the EXE or DLL file containing the source for the object. The Microsoft Common Dialog Control is contained in the file comdlg32.ocx, for example, so this is what is listed for its InprocServer32. ActiveX EXEs will have an entry for LocalServer32. The value for this key will be the full path and filename to the EXE. ActiveX DLLs have an InprocServer32 key, which is short for "in-process server." The value for this key will be the full path and filename for the DLL.

Sub-keys such as Control and Programmable are used by the operating system when the user is browsing the entries in the Registry. When you choose Components from the Project menu to add a new control to your project, VB5 looks through the Registry to find all the entries with the sub-key Control. The dialog box presented to you lists these controls. The Programmable key serves much the same purpose, but for the References list. In addition, for controls, the ToolboxBitmap32 sub-key identifies the file and the location in that file for the bitmap used by VB5 and other environments.

The TypeLib key defines the location of the Type Library for this object. The Type Library is the listing of all the properties, methods, events, and sub-objects of this object. This is the information displayed in the Object Browser for this object. The InprocHandler32 key identifies the DLL that services Automation accesses. For local programs, this is always OLE32.DLL. The ProgID is used as a pointer back to the listing of the programmatic identifier elsewhere in the Registry. Finally, the Version key is used to determine whether a setup program should overwrite this control.

If you are using Remote Automation or DCOM, there may be other entries as well. For Remote Automation or DCOM, the `LocalServer32` is replaced with `_LocalServer32`. This prevents programs from accessing the local copy of the ActiveX Object. Remote Automation adds other keys, such as `AuthenticationLevel` and `NetworkAddress`. These are used to locate the appropriate server for the object. Finally, the `AppID` key identifies the application for DCOM. This points to another key under HKEY_CLASSES_ROOT that contains information on the server hosting the DCOM component.

Registering Controls—Automatically

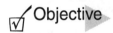 Normally, VB5 handles the registration of new ActiveX Objects automatically, as shown in Table 26.1. Running, compiling, or installing a project containing ActiveX Objects will normally register those objects.

Table 26.1

Automatically Registering Controls	
Action	Effect on the Registry
ActiveX Objects executed in VB5 editor	A temporary GUID created to register the ActiveX Objects.
ActiveX Objects are compiled into an EXE or DLL	A permanent GUID written to the Registry.
ActiveX Objects are installed using a distribution package such as one created by the Setup Wizard (see Chapter 24, "Using the Setup Wizard to Create an Effective Setup Program")	The installation package creates entries in the Registry for the new ActiveX Object.

Temporary Registration

Running a project containing an ActiveX Object in the VB5 IDE creates a temporary GUID. The ProgID is registered, with the CLSID sub-key as normal. However, the CLSID points at the VB5.EXE file as its `LocalServer32`. This identifies the VB5 IDE as the object that will respond to any object attempting to automate this object. It is in fact acting as a proxy for the actively running object. The temporary GUID is otherwise the same as a normal ProgID/CLSID entry pair. The GUID is destroyed when the project containing the ActiveX Objects is ended.

Compiling

When an ActiveX EXE or ActiveX DLL is compiled, the GUID for this object is permanently written to the Registry. The ProgID will be a combination of the project and class names. If the project was called TestObject and one of the publicly available classes was `Class1`, for example, the ProgID would be `TestObject.Class1`. Each publicly available class in the project will have a ProgID created.

Each of the ProgIDs generated for an ActiveX Object will be associated with a unique CLSID. The `InprocServer32` (for ActiveX DLLs) or `LocalServer32` (for ActiveX EXEs) sub-key of this CLSID will point to the compiled EXE or DLL. Other sub-keys will also be generated as described previously.

When you create an ActiveX EXE or DLL for the first time and compile it, the GUID is stored in the Registry. Later compilations may create a new GUID, however. This is determined by the types of changes you make to the object under development, as well as the current setting in the Compatibility settings in the Project Options dialog box. Compatibility can be set to be one of the following:

- ▶ **No compatibility.** Every time you compile this object, it will get a new CLSID. This can lead to a great deal of duplication in the Registry because old ProgIDs and CLSIDs are not removed. They must be manually removed.

▶ **Project compatibility.** This is the default compatibility setting for ActiveX Objects. It acts like no compatibility when you are creating actual objects. However, when used in the VB5 IDE, the Type Library information is maintained. This enables you to continue to use test programs in the same project or project group.

▶ **Binary compatibility.** This is true compatibility. A new CLSID will only be generated if necessary. This will only be necessary if the structure of the ActiveX Object changes fundamentally (for example, if the Class name changes). To use this, however, you need a stable reference copy of the object to compare with.

To avoid multiple CLSIDs for an ActiveX Object, compile the first time with Project compatibility. After the structure of the ActiveX Object has stabilized, set the compatibility to Binary compatibility, and point the reference copy at a previously compiled version of your ActiveX Object.

Using the Setup Wizard

One of the most important reasons for using the Setup Wizard is to register ActiveX Objects. During the installation of a program, the Setup Wizard can be used to register the program itself or any ActiveX Objects that will be used by the program. This is done for those ActiveX Objects that are self-registerable. This happens in the last phase of the installation, after all files have been copied to the hard drive.

For an ActiveX EXE to be considered self-registerable, it must support the use of the command-line parameters, /RegServer and /UnRegServer. When /RegServer is passed to the ActiveX EXE during installation, it writes its Registry information. All ActiveX EXEs created by VB5 recognize this command-line parameter. Similarly, when an ActiveX EXE is uninstalled, /UnRegServer removes any Registry information for the object.

For an ActiveX DLL to be considered self-registerable, it must have two functions exported. Exported functions are those functions the DLL exposes to the outside world. The Setup Wizard calls these functions during installation. `DLLRegisterServer` is called to insert Registry information for the object. `DLLUnRegisterServer` removes the Registry information for the object.

Compiling and Distributing Remote Automation/DCOM Clients

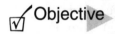 **Objective**

The Enterprise edition of VB5 includes the capability of creating distributed applications. This is done in one of two ways: Remote Automation and DCOM (see Figure 26.6).

Figure 26.6

Remote Automation and DCOM configuration.

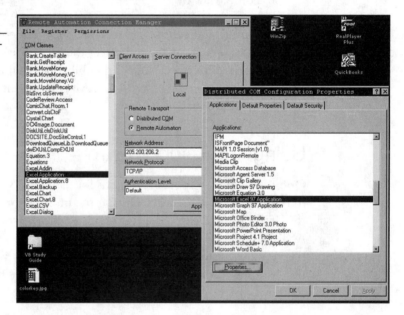

Remote Automation

Remote Automation is a technology that originated with VB4. It allows one ActiveX Object to call another on a different computer. This is done via a pair of proxy agents, one on the client and one on the server. The ActiveX Object on the client computer does not directly communicate with the ActiveX Server. Instead, a proxy DLL (autprx32.dll) receives the Automation request. This proxy DLL then looks up information in the Registry to identify the computer, protocol, and security mechanism to communicate with the actual ActiveX Server. This Registry information is stored in keys under the CLSID key for the ActiveX Objects, and includes the following keys:

- ▶ **NetworkAddress.** The name or network address for the server computer.

- ▶ **ProtocolSequence.** The RPC (Remote Procedure Call) protocol or protocols to be used for the communication (for example, ncacn_ip_tcp for communication across TCP).

- ▶ **AuthenticationLevel.** The type of security used for the communication.

The proxy DLL then uses this information to pass the request on to a proxy program running on the server. This program is the Remote Automation Connection Manager (AUTMGR32.EXE). It receives the Automation request and passes it to the real ActiveX Object. Any response from the ActiveX Object is then passed back through the chain to the client.

DCOM

DCOM (Distributed Common Object Model) is a newer communication mechanism developed as an extension to COM (Common Object Model). COM is the communication mechanism for OLE/ActiveX. DCOM is built into Windows NT 4 and is available as a download for Windows 95. It allows for more transparent communication between ActiveX Objects on remote computers than using Remote Automation. With DCOM, the proxying of the Automation request is handled by the OLE subsystem itself. The only information required is the remote server that will receive the request. Security is configured on that server by using dcomcnfg.exe.

Creating and Registering a Remote Server

To allow a program to be automated remotely (using either Remote Automation or DCOM), it must be compiled and registered as a remote server. To compile an ActiveX Object as a remote server, check the Remote Server Files check box on the Component page of the Project Properties dialog box, as seen in Figure 26.7.

Figure 26.7

Identifying the project as a remote server.

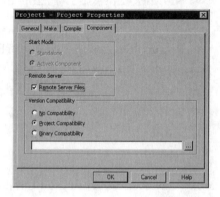

Note that this check box is only available for projects that contain at least one public class module. Compiling the project creates an additional file. This file is named with <Projectname>.VBR extension. It contains the Registry information required to identify this server as well as the intermediate DLLs used. Here is an example of a VBR file:

```
VB5SERVERINFO
VERSION=2.0.1
APPDESCRIPTION=F1 Group message logger
HKEY_CLASSES_ROOT\Typelib\{9313419E-666F-11D0-96AD-
➥00A0C91ED471}\d.0 = F1 Group message logger
HKEY_CLASSES_ROOT\Typelib\{9313419E-666F-11D0-96AD-
➥00A0C91ED471}\d.0\0\win32 = Logger.dll
HKEY_CLASSES_ROOT\Typelib\{9313419E-666F-11D0-96AD-
00A0C91ED471}\d.0\FLAGS = 0
```

```
HKEY_CLASSES_ROOT\F1Logger.Logger\CLSID = {2457C847-C7AD-11D0-
➥9767-00802965DCEE}
HKEY_CLASSES_ROOT\CLSID\{2457C847-C7AD-11D0-9767-
➥00802965DCEE}\ProgID = F1Logger.Logger
HKEY_CLASSES_ROOT\CLSID\{2457C847-C7AD-11D0-9767-
➥00802965DCEE}\Version = d.0
HKEY_CLASSES_ROOT\CLSID\{2457C847-C7AD-11D0-9767-
➥00802965DCEE}\Typelib = {9313419E-666F-11D0-96AD-00A0C91ED471}
HKEY_CLASSES_ROOT\CLSID\{2457C847-C7AD-11D0-9767-
➥00802965DCEE}\LocalServer32 = Logger.dll
HKEY_CLASSES_ROOT\INTERFACE\{2457C846-C7AD-11D0-9767-
➥00802965DCEE} = Logger
HKEY_CLASSES_ROOT\INTERFACE\{2457C846-C7AD-11D0-9767-
➥00802965DCEE}\ProxyStubClsid = {00020420-0000-0000-C000-
➥000000000046}
HKEY_CLASSES_ROOT\INTERFACE\{2457C846-C7AD-11D0-9767-
➥00802965DCEE}\ProxyStubClsid32 = {00020420-0000-0000-C000-
➥000000000046}
HKEY_CLASSES_ROOT\INTERFACE\{2457C846-C7AD-11D0-9767-
➥00802965DCEE}\Typelib = {9313419E-666F-11D0-96AD-00A0C91ED471}
HKEY_CLASSES_ROOT\INTERFACE\{2457C846-C7AD-11D0-9767-
➥00802965DCEE}\Typelib\"version" = d.0
```

After the ActiveX Object is ready, the Setup Wizard can create a setup package that allows the object to be remotely automated. Remove any such objects from the list of local servers and add them as remote servers. Select the VBR file created when the project was compiled. This step in the Setup Wizard should appear similar to Figure 26.8. For Remote Automation, all information needs to be completed; for DCOM, on the other hand, only the server name needs to be filled in. If this information is not completed during the Setup Wizard, the user will be prompted for it during the install.

Figure 26.8

Setting up Remote Automation in the Setup Wizard.

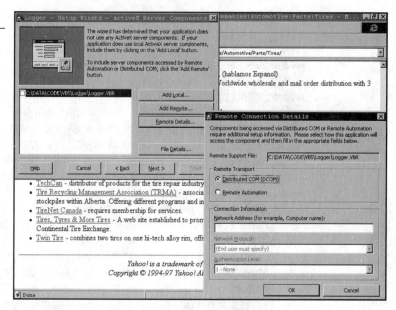

Registering Controls—Manually

 **Objective**

Manual registration of an ActiveX Object may be necessary if it does not register itself automatically. In addition, previously registered objects may need to be removed. Uninstalling ActiveX Objects from the Registry can be a manual process.

ActiveX EXE Files

VB5-created ActiveX EXE files are self-registerable, as described previously in the section on automatic registration. As such, they all recognize two command-line switches: /RegServer and /UnRegServer. Executing the ActiveX EXE with /RegServer on the command line will add the information for the ActiveX EXE into the Registry. Executing the ActiveX EXE with /UnRegServer on the command line will remove the information. This is useful during uninstallation of a component.

ActiveX DLL Files

Obviously, you cannot register an ActiveX DLL just by executing it. Another program is required to register the ActiveX DLL.

That program is regsvr32.exe. Regsvr32.exe runs the `DLLRegisterServer` function in the ActiveX DLL that loads the information into the Registry. It is supplied on the VB5 CD, in the \Tools\RegUtils directory. This executable is used to register any ActiveX DLL that supplies the `DllRegisterServer` function. These DLLs are termed self-registerable. You run the regsvr32 executable, and pass the name of the DLL to register on the command line. If the registration works, you should be presented with a dialog box, as in Figure 26.9. Examining the Registry will show the entries for the DLL are loaded.

Figure 26.9

Successful registration of an ActiveX DLL.

Unloading the Registry information is the same. Run the regsvr32 executable, passing the name of the DLL to unregister and "/u" on the command line. For example:

```
regsvr32 MyDLL.DLL /u
```

This executes the `DLLUnRegisterServer` function in the DLL, removing the Registry information and displaying the message box in Figure 26.10.

Figure 26.10

Successful unregistration of an ActiveX DLL.

There is a second command-line parameter available with regsvr32. If the "/s" parameter is used, no message boxes will be presented on registration or de-registration. This would be useful when installing controls on a machine where there would be no user to clear the dialog box, or as part of an installation program.

If you de-register a control, it is no longer available for automation. It will not appear in the References list in VB. In addition, any programs that use this DLL will fail when they attempt to create an object defined in the DLL. This leads to the trappable run-time error 429, as shown in Figure 26.11.

Figure 26.11

Error creating unregistered object.

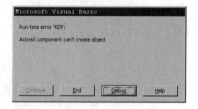

ActiveX Control Files

An ActiveX Control file is a special case of an ActiveX DLL. It is loaded into memory in the same way as an ActiveX DLL, but it also has a visual aspect. As far as the Registry is concerned, the two are also similar. However, an ActiveX Control requires certain extra sub-keys to be available under its CLSID. These extra sub-keys include the following:

> ▶ Control The most important of the sub-keys. This identifies this object as an ActiveX Control. Objects with this sub-key are listed in dialog boxes used to insert ActiveX Controls in various host programs, such as VB5.

> ▶ ToolboxBitmap32 Identifies the source and location of the bitmap used by any host program to display this control in its tool palette.

Therefore, registration of an ActiveX Control must also insert these sub-keys. This is done with the regocx32.exe program. This program can be found on the VB5 CD-ROM in the \Tools\RegUtils subdirectory.

Registering an ActiveX Control with regocx32 is a simple matter. Run regocx32 and pass the name of the OCX as a command-line parameter. Unfortunately, regocx32 does not have an option to unregister an ActiveX Control.

Remote Server Files

Manual registration of remote server files is similar to the automatic registration. Before you can manually register a remote ActiveX Object, the VBR file for the object must be created. This VBR file contains the information necessary for the correct functioning of the remote server. Create this VBR file as described in the automatic registration, listed previously.

The actual manual installation of a Remote Automation or DCOM server can be done with a utility called clireg32.exe. This utility is installed with the Enterprise edition of VB5, under the CliSvr directory.

Note

> The clireg32.exe utility is only available for users of the Enterprise edition of VB5.

Clireg32 allows for the registration of objects as either Remote Automation or DCOM servers. It is a command-line utility and each of the parameters required for either DCOM or Remote Automation are set with various command-line parameters. If any of these parameters are skipped, dialog boxes will prompt for the missing information. Table 26.2 lists some of these parameters.

Table 26.2

Command-Line Parameters for CliReg32

Parameter	Purpose
-s <Network Address>	Identifies the remote server for the ActiveX Objects
-p <Protocol>	Identifies the protocol for communication (Remote Automation only)
-a <security level>	Identifies the security level for the communication (Remote Automation only)
-t <typelib file>	Identifies the TypeLib file
-d	Register the ActiveX Objects for DCOM
-u	Uninstall the object
-q	No dialogs presented

The command line should also include the VBR file. This will load the appropriate Registry information for Remote Automation or DCOM.

Storing Information in the System Registry

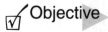 Objective ▶   VB5 adds functionality that allows for saving information about a program in the Registry. This can be useful to save user settings or preferences about your program. This functionality is in the form of a number of VB5 functions and statements, as shown in Table 26.3.

Table 26.3

Registry Functions Available in VB5	
Function	**Purpose**
GetSetting	Allows for the reading of previously saved values for a given key.
SaveSetting	Allows for the creation of new sub-keys and values. In addition, this statement can update existing values for a given key.
DeleteSetting	Removes a single value or sub-key from a given key.
GetAllSettings	Returns all the sub-keys and their associated values from a given key.

This information gets stored in a sub-key of HKEY_CURRENT_USER\Software\VB and VBA Settings (see Figure 26.12). As it is stored under HKEY_CURRENT_USER, this information is independent of any other user's information, when there is more than one user profile.

SaveSetting

SaveSetting is used to create or change Registry settings. If the key does not exist before the first call to SaveSetting, it will be created. If it does exist, the value associated with the key will be changed. The SaveSetting routine has the following syntax:

SaveSetting AppName, Section, Key, Setting

The first two parameters are the same for each of the Setting routines:

AppName is the sub-key under HKEY_CURRENT_USER\ Software\VB and VBA Settings that will be used. This is analogous to the individual INI files you may have used in the past.

Section is a sub-key that, analogous to the sections in an INI file, enables you to break down the information in the Registry further.

Figure 26.12

VB and VBA Program Settings in the Registry.

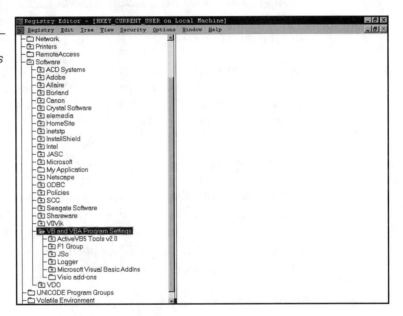

A program called "MyProgram", for example, could have the following sections:

▶ **Window.** Defining the positioning of the main window on the screen

▶ **Directory.** Defining the default directory for saving files or that will be used for user files

▶ **Plug-ins.** Defining the add-on programs installed later

▶ Any other data you may want to keep persistent for each user, such as colors or last file opened

Breaking down the information in the Registry like this enables you to more easily find the configuration information later.

The last two parameters are described as follows:

Key is the actual item you are saving information for, such as WindowHeight, DefaultPath, or Plugin1.

Setting is the parameter that is the value to be saved.

Each individual value needs to be saved one at a time. Therefore if you needed to save (for example) the position of the main window for your program for later use, this could be accomplished with the following code:

```
SaveSetting "MyApp", "Window Section", "Left", Me.Left
SaveSetting "MyApp", "Window Section", "Top", Me.Top
SaveSetting "MyApp", "Window Section", "Width", Me.Width
SaveSetting "MyApp", "Window Section", "Height", Me.Height
```

GetSetting

GetSetting is a function that retrieves information from the Registry. The function allows for a default value that will be returned if the information requested does not exist. Thus, information will be returned even if the key has not been created. The syntax of the GetSetting function is as follows:

```
GetSetting(AppName, Section, Key[, default])
```

The AppName, Section, and Key parameters are the same as for the SaveSetting statement. The default parameter is optional. If used, it will be returned if either the Key or the Section does not exist. If there is no default, a null string ("") will be returned. To recover the window positioning information stored in the preceding example for SaveSetting, you could put the following in the Load event of the form:

```
Me.Left = GetSetting("MyApp", "Window Section", "Left", 0)
Me.Top = GetSetting("MyApp", "Window Section", "Top", 0)
Me.Width = GetSetting("MyApp", "Window Section", "Width", 3600)
Me.Height = GetSetting("MyApp", "Window Section", "Height", 3600)
```

Tip

Including a default for all your calls to `GetSetting` can help prevent errors. If there is no default, an empty string will be returned. This can lead to errors if you are attempting to set the value of a numeric variable. If you pass the value returned from `GetSetting` directly to a numeric variable, you should include a reasonable default.

DeleteSetting

The `DeleteSetting` statement removes specific keys or entire sections from the Registry. The syntax for this command is as follows:

```
DeleteSetting AppName, Section[, Key]
```

The values for the parameters are as described previously for `SaveSetting` and `GetSetting`.

If there is a value for the key parameter, only that key and its associated setting will be deleted. If there is no key listed, however, the entire section will be deleted. To delete the entire section from the preceding examples, you could use the following code:

```
DeleteSetting "MyApp", "Window Section"
```

Caution

It should go without saying that `DeleteSetting` can be a dangerous routine to call.

If the section or the key does not exist, no error occurs.

The `DeleteSetting` statement is useful in a number of situations. You may have released a new version of your program, for example, that has organized its Registry information in a different way. You could use `DeleteSetting` to clean up the older keys to avoid confusion. Another possible use for the `DeleteSetting` could be if you are using a Registry setting as a simple locking mechanism for a file or other resource. You could place a setting identifying the user that has that file in use. When the user is done using it, you could delete that key, allowing others to open the file.

GetAllSettings

The GetAllSettings function is similar to the GetSetting function. Rather than getting a single Key/Setting pair, however, GetAllSettings returns all the Key/Setting pairs in the section. This can be useful when there are a number of related entries or a large number of entries to process. A single hard drive read returns all the entries rather than one for each entry. You are, of course, responsible for dealing with the results. This is made easier by the fact that the GetAllSettings function returns the keys and their associated settings in a two-dimensional array of values: If the section does not exist, GetAllSettings will return an empty variant.

GetAllSettings(AppName, Section)

To read a series of "Most Recently Used Files" from a section in the Registry called "Registry Exercise", for example, you could do the following:

```
Dim vntRegInfo As Variant
Dim I As Integer, J As Integer
vntRegInfo = GetAllSettings("Registry Exercise", "MRU List")
For I = LBound(vntRegInfo, 1) To UBound(vntRegInfo, 1)
    For J = LBound(vntRegInfo, 2) To UBound(vntRegInfo, 2)
        MsgBox vntRegInfo(I, J)
    Next
Next
```

This displays each of the keys, followed by the value.

Note

GetSetting, SaveSetting, and GetAllSettings only allow access of the VB and VBA Settings sub-key of HKEY_CURRENT_USER. In addition, they only allow for the creation and viewing of REG_SZ (string) data stored in the Registry. To access the full functionality of the Registry, you must use the Registry API calls. These APIs are listed in the API Viewer that comes with VB5. They can be identified: All of them begin with the characters "Reg". Some of the more useful ones include RegConnectRegistry, RegOpenKeyEx,

`RegQueryValueEx`, and `RegCreateKeyEx`. There are also a number of useful constants in the API viewer. These also begin with the characters "REG".

Exercises

Exercise 26.1:   Find the Registry Information for an Object

To locate the information for an ActiveX Control in the Registry, complete the following steps:

1. Run the Regedit.exe program (or Regedt32.exe under Windows NT).

2. Open the HKEY_CLASSES_ROOT hive.

3. Scroll down (or search for) the entry for the Microsoft Common Dialog Control. This should be called MSComDlg.CommonDialog. Note the CLSID and CurVer Keys under it.

4. Find the key listed as the current version of the Microsoft Common Dialog Control. This should be MSComDlg.CommonDialog.1. Note that the CLSID matches the one for the non-version dependent entry above it.

5. Find the CLSID for this control under the CLSID key. Note that it has a Control sub-key, and that there is an associated pointer to the ProgID above it.

Exercise 26.2:   Create a Simple ActiveX EXE and Register It

To create a simple ActiveX EXE and a program to test it, complete the following steps:

1. Create an ActiveX EXE project in VB5.

2. Rename the class module **clsCtoF**, and the project **Convert**.

3. Add two public functions to convert a temperature between Celsius and Fahrenheit. These should look similar to this:

```
Public Function CtoF(Celsius As Double)
➥As Double
    CtoF = (Celsius * 9 / 5) + 32
End Function
```

```
Public Function FtoC(Fahrenheit As
➡Double) As Double
    FtoC = (Fahrenheit - 32) * 5 / 9
End Function
```

4. Compile the EXE and execute it. It should now be registered. Confirm that the `Convert.clsCtoF` object is in the Registry.

5. Create a new Standard EXE project. Do not create a project group.

6. Add a reference to the ActiveX EXE project to this new project.

7. Add two `Labels`, `TextBoxes`, and `Command` buttons to the form. These controls should have properties set as in Table 26.4.

Table 26.4

Controls in the ActiveX EXE Exercise

Control	Property	Value
Form	Name	frmConvert
	Caption	Test Convert.EXE
Label1	Name	lblCels
	Caption	Celsius
Label2	Name	lblFahr
	Caption	Fahrenheit
TextBox1	Name	txtCels
	Text	blank or number
TextBox2	Name	txtFahr
	Text	blank or number
CommandButton1	Name	cmdCtoF
	Caption	-> &F
CommandButton2	Name	cmdFtoC
	Caption	-> &C

continues

Exercise 26.2:   Continued

---

8. Add a form-level variable representing a `Convert` object. Set this variable to a newly created `Convert.clsCtoF` object in the `Form Load` event:

```
Private objConvert As Convert.clsCtoF
Private Sub Form_Load()
    Set objConvert = New Convert.clsCtoF
End Sub
```

9. Add code to the two buttons to convert the temperatures listed in the two text boxes when clicked:

```
Private Sub cmdCtoF_Click()
    txtFahr.Text =
    ➥objConvert.CtoF(CDbl(txtCels.Text))
End Sub
Private Sub cmdFtoC_Click()
    txtCels.Text =
    ➥objConvert.FtoC(CDbl(txtFahr.Text))
End Sub
```

10. Run the program and confirm that it works. It should look similar to Figure 26.13. Compile it for later use.

Figure 26.13

An ActiveX EXE exercise.

Exercise 26.3:   Unregister the ActiveX EXE Using the Command Line

---

To unregister the ActiveX EXE created in Exercise 26.2, complete the following steps:

1. Open a Command Prompt and locate the ActiveX EXE created in Exercise 26.2.

2. Run the ActiveX EXE with the /UnRegServer command-line parameter:

```
Convert /UnRegServer
```

3. Try to run the test program created in the second half of Exercise 26.2. You should receive an error.

To register the ActiveX EXE again, complete the following steps:

1. Open a Command Prompt and locate the ActiveX EXE created in Exercise 26.2.

2. Run the ActiveX EXE. To prevent an EXE with a user interface from starting, use the /RegServer command-line parameter.

3. The test program should run again. Compile it to create an executable for the following exercise.

Exercise 26.4: Create a Simple ActiveX DLL and Register It

To create a simple ActiveX DLL and a program to test it, complete the following steps:

1. Create a new ActiveX DLL project.

2. Change the name of the project to **RevDLL**, and the class module to **clsReverse**.

3. Add code to the class module to create a `Public` property, `Word`. This will be a string:

```
Public Word As String
```

4. Add code to create a read-only property that will return the reversed string held in `Word`:

```
Public Property Get Reverse() As String
    Dim sTemp As String
    Dim I As Integer
    For I = Len(Word) To 1 Step -1
        sTemp = sTemp & Mid$(Word, I, 1)
    Next
    Reverse = sTemp
End Property
```

5. Compile the project to create a DLL.

6. Add a new Standard EXE, creating a project group. Set this new project as the Startup.

continues

---

7. Add a `TextBox`, `Label`, and `CommandButton` to the form. Set the properties for the controls as in Table 26.5.

Table 26.5

Controls in ActiveX DLL Exercise

Control	Property	Value
Form	Name	frmTestRev
	Caption	Test Reverse.DLL
TextBox	Name	txtWord
	Text	blank
Label	Name	lblRev
	Caption	blank
Command Button	Name	cmdReverse
	Caption	&Reverse

8. Add a reference to the ActiveX DLL project.

9. Create a form-level instance of the `RevDLL` object in the form, and assign it to a newly created copy of the class during the `Form Load` event:

```
Dim objRev As RevDLL.clsReverse

Private Sub Form_Load()
    Set objRev = New RevDLL.clsReverse
End Sub
```

10. Add code to cmdReverse to reverse the text in `txtWord` and assign the reverse to `lblRev`:

```
Private Sub cmdReverse_Click()
    objRev.Word = txtWord.Text
    lblRev.Caption = objRev.Reverse
End Sub
```

11. Execute the program to confirm it works. It should appear similar to Figure 26.14. Compile it to create an executable for the following exercise.

Figure 26.14

The ActiveX DLL exercise in action.

Exercise 26.5: Unregister the ActiveX DLL Using the Command Line

To unregister the ActiveX DLL created in Exercise 26.4, complete the following steps:

1. Open a Command Prompt and locate the DLL created in Exercise 26.4.

2. Run the regsvr32.exe program, passing the parameters "/u" and the name of the DLL:

   ```
   regsvr32 /u revdll.dll
   ```

3. Try to run the test program EXE, created in Exercise 26.4. You should receive an error message.

To register the ActiveX DLL again, complete the following steps:

1. Open a Command Prompt and locate the DLL created in Exercise 26.4.

2. Run the regsvr32.exe program, passing the name of the DLL as a command-line parameter:

   ```
   regsvr32 revdll.dll
   ```

3. Try to run the test program EXE, created in Exercise 26.4. The program should run as expected.

Exercise 26.6: Create a Program That Saves and Loads Configuration Information from the Registry

To create a program that uses the Registry to save information, complete the following steps:

1. Create a new Standard EXE project.

2. Add a Common dialog object to the project.

continues

3. Add Common dialog and Command Button controls to the form. These controls should have properties set similar to those in Table 26.6.

Table 26.6

Controls in SaveSettings Exercise

Control	Property	Value
Form	Name	frmRegistry
	Caption	Save information in Registry
	BorderStyle	Sizable
Common Dialog	Name	dlgColor
Command Button	Name	cmdSetColor
	Caption	&Set Backcolor

4. Add code to the Command button to display the Common color dialog box and set the background color of the form to the chosen color. This code should appear similar to this:

```
Private Sub cmdSetColor_Click()
    With dlgColor
        .ShowColor
        If .Color Then BackColor = .Color
    End With
End Sub
```

5. To make saving and loading information to the Registry easier, create two form-level constants. These constants will represent the Application name and Section name in the SaveSetting and GetSetting calls:

```
Const APP_NAME As String = "Registry
➥Exercise"
Const SECTION_NAME As String = "Window"
```

6. Add code to the Form Unload event to save information about the form's size and color:

```
Private Sub Form_Unload(Cancel As
➡Integer)
    SaveSetting APP_NAME, SECTION_NAME,
    ➡"Left", Left
    SaveSetting APP_NAME, SECTION_NAME,
    ➡"Top", Top
    SaveSetting APP_NAME, SECTION_NAME,
    ➡"Width", Width
    SaveSetting APP_NAME, SECTION_NAME,
    ➡"Height", Height
    SaveSetting APP_NAME, SECTION_NAME,
    ➡"Backcolor", BackColor
End Sub
```

7. Add code to the `Form Load` event to load the information saved when the form was unloaded:

```
Private Sub Form_Load()
    Left = GetSetting(APP_NAME,
    ➡SECTION_NAME, "Left", 0)
    Top = GetSetting(APP_NAME,
    ➡SECTION_NAME, "Top", 0)
    Width = GetSetting(APP_NAME
    ➡SECTION_NAME, "Width", 3600)
    Height = GetSetting(APP_NAME,
    ➡SECTION_NAME, "Height", 3600)
    BackColor = GetSetting(APP_NAME,
    ➡SECTION_NAME, "Backcolor", &HC0C0C0)
End Sub
```

8. Run the program (see Figure 26.15), notice the window size and color. Move the window on the screen; change its size and color.

Figure 26.15

SaveSetting exercise when first run.

continues

Exercise 26.6:   Continued

9. Stop the program by clicking on the *X* in the top-right corner. Run it again (see Figure 26.16). You should see that it is in the same spot it was before the program ended, and that the color is the color you set it to previously.

Figure 26.16

SaveSetting exercise after saving settings.

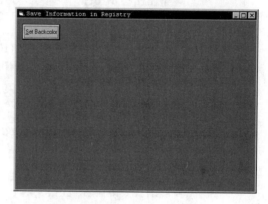

Review Questions

1. Which hive stores information about the objects installed on the computer?

   A. HKEY_CURRENT_USER

   B. HKEY_CLASSES_ROOT

   C. HKEY_ALL_OBJECTS

   D. HKEY_INSTALLED_OBJECTS

2. Where in the Registry does `SaveSetting` save the information for a program?

   A. HKEY_LOCAL_MACHINE\Settings

   B. HKEY_CURRENT_USER\Settings

   C. HKEY_LOCAL_MACHINE\Software\VB and VBA Settings

   D. HKEY_CURRENT_USER\Software\VB and VBA Settings

3. Which of the following are valid types for Registry settings? (Select all correct answers.)

   A. REG_SZ

   B. REG_DWORD

   C. REG_BINARY

   D. REG_WORD

4. Which of the following can be used to manually register an OCX?

   A. CliReg32

   B. OCXReg

   C. RegOCX32

   D. OLEReg32

5. What must you do to register an ActiveX DLL installed using Setup Wizard before using a program that needs that control?

   A. Nothing. The control will be registered when you first call it.

   B. Nothing. The Setup Wizard registers the control.

   C. Register the control with RegSvr32.

   D. Run the program once to register all ActiveX DLL that it uses.

6. Which is a valid GUID?

   A. MyServer.MyClass

   B. 112-1111111

   C. {2457C847-C7AD-11D0-9767-00802965DCEE}

   D. Excel.Application.8

7. Which compatibility mode ensures that your ActiveX Object will always use the same GUID?

   A. Binary Compatibility

   B. GUID Compatibility

   C. Program Compatibility

   D. Project Compatibility

8. Which would unregister an ActiveX EXE object? (Select all correct answers.)

   A. Deleting the ActiveX EXE

   B. Uninstalling the ActiveX EXE using Add/Remove Programs from the Control Panel

   C. Running the program with the /UnRegister command-line parameter.

   D. Running the program with the /UnRegServer parameter.

9. You want to save the last user of your program to the Registry. Which of the following would do that?

    A. `WritePrivateProfileString "MyProgram", "Users", "Last", UserID`

    B. `WriteSetting "MyProgram", "Users", "Last", UserID`

    C. `SaveSetting "MyProgram", "Users", "Last", UserID`

    D. `PutSetting "MyProgram", "Users", "Last", UserID`

10. What will happen when the following line of code executes if there is no "Window" section?

    `SomeVar = GetSetting("MyApp", "Window", "Left", 100)`

    A. A trappable runtime error will occur.

    B. SomeVar will hold the value 100.

    C. SomeVar will hold a null string ("").

    D. SomeVar will be empty.

11. Which of the following actions would not register a self-registerable component?

    A. Running an ActiveX EXE outside of VB

    B. Adding an ActiveX Control to the Components dialog using the Browse button

    C. Running an ActiveX DLL project in the VB5 IDE

    D. Opening an ActiveX DLL project in VB5

12. What is a program you can use to edit the Registry? (Select all that apply.)

    A. Notepad

    B. Regedit

    C. Editreg

    D. Regedt32

Answers to Review Questions

1. B. The HKEY_CLASSES_ROOT hive stores all the information about installed objects. For more information, see the section titled "Storing Class Information in the System Registry."

2. D. SaveSetting stores information for each user individually under HKEY_CURRENT_USER\Software\VB and VBA Settings. For more information, see the section titled "SaveSetting."

3. A, B, C. Types of Registry values include REG_SZ, REG_DWORD, REG_BINARY, REG_EXPAND_SZ, and REG_MULTI_SZ. For more information, see the section titled "Information Types."

4. C. RegOCX32 is used to register an OCX (ActiveX Control). It adds all appropriate Registry entries for the control. For more information, see the section titled "Registering Controls—Manually."

5. B. One of the main reasons for using Setup Wizard is to properly register all ActiveX components. For more information, see the section titled "Registering Controls—Automatically."

6. C. A GUID is a 128-bit value that uniquely identifies an object. It is usually represented as a 32-digit value. For more information, see the section titled "Storing Class Information in the System Registry."

7. A. Setting the compatibility mode to Binary Compatibility ensures that your component will always use the same GUID. For more information, see the section titled "Compiling."

8. B, D. Using the /UnRegServer parameter when running an ActiveX EXE removes the Registry information for the component. This information is also removed when the component is uninstalled. For more information, see the section titled "Registering Controls—Manually."

9. C. The `SaveSetting` command is used to write information to the Registry. For more information, see the section titled "`SaveSetting`."

10. B. The last parameter in the call to `GetSetting` is a default value that will be returned if there is no value for the requested item or if the item doesn't exist. For more information, see the section titled "`GetSetting`."

11. D. Just opening an ActiveX DLL project will not register it. For more information, see the section titled "Registering Controls—Automatically."

12. B, D. Under Windows NT, Regedit.exe and Regedt32.exe can be used to edit the Registry. Under Windows 95, only Regedit.exe is available. For more information, see the section titled "Understanding the System Registry."

Answers to Test Yourself Questions at Beginning of Chapter

1. A ProgID is a programmatic identifier. It is a human-friendly name for an object. A CLSID is a 128-bit value that uniquely identifies an ActiveX Object. The computer uses it to create an instance of the ActiveX Object. See "Storing Class Information in the System Registry."

2. Clireg32.exe is used to manually register remote automation components. See "Registering Controls—Manually."

3. Sub-keys of a CLSID include `ProgID`, `Control`, `Programmable`, `Shell`, and `InProcServer32`. See "Storing Class Information in the System Registry."

4. The VBR file contains registration information for remote server objects. See "Registering Controls—Automatically."

5. A GUID (Globally Unique IDentifier) uniquely identifies an object. No two objects, regardless of manufacturer, should have the same GUID. See "Storing Class Information in the System Registry."

6. One or more of the objects were not registered correctly. Use the Setup Wizard to install the program, or manually register the objects. See "Registering Controls—Manually."

7. The `GetAllSettings` function returns a two-dimensional array containing all the values from one section of the Registry. See "Storing Information in the System Registry."

8. The Compatibility option for the project is not set to Binary Compatibility. See "Registering Controls—Automatically."

Distributing an Application over the Internet

This chapter helps you prepare for the exam by covering the following objectives:

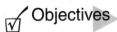 Objectives

▶ Prepare for component downloading

▶ Make use of digital signing

▶ Guarantee the component is safe

▶ Understand your licensing options

Test Yourself! Before reading this chapter, test yourself to determine how much study time you will need to devote to this section.

1. Describe the process that the browser goes through when it finds a reference to an ActiveX component in the HTML page it is rendering.

2. What two key things does a digital signature provide?

3. Describe what "Safe for scripting" means. How is it different from "Safe for initialization"?

4. What is a file that contains all the license keys for all the licensed ActiveX components on a particular HTML page?

Answers are located at the end of the chapter...

In this chapter, you will discover how to package your ActiveX executable code, be it Controls, EXEs, DLLs, or Documents, so that they may be easily and automatically downloaded by the browser. You will also run head-on into a number of security and safety issues that occur with this new method of distributing application code.

This chapter discusses the bundling of ActiveX executable code for use in a runtime HTML environment. If you want to provide your controls for use by developers at *design-time* in Visual Basic or other application development environments, see Chapter 25, "Creating a Setup Program That Installs and Registers ActiveX Controls."

For more information on creating a more traditional setup program to install standard applications from a floppy disk or CD-ROM, see Chapter 24, "Using the Setup Wizard to Create an Effective Setup Program."

This chapter covers the following topics:

▶ Preparing for component downloading

▶ Making use of digital signing

▶ Guaranteeing the component is safe

▶ Understanding your licensing options

Preparing for Component Downloading

 The Professional and Enterprise editions of Visual Basic enable you to create ActiveX Controls, ActiveX EXEs, ActiveX DLLs, and ActiveX Documents. After they are created, any of these may be placed on a web page to use as part of a web application. But distributing executable code in this way takes some extra care and consideration.

By the way, Visual Basic Internet distribution of ActiveX Controls, ActiveX EXEs, ActiveX DLLs, and ActiveX Documents all works about the same way. Therefore, whenever this chapter refers to *ActiveX code* or *ActiveX components*, you should understand that what is said applies to any of these.

Understanding the Automatic Download Process

Internet Explorer 3.0 or higher understands how to use ActiveX along with your web page. If the browser sees from the HTML that an ActiveX Control is to be a part of this page, for example, it will automatically check to see whether the user already has this control. If the user does not, the browser will go to the URL address specified in the HTML and download the ActiveX Control.

The browser also looks to see whether any other associated controls or files are needed and downloads those if necessary. Finally, after the control and everything it needs is downloaded and installed on the user's machine, the control is rendered on the page.

Making the Automatic Download Happen

Before all this magic can happen, you have to do some preparation. The Visual Basic 5 Setup Wizard has been extended to help you do that magic.

As with other installation procedures, your ActiveX code and the files that go with it are bundled together and compressed into a *cabinet* (.CAB) file. Included in the .CAB file is all the information necessary to download, install, and get your ActiveX code working.

That is not to say that every component or DLL that your code depends on is included in the .CAB file. All ActiveX code you create with Visual Basic requires the Msvbvm50.dll, for example, but this will not be a part of your .CAB file. Instead, the browser will see that this file is necessary and check to see whether the user already has it. If not, the browser will go out and download it separately.

You can choose to have the browser download support files such as these either from your own site or from Microsoft's site. It is always a good idea to choose Microsoft's site. This has the following several advantages:

▶ The load on your server is reduced.

▶ The user will always get the latest version of the component or DLL.

▶ The browser, when it requests these support components or DLLs, will send along information about the user's OS and version so that the user will get exactly the components he or she needs automatically.

The only time you will want to tell the browser to download support files from your web site is when your are providing web pages to an intranet that can't easily access or download files from locations outside the firewall.

Making Use of Digital Signing

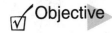 Objective

When you go into a software store and buy a package off the shelf, you usually aren't too concerned about installing the software on your PC. Although there is an outside chance that the software might contain a virus or might actually be written to do harmful things to your PC, you don't usually give it a second thought. Why? Because the company that produces it has a reputable name and because the software is shrink-wrapped at the factory no one else has had the chance to tamper with it.

Digital signing provides a sort of electronic shrink-wrap for your software. It does the following two things:

▶ It identifies that you were the creator of the software. This may mean that you accept certain legal responsibilities for doing so.

▶ It ensures that no one has tampered with the software since you bundled it together and sent it out.

How You Use Digital Signatures

Four different types of files available in VB5 may have a digital signature:

▶ .EXE files

▶ .DLL files

▶ .OCX files

▶ .CAB files

Notice that not only can you sign your ActiveX component, but you can also sign the compressed .CAB file that contains the component and other files. Which should you sign? Both!

So how do you get a digital signature? Digital signatures are purchased from a firm called a *certificate authority*. After you have purchased your signature, you can then apply that signature as you see fit to your software components and .CAB files. If there is ever a legal dispute about one of your components, the certificate authority can become an identity witness to verify that a component did, in fact, come from you (based on its signature).

Actually, many companies don't even keep their digital signature file on site. It is much safer to keep the file at the certificate authority and to send files there to be signed. If you do keep your signature file on site, you must have tight controls to ensure that no unauthorized signatures are made.

If you don't have the ongoing need to obtain your own signature, it is possible to work with a third-party company that has their own signature and borrow theirs. Of course, because they will be responsible, they will probably want to review the source code and ensure that it is safe, compile it on their site, and then apply the signature themselves.

If you do choose to purchase your own digital signature, you can use the software and documentation in the ActiveX SDK to apply it to your components.

What Makes Digital Signatures Work

Digital signatures are typically done with a technology called *Authenticode*. Authenticode is a technology based on the concept of public-key encryption algorithms.

You don't need to know all the complex details about how public-key encryption works, but there are some basic principles you should understand.

In public-key encryption, there are two keys: a *public key* and a *private key*. A file is encrypted using the private key and decrypted using the public key. The public key is available to anyone who wants to see the information in the file. The private key is kept a secret.

Encrypting an entire file's worth of information takes a lot of time and isn't really necessary. So instead, only the signature file, which holds the information about you, is encrypted.

That signature file information is encoded with a private key producing an encrypted file. That file can be decrypted using the public key so that anyone can see whose company name is associated with this product.

But the opposite is *not* true. You cannot turn around and use the public key to apply that company name to *another* product. You must have the private key to apply the signature to a new product and create a new encrypted file. This ensures that only the owner and the certificate authority, who have the private key, can make new encrypted files.

In addition to encrypting the signature information, one other piece of information is encrypted—a *hash number*. The hash number works similarly to a Cyclical Redundancy Check (CRC) and more or less uniquely represents this file. If the file is tampered with in any way, the hash would no longer match the file and it would make the tampering obvious.

Together the encrypted signature and encrypted hash ensure the following:

▶ This file was created by you and you alone.

▶ This file is exactly as it was when you signed it—it has not been tampered with.

Guaranteeing the Component Is Safe

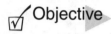 In the process of using the Setup Wizard to create the .CAB file for your ActiveX code, you will be asked to check off two important check boxes (see Figure 27.5 later this chapter). These check boxes ask the following two simple questions:

▶ Is this component safe for initialization?

▶ Is this component safe for scripting?

The first question asks you to verify that this component will not do anything *bad* as a result of initialization parameters that are specified (using the PARM tag in HTML). Of course, your first question is, "What does *bad* mean?" You will get to that in a minute (in the next section). Right now, just use your imagination.

The second question asks you to verify that this component will never do anything bad as a result of script that is written making use of this component. Although the script in *your* web page may not make use of your component in a bad way, someone else might write a script that would.

This is a more rigorous test and asks you to verify all runtime properties and methods.

Understanding What *Bad* Means

Okay, so what is meant by *bad*? Well, it is a broad definition. Perhaps the best way to get the full scope of it is to look at the differences between the Visual Basic language and the VBScript language. One of the major driving factors in creating VBScript was to ensure that it was *safe*. And here, *safe* means *not bad*.

In general *bad* refers to things that cause harm to the computer, the operating system configuration, or the software on the computer. It also refers to things that steal information from that computer.

One example of a *bad* thing is creating or reading files using a filename specified *outside* the component. In other words, if a component method receives a filename as an argument and passes back the contents of the file, that would be bad. Or if an initialization parameter enabled you to specify a filename that would be created on the user's hard drive, that's bad.

If the component internally creates its own temporary file—using its own filename, not one specified outside the component—to keep track of information as it runs, this may not be bad.

Likewise, getting information from the Registry or writing information to the Registry is bad if the information is specified by a script or an initialization parameter.

But again, the component might create its own section in the Registry to temporarily hold data while it's running. As long as this is not controlled by script, it is probably not bad.

The same rules apply to INI files.

In addition, getting information about the user or the user's machine and providing it to the script writer in the form of property values or values returned from methods may seem harmless, but it definitely falls into the *bad* category.

There is one key factor with each of these situations: Bad behavior is triggered by either an initialization parameter or a script.

The component may do things that are undesirable. It may format the hard drive after it is used three times. But this control may still be considered safe for initialization and safe for scripting. Because the formatting was in no way related to scripting or initialization, these two questions can be answered truthfully: Yes.

Of course, if this hard-drive formatting component has your digital signature, you may still be held legally liable for its actions, regardless of your truthfulness!

Documenting Your Assertions

The issues of safety and reliability are not trivial. Therefore, when you make these two assertions under your digital signature, you must be sure that what you say is true.

One way to help you verify the truth is to make two lists—one of all the methods, events, and properties of your component; the other of all the files opened, Registry and INI calls made, user information gathered, and API functions called. Then look carefully to see whether there are any dependencies, links, or data transferred between these two lists. If there are, you may very well have a bad situation that needs to be addressed.

Understanding Your Licensing Options

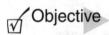 Objective

Licensing is a very important issue when creating ActiveX Controls. Because developers spend many hours creating useful, reusable components, they need to be compensated for their work. The Internet throws a wrench into the works that makes necessary a new licensing scheme that works a little differently than the one traditionally used for ActiveX Controls in standalone applications.

Using the Traditional Licensing Scheme

In Chapter 25, you discovered how ActiveX components are used in applications but are protected from reuse at design time by license files.

To summarize, ActiveX Controls are created and distributed with a license file that contains a number called the license *key*. This key is required for the control to be created.

This design enables the developer to use the control in a standard development environment such as Visual Basic or Visual C++. When an application is created using an ActiveX Control, however, that application is distributed *without* the license file. Instead, the necessary license key is built into the executable itself and passed to the ActiveX Control when the control is created. This enables the user of the application to make use of the control in the application, but not anywhere else. Because the user doesn't have the license file, he cannot use the ActiveX Control to create his own applications.

This system works well for standalone applications and standard development environments such as Visual Basic, Visual C++, and others.

This system does *not* work well, however, with Internet Explorer and ActiveX Controls on the Internet. That is because web pages aren't created in traditional development environments. In fact, they can be created in Notepad or any other simple editor. And when a page is viewed in a browser, all its "source code" can be easily copied and manipulated. Because of these differences in how web applications work, the traditional licensing mechanism for ActiveX Controls really doesn't work well. If the license key was included right in the web page, it could be easily copied and stolen.

Using the New Runtime Licensing Scheme

To address these problems, Microsoft created a new runtime licensing mechanism. It works like this: For each page that you create that includes licensed ActiveX components, you also create a license *package*. The license package is a file with an .LPK extension. The license package is basically a normal ASCII text file and has the following four sections:

▶ *The header.* Identifies the type of file this is. Contains the text "LPK License Package."

▶ *The copyright notice.* This text is used to discourage copying, reverse-engineering, or otherwise hacking this file.

▶ *LPK GUID.* A unique identification number for this license package. It identifies the beginning of the licensing data.

▶ A uuencoded (Base64) series of Class ID and license key numbers, one for each ActiveX component on the page.

Don't worry. You don't have to create this file by hand. Microsoft has created a utility, which it creatively refers to as LPK_TOOL.EXE. You can find this utility in the Internet Client SDK. It is a very straightforward application that lists all the controls registered on this computer on the left and enables you to pick from among those that should appear in the license package. After you have identified them all, you just click on the Save & Exit button to generate the .LPK file. It is a good idea to name the .LPK file using the same name as the associated HTML file so that it is clear that they go together.

After the file is created, it is placed on the server. Often the .LPK is placed in the same folder where its associated HTML page is found.

The only thing remaining is to identify the license package on the web page. You can do this within the OBJECT tag of the first licensed ActiveX Control on the page. All you have to do is add a PARAM tag:

```
<OBJECT CLASSID="clsid:3220CB33-C77D-11fg-B667-00XX00X28834">
   <PARAM NAME="LPKPath" VALUE="game.lpk">
</OBJECT>
```

Remember that the license package contains all the license keys for all the licensed ActiveX components on the page. Therefore, there should be only *one* .LPK file for each HTML file. If you refer to more than one .LPK file in your HTML, only the first one referred to is used.

Exercises

Exercise 27.1:   Creating an ActiveX Component .CAB File

In this exercise, you use the Microsoft Visual Basic Setup Wizard to bundle together the files you need to create an automatically downloadable ActiveX Control you can use in a Web page.

To create an ActiveX .CAB file, follow these steps:

1. Open the Application Setup Wizard from the Programs/ Microsoft Visual Basic 5.0 folder in the Start menu. The Setup Wizard Introduction window appears, as shown in Figure 27.1.

Figure 27.1

The Application Setup Wizard's Introduction window.

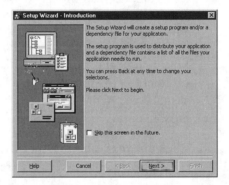

This window is just an introduction to the Setup Wizard. It may not even appear if someone has clicked the Skip This Screen in the Future check box. If it does appear, read through the text. Otherwise, you should see the window pictured in Figure 27.3. Skip to step 3.

2. Click on the Next button. The Select Project and Options window appears, as shown in Figure 27.2.

3. Click on the Browse button. Locate the project file (extension .vbp) associated with the ActiveX component you want to distribute. Click to select the project file, and then click on OK. The path appears in the edit on the Select Project and Options window.

continues

Exercise 27.1: Continued

Figure 27.2

*The Select
Project and
Options window.*

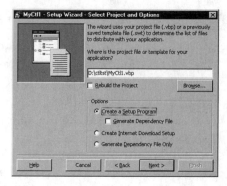

4. If you want to rebuild the project before bundling it up in a .CAB file, click on the Rebuild the Project check box.

5. Click on the Create Internet Download Setup radio button in the Options group box. When you do, the What's New button appears on the left. This button links you to a page on Microsoft's Web site with a list of links to all the Microsoft Visual Basic ActiveX Controls in .CAB file format on Microsoft's site.

6. Click on Next. The Internet Distribution Location dialog box appears, as shown in Figure 27.3.

Figure 27.3

*The Internet
Distribution Loca-
tion dialog box.*

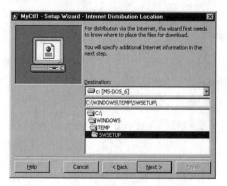

7. Identify a drive and a folder where the completed ActiveX component .CAB file should be placed.

8. Click on Next. The Internet Package dialog box appears, as shown in Figure 27.4.

Figure 27.4

The Internet Package dialog box.

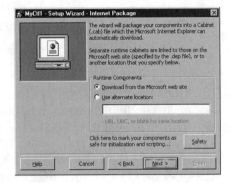

9. Your component depends on other components or Visual Basic files. If the user doesn't already have these files, they must be downloaded, too. In this dialog box, you decide where those files should be downloaded from—Microsoft's web site or someplace else (such as your own server).

   Whenever possible, it is best to choose Microsoft's Web site. See "Making the Automatic Download Happen" earlier in this chapter for a list of reasons and more discussion on this topic.

10. Click on the Safety button. The Safety dialog box appears, as shown in Figure 27.5.

Figure 27.5

The Safety dialog box.

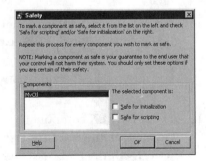

continues

Exercise 27.1: Continued

11. Your ActiveX component and any others it depends on that you have created appear in the list box on the left. You can click on each component in turn and then check off the Safe for Initialization and Safe for Scripting boxes.

    Checking off these boxes indicates a promise of a certain level of safety for those who use this component. It may also make you liable if your component is not, in fact, safe. See "Guaranteeing the Component Is Safe" earlier in this chapter for more information.

12. Click on OK to return to the Internet Package dialog box.

13. Click on Next. The ActiveX Server Components dialog box appears, as shown in Figure 27.6.

Figure 27.6

The ActiveX Server Components dialog box.

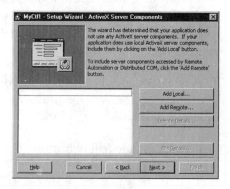

14. Any ActiveX server components that you use will appear in the list box on the left. You can add more by using the buttons on the right.

15. Click on Next.

16. If your ActiveX component uses other ActiveX components, you may see the Confirm Dependencies window. (If your ActiveX component does *not* use other ActiveX components, you will not see this window. Skip to step 19.)

17. Verify or change the dependencies presented as necessary.

18. Click on Next.

19. The Working window appears. A series of messages will appear at the bottom of the window as your distribution files are generated.

20. You may see a window asking whether you would like to include a Property Page DLL. This DLL is necessary if you intend to allow others to use the control in a design-time environment such as Visual Basic or Visual C++. Click on Yes or No.

21. The File Summary dialog box appears, as shown in Figure 27.7.

Figure 27.7

The File Summary dialog box.

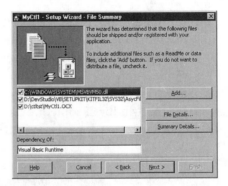

22. All the files that the wizard thinks you will need appear in the list box on the left with a check mark beside each. You can add additional files, such as a readme.txt, by using the Add button on the right. The File Details button gives you a lot of information about whichever file is selected in the list box. The Summary Details button provides summary information about all the files.

    Note that not all these files will be bundled into your .CAB file. Many of them, if they aren't already on the user's hard drive, will be downloaded separately. For more information on this, see "Making the Automatic Download Happen" earlier in this chapter.

23. Click on Next. The Finished! window appears, as shown in Figure 27.8.

continues

Exercise 27.1: Continued

Figure 27.8

The Finished! window.

24. If you want to save all the information you have entered in this wizard as a template for the future, click on the Save Template button. Otherwise, click on Finish. A processing window appears for a few seconds, and then a final confirmation window appears, as shown in Figure 27.9. (You may not see this window if someone has previously clicked on the check box that appears on it. If that's the case, skip to step 26.)

Figure 27.9

The Setup Wizard confirmation window.

25. Click on OK.

26. In the folder you specified, you will now find two files and a folder. The files will have the .CAB and .HTM extension. The .CAB file is the compressed file the wizard generated for you. The .HTM file is a web page that demonstrates the OBJECT tag syntax you will use to include the ActiveX Control in a page for both licensed and unlicensed controls.

    In the folder, named Support, you will find the files used to create the .CAB file—just in case you ever need them.

Review Questions

1. What files will be included in your .CAB file when you create it? Choose one.

   A. The component and all the information necessary to get it installed and working

   B. The component and all the components it is dependent on

   C. The component and Msvbvm50.dll

   D. Only the component

2. Digital signing does what two things?

   A. Identifies the creator of the software

   B. Ensures that the file cannot be copied

   C. Ensures that no one has tampered with the file since it was created

   D. Removes all viruses from the software

   E. Confirms that the software will not do anything bad to the user's machine

3. To which file types can you apply digital signatures? (Choose all that apply.)

   A. .EXE and .DLL files

   B. .OCX files

   C. .VPR files

   D. .BAS files

   E. .CAB files

4. The certificate authority does what? (Choose all that apply.)

    A. Acts as an identity witness to verify a component's creator

    B. Certifies that software is safe

    C. Applies the digital signature to a file

    D. Sells digital signatures

    E. Provides proof that a component is virus-free

5. Which statement correctly describes how public and private keys work together?

    A. Both the public and private key are necessary to both encode and decode a file.

    B. The public key encodes the file, but you must have the private key to decode the file.

    C. The private key encodes the file, and the public key decodes the file.

    D. Both keys are necessary to encode a file, but neither is needed to decode the file.

6. What is the hash number used for?

    A. Verifying that the file has no viruses.

    B. Ensuring the file hasn't been tampered with.

    C. Identifying the creator of the file.

    D. It labels the component as safe.

7. "Safe for scripting" means what?

    A. This component will not do anything bad.

    B. The component will work in this page with its script without doing anything bad.

    C. No matter what script you write, there is no way you can make this component do anything bad as a result of the script.

    D. Viruses cannot be written using scripting code.

8. Which of the following would *not* be considered bad? (Choose all that apply.)

    A. Receiving a filename as an argument to a method and then reading that file

    B. Creating a file that is always named temp.txt

    C. Accessing a specified key in the Registry and returning the value

    D. Writing to an INI when a component is initialized with the INI filename specified in a parameter

9. Which of the following is *not* true of a license package? (Choose all that apply.)

    A. It contains a copyright notice.

    B. It holds the license key for only one licensed ActiveX component.

    C. It has a unique identification number.

    D. It is strongly encrypted so that the license keys may not be discovered.

    E. It must be created by hand.

Answers to Review Questions

1. A. The dependent files are downloaded separately, usually from the Microsoft web site. For more information, see the section titled "Preparing for Component Downloading."

2. A, C. It just identifies the creator and ensures that it has not been tampered with. It doesn't represent anything more than a promise from the creator. For more information, see the section titled "Making Use of Digital Signing."

3. A, B, and E. There would be no need to add digital signatures to source code files because they are not distributed. For more information, see the section titled "How You Use Digital Signatures."

4. A, C, and D. Their primary job is to sell the signatures, but if called on, they can be a witness. Also, when requested, they can apply signatures for a company that doesn't want to keep the signature file locally. For more information, see the section titled "How You Use Digital Signatures."

5. C. The private key is kept a secret between the certificate authority and the signature owner. They are the only two entities, therefore, who can sign a file. Anyone who wants to, however, can use the public key to access the information. For more information, see the section titled "What Makes Digital Signatures Work."

6. B. The hash number works in a way similar to a Cyclical Redundancy Check and ends up holding a number that more or less uniquely identifies the file. If the file is changed in any way, the hash would no longer match up and the tampering would be obvious. For more information, see the section titled "What Makes Digital Signatures Work."

7. C. It may be safe with the script on this page, but to mark it "Safe for scripting" it must be safe with any script. It should not do anything bad as a result of scripting. For more information, see the section titled "Guaranteeing the Component Is Safe."

8. B. Any time the specific filename or key is identified by the script, it is bad. For more information, see the section titled "Understanding What *Bad* Means."

9. B, D. The license package holds the license keys for all the licensed components on a page. The keys are uuencoded to keep the casual hacker at bay, but it certainly couldn't be called strongly encrypted. For more information, see the section titled "Using the New Runtime Licensing Scheme."

Answers to Test Yourself Questions at Beginning of Chapter

1. The browser first checks to see whether the component exists on the user's hard drive. If it does not, the component is downloaded. It then checks to see whether any other files or components are necessary to use this one. If there are, those files or components are also downloaded. Finally, all the files and components are installed and the ActiveX component is rendered on the page. See "Understanding the Automatic Download Process."

2. Information about who created the component and a hash that ensures that the file hasn't been tampered with since it was signed. See "What Makes Digital Signatures Work."

3. "Safe for scripting" means that under no circumstances will this component do something bad (such as create a specified file or write to a specified key in the Registry) as a result of a script interacting with the component. "Safe for initialization" means that the component won't do something bad as a result of setting certain initialization parameters. See "Guaranteeing the Component Is Safe."

4. The file is called a *license package*. It is designed to provide licensing information for all the components on a page, not just a single component. See "Using the New Runtime Licensing Scheme."

Where to Go from Here

This book has covered what you need to know to pass the Visual Basic exam, but there is always more to learn. Often you will need to accomplish more complex tasks than standard Visual Basic code enables. You may need to trap window events not exposed by Visual Basic's form object; this can be done through the Windows Application Programming Interface (API). Maybe you have a function that just isn't fast enough in Visual Basic, no matter what you do; creating a custom component in Visual C++ could be the answer. The accounting department has many complex spreadsheets in Microsoft Excel that they want to combine into some form of application; Visual Basic for Applications (VBA) could be a simple way to solve the problem. If it has not happened already, it won't be long before your boss or your client asks you to build an application that works with the Internet. What should you use? Active Server Pages (ASP), VBScript, ActiveX Controls, and Java are all potential methods; but which one is best? When these situations occur, you—as the expert programmer—will be expected to know what to do.

This chapter helps prepare you for those situations and others. You will not become an expert in any of these topics just by reading this chapter, but you will gain a general understanding of how that technology relates to Visual Basic and how it could benefit you. This chapter briefly covers each of the following technologies:

▶ The Win32 API

▶ Visual Basic for Applications

> ▶ Visual C++

> ▶ Internet Programming (Active Server Pages, VBScript, ActiveX Controls and Java)

Using the Win32 API from Visual Basic

The 32-bit Windows Application Programming Interface, or Win32 API as it more commonly known, is provided by the operating system (Windows) to enable programmers access to its various features and functions. Whenever a program needs to display a new window, a message box, or even a menu, it does so through the API. The code for these calls is contained in certain operating system DLLs, and can be accessed by any program. This is why almost every application you run has the same windows, the same toolbars, menus, and they even share many common behaviors (such as the capability to minimize and maximize windows). Programs written in Visual Basic are no exception; you may only have to execute a form's show method (form1.show) but, at some point, a call is made to the API function ShowWindow. Why didn't you have to make the API call yourself? You didn't because Visual Basic took care of it for you, converting your call to the form's show method into the required series of API calls.

Visual Basic's main function (and the main function of most development environments) is to shield you from the complexity of the Win32 API, to give you easier, friendlier ways to accomplish the same things. The Form object is a good example of Visual Basic's attempt to simplify your programming. A form is essentially just a standard object known as a window. There are API calls to manipulate every feature of a window, enabling you to change its caption, size, position, and other properties. By wrapping the standard window in its Form object, Visual Basic enables you access to all the same information through easy-to-use properties. Overall, this simplification enables you, as a programmer, to develop applications much quicker than would normally be possible. Most of the functionality of the API is provided for you through Visual Basic objects. Occasionally, however, you need to go beyond the basics. Using the API is the first and most common method of extending the functionality of Visual Basic programs, so this topic is covered in more detail than the others in this chapter.

To illustrate some of the concepts involved in working with the Win32 API, a detailed sample problem is presented in this section along with an examination of each of the steps involved in solving it.

Your client, or supervisor, has just reviewed your latest application, and has only the following few small requests:

▶ Add tool tips to all your buttons and your application's toolbar

▶ Add a status bar to your main window that gives the user feedback on what the program is doing

▶ Display text (using the status bar) to describe what each menu option does, as the user highlights it, just like Microsoft FrontPage (see Figure 28.1)

Figure 28.1

FrontPage displays status information as the user selects each menu item.

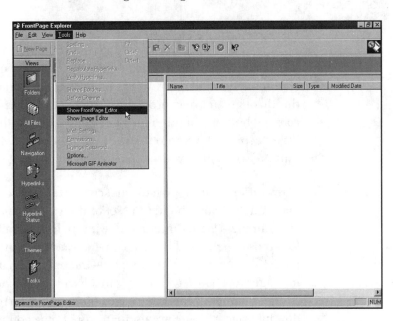

"No problem," you say, and head back to your desk, full of joy at so few requests. You quickly go through the first request, modifying each button's `ToolTipText` property to hold appropriate bits of text. First request completed, no sweat.

The status bar is added by dragging it off your toolbox window into your main form, adding code to display some informative messages during several key procedures takes another hour and then you are almost done—only one thing left: menu-specific status messages. You are not quite sure how to accomplish this one, but how difficult can it be? A quick pass through the Help reveals no `MouseMove` event for menus. In fact, the `click` event is the only event a menu control has. Search as long as you like, there is no way, built in to Visual Basic, to accomplish the user's request. You could go back to the client and inform him that it can't be done. You know what he'll say, however: "But I have seen lots of programs do it, why can't yours?" If that is okay with you, you will probably never think about it again. If, on the other hand, you don't like disappointing your client or if you don't have that option, you need to figure it out. This is where the Windows API comes in. If it can be done, it is probably through the API.

Window Messages

What you need to do is to execute some code whenever a user chooses a menu item. In Visual Basic, you would normally handle this through an `Event` procedure (such as the `click` event of a `command` button); but there isn't one. If you are willing to dig a little deeper—down into the world of window messages—you can find the solution to your problem.

Many different things occur on a computer that some program may want to know about. One set of things of particular interest to programmers is user interaction with their program's windows. When user-generated things happen—such as button clicks, mouse movements, or key presses—the operating system sends messages to whatever window is involved in the action. There are a huge number of those messages (generally referred to as window messages). Some are useful to you. Some you may never need to use. When a window receives one of these messages, it passes it to a piece of code called a *window procedure*, which takes whatever action is necessary. Windows provides default code for this purpose, which handles the common window actions such as resizing, moving, and redrawing as required. It is possible to override this default procedure with a custom one, enabling you to trap a certain message and perform an appropriate action.

Visual Basic programmers usually don't have to worry about these things because VB is already overriding the window procedure for them. When it receives certain messages, it can then call the corresponding Visual Basic event, which, in turn, executes your code. As part of Visual Basic's attempt to simplify programming, only the most commonly used messages are trapped. If, as in this case, you need to trap a message not handled by Visual Basic, you need to override that window procedure yourself.

Subclassing

When you override the current functionality of an object with your own, it is known as *subclassing*. The term comes from the fact that you are, in some respects, creating your own version (or subclass) of the object by changing its behavior. Overriding a form's window procedure provides access to all the messages received by that form, and is the path to implementing many types of advanced functions in Visual Basic.

To subclass a window, the first thing you need to do is create a function to replace the window procedure. This function has to have a certain format because it has to accept the same parameters as the one it is replacing (see the following code). Next, you will use an API call, SetWindowLong, to place the address of this new function in place of the existing one.

 Note

Subclassing a window requires the address of a procedure, as do many useful API calls. Until Visual Basic 5, and its addressof operator, these functions were not possible without using some form of OCX or VBX. The addition of this one small feature enables Visual Basic programmers to use almost all the available API calls.

The return value from this procedure is important because it is the handle to the procedure you are replacing. You need to keep the handle to the old procedure around for two reasons: to put back when you are done subclassing the window, and to use in your own window procedure (as you will see next). All you want to do in your procedure is to trap the few messages Visual Basic isn't handling for you. What do you do with all the others? You don't want to write code to handle every possible event, especially because it has already been done for you by Microsoft. After you have done your own processing on a message, you will just pass it on to the original procedure, thereby guaranteeing it will be handled appropriately. To do this, you will be using another aptly named API call, `CallWindowProc`. You may choose not to pass on some messages—to filter out things you do not want to happen—such as mouse click or key press. Never filter them all, however, because this could cause your window to behave incorrectly.

 Note

Declaring and using API calls is not any different than making calls to DLLs, but finding the right call can be. Many books are available that document the Win32 API (the best of which is Dan Appleman's *Visual Basic 5.0 Programmer's Guide to the Win32 API* from ZDPress, ISBN: 1-56276-446-2), and Microsoft makes a reference available online at `http://www.microsoft.com/msdn`, so there are plenty of places to start your search. These references will also contain at least a partial list of the many available Window Messages.

The following sample code shows three functions: `WindowProc`, `Hook`, and `Unhook`. To make the example work, you must call `Hook` from the `load` event of the form you want to subclass, and `Unhook` from the `unload` event. Because `addressof` works only with procedures located in standard modules (.bas files), that is where you should place the three procedures and their associated declarations. The `WindowProc` procedure in this example does not actually do any work; it is just a placeholder for you to use as needed:

```
Declare Function CallWindowProc Lib "user32" Alias _
"CallWindowProcA" (ByVal lpPrevWndFunc As Long, _
ByVal HWND As Long, ByVal Msg As Long, _
ByVal wParam As Long, ByVal lParam As Long) As Long
```

```
Declare Function SetWindowLong Lib "user32" Alias _
"SetWindowLongA" (ByVal HWND As Long, _
ByVal nIndex As Long, ByVal dwNewLong As Long) As Long

Public Const GWL_WNDPROC = -4
Public lpPrevWndProc As Long
Public gHW As Long

Public Sub Hook(MyHwnd As Long)

    lpPrevWndProc = SetWindowLong(MyHwnd, GWL_WNDPROC, _
    AddressOf WindowProc)

End Sub

Public Sub Unhook(MyHwnd As Long)

    Dim temp As Long
    temp = SetWindowLong(MyHwnd, GWL_WNDPROC, lpPrevWndProc)

End Sub

Function WindowProc(ByVal hw As Long, ByVal uMsg As _
        Long, ByVal wParam As Long, ByVal lParam As Long) As Long

On Error GoTo windowproc_err

'Insert your message handling code here.

    WindowProc = CallWindowProc(lpPrevWndProc, hw, _
    uMsg, wParam, lParam)

    Exit Function

windowproc_err:

    Err.Raise Err.Number, "WindowProc", Err.Description

    Exit Function

End Function
```

The benefits of subclassing do not come without some negative aspects: there are dangers involved in using this technique. When you provide your own window procedure for a form, every message that window receives causes your code to execute. This causes a problem, however, when you use Visual Basic's break mode. When a Visual Basic application is in break mode, your forms still exist and therefore are still receiving messages. When a message arrives, the form attempts to execute your window procedure—which is no longer available because you are in break mode. A General Protection Fault (GPF) usually results within a few seconds. The overall result of this sequence of events is that if you go into break mode while you have a window subclassed, Visual Basic may crash, and you will lose any work you haven't saved. Always save your work before running an application that uses subclassing, and use alternative methods of debugging such as debug.print commands and message boxes, when necessary.

 Tip

It is sometimes easier to just comment out the Hook and Unhook procedure calls until you are done debugging your application.

Trapping the Menu Selection Message

Returning to the original problem—displaying status information for menu options as the user highlights them—you need to create a sample form and project. Create a new Standard EXE project in Visual Basic, add a new module, and enter the code from the "Subclassing" section. Now, with the default form provided, add some sample menus and a status bar (see Chapters 3 and 4). It doesn't matter what the menus look like because this is just a sample. Note that the status bar Type property must be set to "Simple Text" for the provided code to work correctly.

To actually subclass the form, add the following code to its Form_Load and Form_Unload events:

```
Private Sub Form_Load()

    Hook Me.HWND
```

```
End Sub

Private Sub Form_Unload(Cancel As Integer)

    Unhook Me.HWND

End Sub
```

At this point, you can run the application and your form will be
displayed. You are subclassing the form, but nothing special is
happening because you are not doing anything inside your window
procedure. Your window procedure receives four parameters: hw,
the handle to the window that received the message; uMsg, the
window message received; and two parameters called wParam and
lParam. The meaning of the last two values is different depending
on the message sent. Using the API Viewer, find and copy the
constant declaration for the Menu Select window message
(WM_MENUSELECT). This message is fired whenever the user selects
(highlights) a menu option. Paste the declaration into your code.
Now you can add a simple If statement to your window procedure, comparing the value of uMsg to the constant WM_MENUSELECT.
If the two values match, a menu selection has occurred and you
need to process it. For now, just add a debug.print statement that
prints out that a menu selection has occurred and the values of
wParam and lParam. Your code should look similar to the following:

```
Option Explicit

Public Const WM_MENUSELECT = &H11F


...
[Other Declarations and Procedures]
...

Function WindowProc(ByVal hw As Long, ByVal uMsg As _
        Long, ByVal wParam As Long, ByVal lParam As Long) As Long

On Error GoTo windowproc_err

'Insert your message handling code here.
```

```
        If uMsg = WM_MENUSELECT Then

            Debug.Print "Menu Selection!!"
            Debug.Print "WParam: " & wParam
            Debug.Print "LParam: " & lParam

        End If

        WindowProc = CallWindowProc(lPrevWndProc, hw, _
        uMsg, wParam, lParam)

        Exit Function

windowproc_err:

    Err.Raise Err.Number, "WindowProc", Err.Description

    Exit Function

End Function
```

Test the code by running the project and then arranging the form and Visual Basic's windows so that you can see the Immediate window during testing, as in Figure 28.2. Watch the values displayed as you select the various menus. Notice that the values are different for each menu item selected. If you close the program (using the form's Close button) and then run it again, however, the values—although they are still different for each menu item— are not the same as they were the first time.

Because their values are not consistent for a menu item, the two

Figure 28.2

Using the Immediate window and **debug.print** *to view your message parameters.*

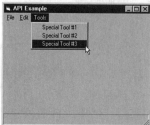

parameters do not directly provide you with enough information to determine what text to display in your status bar. You can use those parameters to get the information you need, however, through a series of other related API calls. The following, full code does this—as a procedure that takes the handle of your status bar, your form, and the two message parameters. Another procedure, GetMenuTag, is then used to find the corresponding Visual Basic menu control and return the text contained within its Tag property. This text is then placed into the status bar. The procedure places a blank value into the status bar if the parameters indicate that the current menu selected opens a submenu or that the user has deselected the menu bar:

```
Private Sub HandleMenuSelection(sBar As StatusBar, _
    CurrentForm As Form, _
    wParam As Long, _
    lParam As Long)

Dim sOutput As String
Dim lMenuHandle As Long

Dim lResult As Long
Dim sTmp As String

Dim LoWord As Long
Dim HiWord As Long

    sOutput = ""

    sTmp = Space(255)

    'Get handle of menubar
    lMenuHandle = GetMenu(CurrentForm.hwnd)

    'Get Low and High Words of wParam
    LoWord = wParam And 65535
    HiWord = CLng("&H" & Left(Hex(wParam - LoWord), 4))


    'If it is a not an actual command item, do nothing
    If Not (HiWord And MF_POPUP) Then
```

```
                        'Get Menu Caption
                        lResult = GetMenuString(lParam, LoWord, _
                        sTmp, 255, 0&)

                        'Trim off the null at the end
                        sTmp = Left(sTmp, lResult)

                        sOutput = GetMenuTag(CurrentForm, sTmp)

                End If

                sBar.SimpleText = sOutput

        End Sub

        Private Function GetMenuTag(CurrentForm As Form, _
        sCaption As String) As String
        Dim X As Control

        For Each X In CurrentForm.Controls
            If TypeOf X Is Menu Then
                If X.Caption = sCaption Then
                    GetMenuTag = X.Tag
                    Exit For
                End If
            End If
        Next

        End Function
```

It is necessary to modify your replacement window procedure so that it calls the preceding (new) code. See the following code:

```
Function WindowProc(ByVal hw As Long, _
    ByVal uMsg As Long, _
    ByVal wParam As Long, _
    ByVal lParam As Long) As Long

On Error GoTo windowproc_err

'Insert your message handling code here.
Dim lMenuPicked As Long

    If uMsg = WM_MENUSELECT Then
```

```
        Debug.Print "Menu Selection!!"
        Debug.Print "wParam: " & wParam
        Debug.Print "lParam: " & lParam

        HandleMenuSelection frmSamp.sbInfo, _
        frmSamp, wParam, lParam

    End If

    WindowProc = CallWindowProc(lpPrevWndProc, hw, _
    uMsg, wParam, lParam)

    Exit Function

windowproc_err:

    Err.Raise Err.Number, "WindowProc", Err.Description

    Exit Function

End Function
```

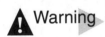 **Warning**

An important limitation of this method is that your menus must have distinct captions. If they do not, the wrong status information might be displayed.

With the addition of these new pieces of code, and after you have placed some values into the Tag property of your menu items, your sample program is complete. A screenshot of the completed application shows the status bar text being displayed as the user selects a specific menu item, as shown in Figure 28.3.

Figure 28.3

The completed program showing status bar information for a specific menu selection.

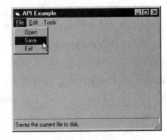

This has been an example of a more complex application of API programming in Visual Basic, but there are also many simple uses for this type of code. Whenever you need to perform a task that other programs commonly perform, it is likely to be done through one or more Win32 API calls. Determining the path to the user's Windows directory (`GetWindowsDirectory`), checking available hard drive space (`GetDiskFreeSpace`), or even shutting down Windows itself (`ExitWindows`) can all be done through the API. As you build more and more applications, using API calls will become a common way to solve problems and is your first method of expanding the power and flexibility of Visual Basic.

Visual Basic for Applications (VBA)

The capability to create scripts and macros for computer applications has been a common feature for many years; it is nothing new. Visual Basic for Applications (VBA), is different. Microsoft has taken the whole concept of a macro language to another level, providing a level of power and flexibility normally found only in full-development environments.

Before VBA, when you needed to develop with a Microsoft Office application such as Word or Excel, you had two choices: work in the application's own built-in language, or use a separate product such as Visual Basic. Built-in languages lacked the features of a true development product, and the programming environments were usually only one step above a text editor (but were generally easier to integrate with the main application). Macros could easily be assigned to a toolbar item or a menu option, making them seem like part of the main application itself. VBA gives you the best of both worlds, the flexibility and power of Visual Basic 5 along with a nearly identical development environment, while still providing easy integration. The languages themselves are virtually identical, so your programming knowledge, as well as actual code, can be transferred between the two environments with no changes required. The following code, for example, opens a database connection, retrieves a recordset, and loops through its records; it is also 100% VB and VBA compatible. If you need to use VBA, you won't be starting from scratch.

The following identical code can used in both VBA and VB, with no changes required:

```
Public Sub RecordLoop()

Dim DB As Database
Dim RS As Recordset
Dim DBPath as string


DBPath = "E:\Program Files\Microsoft Office\" & _
"Office\Samples\Northwind.mdb"

    Set DB = Workspaces(0).OpenDatabase(DBPath)
    Set RS = DB.OpenRecordset("Select * From Customers")

    Do While Not RS.EOF

        Debug.Print RS("CompanyName")
        RS.MoveNext

    Loop

    RS.Close

End Sub
```

Note For those situations when you don't want to just transfer the code, VBA also supports COM, enabling you to access ActiveX DLLs and EXEs created in Visual Basic or any other language.

Because it is possible to access Microsoft Office applications from both VB and VBA, many tasks can be performed with either language. You need a way to determine what type of development is best for a particular situation. In general, you should use VB if you are building an application that uses the Office application as a tool to perform a specific function, and VBA if you are building a tool to be used from within the Office application. One example of the first type of program would be a database program that uses Microsoft Excel to create its reports. On the other hand, developing a function to perform a complicated interest calculation when the user clicks a toolbar button would be better done in VBA.

Programming with Visual C++

Some of you may be Visual C++ programmers already, some of you may wish you were, and the rest probably grow a little weak at the sight of it. Regardless, it is important to understand what it is and how it can be used to help your Visual Basic applications.

Visual Basic 5 has removed two of the main arguments for using Visual C++:

▶ *Speed.* Pure code execution speed in Visual Basic 5 is comparable to that of Visual C++.

▶ *Better access to the Windows API.* The new `addressof` operator that enables your program to use callbacks makes almost all API calls available to you directly from Visual Basic.

So why would you bother? Well, there still are reasons. Despite the improvements in Visual Basic 5, Visual C++ applications are still faster. Although your code, when natively compiled, can execute almost as fast as similar Visual C++ code, that is not the only factor determining the overall speed of an application. Visual Basic programs have more overhead than ones created in Visual C++, making them load more slowly and require more memory. Visual Basic also suffers from performance problems when drawing controls, windows, and other graphics objects—operations performed almost constantly in the majority of Windows applications. Generally you should use Visual C++ when memory usage and performance considerations outweigh the increased development time required.

Internet Programming

As the Internet becomes more and more of a major part of business life, it is increasingly likely that you will need to understand how to develop applications for it. Many different technologies are available, but this section is going to focus on the ones that are the most related to Visual Basic: VBScript; ActiveX; Active Server Pages; and the one you have probably heard the most about, Java.

Client-Side Versus Server-Side

In Internet development, there are two main types of programming. The defining factor of these types is where the code is executed. In client-side programming, the code runs on the end-user's machine. In server-side, all execution takes place on the actual web server. Each has advantages and disadvantages, and there is currently no clear winner between the two types. In server-side programming, web pages are created when requested, using parameters to determine what information the client wants. These pages, once created, are then returned to the client for display. The types of operating systems and browsers used by the client don't affect the processing of the pages, although they may be used to determine how the results are formatted. Active Server Pages (ASP) and Common Gateway Interface (CGI) applications are examples of server-side programming.

Client-side programming is creating scripts and objects that are executed on the users' machines. This means that the client's choice of browser, operating system, and even his system configuration can affect how the code is executed. That fact alone makes it seem to be the less desirable method for creating a web application, but it is still necessary. Java Applets, ActiveX Controls, and other client-based technologies are currently the only way to produce interfaces comparable to standard applications. Putting up dialog boxes, displaying complex controls, and even simple animations all require some client-side code. Server-side and client-side programming is not an either-or choice: You can create an Active Server Page script that generates web pages containing client-side code, enabling you the best features of both types of development.

As greater functionality is added directly to the browsers—such as the addition of Dynamic HTML to Netscape Communicator and IE 4.0—it will become possible to use little, or no, client-side code and still produce fully functional applications.

VBScript

VBScript is a limited dialect of Visual Basic designed primarily for use in Internet applications. Unlike Visual Basic for Applications, another Visual Basic derivative (see the section titled "Visual Basic for Applications"), VBScript supports only a subset of the complete language. Its main restriction is that it is limited to working with the object model of the application hosting it (such as Internet Explorer). This prevents you from directly accessing external DLLs and using Win32 API calls from VBScript, unless those features are available through the objects provided by the environment. This is an intentional limitation, designed to prevent security problems when using VBScript as a client-side scripting language. By limiting it to the host's objects, all security can be handled by the browser. Despite its limitations, it is still very similar to Visual Basic, enabling you to easily transfer your existing programming skills, making it a likely choice for your Internet projects. Its capability to do what you need really depends more on the hosting application than on VBScript itself. If the object model provided by an application is limited, you will be, too. Several different applications can host VBScript code; Internet Explorer uses it for client-side scripting, the Active Server Pages engine supports VBScript for generating pages, the latest version of the Microsoft Exchange Server and its Outlook client use VBScript as their internal scripting language, and Windows itself plans to incorporate it to enable users to script the operating system.

JavaScript

JavaScript, or JScript, is another scripting language, almost identical to VBScript in its purpose and restrictions. One of its major differences is that it is a subset of Java, not Visual Basic, making it a little more difficult for you to start using, but giving it similar functionality. The other major difference—and this becomes the reason why you should consider learning it—is that it is supported in both Netscape and Microsoft browsers and on most operating systems. When building any form of client-side web application, you need to consider your audience. If you use VBScript to script your pages, you will be preventing over half the Internet from using your site. Choosing JavaScript still limits you to people with more recent browsers, but allows a much greater number of users than would be possible with VBScript alone. Similarly to VBScript, JavaScript is available for both client-side and server-side programming because it can also be used with Active Server Pages.

ActiveX Controls

This topic is discussed in detail in Chapter 13, "Creating and Using ActiveX Controls," and Chapter 14, "Creating and Using ActiveX Documents." Therefore, this chapter provides only the essential details. ActiveX Controls are client-side objects that you can create in Visual Basic or Visual C++. They provide the quickest way to transfer a Visual Basic application to the Internet because you can just modify the code and forms to create a valid user control or document object. The negatives of using this technology are the general problems of client-side development: dependence on the client's system and configuration. ActiveX Controls are only supported natively in Internet Explorer, limiting your clients in the same way as using VBScript. Controls are usually combined with some form of client-side scripting (JavaScript or VBScript) to manipulate their properties or handle the results of user interaction with the control.

Java Applets

It would be incorrect to say that an applet is just like an ActiveX Control. They do have many different properties and capabilities, but in general that is the case. Anywhere you could use an ActiveX Control, you can usually replace it with an applet; the reverse is also true. Similar to the previous comparison of VBScript with JavaScript, applets have the advantage over ActiveX Controls in that they are supported by more browsers and therefore have a much wider audience. Applets are written in Java, which has much more in common with a language such as C++ than Visual Basic, creating a greater learning curve than ActiveX Controls. If you are serious about creating client-side web applications, this is what you should learn (at present).

Active Server Pages

The last topic to discuss is the only server-side technology being covered: Active Server Pages (ASP). ASP is a Microsoft product that allows the generation of web content at the server level. This technology is an integral part of the new Active Server Platform that consists of IIS 3.0 + and Windows NT Server 4 +. Script files (.asp) are created that contain the code needed to generate a web page, and then these files are executed by the web server when the page is requested by a browser. The files themselves can be written with any ActiveX scripting language (which currently includes JavaScript and VBScript) to produce the results, and have access to a powerful built-in object model. A major feature of the Active Server Pages object model is the capability to create external COM objects through a version of the VB `CreateObject` function. This feature allows Active Server Page-based applications access to COM objects, including ActiveX DLLs created in Visual C++ or Visual Basic. The ASP object model also allows access to information submitted from HTML forms, information on the requesting browser (enabling customization based on what features are supported on the receiving end), and a large number of other useful HTTP-oriented functions.

As a server-side technology, ASP is perfectly suited to creating applications that are completely browser independent, while still enabling you to reuse existing Visual Basic code or components. Because the script files are straight text, no development environment is necessary. If something beyond a text-editor is desired, however, Visual InterDev is available.

P a r t **5**

Appendixes

Appendix

Overview of the Certification Process

You must pass rigorous certification exams to become a Microsoft Certified Professional. These certification exams provide a valid and reliable measure of your technical proficiency and expertise. The closed-book exams are developed in consultation with computer industry professionals who have on-the-job experience with Microsoft products in the workplace. These exams are conducted by an independent organization—Sylvan Prometric—at more than 700 Sylvan Authorized Testing Centers around the world.

Currently Microsoft offers five types of certification, based on specific areas of expertise:

▶ **Microsoft Certified Professional (MCP).** Qualified to provide installation, configuration, and support for users of at least one Microsoft desktop operating system, such as Windows NT Workstation. In addition, candidates can take elective exams to develop areas of specialization. MCP is the initial or first level of expertise.

▶ **Microsoft Certified Systems Engineer (MCSE).** Qualified to effectively plan, implement, maintain, and support information systems with Microsoft Windows NT and other Microsoft advanced systems and workgroup products such as Microsoft Office and Microsoft BackOffice. MCSE is a second level of expertise.

▶ **Microsoft Certified Solution Developer (MCSD).** Qualified to design and develop custom business solutions by using Microsoft development tools, technologies, and platforms, including Microsoft Office and Microsoft BackOffice.

MCSD is a second level of expertise with a focus on software development.

▶ **Microsoft Certified Professional—Specialist: Internet (MCP-SI).** Qualified to plan security, install and configure server products, manage server resources, extend service to run CGI scripts or ISAPI scripts, monitor and analyze performance, and troubleshoot problems. Expertise is similar to that of an MCP with a focus on the Internet.

▶ **Microsoft Certified Trainer (MCT).** Instructionally and technically qualified by Microsoft to deliver Microsoft Education courses at Microsoft-authorized sites. An MCT must be employed by a Microsoft Solution Provider Authorized Technical Education Center or a Microsoft Authorized Academic Training site.

 Note

For up-to-date information about each type of certification, visit the Microsoft Training and Certification World Wide Web site at `http://www.microsoft.com/train_cert`. You must have an Internet account and a WWW browser to access this information. You also can call the following sources:

▶ Microsoft Certified Professional Program: 800-636-7544

▶ Sylvan Prometric Testing Centers: 800-755-EXAM

▶ Microsoft Online Institute (MOLI): 800-449-9333

How to Become a Microsoft Certified Professional (MCP)

Becoming an MCP requires you to pass one operating system exam. The following list shows the names and exam numbers of all the operating systems from which you can choose to qualify for your MCP certification:

▶ Implementing and Supporting Microsoft Windows 95, #70-064 (also #70-063 until retirement)

- ▶ Implementing and Supporting Microsoft Windows NT Workstation 4.0, #70-073

- ▶ Implementing and Supporting Microsoft Windows NT Workstation 3.51, #70-042

- ▶ Implementing and Supporting Microsoft Windows NT Server 4.0, #70-067

- ▶ Implementing and Supporting Microsoft Windows NT Server 3.51, #70-043

- ▶ Microsoft Windows for Workgroups 3.11-Desktop, #70-048

- ▶ Microsoft Windows 3.1, #70-030

- ▶ Microsoft Windows Architecture I, #70-160

- ▶ Microsoft Windows Architecture II, #70-161

How to Become a Microsoft Certified Professional—Specialist: Internet (MCP-SI)

Becoming an MCP with a specialty in Internet technology requires that you pass the following three exams:

- ▶ Internetworking Microsoft TCP/IP on Microsoft Windows NT 4.0, #70-059

- ▶ Implementing and Supporting Microsoft Windows NT Server 4.0, #70-067

- ▶ Implementing and Supporting Microsoft Internet Information Server 3.0 and Microsoft Index Server 1.1, #70-077

How to Become a Microsoft Certified Systems Engineer (MCSE)

MCSE candidates must pass four operating system exams and two elective exams. The MCSE certification path is divided into two tracks: the Windows NT 3.51 track and the Windows NT 4.0 track.

The following lists show the core requirements (four operating system exams) for both the Windows NT 3.51 and 4.0 tracks, and the elective courses (two exams) you can choose from for either track.

The four Windows NT 3.51-track core requirements for MCSE certification are as follows:

▶ Implementing and Supporting Microsoft Windows NT Server 3.51, #70-043

▶ Implementing and Supporting Microsoft Windows NT Workstation 3.51, #70-042

▶ Networking Essentials, #70-058

▶ Microsoft Windows 3.1, #70-030

  OR Microsoft Windows for Workgroups 3.11, #70-048

  OR Implementing and Supporting Microsoft Windows 95, #70-064 (also #70-063 until retirement)

The four Windows NT 4.0-track core requirements for MCSE certification are as follows:

▶ Implementing and Supporting Microsoft Windows NT Server 4.0, #70-067

▶ Implementing and Supporting Microsoft Windows NT Server 4.0 in the Enterprise, #70-068

▶ Networking Essentials, #70-058

▶ Microsoft Windows 3.1, #70-030

  OR Microsoft Windows for Workgroups 3.11, #70-048

  OR Implementing and Supporting Microsoft Windows 95, #70-064 (also #70-063 until retirement)

  OR Implementing and Supporting Microsoft Windows NT Workstation 4.0, #70-073

For either the Windows NT 3.51 and/or the 4.0 track, you must pass two of the following elective exams for MCSE certification:

▶ Implementing and Supporting Microsoft SNA Server 3.0, #70-013

   OR Implementing and Supporting Microsoft SNA Server 4.0, #70-085

▶ Implementing and Supporting Microsoft Systems Management Server 1.0, #70-014

   OR Implementing and Supporting Microsoft Systems Management Server 1.2, #70-018

▶ Microsoft SQL Server 4.2 Database Implementation, #70-021

   OR Implementing a Database Design on Microsoft SQL Server 6.5, #70-027

▶ Microsoft SQL Server 4.2 Database Administration for Microsoft Windows NT, #70-022

   OR System Administration for Microsoft SQL Server 6.5, #70-026

▶ Microsoft Mail for PC Networks 3.2-Enterprise, #70-037

▶ Internetworking with Microsoft TCP/IP on Microsoft Windows NT (3.5-3.51), #70-053

   OR Internetworking with Microsoft TCP/IP on Microsoft Windows NT 4.0, #70-059

▶ Implementing and Supporting Microsoft Exchange Server 4.0, #70-075

   OR Implementing and Supporting Microsoft Exchange Server 5.0, #70-076

▶ Implementing and Supporting Microsoft Internet Information Server 3.0 and Microsoft Index Server 1.1, #70-077

   OR Implementing and Supporting Microsoft Internet Information Server 4.0, #70-087

▶ Implementing and Supporting Microsoft Proxy Server 1.0, #70-078

OR Implementing and Supporting Microsoft Proxy Server 2.0, #70-088

▶ Implementing and Supporting Microsoft Internet Explorer 4.0 by Using the Internet Explorer Resource Kit, #70-079

How to Become a Microsoft Certified Solution Developer (MCSD)

MCSD candidates must pass two core technology exams and two elective exams. The following lists show the required technology exams and the elective exams that apply toward obtaining the MCSD.

You must pass the following two core technology exams to qualify for MCSD certification:

▶ Microsoft Windows Architecture I, #70-160

▶ Microsoft Windows Architecture II, #70-161

You also must pass two of the following elective exams to become an MSCD:

▶ Microsoft SQL Server 4.2 Database Implementation, #70-021

OR Implementing a Database Design on Microsoft SQL Server 6.5, #70-027

▶ Developing Applications with C++ Using the Microsoft Foundation Class Library, #70-024

▶ Microsoft Visual Basic 3.0 for Windows-Application Development, #70-050

OR Programming with Microsoft Visual Basic 4.0, #70-065

OR Developing Applications with Microsoft Visual Basic 5.0, #70-165

- Microsoft Access 2.0 for Windows-Application Development, #70-051

  OR Microsoft Access for Windows 95 and the Microsoft Access Development Toolkit, #70-069

- Developing Applications with Microsoft Excel 5.0 Using Visual Basic for Applications, #70-052

- Programming in Microsoft Visual FoxPro 3.0 for Windows, #70-054

- Implementing OLE in Microsoft Foundation Class Applications, #70-025

Becoming a Microsoft Certified Trainer (MCT)

To understand the requirements and process for becoming a Microsoft Certified Trainer (MCT), you must obtain the Microsoft Certified Trainer Guide document (MCTGUIDE.DOC) from the following WWW site:

```
http://www.microsoft.com/train_cert/download.htm
```

On this page, click on the hyperlink MCT GUIDE (MCTGUIDE.DOC) (117K). If your WWW browser can display DOC files (Word for Windows native file format), the MCT Guide appears in the browser window. Otherwise, you need to download it and open it in Word for Windows or Windows 95 WordPad. The MCT Guide explains in detail the following four-step process to becoming an MCT:

1. Complete and mail a Microsoft Certified Trainer application to Microsoft. You must include proof of your skills for presenting instructional material. The options for doing so are described in the MCT Guide.

2. Obtain and study the Microsoft Trainer Kit for the Microsoft Official Curricula (MOC) course(s) for which you want to be certified. Microsoft Trainer Kits can be ordered by calling

800-688-0496 in North America. Other regions should review the MCT Guide for information about how to order a Trainer Kit.

3. Pass the Microsoft certification exam for the product for which you want to be certified to teach.

4. Attend the Microsoft Official Curriculum (MOC) course for the course for which you want to be certified. This must be done so you can understand how the course is structured, how labs are completed, and how the course flows.

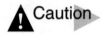 **Caution**

> You should consider the steps in this appendix as a general overview of the MCT certification process. The precise steps that you need to take are described in detail in the MCTGUIDE.DOC file on the WWW site mentioned earlier. Do not misconstrue the steps outlined here as the actual process you need to take.

If you are interested in becoming an MCT, you can receive more information by visiting the Microsoft Certified Training (MCT) WWW site at `http://www.microsoft.com/train_cert/mctint.htm`; or call 800-688-0496.

Appendix

Study Tips

B

Self-study involves any method that you employ to learn a given topic, with the most popular being third-party books such as the one you hold in your hand. Before you begin to study for a certification exam, you should know exactly what Microsoft expects you to learn.

Pay close attention to the objectives posted for the exam. The most current objectives can always be found on the WWW site `http://www.microsoft.com/train_cert`. This book was written to the most current objectives, and the beginning of each chapter lists the relevant objectives for that chapter. As well, you should notice at the beginning of the book a handy tear-out card with an objectives matrix that lists all objectives and the page you can turn to for information on that objective.

If you have taken any college courses in the past, you have probably learned what study habits work best for you. Nevertheless, consider the following:

▶ Study in bright light to reduce fatigue and depression.

▶ Establish a regular study schedule and stick as close to it as possible.

▶ Turn off all forms of distraction—including radios and televisions—or try studying in a quiet room.

▶ Always study in the same place so that your materials are always readily at hand.

▶ Take short (approximately 15-minute) breaks every two to three hours or so. Studies have proven that your brain assimilates information better when these rest periods are taken.

Another thing to think about is this: Humans vary in their learning styles. Some people are visual learners, others are tactile, and still others learn best from aural sources. However, there are some basic principles of learning that apply to everyone. Students who take notes on lectures have better recall on exam day—even if they did not study the notes later—because they encoded the information as well as decoded it. They processed it in a deeper, more active fashion than those who just listened to the lecture.

Hence, use the study techniques that you know work for you, but also take advantage of more general principles of learning. If you are a visual learner, for example, pay special attention to the figures provided in this book. Also create your own visual cues by doing things such as diagramming processes and relationships. Another general principle of learning that you might take advantage of has to do with studying the organization and the details of information separately. Cognitive learning research has demonstrated that if you attempt to focus on learning just the organization of the information, followed by a focus on just learning the specific details, you will retain the information better than if you attempt to take in all the information at once.

Pre-Testing Yourself

Before taking the actual exam, verify that you are ready to do so by testing yourself many times in a variety of ways. Within this book, questions appear at the beginning and end of each chapter. The accompanying CD-ROM contains an electronic test engine that emulates the actual Microsoft exam and enables you to test your knowledge of the subject areas. Use this repeatedly until you are consistently scoring in the 90% range (or better).

 Note

This means, of course, that you can't start studying five days before the exam begins. You need to give yourself plenty of time to read, practice, and then test yourself several times.

The New Riders' TestPrep electronic testing engine, we believe, is the best test preparation tool on the market, unparalleled by most other engines. TestPrep is described in detail in Appendix D, "All About TestPrep."

Hints and Tips for Doing Your Best on the Tests

When you go to take the actual exam, be prepared. Arrive early and be ready to show two forms of identification, and then sit before the monitor. Expect wordy questions. Although you have 75 minutes to take the exam, there are 60 questions you must answer. This gives you just over one minute to answer each question. This may sound like ample time for each question, but remember that most of the questions are lengthy word problems, which tend to ramble on for paragraphs. Your 75 minutes of exam time can be consumed very quickly.

It has been estimated that approximately 85 percent of the candidates taking their first Microsoft exam fail it. It is not so much that they are unprepared and unknowledgeable. It is more likely that they don't know what to expect and are immediately intimidated by the wordiness of the questions and the ambiguity implied in the answers.

Things to Watch For

When you take the exam, read the questions closely to determine the number of choices you need to select. Some questions require that you select a single answer; other questions have more than one correct answer. When you see radio buttons next to the answer choices, you can expect that the answers are mutually exclusive and there is but one correct answer. On the other hand, check boxes indicate that the answers are not mutually exclusive and there are multiple correct answers.

Also, read the questions fully. With lengthy questions, the last sentence often dramatically changes the scenario. When taking the exam, you are given pencils and two sheets of paper. If you are uncertain of what the question is saying, map out the scenario on the paper until you have it clear in your mind. You are required to turn in the scrap paper at the end of the exam.

Marking Answers for Return

You can mark questions on the exam and refer back to them later. If you encounter a wordy question that will take a long time to read and decipher, mark it and return to it when you have completed the rest of the exam. This will prevent you from wasting time on it and running out of time on the exam—there are only 75 minutes allotted for the exam and it ends when those 75 minutes expire, regardless of whether you are finished with the exam.

Attaching Notes to Test Questions

At the conclusion of the exam, before the grading takes place, you are given the opportunity to attach a message to any question. If you feel that a question was too ambiguous, or you were tested on knowledge you do not need to know to work with the product, take this opportunity to state your case. Unheard of is the instance in which Microsoft changes a test score as a result of an attached message. However, it never hurts to try—and it helps to vent your frustration before blowing the proverbial 50-amp fuse.

Good luck!

Appendix

What's on the CD-ROM

This appendix is a brief rundown of what you will find on the CD-ROM that comes with this book. For a more detailed description of the newly developed TestPrep test engine, exclusive to Macmillan Computer Publishing, please see Appendix D, "All About TestPrep."

TestPrep

TestPrep is a new test engine developed exclusively for Macmillan Computer Publishing. It is, we believe, the best test engine available because it closely emulates the actual Microsoft exam, and enables you to check your score by category, which helps you determine what topics you need to study further. Before running the TestPrep software, be sure to read CDROM.HLP (in the root directory of the CD-ROM) for late-breaking news on TestPrep features. For a complete description of the benefits of TestPrep, see Appendix D.

Exclusive Electronic Version of Text

Also contained on the CD is the electronic version of this book. You can use this to help you search for terms or areas that you need to study. The electronic version comes complete with all figures as they appear in the book.

Copyright Information and Disclaimer

Macmillan Computer Publishing's TestPrep test engine: Copyright 1997 New Riders Publishing. All rights reserved. Made in U.S.A.

All About TestPrep

The TestPrep software included on the CD-ROM accompanying this book enables you to test your Visual Basic 5 knowledge in a manner similar to that employed by the actual Microsoft exam. There are actually three applications included: Practice Exams, Study Cards, and Flash Cards. Practice Exams provide you with a simulated multiple-choice test. Study Cards provide the same sorts of questions (but enable you to control the number and types of questions), and provide immediate feedback. This format enables you to limit your testing to topics on which you need further study. Flash Cards require short-answer or essay answers to their questions; you are not prompted with multiple-choice selections or cued as to the number of correct answers to provide.

Although it is possible to maximize the TestPrep applications, the default is for them to run in smaller mode so that you can refer to your Visual Basic 5 desktop while answering questions. TestPrep uses a unique randomization sequence to ensure that each time you run the programs, you face a different sequence of questions; this enhances your learning and helps prevent you from merely memorizing the expected answers over time without reading the question each and every time.

Question Presentation

TestPrep Practice Exams and Study Cards emulate the actual Microsoft "Developing Applications with Microsoft Visual Basic 5" exam (#70-165) in that radio (circle) buttons are used to signify only one correct choice; check boxes (squares) are used to indicate multiple correct answers. Whenever more than one answer is correct, the number you should select is given in the wording of the question.

Index

R

S

U